CADOGAN
ISLAND GUIDES

CYPR

D1500517

Cadogan Books plc
London House, Parkgate Road, London SW11 4NQ

The Globe Pequot Press
6 Business Park Road, PO Box 833, Old Saybrook,
Connecticut 06475–0833

Copyright © Barnaby Rogerson 1994
Illustrations © Angela Culme-Seymour 1994

Book design by Animage
Cover design by Ralph King
Cover illustration by Povl Webb
Maps © Cadogan Guides, drawn by Thames
Cartographic Services Ltd

Proofreading maps and text: Eric Smith, Peter Casterton, Linda McQueen
Indexing: Jane Wregg
Production: Book Production Services
Mac Help: Jacqueline Lewin, Alex Manolatos

Editing: Rachel Fielding and Tanya Colbourne
Series Editors: Rachel Fielding and Vicki Ingle

A catalogue record for this book is available from the British Library
ISBN 0 947754 20 2

Library of Congress Cataloging-in-Publication-Data
Rogerson, Barnaby.
     Cyprus/Barnaby Rogerson
        p. cm. -- (Cadogan guides)
     "A Voyager book."
     Includes index.
     ISBN 1-56440-177-4
     1. Cyprus--Guidebooks. I. Title. II. Series
     DS54.A3R64 1993
     915.69304'4--dc20   93-5568 CIP

The author and publishers have made every effort to ensure the accuracy of the information in this book at the time of going to press. However they cannot accept any responsibility for any loss, injury or inconvenience resulting from the use of information contained in this guide.

Typeset in Weidemann and entirely produced on Apple Macintosh with Quark XPress, Photoshop, Freehand and Word software.

Printed and bound in Great Britain by The Lavenham Press, Suffolk, on Jordan Opaque supplied by McNaughton Publishing Papers Ltd. Output by Cooling Brown.

About the Author

Barnaby Rogerson was born and finished his education in Fife, Scotland, but now lives in a warm flat in London. He is a historian, would-be icon painter and zealous tourist who has written a number of guides to the Islamic countries of the Mediterranean. He was named after St Barnabas, the patron saint of Cyprus, who is credited with saving his father from a rocket attack in the 50s.

Acknowledgements

I would like to thank my brother James, then serving in the UN forces on the island, for arranging an initial introduction to both sides of the island. I am also indebted to Barnabas White-Spunner who has generously shared his wide knowledge of the island and its literature; his friends in the British High Commission in Nicosia, Richard Potter and Christopher and Lottie James, proved equally hospitable and informative. I was also fortunate to be put up by both Joumana and Jim Muir in Strovolos and Adrian and Penny Akers-Douglas, and to share some of their passionate enthusiasm for their adopted country. Among the many others who have helped, shared meals, enthusiasm or walks I would like to thank Charlie and Kate Boxer, Anne Baring, Nicholas and Sue Kay in Lefke, Anne Cryer, Aluine and Lothar Gerner, Tony Kay, John and Mary Burgess afloat in Larnaca, Alistair Gordon, Renofs Loizou, Stewart Swiney, Artemis Yiordamlis, Edgar Peltenberg and Gordon Thomas, who sent me a copy of his unpublished archaeology doctorate. The tourist offices of both the Republic of Cyprus and the Turkish Republic of North Cyprus have been invariably informative and helpful. In particular I would like to thank Lillian Panayi for providing a car and a museum pass and Ozkan Irfanoğlu for arranging accommodation.

I am also indebted to the shared labour of Rachel Fielding at Cadogan Books, Tanya Colbourne, a freelance editor who was driven to near distraction by my enthusiastic use of every variant Cypriot spelling, Eric Smith, who oversaw the production of the maps, to my father for writing about the flowers, birds and bees, and to Angela Culme-Seymour who created the enchanting illustrations.

Olive, cypress and eucalyptus trees

Contents

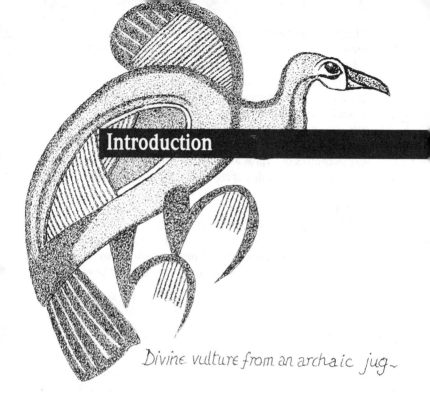

Introduction

Divine vulture from an archaic jug

Cyprus is an island unto itself, whose distinct identity has been formed by a fusion of the great cultures of the Eastern Mediterranean. It is neither wholly of the Levant, of nearby Turkey nor yet an outlying part of Greece. Lit by the burning sun of the Near East, its intriguingly complex culture is expressed in both landscape and architecture. Cyprus is a land of palm and pine, of pale hillsides covered in vines and irrigated valleys covered in citrus orchards. It has goat-grazed hillsides, intensively worked ploughland, a wind-blown dusty plain, silent cedar forests and patches of ancient olive and carob groves. In any one day it is easy to pass a Gothic cathedral, an Ottoman minaret, Venetian fortifications, Roman mosaics, a British postbox, excavations into a Bronze-Age city, a Crusader castle and a working Orthodox church founded in the days of the Byzantine Empire.

This cross thread of cultures, which historically has provided so many commercial and tactical advantages, is not without its negative side. Cyprus was one of the first victims of the rising tide of ethnic conflict that has gripped the late 20th-century world. Twenty years ago it was riven in two by ethnic loyalties focused on distant capitals. These political scars are more than matched by the self-inflicted wounds of recent prosperity. Most of the urban centres of Cyprus are possessed by new apartment blocks, surrounded by a spreading sea of suburban villas. Much of the shore has now been disfigured by brash high-rise hotels that provide hundreds of thousands of holidays in the sun for the package tourist trade. It is however easy enough to peer beneath these discouraging first impressions, and head out from the coastal resorts, to find a still lovely isle, renowned as the Island of Love.

Guide to the Guide

Divided Cyprus

The one essential fact to bear in mind is that Cyprus is divided. Since 1974 the northern third of the island has been Turkish and the southern two-thirds has been Greek (The Republic of Cyprus). Before this an educated Cypriot was often trilingual in Greek, Turkish and English, but since 1974 an entire generation has grown up in ignorance of the language and culture of the 'other side'. This separation may yet be healed, but after twenty years of failed peace negotiations there is a discernible pessimism and a reluctant acceptance of the status quo. Fortunately this has had next to no effect on the easy charm and hospitality of the islanders on both sides of the border. The Cypriots, with over a century of experience, are also particularly skilled at defrosting Anglo-Saxon reserve. They themselves tend to exist in an intricate but far-flung web of family loyalties and friendships that extends over most of the island and a good portion of the globe. This can at any moment be stretched to include a passing visitor.

If you choose to holiday in the Turkish north (whose government has only been recognized by Turkey and North Korea) you are not permitted to cross into the Greek south. If you holiday in the Greek south you can cross over into the north by foot, for the day, but only from the border post beside the old Ledra Palace Hotel in Nicosia.

South or North?

Which part of Cyprus you choose for a holiday may already be determined by your affection for Greek or Turkish culture. Those who admire both (they have so much in common that at times they seem to be but two faces of a single coin) can decide on two holidays… but make a small saving by buying only one guidebook.

The **Turkish north** receives about 4 per cent of the tourists that pack into the southern resorts. It is a much more attractive destination if you are looking for quiet swimming, small village tavernas and calm walks amongst a relatively undisturbed Mediterranean landscape. It has many of the most famous landmarks of Cyprus, such as Bellapais Abbey, the Gothic Cathedral in Nicosia, the ruins of Romano-Byzantine Salamis, the hill-top castles of St Hilarion, Buffavento and Kantara and, last but by no means least, the walled city of Famagusta stuffed with Gothic monuments. It also contains a disturbing number of Turkish army posts and is touched by a lethargy which is partly charming but is also a reflection of its commercial, cultural and political isolation from the world community.

Greek Cyprus, the southern two-thirds of the island, is a much busier, bustling place with all the natural vivacity, charm and sharp business sense that you expect from the Greeks. Be prepared to fly into a fully 20th-century landscape, complete with motorways, extensive new suburbs and town centres that have been partly decimated by a rash of modern office blocks and high-rise apartments. If you are looking for a summer beach holiday with a bit of a buzz, water sports, bars and discotheques, you will be served by the resorts of Ayia Napa, Protaras, Larnaca, Limassol or Paphos which now dominate about a quarter of the coastline.

For those looking for a more individual holiday there are still a large number of empty beaches but only about two dozen hotels sympathetic to an independent traveller (listed both in the text and under 'Where to Stay' on p. 29). It will make all the difference to your holiday to make one or two reservations before your arrival. Despite the booming resorts there is still much of interest to be discovered in the towns and along the coast, such as the mosaics and the tombs of the kings at Nea Paphos, the ruins at Kourion, Kolossi Castle, Hala Sultan Tekke, the Pierides Museum and Ayia Napa Monastery. Nicosia, aside from its interesting assortment of architecture, is worth a visit simply for either the Cyprus Archaeological Museum or the Byzantine (Icon) Museum. The rural hinterland and central mountains are almost entirely untouched by package tourism. They are perfectly suited to walks, long meals and gentle explorations in a network of quiet villages, forest tracks and under-visited sites. This area contains almost all of the island's important frescoed Byzantine chapels, whose international importance has only recently been recognized.

The Republic of Cyprus: the Greek South

Beaches Lara, Evdhimiou, Kourion, Lady's Mile.

Painted Churches Asinou, Stavros tou Ayiasmati, Ayios Nikolaos tis Steyis/St Nicholas of the Roof, Panayia tou Araka at Lagoudera, Ayios Neophytos Monastery (outside Paphos) and Ayios Ioannis Lambadhistis.

Castles Kolossi, Limassol.

Classical and Early Byzantine Ruins Kourion, Nea Paphos.

Museums The Cyprus Museum in Nicosia, the Byzantine (Icon) Museum in Nicosia, the Pierides Museum in Larnaca.

Folk Art Phikardou, Eliades Museum in Paphos, Limassol Folk Art Museum, Yeroskipou, Omodhos, Pano Lefkara.

Following the myth of Aphrodite Petra tou Romiou (the birthplace), Palea Paphos (the Paphian temple), Yeroskipou (the sacred garden), the Baths of Aphrodite (an Italian poetic fiction), Tamassos (site of a temple and the fountain of youth), Idalium (site of a temple), Kition (excavated foundations of an ancient temple site).

Curiosities St Nicholas of the Cats, the Tombs of the Kings, Cedar Valley, Pyla village, Khirokitia excavations and Green Line in Nicosia.

Turkish Northern Cyprus

Beaches Salamis, Yeşilırmak, Yenierenköy, Lara.

Painted Churches Antiphonitis and Iskele (Trikomo).

Castles St Hilarion, Kantara, Buffavento.

Gothic Monuments Bellapais Abbey, Cathedral-Mosque and Haydarpaşa/ St Catherine's in Nicosia, Cathedral-Mosque and St George of the Latins in Gazimağusa (Famagusta).

Classical and Early Byzantine Ruins Salamis, Soli and Vouni.

Museums Kyrenia Ship Museum, Dervis Paşa Mansion.

Ottoman Architecture Sultan Mahmud's library, Büyük Han, Büyük Hammam, Mevelevi Tekke Museum.

Travel

By Air

From Britain

The old international airport of Nicosia remains embedded in the Green Line, the UN-patrolled strip of territory that divides Cyprus. After 1974 the simple airstrip established in the middle of the Larnaca salt lake was rapidly expanded and developed into the new international airport for the south. Since 1983 it has been assisted by a lesser airport established at Paphos.

Cyprus Airways and British Airways run regular scheduled flights between Larnaca and London. Cyprus Airways also flies to Paphos from London and Manchester. For information and bookings visit the smart new **British Airways** travel centre at 156 Regent Street, London W1, ℂ 0345 222111, or **Cyprus Airways** at Euston Centre, 29–31 Hampstead Road, London NW1 3JA, ℂ (071) 388 5411.

Charter flights leave from Gatwick, Stansted, Luton, Manchester and Birmingham. They can be almost half the price of a regular scheduled flight, but have certain disadvantages: they do suffer from almost routine delays, odd departure times, a pay bar and reduced leg room. Charter flights are supposed only to be taken with a package holiday and, though this is a polite fiction in most of the travel industry, the Cypriot Aviation authorities, keen to boost the earnings of the national carrier, have instituted occasional but well publicized clampdowns. A few unfortunate travellers with either fictitious or no hotel bookings have been known to be held in the transit lounge and sent back from whence they came.

From North America or Australasia

Despite the sizeable communities of emigrant Cypriots there are no direct flights to the Republic of Cyprus (the Greek South) from Australia, Canada, New Zealand, South Africa or the USA. Rather than head for some geographical neighbour it is much cheaper and usually quicker to head for Britain first and then pick up a connection for Cyprus. Britain still provides the vast majority of Cyprus's tourists and the holiday industry in Britain is one of the most competitive in the world, which keeps the prices honed down.

By Ferry

From Greece, Israel or Italy

Poseidon Lines runs a regular ferry service from Piraeus (the port of Athens) that leaves on Monday evening and arrives at Cyprus's Limassol harbour on Wednesday morning having stopped en route at either Rhodes or Crete's Herakleon harbour. This boat continues on to Haifa (the main ferry port for Israel) and returns back from Haifa on Thursday evening calling at Limassol on Friday morning before continuing back to Piraeus. The Poseidon Line office is at Alkyonidion, 32 Voula, Athens, © (01) 9658300; Jacob Caspi is their agent in Haifa at 76 Haatzma'ut Road, © (04) 674444.

In the summer months, from April to September, the choice of boats and departure days is greatly expanded by other Piraeus-based companies such as Arkadia, Afroessa and Vergina. For those looking for an even more individual route to Cyprus, Marlines runs a ferry (in July and August) from Ancona in Italy which leaves on Friday and arrives in Limassol on Tuesday.

There are no ordinary ferries from the Arab Middle East to Cyprus, though you can take a return passage on a package cruise which leaves from Limassol (*see* text) to Egypt's Port Said, so long as it is not already booked up. Despite the evidence of current maps and other guide books there are no ferries operating out of Larnaca, and direct connections have not yet been re-established with either Syria or Lebanon.

By Car

Driving to Cyprus is an eccentric option, particularly given the current situation amongst the warring nations of old Yugoslavia and the ease of car rental on the island, though for potential emigrants or those taking up a foreign posting it may be a justifiable choice. Car ferries depart from Piraeus, the port of Athens, for those bound for the Republic of Cyprus (the Greek South). You might think about crossing the Adriatic from one of the ports of Southern Italy (such as Bari, Brindisi or Ancona) in order to land at Igoumenitsa in western Greece.

Tour Operators

Practically every one of the 60 or so major tour operators in Britain features the Republic of Cyprus (the Greek South) in their brochures. Five agencies interested in the more individual side of the market, with villas and village houses to rent, are:

> **Cypriana**, 31 Topsfield Parade, Crouch End, London N8 8PT, © (081) 348 8211;
>
> **Libra**, 343 Ballards Lane, London N12 8LJ, © (081) 446 8231;
>
> **Manos**, 168/172 Old Street, London EC1V 9BP, © (071) 216 8000;
>
> **Olympic Holidays**, Olympic House, 30-32 Cross Street, London N1 2BG, © (071) 359 3500;
>
> **Sunvil Holidays**, 7/8 Upper Square, Old Isleworth, Middlesex TW7 7BJ, © (081) 568 4499.

Other Cyprus specialist operators offering a wide range of accommodation include:

> **Amathus Holidays**, 51 Tottenham Court Road, London W1P 0HS, © (071) 636 9873;

Cyplon Holidays, 561 Green Lanes, Haringey, London N8 0RL, ℂ (081) 340 7612;

Cyprair Holidays, 23 Hampstead Road, London NW1 3JA, ℂ (071) 388 7515.

For details of other specialist companies which operate holidays to Cyprus, and a free directory, contact **AITO** (The Association of Independent Tour Operators), 133a St Margaret's Road, Twickenham, Middx TW1 1RG, ℂ (081) 744 3187.

For those interested in a holiday of walks, wild flowers and bird-watching in the Akamas, Anne Cryer puts together a spring and autumn programme: details from **Wildlife Travel**, Dudwich House, Buxton, Norwich, NR10 5HX, ℂ (0603) 278296. For a holiday based around coarse fishing, contact **Cyprus Angling Holidays**, 3 The Drive, Sevenoaks, TN13 3AB ℂ (0732) 450749.

You can also get the Cyprus Tourist Office at 213 Regent Street, London W1R 8DA, ℂ (071) 734 9822, to forward you their information pack and brochures.

Getting to North Cyprus

By Air

From Britain

The old Nicosia international airport, to the west of the city, is occupied by UN forces and is inaccessible. North Cyprus is now served by Ercan (Tymbou) airport which is a 23km drive east from Nicosia. It is named after a Turkish pilot who died during the invasion, and is making a gradual evolution from a military airstrip to a civil airport. Geçitkale (Lefkoniko) airport is now exclusively military but is still available as an emergency standby.

The Turkish Republic of North Cyprus is only recognized by Turkey and North Korea. There are, theoretically, no direct international flights though in practice Istanbul Airlines, Onur Air and Cyprus Turkish Airways (a branch of Türk Hava Yolari, the Turkish national airline) offer flights to North Cyprus from Frankfurt, Vienna and London-Heathrow. The airlines get around this restriction by changing planes at Istanbul or by a simple touchdown at Izmir. The latter can take anything between one and three hours before the flight is renumbered, the stewardesses change uniform and the airplane continues on to its destination. Passengers do not normally have to disembark. A **Cyprus Turkish Airlines** return flight to London via Izmir costs around £250, and can be purchased either through travel agents or direct from the office at 41 Pall Mall, London SW1Y 5JG, ℂ (071) 930 4853, fax 930 1046. **Istanbul Airline** tickets can be acquired from President Holidays, 542 Kingsland Road, London E8 4AH, ℂ (071) 249 4002 and **Onur Air** from TK Air Travel, 46 Newington Green, London N16 9PX, ℂ (071) 359 9214.

There are daily flights from Ercan to Istanbul and Ankara with less frequent services to Adana, Izmir and Antalya. A return flight to Istanbul, Izmir or Antalya costs around £80, less for Ankara and Adana. Tickets can be bought from the airport or from offices in Nicosia and Girne (Kyrenia), listed under these towns in the text.

Note that it is essential to confirm your return flight from Northern Cyprus. Make sure that your ticket has been stamped by the relevant airline office and do this as early as possible, as flights are often overbooked.

From North America or Australasia

There are no direct flights to Turkish North Cyprus from Australia, Canada, New Zealand, South Africa or the USA. You are faced with a choice of flying to Britain (or Germany or Austria) to pick up the connection listed above, or direct to Istanbul from where there are frequent flights to North Cyprus. If you have time to explore Istanbul the latter is the more enticing option, though if you are looking for the cheapest option, fly to Britain. Coming from North America there are four weekly THY flights from New York to Istanbul, coming from Australasia there are two weekly THY flights from Singapore to Istanbul.

By Ferry

From Turkey

There is an all-year-round passenger and car ferry service from Mersin, the largest port on the southern coast of Turkey, to North Cyprus's Gazimağusa (Famagusta). In summer a cheaper and much quicker connection (6 as opposed to 24 hours) operates between North Cyprus's Girne (Kyrenia) to the Turkish harbour of Taşucu which serves the nearby town of Silifke (*see* p. 316). There may also be a hydrofoil (passenger only) in operation between Taşucu and Girne (Kyrenia), though this service (currently run by Kibris Expresi) chops and changes every few years. Many maps and guide books still record a ferry link between Gazimağusa (Famagusta) and the Syrian port of Latakia or Jounié in the Lebanon, though these links have been closed for years.

By Car

For those bound for Turkish North Cyprus there are car ferries on the Turkish mainland at Taşucu-Silifke and Mersin and connections from Ancona, such as the Turkish Maritime Lines weekly journey to Izmir (a 60-hour passage) or Minoan Lines which stops at Piraeus on its way to Kuşadasi in western Turkey.

Tour Operators

A pick of the agencies would begin with **Cricketer Holidays**, 4 White House, Beacon Road, Crowborough, East Sussex TN6 1AB, © (0892) 664242, fax (0892) 662355 who know the area intimately and arrange a number of specialist tours. There are also, amongst others: **CTA Holidays Ltd**, 28 Cockspur Street, London SW1Y 5BN, ✆ (071) 930 4853, fax 930 1046; **Celebrity Holidays and Travel**, 18 Frith Street, London W1V 5TS, ✆ (071) 439 1961, fax 439 2026; **President Holidays**, 542 Kingsland Road, Dalston, London E8 4AH, ✆ (071) 249 4002, fax 923 2602 and **Mosaic Holidays**, Patman House, George Lane, South Woodford, London E18 2LS, ✆ (081) 532 9050.

Entry Requirements

Passports and Visas

All persons arriving in the Republic of Cyprus (the Greek South) must hold a valid passport. Visas are not required from American, Canadian, Australian, New Zealand, British or EC citizens, who are issued with a three-month visitor's permit by the immigration authorities on arrival. The same conditions apply for entry into Turkish North Cyprus. To prolong your stay in the south you can take a boat trip from Limassol to Israel or Egypt and collect another three-month permit on your return. The same policy applies to the north where a short trip to mainland Turkey from either Girne (Kyrenia) or Gazimağusa (Famagusta) allows you to collect another three month stamp on your return. Residency Permits are acquired from the Aliens Department in Nicosia with six passport sized photographs, evidence of a residence and sufficient funds.

Note well that any evidence of a visit to Turkish North Cyprus in your passport will mean that you are prohibited from entering the South. This fate is avoided by having your entrance visa stamped onto a loose sheet of paper, which is almost routine practice at the immigration booths at Ercan airport.

Customs

Cameras, sporting equipment and even cars are allowed to be imported duty-free for three months, providing they are for personal use and not for resale. In addition you are permitted the usual duty-free allowances as you enter Cyprus (both South and North); 200 cigarettes or 200 grams of tobacco, a ¾ litre of wine, a litre of spirits, a ⅓ of a litre of scent and C£50 worth of presents. The export of antiquities is strictly prohibited.

Getting Around

All communication within Cyprus is by road and track. There are no longer any trains (a line used to run from coast to coast across the Mesaoria plain between 1905–1951) and there are no internal flights or passenger boats between the ports. The bulk of tourists move around the island by hiring their own vehicle, though there is a perfectly good public transport system assisted by a plentiful supply of local taxis. Detailed travel information is given in each chapter.

By Car

You can rent a car in any major town, resort or airport. All rental cars (in the South) come with a distinguishing red number plate and are usually not in the first flush of youthful power. You will need to be over 21, possess a valid driving licence and be able to leave a deposit either in cash or on a credit card. Car-hire agencies offer a range of models and a printed tariff to which will be added local taxes, the price of a full tank and usually some extra insurance cover.

Republic of Cyprus: driving in Southern Cyprus is on the left as in Britain. There are international road signs in Greek and English. Distances in the South are now almost all marked up in kilometres but there are still a few mile posts around since they only went metric in 1987. The only local oddities to watch out for are the frequent use of the horn (often as a greeting), the comparative lack of indicating for a turn, the habit of accelerating if threatened by a car intending to overtake, and the close positioning of signposts to the actual turn. On a narrow road you should pull in to allow others to pass, but keep a watch out for abrupt verges. If you are unused to mountain roads watch out for patches of gravel which can act like ice when you break. Speed limits are 110km/hr on the motorways, 80km/hr on lesser roads and 50km/hr in built up areas. Petrol stations in the South are well distributed along the coast road and major towns. They are open from 7am–6pm from Mon–Fri and close an hour earlier on Saturday. Try to avoid running out of petrol in the hills and on Sundays or public holidays.

Turkish North Cyprus: in the North they also drive on the left but have very few signs of any sort (those that do exist are marked up in miles) but this inconvenience is partly compensated for by many fewer cars on the road. Petrol stations are only found on principal highways or in major towns but they are cheaper than those in the South and are generally open from 7am–8pm Mon–Sat. In the North it is 60mph on the highways, 40mph on lesser roads and 30mph in built up areas. Main roads are in good condition but minor roads can be narrow and twisting.

By Bus

A bus network connects the major towns and the surrounding suburban villages. It is less useful for getting around the country as the village buses leave at around 6am and return home later that afternoon. Full details are given in each chapter.

By Service Taxi

Republic of Cyprus: the simplest way to travel is to take one of the half-dozen seats in shared or service-taxis that connect the four towns of Southern Cyprus:

Nicosia, Limassol, Larnaca and Paphos. Places can be booked by telephone, and you are collected and dropped wherever you wish. Service taxis operate every half-hour from 6am to 7pm with a very reduced service on Sunday and public holidays.

Northern Cyprus: the only route links Northern Nicosia and Girne (Kyrenia).

By Taxi

For more individual routes and personal flexibility, take a cab. In the South they have meters, in the North they have a printed tariff. Telephone numbers, taxi rank locations and price-guidelines are given where appropriate in each chapter.

Disabled Travellers

Larnaca Airport has installed a mobile lift to receive wheelchairs and there is a special bus that can be booked through tour operators with a ramp and wide doors that can take 25 wheelchairs if you are planning a group trip.

Crossing the Green Line

Foreign visitors may only cross the Green Line into Northern Cyprus at the Ledra Palace hotel crossing in central Nicosia. It is only possible to do this for day trips from the South into the North. The checkpoint is open from about 8am and the Greek Cypriot officials at the frontier post will instruct visitors to return by a designated time in the afternoon, usually between 4–7pm. At times of international stress or border tension even this limited flow may be halted for weeks at a time.

There is no land crossing from Turkish North Cyprus into the South; visitors who arrive at the Ledra Palace hotel checkpoint will politely be refused entry into the South on the grounds that they have entered the country through an illegal port or airport. There is however a laborious maritime route that will only appeal to ferry-loving travellers who have kept their North Cyprus entrance and exit visas on a separate slip of paper and off their passports. Take the £16 ferry at noon from Girne (Kyrenia) to Taşucu in Turkey with enough time for a meal and a walk, before catching the 8.30 overnight bus to Marmaris from the neighbouring town of Silifke, a 15-hour journey for £10. At Marmaris Greek and Turkish ferries cross over to Rhodes five days out of seven, in about four hours. You might make it onto the mid-afternoon Greek ferry, but more likely you will have to stay the night in Marmaris and catch the 9am Turkish ferry the following morning. A return ticket to Rhodes costs £35 and you will be asked by the Turkish immigration authorities to submit your passport when booking your ticket; it will be returned to you just prior to departure. At Rhodes you can then pick up the ferry to Limassol, which in summer leaves on Friday at 4pm, Tuesday at 12noon and Saturday 8am (cheapest one-way deck ticket around £50). A faster, more expensive route involves flying from Ercan in Northern Cyprus to Istanbul, Istanbul to Athens and Athens to Larnaca.

Practical A–Z

Spring (March and April) is the ideal time to visit Cyprus, when the flowers are out in force and it is warm enough to swim and picnic outdoors. By May it is already starting to get hot and by midsummer (July and August) temperatures can reach 38°C inland and 30°C on the coast. It is then too hot to contemplate much walking or sightseeing. The autumn (September and October) is more pleasant and the sea remains surprisingly warm and inviting. If you are lucky some light rain can produce a second springtime for flowers. From November to April it is cooler, with shorter days. The rains usually occur in December, January and February but are unpredictable. Several years of near drought can suddenly be broken by an intemperate week-long flood which will fall as snow on Mount Olympos between mid January and early March, when skiing is possible.

	Jan	Feb	Mar	Apr	May	Jun	July	Aug	Sept	Oct	Nov	Dec
Average temperature °C	14	14	15	18	21	24	29	29	25	23	18	13
Average max temperature °C	16	17	19	23	27	34	37	38	32	28	22	17
Average hours of sunshine	169	197	255	285	355	379	399	358	321	277	231	175
Average no. of rainy days	12	8	7	4	4	1	0	0	1	3	6	11
Average sea temperature °C	16	17	19	21	24	26	28	27	25	22	19	17

Cyprus in London

The British Museum houses its ancient Cypriot artefacts on the upstairs floor in room 72, named the 'A. G. Leventis Gallery' in acknowledgment of the gifts of that Greek Cypriot philanthropist. It is a well-balanced collection of coins, jewellery, ceramics and limestone sculpture which has been displayed thematically. Exceptional exhibits (which are sadly not duplicated in any Cypriot museum) include the 5th-century Golgoi sarcophagus, with its low relief carving of hunting hoplites, a 12th-century BC carved ivory gaming box for playing Tjau and Senet and a series of limestone statues from Idalion, including a 3rd-century BC temple boy and a 5th-century Melkarth-Hercules. The British Museum has published a 70-page colour guide to its Ancient Cyprus collection which is for sale in the museum gift shops. The British Museum is on Great Russell Street, London and is open Mon–Sat 10am–5pm Sun 2.30–6, admission free.

The Camden Cypriot Festival, usually held in late October, draws together the various strands of the islands disparate artistic communities with film shows, art and architectural exhibitions and concerts. One of the more awesome events is the celebration of Byzantine Church Music at All Saints Greek Cathedral, Camden, London NW1. Gallery K at 101–103 Heath Street, Hampstead, London NW3 6SS, run by George and Ritsa Kyriacou, should be visited by anyone interested in modern trends in Greek and Cypriot art. Other centres of information are the two specialist London bookshops: Zeno's at 6 Denmark Street, WC2 and the Hellenic Book Service at 91 Fortress Road, NW5 1AG.

Electricity and Measurements

Electricity is supplied throughout the island at 240 volts AC and standard fittings are the three point 13 Amp fused plug as used in Great Britain. It, like the sewage from Nicosia, knows no boundaries and flows freely across the Green Line.

Although the Republic of Cyprus (the Greek South) adopted the metric system in 1987 there are still as many gallons as litres, miles as kilometres, Fahrenheit as Celsius around, while land is still registered in Ottoman dounums (about a third of an acre) and food is often weighed in okes (1.268kg or 2.8 lbs). The sway of the metric system is even less pronounced in the Turkish North.

Embassies and Consulates

All the diplomatic, journalistic and information-gathering communities are based in Nicosia. The ports of Limassol and Larnaca have their consuls but they are now honorary, if not exclusively social positions, awarded to prominent Cypriots.

In the Republic of Cyprus

British High Commission: Alexander Pallis Street, ✆ (02) 473131

Australian High Commission: 4 Annis Komninis Street, ✆ (02) 473001

American Embassy: Dositheos and Therissos Street, ✆ (02) 465151

Canadian Consulate: 3 Them Dervis Street, ✆ (02) 451630

In North Cyprus

British High Commission (consular section): ✆ (020) 71938
      (*7.30am–1pm Mon–Fri*)

Australian High Commission: Saray Hotel, ✆ (020) 77332
      (*9am–12.30 Tues and Thurs*)

American Centre: Guner Turkmen Sokağı, ✆ (020) 72443
      (*8am–5pm Mon–Fri*)

Cypriots have a marked affinity for holidays whether secular public celebrations, religious anniversaries and even the humble weekends which are enjoyed with undiminished enthusiasm in a series of parades, lunches and family picnics.

Republic of Cyprus (the Greek South)

1 January	New Year's day
6 January	Epiphany
19 January	Name day of Makarios
Green Monday	50 days before Easter
Easter	Good Friday through to Easter Monday
25 March	Greek National day
1 April	Independence Struggle day
1 May	Labour day
3 August	Anniversary of the death of Makarios
15 August	Dormition of the Virgin
1 October	Independence day
28 October	Greek National day
24, 25, 26 December	Christmas Eve, Christmas Day, Boxing Day

North Cyprus

1 January	New Year's Day
23 April	National Sovereignty and Children's Day
1 May	Labour Day
19 May	Youth and Sports Day
20 July	Peace & Freedom Day (biggest annual celebration)
1 August	TMT day (foundation of Turkish Cypriot Resistance Movement)
30 August	Victory Day
29 October	Turkish Republic Day
15 November	Proclamation of Turkish Republic of Northern Cyprus.

Turkish Cypriots celebrate a number of secular anniversaries and recent political achievments with speeches and parades followed by picnics or banquets. In addition there are the religious feasts but these have no fixed date. The Muslim calendar is based on a 354- or 355-day lunar year and so slips ten or eleven days behind the solar based Gregorian calendar which is based on a 364- or 365-day year. *Ramadan*, the month of daylight fasting, is not ostentatiously followed but the four-day holiday preceding it, the *Kurban Bairam*, and the three-day holiday following it, the *Ramazan Bairam*, are. *Mouloud*, the prophet's birthday, falls in September for 1994/5 and *Muharram*, the Muslim New Year, in June.

Panayiria and Easter and Lent Celebrations

Although there are a variety of cultural events organised in the principal towns and resorts over the summer months, which are listed in each chapter, there are really only two sorts of popular festivals in Cyprus: the local *panayiria* and the Easter and Lent celebrations, which are taken much more seriously in the Orthodox East than in Western Europe or America.

Apokreo, Carnival, is in the two weeks before the fifty-day fast of Lent that proceeds Easter. The first week of carnival is known as Kreatini (meat), the second as Tyrini (cheese). The Thursday of meat week, Tsiknopefti, kicks off the action with barbecues, the arrival of King Carnival, followed by a succession of fancy dress trickster visits by children, masked balls and dinners with satirical and lewd songs which culminates in the first Sunday of cheese week. The big day for feasting parade is held on Sunday of cheese week but with subsidiary action from children in masks and fancy dress with trickster visits and satirical songs. Green Monday, which has nothing to do with the Green Line, is a day of family picnics that marks the beginning of fifty-day Lent period before Easter.

The *panayiria* are village and monastery festivals that celebrate the local Saint's Day. They can be considered a sort of communal birthday party spread over two or three days, with a happy combination of fairs, processions of icons, solemn services, family picnics, song, recitals and dances. They occur throughout the year but with a particular concentration around the Dormition of the Virgin, on 14 and 15 August, the Birth of the Virgin on 7 and 8 September and the Raising of the Cross on 13 and 14 September. Most of the more popular and accessible of these are listed in the relevant chapters.

Food and Drink

Coffee at the Café

A cup of coffee and a copper *imbrikia*

Coffee is at the centre of Cypriot life, both in the office and the male-dominated café, which stands shaded under a tree of idleness at the social centre of every village. If you want assistance in finding the key to a church or a path up into the hills, don't barge into the gathering immediately with your questions but take time for a coffee and a gently framed request. Though you may be offered Nescafé, which has become a generic name for all instant coffee powders, ask for the real thing cooked up with water and sugar in the distinctive copper pots with long handles, known as *Imbrikia*. This brew used to be known as Turkish coffee, but since 1974 it has fallen victim to nationalism, and is now known as Greek or Cypriot coffee in Southern Cyprus. It is served with a glass of water and in three forms; without sugar (*sketos* in Greek, *sade* in Turkish), medium sweet (*metrios* in Greek, *orta* in Turkish) or plain sweet (*glykos* in Greek, *sekerli* in Turkish). The bottom quarter of your small cup will remain filled with grounds which can be inverted, by those with the power, to reveal your inclinations and possible futures.

Beer, Ouzo or Brandy at the Bar?

The local lager-like beer is brewed from imported malted barley and kept cold in large bottles. It, like all other drinks at a proper Cypriot bar, will be served with an accompanying saucer of nuts. *Ouzo*, or its Turkish equivalent *Raki*, is another popular drink. It is a clear aniseed-flavoured spirit that turns a cloudy milky white when mixed with water in a long glass. It can be drunk as an aperitif but does not mix well with other drinks: once you have started it is best to stay with it the whole evening. Brandy completes the trinity of favourite local drinks. Some of the better brands can be drunk neat though it is common practice in Cyprus to dilute it with soda or water. For the visitor there is no better introduction to an evening in Cyprus than a brandy sour, made in a long glass half filled with ice into which are poured two parts brandy and one part fresh lemon juice (slightly sweetened), with a dash of angostura bitters and a generous splash of soda.

Eating Out

Cyprus should have a fascinating cuisine as it has been occupied by three cultures renowned for their cooking: the French, the Italians and the Ottomans. Though these influences can be detected they have been overlain by the malign culinary influence of the British, manifested in the 'cold beer and chips with everything' doctrine. Cook shops serving chips, fried eggs, chops, hamburgers, doner kebabs and steaks can be found doing a thriving trade in every coastal resort. This is given variety by Chinese, Indian or Mexican establishments and the odd half-pretentious place with its familiar international hotchpotch of a menu. Fortunately it is also easy to come across dozens of good Cypriot tavernas which seldom charge more than C£6 for a meal. Restaurants have been divided into three categories based on the price of a filling three-course meal with drinks and coffee.

cheap: Anything under C£5 a head.

moderate: Between C£5 and C£15 a head (the great bulk of taverna recommendations fall into this category).

expensive: Those few restaurants which, on average, charge more than C£15 a head and which require some degree of dressing up.

The Cypriot **meze** or **mezedhes** (little delicacies) is the most distinctive island offering. It comprises a succession of appetizers, sometimes as many as 20 which change with each patron and season. At its best it is an almost embarrassingly opulent feast which should be consumed as slowly as possible. A true Cypriot takes just a passing taste at the various dishes in order to do justice to them all. You make no decisions—everything is up to the proprietor—though there is an established order. First come small saucers of olives swimming in a rich garlic, oil and lemon dressing accompanied by fresh bread and a village salad enlivened with local herbs such as rocket with its lemon and olive oil dressing offset by roasted cracked wheat. Then come plates of *tahini* (sesame paste), *taramasalata* (cod's roe with olive oil paté), *melintzanosalata* (mashed, roasted aubergine flavoured with garlic and lemon) or *humous* (chick pea with sesame oil, garlic and cayenne). These might be followed by cold pickled vegetables, usually capers, cauliflowers or beans. Then there is the possibility of *dolmadhes* (small packages of rice and minced lamb rolled in vine leaves), slices of *loukanika* (sausage soaked in red wine, smoked and often served hot from the grill), *lountza* (smoked pork) or *hiromeri* (locally cured ham), fresh or fried *halloumi* (a soft sheep's milk cheese peculiar to the island), *keftedes* (lightly spiced meat balls), *bourekia* (fried pastry rolls filled with mince or cheese) and *sheftalia*, a generic name for the local sausages made from gut stuffed in a hundred different ways with pork, mutton and lites. This is succeeded by either *moussaka* (the familiar Greek mainland baked dish of layers of aubergine, potatoes and mince with bechamel sauce), *afelia* (pork stewed in red wine and coriander), *stifado* (beef or hare casseroled on the bone with onions), *souvlaka* (spit roasted kebabs of lamb or pork often served on pitta bread dressed with tomatoes and onions) or *kleftiko* (lamb roasted in a sealed pot). After a decent interval this can then be followed by a few rich pastries such as *baklava* and the shredded wheat like *kadeifi* (both filled with ground walnuts, almonds and a rich cinnamon-flavoured syrup), *halva* (sesame cake), *daktyla* (almond-filled pastries) and *amygdalota* (almond paste).

Every meal should be concluded with **fruit** for which Cyprus is deservedly famous. For those who have only known imported stuff, it is astonishing treat to taste fruit fresh from the trees. Oranges, melons, cherries, lemons, pears, plums, grapes, figs, loquats, tangerines, pomegranates, peaches, apricots, prickly pears, peaches and apples come cascading down from the orchards to fill the market stalls and pudding plates in a calendar of changing tastes. Dried apricots, cherries, raisins, sultanas and prunes are available throughout the year as is the Cypriot delicacy of *glyko*, fruit preserved in syrup.

Meze is not something that your stomach should be expected to digest every night. On non-*meze* nights, pick out your favourite course, preceded by **soups** like *faki* (lentil), *avgolemono* (chicken broth with rice, egg and lemon), *hortsoupa* (house vegetables) or *trakhana* (stock with crushed wheat and yoghurt). In addition, there is a whole domestic tradition of pilafs, spinach pies, stuffed vegetables, macaroni-like pasta dishes, varied casseroles and imaginative combinations of spiced vegetables and pulses which never reach a taverna or restaurant table. It is an enormous pity and you must continually struggle to correct this imbalance, formed by decades of 'chips with everything', by enthusiastically consuming everything Cypriot and avoid restaurants serving insipid British fare.

One of the great culinary secrets of the island of Cyprus is that there is very little fresh **fish**. The waters around the island are almost completely fished out, and the cluster of states in this corner of the Near East are unable to impose a common conservation policy. Most of the dazzling succession of plates offered in a fish restaurant or a fish *meze*—prawns swimming in hot garlic butter, prawns baked in paprika, fish cakes, kalamari (squid rings deep-fried), octopus grilled or cooked in a sauce of its own ink, crabs, lobster or the dozens of varieties of fish charcoal-grilled, olive-oil-fried or coated in batter—come directly from the Atlantic or Western Mediterranean. The empty boxes of frozen and salted fish from Portugal, Spain and Scotland are usually pushed deep into the rubbish bins in order not to spoil the atmosphere for the tourists. Don't let this put you off ordering fish, but there is no point in pestering the waiter with inquiries as to its freshness.

There is a small quantity of locally caught fish but it is periodic and much sought after. If you are lucky to find a restaurant with a good source you will probably be served *woppa* or *marida*, a sort of local sardine which is fried and eaten on the bone. The distinctive *barbounia* or red mullet is also cooked in the same way. Catfish and dogfish are often neglected by other nations but an enthusiastic Cypriot cook will skin and fillet them and perhaps enhance the muddy flesh by baking it in a sauce. *Menari*, a big barracuda like fish, can also be skinned, filleted and fried to come out looking like a sword-fish steak.

Foreign Residents

There are about 10,000 British, including military personnel, in residence at any given time in the Greek South and about 500 in North Cyprus. Property may be bought freehold or leasehold, and must be recorded at the Land Registry. Until such times as a peace agreement is worked out, it may be wise to acquire land only from those in clear possession of it from before 1974. Pensions may be remitted with ease via the international banks and for your tax liabilities as an expatriate you should inquire from the Inspector of Foreign Dividends, Lynwood Road, Thames Ditton, Surrey, (081) 398 4242 or Claims branch, St John's House, Merton Road, Bootle, © (051) 922 6363.

Health and Medicine

Chemists (FARMAKEIO, *farmakío*) in Greek, *eczane* in Turkish) in Cyprus are well qualified, courteous, speak perfect English and are fully aware of the frailties of their summer guests like sunburn, stomach upsets and dehydration. In the South they are indicated by a large green cross on white and operate a late-night rota and a Sunday opening. These extended opening hours are usually posted on the front door of the pharmacy, in the pages of the Cyprus Mail and can also be found out by telephoning 192, or the emergency number 199.

Media

British, American and European newspapers are available in all the big towns a day after printing and can be supplemented by the *Cyprus Mail*, the local English language daily and at the weekend the *Cyprus Weekly*. The service in North Cyprus is more haphazard but an English language weekly, *Cyprus Today*, is published on Saturday morning.

The *Cyprus Mail* lists the frequencies of various radio programmes, including the BBC world service and the local BFBS (British Forces Broadcasting Service), as well as the satellite TV channels picked up from Greece and other European nations. In addition the Cyprus Broadcasting Corporation, established in 1959, provides a daily diet of Greek-language programmes and news supplemented by special tourist broadcasts in the summer. In North Cyprus there are two local radio channels. Television is beamed in from Turkey and supplemented by four hours of homegrown, government funded BRT, Bayrack Broadcasting Television.

Money and Banks

The Cypriot pound is divided into 100 cents. There are 50 cent, C£1, C£5, C£10 and C£20 notes and 1, 2, 5, 10 and 20 cent coins. The exchange rate is fixed by the government-controlled Central Bank, which means that it is a soft or protected currency which is not allowed to float free and be traded on the international markets. Like most soft currencies it has hedged around with some protective restrictions and you are not allowed to import or export more than C£50 or exchange back more than you can prove to have converted (in other words keep some of your exchange slips) but you are free to bring in and take out as much foreign currency and travellers cheques as you like.

The Turkish Republic of North Cyprus, which has no separate currency, uses Turkish lira (TL) which is passing through a period of inflation. Rates of exchange for the Turkish lira have been changing daily, to create a noticeable difference within a fortnight holiday. Many prices are posted in foreign currency which is usually freely accepted and can be brought into North Cyprus without restriction.

Banking hours in Southern Cyprus are Mon–Fri 8.30–12 though there is a rota operating in the busier tourist resorts to allow a Saturday morning and afternoon service. There are four main banks on the island, the Bank of Cyprus, Hellenic

Bank, Popular Bank and Co-Operative Bank, which are well distributed and backed up by Barclays with its familiar and unattractive plastic blue signs.

The same banking hours operate in the North, though they have elaborate, slow procedures and charge a handling commission. For cash and traveller's cheques it is quicker and easier to use the money exchange kiosks, hotel reception desks or car hire firms, who will look up the exchange rate in the daily paper.

Nightlife

Each of the big coastal resorts, Ayia Napa, Protaras, Larnaca, Limassol and Paphos, have a nightlife centre where you can find a selection of late-night cocktail bars and discotheques built to appeal to tourists. There are also a chain of fairly seedy Floor Show clubs where foreign women strike attitudes and a predominately male clientele consume expensive drinks. There are also a number of taverna on the island that arrange live music for the weekends and the summer holidays. This is supplemented by the more dedicated Greek audiences that visit the small network of late-night music bars that are scattered around the island.

Opening Hours

Public holidays and important festivals are enthusiastically observed in Cyprus when the whole island can close up shop. The more ambitious shops in the heart of a tourist strip might aspire to be open from 8am–7pm but this is only achieved by a small minority of stores. The majority of shops take a lunch break and will close earlier in the winter to give opening hours from about 8am–1pm, 2.30–5.30pm. A much longer lunchtime siesta in the summer gives opening hours of around 8am–1pm and 4–7pm, Wednesday and Saturday are half days, with the doors shutting around 1pm. Nothing happens on Sunday. In North Cyprus it is even more relaxed, with few stores staying open after 6pm.

Opening times of museums and archaeological sites are listed in the relevant text.

Packing

The puckered rocks along the foreshore and the eroded limestone hills in the interior can make for some rough walking so pack a stout pair of shoes, or better still some boots. Ankle boots also give you more confidence if you should meet a snake out walking. You will need a hat, strong sun oil and sunglasses to protect you from the sun's rays even on a holiday in the spring, let alone the summer. A sweater will allow you to sit out and enjoy the cool nights but for the days you will need nothing more heavy than light cotton. Pack long trousers or a long skirt with a shirt with full-length sleeves if you want to be dressed sympathetically for visiting the island's monasteries and churches. No Cypriot taverna would dream of turning away a guest for sartorial failings, but some of the expensive hotels are beginning to toy with dress codes. Bring at least one outfit in which you can look suitably smart whilst you sample a cocktail in a hotel foyer.

On a more pragmatic note you might also include a suction basin plug, some travel-wash for rinsing out your smalls, a torch, a corkscrew, a tin opener, a packet of Immodium (or some other diarrhoea blocker) and something to diminish the activity of mosquitoes.

Photography

Film is available everywhere and can easily be developed in Cyprus. Photography is banned around every military installation on the island, including the entire length of the Green Line. The division of the island in 1974, its proximity to the stormy politics of the Middle East and the attraction to the IRA of a pair of British military base have all worked up a considerable amount of security consciousness. This prohibition should be taken seriously but is seldom cause for an aesthetic regret, though the Green Line in Nicosia has a certain magnetism.

It is also usually forbidden to photograph the interior of churches and monasteries. This banning of the exploding white glare of the flash attachment is both to protect the frescoes physically and as an emotional expression of reverence.

Police and Other Uniforms

The police in Cyprus tend to keep themselves to traffic duties or cosy chats in the barracks. The army, stiffened by professionals on secondment from Greece, mans the southern frontier of the Green Line but is a National Guard type force that frequently returns home to sleep and eat. It has, however, spread the habit of wearing camouflage military clothing all over the island. The various contingents of the UN forces; mostly Canadian, British and Danish, wear their own national uniforms with the addition of a pale blue beret. There are also units of the British army to be seen in their two Sovereign Bases of Dhekelia, east of Larnaca and Episkopi, west of Limassol, with the frontiers guarded by locally recruited base policemen. This familiar dark blue serge can also be seen on the police in Northern Cyprus, who are usually only met directing traffic in the three main towns. The Turkish army and its own white-helmeted ASIZ police force is a much more conspicuous feature of the landscape.

Post Offices and Telephones

Post Offices

In the South: Post offices are open 7.30am–1pm Monday to Friday and 3–6pm on Thursdays; district post offices in main towns also open for a couple of hours in the afternoon on Mondays, Tuesdays and Fridays from 4–6pm in summer and

3.30–5.30pm in winter, and on Saturday mornings from 9–11am. Stamps can be bought from post offices, hotels, news-stands and kiosks. The price of a stamp for a postcard is 21c to the UK, 26c to North America and 31c to Australia and New Zealand; for a letter, 31c, 36c and 41c respectively. Poste-restante services are available in main post offices in city centres, which are listed in the guide.

In the North: The post offices in the four principal towns are open 8–1, 2–5 from Monday to Friday and 9–12 on Saturday. Incoming and outgoing mail is routed via Turkey because of the international postal union boycott. Northern Cyprus issues its own stamps (occasionally also available from postcard salesmen).

Telephones

Cyprus Inland Telecommunications Authority (CITA) runs an efficient operation in the **Republic of Cyprus**. The public telephone boxes are green and can be fed with combinations of 10 and 20 cent coins or with C£2, £5 or £10 phone cards brought from the post office. To ring the UK you will need at least 50c, the code from Cyprus is 00 44 and you should drop the first 0 in the British local code. Ireland is 00 353, Australia is 00 61 and Canada and the USA are 001. You can dial almost anywhere in the world direct with the exception of North Cyprus and Turkey. Local Cypriot codes are given in brackets throughout the guide.

Nicosia district	(02)
Limassol district	(05)
Larnaca district	(04)
Paphos district	(06)
Ayia Napa district	(03)
Polis	(06)
Directory enquiries	191
International operator	194 or 198
Emergency services (police, fire, ambulance)	199

In **Turkish North Cyprus** brass disks of three different values are sold beside the various telephone kiosks that are found outside post offices. Use the same dialling codes for external calls but when telephoning from the United Kingdom to North Cyprus the code to use is (01 090) plus the local dialling code plus the number. Within this guide local codes prefix all numbers and have been placed in brackets.

North Nicosia (Lefkoşa)	020
Girne (Kyrenia)	081
Gazimağusa (Famagusta)	036
Güzelyurt (Morphou)	071
Boğaz	02316

It is disrespectful to enter a church or mosque inadequately dressed. Cypriot men would not dream of entering a holy place in less than trousers and a short sleeve shirt, and while a full skirt or dress is *de rigueur* for local women foreign women can often get away with trousers.

You should take your shoes off before entering a mosque and place them in racks at the back of the prayer hall. Do not enter while prayers are being performed but you are free to explore the prayer halls at any other time.

You are welcome to enter an Orthodox Church while a service is in progress, and may stay for as much or as little as you wish, but don't wander around gaping at the frescoes like a tourist. Even outside a service it is considered rude to stare too critically at an icon, for they are perceived as windows to the divine (for more on icons *see* p. 118). Instead buy some candles to light in honour of friends or relations in need of help, approach an icon and cross yourself (thumb and index finger move to right shoulder, left shoulder, forehead and breast) before stooping to kiss the lower corner of the icon, which is now often protected with glass.

The Orthodox monasteries used to offer accommodation to visitors but since the development of the tourist industry on the island their hospitality was abused by those who had no interest in their faith and life's work. If you are a genuine pilgrim you will still find hospitality; if you are a mere traveller or tourist find yourself a hotel bedroom.

Sex

Cypriot men still expect to marry a virgin bride who is approved of by their family. The lack of pre-marital sex is corrected by a summer season that brings thousands of uninhibited northern women to the shores of Cyprus. In addition there is a red-light area in the centre of Nicosia and a substantial community of independent-minded Asian cabaret dancers who work in nightclubs throughout the coastal resorts. Homosexual sex is theoretically illegal in Greek Cyprus. This contravention of human rights will have to be removed if Cyprus is to join the European Union, but the Cypriot government are currently offering only a commitment never to prosecute. It would be wise in the island of love to travel with a pack of condoms (*profilaktika* in Greek, *preservatif* in Turkish). These can be brought at the airport or in Cypriot pharmacies.

Shopping

Some of the happiest shopping is in the covered markets of the town centres where you can assemble hampers for a succession of Cypriot picnics or a feast for friends on your return home. Here you can pick out decorated **gourds**, rough earthenware **flasks** and plaited grass **cones** amongst the assortment sturdy **raffia** baskets and containers. These can then be gradually filled with pots of honey, bottles of lemon juice, local cheeses, dried nuts, dried fruit, bottled fruit, candied fruit, Turkish delight, fresh fruit and a selection of wine, brandy and Commandaria.

Sturdy wooden **chairs** with plaited raffia seats are produced cheaply on the island but prove quite tricky to take back onto an aeroplane as hand luggage. The distinctive tin-lined **copper coffee ladles** are a more convenient size and, though they are often fashioned on the island, it is slightly disappointing to realize that copper is no longer mined in Cyprus and hasn't been smelted here since early medieval times. You can also shop around for **fabrics**, brightly woven **rugs**, rag rugs and stripy runners as well as for the coloured **embroidery** and much touted island **lace**, in particular Lefkara lace, though first think hard where these traditional lozenge designs are going to be used in your house or whether you will condemn them to imprisonment amongst the crisply ironed piles of your linen cupboard. The island's **jewellery** can be very fine, especially if you share the Greek taste for swaggeringly Baroque silverware. For **silver** you should also look in at the Leventis museum shop in Nicosia, which has some good-quality Byzantine reproductions. Printed **icons**, framed in metal or pasted onto a thick wooden board, can be bought in bazaars throughout the island for a few pounds. The considerably more costly originals can be sought out at monasteries like St Yeoryios Alaminos outside Limassol and Ayia Varvara, on the road up to the monastery of Stavrovouni. Original modern **paintings**, produced from the lively world of Cypriot contemporary art, can be acquired in the galleries of Nicosia and Limassol; their addresses are listed on pp. 126 and 202. Last, but by no means least, there is the island **pottery** which has good cause to be considered the most enduring and by far the most distinctive and exceptional Cypriot art form, as even the briefest tour through any of the museums will reveal. A number of fine potters display their work in their own studios, or mixed in among more brightly coloured imports in galleries thoughout the island (listed in each chapter).

Northern Cyprus is not a shopper's paradise though there are a few places listed in the sections on Kyrenia (Girne) and North Nicosia which are worth a browse before you find the Dizayn 74 pottery on the road west from Kyrenia.

Snakes and Other Dangerous Things

There are half a dozen snakes indigenous to Cyprus. You might come across any of them while walking in the spring and early summer; in midsummer they are relatively inactive during the heat of the day and they hibernate over the winter. They are not aggressive but will defend themselves if disturbed. The bite of the Cypriot blunt-nosed viper (*Vipera lebetina lebetina*), a well camouflaged fat-looking snake with a distinctive horny tail, is the one to avoid. Should you be bitten, use a tourniquet to stop the poison working its way to the heart and then get to hospital as quickly as possible to receive an antidote. However, avoid violent physical exercise as this will circulate the poison. Fortunately you are much more likely to come across one of the Whip snakes, such as the Balkan, Ravergiers or the Large Whip snake. The latter has a striking black back and a very determined movement which can exaggerate its length, known to exceed 6 foot. It can climb trees but is a comparatively welcome sight as it is not venomous.

There are also scorpions, though the sting of the Cypriot variety should only give a painful swelling to a healthy adult. The poisonous spines of the weever fish should also be avoided. Fortunately the weever is quite rare, for its habit of burying itself in tidal sands puts it within reach of practically every holidaymaker. Its venom is agonising and highly toxic and you should seek medical aid immediately. First aid treatment is to immerse the bite in very hot water, as hot as the patient can bear, which both relieves the pain and diminishes the venom.

Sports

In winter there is skiing on Mount Troödos, *see* p. 175. There are a large number of suggested walks in each chapter which take you through some of the best areas for bird watching, botanising, sketching and swimming off deserted coves. Riding is organized throughout the year at a number of stables outside Limassol, *see* p. 203 and weekend race meetings are held at Nicosia, *see* p. 128. All the big resorts, such as Limassol, Ayia Napa, Larnaca, Paphos, as well as smaller places such as Kyrenia and Polis offer every possible variety of water sports in the summer months, including paragliding, water-skiing, snorkelling, windsurfing, canoeing, pedalo-ing, yachting and the more demanding scuba diving training courses. Details are listed in the text. Most of the large hotels have their own tennis courts. In the main towns you will find public tennis courts, squash, badminton, go-carts, bridge clubs and bowling alleys aside from the island obsessions like football and rough shooting.

Tipping

Although there is usually a 10% service charge added to your bill, you should try to look on this as a cover charge and, providing you are happy with your meal, add a bit extra. Taxi drivers like an additional something, but seldom seem to make much of an effort to give you your change before you can make a gift of it. The drivers of service taxis are a different numerical breed and pass exact change to half a dozen passengers as they drive.

Time

Cyprus time is two hours ahead of Greenwich Mean Time and does not alter in the summer.

Toilets

The typical Cypriot lavatory or water closet is not a sturdy porcelain affair with a dangling chain that lets loose a resounding torrent. It is usually a quite inglorious compromise, as is only natural for a hot country with never enough rainfall. They are commonly equipped with a 'rat-trap' plastic seat that can never be persuaded to stand up, a weak head of water and a discreet plastic bin in which to put your soiled paper.

Tourist Information Offices

The Republic of Cyprus (Greek South)

The Cyprus Tourist Office in London is at 213 Regent Street, W1R 8DA, ✆ (071) 734 9822, where three strong-minded women will shower visitors with a plethora of free maps and brochures on request. In the USA their office is at 13 East 40th Street, New York 10016, ✆ (212) 2139100. There are no offices in Canada, Australia, New Zealand or South Africa. In the Republic of Cyprus (the Greek South) there are information offices in the Laiki Yitonia quarter of Nicosia; in Limassol town, Limassol beach and Limassol port; in Larnaca airport and in Larnaca town: in Paphos town, and Paphos airport; in Ayia Napa and (in the summer) in the hill resort of Pano Platres. They can book hotel rooms and point you towards buses or taxis, as well as loading you up with more pamphlets.

TRNC (Turkish North Cyprus)

In London the tourist office for Turkish Republic of North Cyprus is at 28 Cockspur Street, SW1 5BN, ✆ (071) 930 5069, on the south side of Trafalgar Square. It is presided over by the genial, smiling figure of Mr Ozkan Irfanoglu who provides visitors with brochures and directions to the nearby Turkish Cyprus Airways. In North Cyprus the tourist information office at Nicosia, ✆ (020) 75051, is hopelessly out of any visitor's way on the Girne road. The Girne (Kyrenia) office, ✆ (081) 52145 is conveniently placed in an attractive building on the old harbour at 30 Kordon Boyu. There is also a branch at Gazimağusa (Famagusta), ✆ (036) 62864, which is sometimes found open, at 5 Fevzi Cakmak Street, just south of the Venetian Walls.

Water

Tap water in Cyprus is safe to drink and bottled mineral water is available in most restaurants. There is a continual water crisis, and decades of overuse of artesian supplies is gradually drying up springs and lowering the water table. You will find adhesive labels by practically every basin, shower and bath in the country requesting sparing use of water. Solar heating panels are widespread throughout the island. If you intend an early morning or evening wash, hunt for the standby immersion switch which should be turned on a quarter of an hour before use.

Where to Stay

Where to stay in Cyprus, particularly the South, is a problem that requires some advance planning. This is a sad state of affairs, for there are literally hundreds of hotels in Cyprus, but the vast majority of these are soulless concrete blocks run up for the package trade. They are well appointed but apart from the staff that run them they have nothing to do with the island's culture.

For the Cadogan-Guide-reading traveller Cyprus has a very disappointing stock of hotels. There are less than a dozen hotels of character, of which only a couple have entered into that circuit of whispered confidential recommendations among travellers. Nothing has been held back from you, and in addition to the chapter listings a short hit-list of recommended hotels has been given below to help you organize your bookings. This only covers the South, for there is a greater range in the North and not nearly so much pressure on the available rooms.

Hotels in have been listed under three categories:

expensive:	over £35
moderate:	£20–35
cheap:	under £20

The prices are taken for a double room in high season with breakfast. Hotels in the expensive and moderate price range will include a private toilet and bath/shower; not so for the cheap. If you are travelling alone you will be charged single occupancy which is usually fixed at 80% of the double room price. In case of three persons occupying a double room, the third person gets a 20% discount. Children from 1–5 get a 50% discount, from 6–10 a 25% discount if they are occupying the same room. Some hotels offer a winter discount between November and march which ranges from anything between 10 to 50%. Guests are entitled to use their room until 12 noon, with half-rates offered to 6pm, after which a full room rate is payable.

There are hundreds of hotels in the Republic of Cyprus (the Greek South) but only about two dozen with an individual atmosphere or a pleasantly isolated position to appeal to an independent-minded traveller. These can get booked up, particularly in the summer months, so it may be advisable to plan ahead and book, especially if you wish to avoid ending up in one of the more bland and featureless hotels run up for the package trade.

Recommended Hotels

Larnaca: the Sandbeach Hotel or the Four Lanterns for those on a moderate budget, and the Maison Belge and Harry's at the cheaper end of the scale. A trip out to the Lefkarama Hotel in the mountain village of Pano Lefkara is strongly recommended.

Southern Nicosia: Try and stay in the Kennedy, or the cheaper but adjacent Venetian Walls Hotel. In the mountains there is a wider choice with a number of moderately priced hotels in both Pano Platres, Pedhoulas and Troödos, with the isolated Rodon outside Agros making a fine base for the eastern half of the region.

Limassol: In the town centre the Curium Palace Hotel, the Continental and Ellas Guest House cover most price ranges. To the east of Limassol, the village of Pissouri offers the expensive Columbia Pissouri Beach Hotel and the smaller, moderately priced Bunch of Grapes Inn.

Paphos: Try to secure a room in the Axiothea. Out of town there is a wider choice including the Drousha Heights, or one of the smaller, cheaper establishments in the coastal villages of Ayios Yeoryios-Cape Drepanum, Kato Pyrgos or the hill village of Pano Panayia.

In **Turkish North Cyprus** there is not so much demand for hotel rooms, and you can be more relaxed about planning the shape of your holiday. It would be wise to secure an initial base in Girne (Kyrenia), *see* p. 328, before planning trips out to the Soli Inn on the west coast with a variety of accommodation available at Boğhaz, Salamis Bay and Gazimağusa (Famagusta).

To rent a villa or a restored village house inquire from the specialist agencies listed under travel agents.

In the **mountains** there is a much wider choice in a range of prices. A full listing is given in the chapter but a possible itinerary would take you to the New Helvetia in Pano Platres, the Troödos in Troödos, with the Rodon at Argos providing a good base from which to explore the eastern half of the region.

Updated Listings

The Cyprus Tourist Organisation publishes an efficient 100-page 'Cyprus Hotels Guide'. It is updated annually to include room numbers, star ratings, address, telephone, fax numbers and all relevant price details. The North Cyprus Tourist Office provides a similar but less comprehensive service with their 24-page glossy 'Hotels of North Cyprus' brochure.

The island of Cyprus first emerged in that slow dance of continents that is charted in tens of millions of years. From deep within the earth's crust molten rock poured out onto the floor of the Tethys Ocean. In this submarine environment the mineral-rich magma cooled rapidly into distinctive pillow-like folds that piled up like whipped cream into future mountains. About 20 million years ago enormous forces were created by the collision of the African and Eurasian continental plates which created the Alps and also lifted Cyprus up from the sea bed. The island of Cyprus, just like her future goddess, Aphrodite, was foam-born from the salt spray of the Mediterranean.

History and Culture

Hunter-Gatherers and the Neolithic Revolution

A cave to the west of Limassol, piled high with the bones of defenceless elephants and hippopotami, mixed in with stone tools and burnt shells, attest to man's first arrival, in about 8000 BC. Though the evidence is sketchy it now seems that visiting bands of hunter-gatherers, in an orgy of feasting, exterminated the island's unique fauna. The hunters, perhaps haunted by the ghosts of the defenceless animals, did not make a permanent settlement.

At about the same time a great revolution was occurring in the high plateau of Anatolia (eastern Turkey). The invention of agriculture transformed mankind from family groups of mobile hunter-gatherers into permanent communities of farmers. It led to a rapid growth in population and a consistent pattern of emigration which steadily diffused the new techniques. By 7000 BC soil and forest exhaustion in Anatolia escalated the pressure for new land. Refugees from the ensuing conflict were forced onto the unhealthy marshy coast of Syria and Turkey and some then moved on to Cyprus, visible on a clear day.

The First Settlers: the Khirokitians

The first settlers landed on the Karpas peninsula and spread slowly out along the coasts but never settled the central plain or the western third of the island. They brought with them a highly developed culture, described as **Aceramic** (non-pottery-using) **Neolithic**, which lasted from about 7000–5300 BC. We know quite a lot about their habits, for 17 of their settlements have been identified. The excavations at Khirokitia (*see* p. 89) date from this period, as well as less visited sites such as Kastros-Cape Apostolos Andreas, Kalavassos-Tenta and Troulli. The later villages were all carefully positioned, within sight of the sea and on the 400m contour, the natural frontier between farming and herding land. Their diet differed little from ours, for they grew barley, beans, peas, lentils and two varieties of wheat. They herded sheep, goats and pigs; hunted deer, birds and fish; and gathered figs, wild olives, vetch and pistachio. Although they did not use pottery they were skilled craftsmen in stone: polished river boulders were fashioned into bowls, and blades were made from obsidian, a black rock from eastern Turkey.

The Pottery-Using Neolithic and Chalcolithic: 4500–2500 BC

There is a thousand-year gap between the end of the Khirokitian culture, in about 5700 BC, and the beginning of the next, the **pottery-using Neolithic**, in 4500 BC. Prolonged isolation and inbreeding had produced a weakened human stock that was exterminated by disease. However, a similiar range of settlement, the re-use of old sites and some enduring customs (the deliberate flattening of the back of the skull, and the sacred outer walls for each village) link the two cultures.

The new settlers used pottery, whose shapes were largely based on natural containers such as gourds and eggs. They also imported the grapevine to Cyprus. Their villages seldom extended beyond 50 huts and they no longer buried their dead beneath the floor but in separate cemeteries. The violence that forced their original migration from the mainland is reflected in their initial choice of defensible sites reinforced by walls, but these precautions were later abandoned in favour of open, gently sloping farm land and a later group of immigrants were peacefully integrated.

The most noticeable change, in 3900 BC, was caused by a shattering earthquake. The survivors moved from old villages to establish smaller hamlets, and also began to occupy the hitherto empty west. At Lemba, outside Paphos, an archaeological team has recreated a group of three huts which provide a vivid insight into the living conditions of this period. The labelling of this post-earthquake society as the **Chalcolithic** (Copper Age), on the basis of half a dozen pieces of copper, may at first seem presumptuous. However, these fragments of chisels and jewellery indicate a developed understanding of the uses of metal. The Chalcolithic culture is more famous, however, for its unique crucifix idols carved from blue-green picrolite. They appear to have been used as pendants, hanging from the shell necklace placed with the especially honoured dead. Beliefs were centred around the maintenance of the fertility of the earth which was conceived as the Great Goddess. She, like the fields, only gave birth to new life after she had been fertilized with some of the old. Youthful male deities, doomed to an annual sacrifice, as crops were doomed to the harvest, were an expression of this recurring cycle.

The Cypriot Bronze Ages: Early and Middle

The Bronze Age in Cyprus witnessed the growth of a literate, urban culture which communicated with the three sophisticated civilizations of the era: Egypt, Minoan Crete and Hittite Anatolia. It is one of the island's great periods of creativity, when it loomed large in the affairs of the civilized world. Cyprus's importance was as a producer of copper, which mixed with tin to make bronze, a vital resource for any state.

The six centuries of the **Early Bronze Age** began in 2500 BC when a war on the Cilician coast of Turkey brought a group of skilled emigrants to the northwestern corner of the island. They destroyed most of the old settlements and founded new centres, apparently ruling over the indigenous population to whom they introduced cattle, horses, bronze-making, new burial habits and an exuberant ceramic style. Their culture is known almost entirely from its chambered tombs, especially those found at Vounous and Lapithos near Kyrenia. These were generously furnished with food and a rich, imaginative and humorous gallery of pottery grave goods. The introduction of plough animals greatly increased the area of cultivation and the lack of village sites has been tentatively explained by the use of wattle huts or wood-framed tents. There is evidence of a small but growing trade with Crete, Syria and Egypt and no doubt further afield, for though there are several sources of copper ore in the Mediterranean, tin is only found in Eastern Anatolia.

The three centuries of the **Middle Bronze Age**, 1900–1600 BC, saw the spread of this culture away from its base in northwestern Cyprus. The developing copper trade brought increasing friction between communities for control of the inland mines, as revealed by weapons in the warriors' graves, hill forts and a decline in artistic expression. By the end of the period the new harbour towns along the south and east coast, such as Enkomi-Alasia near Famagusta, and Hala Sultan Tekke near Larnaca, were dominant. The old fertility goddess kept her undisputed primacy in religious life but the various male deities—who were both her sons or lovers and a sacrifice to her—grew in complexity with the culture. As well as the young god of the harvest, there is one representing the flocks, the merchants' boats and the continuing prosperity of the copper mines and forges.

The Late Bronze Age: 1600–1050 BC

By 1600 BC there were half a dozen harbour towns all prospering from the rich export trade in copper. The rival Hittite and Egyptian Empires seem to have exercised intermittent authority over the rulers of the Cypriot cities, who sent tribute and may have had to accept the presence of alien garrisons on the island.

The first crude smelting of the copper ore in charcoal furnaces occurred by the mines, which were on the periphery of the forested Troödos mountains. The copper extraction was controlled by a number of inland centres, such as Athienou, Tamassos and Kalavassos, which were sited halfway between the upland mines and the sea. Further smelting occurred at the harbour towns where copper was cast into oxhide-shaped ingots. The ingots were usually shipped, with other goods like pottery and opium, to Ugarit on the coast of Syria, the great entrepôt of the period. Ugarit traded with both Egypt and Mesopotamia and so was familiar with both of the ancient forms of writing: cuneiform and hieroglyphics which were the models from which the so called **Cypro-Minoan script** of Cyprus was developed. It was in widespread use but none of its 80 signs have yet been decoded, so the inscriptions on hoards of baked clay tablets, dated between 1500–1050 BC, remain unread in museum vaults. Rectangular courtyards and rooms replaced the old taste for circular huts and sanctuaries. This new linear awareness is reflected by the distinctive base ring and white slip ceramic ware of the period which was, for the first time, designed to be stood on a flat surface. Most of the important structures, such as palaces, city gates and temples, were built from ashlar, specially dressed blocks of stone. Simple houses were constructed on a low ragstone foundation wall with mudbrick walls and a flat roof, which remained the basic housing unit until this century.

Mycenaean Rule: 1200–1050 BC

In the 14th century BC the distinctive vases of the Mycenaeans painted with such characteristic symbols as charioteers and octopuses, begin to appear in Cyprus. The **Mycenaeans** (also known to us as the Achaeans through the pages of Homer) were free-ranging warrior-merchants from the coast of Greece. Their influence in Cyprus remained mercantile until they were threatened in their own Greek homeland by barbarian invasions from the north. The Mycenaeans, allied with other disaffected groups, took to raiding the wealthy cities of the Near East. Surviving Egyptian records from this period are full of references to the piratical fleets of the 'Sea Peoples'. In 1200 their fleets fell upon Cyprus and devastated the rich Late Bronze Age palaces and cities. These were left smoking ruins, at about the same time that a much more famous group of Sea Peoples were besieging Priam's Troy. At one or two sites, such as Enkomi and Kition, the sacked cities were later rebuilt and strongly fortified as centres of Mycenaean power. These Cypriot city states, ruled by a Greek-speaking upper class, have produced some of the more inspiring architecture (whose slight remains may be seen at Kition and Enkomi) as well as the fabulous material objects of the Late Bronze Age that are displayed in the Cyprus Museum at Nicosia, such as the horned god of the ingot.

The Coming of Iron, the Dorians and a Dark Age: 1050–850 BC

It was a glorious but short swan-song, for 150 years later further waves of sea-borne Greek-speaking invaders, now armed with fearful **iron** weapons, followed in the wake of the Mycenaeans. These settlers, each apparently more barbaric but better armed than the last, are collectively known as the **Dorians**. Between 1075 and 1050 they destroyed the literate cosmopolitan culture of the Late Bronze Age city states and permanently introduced Greek to the island. Apart from their wheel-produced pottery (labelled Cypro-Geometric after its strict circular decoration) the two centuries following the Dorian conquest are a virtual blank. It was a cultural **dark age**, filled by heroic warring chieftains who fought over the recently conquered land from dozens of fortified citadels.

The Phoenician-led Renaissance: 850–750 BC

Phoenician merchants were responsible for the restoration of trade routes and cultural contacts that had been severed during the fall of the Late Bronze Age civilizations. The Phoenician homeland was a loose confederation of half a dozen cities along the coast of Lebanon. Nearby Cyprus with her rich woods and copper mines was one of their first ports of call. By the mid-9th century BC a Phoenician colony was already well established at Kition (modern Larnaca), with small but influential trading communities in the other emerging towns. As well as luxury goods for the royal courts, such as fine textiles, engraved gemstones, carved ivories, metalwork, glass, paper and their famous purple cloth, the Phoenicians brought with them another of their inventions, the **alphabet**. This form of writing, based on just 20 or so notations for different sounds, remains in use today and is endlessly adaptable. Within a century of its importation to Cyprus it was being used by the Greek-speaking settlers and those who still spoke the language of the Cypriot Bronze Age. Amathus and Palea Paphos were the strongholds of the latter, and retained their shrines to the old fertility goddess of the island, who was addressed as Astarte by the Phoenicians and Aphrodite by the Greeks.

The Golden Age of Archaic Cyprus: 750–475 BC

By the middle of the 8th century BC Cyprus was once more the home to a sophisticated culture. Through its exports of copper and wood, its ships and its central position in the eastern Mediterranean, it was an important entity in the affairs of the civilized Near East. As well as sharing in the cultural exchanges of the period it had a distinctive cultural identity of its own. The **free field** pottery of this period is painted with markedly individual spiritual images, such as the sacred birds of the goddess, the budding lotus of spring, the pre-ordained sacrifice of the bull and the swastika (which expresses the inter-connection of the four seasons). The stone carvings—the luxuriant poses of temple-boys, the bejewelled panoply of a bare-chested high priestess and the patrician with his coiffured beard—are all possessed by an alluring combination of sensuality and spiritual calm.

Archaic Cyprus also served as an important melting pot or conduit for the various Mesopotamian, Syrian and Egyptian forms from which the classical architecture of the Greeks would emerge. The island enjoyed a remarkable linguistic variety in this period: there was Phoenician, at least two distinct island forms of written Greek as well as Eteo (true) Cypriot, the language of the indigenous islanders. Politically, Cyprus was divided between a dozen city-states each ruled by its dynasty of high-priest kings, though due to temporary annexations the number of Cypriot kingdoms varies between seven and twelve in any of the ancient lists.

The Twelve Kingdoms: 707–325 BC

In the three centuries between 707 and 325 BC Cyprus passed under the suzerainty of a dazzling succession of Near Eastern Empires. The Assyrian King Sargon II appears to have been the first to collect tribute from the Cypriot kingdoms in 707. Assyrian hegemony was replaced by that of Egypt in 570 followed by that of Persia in 521. The two hundred years of Persian rule, studded with intrigues and failed revolts, only ended when the entire Persian Empire was conquered by Alexander the Great at the end of the 4th century BC.

For the most part these distant empires were content to rule through the existing kingdoms which provided occasional tribute and naval assistance. Beneath this apparent order the local politics of the island buzzed with the rivalries and ambitions of the dozen city states, which formed and reformed into a bewildering assortment of factions and temporary alliances. By the 5th century BC the internal island politics was dominated by the rivalry between the two leading cities: **Salamis** (just north of Famagusta) with its predominately Greek culture and Phoenician **Kition** (modern Larnaca) which tended to be pro-Persian. The three cities in the interior, **Tamassos** (Politiko village), **Idalion** (Dhali) and **Golgoi** (Athienou), prospered from their proximity to the mines but were overawed by either Kition or Salamis. The seven other cities on, or just in from, the coast were more assertively independent but consumed by fierce rivalry with a neighbour. In an island-wide dispute **Marion**, **Amathus** and the two Phoenician settlements of **Lapithos** and **Kyrenia** tended to join Kition's pro-Persian party while **Soli**, **Kourion** and **Palea Paphos** supported Salamis and the pro-Greek league.

The Cypro-Classical Period: 475–323 BC

The succession of revolts by various Cypriot cities against Persian rule (beginning with the **Ionian revolt** of 499) was both a mixture of Greek military adventurism and a reflection of the growing Hellenic culture of the island. From the 5th century BC the island's indigenous Archaic culture was gradually superseded by sophisticated Greek imports, most noticeably the glorious red and black figured vases from Attica and the graceful stone carvings of Ionia. **King Evagoras**, one of the most dynamic rulers of Salamis, pushed through an intensive Hellenization of his state at the end of the 4th century BC and was the first to use the Greek alphabet and coinage. His attempt to create a unified Greek kingdom of Cyprus seemed on the point of succeeding in 381 BC when he lay siege to Kition, the only city that still defied him. However, the destruction of his navy, in a battle fought within view of the besieged walls of Kition, completely destroyed this scheme.

Two generations later, the kings of the two most militantly Greek cities in Cyprus, Salamis and Soli, were enthusiastic allies of **Alexander the Great**. Their navies assisted in the siege of Tyre, the celebrated island-mother-city of the Phoenicians, that alone defied the young conqueror. The **destruction of Tyre** in 332 BC brought enormous rewards to the kings of Salamis and Soli, but it also signalled a new authoritarian order. The next year Alexander abolished the individual coinage of the dozen cities and issued coins for the whole island under his name. The old system of weights and measures was also replaced by his new Imperial system based on that of Athens.

Hellenistic Rule: 323-31 BC

The Hellenistic Period witnessed the destruction of Cyprus' institutions and its independent identity as it was transformed into an efficiently run province.

On the death of Alexander the Great in 323 BC his Empire was divided amongst his generals who fought over the spoils in the **War of the Diadochi**, 'the successors', which intermittently raged from 323 BC–280 BC. Cyprus was poised on the frontier between Ptolemy's Egypt, Seleucus's Middle East and the Antigonid fleet commanded by **Demetrius Poliorcetes** (the conqueror of cities). The island briefly passed under Antigonid control after Demetrius' great naval victory outside Salamis in 306 BC but it later fell to the Ptolemy. The dozen cities of Cyprus had divided in customary fashion: the old Salamis-pro-Greek faction supported **Ptolemy** and the old Kition-pro-Persian faction supported the Antigonids. But the rules had changed. During the fighting, Kition, Lapithos, Kyrenia and Marion were ruthlessly destroyed by the army of Ptolemy and their populations enslaved.

Nor were the allies of Ptolemy safe. Within a few years of the official annexation of the island in 294 BC the ancient ruling dynasties of Palea Paphos, Amathus and Salamis had been exterminated. The old ruling class was replaced by a professional body of non-Cypriot officials, appointed from the Ptolemaic capital of Alexandria which had been recently founded to give a Greek identity to Egypt. All the old languages and scripts were forbidden and replaced with standard Ionian Greek. Governors were appointed over each city and the island divided into four provinces. The *strategos*, a Macedonian governor-general, assumed complete control, which extended even to religious cults. He was assisted by the *anti-strategos* who controlled the island's copper mines and a pair of *grammateis* who ran separate army and navy establishments. Greek theatre, musical and athletic contests were encouraged alongside official Ptolemaic cults in honour of the ruling dynasty and of Serapis, a deity that synthesized elements of Greek and Egyptian religion. The pottery and carvings of the period reflect a growing conformity with the wider Hellenistic world that stretched all the way east to modern Pakistan.

Rome: the Heir to the Hellenistic Monarchies: 168–31 BC

The **Seleucids** (another dynasty descended from one of Alexander's generals who ruled over Syria) seized control of Cyprus in 168 BC. This coup was, however, reversed by decree of Rome which had begun to exercise an unofficial 'protectorate' over Ptolemaic Egypt. Rome's actual annexation of Cyprus in 58 BC from her client state was inevitable, though the timing of the decision was purely based on mercenary Roman party politics. The annexation of Ptolemaic Cyprus was organized by Clodius Pulcher, an aristocratic urban-terrorist, who was one of the chief supporters of **Julius Caesar**. Caesar and his friends were always strapped for cash and they netted 7,000 talents, a vast sum, from the confiscation of the Ptolemaic treasure on Cyprus. The island was later given to **Cleopatra** as a thank-you present from Julius Caesar after she gave birth to his child Caesarion. In 31 BC Octavian, better known by his later title of the **Emperor Augustus**, conquered Egypt. A year later he ordered the murder of the young prince of Cyprus, Caesarion, the son of Julius Caesar and Cleopatra, the last of the Ptolemys.

A Province of Rome: 31 BC–AD 325

The rule of Rome is one of the least exciting but most prosperous periods in Cypriot history. There is no evidence of colonial settlement or any attempt to impose Latin or an alien creed on the island. There is ample evidence of the Imperial restoration of many of the island's famous sanctuaries as well as the overhaul of the island's road network, harbours and water supply. In terms of population, civic amenities and fertility, this period has yet to be equalled.

After the island had been annexed to the Empire by Augustus in 31 BC it was demilitarized; apart from that little was changed. Nea Paphos remained the seat of government and the island, just as in the Ptolemaic period, was divided into the four districts of Salamis, Nea Paphos, Amathus and Lapithos (which fit curiously well with the modern districts of Famagusta, Paphos, Limassol and Kyrenia).

The governor or *proconsul* was only appointed for a year at a time and was assisted by a financial expert, the *quaestor provincae*, with a legate as his deputy. He collected taxes, oversaw the road network, water supply and major civic projects. A separately appointed procurator looked after the mines that were owned by the Emperor and also served to keep an eye on the ambitions of the proconsul. The *curator civitatis* kept an eye on the municipal administration of the 12 cities, for then, just as now, local city authorities were always being accused of over spending. The *limenarcha Cypri* supervised the conditions of the harbours. Popular assemblies in each city elected their own magistrates and town council, which approved the appointment of professional officials. There was no island-wide elective council, though the **Koinon Kyprion**, which oversaw the cults of the deified emperors, various common festivals and issued the lower denominations of the coinage, came close to acting as one.

The most famous event of the Roman period is the missionary journey of **St Paul** and **St Barnabas** in AD 45, as recorded in the *Acts of the Apostles*. They took boat from Antioch to Salamis, Barnabas's home town, before proceeding across the island to Paphos. Their surprising conversion of the proconsul **L. Sergius Paulus** has recently been given independent corroboration. For their next destination after Cyprus was the Roman colony of Pisidian Antioch, hundreds of miles into the Anatolian interior. It appeared a bizarre choice for a pair of Jewish missionaries until inscriptions revealed that the Sergi Pauli, the family of the proconsul of Cyprus, owned vast estates in the area and were prominent in local politics.

The second most famous event of the period appears to have undone the first. In AD 116 a **Jewish insurrection** broke out throughout the Levant and the Jews in Salamis, led by one Artemion, seized control of the city. The lack of a permanent garrison on the island allowed the revolt to spread and it was only finally crushed in a bloody campaign after a veteran cavalry commander (a classical Othello, in that he was a Moorish prince who had taken service under Rome to fight the eastern Empire of Parthia) landed on the island. Some 240,000 are reported to have died (certainly an exaggeration) but this seems to have included the island's nascent Christian community which would have appeared as just a group of Jews.

Early Byzantine Period: AD 330–649

The accession of the **Emperor Constantine,** and his foundation of Constantinople as the avowedly Christian capital of the Roman Empire in AD 330, heralds the coming of **Byzantium** to the eastern Mediterranean. In Cyprus there appears to have been a very gradual transformation. Excavations have yet to reveal any church before the 4th century, whilst gorgeous pagan mosaics and temples to lustral Zeus were still being created as late as the 6th century.

St Spyridon, the rigidly Orthodox Cypriot bishop, was a powerful early influence. At the first Council of the Church, at Nicea in AD 325, he was one of only three Cypriot bishops. By AD 400 there were 15, one for every major town. This body of men was under the authoritarian control of **St Epiphanius**, the energetic Archbishop of Salamis (renamed Constantia in this period), who dominated the Cypriot church from AD 368 to his death, aged 90, in 403.

A series of devastating **earthquakes** (Paphos was the first to be hit, in 332, then Salamis in 342, followed by Kourion in 365) diminished the principal cities of the island. It marked the changing of the era's as the erection of substantial new cathedrals over the earthquake rubble allowed Christianity to physically dominate the cities, whose classical edifices—the temples, theatres and stadium—were left in ruin. In the 5th century the miraculous discovery of the tomb of St Barnabas allowed the Church of Cyprus to prove its apostolic foundation and gain its independence from the Patriarch of Antioch.

By the 7th century the island was an oasis of calm and order. It had grown prosperous from the profits of the new silk industry and had been chosen as temporary headquarters by the **Byzantine Emperor Heraclius**, in preference to any of the mainland cities which had been devastated by the long Persian wars.

A Second Dark Age: AD 649–965

This all ended in 649 when a Saracen army led by Muawiya sacked the island and destroyed its walled cities. He returned again in 653 to plunder the miserable survivors, but this time left a garrison of 12,000 men to control them and encourage Muslim settlers. In 688 **Emperor Justinian II** and **Caliph Abdel Malik** agreed to demilitarize the island and share the taxes extracted from the mixed communities of Muslims and Christians. For the next 300 years the chronicles record only a botched attempt at compulsory Christian emigration in 690, a brief attempt by Basil I to reoccupy the island and a succession of raids and naval battles between the Byzantine Empire and the Caliphate, which accused each other of being the first to break the truce. Urban life in the island was finished, the coast deserted and the population moved inland to the safety of the hills and forests.

Return to Byzantium: AD 965–1191

The Byzantine Emperor **Nicephorus Phocas**, having conquered the neighbouring coast of Cilicia and defeated an Egyptian fleet, was able to reoccupy Cyprus peacefully in AD 965. In order to secure the island against the Saracen threat the Muslim inhabitants were encouraged to convert or emigrate. A series of mountain fortresses above the northern coast were built to give early warning of raiders to the permanent garrison. Secure inland headquarters were created with the foundation of Nicosia (Lefkoşa) where three high officials set up their rival courts. The *doux*, the military governor was the paramount official, a man of high standing, often closely connected to the court at Constantinople, who enjoyed additional prestige as the protector of pilgrims visiting the Holy Land. The *protospatharius* was in charge of all financial and judicial affairs and tended to be a professional administrator who also kept a weather eye on the ambitions of the governor. At near permenant loggerheads with either or both of these officials was the **archbishop**, who tried to protect the island from the more outrageous tax demands. The Byzantine Empire was rigidly thorough in its tax collection but it also gave much back to the people in firm government and in its building programmes. The 10th-century churches of St Lazarus, in Larnaca and St Barnabas, outside Salamis, though they are much diminished by age and clumsy restorations, are still the proudest Orthodox buildings on the island. The astonishing elegance of the frescoes that survive from this period is alone sufficient to assure that it is one of the great periods of Cypriot history.

The success of the **First Crusade** at the end of the 11th century increased the prosperity of the island which benefited from the new markets for its produce on the coast of Palestine and the increased pilgrim traffic. However, by the mid-12th century the military decline of Byzantium was obvious. In 1184 **Isaac Comnenus**, who was also a member of the ruling Byzantine dynasty, imposed himself as *doucas*, governor, and then later announced himself as ruler of an independent Cyprus. Isaac proved to be avaricious and tyrannical and was hated by both the church and the people. He managed to make good use of his Norman brother-in-law, William II of Sicily, who helped him beat off an Imperial attempt at reconquest. However, even if Isaac Comnenus had been the most wise and beloved ruler it is doubtful if he could have preserved the fragile independence of the island. Though the Crusader conquest of Cyprus appears almost accidental, it was in fact part of the process that had begun with the schism between the Catholic and Orthodox Churches and which was to end 13 years later with the sack of Constantinople by the **Fourth Crusade**.

The Year of Four Rulers, 1191–92

Saladin's victorious battle of the Horns of Hattin in 1187 had virtually destroyed the Crusader kingdom of Jerusalem and to recover it the armies of the Third Crusade (led by Philip II of France, Richard I of England and the German emperor, Frederick Barbarossa) desired a secure base. Isaac's shifty treatment of King Richard's sister and future wife, who had been separated from the English Crusader fleet as it sailed to Cyprus, provided a pretext for the invasion and conquest.

King Richard appointed English bailiffs to govern Cyprus before proceeding to the main business of the Crusade and landing at Acre in Palestine. Hearing of a revolt in Cyprus in his absence he struck a deal with the **Knights Templars**. They bought Cyprus for 100,000 dinars with a cash deposit of 40,000.

The Knights were fine bankers but made such a mess of ruling—massacring an Easter crowd at Nicosia which they feared might be rebellious—that they soon withdrew from the contract. Richard then offered it to **Guy de Lusignan**, who had been his second-in-command during the conquest of Cyprus and was proving an increasingly inconvenient figure in Palestine. Guy was good looking and honourable but not from the top echelons of the nobility. The younger son of a baron from Poitou, he had risen to become king of Jerusalem, after falling in love and marrying Sybil, its heiress. In command at the disastrous battle of the Horns of Hattin, where he had been captured, he had lost credibility and his position became more difficult after Sybil's death. There was general relief when he accepted the fief of Cyprus from Richard I and made the way clear for a new king of Jerusalem. All that was left was for Guy to raise a loan of 40,000 dinars from some local bankers, to pay back the money the Templars had advanced to Richard.

The Lusignan Crusader State: 1192–1489

The 300 years of Crusader rule has given the island a magnificent heritage of Gothic buildings whose soaring vaults, exquisite stone carving and crumbling battlements provide it with some of its most striking monuments. The language, religion and culture of this period has been completely extirpated but the tales from the lives of the kings and queens of Cyprus still haunt the land.

Guy (1192–4) and his brother **Aimery** (1194–1205) were energetic rulers and established the pattern of Lusignan authority. Guy was able to attract to Cyprus 300 knights and 200 mounted sergeants from those Crusader families who had lost their lands in Palestine. This body of fighting men constituted the basic power of the regime. Though almost all of French origin, some of them were the fourth generation to have lived and fought in the Near East. They were imposed as a landed upper class over the Greek-speaking villages. This Crusader nobility was allowed to build defensible tower houses (such as can be seen at Pyla and

Alaminos) but the **eight great fortified castles** of the island (at Nicosia, Famagusta, Paphos, Limassol, Kyrenia, St Hilarion, Buffavento and Kantara) were all held by the crown. The Assizes of Jerusalem, which had defined the relationship between the ruler, nobility and burghers in Crusader Palestine, was adopted as a constitution. It provided for a High Court of barons and a Low Court of merchants to check arbitrary rule, though the ever-present threat of Saracen invasion or Cypriot rebellion kept the ruling class united. The rival authority of the Orthodox Church was diminished by a series of repressive decrees over the 13th century. The twelve Orthodox bishoprics were reduced to four, banished to the countryside and made officially dependent on the four Catholic bishops of Nicosia, Paphos, Limassol and Famagusta. Aside from a few privileged Greek merchants and artisans in the towns, the natives were divided into three classes. The *paroikoi* were serfs bound to the land they worked. They gave a third of their produce to the lord of the manor, worked two days a week for him as well, submitting to the fines and judgements of his manorial court. The *perpariari* paid an annual sum in lieu of labour, but in dignity were much eclipsed by the *lefteroi,* who were free men holding land by tenure or lease.

The capstone to this state was provided in 1196 when Aimery did homage to the Holy Roman Emperor and in return had his status raised from lord of Cyprus to king. The next year, by marrying Isabel the heiress of Jerusalem, he added another crown to his coat of arms, though by this period the kingdom of Jerusalem comprised only the port of Acre.

The Golden Age of Lusignan Cyprus: 1205–1372

However, the Lusignan state was soon to be severely tested. In 1218 **Hugh I** died leaving as heir a nine-month-old baby. Queen Alice, who was a member of the eminent Crusader family of **d'Ibelin**, held the regency with the assistance of her two brothers, Philip and John. In a desperate civil war from 1229–33 they succeeded in fighting off the attempt by the German emperor, **Frederick Hohenstaufen**, to take control of Cyprus.

The young **King Henry** showed little evidence of his maternal inheritance. He was fat, pacific and indolent, but managed to father a child just a few months before he died. His wife, Queen Plaisance, ruled for 14 years as regent until the death of her son, when the succession passed to a cousin, **Hugh III** (1267–84). He is remembered for his attempts to prop up the crumbling Crusader presence in Palestine, undermined by the ferocious rivalry between Venetians and Genoese and between the Knights Hospitallers and the Knights Templars.

His son **Henry II** (1285–1324) is one of the more intriguing Lusignan monarchs for though he was a brave, pious and courteous man he was also afflicted with epilepsy. His scheming younger brother imposed his rule for a few years but Henry was later returned to power. At the fall of Acre (the last remnant of

Crusader Palestine) to a Saracen siege in 1290 he proved his courage when he supervised the evacuation and was the last to take ship from the embattled harbour. This apparent catastrophe was in fact a boon for Cyprus, as she was both relieved of the heavy expense of Palestine and became the central entrepôt of the enormously profitable Near Eastern trade. **Hugh IV** (1324–59) presided over this halcyon period of prosperity when many of the finest Gothic churches were built. The king loved literature and hunting equally and lived contentedly at peace with his Muslim trading neighbours.

The reign of the amorous **Peter I** (1359–69) brings Lusignan Cyprus to its swashbuckling zenith. Peter, who was obssessed with relaunching the Crusades, is approvingly referred to in the lines of Chaucer, Villon, St Peter de Thomas and numerous island bards. An early raid on the Cilician coast, where he massacred the inhabitants of a defenceless port, wetted his appetite for a bigger campaign. After a 3-year fund-raising trip around the palaces of Europe, he launched an attack on Alexandria in 1365. He captured this great city but proved the bankruptcy of the Crusader ideal by massacring the population and sailing away, like any barbarian looter, with his ships piled high with booty. Peter's tyrannical behaviour and wide-ranging adulteries led to his assassination in Nicosia three years later. His 12-year-old son **Peter II** (1369–82) succeeded to the throne.

Italian Influence over the Lusignan State: 1372–1489

The coronation of the young King Peter at Famagusta in 1372 deteriorated into a riot which ended with the sacking of the Genoese quarter of the city. The next year, a Genoese army returned to ravage the island so thoroughly that only a few castles and guerilla bands remained to oppose them. The weak Lusignan resistance was further weakened by a murderous feud between the widowed Queen Eleanor of Aragon and her brother-in-law the regent, Prince John of Antioch. (*see* p. 340).

King James I (1382–98) began the first three years of his reign as a Genoese prisoner and was only permitted to land on Cyprus in 1385 after he had ceded the port of Famagusta and all custom dues to Genoa. In 1393 he inherited the additional title of king of Armenia, an honorific sop for a monarch with a precarious enough hold on his own nation. His son **Janus** (1398–1432) dedicated himself to the struggle against Genoa and twice laid siege to Famagusta. He failed on both occasions but faced a much greater humiliation when his entire army was destroyed by the Egyptians at the **battle of Khirokitia** in 1426 (*see* p. 90). Janus was captured, mocked through the streets of Cairo and only allowed to return to Cyprus two years later, after he had accepted the overlordship of the sultan and agreed to pay an annual tribute. The king slowly withered away with grief and handed control over to his handsome, effeminate and lustful son, John.

King John's reign (1432–58) was a time of assimilation between the hitherto separate cultures of the Orthodox Greeks and the Catholic Crusaders. In both architecture and language this period produced a curious hybrid of Greek, French and Italian influences. This mingling of cultures was also reflected in the powerful women who occupied the king's bed. His first wife, Medea Palaeologi, his second wife, Helena Palaeologina (the granddaughter of a Byzantine emperor) and even his mistress, Marietta of Patras, were all Greek and intensely proud of it.

The accession of John's only legitimate child, his daughter Charlotte, in 1458 was quickly challenged by her illegitimate and charismatic half-brother, known either as **James II** (1460–73) or James the Bastard. James patched together an alliance between Venice and Egypt which gave him temporary use of a fleet of 80 ships and an army which landed at Ayia Napa in 1460. Within four years he had subdued his sister's last castle and finally expelled the Genoese from Famagusta. For nine years he presided over a united and independent Cyprus, but this renaissance was not to last. Within a year of his marriage to the Venetian **Caterina Cornaro** he was dead and his posthumous son, **James III**, the last Lusignan monarch, followed him to the grave a year later.

A Province of Venice: 1489–1571

Queen Caterina officially reigned for 13 years after the death of her husband but all power was exercised by her Venetian advisers. Even this pretence was abandoned in 1489 when her brother was sent to persuade her to abdicate in favour of the Venetian Republic. The terms he agreed with his sister would have tempted anyone into early retirement. Caterina departed with royal salutes and was given the little Italian city of Asolo to rule over, assisted by a regal pension and a palace in Venice.

The Venetian Senate appointed a governor, or *proveditor*, assisted by two councillors who together were known as the three rectors. They were the chief judges, generals, tax collectors and administrators of Cyprus, though their ambitions were checked by their two year appointment and by the captain in charge of the permanent garrison on the island. The three rectors disbanded the Assizes of Jerusalem, and the landed estates of the old Crusader families increasingly passed into the hands of Italians. As a graphic illustration of the changed order, the old royal castles were slighted and only Kyrenia, Nicosia and particularly Famagusta prepared for the challenge of artillery warfare.

Though there are examples of assimiliation at the top reaches of society, the mass of the Cypriot population remained down-trodden serfs. The Venetians recognized the essential unpopularity of their rule and did not allow any Greeks to serve in their army. The military, rather than commercial, nature of Venetian rule was paramount, and while they prepared the island for defence they were scrupulous not to cause the Ottomans any offence. They continued to pay the tribute agreed by the captive King Janus to the Mameluke sultan of Egypt.

The Ottoman Conquest: June 1570–July 1571

From the late 15th century the Ottoman Empire began to extend its control over the Greek islands. The conquest of Egypt in 1517 and of Rhodes in 1522 put Cyprus on the front line. The delay in the Ottoman invasion was thanks to embroilment on other frontiers and to Venice's punctual payments of tribute. The accession of **Selim II** in 1566 saw a switch in Ottoman priorities due, according to a mischievous folk tale, to the Sultan's obsessive fondness for Cypriot wine.

In planning the invasion of Cyprus, the Ottoman high command was more wary of the Christian fleet than the fortifications in Cyprus. An alliance between Spain, Venice and the Papacy had put a fleet of 200 ships into the eastern Mediterranean. In the spring of 1570, the Ottoman fleet divided into three squadrons, criss-crossed the Aegean to hide its intention and then united to carry the invasion force across to the southern coast of Cyprus. The epic sieges of Nicosia and Famagusta are described on p. 123 and 353, but in the background was the continuous expectation on both sides of intervention by the Christian fleet based at Crete. It came in October 1571 when virtually the entire Ottoman fleet was destroyed at Lepanto 10 weeks after Famagusta had fallen to a 13-month siege. At the peace negotiations two years later the grand vizier told the Venetian ambassador, 'by conquering Cyprus we have cut off one of your arms, but by defeating our fleet you have only shaved our beard. You can't expect another arm to grow to replace the cut one, whereas the shaven beard always grows again and even more abundantly'.

Ottoman Liberation and Turkish Settlement

The conquest of 1571 was a liberation for the bulk of the Greek Orthodox population. Indeed in some areas, such as Lefkara, there had been local risings against the Venetians in support of the Ottoman invasion. Serfdom was abolished and the peasant families were given the freehold of the land they had worked for centuries. The Orthodox Church was also freed from centuries of control by the Latin hierachy and its previous tradition of independence reasserted under a revived archbishopric. On the other hand, the Catholic Church of the Crusader and Venetian rulers was destroyed. Its buildings were confiscated and converted into mosques, warehouses or sold to the Orthodox Church. Catholics on the island were given the choice of conversion (either to Islam or Orthodoxy) or exile.

At the same time a number of soldiers, assisted by drafts of colonists from Anatolia, were settled on the island. Apart from a reservation within the walls of Famagusta, there was no strategic placement of these immigrants, and they were fairly evenly distributed around the island. This policy was energetically pursued until about 30,000 Muslim Turks had been settled on the island amongst an indigenous population of perhaps 150,000 Greek Cypriots. This proportion, around 1:5, is still true today.

Ottoman Cyprus in the 17th and 18th Centuries

The Ottoman conquest of Cyprus coincided with the gradual stagnation of the Near Eastern economy due to the discovery of the Atlantic trade routes in the mid-15th century. Within a century, the busy waters of the eastern Mediterranean had become a neglected backwater. Many of the island's most profitable crops, such as sugar, were also ruined by American competition in the 17th century. This was partly offset by cotton plantations which tied in well with a tradition of producing fine textiles. Morphou exported linen, the Marathasa valley was known for its woollens and Nicosia famed for its silks and gold embroidery.

Throughout this period there was a series of armed tax revolts which often united both Greek and Turk against an especially avaricious governor or an over-mighty community leader. The system of selling the office of governor (*paşa*), the collection of taxes by ethnic group or *milet* and the farming, or auctioning, of taxes, helped establish a powerful body of community leaders on the island. The actual governor of the island, though he commanded a small garrison of 3,000 troops, was relatively powerless. He held authority for a brief period and was principally concerned with recouping the purchase of his office with the minimum of fuss and maximum profit. He was only able to do this through the *aghas* (uncles) of the Turkish community and the bishops of the Greeks. The archbishop grew particularly influential, and in 1660 became recognized as the official representatives of the Greek Cypriots, with rights of direct access to the sultan's palace in Istanbul. In 1754 the archibishop was made responsible for the collection of taxes and later gained the right to appoint the dragoman of the serai, who was the head of the civil service. By the early 19th century the archbishop had almost become of greater consequence than the governor.

The 1821 Greek War of Liberation and the mid-19th Century

These gradual and promising developments were reversed in 1821. In 1818 **Archbishop Kyprianos** became a member of the *Philike Hetaireia*, a secret society that planned to establish an independent Greek state out of the Ottoman Empire. Kyprianos was fully aware of Cyprus's isolated position and its resident Turkish garrison, and only felt able to promise financial and material support.

In 1821 revolts broke out all over the Greek-speaking provinces of the Ottoman Empire and the Turkish governor of Cyprus, having previously requested reinforcements from Syria, received permission from the sultan to launch a campaign of terror. First the archbishop was hanged and the next day the other Greek chief clerics, officials and merchants in Nicosia were beheaded. Detachments of soldiers were despatched to the districts in an organized campaign of looting and lynching. This was repeated later in the year with greater and more widespread violence with the arrival of more Ottoman troops from Egypt.

The terror campaign effectively destroyed Cyprus's chance of joining the Greek rebellion. It also indelibly stamped Greek Cypriots with a loathing of the Ottoman administration and a desire for *enosis*, or union with the independent Greece that was born of this traumatic period.

After the peace of 1830, the Ottoman sultan, Mahmud II, and his son, Abdul Mejid I, made an attempt to reform the Empire's administration. Taxes were now collected directly, but few of the well-intentioned new laws that aspired to turn the Ottoman Empire into a multi-ethnic commonwealth were put into practice.

The British Period: 1878–1960

Apart from a few eccentric travellers and a medieval king, Britain had had no involvement with Cyprus before 1878. But the island's sudden and peaceful absorption into the British Empire is not difficult to explain. The keystone of British imperial policy in the 19th century was to protect the sea route to India, and to support the Ottoman Empire against the ambitions of an ever-expanding Russia. The Crimean War of 1853–6 had been fought for just such a purpose.

In 1875 British policy took a vital shift when Disraeli purchased a key block of Suez Canal shares. Three years later the Congress of Berlin was convened to defuse another crisis caused by Russian ambitions over the disintegrating Ottoman Empire. While Bismark skillfully assumed Britain's old role as the Ottoman Empire's honest broker, the British prime minister began to show signs of a distinctly predatory interest in the area nearest the Suez Canal. During these negotiations in 1878 Cyprus was acquired by Britain as a 'Place of Arms' in order to better enable Britain to assist the Ottoman Empire. The nature of that assistance was to be more fully revealed four years later, in 1882, when Britain absorbed into her own Empire the old Ottoman province of Egypt. Cyprus had been a mere stepping stone to the greater prize and within four years of its occupation by Britain, the island had become a colonial backwater. It had no deep-water port, which made it virtually useless to the Royal Navy. On the agenda of the British Empire, Cyprus, the third largest island of the Mediterranean, ranked considerably lower than the rock of Gibraltar or little Malta. The island remained under the nominal sovereignty of the Ottoman Empire until it was formally annexed in 1914 and given the status of a colony in 1925.

The Achievements of the British Period

The efficient staff of the Colonial Office ruled Cyprus for 83 years, leaving as a legacy the use of English language, law and adminstration. The physical evidence of this period is a humdrum matter of dams, drains, hospitals, government offices, harbours, piers and the best road network in the Levant. The triple curses of the countryside, malaria, locusts and usury, were speedily removed and Cyprus's position within the Imperial tariffs produced a ready market for its fruit and wine. Improved sanitation, water supplies and medical care is reflected in the population growth which, despite substantial emigration, increased from 186,000 in 1878 to 600,000 in 1960. Another great achievement of the colonial period was the re-afforestation of great swathes of the central Troödos mountains and the preservation of the indigenous Cyprus cedar. The Cyprus Forestry Service achieved this gradually, against the ingrained traditions of goat herders, woodmen and charcoal burners, and on the most slender of budgets.

The Failings of British Rule

Parsimony and a dangerous lack of imagination were the chief failings of the British rule. Apart from cheap administration, they had no policy. There was no attempt to inculcate an Imperial or national ideal. Cyprus was neither offered a fitting place within the British Commonwealth nor gradually prepared for independence. This political limbo was assured when an early attempt to create a unified English educational system was abandoned. It could have healed the differences between Greek and Turkish Cypriots, assured the islanders opportunities in the English-speaking world and helped create a Cypriot identity, distinct from that of mainland Greece and Turkey. Instead, right from the earliest age, a Cypriot child was either taught in Greek or Turkish by teachers who seldom failed to stress the differences between the two antagonistic motherlands. This lack of political imagination was also reflected in a cultural limbo. The British established no university, no theatre and not a single public building of architectural interest, though there are numerous cases of pitiless philistinism. The medieval palace of the Lusignans in Nicosia was demolished to make room for prefabricated colonial huts; the ancient acropolis of Kition was bulldozed to fill in a swamp; and the dormitory wing at the great abbey of Bellapais was used as road rubble.

The Struggle for Enosis

The desire for *enosis*, union with Greece, was held by the majority of the population throughout the period of British rule. In 1878 the first British governor, Sir Garnet Wolseley, received an enthusiastic welcome from the Orthodox Church, including a famous statement from the Bishop of Kition that 'we accept the change of government in as much as we trust Great Britain will help Cyprus, as it did the Ionian Islands, to be united with Mother Greece, with which it is naturally connected'. This request was to be annually repeated and ignored, though the island, after the British acquisition of Egypt in 1882, had no strategic value or commercial importance to the British Empire. Gladstone in 1880 and 1897, and Winston Churchill in 1907, all spoke in favour of allowing Cyprus to join Greece though what they said while in opposition was not reflected by anything they did while in power. That there was no underlying principle against *enosis* was made clear in 1915 when the British government secretly offered Cyprus to Greece as an inducement to enter the First World War on her side. This tempting offer was rejected and then speedily withdrawn.

In 1931 internal pressure for *enosis* exploded in a riot in which the governor's house was burned down. The British reacted by banning political parties, censoring the press and prohibiting the flying of the Greek flag. In the Second World War, domestic politics were buried in the common fight against Fascist Italy and Nazi Germany, whose control of Rhodes and Crete brought the enemy close to hand.

Archbishop Makarios III, Ethnarch and first President of Cyprus.

In 1945 a well-meaning plan was produced by the British Labour Party for an elected Cypriot parliament and a ten-year development programme. The plan was rejected by Cyprus in a storm of protest. It was seen as a plot to frustrate full *enosis* and was considered deeply patronizing in the light of full independence then being granted to India and Pakistan. In 1950 a plebiscite organized by the Orthodox Church produced a 96% vote for *enosis*. In the same year Mikhail Mouskos, the 37-year-old Bishop of Kition, was elected archbishop and took the name **Makarios III**. He continued the well-established Cypriot tradition of using his spiritual office to articulate the political demands of his people to their rulers.

A new intensity was engendered by a foolish speech by the British colonial minister, who declared in July 1954 that some territories 'can never expect to be fully independent' and that 'British sovereignty will remain' over Cyprus. Those who had hung back from the use of violence now saw no other avenue of communication with Britain. On 1 April 1955 a series of explosions across the island ushered in the armed struggle for *enosis* led by **EOKA** (the National Organisation of Cypriot Fighters). EOKA was organized and led by **Lt-Colonel George Grivas**, who operated under the name of a Byzantine folk hero, Dighenis. Grivas was a native of Cyprus, but had pursued a career in the Greek Army and had had a decade of experience from his leadership of armed bands of right-wing extremists in both the Second World War and the 1945–9 Greek Civil War. Within the first year of EOKA activity, backed by a parallel political campaign, there was a tripartite conference on the future of Cyprus, attended by Turkey, Greece and Britain, and an offer of self-government. It was too little, too late, and any promising atmosphere that had developed during these talks was then destroyed by the foolish decision to exile Makarios to the Seychelles.

A more sinister element of British policy (directed by Anthony Eden and then Harold Macmillan) had been the deliberate stirring up of Turkish interest in Cyprus as a way of frustrating *enosis*. This was coupled with the employment of

Turkish Cypriots in the police and in the paramilitary units used to suppress EOKA and control Greek Cypriot demonstrations. By 1957 an alarming animosity had been created between the island's two communities and between Greece and Turkey. There was talk of 'double *enosis*', the divison of Cyprus between the two mainland powers.

That same year the **TMT** (Turkish Defence Organisation) was formed to protect the Turkish Cypriots from a Greek backlash. It, like EOKA on which it was modelled, was strongly right-wing and began its 'protection' with a purge of liberals, union leaders and communists in its community. By September 1958 the five principal towns on the island had been divided into Greek and Turkish areas. The death toll after four years of armed struggle has been estimated at around 600.

Against the growing threat of partition, Makarios began to accept the idea of independence rather than *enosis*. A meeting at Zurich led to the Lancaster House settlement of February 1959. Britain was to maintain two sovereign military bases, with a combined area of 99 square miles; the rights of the Turkish-Cypriot minority were written into the constitution; and Cyprus's independence was to be guaranteed by all three powers. Archbishop Makarios was elected to the Greek-Cypriot post of president while Dr Fazil Kuchuk was elected to the vice-presidency reserved for the Turkish Cypriots.

The Republic of Cyprus: 1960–74

Independence was celebrated at the stroke of midnight, **16 August 1960**, but the brand-new republic came into the world heavily burdened. There were 199 articles in the constitution to serve a population of just 600,000, and little good will to put this complicated legal morass into operation. Most Greek Cypriots saw independence as a step towards *enosis*, while Turkish Cypriots defended the constitutional demarcations and job quotas with unbending and unworkable zeal. Disputes over the army, taxes, civil-service recruitment and presidential powers soon paralysed central government. Communal tension was not eased by **Polycarpos Yorgadjiis**, who ran the Ministry of the Interior as a continuation of EOKA, and by Markarios's celebration of *enosis* martyrs in state festivals.

In November 1963 Makarios proposed to the Turkish Cypriots 13 constitutional amendments. It was a tactless presentation, for each amendment was designed to strengthen Greek-Cypriot control of a streamlined central administration and there was nothing to quieten Turkish-Cypriot fears for the future. It was rejected and a few weeks later a major attack was launched on the Turkish Cypriots by Greek-Cypriot para-military forces. Hundreds died and 20,000 Turkish Cypriots fled to the safety of their principal enclaves around Nicosia and Kyrenia. Faced with the threat of Turkish military intervention, Makarios agreed that the British should intervene. The **Green Line** separated the two communities in Nicosia, but fighting continued in the villages requiring the presence of a UN force which arrived in March 1964. Later that year Makarios formed a National Guard which under the command of Grivas launched an attack on **Kokkina**, where the Turkish Cypriots were receiving military supplies from the mainland. Grivas's assault was only repelled by the intervention of the Turkish airforce. Makarios had in his turn called for the support of the Greek airforce but Cyprus was beyond its range. The strategic implications of the island's geography, so near to Turkey, so far from Greece, had a sobering effect on the Greek-Cypriot leadership.

By the end of 1964 the Turkish Cypriots were concentrated in a dozen enclaves: a state within a state, protected by its fighters and governed by its own councils. The Greek Cypriots at first tried to blockade them into submission, but intervention by the UN and the Red Cross led to a growing acceptance of the situation. In 1967 the spirit of toleration was further encouraged by the coup in Greece which replaced democracy in Athens with a junta of colonels. *Enosis* with this authoritarian regime seemed less attractive, and Makarios became resigned to an independent Cyprus. He tried to create a more personally dependable paramilitary force to balance the power of the 30,000 strong Greek-officered National Guard. Grivas opposed this increasingly equivocal attitude to *enosis* and in the winter of 1967 launched a terror campaign against the island's well-established left-wing parties and attacked the Turkish-Cypriot Kophinou enclave. Despite these actions, a series of bilateral talks between 1968–74 seemed to offer some hope.

By 1973 Makarios was so isolated that his only chance of personal victory lay in making a lasting peace with the Turkish Cypriots and hence with Turkey. In 1970 the Greek military government's enmity towards him had been graphically revealed when his helicopter was shot down. Makarios miraculously survived, and a week later the minister of the interior, heavily implicated in the Athens-directed coup, was murdered. In 1971 Grivas re-established an *enosis* terror group, **EOKA-B**, and in 1973 rival bishops attempted to unfrock Makarios. The president's association with the non-aligned group of nations, his easy relationship with local communists and flirtatious diplomacy with the Soviet bloc had further estranged him from the Western powers.

The Events of 1974 and their Repercussions

The death of Grivas in January 1974 meant all the pro-*enosis* groups were directed by the junta in Athens. Makarios, aware of plans for a second coup, called for the withdrawal of Greek army officers from Cyprus in early July. On 15 July the National Guard attacked the presidential palace, though once again Makarios escaped with his life. The announcement that **Nikos Sampson** (a notorious EOKA gunman associated with some of the worst excesses of the intercommunal violence) was to be the new president completely discredited the coup in international eyes.

The Turkish leader, **Bulent Ecevit**, immediately flew to London to request British intervention, as guarantor under the Lancaster House settlement. The British, reluctant to involve themselves again in Cyprus, refused.

On 18 July Bulent Ecevit demanded that Athens withdraw its forces from Cyprus and remove Nikos Sampson. Athens did nothing and at dawn on 20 July units of the Turkish army, supported by air strikes, landed on the coast near Kyrenia.This was met with fierce resistance, and throughout the island old scores were settled in a number of pitiless massacres that have never been fully examined. For a few terrible days it seemed that the fighting in Cyprus would escalate into a general war between Greece and Turkey, but on 23 July the Greek field army toppled the junta and allowed the return of democracy. A ceasefire and peace conference was arranged for the first fortnight of August. Negotiations collapsed in the early hours of 14 August, and within an hour the Turkish army was on the offensive. Its grip over the narrow Kyrenia-to-Nicosia corridor widened into an occupation of the northern 36% of the island. While guaranteeing the security and bargaining position of the Turkish Cypriots, this aggression reversed international sympathy. In July it had been in favour of the Turkish Cypriots, but by September it was behind the 160,000 Greek Cypriots being forced from their homeland by foreign troops.

A Divided Island

By the end of 1974 UN forces had been inserted between the battle lines and an exchange of populations turned southern Cyprus into the Greek-Cypriot zone and northern Cyprus into the Turkish Cypriot zone. At the cost of several thousand dead and missing and the loss of some 200,000 homes, the island enjoyed peace for the first time in two decades.

Little has changed, and today there is little love left between the two communities. The division of the island into two ethnic zones is an accepted political fact, whatever the rhetoric, and one which is further marked by the booming economy of the south and the stagnant one of the north. The latter is entirely dependent on Turkey for its survival, both financially and militarily. In 1983 the Turkish Cypriot government altered its status from the mere Turkish Federated State of Cyprus to the **Turkish Republic of Northern Cyprus (TRNC)**. Both sides of the island have an elective presidency and a small legislative assembly of around 50 members, who are chosen in quite separate elections. There is lively democracy, an active media and stormy politics, but no party, not even the well-established Cypriot Communists (AKEL), transcends the division of the border.

Negotiations to reunify the island have been pursued under UN auspices for the last 20 years, but it has not always been clear that a solution has been wanted by either side. Until recently, the Greek-Cypriot leadership (Presidents Archbishop Makarios (1974–7), **Spyros Kyprianou** (1977–88) and **George Vassiliou** (1988–93)) has concentrated on internationalizing the problem, pillorying Turkey and its dependent TRNC through the world media and the UN. They have succeeded in notching up an impressive number of UN resolutions in their favour while the TRNC is still not recognized by any international body and remains isolated from world scholarship, aid and trade. However, the new president, **Glafkos Clerides**, who was elected in 1993, has consistently championed a low-key, pragmatic approach to negotiations. He sees a united Cyprus, with membership of both the EC and NATO, as the key to security and harmony in the future. Rauf Denktas, the president of the TRNC, has been the dominant figure in Turkish Cypriot politics for thirty years and is unlikely to unmake the Republic he has founded. He announced his intention to resign from his leadership in 1995.

The Four Big Issues to be Resolved in Negotiation

Federal Government. The role and powers of a new federal government are crucial. The Greek South wants a strong central government, which it will necessarily dominate with its greater population and wealth. The Turkish North wants federal window-dressing, with most power left in the hands of existing regional administrations. Recent talks suggested a Lower House elected proportionally, with an ethnically balanced Upper House and Supreme Court. The presidency, alternating between the two communities, would direct foreign affairs and finance.

Land and Immigrants. The current frontier which gives the Turkish Cypriots (who number about 20% of the population) about 36% of the island will have to be adjusted in favour of the Greek South. A possible compromise would be the return of Varosha (the abandoned southern suburb of Famagusta) and about half the Mesaoria plain to the south, reducing the north to about 28% of the island. Many of the Greek refugee families would then be able to return home. All others, both Greek and Turkish, could be compensated in a final settlement. A more contentious issue is the fate of the 40,000 or so immigrant farmers from mainland Turkey who have been settled in the north since 1974. The Greeks demand their expulsion, the Turks their retention.

Future Ownership. Another difficult issue is over future land ownership. Open borders between the two regions would seem to be an absolute necessity of union (even if they may have to be policed for a period of transition), but would Greeks be allowed to establish businesses and own land in the north? The Greeks argue that it would be an infringement of natural liberty and an ethnic apartheid to deny them this right; the Turks fear that they would soon be swamped by the greater wealth of the south and reduced to an endangered minority again.

Protection. The Turkish Cypriots want some elements of the Turkish army to remain to guarantee their protection in a united Cyprus; the Greeks demand that all foreign forces leave the island. It may be possible to resolve this dispute by scheduling a transition period, during which there is a gradual reduction in forces. A few Turkish units could then be placed under a UN (or eventually NATO) flag.

Larnaca and District

Ayios Lazarus ~ Larnaca ~

55

The first view of Cyprus, for most visitors, is of the
Larnaca shore framed by the oval porthole of a
descending aeroplane. It can make a shocking
introduction to the island of Aphrodite. The
delicate footprints of the goddess of love
seem to be totally submerged under an
expanding layer of fresh tarmac
and ferroconcrete. A
sprawl of suburbs
and new

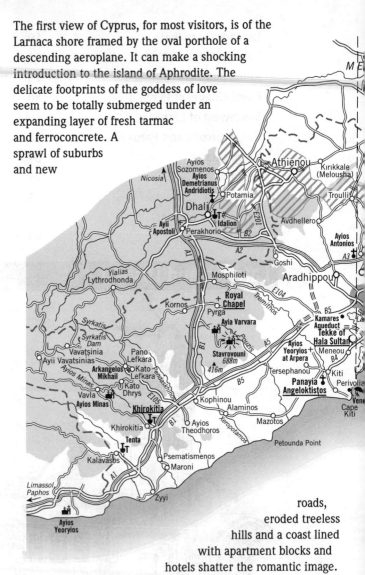

roads,
eroded treeless
hills and a coast lined
with apartment blocks and
hotels shatter the romantic image.
On a hitherto barren and unprofitable shore the Cypriots provide
food, drink, rooms and a hint of sex in the sun for tens of
thousands of victims of the climate of northern Europe.

KEY

-----	Sovereign Base (UK)
▧	Demilitarized Zone
	Land over 200m
— —	Provincial Boundary
⚹⚹⚹	Road barred

Moving east from the town of Larnaca is a necklace of resorts strung unevenly along the shore: Larnaca Bay, Nissi Beach, Ayia Napa, Protaras and Paralimni. They can have something of a carnival air about them, but are more markedly touched by the suffocating blandness of packaged tourism. Yet there are good reasons not to head straight out of the district, but to relish a few nights in Larnaca. Against this unpromising backdrop are a dozen mysterious and intimate places, such as the four-millennia-old temple of the goddess, the tomb of the twice-dead Lazarus and the haunting lakeside shrine of the Tekke of Hala Sultan (which you might recognize from the cover). A short trip out of town can take you to the mosaic built by angels at Panayia Angeloktistos; the holy, male-only mountain top of Stavrovouni; the Stone-Age village of fearful Khirokitia; the tiny painted chapel at Pyrga commissioned by a doomed, bankrupt medieval king; and the village of Pyla where you can look directly into Cyprus's divided past. Empty beaches still exist to the west of Larnaca for picnics and swims, and when you have had your fill of dining beside the sea you can then take a few days off for some quiet walking in the forested hills around Pano Lefkara.

Festivals

The *panayiri* of Ayia Napa monastery, on 24 and 25 March, celebrates the **Annunciation**. Larnaca cannot hope to compete with Limassol over its **carnival** parades, but it does organize a street party on the first Sunday of carnival (the date fluctuates with that of Easter), with live music on the seafront promenade outside the town hall. In the middle of April the town celebrates a week of **classical music** with concerts performed by local students and foreign talent. On 18 April a **special mass** is held in Ayios Lazaros church, after which an icon of St Lazarus, the patron saint, is paraded through the principal streets of Larnaca. **Ayios Yeoryios** monastery celebrates its saint's day on 22 and 23 April, and Dherinia has its *panayiri* on **St Constantine and St Helen's Day**, on 20 and 21 May. Ayia Napa has adopted International Children's Day on 2 June as its own, with appropriate mime, dancing, music and parties for and by children.

Kataklysmos Day on 15 June used to be an event specific to Larnaca, but has now spread to all the coast towns. The water fight on the first Monday after the 15th has pagan origins but is now considered to commemorate Noah's survival of the flood and the cleansing from corruption in the earth's great baptism. The celebration now extends over a whole week of boat races, swimming, water fights, dancing and formalized *tchattista*, originally a competition between bards who sang improvised verses which exceeded each other in dizzy flights of verbal fancy.

Larnaca arranges a **summer festival** which brings exhibitions to the fort and a number of evenings of music, theatre and dance during July and August. The **Dormition of the Virgin**, on 14 and 15 August, marks the *panayiri* at Liopetri village; the **Festival of the Holy Cross** on 13 and 14 September that of Lefkara. On 18 October, the village of Aradhippou celebrates the feast day of its patron **St Luke** with a large fair. November is **fine arts month** with a number of exhibitions and lectures organized at the Larnaca town hall, ✆ (04) 653333.

History

Larnaca, which looks so brash and modern at first glance, has more than 3000 years of urban history. Twice the city was completely devastated; it lay in ruins from 1050–850 BC, and then again from AD 649–985, however both periods were succeeded by cultures that stressed an essential continuity. The city was so surrounded by the tombs of its past citizens that by the 16th century it had become known as Larnax (the Greek word for sarcophagus), from which the present name of Larnaca is derived. In addition to tombs it has also collected names: it is Chittim in the Bible, Kittim in inscriptions, Phoenician Kition, Greek Cition and Roman Citium; in medieval times the ancient ruins were known as Bamboula.

By the 13th century BC Larnaca was already a walled town with its own temples, bronze foundries, workshops and docks. After a minor earthquake around 1200 BC it was rebuilt on a larger and regular scale in the period when the **Mycenaean** warrior-traders of the Greek coast were growing in influence. The excavated temple area dates from this period. The old mudbrick walls were replaced by an *enceinte* of massive dressed stone and reinforced by rectangular towers. Some alterations 50 years later might indicate the consolidation of Mycenaean influence. The city was weakened by an earthquake in 1075 BC, but it was the succession of seaborne invasions by bands of iron-using warriors a generation later that destroyed both the city and the old Bronze-Age civilization.

For two centuries the city lay windblown and empty in the anarchy of a dark age. Fortunately, the tools of urban civilization had been preserved and augmented in the half-dozen trading cities of Phoenicia, on the nearby coast of Lebanon. Kition was colonized by the Phoenicians in the 10th century BC. The ancient temple was cleaned of its desecration, lovingly restored and rededicated to the goddess Astarte. Its local prestige is reflected in a number of prophetic references to Chittim in the Old Testament: Daniel foretold that its ships would advance against the kings of the north, Balaam that it would afflict Assyria, and Isaiah saw conflict with Tyre. It was all wishful thinking, for canny Kition was content to trade under the loose suzerainty of first the Assyrian and then the Egyptian Empire, and went on to become the trusted ally of Persian hegemony in Cyprus. Only Kition held out against the army of **Cimon** in 450 BC, when this celebrated Athenian general came to 'liberate' Cyprus and add her wealth to the tribute lists of the Athenian Empire. Cimon died during the siege, his mission collapsed and Kition was rewarded by a grateful Persia with the annexation of the neighbouring city of Idalion and its valuable copper mines. The destruction of Tyre, the Phoenician mother city, and the conquest of Persia by **Alexander the Great**, was the writing on the wall for Kition. When the **Ptolemies** took control of

Cyprus in 312 BC they set out to humble Kition; its temples were levelled and Pumyathon, the last Phoenician king of the old dynasty, was publicly drowned.

Kition declined into a minor provincial town during the Hellenistic and Roman periods, from 317 BC–AD 750. Its history is enlivened by the presence of two extraordinary men, the philospher Zeno and St Lazarus.

Zeno

By one of those quirks of fate, just as Greece triumphed over Phoenician Kition, a Phoenician from Kition triumphed in the heart of Greece. Zeno was born in 336 BC into a family of Kition merchants, but became interested in philosophy during an early trading visit to Athens. He returned to study and later taught in the *stoa*, a shaded colonnade that encircled the Athenian marketplace and which gave the name Stoic to the enormously influential school of philosophy he developed. His teaching stressed a personal struggle for virtue in a heartless materialistic world and his ethics are recorded in the writings of three later disciples: Seneca, Epictetus and Marcus Aurelius—a minister, a slave and an emperor. He died by his own hand in 264 BC. His marble bust can be seen at the junction of Leoforos Grigori Afxentiou and Nikodimou Mylona street.

Lazarus

Lazarus and his two sisters Martha and Mary were among Jesus's most treasured friends. The raising of Lazarus, after he had been dead for four days and was already stinking, from the cemetery of Bethany is the most marvellous of all Jesus's miracles. Though the Gospels are silent, tradition recalls that Lazarus, with the three Marys, was forced into exile by the persecution that claimed the deacon Stephen as the first martyr. They fled by boat from the Phoenician shore to the quiet town of Kition, where Lazarus was later ordained bishop during the visit of the apostles Paul and Barnabas. He was never known to smile, for his experience of the other world had scorched away his sense of humour. His one attempt to crack a joke—he quipped 'clay steals clay' when he saw a man steal a pot—had such a depressing effect on his listeners that he never tried again. He presided over the church of Kition for 30 years before he returned to the tomb. After the destruction of Kition by Saracen raids his shrine was lost amongst the rubble for two centuries. It was rediscovered in AD 890 and the holy relics were sent to Constantinople for safe keeping. A great church was erected over the tomb when the Byzantine Empire recovered Cyprus at the end of the 10th century.

The shrine of St Lazarus was an essential stop on the pilgrims' tour of the Holy Land. The surrounding area was known as **La Scala**, the landing stage, or the marina. **Salines** was a separate inland town and base for the profitable local industry in salt extraction from the neighbouring lake. Throughout the high days of the Lusignan kingdom it was overawed by Famagusta, but gradually acquired an increasing share of trade as its rival ossified into a military base. Within a few decades of the Ottoman conquest it had emerged as the principal port of Cyprus and one of the centres of the Levant trade in silk and dried fruit.

By the 17th century all the trading nations were represented in Larnaca by consuls, who combined a spirit of untrammelled free enterprise with a preoccupation for etiquette and rank to match a European court. When not trying to ruin each other in business, the consuls filled their year with elaborate courtesy visits, receptions, galas and a summer season taken in the village of **Ormidhia**. They were a distinctive feature of the local landscape with their gilded canes, plumed hats and burnished carriages. By the mid-19th century trade was at its height and Larnaca's population of 13,000 exceeded even that of Nicosia.

Larnaca's consular era ended in the summer of 1878 when two young officials, Harry Rawson and Walter Baring, were rowed ashore from *HMS Minotaur*. They landed, debriefed the local consul and then rode inland to transfer Cyprus from the Ottoman to the British Empire. Thereafter the city seemed set on a slow, graceful and irreversible decline, as first Nicosia took over its administrative functions and then, despite a new harbour, both Famagusta and Limassol overtook it commercially. The invasion of 1974 gave Larnaca an unexpected renewal as refugees poured in, a yacht marina and international airport were built, and a tourist industry was created from virtually nothing.

Getting Around

By Air

Larnaca International Airport, ✆ (04) 654389, lies 6km southwest of Larnaca and 50km from Nicosia. It handles a busy international schedule of flights to the principal cities of Europe and the Middle East. Side trips on **Cyprus Airways** include flights to Athens, Heraklion, Tel Aviv, Damascus and Cairo. These can be booked through any travel agent or at the Cyprus Airways office at 21 Alkeus Street, Nicosia, ✆ (02) 443054. There are regular connections to Amman on **Royal Jordanian Air**, ✆ (02) 452124; and Beirut on **MEA**, ✆ (02) 443132.

By Bus

Buses are reasonably cheap; a ticket from Larnaca to Nicosia, for example, is under C£1. In general they run from 6am–5pm on weekdays, stop shortly after lunch on Saturday and do not operate on Sunday.

Bus nos. 21 and 19 provide a frequent service between the airport and the sea promenade in the town centre. The latter service also continues west to pass by the Tekke of Hala Sultan on its way to Meneou village. The no. 20 follows the coast road south to the Mackenzie beach area; the no. 18 north takes you along the Larnaca Bay beach strip. From the Kallenos or Eman bus stop on the sea promenade, there are 11 daily departures for Nicosia (1hr), 7 for Limassol (1hr 15min) and 17 for Ayia Napa (45min).

For Kiti village, Faros-Perivolia (Kiti beach) or Lefkara you leave from Ayios Lazaros square. The no. 6 bus does the journey to Kiti a dozen times a day; the Perivolia bus five times a day; the Lefkara bus only once a day, leaving Larnaca at 1pm and returning the following morning.

By Taxi

It costs about C£2 for a taxi from the airport to a hotel in the centre of Larnaca, about C£12 to Nicosia or Ayia Napa, a few pounds more to Limassol, and around C£25 to Paphos.

By Shared or Service Taxi

This is by the far the most convenient way to travel to any one of the other three major towns—Nicosia, Limassol or Paphos. Service taxis operate between 6am and 6pm on weekdays, with a reduced service on Sundays and minimal cover over public holidays. A seat, currently costing under C£2, can be booked by phone, and a taxi will usually be able to collect you within half an hour. The fetching and delivery of the half-dozen other passengers can offer revealing urban insights but can also be time-consuming. **Kyriakos** at 2C Ermou street, ✆ (04) 655100, just does the Nicosia run; **Acropolis**, on the corner of Leoforos Gregori Afxentiou and Leoforos Archiepiskopou Makariou III, ✆ (04) 655555, and **Makris** at 13 Plateia Vasileos Pavlou, ✆ (04) 652929, both cover Nicosia and Limassol. You will have to change at Limassol for Paphos.

Car Hire

There are half a dozen car hire companies that run booths at the airport. Those who want to drive straight away can choose at random from: **A. Petsas** (who also runs **Budget**), ✆ (04) 657850; **Hertz**, ✆ (04) 622388; or **Thames**, ✆ (04) 657844. Think in terms of around C£100 for a week's hire of a 1000cc Austin Metro and double that for a four-wheel-drive Suzuki Jeep. If you have time to hunt around for a bargain, try the cluster of local firms just east of the high-rise Lordos Sea Gate Hotel on the south end of Piyâle Paşa street, e.g. **F. Apollo**, ✆ (04) 656592; **Loucas**, ✆ (04) 656763; or **Cycar**, ✆ (04) 656661.

In the winter months the marina is filled to capacity, with all 400 berths taken and a number of yachts up on chocks. Boat people may enquire into the availability of berths and charges on ℂ (04) 653110, fax (04) 624110, and can clear Customs and Immigration within the harbour. The entrance is well guarded; genuine visitors are required to name a boat and its owner and leave their passport at the gate.

Coach and Boat Excursions

National Tours, ℂ (04) 654404, is run by the Louis Agency, but a seat on this or any other coach trip can be booked through any travel agent or large hotel. There are weekly trips to **Nicosia**, to **Troödos** and **Kykko**, to **Paphos**, to **Lefkara** and **Limassol**, to **Kakopetria** and **Platres**, and boat trips from the harbour.

Andreas Constantinou-Dornos runs **Ayia Napa Sea Cruises** from the marina pier in the summer, ℂ (04) 653110. He either heads east to spend the day off **Ayia Napa**, or west to **Cape Kiti**; but he will also consider longer trips for a group. Prices, at around C£10 a head, include a lunch-time barbecue and the opportunity for water sports.

Tourist Information

The **tourist information office** (CTO) is just up from the marina pier on the corner of Plateia Vasileos Pavlou (Dhimokratias). Just around the corner, where the street bends north, is the central **post office**, ℂ (04) 657075. The palm-tree ornamented sea promenade, which is also known as Leoforos Athinon (Athens avenue), stretches in a newly embellished form between the yacht marina and the fort. It and the parallel Zinonos Kitieos street mark the centre of town, where you will find a large selection of **banks**, taxi stands, hotels, shops and bars.

The City

Larnaca Fort

Open 7.30am–7.30pm every day except Sun; adm.

Only the seaward-facing wall with its artillery casemates and portals survives from the original rectangular stone fort built by the Ottoman governor in 1625. The land walls are composed of a simple parapet to the north and a domestic clutter of red-tiled buildings that used to house the small janissary garrison. A grass court-yard, partly shaded by pine trees, is decorated with a small collection of rusting cannon. To the left of the gate is a collection of **tombstones** carved with the scripts of the various religions in Cyprus: the Latin of Catholics, the Arabic script of an Ottoman Muslim, Hebrew for Jews and Greek for the Orthodox. An **upstairs gallery** has a photographic exhibition of Byzantine architecture, a few fragments from early Christian churches, four cases of sgraffito ware (*see* p. 409), a case of Islamic pottery, a collection of Ottoman kitchen and tableware, and some assorted 18th- to 19th-century muskets, swords and armour.

The Cami Kebir (Grand Mosque)

Just inland from the fort, the Grand Mosque of Larnaca stands on an elevated terrace supported on either side by buttresses that lean across the side streets. Five arches support an open colonnade to the west, to give an imposing entrance to the simple rectangular prayer hall. Visitors are welcome (just after prayer hours) to tiptoe across the creaking balcony (an area traditionally set aside for the female congregation) and climb up the minaret for a view out over the old Turkish quarter with its low houses and red terracotta roofs. The tomb of **Seyit Elhac Mehmet Aǧa**, who rebuilt the original 16th-century mosque during his governorship in 1835, is at the rear, whilst the graves of lesser officials cluster around the front. Turbans were carved on tombstones until 1826 when Mehmet II signified his reform of the Ottoman Empire by decreeing the use of the fez, a hat which did not reveal the wearer's religion.

The **Zohour mosque** is 100m northwest of the Grand Mosque, off Dionysou street. It overlooks the remains of the old Bedestan, an enclosed courtyard for the use of merchants

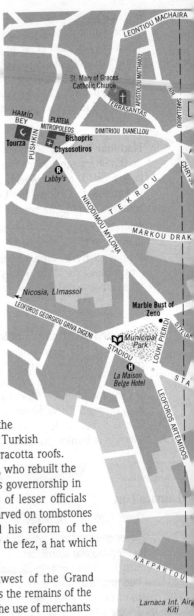

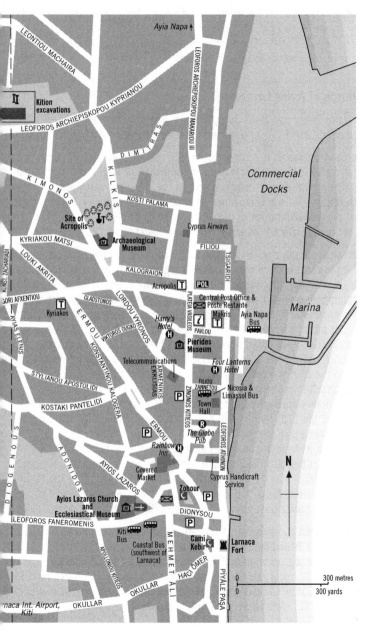

and travellers. The minaret has fallen but the mosque has a handsome aspect with its shady arcade, strong pair of domes and green shutters contrasting pleasantly with the local yellow stone. The arcades of the associated lodge are now half filled in, and the building serves as a youth hostel.

The Church of Ayios Lazaros

Open every day 8–12.30; afternoon hours in summer 3.30–6.30; in winter 2.30–5. No adm charge but leave a donation and light a candle.

The church of St Lazarus is easily recognized by its bold, four-storey bell tower of elaborately carved pale stone. It is perhaps ironic that the largest and most venerable Byzantine church in Cyprus should be strongly associated with a late-19th-century Italian campanile. At dusk the cultures seem even more entwined as pigeons flirt through the windows, electric bulbs are switched on and the call of the muezzin echoes across from the minaret of the Grand Mosque.

The open-arched south cloisters are also a later addition, but once you step down into the triple-aisled body of the church you are in an ancient Byzantine basilica. According to tradition this was built in AD 890 on the orders of Emperor Leo VI, the Wise, though it would seem doubtful that such a substantial church would have been completed before the Byzantine Empire regained control over Cyprus in 965. Four massive stone piers stand at the centre and support a succession of great stone barrel vaults. Classical cornices have been reused to cap the walls and antique capitals have been set in corners as springs for the transition from the vertical wall to the arch of a barrel vault. It is a distinctive form of early Byzantine decoration that allows the stresses within a building to be instantly understood. Three great domes once gave even greater height and space to the central nave but they fell in the 17th century and have never been replaced. The bare unplastered stone gives a fine contrast to the richly carved furniture and the glittering iconostasis with its famous icon of **St Lazarus**. A short flight of steps leads down to a simple crypt beneath the altar and the sarcophagus of the saint. His relics were taken to grace first the city of Constantinople and then, after the Fourth Crusade, they were stolen in the looting of the city and reappeared in Marseille. The church kept back a bone or two, which are exhibited in a reliquary.

St Lazarus has been home to many faiths. After the Crusader conquest, St Lazarus was turned into a Benedictine monastery, before passing to the Armenians and back to the Catholic Church in time to be confiscated by the Ottomans in 1571. After a 400-year hiatus, it was finally sold back to the Orthodox Church in 1589 for 3000 coins. European residents were allowed to use the chapel in the north aisle for services, but were ejected in 1784, as they had become too possessive. A

Catholic altar and a Latin cross above the north door have been left as souvenirs of a troublesome history. Today, services here have a powerful solemnity.

A small ecclesiastical museum has been established in the old school house of the churchyard (*open Mon–Sat 8–1 and, except on Wed and Sat, 2.30–5; adm*). Among the 19th-century plate, regalia and *ex voto* icons, look out for the contemporary piece by **George Matsangides** of Leo the Wise offering the church to St Lazarus; a wooden apse with its rustic painted decoration; and the 17th-century *Descent from the Cross* icon in the second chamber.

In the northwest corner of the church precincts is a collection of Protestant tombstones from the old English and Dutch cemetery which used to stand here. There are some characteristically verbose inscriptions, such as the one to William Balls erected by his shipmates on board *HBMS* (Her Britannic Majesty's Ship) *Volage*.

Consular Crooks

The Larnaca that was dominated by foreign consuls survives in a number of contemporary travelogues and memoirs which vividly recall the antics and scandals of the day, like the worrying number of young men in the 1830s who had taken to walking the streets in drag. Some consular careers have an almost fictional quality—Thackeray would have relished Treadway, and George Macdonald Fraser must have toyed with the idea of placing di Cesnola in a Flashman adventure.

Mr Treadway was easily the most hospitable, courteous and popular of the British 18th-century consuls, but after a few years he had tapped everyone in town for a loan. Not only was he running out of credit but he began to be pressed for payment. He made plans for a great banquet which was to precede the complete settlement of his considerable debts. The whole town watched the elaborate preparations of the expected feast with such relish that, in their enthusiasm, they failed to notice the consul quietly slipping all his valuables on board the ship of a friendly naval officer. By the time Mr Treadway's hungry guests had pushed their way into an enticingly lit but empty dining room, he was already a speck on the horizon.

Luigi Palma di Cesnola, a veteran general of the American Civil War, arrived at Larnaca in 1865 as the consul of both America and Russia, a unique double billing. He bullied and bribed the local Ottoman officials in order to proceed with his rapid and devastatingly extensive excavations. Di Cesnola was halfway in the evolution from tomb robber to archaeologist. He identified 65 ancient cemeteries and opened over 60,000 tombs. He was not beyond fabricating evidence or stimulating auctions between rival collectors, yet he was a careful observer, an enthusiast and an educator.

The Pierides Museum

Open every day except Sun 9–1; adm; 4 Zinonos Kitieos street, © (04) 622345.

The worn and graceful exterior of the Pierides Museum, bearing the shield of the Swedish consulate, stands opposite what used to be the old Ottoman bank and clubhouse. It has the intimate, dusty atmosphere of a private art collection, with worn carpets, creaking floorboards and the high, peeling ceilings of an old 19th-century family house. A library just to the right of the entrance, filled with books on art and archaeology, is available to interested members of the public. The collection has been assembled over the last 150 years and is presided over by the elegant Madame Pierides, the sixth generation of family curators. She lives on the private first floor, which is almost as filled with old maps, icons, cabinets of medals and medieval pottery as the ground floor is with ancient ceramics.

Though the collection is arranged chronologically and covers all the recognized cultural periods, few of its objects can be traced to specific sites. It should be treated as a gallery of ancient art, and one especially strong in the themes of the **Cypro-Archaic period**, rather than as an archaeological display. (For a general stylistic introduction *see* p. 408.)

The collection is divided into four rooms. The first room holds objects from the Neolithic to the Iron Age, and is dominated by the unique figure of an enthroned deity from the Copper Age. Liquid poured into his skull splashes from his mouth and can be drunk from his penis. The second room, filled with Cypro-Archaic figurines and pots, comprises the heart of the collection. Roman and Hellenistic objects, including Phoenician glass, trading beads and some delightful Attic black figure ware, are displayed in rooms three and four. The hallway is decorated with island embroideries, inlayed furniture, carved dower chests (*see* p. 193) and some of the finest sgraffito ware on the island.

Larnaca Archaeological Museum

Open every day except Sun 7.30–1.30; adm; on the corner of Kimonos and Kilkis streets, © (04) 630169.

An antique olive press, corn mill and a circular mosaic formed from black and white tesserae in the Italian taste embellish the exterior of this museum, which has a pair of Phoenician sarcophagi beside the ticket desk. (For a general overview of the different stylistic periods of ancient pottery and carving, *see* p. 405.)

The **first gallery** houses the products of the indigenous Neolithic and Early Bronze Ages, as well as imported Egyptian alabaster and Minoan craters. They were discovered in late Bronze-Age cities, alongside such ingenious local devices as a ceramic torch and foot warmer. The **second gallery** begins with two cases of imported Mycenaean pottery, but is otherwise dominated by relics from the excavations at Kition, such as the carved ivory plaque of a divine warrior and three figurines of the fertility goddess Astarte (the Syrian Aphrodite). The **third gallery** is furnished with clay figurines and some Phoenician inscriptions, which are overawed by the carved female figures of Archaic Cyprus, with their characteristic hint of a divinely knowing smile and attenuated painted eyes, set above a bejewelled but bare torso. The last room is devoted to the Hellenistic and Roman periods, beginning with the full glory of painted Attic vases before declining into plain slipware, when glass and metal took the leading role in artistic expression.

In the courtyard behind, the more durable architectural pieces and tomb fragments are exhibited in an outdoor sketching gallery. The wooded area to the north is known as Bamboula, the site of the **acropolis of Kition**, which was levelled by the well-meaning but ignorant British colonial administration for hard core with which to fill the ancient harbour site. They killed a breeding ground for mosquitoes, but also several millennia of buried history.

Kition Excavations

Open Mon–Sat 7.30–1.30; adm; located in Larnaca suburbs and best approached from the north, off a turning on Leontiou Machaira street.

Only a small fraction of the ancient city has been excavated, and an even smaller area made available to the public. From the ticket hut a 50m-long wooden walkway allows you to view a small section of the city that was tucked inside the north wall. It is a sunken dun-coloured area surrounded by reeds, with a confusing trail of knee-high foundation walls and ruined buildings spanning four different eras of occupation. However, from these scant traces it is possible to tease out a fabulous, near mythical past.

The Temple of the Goddess

Walk halfway along the boardwalk and look west (to your right) over an open area dotted with pits and regular rows of column bases. This is the enclosed garden of the great goddess, who, under a thousand different names and attributes, has reigned over all the world's early agricultural societies. The memory of the sacred rites performed in her gardens has provided all the monotheistic religions with their ideal of paradise. Even the English word 'paradise' is a direct transliteration of the Old Persian *pairi* (around) and *daeza* (wall). The pits, which predate any existing Bronze-Age building in this city, are associated with a grove of sacred trees that were watered by a channel fed from a well beneath the temple's inner sanctum. Within the garden was an ornamental pool carved from the bedrock, which one imagines was filled with dark eels nibbling hand-held gifts of eggs. Add the tinkle of cymbals and bells, the perfumed scent of sacrifice and the flutter of ornamental birds to create a garden of earthly delights.

To the south a covered way created a solemn processional avenue to the three chapels at the west end of the garden where the goddess could be worshipped in her three manifestations: Maiden, Mother and Crone. To the east of the garden were two open courtyards where the business of religion, like the burning of offerings, animal sacrifices and the dedication of pottery statuettes, would take place. A horn of consecration, a stylized bull's skull that was developed in Minoan Crete, and an area of fire-blackened clay can still be seen. The next-door courtyard was dominated by a pair of free-standing columns thought to be associated with the youthful lover of the goddess, who, like the vegetation and crops, is fated to die and to be reborn in the spring. Further east, built against the city wall, is another temple. This used ancient anchors—stone slabs with holes in them—for its foundations. The essentially commercial nature of copper-exporting Kition, when added to the opium pipe and a statuette of Bes that was found here, combine to suggest the sort of deity that might have inhabited this sanctuary. The Egyptian deity Bes was a cunning trickster who is often depicted as a bow-legged dwarf, and was the favourite figurehead on most ancient merchant ships.

Return your gaze to the garden of the goddess and the neat rows of unexplained column bases. After the destruction of the city at the beginning of the Iron Age it lay empty for 200 years, until Phoenician colonists settled here around 850 BC. They scrupulously tidied the ruins, carefully burying the old broken offerings in pits, and reused the old altars and walls. The garden was converted into the covered temple of Astarte, the Phoenician name for the ancient fertility goddess of their homeland, also referred to as Syrian Aphrodite. The first wooden structure burnt down in 650 BC, but it was replaced by one of stone. This survived until 312 BC when Ptolemy I, the Macedonian ruler of Egypt, ordered the execution of Pumyathon, the last Phoenician king of Kition, and the destruction of the city's holiest temple. Traces of commercial cisterns from the Ptolemaic period, in the southeast corner of the excavations, should not be honoured with a second glance.

Salines

About 600m west of these ruins the position of the medieval town of Salines is remembered by the **Bishopric** and the **Tourza mosque**. The former is a new loggia-style palace with an attached conference room and the chapel of Khrysosotiros. The latter is 150m further west, on the corner of Pushkin and Hamid Bey streets, and is surrounded by cedars and palms and dominated by the warped silhouette of its minaret. The mosque was built over an old Gothic chapel and has a heavily buttressed back arcade partly formed from Roman columns. If you are hungry there is a run-down Greek-speaking taverna in the nearby market square of the butchers, opposite the big Catholic church on Terrasantas street.

The Tekke of Hala Sultan

Open every day 7.30–sunset; no adm but tips to custodian; the approach road to the Tekke of Hala Sultan (the monastery of the Holy Lady) is 800m southwest of the airport entrance.

The Tekke was built around the 7th-century tomb of **Umm Haram**, which translates as the 'Pious Woman', and is the most revered Muslim sanctuary in Cyprus. Local enthusiasm has, with fearless exaggeration, promoted it as the third-holiest pilgrimage place in all Islam. The minaret and dome of the mosque sit by the shore of the **Salt Lake**, shaded by a garden of cypress and palm trees surrounded by a lemon grove. A couple of water tanks linked by irrigation trenches echo the chatter of birds, but otherwise it is distinguished by a reflective air that borders on a spiritual serenity—despite its proximity to the airport. A Late-Bronze-Age archaeological site, of the city of Vyzakia, and an Ottoman aqueduct are both within walking distance of the mosque, as is the **Flamingo restaurant** (*see* p. 78).

The Story of Umm Haram

Only 17 years after the death of the Prophet Mohammed, the caliph **Othman** presided over an enormous Muslim Empire, which was annually extended by the Arab cavalry armies posted on its borders. Moawiya, the caliph's deputy in Syria, was constantly requesting permission to launch raids into the Byzantine Empire, to test his newly constructed fleet. Othman did not trust the sea and could not be persuaded that it was safe to put an army in boats until Moawiya, keen to display his complete confidence in the venture, offered to take all his wives and children with him. His senior officers respectfully followed suit, which was how, in 649, Umm Haram landed with the Arab army that came to plunder Byzantine Cyprus. She rode on a mule which stumbled at the lake shore and, in the words of the historian Ibn Al Attir, 'broke her pellucid neck and yielded up her victorious soul, and in that fragrant spot was at once buried'. She was buried beneath the three stones of an ancient menhir, a suitable headstone for this distinguished, first casualty of the invasion. Umm Haram Rumeysha bint Milham, 'the beautiful, pious lady with light brown eyes, the daughter of Milham', was one of the earliest Muslim believers, a member of a small group who had endured years of derision and persecution. Her friendship with the **Prophet Mohammed** was strengthened by her nephew Anas, who served as his private secretary. Her first husband, Ohod, was an early Muslim martyr, and her second was a scholar who served as the *cadi* (the chief judge) of Palestine. Umm Haram had long known the instances of her death from a revelatory dream of the Prophet, who had fallen asleep in her lap whilst she had been combing his hair for lice. He awoke and told her the future, which included the welcome news that she was among those destined for paradise.

The Sanctuary

After the Byzantine reconquest of the island in the 10th century the tomb fell into neglect, but it was never forgotten and after the Ottoman conquest its fame revived. Generations upon generations of Turkish girls were named in her honour, pilgrims visited her grave to request her intercession and ships approaching Larnaca were careful to salute the shrine. In 1787 a *tekke*, an informal Ottoman monastery, was established beside the tomb, though none of the existing buildings dates from before a full-scale reconstruction job in 1816.

Pots of local honey and bottles of lemon juice are sold by the entrance arch from where steps lead down through the garden to the *şadirvan*. This hexagonal kiosk shelters eight marble stools for the ritual washing required before prayer, though non-Muslims are asked only to remove their shoes before entering the mosque. A circle of eight arches carries the dome of the prayer hall (the same arrangment as for the ArabAhmet mosque in Nicosia), with its carved *mihrab*, or prayer niche, indicating the direction of prayer towards Mecca. The pulpit-like *mimber* is used for the Friday sermon. The shields that hang from the walls announce the name of the Prophet and the first four rightly-guided caliphs of Sunni Islam.

The custodian leads visitors into the tomb room, pointing out on the way the grave of **Hatidje**, the wife of King Hussein of Hejaz and the grandmother of King Hussein of Jordan. She was born in Istanbul, the granddaughter of a grand vizier, who must have had mixed feelings about the assistance the British, in the guise of T. E. Lawrence, gave to her husband's Arab revolt against the Ottoman Empire. She died in 1929 in exile. Umm Haram's tomb is a dark cube wrapped in green, the ancient menhirs obscured by the holy gloom and various whitewashed restorations. The pious believe that the stones flew here from Mecca on the night of her death, and that in the greater faith of past centuries the stone crossbar hovered miraculously above the two uprights.

Vyzakia and Kamares Aqueduct

The site of the Late Bronze Age city of **Vyzakia**, also known as Hala Sultan Tekke, is 200m northwest of the sanctuary. A fenced area to the left of the lakeside track is currently being excavated, and though it is not open to the public, you can view from outside the street plan, cisterns and houses of this ancient community. It rose to prosperity at the end of the Bronze Age when, after the destruction of the settlements at Kalavassos and Maroni, there was room for a new port and metal-working centre to benefit from the inland copper mines. During that period the Salt Lake was a sheltered lagoon open to the sea, and Vyzakia engaged in profitable trade with the Egypt of Rameses II, the Syrian cities such as Ugarit and the palaces of Minoan Crete. It was destroyed in 1175 BC and later used as a cemetery, which may have provided the menhir besides which Umm Haram was to be buried.

About 2km northwest of Vyzakia there are four stretches of arches from the **Kamares aqueduct**. The most impressive stretch is just south of the Nicosia road out of Larnaca. The aqueduct, despite many local tales, dates from the Ottoman not from the Roman Empire. It was built around 1745 by **Abu Bekir Paşa**, during his period as governor of Cyprus. He had wells sunk around the village of Arpera (of which only the chapel of **Ayios Yeoryios** remains; *see p. 86*) and the spring water collected for its 10km journey to the public fountains in Larnaca. The aqueduct was maintained by a special charitable trust established by the paşa until replaced by pipes in 1939.

Just North of Larnaca

North of Larnaca pale treeless escarpments shelter decaying agricultural villages with outlying patches of olive groves. The **Green Line** runs through this district, separating it from the Mesaoria plain; and turning many former through-roads into cul-de-sacs. **Pyla village**, the **Pyla tomb** and the 11th-century paintings in **Ayios Antonios at Kellia** are the principal attractions. The latter can be reached on a no. 8 bus from Larnaca.

Livadhia, Kellia and Troulli

Leaving north from Larnaca, turn left just after the petrol refinery up the E301 to **Livadhia**, which has been much expanded by refugees. The traditional industry of basket weaving from split canes is still practised in this village. After a coffee in the central café, stroll across to admire the **church of St Paraskeva**, with its fine collection of icons and three-storey limestone bell tower carved in the 19th century.

The hamlet of **Kellia** is 3km north of Livadhia. It was once a pretty Turkish village, but now only a few decaying palm- and fig-shaded gardens and a couple of handsome Ottoman street fountains remain amongst the neat villas built after 1974 for Greek-Cypriot refugees. The Byzantine **church of Ayios Antonios** (St Anthony's) stands on a hillock on the western edge of the hamlet. (*To visit it you will need to stop for a drink at the café by the bus stop and ask for the custodian.*) It was built around AD 1000 as a simple cross-shaped chapel for a community of hermit-like monks. After the Mameluke devastation of 1425 it was rebuilt as a parish church and given a narthex, a verandah and the rather odd-looking barrel-vaulted dome. A recent restoration programme has revealed a number of 11th- and 13th-century paintings that survived on the central piers.

There are three separate depictions of the red-cloaked *St George* on his white horse, the *Virgin* seated on a great imperial throne and an early, eastern-influenced *Crucifixion* (on the south pier of the central apse), with Christ addressing his mother and St John wearing a white toga. The open-arched verandah on the south face has also been sympathetically restored using traditional Cypriot materials: thin beams, a woven-cane ceiling and terracotta pantiles. It shades the firmly riveted south door which stands below a sunburst shield carved on the marble lintel, the arms of the Gourri family.

North of Kellia the hills are stained with a rich palette of mineral leachings which were once quarried for their colours as well as for iron. The ruined **monastery of Ayios Yeoryios** is 1.5km from the E301 road, but it is not a good area for walking as it is also dotted with army posts. The village of **Troulli** marks the end of the road. The 16th-century barrel-vaulted church of St Mamas in the village centre is now dwarfed by a neo-Byzantine monster of a church, a new home for the miracle-working icon of **St Mamas**, which is especially efficacious in the cure of sore throats. From Troulli there is a track west to the hamlet of Avdhellero, where you can pick up the road to Athienou in order to make a round-trip.

Pyla Village and Tomb

The odd frontiers of the **British Sovereign Base of Dhekelia** and an impartial UN police force have preserved Pyla as the island's only surviving mixed village. Post-1974 politics have done nothing to make the relationship between Greek and Turkish Cypriots any easier but here, as if in aspic, is the old situation. Different schools proudly fly either the Greek or Turkish flag, the bell tower and minaret mark the separate places of worship, and a pair of opposing cafés allow the two communities to share the streets, but very little of each other's lives. The simmering animosity is made tangible by the ring of Turkish army posts on the hills to the west, and the Greek-Cypriot army and police who whisper advice to visitors not to buy clothes, or even food from a Turk.

The village is centred around a small square overlooked by the graceful arched colonnade of the old Turkish café, its modern Greek rival, the Trokos fish taverna and a UN police post. Behind the post office there is a small chapel dedicated to the archangel Michael. Uphill is a partly ruined three-storey medieval **tower house**, built by John de Brie, Prince of Galilee in the 14th century, and now occupied by pigeons. It was originally entered through the first floor along a precarious drawbridge overlooked by a projecting balcony. The back streets are filled with traditional mudbrick houses built up from stone foundations, and with projecting wooden balconies. There is a good view from the summit of the recently constructed minaret. (*Ask for the key at the Turkish café or from the custodian in his sportswear shop on the corner before the medieval tower; tips expected*).

The 5th-century BC **Pyla tomb** is one of the finest of its period and lies to the southeast of the village. Approaching Pyla from the coast, turn right between a taverna and the Turkish school, carry on past the Greek school and then continue along a dirt road for 800m and take the third right turn, opposite a grove of oranges, lemons and figs. The tomb is 100m on the right, surrounded by a barbed-wire enclosure covered in asphodel and wild fennel. Fourteen steps descend below ground to a vaulted hall with three doors leading off into tomb chambers. The doorway of the central tomb is carved with protective spirits set to guard the now-broken sanctity of the shattered sarcophagi. A pair of finely detailed sphinxes with crowned heads flank an Archaic wild-eyed face with splayed nose, prominent ears and protruding tongue. If you have brought a chisel, stay your hand, for these are casts from the originals on show in the Cyprus Museum in Nicosia.

A 2.5km walk southeast from the tomb brings you uphill past the **Pogazoudi escarpment** to the heart-shaped **Kokkinokremos plateau**, which overlooks the shoreline 800m to the south. This was the site of a Late-Bronze-Age fortified town which compensated for its lack of a fresh water spring by using large sunken storage jars. The discovery of a hurriedly hidden stash of jewellery, ingots, sheet gold and remnants of a warning beacon tell of its sudden destruction in 1190 BC.

Shopping

Go to Estia's general store on Plateia Vasileos Pavlou for **English language** books, foreign newspapers and writing paper. The **covered market** off Ermou street is a fertile ground for **picnic provisions** and presents. Here you'll find cane, raffia and grass baskets and trays; fresh fruit, dried fruit, pickled fruit and candied fruit; bottles of wine and heavy earthenware decanters. Walking south from the market towards Ayios Lazaros you'll pass chair makers and **souvenir shops** selling copper coffeepots amongst the tackier goods. There is also Cyprus **raku ware** with its silver lacelike appliqué set on a salt glaze produced by Vassos, a local potter, at Andreas Charamanos's smart jewellery shop at 37 Nicolaou Rossou street, © (04) 655089.

Going out of Larnaca, **local pottery** can be bought at the villages of Kornos, Kophinou and Mosphiloti. Pano Lefkara is famous for its **lace** and **silver jewellery**, and you can acquire an **icon** from the studio of Father Kallinikos at the Ayia Varvara monastery on the way up to Stavrovouni. (For further details *see* the 'South of Larnaca' section.)

Laundry

In Larnaca, laundry can be picked up from your hotel by **Michael Panagi**, © (04) 644050, or taken to **Artemis Washing** at 12 Armenikis

Ekklisias street, ✆ (04) 625454, or the **New London Laundry** at 34 Nikodimou Mylona, ✆ (04) 652178.

Religious Services

An evening service at **Ayios Lazaros** will give you a powerful insight into the enduring beauty of the Orthodox church. The foreign communities are also well represented by **St Helena's Anglican church**, ✆ (04) 622327; the **American church**, ✆ (04) 654435; the International Evangelical church, ✆ (04) 657057; and **St Mary of Graces Catholic church** on Terrasantas street, ✆ (04) 652858, which celebrates mass on Sunday at 8am and 9.30am.

Sports

For **water sports** go to the Larnaca beach strip, between 9 and 12km north of the town. The **National Windsurfing School** is located between the Karpasiana and Lordos beach hotels. For **sub-aqua** training courses and equipment-hire try Louis Koizou at 33D Evanthias Pieridou street, ✆ (04) 627091; Octabus at 2 Ayiou Neophytou, ✆ (04) 621266; or, during the summer months, a hut opposite the Palm Beach Hotel, ✆ (04) 635571. The **Larnaca Tennis Club** has four all-weather courts, ✆ (04) 656999, and offers a short-term membership deal.

The **18-hole golf course** at Dhekelia is in good condition considering the chronic lack of water. It is in the precincts of the British Sovereign Base, so you can play only if you can first find a military friend to provide a pass. In practice, this means that interested expatriates and locals can play here but visitors cannot. For **bridge** partners you can advertise on the hotel notice boards or try the Larnaca Bridge Club at 6 M Parides street, ✆ (04) 652814.

Where to Stay

In addition to the hotels in central Larnaca, the district could be explored from two other moderately priced hotels: the **Three Seas** at Faros near Perivolia or the **Lefkarama Village** in Pano Lefkara (both listed in the South of Larnaca section).

moderate

The Four Lanterns, ✆ (04) 655012, fax (04) 626012, is one of the few old buildings left on the seafront. It has a number of balconied bedrooms overlooking the promenade from a prime position at 19–24 Leoforos Athinon (Athens street). It has a worn but still comfortable air, and features a ballroom and the Vienna café on the ground floor, where musicians play on Wednesdays and Sundays. The whitewashed and machicolated **Sandbeach Castle**, ✆ (04) 655437, is one of the few hotels in Larnaca to be washed by the sea. It is in the area known as Mackenzie beach, at the southern end of Piyâle Paşa street, 3km south along the coast from the marina.

cheap

La Maison Belge at 103 Stadiou street, ✆ (04) 654655, is at the top end of this price range. It is a small 16-room hotel situated 1km inland from the touristy seafront, opposite the triangular municipal park. The hotel is quietly and efficiently run by its owner, Mr Pavlos Evangelides. The smaller **Harry's Hotel** is like entering the world of Anthony Burgess's Enderby, with its interior of stacked suitcases and piles of paper. It is in the centre of town at 2 Thermopylon street, ✆ (04) 654453, but can be surprisingly hard to find. If you walk inland from the marina pier and take the fourth turning on your left you should spot it. If full you could try the **Rainbow Inn**, ✆ (04) 655874, on the west corner of Zinonos Kitieos street. There is also a handful of cheap guesthouses around Ayios Lazaros, like the **Pavilion**, **Makaria** and the **Ayios Lazaros Inn**, but they tend to be open only during the summer months.

Eating Out

There is a massed selection of bars and restaurants along the promenade, though the cooking gets progressively more Cypriot and interesting as you progress south. You can enjoy a cheap meal for under C£5 at most of these places, or an expensive one if you choose seafood from the menu.

The Monte Carlo, ✆ (04) 653815, is on the Piyâle Paşa section of the coast road, beyond the fort with a white balustraded terrace that is lapped by the waves. It offers one of the best and cheapest *mezedhes* in town. **Militis** is right next door to the Monte Carlo at 42, Piyâle Paşa street, ✆ (04) 655867. Do not be put off by its plate glass and kitsch village exterior; it has a strong local following and three outdoor ovens that, with the crushed wheat on your salad and the aroma of casseroles, indicate a traditional Cypriot kitchen.

Going further west there are two beach tavernas overlooking the fishing shelter where you can dine outdoors, touched by the evening sea breeze and the sound of boats bobbing up and down. Sit at **Zephyros**, ✆ (04) 57198, or the seasonal **Psarolimano**, ✆ (04) 655408.

The Tudor Inn, ✆ (04) 625608, is a steakhouse run by an English and Cypriot couple who serve fillet steaks in seven different ways from 7.30–10 every day except Sun and Mon. It is on Kala Mustafa Paşa street, which lies just off the Piyâle Paşa stretch of the coast road. A step up from the Tudor Inn in its menu and price, but with a noticeably English pudding trolley, interior and clientele is **Labby's**, tucked away at 10 Nikodimou Mylona street, ✆ (04) 626110. It is open from 7pm, closed on Sun and Mon. Reservations are often required.

The **Pyla** taverna, ✆ (04) 653990, is situated off the coast road east of the Larnaca Bay strip but before the Dhekelia barracks. It overlooks the sea on its own promontory with an agreeably shabby interior, and serves charcoal-grilled or fried fish.

The Flamingo restaurant and café is run by Peter of Famagusta, and is situated beside the Tekke of Hala Sultan, ✆ (04) 655660. Despite its position next to a major tourist attraction, it maintains its own high standards of Cypriot cooking. Look out for the malika tawny soup with its richly flavoured stock, or pot specials like *tavha*, a fusion of lamb, marrows, artichokes and onions roasted with cumin. Order your wine early as the service can be erratic.

Bars and Nightlife

The Globe is one of the most popular pubs with its mixed clientele of yachtsman, locals and expatriates. **Cloud Nine**, beside the Calabash beer garden, is a smart new neon and chrome disco-bar in the centre of town. The larger and tackier **Stringfellows** is out on the Larnaca beach strip. For a floor show and higher-priced drinks head for **Pussycat** disco-night-club, which is staffed by Danish girls. Its illuminated sign is easily spotted in the dock quarter along Leoforos Archiepiskopou Makariou III avenue, almost opposite the tall Avenue Hotel Apartments.

For Cypriot food, music, lavish hospitality and pink-uniformed waiters, go out to the cavernous **Romantzo** overlooking the sea halfway along the coast road east of Larnaca.

If you are wandering around the illuminated Ayios Lazaros in the evening you might be drawn to the intimate upstairs bar of the **Black Turtle** taverna, occasionally visited by local musicians. **Barabende**, ✆ (04) 628462, is even more removed from the lager-swilling scene on the beach strip. It is a small music bar, devoted to Greek folk music, that opens late in the evening and is found near Ayia Phileromeni (Faneromeni) church.

North and Due West of Larnaca

Northwest of Larnaca the land rises slowly, separating the coast from the Mesaoria plain with a pale line of eroded limestone hills. It is an ancient and largely unimpressive landscape, but one that is speckled with quiet villages, frescoed chapels, lone ruins and minor archaeological sites. With the exception of the **Stavrovouni monastery**, with its magnificent view, the area is usually empty of tourists, and there are no hotels. The 15th-century frescoes in the **Royal Chapel** at Pyrga, the 12th-century frescoes in the **Ayii Apostoli** chapel at Perakhorio and the melancholy ruins of **Ayios Sozomenos** are the other principal attractions. The sites of the ancient cities of Idalion and Golgi, outside the large but quiet villages of Dhali and Athienou, are only for those who want to immerse themselves in Cypriot history.

Stavrovouni (The Mountain of the Cross) Monastery

> *I, the unworthy, worshipped this holy and miraculous thing, and saw with my sinful eyes the Divine favour which rests upon this place.*

Abbot Daniel, a 12th-century pilgrim from Russia

(Open, to men only, on the morning and afternoon of Mon, Wed, Fri and Sun. Women are not allowed within the monastery precincts except to join church services on Sunday or on 13 and 14 September, the annual festival of the Exultation of the Cross. No cameras.)

The 19th-century monastery buildings crown an isolated mountain top 40km west of Larnaca, an ancient holy place that is halfway between God and man. Some of its grandeur is diminished by a steady trickle of hire cars whose occupants often seem disappointed to discover there is no toilet or café to match the view. The approach road is signposted off the old Limassol to Nicosia road, not the motorway, and twists up through the wooded hills to pass, at the foot of the mountain, the **Ayia Varvara (St Barbara) monastery**, which acts as a base camp for isolated, windswept Stavrovouni. St Barbara has its own chapel inside the residential courtyard and a cluster of farm sheds, workshops and the famous icon and fresco studio of Father Kallinikos. Visitors are welcome into the studio, which has a shop which sells framed reproductions for C£10, while the more desirable hand-painted icons cost around C£130.

History and Tradition

The mountain summit has long had religious significance and was visited by pilgrims centuries before Christianity. A temple to Aphrodite, reproduced on some of the island's coins, stood on the summit of this lone 690m-high mountain. It was known as Mount Olympos until **St Helena**, the mother of Constantine, the first Christian emperor, called in at Cyprus in AD 325, on her way back from her archaeological investigations into the holy places around Jerusalem. The traditions record that after a picnic lunch by the coast she fell asleep and received an inspirational dream to build a church on the island and furnish it with one of her many relics. Before she could settle on a site, the cross of Olympas (the good thief also known by the name of Dysmas) miraculously transferred itself to the mountain of similar name. St Helena was thrilled, but she was also canny of her holy store of relics. She swopped crossbeams with the cross of Gesmas, the bad thief, but generously contributed a nail and a fragment of the True Cross.

The earliest documentary mention of the monastery is in 1106, by which time it was firmly established on the medieval pilgrimage route. The good thief's cross, wrapped in gold, was housed in a chapel behind the high altar where it appeared, to the pious at least, to float in mid-air. A Catholic Benedictine community ousted the Orthodox after 1191; the monastery was destroyed and the precious cross carried off during the Mameluke raid of 1426. The fragment of the True Cross was hidden and twice escaped destruction, during both the Ottoman invasion of 1570 and the 1821 terror campaign.

None of the existing buildings dates from before the late 19th century, when the monastery was re-established. It is built from local stone which gives it, and especially the surrounding garden terraces, an organic relationship to the mountain. It seems almost to have grown out of the mountain, though the rough texture and metallic colours of the stone also create a grim, forbidding exterior. The terraces below the terracotta-domed church provide a celebrated panorama over the southern coast and inland to the broken forested hills with their hidden mine workings. The church interior is surprisingly small and its intimacy enhanced by a clutter of *ex voto* silver lamps and eggs. The small gilt reliquary that contains the fragment of True Cross is not always on display, but in the right-hand niche of the iconostasis is a cross carved in the 15th century, to replace the relic that had been carried away into Egypt by the Mamelukes. It is now embossed in silver worked with scenes from the *Life of Christ*. The church and the oratory chapel by the car park are being furnished with a complete body of traditional frescoes lovingly created by the studio at St Barbara.

The Royal Chapel at Pyrga and the Village of Kornos

The hamlet of Pyrga is just east of the Limassol-to-Nicosia motorway (turn off at junction 11). At the entrance to the village a large modern parish church stands beside the road and overlooks a wire-enclosed blockhouse made from ragstone. It is something of a surprise to discover that the latter, a modest, rectangular building, only 6m by 4m, turns out on closer inspection to be the famous 15th-century **Royal Chapel**. Though originally dedicated to the Virgin, it is now known as Ayia Ekaterini, or St Catherine's. It was built in 1421 by King Janus as the chapel of a royal manor house, and is a world removed from the soaring

Gothic chapels, rich cloisters and cathedrals that his family had erected in the previous century, before the Genoese invasion impoverished the kingdom.

The frescoes in the interior of the chapel, which combine Byzantine and Italian traditions with French inscriptions, have a poignant delicacy. The *Crucifixion*, and three other scenes from the Passion, fill the east wall below three high windows. The Virgin faints to the left of the Cross, and St John and the good centurion stand to the right, while King Janus and his Queen, Charlotte of Bourbon, can be seen praying at its foot. The groins of the vaulting are painted with details from the royal arms—the lions of Cyprus and Armenia with the Cross of Jerusalem. Within a year of the chapel's completion the queen was dead; within five years King Janus was a prisoner, tied backwards on a hobbled ass and paraded through the jeering streets of Cairo, having witnessed the death of his brother and the annihiliation of his army at the battle of Khirokitia.

Amongst other fresco panels, *St Damien* and *St Cosmo* can be recognized in the eastern corners with the *Ascension* and *Pentecost* on the south wall, the *Raising of Lazarus*, the *Triumphal Entrance into Jerusalem*, the *Last Supper* and the *Washing of Feet* on the north wall. In the western half of the chapel Peter and Paul are painted above the eponymous *St Catherine*, by the south door, and continuing clockwise, there is *Gabriel*, *St Constantine* and *St Helena*; above the west door, the *Virgin Enthroned* and the *Dormition of the Virgin*.

Just west of the motorway from Pyrga is the village of **Kornos**, overlooked by granite plugs that have eroded to provide beds of good-quality clay. A number of potters are still active in the tightly-packed streets of the village centre. The village was famous for its earthenware jars, huge red flasks made not on a potter's wheel but built up by hand. These *pitharia* used to store water, oil, wine and grain, but now serve as garden ornaments. The demand has gone, so you are more likely to find small jugs embellished with fritted brims, swirls, imprints and modelled birds that seem touched by a hint of ancient Cyprus. For older pieces of earthenware, browse at the **Mosphiloti flower shop** at the turning to Mosphiloti village from the old Nicosia road. It is like an open-air folk museum filled with desirable farm carts, trees, mills and jars—all far too big to be squeezed onto the flight home.

The Chapel of Ayii Apostoli at Perakhorio

The motorway thunders within a stone's throw of the delicate 12th-century frescoed chapel of Ayii Apostoli, or Holy Apostles. Situated on a hill just west of the village, it is approached from the Perakhorio turning off the old Nicosia road. To find the key-bearing custodian, either ask at the modernist village café or at 12 Apostles Road, which leads west from the village centre to the cemetery now surrounding the chapel. Once your eyes become accustomed to the dark you can pick out the benign *Christ Pantocrator* that blesses visitors from the dome of the church. Against the aged blue background of the altar apse the *Virgin* is depicted in the Blacherniotissa pose (hands raised in blessing and the Christ Child framed in a medallion). She is flanked by St Peter and St Paul, not her usual archangel escorts. An *Annunciation* can be admired above her, whilst below, frowning angels guard the altar canopy for the *Communion of the Apostles*, with presiding prelates in assorted vestments on the ground level. The paintings on the south wall are noticeably cruder, but the apse sequence was painted when Cyprus was still a province of the Byzantine Empire. The paintings have been dated around 1170, for stylistically they closely follow the classicizing trend associated with the Comnenian court at Constantinople.

Dhali, Ancient Idalion and Potamia

The village of **Dhali** sits on the south bank of the Yialias riverbed. It is approached from Larnaca on the B2, or off the Nicosia motorway, about 4km to its west.

The ruins of the city of **Idalion** are not marked. Coming from Larnaca you will reach the statue of an *enosis* hero on the southern edge of Dhali. Turn west here (to your left) and 200m later turn south (left again) onto a bumpy track leading uphill to the site of the ancient city of Idalion, in a valley formed by three pale limestone hills. It was much looted by di Cesnola and other turn-of-the-century stone hunters, so its temple carvings and inscriptions are well represented in foreign museums. Recent work is just beginning to confirm the haphazard 19th-century reports. Idalion was founded in the Late Bronze Age, then re-established in the Archaic period, when it was one of the dozen independent city-states of the island; but it perished in the 4th century BC, a victim, like Kition, of the new Hellenistic order.

Excavation trenches at the foot of the eastern hill have exposed some of the finely dressed stone walls and towers that defended the town in the 5th century BC. The summit was once graced by an acropolis which enclosed a great temple to Aphrodite. Now all that remains visible are the scars of old excavations, together with the dugouts and emplacements of an abandoned Greek-Cypriot military post. To the northeast stands the handsome 13th-century domed cruciform chapel of **Ayios Yeoryios** (St George), whose walls are built of fragments from Idalion. On the slopes of the two western hills stood temples to the Virgin Athene and Aphrodite Kourotrophos, with the shrine to Apollo in the centre of the valley. The latter was probably associated with the city's Adonis cult, the young god and lover of the goddess, whose annual sacrificial death and rebirth mirrored the miracle of the seasons and assured the growth of future crops.

From the centre of Dhali take the road following the riverbed and continue 3km northeast to **Potamia**. As you leave Dhali, you pass a cemetery on your left, served by a distinguished-looking chapel, the broad-naved and high-vaulted

St Mamas. This is a rare example of a 16th-century Venetian church. Elsewhere on the island the Venetians are better known for ruthlessly demolishing churches and using the stone to build fortresses.

The domed church of **Ayios Demetrianus Andridiotis** stands alone, halfway between Dhali and Potamia. Inside is the portrait of Mr and Mrs Michael Katzourobis, the medieval donors who renovated the church in 1317, or, as the inscription has it, in the 6825th year of creation. There are three other fine 14th-century frescoes: a *Holy Tile* above the west door, a *Holy Handkerchief* above the south door and an unusual *St Kyriaki*, accompanied by figures representing the days of the week, on a northern pier.

Ayios Sozomenos

The empty village of Ayios Sozomenos lies 3km north of Potamia. As you pass by Potamia village there is a mound, just to the left as you cross the Yialias riverbed, which contains the ruins of the chapel of **Ayia Ekaterini** (St Catherine's). This served as the private chapel of the royal Lusignan manor house of Potamia, the foundations of which can be seen 50m south. It was once surrounded by a famously elegant medieval garden much praised for its tranquillity.

Ayios Sozomenos was a Turkish village. It is now empty and in ruins; the earth-brick walls of the village houses have lost their protective white plaster and are eroding back into the soil. It was heavily fought over in the intercommunal violence of the early sixties. The Turkish-Cypriot dead are recorded in the striking photographs of Don McCullin that were syndicated around the world. In his autobiography he recalls the devastation:

> *There was silence. I turned the handle and opened the door. The early morning cold syphoned out warm sticky air. It was a sticky carnage that I saw. The floor was covered in blood. A man was lying on his face, another flat on his back. I could smell something burning. In another room I found a third man dead. Three men dead, a father and two sons. Suddenly the door opened and people came in led by what I later learned was the wife of the youngest man. They had been married only a few days. All the presents were laid out in the front room, all shot up in the gun battle. The woman picked up a towel to cover her husband's face and started to cry... An older man said, 'Take your picture...'*

In the centre of the village stands the ruined Gothic church of **St Mamas**, built from golden yellow stone. The finely carved details on the west door date back to the early 15th century. The high south wall contains twin tomb niches. The nave, which is divided into three aisles, may originally have been intended to support a central dome, which would explain the taller and broader central arches. It may have never been finished before the Mameluke invasion of 1426 brought it to ruin. It stands, like its more famous namesake at Morphou, as testimony to the gradual fusion of Byzantine and Gothic culture at the end of the Lusignan period. Beside it is a simple village church with a painting of the Panayia (Virgin Mary) under its terracotta-tiled roof. The track leads up past the bullet-splattered walls of a roofless mosque and Muslim cemetery under a eucalyptus grove, to a rock-cut chapel. This, with its fragile paintings, was added to the hermit's cave and tomb of St Sozomenos, which he dug out of the golden escarpment above the village.

Athienou and the Excavations at Golgoi

The turning to **Athienou** village is 15km northwest of Larnaca, off the main Nicosia road at Goshi. You can also approach the village on a 15km dirt road north from Aradhippou, passing through open country and the hamlet of Avdhellero.

Athienou was home to 150 families of Kiraji muleteers, who ran the trade route between Nicosia and Larnaca. Their only competitor was the village of Aradhippou, which relied upon camels. The Kiraji were distinguished by their honesty and efficiency. They claimed to be descended from a band of Italian nobles who survived the fall of Famagusta in 1571. They were too poor to have any hope for a ransom but the Turks nevertheless spared them, so tired had they become of spilling blood. Like the aristocratic White Russians who took to driving cabs in Paris after the Bolshevik revolution, the Kiraji also took to earning a living on the road. Athienou's role was ended by the construction of permanent roads by the British colonial administration which bypassed the town. It is now even further isolated by the close grip of the **Green Line**.

Just 600m northeast of the village, along the road to Kırıkkale (Melousha) is the site of the ancient city of **Golgoi**. Here, in 1860, the tomb-robbing foreign consul, di Cesnola, unearthed massive sculpted heads and Archaic statues from the temple area. These are now exhibited in the Metropolitan Museum of New York. Access to Golgoi is sometimes restricted; if you do not feel like rushing off, then have a walk through the village (which is itself built over an Early-Bronze-Age settlement) and admire the traditional exterior of the preserved Zanettis' house.

Southwest of Larnaca

The three principal sites to the southwest of Larnaca are the **mosaic of the Virgin** in Kiti, the **Neolithic village** at Khirokitia and the hill town of **Pano Lefkara**. However, it would be a pity not to explore this area in greater depth. It is dotted with a dozen compact agricultural villages and a coast which is virtually empty, scoured clean of human settlement by centuries of seaborne raids. Few of the villages boast anything more elaborate than the ubiquitous café for the entertainment of passing visitors. Rough farm tracks lead south from the villages to the coast, which has a predominately rocky shore broken by strips of pebble beach. It is an area for picnics, walks and swims. You can stay and eat at either Perivolia-Cape Kiti on the coast, or in Pano Lefkara which is tucked up in the hills, with additional good meals awaiting at Vavatsinia and Zyyi.

Kiti, Perivolia and Faros

The church of **Panayia Angeloktistos** (*open weekdays 8–4, Sat 10–4, Sun 9–12, 2–4*), which literally translates as 'Our Lady built by angels', is named after the Byzantine mosaic in its apse. It is on the northwest edge of the village of **Kiti**, just before the Venetian bridge that spans the Tremithos riverbed, 5km southwest of Larnaca airport. The village is traditionally considered to have been founded by Kittim, the great grandson of Noah, though a more modest lineage traces its foundation to refugees from Kition. The church was built in the 11th century using the ruins of a much older church, of which only the apse with its 'angel-built mosaic' survives. The entrance is through the southern porch, which bears three coats of arms below the bell arch. The lion quartered with the Cross of Jerusalem is that of the Lusignans, probably in reference to a cadet branch of the royal family who occupied the castle of Le Quid at Kiti. The shield with three lions around a cross is that of the de Gibelet family, who originally built this vaulted porch as a separate Catholic chapel beside the older Orthodox church. In the apse a collection of portable icons is displayed, and the medieval tombstone of Lady Simone Guers, wife of Sir Renier de Gibelet, can be seen on the west wall. The main body of the church has suffered from well-meaning restorations, which have exposed fragments of frescoes like the 13th-century *St John* on the south central pier.

The great glory of the church, and indeed of Cyprus, is on the wall of the sanctuary apse. It is dated to either the 6th or 9th century by scholars who depend on comparisons with the securely dated Byzantine mosaics at Ravenna and Istanbul. Peer over the iconostasis door and above the altar to admire the glittering golden mosaic inscribed *Hagia Maria* (St Mary), and set within a symbolic frieze composed of a cross, a pair of white harts and three crystal chalices wrapped in intricate blue and green foliage. The Virgin, dressed in the stripy home-spun red and white cloak that is still worn in Palestine, holds the infant Jesus, represented as a fair-haired prince, clad in a gilded toga and sandals. The Holy Mother of God stands on a bejewelled footstool, but her face is filled with quiet maternal anxiety, whilst her eyes stare straight ahead and shame the onlooker with her absolute purity.

On either side of her a pair of peacock-winged archangels approach, Michael on the left, Gabriel on the right, offering orbs, the golden apples of dominion. They are dressed in white togas that have a broad gold stripe of rank, and clutch the rods of authority used by the ushers in the Imperial Palace at Constantinople. These ceremonial accoutrements of Byzantium survive on in Britain, where an ash rod indicates the Lord Chancellor and the eponymous Black Rod marshals the peers in the House of Lords.

South from Kiti

Perivolia village lies 3km southeast of Kiti. It has a markedly commercial air, with restaurants, banks, car hire agencies and a supermarket, all fuelled by the villa apartments growing on its outskirts. There are two churches, **Ayia Irini** and **Ayios Leondios** (St Leontios). The latter, with its pretty bell tower, is found along the cemetery-beach road west of the village. St Leontios is one of Cyprus's 300 lesser-known saints; he was the biographer of St John the Almoner, who lived and worked in Cyprus at the end of the 6th century, though both Perivolia and Amathus claim him as a local.

South of Perivolia a road leads to **Faros**, the stumpy lighthouse on the slight promontory of Cape Kiti, which stands on the site of a 6th-century BC Phoenician temple. The limestone escarpment hides a shore lined with grey sand or black and white pebbles. A farm track beside the shore allows for an easy 2km stroll to the two-storey **Venetian watchtower**, which crowns an inland knoll. It was built in 1500 and has a pleasing silhouette formed by the machicolations and projecting brackets that once supported a wooden upper gallery. A ladder and rope allow for a strenuous ascent to the first floor door. The door lintel is decorated with a sword holding the Lion of St Mark between two shields. The upper chamber has a groined vault and skylight up to the roof.

Where to Stay in and around Perivolia

The Three Seas, © (05) 321975, is an uninspiring concrete rectangle, but has a pleasantly isolated position near the lighthouse-guarded head-land, south of Perivolia. It is moderately priced, efficiently run and dominated by *sportif* French tour groups.

If you are looking for something cheaper, ask for rooms at the roadside **Mangas** taverna in Perivolia, or rent one of the flats behind the Kastania Disco, © (05) 422629.

The Chapel of Ayios Yeoryios at Arpera

The lone chapel of Ayios Yeoryios at Arpera is all that remains of a medieval village that flourished in the 18th century. It has a melancholic atmosphere further enhanced by a few straggling palms, ruined arches and the earthen ramparts of a nearby dam. The chapel is associated with the village of Tersephanou, though it is more easily reached from Kiti. Travelling west from Kiti, turn right immediately after crossing the bridge over the Tremithos stream and continue 3km up the track. Ask for the keys to the chapel from the farmhouse nearby with its surprisingly approachable Alsatian dogs.

The barrel-vaulted chapel of Ayios Yeoryios was built in 1745 from the ruins of a Catholic church by Christophakis Constantinou, the dragoman of the saray, interpreter to the Ottoman governor. The dragoman had an extremely powerful but vulnerable position, like the prime minister who serves a modern president. Christophakis built the church as a thanks offering, but before he could finish its decoration he was murdered. The villainous one-eyed Haji Baki Agha, whom he had sacked from his judicial post at Larnaca, employed assassins to strike him down as he approached the church on the Easter morning of 1750. Above the north door is an accurate portrayal of Christophakis and his family, dressed entirely in the Ottoman style, listening to a tonsured preacher. Christophakis wears the *qalpaq*, a busby made of marten skin, that was reserved for his high office. To the north of the iconostasis is a vivid portrayal of *St George*, with both the princess rescued from the dragon and his coffee-bearing page riding pillion. A large *Archangel Michael* is on the wall beside the double icon of *St George*, along with the curious lupine-faced *St Christopher Kynokephalos.*

Mazotos, Alaminos and Kophinou (Afinou)

Mazotos is a sleepy village surrounded by fields fringed with small groves of olive and carob trees. A few villas have been built and in summer there is a chance of renting a room; ask at the café or supermarket by the modern church of Ayios Yeoryios. **Petounda Point** is 3km south of the village, and most of the tracks leading to it peter out before you actually reach the shore. Those who persevere will discover a **pair of chapels** to the Panayia (Virgin Mary), standing on what was the acropolis of a Roman town.

Alaminos is caught in the fold of hills and divided by the Xeropotamos 'no water' stream, which used to separate the village into Greek and Turkish quarters. On the east side, in what used to be the Turkish quarter, stands a **medieval tower**, a simple three-storey structure which was entered via a drawbridge on the first floor. It was a minor possession of the d'Ibelin, one of the most powerful and well-connected of the Crusader families. On the other side of the valley is the lone whitewashed church of **St Mamas.**

Kophinou, also known as Afinou, is at the junction of the Larnaca road and the main Limassol to Nicosia highway, but only a rough taverna with a sand floor remains of this old truck stop. The main village is just south of the main road, and its strategic position may partly explain the brutal attack on its Turkish inhabitants by Grivas's EOKA B in the winter of 1967. The decaying houses around the boarded-up mosque stand like some mute witness. Skoutari earthenware can be bought direct from the **pottery studio** at No. 202, which has the widest choice of mugs, censers and bowls.

Ayios Theodhoros, Psematismenos and Maroni

Ayios Theodhoros is a village 3km south of the main Limassol-to-Larnaca road and the starting point for an 8km walk to the sea. Follow the track south down the valley, passing the chapel of **Ayii Anagrii** halfway. Continue on, keeping left at the next two junctions, to enter a large orange grove and on past the ruined churches of **Ayios Athanasos** (St Anthony) and **Ayios Yeoryios** (St George), which mark the site of the old coastal village of Pendaskhinos. The isolated **Kentpon** fish taverna stands by the pebble beach like an undeserved reward.

The villages of **Psematismenos** and **Maroni** are strung along the **Ayios Minas valley** south of the main highway. They both contain a number of handsome stone-built houses in the narrow streets of the village centres. The Ayios Minas valley, which boasts Khirokitia upstream, amongst numerous other ancient sites, could almost be turned into an archaeological park. Excavations at **Vournes**, a low hill situated 500m from the sea beside a track running southeast from Maroni, have revealed a square stone building which was built in the Late Bronze Age. It received tribute from the surrounding area, but there is no knowing if it was the palace of a local lord or whether it had a religious function. It lay in ruins for 500 years, before it was reoccupied in the 7th century BC to serve as an Archaic shrine to the goddess. Her particular local aspect, as the protector of agricultural fertility, meant that she was addressed as Demeter in the Hellenistic era.

Zyyi

The E107 turn-off from the motorway leads south to **Zyyi** and north to **Kalavasos**. Zyyi is the small sister to the port of Vasilikos, where mining companies used to run trains full of ore down from the hills to piers that stretched out from the shallow shore. Warehouses, disused railway tracks and a radar post still give Zyyi a slightly shabby industrial air, which help camouflage some Cypriot holiday apartments and a number of good restaurants from overuse.

Eating Out in Zyyi

The fish taverna in front of the old pier, **Psaro Yiotis**, ✆ (04) 332424, run by Marios and George, is the most immediately attractive-looking establishment in Zyyi, though the more modest **H EXAPA** taverna run by Charlie the musician, ✆ (04) 332922, has its own charm. **Santa Elena** concentrates on kebabs, grilled meat and fresh salads.

Just north of the Limassol-to-Nicosia motorway, a barn-like hangar has been erected over the **Tenta-Kalavasos excavations** where a Neolithic village of circular mud and stone houses has been unearthed. It is from the same pre-ceramic Neolithic culture as Khirokitia that flourished from around 7000 BC, but mysteriously perished 1700 years later. It is not yet open to the public but the site can be appreciated through the fence and is best approached from the old main road that runs beneath the motorway.

Another local dig, known as **Kalavasos-Ayios Dhimitrios**, has revealed a Bronze-Age palace which had an upper storey and a tribute hall filled with 47 *pithoi*. It was suddenly destroyed and burnt in 1200 BC, but the fire did have one beneficial side effect, for it baked and preserved a number of Cypro-Minoan inscriptions scratched onto five clay cylinders.

Khirokitia Neolithic Village

Open daily 7.30am–7.30pm; adm.

The entrance to the Neolithic site, one of the earliest settlements on the island, is just over the bridge as you approach the modern village of Khirokitia from the old main road, where there are a pair of café-tavernas beside the petrol station. Only a small portion of the village has been revealed by the excavations which started in 1936. Various layers from later cultures were carefully stripped away to expose the low foundation walls of the oldest settlement belonging to the Aceramic Neolithic culture which occupied this hilltop village between 7000 and 5300 BC. A stairway allows visitors to safely view three fragile areas of excavation, where the confused patterns from the foundations of a mass of circular stone huts cling to the steep slope of the hill.

The huts are packed around what at first looks like a raised road, but is in fact the wide perimeter wall. The village was established on the eastern end of the escarpment, which is enclosed by the serpentine bend of the river, except on the west face, where the perimeter wall was built. As the village grew, an extension to the wall was made (on the summit at sector D), but through pressure of numbers the population soon spilled out even further west of this addition. No weapons have been found, and the wall is considered to have been as much a spiritual barrier as protection against wild animals or neighbouring villages. Within the wall the villagers may have felt themselves part of a privileged community which maintained a collective relationship to a protective deity.

Life in the Village

The huts were fitted with plaster floors, warmed by a central hearth with platforms for sitting and eating. The stone walls were plastered and whitewashed in and out and possibly embellished with designs in red ochre. The larger ones have basins and stone piers (like the hut marked 1a) which upheld a small loft. They are no longer considered to have been capable of supporting a dome, like the famous beehive houses of the Trulli villages of southern Italy, but probably bore a flat roof of thick branches covered in reeds and sealed with a mud plaster. The huts were probably arranged in clusters of an extended family, with the dead buried beneath the floors in a fetal position as if returning to the womb. A number of stone querns can be seen outside the huts where the crops of wheat and barley were milled into flour. Deer, sheep, goat and pig bones testify to a varied diet but the villagers seem to have avoided shellfish. They made clothes from sewn leather, and ornaments and tools from reed, wood and stone, though only the stone has survived the millennia. Their flint blades, gaming pieces, shell and cornelian jewellery, polished axes, bowls and figurines, carved from grey-green andesite river-boulders, are displayed in the Cyprus Museum in Nicosia.

The Battle of Khirokitia in 1426

The modern village of Khirokitia is perched on a long escarpment of rock. This natural defensive position is further fortified by the serpentine bends of the Ayios Minas river that flows to its north. The gently sloping fields to the southwest, dotted with old olive trees, is the site of the Battle of Khirokitia, which broke the spirit and the substance of the medieval kingdom of Cyprus. The Mamelukes invaded in 1426, partly to revenge the Cypriot sack of Alexandria, but also to negotiate a peace that would halt further raids and re-establish trade. However, the Christian knights of Cyprus amused themselves by torturing the envoys to death. This horrifying breach of civilized conduct was avenged at Khirokitia on Sunday 7 July. The Lusignan army had begun the day by rioting before the old Templar tower over the lack of strong drink. For as one soldier complained, 'Where are we to get wine to drink that we may face our enemies?' They retreated in disorder after the first charge. King Janus was taken captive to be mocked by the urchins of Cairo, while his brother, the Prince of Galilee, and most of the army were slain.

The Church of Panayia tou Kambou and Khirokitia Tower

On the road to Vavla, which skirts Khirokitia village, go down the white dirt track almost due west of the village bell tower which leads to the small church of **Panayia tou Kambou** where King Janus was captured. It was built from the large, dressed stones of an older chapel, and above the west door are fragments of reused Gothic carvings, such as a green man, whose face peers out from its surrounding foliage. A few patches of painting survive, like *St George* in a niche on the north wall and beside him, on a buttress, *St Helios* with a black-robed donor wearing the Cross of St John of the Knights Hospitallers. A field away to the west is a vaulted basement, all that remains of **Khirokitia tower** which was so crucially empty of wine on the morning of battle. It was built by the Knights Templars, but passed into the hands of the rival Hospitallers when the Templars were suppressed for heresy in the early 14th century.

Lefkara

This picturesque hill town, 50km from Larnaca, is a maze of narrow streets and alleys lined with houses all built from thin slabs of pale local stone. Lefkara is divided into an unequal pair of adjoining villages. **Pano** (upper) **Lefkara**, the main tourist centre, is larger and uphill, whilst **Kato** (lower) **Lefkara** is decayed and downhill. Both are approached off the E105, which twists uphill 10km north of the Limassol-to-Nicosia highway. Walks in the surrounding mountains, a frescoed chapel, a family-run hotel, a folk museum, traffic-free streets and the quiet starry nights are reasons enough for a long stay.

Lefkara is also a popular day trip for hundreds of coach-borne excursionists, who come to admire its cottage industry of **lace-making**. *Lefkaritika* lace has been esteemed for centuries—Leonardo da Vinci is recorded to have bought an altar cloth for Milan Cathedral during his visit in 1481. The pure lacework, using the island's own cotton, has not been made for generations. Now the town mostly produces a thicker lace, in white or brown thread on a backing of imported Irish linen. The flourishing souvenir trade in lace, **Turkish delight** and **jewellery** keeps the town commercially alive. Visitors are routinely lured into one of the dozens of lace-making houses. Free drinks, demonstrations and easy chat can represent the highest level of salesmanship, where conversation flows seamlessly into a sale, but it can also descend into an arch routine not far removed from hassle.

History

Lefkara is a Byzantine foundation. Like many of Cyprus's inland towns, it was established in the 7th century when the old coastal cities were destroyed by Saracen raids. In some recognition of its importance, and its remoteness, the Orthodox Bishopric of Amathus and Limassol (one of only four permitted to the Greeks by the Crusaders) was exiled here from 1222 to 1470. The resentment against its Catholic overlords remained, and in a famous incident during the Ottoman invasion of 1570, a local Orthodox priest escorted a detachment of Turkish troops up from the coast to take possession of Lefkara. The Venetian governor, concerned that this rebellion might spread, reacted with deliberate brutality. A detachment of cavalry was sent out from Nicosia to slaughter all the inhabitants of Lefkara and burn the town to the ground.

As some compensation for the devastation, the town was treated as an ally, not a conquered subject, by the Ottoman government and excused its poll tax. Prosperity was gradually restored, as the women settled down again to their lace-making activities and their products were hawked abroad by the men, who developed a reputation for driving a hard bargain. This tradition is exemplified by Reo Stakis, who emigrated to Britain in the depression of the thirties and now presides over a large chain of Scottish hotels and casinos.

The Town

The centre of **Pano Lefkara** has a school, post office, the colonnaded **George's café** and half a dozen lunch-time restaurants, and is immediately below the new car park at the town's northern entrance. The sturdy **bell tower** carved with Gothic arches and lunettes is the most handsome feature of the late 19th-century parish church of the Holy Cross. Signs point the way to the **Museum of Folk Art**, recently established in the restored **House of Patsalos**, where the traditional embroidery and silversmithing of Lefkara are on display (*open every day except Sun, 10–4; adm*). The poorer houses of the old Turkish quarter and its two closed mosques stand to the north of the town where a path wiggles down, past the clean structural lines of the medieval chapel of **Ayios Timotheos** (St Timothy), before reaching the decaying village of **Kato Lefkara**. Standing alone to the southwest of the village is the chapel of **Arkhangelos Mikhail** (Archangel Michael), with some fine 12th-century frescoes preserved in the altar apse. On the ground level are six presiding prelates with their attentuated foreheads, holy script and richly depicted cross-emblazoned cloaks. Immediately above is the *Communion of the Apostles*, where Jesus administers wine to the beloved John, followed by Mark, a beardless Thomas, Simon, James and Bartholomew, all set against a serene blue background. There are traces of prophets in the drum of the dome and a striking *Holy Handkerchief* decorates the lintel of the south door, above which is a faded *Baptism*. The *Anastasis*, known in the west as the *Harrowing of Hell*, in the arch of the west vault, was probably painted 300 years after the apse, whilst the large and crude *St Michael and St George* could have been executed any time within the last 100 years.

Where to Stay in Lefkara

The Zacharia family run the **Lefkarama Village**, ℂ (04) 342000, a small, calm, moderately priced hotel tucked away in an unobtrusive side street in the centre of the village. It was recently constructed by converting a traditional house to make one large dining room and an interior courtyard, around which are arranged 10 spruce bedrooms. The 10th-century chapel of St Mamas was restored at the same time. It is an admirable example of a type of hotel of which Cyprus still has far too few.

Walks around Pano Lefkara

From the old **Turkish quarter** of Pano Lefkara, a track winds almost due north through the wooded hills. After about 4km it passes the drive to the new **Syrkatis dam** and shortly afterwards a right turn to Kornos (which you can ignore), before climbing for another 4km through the **Aetomouti forest** to reach the pass below **Vulture Point**. From here the track descends 3km down to the E103 road at the village of **Lythrodhonda**, where you will have arranged for a friend or taxi to meet you. The village was one of the old haunts of the Linobambakoi.

Almost opposite the Kato Lefkara turning off the E105 there is a tarmac road that twists west towards Kato Dhrys and Vavla. Between these two hamlets, just after the Demetrious Brothers' taverna, which is about 6km from Lefkara, is the entrance arch to the convent of **Ayios Minas** (*closed in the afternoon during the summer months*). Here you can buy a pot of honey or a souvenir icon from the porter's lodge, before admiring the two-storey courtyard which encloses the nunnery church with its fresh carved iconostasis.

The E105 road continues 10km northwest of Lefkara to **Vavatsinia**, a red-roofed mountain hamlet astride a highland stream which overlooks a few terraced beds shaded with fruit trees, olive and poplars. Just the other side of the stream in Vavatsinia is the old village church which is also dedicated to the Panayia (Virgin Mary). It is a characteristic example of a steep-roofed mountain chapel with a fine wood-carved interior that includes a loft and a gilded iconostasis.

> Beside the new church of Ayios Yeoryios is the **O Meykos** family restaurant, © (04) 342640, which serves traditional Cypriot oven-cooked stews, homemade pasta, fresh salads and grilled meat in a stove-heated dining room in winter or in the dappled shade of the garden in summer. Book a table in the morning and work up an appetite by walking any of the surrounding tracks.

East from Larnaca into Free Famagusta

The big, brash, new resorts of Ayia Napa, Protaras Beach-Fig Tree Bay and Paralimni are all packed into the triangle of territory that is all that remains to the Greek Cypriots of the old District of Famagusta. The presence of the British Sovereign Base at Dhekelia was a crucial factor in the halting of the Turkish army's advance to the sea in the summer of 1974.

If you are already booked into a hotel here, you might care to explore some of the inland villages which have a quiet charm, especially when contrasted with the overdeveloped coast. If you are not, avoid this area. A ruthless itinerary would insist on an early start in order to see the **monastery of Ayia Napa** without crowds, followed by a **walk** at Cape Greco or by Xylophagou river, and a look at some of the **village churches**, like Ayios Yeoryios at Xylophagou, on your way back. If you have children you might want to try the **go-cart track** near Ayia Thekla. If you are single or merely thirsty then head to **Ayia Napa** at dusk, where there are plenty of pubs, cocktail bars and discos encircling the monastery.

Dhekelia Sovereign Base Area

Only a few police-manned kiosks, some no-entry signs to dull red-brick barrack compounds, barbed wire and sports fields serve to distinguish the Dhekelia Sovereign Base Area from the rest of Cyprus. The base was created in 1954 to provide security and support for the Ayios Nikolaos listening post, just inland of Famagusta, where a British Signals Regiment assisted by some American 'colleagues' have been quietly and industriously tapping into the communications of the Middle East. It is normally kept out of the news, but the British government managed to publicize its role during the prolonged, but unsuccessful, trial of seven British servicemen from GCHQ for espionage in 1985.

Xylotymbou

Xylotymbou is a sprawling village, swollen by refugees, which is reached by turning north onto the E303, before the Dhekelia barracks. It has a good taverna called the **Bambos** on the main street, for a lunch of home-made moussaka and fresh bread, washed down with cold lager.

Xylotymbou has recently been provided with a bypass to the west of town, which takes you conveniently close to its two attractions, a pair of 15th-century painted chapels dedicated to **Ayia Marina** (St Marina) and **Ayios Vasileos** (St Basil). The turning to St Marina is the second left as you trundle along the bypass. The barrel-vaulted church is enclosed within the outbuildings of a new monastery . The chapel contains a number of smoke-blackened 15th-century paintings, the best preserved of which, like the *Crucifixion* and *Descent from the Cross*, are in the top register of the middle section. The *Betrayal* scene on the south side reveals strong western influences in the lively movement of its figures and strikingly breaks from the canon with Judas kissing his master's feet rather than his cheek. Above the south door are the *Two Marys Visiting the Empty Tomb* and an *Anastasis*, a classically Byzantine version of the western *Harrowing of Hell*.

The whitewashed, barrel-vaulted chapel of *St Basil* is from the same period, and is just the other side of a shallow valley, but can also be approached from the next turning off the bypass. Soot and whitewash have left only a few fragments of painting, the best preserved of which can be peeped at in the apse behind the iconostasis.

2km north of the village the road meets the **Green Line** and runs along the frontier towards the **Ayios Nikolaos** listening post, providing a melancholy view of the empty village of Düzce (Athna). The 16th-century monastery of Ayios Kendeas is not worth the drive, as it is currently a Greek-Cypriot army post.

Xylophagou Village and River

The main coast road from Larnaca to Ayia Napa, the B3, passes through the village of Xylophagou and past its large, modern parish church which overawes the smaller church of **Ayios Yeoryios**. It is a simple 15th-century barrel-vaulted church with a stumpy bell tower encrusted with several centuries of whitewash, but it preserves some wall paintings in its candle-blackened interior. The scenes from the *Life of Christ* on the western vault are the best preserved, though there is an imposing figure of a reclining Jesse in the *Tree of Jesse* mural on the north face of the central bay. The *St George* surrounded by scenes of his martyrdom on the south wall and the colossal *Archangel Michael* on the north wall are more in the realm of folk art. If youare hungry or thirsty, there are a couple of good tavernas and bars in the centre of Xylophagou, such as the **Fame** or **La Dolce Vita**.

4km east of Xylophagou on the Ayia Napa road there is a turning down to **Xylophagou river**. It is a raffish, muddy place, lined with wooden jetties, bobbing fishing craft and, on the east side of the estuary, the lone **Amphitrion** fish restaurant with a good view out to sea. If you want to work up an appetite, walk past the rough chapel of Ayios Yeoryios (St George) entwined in the prayer strings of women supplicants. The coastal track peters out in about 2km, leaving you to walk through another 3km of heathland to the hillock of New Pyla, and the remains of a **Venetian watchtower**, a scruffy sister to the better-preserved tower at Cape Kiti. A cave on this shoreline filled with bones was long venerated as that of the Forty Martyrs, until scholarly analysis by an Orthodox bishop revealed them to belong to the pygmy hippopotamus, a unique creature indigenous to Cyprus which may yet be considered a form of martyr to early man (*see* p. 401).

Ayia Napa

The Larnaca road turns into Nissi avenue as you enter Ayia Napa. Turn left as this meets Leoforos Archiepiskopou Makariou III, and continue 400m uphill to **Seferis square** in the centre of town. A few decades ago this was the quiet heart of a small fishing village, but it is now the lively centre of a growing resort. The streets around are lit by a proliferation of neon signs offering Mexican, Chinese, Indian and Greek food, and the whole town abounds with well-lit jewellery, leather and tourist bric-a-brac bazaars, pubs, cocktail bars, money changers and discos. Traditional folk dancing and music are staged every Sunday from April to October, with a week-long spectacular in the last week of September.

Ayia Napa's tourist information office, ℂ (03) 721796, is just below Seferis square on Leoforos Archiepiskopou Makariou III, where you will also find **banks** and **pharmacies**. From the square take the first right and walk 100m uphill to find the **post office**, ℂ (03) 721550.

Getting Around

By Bus

A direct bus from Ayia Napa to Nicosia leaves from the blue Eman bus stop at Seferis square, or on Leoforos Archiepiskopou Makariou III avenue, departing at 8am and returning at 3pm, weekdays only. The Eman bus company, ℂ (03) 721321, also runs 10 buses a day from Ayia Napa to Larnaca, from 6.30–5. There is an hourly service from Ayia Napa to Paralimni from 9–5, and seven buses a day leave from a bus stop west of St George's in Paralimni village to the Protaras beach resort.

By Taxi

There are no service taxis until you get to Larnaca, but plenty of private taxis will charge around C£10 for the 40km trip to Larnaca, C£20 for the 88km drive to Nicosia, and only a couple of pounds to an inland 'red village' or beach of your choice.

Ayia Napa Monastery

Nothing about this brash new beach resort prepares you for the quiet beauty and charm of the monastery of Ayia Napa (the Holy Handkerchief). The **Holy Handkerchief**, the Mandylion, was one of the most precious relics of the Byzantine Empire and is frequently painted over the lintels of church doors in Cyprus. The monastery is first mentioned in the 14th century, but local traditions recall a 10th-century chapel established around a miraculous image of the Virgin found in the grotto, and whisper of a previous association with a Virgin Lady of the Forest, an Artemis-like deity. Most of the existing buildings date from the late 16th century when it was the Catholic nunnery of Santa Napa, after which the Venetians named the great southeastern bastion at Famagusta. Work was abruptly halted by the Ottoman conquest of 1571, after which itwas handed back to the Orthodox Church. A small community of Calogrie, uncloistered nuns, existed here until 1790, after which it was used as the village church and school. In 1978 it received a new role when it was rededicated as a conference centre for the World Council of Churches. Its extensive land-holdings in the area (it owned most of the land west to the village of Ormidhia) have been efficiently managed by the Orthodox Church.

The Buildings

A two-storey Venetian gatehouse, the only part built of an elaborate scheme to double the size of the monastery with a Renaissance upper storey and balcony, guards the entrance into the cloistered courtyard. The pointed arches of the colonnade are lit by the dappled light that filters through the disorderly garden of sycamore, olive, palm and fruit trees. Below the three elaborately carved upper doors of the gatehouse, an ancient irrigation channel gurgles out through an antique marble boar's head, spilling a tinkling cascade from its snout. In the centre of the courtyard a dome, supported on four open arches that frame stone benches, shades an octagonal fountain pool of travertine marble.

The half-subterranean church, tucked under the natural rock escarpment, seems to take second place to the mystery of the fountain and the half-fulfilled opulence of the gatehouse. Its most celebrated feature is the arch-enclosed petal window above the west door. The usual entrance is through the south door which leads into a passage lined with stone seats and a small chapel set aside for Catholic worship, a return for a similar favour granted in the era of Catholic supremacy. The main body of the church is sunk into the bedrock to bring it to the level of the grotto, though now there is no image of the Virgin older than the 18th century. The decaying bell arch was superseded in the 19th century, when a three-storey bell tower made full use of the extra height offered by the escarpment above. From the courtyard, descend through an arch to the reservoir tank, to the new black and white pebble *kouvlaki* pavement and the terraced gardens that are shaded by a 600-year-old sycamore.

Ayia Napa Beaches

Demand for beach space has outstripped supply, and many hotels have created sunbathing areas of their own. If you like to swim as you sunbathe, choose from one of six crowded beaches.

The 900m-wide **Ayia Napa Bay** just to the east of the fishing harbour is the largest stretch of open sand in the area, and is overlooked by a dozen six-storey white hotels with the dry limestone upland peaking above them. There is a much smaller stretch of sand on the other side of the harbour known as **Sandy beach**. About 4km east of the harbour the Kermia Beach Hotel marks the small sandy **Limnaria beach** halfway between Ayia Napa and Cape Greco. Three km west of the harbour there are two small sandy coves at **Nissi** which are screened from the road by a cluster of large hotels. The Vassos Nissi Plage Hotel marks the first cove, the Adams Hotel the second. Another 1.5km to the west is the **Makronisos peninsula**; follow signs to the Dome or Asterias Hotel, which has three small sandy coves and an even smaller patch of sand 2km further west by the Ayia Thekla chapel.

Sports

The **EMW go-cart track** is lined with old tyres and overlooked by its own black and white striped viewing terrace with a café. It is 6km west from Ayia Napa on the rough road between Makronisos and Ayia Thekla, after the Marinos Hotel Apartments and almost opposite the Axartis restaurant. It is open from 8 am until dusk, and costs C£5 for a 10-minute session. Drivers must be at least nine years of age.

At the fishing harbour there are charter and glass-bottom **boats** for day trips or hour-long cruises and **water-ski** speedboats stand ready for hire. At 26 Leoforos Archiepiskopou Makariou III avenue is the **Sunfish Diving School**, ✆ (03) 721300, where you can check prices before booking yourself onto a **scuba-diving course**. Two other well-established diving schools that also offer a full range of watersports are **Nissi Beach**, ✆ (03) 721021, and **Sunwing**, ✆ (03) 721806.

Where to Stay

There is nothing on this coast that can be wholeheartedly recommended, nor are there any hotels or pensions in any of the inland villages. The enormous and expensive **Grecian Bay**, ✆ (03) 721301, has one of the best positions, directly above the sandy beach of Ayia Napa Bay and just a short stroll from the village centre. **Leros**, ✆ (03) 721126, is central, moderately priced and reasonably quiet in its detached position at the harbour end of Leoforos Archiepiskopou Makariou III avenue. It has two dozen immaculate rooms, and gets quickly filled up in the summer season. Going further downmarket there are a few cheap rooms to let, behind the **5 Kings Bar**, just behind the monastery bell tower.

Eating Out

There are a number of fish restuarants in the harbour, amongst the children's rides, clock golf and whitewashed chapel of Ayios Yeoryios. **Markos** and **Vassos Hambou** are both good for a simple meal, while the larger sea-washed **Esperia** is the place to go for a more elaborate dinner, with live music in the evening.

Cape Greco (Pedalion) and the East Coast

The limestone plateau that marks the southeastern corner of Cyprus was, like most of the headlands, sacred to the island's great goddess. Strabo, who wrote his *Geographia* in about AD 23, records, 'Then Cape Pedalion, over which hangs a steep high hill, sacred to Aphrodite'. The sanctuary site (there are no ruins to identify) is at the centre of the summit, which has a serene view straight down over the low, pale limestone headland that extends out into the choppy Syrian sea. The far end of the headland is occupied by a small lighthouse, the military and the Radio Monte Carlo relay masts.

The first hotels, like the Grecian at Konnos Bay, begin 2km north of Cape Greco and continue for 6km in a long ribbon development known as Protaras-Fig Tree Bay or Paralimni Beach. About 600m after the turning to the Green Bay Hotel, look out for a track going west up to the Panayia chapel and dam. Follow the path on the right-hand side of the valley for about 2km uphill to enjoy some solitude in the curious, deserted cave **chapel of Ayii Saranda**, with its natural skylight encased in a drum dome.

The Capo Bay Hotel, which is only about 1km from the Panayia chapel path, stands on the site of the ancient harbour of **Lefkolla**, where di Cesnola found a colossal head of the goddess Demeter. It was off this shore that the galleys of Ptolemy of Egypt and Demetrius Poliorcetes met in bloody battle in 306 BC to contest the spoils of Alexander the Great's Empire in the third war of the Diadochi, the 'successors'. Just to the north is the modest stretch of sandy beach known as **Fig Tree Bay**, fringed by a rocky shore and protected by an offshore island. Two km north stands the small chapel of **Prophitis Elias** on its rocky promontory, which has been given a new stairway, in keeping with the apartments and hotels that have transformed a shore virtually empty of buildings in 1980. A modern icon inside the chapel shows the *Prophet Elias* sitting anguished on his cloak, about to be fed a wafer, and the *Gift of Prophecy by a Raven*. **Pernera** fishing harbour marks the current edge of development, and from here, the coast is dominated by a mass of windmills pumping up water to feed the market gardens. The **Ayia Trias** chapel marks a small fishing shelter, due east of Paralimni village, which has a slight stretch of sand overlooked by the **Augoutis** fish restaurant.

Ta Kokkinokhoria: The 'Red Villages'

The Ta Kokkinokhoria villages take their name from the fertile red soil which produces early crops of vegetables, like the fine Cypriot potatoes, which are principally exported to Britain. Two generations ago, when the sunbaked mud-brick was the universal building block, the villages visibly lived up to their name and were in strong contrast to the pale houses around Larnaca and the surviving mud-grey villages of the Mesaoria. Now they are built of ferroconcrete and only the medieval churches and unspoilt tavernas in the village centres are of interest.

There are three churches in the centre of **Paralimni**. A brassy, big, modern thing stands beside the elegantly colonnaded church of Ayios Yeoryios with its fading whitewash. However, it is the older stone-built **chapel of the Panayia**, the Virgin Mary, which is worth the journey. It is usually kept locked so you will have to ask at the nearest café for the custodian. The vaults of this domed church, decorated with porcelain plates, have inspired a number of copies, but few can match the dignity and simplicity of this early 18th-century porcelain set into plaster.

Dherinia is closely wrapped up in the Green Line and attracts a trickle of visitors who follow the pink signs to the '**Free Viewpoint Café**' which overlooks the empty, decaying villas and high-rise blocks of **Varosha**, the once-prosperous Greek quarter of Famagusta. Just off the Y-junction at the centre of the village is the medieval cruciform and domed chapel of **Ayios Yeoryios**. It is rendered with an attractive old pinkish-yellow stucco, furnished with a tottering iconostasis and an icon of the saint, which leans against the north wall onto the only surviving wall painting, suitably of *St George*. The whitewashed **church of the Panayia**, packed full of icons, is more easily identifiable with its 19th-century bell tower, southern aisle and colonnade tacked onto the original domed medieval chapel.

Beside the big new church in **Phrenaros** stands the diminutive but charmingly erratic chapel of the **Archangel Michael**. No two of its many-angled roof lines and projections match, and the pair of nipple domes, each supported by cruciform transepts, decline into a bumpy porch. The brass key, kept in the main church, enables you to inspect the dark interior and its large 19th-century painting of the *Archangel* standing to the south of the apse.

There is a nest of three churches in the centre of **Sotira**. The whitewashed church of the **Transfiguration** was originally much larger, and fragments of its old columns and capitals can be seen in the square outside. Some fine 14th-century wall paintings have been uncovered on the four buttresses supporting the dome. *St Peter* and *St Paul* flank the western piers, while a pair of warrior saints and *St Constantine* with the good shepherd are beneath a pair of evangelists on the eastern piers. An old chapel just outside the church has been turned into a small **museum** to house various portable treasures and icons, including a 15th-century *Christ Pantocrator* and *Virgin with Christ Child*. These were taken into safety from three isolated medieval churches (Panayia Chortakiotissa, Ayios Theodhoros and the ruined oratory of Ayios Yeoryios, which is open to the four winds) that mark an old village. They can be seen by the walled cemetery, opposite the football stadium, on the road to Liopetri.

Liopetri was one of the villages of the Linobamaki, the 'linen-cottoners'. They were a poor community of itinerant traders who earned their nickname by freely switching between professing Islam or Orthodoxy, depending on whether the Turkish recruiting officer or Greek taxman was in town. Their cynicism was supposed to derive from compulsory conversion from Catholicism after the 1571 conquest. This is partly corroborated by the 15th-century domed church of **Ayios Andronikos**, on the Sotira road at the eastern edge of the village, which started out as a Catholic chapel.

Southern Nicosia (Lefkosia)

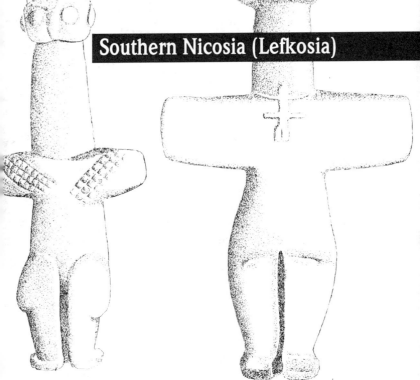

Crucifix shaped idols from the Chalcolithic period

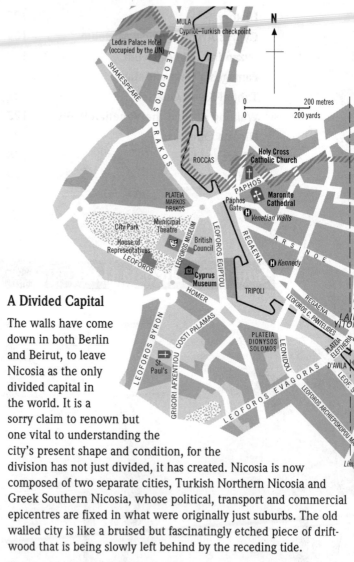

MULA
Cypriot–Turkish checkpoint

Ledra Palace Hotel
(occupied by the UN)

SHAKESPEARE

LEOFOROS DRAKOS

ROCCAS

Holy Cross
Catholic Church

PAPHOS

PLATEIA
MARKOS
DRAKOS

Paphos
Gate

Maronite
Cathedral

City Park

Municipal
Theatre

Venetian Walls

REGAENA

House of
Representatives

British
Council

ARSINOE

LEOFOROS MUSEUM

Kennedy

LEOFOROS

LEOFOROS EGIPTOU

Cyprus
Museum

TRIPOLI

LEDRA

HOMER

REGAENA

LEOFOROS BYRON

GRIGORI AFXENTIOU

COSTI PALAMAS

St.
Paul's

LEOFOROS C. PANTELIDES

LAIKI
YITONI

PLATEIA
DIONYSOS
SOLOMOS

PLATEIA
ELEFTHERIA

LEONIDOU

D'AVILA

Tow

LEOFOROS EVAGORAS

LEOFOROS ARCHIEPISKOPOU MAKARIO

Limass

0   200 metres
0   200 yards

N

A Divided Capital

The walls have come down in both Berlin and Beirut, to leave Nicosia as the only divided capital in the world. It is a sorry claim to renown but one vital to understanding the city's present shape and condition, for the division has not just divided, it has created. Nicosia is now composed of two separate cities, Turkish Northern Nicosia and Greek Southern Nicosia, whose political, transport and commercial epicentres are fixed in what were originally just suburbs. The old walled city is like a bruised but fascinatingly etched piece of drift-wood that is being slowly left behind by the receding tide.

This is especially marked in Southern Nicosia, where the low roof-line within the Venetian ramparts is overlooked by a forest of high-rise office buildings and apartment blocks. The city has grown

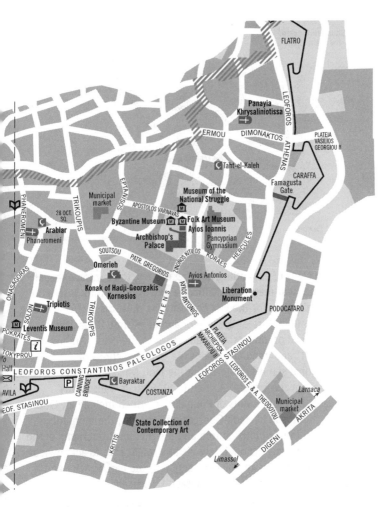

rapidly since independence, fed by a steady stream of villagers leaving the countryside. The stream turned into a flood in 1974 as refugees arrived from North Cyprus and the civil war in Beirut. The city is now the diplomatic, media and communications centre for the Middle East and has an emerging financial role.

This all makes for a discouraging introduction as you approach Nicosia along the constricted roads south of the city, which pass

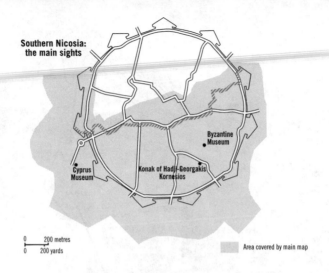

Byzantine
Museum

Cyprus
Museum

Konak of Hadji-Georgakis
Kornesios

0   200 metres

0   200 yards

Area covered by main map

through signs of expanding housing estates, thickening exhaust
fumes and near featureless concrete extrusions. Think instead of
what awaits you, for the city contains the most distinctive cooking,
nightlife and culture of the island; and at teatime it magically
empties itself of tourists, who all return to the coast. Among the
city's most renowned attractions are two collections of
international standing: the Byzantine Icon Museum and the Cyprus
Archaeological Museum. A circuit of Venetian walls neatly
encloses the monuments of the old city, which include an Ottoman
oda in the house of Hadji-Georgakis Kornesios, the monolithic
interior of the Tripiotis church and the medieval remnants of the
Omerieh mosque. Though few visitors might care to acknowledge
it, there is also the ghoulish attraction of the barbed wire and
breeze-block barricades of the Green Line itself.

To enter North Cyprus, you must cross over on foot at the Ledra
Palace Checkpoint. Once across, you can further your understanding of Nicosia by visiting the buildings in the northern half of
the walled city, such as the alluring, conspicuous Crusader cathedral (*see* p. 288). Do not allow the internal politics of Cyprus to
put you off the crossing; you should see the difference between the
North and South, between Turkish and Greek Cyprus, for yourself.

The Green Line, which splits the city and the island in two, has also divided the district of Nicosia in two. Apart from a few minor sites in the suburbs, the southern part of this area is described in the 'Mountain' chapter, but remains an easy day trip from the city.

History

Why Here?

Nicosia sits like a concrete spider in the centre of the Mesaoria plain, often wreathed in a haze of its own creation. In the dry heat of the summer, it can seem quite inappropriately sited. It lacks a central geographical feature—a river crossing, harbour or at least a fortified hillfort—to explain its position. In fact, there is a river of sorts, the Pedhieos, but it is either dry or in spate and is seldom attractive in either state. It twists out of sight just to the west and north of the walls, whose moat it once filled. A small classical town known as Ledra stood beside it, but was insignificant compared with any of the great and ancient cities on the coast. These, however, were completely destroyed by Saracen invasions in the middle of the 7th century AD; 300 years of raids and petty warfare followed, virtually subsuming the island's culture. The surviving population moved to smaller and safer places tucked away in inland valleys.

Byzantine Foundation

When the Byzantine Empire re-established control in AD 964, the first priority of the governor was to establish an effective system of defence. For this purpose Lefkosia (Nicosia) proved to be an ideal base for the Byzantine duke and his rapid-reaction force, for it is equidistant from the vulnerable northern and eastern coasts and within signalling distance of the mountain look-out posts. It was also well placed for administering the medieval pattern of rural settlements which had replaced the ancient coastal cities. The archbishopric also moved inland, though the Orthodox Church kept the memory of the old capital alive by retaining the episcopal title of Constantia-Salamis. A sizeable town rapidly grew around these two great officials, and by the time of the Crusader conquest it had become firmly established as the chief, indeed the only, city of Cyprus.

A Medieval Capital

The French Lusignan monarchs followed in the steps of Byzantium, ruling the island from a pair of Gothic palaces in Nicosia. A great Gothic cathedral was raised, lesser churches built and sectarian chapels added to the proliferation of town houses and walled gardens built by the Frankish burgesses and Crusader nobility. The French-speaking Crusaders called their city 'La Nicosie', which was perhaps a crude attempt to pronounce the Greek name Lefkosia. The bustling city, enriched by the Near East trade, incited the envious praise of every passing European pilgrim. This medieval golden age ended with a triple sacking by the Genoese in 1373, a fate repeated by a Mameluke army in 1426. Each time, the somewhat diminished city managed to recover. It is ironical to note that it was the successor Venetians' attempt to defend the city that caused the greatest destruction. They would have done better to have put their trust in the sea and their coastal fortresses, and left Nicosia an open city. The story of the Venetian defences and the Ottoman siege of 1570 is told as a prelude to a walk around the walls, on p. 123.

An Ottoman Provincial Capital

The power of the Catholic Church and the mixed nobility of Venetians and old French Crusader families was completely destroyed by the Ottoman conquest. The Ottoman Empire abolished serfdom outright and gave those Catholics who had not been killed or captured during the great siege the choice of emigration or conversion to either Islam or Orthodoxy. The dozens of Catholic churches, chapels and monasteries in the city were either converted into mosques, sold to the Orthodox, or put to some secular use.

Even when one includes specific new taxes levied exclusively on the Greek population such as the haratasi, the poll tax and the tax collected in lieu of military service, the Cypriot population was still in a better financial and legal position under the Muslim Ottomans than they ever had been under the domination of the Christian French or Italians. The Greek language and Orthodox Church also rapidly regained their natural prominence. Indeed, the four bishops assisted by a secular hierachy of Greek officials headed by the chief interpreter, the dragoman, performed much of the actual business of government.

Unlike contemporary Nicosia, the city was not divided into exclusive ethnic quarters, and early travellers noted that the streets were filled with an assorted and colourfully dressed population of Turks, Greeks, Armenians and Maronites. It was also renowned for its large number of palm-shaded walled gardens, its frequent religious festivals and its fine mountain views. Camel and donkey caravans awaited outside the city gates, and plied the rough road south to Larnaca to connect the city's merchants, artisans and officials with the wider world.

The British

Sir Garnet Wolseley, the first British governor, rode to Nicosia in 1878 with two mules filled with sixpences to pay the staff he had inherited from his Ottoman predecessor. Though the prompt payment of salaries seemed revolutionary at the time, the twin hallmarks of the 20th century—the internal combustion engine and the plain serge office suit—would effect a greater transformation. During the late 1920s holes were punched through the unbroken circuit of Venetian walls, allowing traffic to disturb the narrow streets of the old city. The bungalows of colonial administrators began to line the roads out of town.

Nicosia continued to lead the political life of the island. Its population, particularly its high-school students, were at the heart of the *enosis* struggle. It was also the first place after independence to be consumed by intercommunal violence. The **Green Line**, which has divided the island as a whole since 1974, has divided the city of Nicosia since 1964. The colour has no political significance, being named from the coloured crayon used by the British major who marked up city maps for the first UN contingent.

Getting Around

By Air

Nicosia International Airport has been closed since 1974, when it witnessed some of the heaviest fighting of the invasion. The dilapidated airfield and its outskirts are inaccessible, as it now functions as headquarters and barracks for UN forces; the runway is still used occasionally by aircraft on UN business.

By Bus

The **Kallenos bus**, ✆ (02) 453560, leaves 34 Leonidou street for Larnaca about a dozen times a day between 6am and 6.30pm, with a reduced service on Saturday and Sunday. Exactly the same conditions apply for the Limassol run which is managed by **Kemek**, ✆ (02) 463985, with four direct buses to Paphos at 7, 9.30am, 12.30 and 3.30pm.

Travelling southwest to Kakopetria is simple but for the rest of the mountains there is a much reduced service. The **Zingas bus**, ✆ (02) 463154, leaves from Leonidou street at 12.15 for Platres via Pedhoulas and returns the next day at 6am. There are about 10 departures a day to Kakopetria with the **Solea bus**, ✆ (02) 453234, leaving from the Costanza bastion. If you are going on to Troödos you will have to catch the 12 noon bus which returns the next day at 6.30am.

By Service Taxi/Minibus

This quick and convenient service operates only to Limassol (80km/50 miles) and Larnaca (47km/30 miles) where you can pick up other connections. **Kyriakos**, at 27 Leoforos Stasinou, ✆ (02) 444114, covers both destinations while their neighbour **Kypros** at 9A, ✆ (02) 464811, covers Limassol. **Acropolis**, at 9, ✆ (02) 472525 and **Makris** at 11, ✆ (02) 466201, cover just the Larnaca run.

By Taxi

These can be flagged down in the street or ordered throughout the day and night. The telephone numbers of the main taxi firms are as follows: **Amazon**, ✆ (02) 455095, **Columbia**, ✆ (02) 441700, **Markos** at 3 Regaena street, ✆ (02) 473010.

Car Hire

Though you will not need a car in Nicosia, one may be vital for exploring the churches in the mountain valleys. Shop around amongst **Airtour** at 4 Naxou street, ✆ (02) 450403, **Budget/Petsas** at 24A–B Costakis Pantelides street, ✆ (02) 444365; and **InterRent** at 54 Leoforos Evagoras, ✆ (02) 442114.

Tourist Information

There is a **tourist information booth**, ✆ (02) 444264, in the Laiki Yitonia area of the walled town, just north of the **post office** between Constantinos Paleologos avenue and the D'Avila bastion. As well as handing out maps and monthly brochures they organize free **walking tours**. The tour of the old city within the walls leaves at 10am on Thursday, with a two-hour bus and walking tour of Kaimakli arranged on Monday at 10am and the Engomi tour on Friday.

Banks are scattered throughout the city and an afternoon service is operated by both the Bank of Cyprus and the Cyprus Popular Bank in Plateia Eleftheria.

For **emergencies**, the police are on ✆ (02) 305115, the hospital on ✆ (02) 451111 and a 24-hour chemist can be found by telephoning 192, or looking in the daily papers.

Orientation

This description begins at the Cyprus Museum, just to the west of the walled city, and then enters the walled city through the **Paphos Gate**, proceeding in a roundabout way to the far northeast corner of the old town before returning along the outside of the walls. If you are only here for a short time, concentrate on three essential sites: the Cyprus Museum, the house of Hadji-Georgakis Kornesios and the Byzantine Museum.

The Cyprus Archaeological Museum

Open in summer Mon–Sat 7.30–1.30, 4–6 and Sun 10–1, in winter Mon–Sat 9–5 and Sun 10–1; adm; © (02) 302189.

This outstanding one-storey museum dressed with a classical façade lies at the corner of Museum street and Homer avenue. It is filled with an astonishingly rich archaeological collection that begun to be assembled in 1883 and was moved into this colonial memorial to Queen Victoria in 1909. The interior and style of display is beginning to look a bit dated but not yet fascinatingly so. The collection is far too large to be seen in one go and short breaks can be taken in the garden café, opposite the entrance, or by browsing in the postcard shop, just inside the porticoed entrance. Below is a brief account of the exhibits displayed in the museum's 14 galleries.

At the lobby, turn right to enter **Gallery I**, which is devoted to the island's earliest known cultures. Aesthetically it is dominated by the extraordinary, and uniquely Cypriot, grey-green stone **cruciform idols** carved in the Chalcolithic age. The sacrifice of a young deity for the common good is one of the oldest concepts in world mythologies; they appear to express a chilling foreknowledge of the Crucifixion. Stylistically the idols share strong similarities with notable contemporaries, such as the stone figures of the Cyclades and the pale clay idols of Canaan.

The **Mosphilia deposit**—an intriguing selection of stone and ceramic idols packed into a bowl with a triton shell and then reverentially buried—occupies the centre of the room. The bowl is considered to be a model of an ancient shrine whilst the presence of the triton shell, a familiar attribute of the classical sea god, hints at the venerable sources of pagan religion. By the door are two enormous cult jars decorated with the bold red designs of the Chalcolithic age. These are considered to have been used for the brewing of sacred ale, consumed as a sacrament which put the worshipper more in touch with the divine. Some scholars have argued that the agricultural revolution was as much concerned with the need to create ritual alcohol as bread.

Gallery II is furnished with an extraordinary variety of designs and experimental forms, which clearly demonstrates that the Cypriot Bronze Age was one of the great eras of ceramic art. There is an inventive genius expressed in this room which is quite overwhelming. The **three pottery models**, however, manage to steal the show, allowing us to go back 4000 years and witness the intensity of belief of our forefathers. In one a human figure stands diminutive and alone behind an offering-vase. The vase is set before a looming, dark trinity of interlinked deities, each crowned with the skulls of sacrificed bulls. The other temple scene is more crowded and familiar with its peeping onlooker, pair of guards, stockaded animals for sacrifice and circle of believers around the deity-priestess seated on the triple throne. The third model, which represents a ploughing scene, is also fraught with the poignancy of ritual. At the birth of spring, a pair of oxen teams stand with their attendant farmers. They wait as a priest prepares the ground for fertility with his mysterious, sacred objects held in a tray.

Gallery III is filled with a treasury of ancient ceramics that takes you from the Late Bronze Age through to the Roman era. They are not arranged chronologically, nor particularly well lit or explained; to understand their significance *see* 'Cypriot Ceramics' on p. 405. The finest pieces to look out for include the **Mycenaean Zeus crater** with its famous chariot scene; a 13th-century BC blue faïence **drinking horn** decorated with exuberant galloping animals pursued by Syrian hunters; and the **Archaic bull** sniffing a lotus. The central cruciform case displays striking imports from Attica: olive-oil jars tastefully embellished with Athena or an olive branch; a more vivid scene is depicted on an urn: an aroused man propositions a beardless youth to the disgust of his two colleagues, who walk away with exclamations of embarrassment.

The convex case in **Gallery IV** is one of the most striking in the museum—a whole wall filled with warrior and bull-mask figurines stares mutely out at the visitor, who may feel as if they have impiously broken into the sanctuary of an Archaic shrine. These figurines, a mere sample of the 2000 found at Ayia Irini-Paleokastro, date from the early Cypro-Archaic period, around 600 BC. They show typically male concerns for success in war which distinguish the competitive post-iron-age societies from the organized fertility cults of the Bronze-Age civilization.

The long hall of **Gallery V** is filled with limestone carvings that trace the transformation of Cyprus: from a dynamic mix of cultures in the Archaic period into a mere Hellenistic province. The oriental, if not Mesopotamian, origins of the Asiatic Heracles from Kition, and the gorgeous 5th-century BC priestesses and crowned queens from Arsos, are replaced by a serene classicism expressed by athletic youths and the distant gaze of **Aphrodite of Soli**.

The corner lobby, **Gallery VI**, is lined with Roman busts and heads. Accurate portraiture, with all the finely observed surface details that reveal character, has replaced the idealization of Greece. A finely observed Caligula and a diffident-looking graduate from Soli overlook the massive bronze statue of the **Emperor Septimius Severus** (AD 193–211). This was found by a ploughman 10 miles east of Nicosia. The body is in disproportion to the head, for it appears that the emperor's serious features were added to the statue of an athlete. This also explains why Septimius is uncircumcised, an impossible aberration for a descendant of an old Phoenician family long settled in Libya.

The **Long Gallery VII**, is devoted to jewellery and metalwork from all ages. Though one half regrets the lack of chronological order, this glittering array does reflect an essential unity of design and taste in ornamentation. Gold, the most easily worked but most incorruptible of metals, survives intact in tombs long after cloth, cabinets and bones have decayed. It has never gone out of vogue.

The Salamis sceptre, the necklace of the high priestess of Aphrodite at Arsos (so accurately portrayed in stone in gallery V), a 14th-century BC silver dish inlayed with a bull and lotus relief, Hellenistic gold-leaf fillets that dressed the brow of the dead, the celebrated 7th-century silver plates from Lapta (whose theme of the battle between David and Goliath specifically refers to the Emperor Heraclius's almost magical victory over the Persians in AD 630) shine out amongst seals, rings, earrings and assorted treasures. Amongst this embarrassment of riches it is easy to overlook still famous but less showy pieces such as the horned ingot gods and bronze, wheeled incense-urn stands found in the temples of the Bronze Age city of Enkomi; the splendid Hellenistic parade-piece helmet with its hair curls and swan-neck-held horsehair plume worthy of a Ptolemy; the Cypro-Archaic capitals; Phoenician glassware from the Syrian coast; carved ivories and Roman mosaics.

Leading off this long gallery are three especially dusty and badly lit chambers. **Gallery IX** is filled with tombstones and **X** is devoted to scripts. Cypro-Minoan was the first script used on the island, from 1400 BC to 1050 BC, but disappeared during the three centuries of the dark age. A distinctive Cypriot Syllabic script appears around 725 BC, which was used to express two separate languages: the Arcado-Cyprian-Greek dialect and the indigenous Eteo-Cypriot. At the same time there was also on offer the Phoenician alphabet, soon to be followed by the Greek. All three remained in use until Ptolemy enforced the sole use of Greek in 312 BC. **Gallery VIII** reconstructs the six major types of ancient tombs and burial practice. Tombs from the Iron Age include evidence of human sacrifice. This custom was retained by the 8th-century kings of Salamis, whose tomb furniture is exhibited in **Gallery XI** (for a description of the burial rites *see* 'Salamis' p. 382). It is a splendid, cosmopolitan hoard with gilded alabasters and exquisite ivory carvings, mixed with the barbaric splendour of a forged-metal throne, chariot fittings and the great **bronze cauldron** decorated with four triple-headed sphinxes. The former would not have looked out of place in Egypt, the latter could have come from the burial mound of some nomadic lord of the Russian steppes.

Next is **Gallery XII**, newly opened to explain ancient metallurgy and some geology; it is stronger on story-board information displays than on actual objects.

Gallery XIII is dominated by the divine shape of Apollo the lyre player, together with other pieces of Roman statuary found at the baths in Salamis. Apollo's statue and those of Zeus, Aphrodite and Isis were found defaced and thrown into the drains (one suspects by Christian monks who specialized in this form of cultural revolution). The clothed figures, and more respectable morals, of Asclepius the healer, Heracles the literary hero and the virgin Artemis could survive the transition, perhaps with some judicious relabelling, into the Christian era.

Gallery XIV displays terracotta figurines discovered in rural sanctuaries. Among them are bird-headed female figures, ram-horned Baal Hamman (the Phoenician Zeus) with attendant lotus-like censers and extremes of taste varying from the exquisite coiffures of Hellenistic heads to a Punch-like figure with a large nose and donkey sized prick. They range from the Bronze Age to the late Roman period, from high art commissioned by royal courts to humble mould-produced models.

Political Quarter

The museum lies in the political and diplomatic quarter of the city with the building of the House of Representatives a further 100m west along Homer avenue. The more distinguished colonnaded exterior of the Municipal Theatre is 100m north along Museum Street, beyond which is the entrance to the Municipal Gardens with its avenue of ivy-clad palms and pigeons cooing from shaded aviaries. A statue of Markos Drakos, a hero of the EOKA struggle of 1955–59 against the British, stands in the roundabout square below the walled city.

The Southwest Quarter of the Walled City

The original **Paphos Gate** is the dark narrow tunnel tucked beside the modern road which cuts through the Venetian walls. The metal-plated doors are now permanently open and above them can be seen the Caliph's Tugra, the formalized signature of the Ottoman rulers. Paphos street, for all its modernity, retains echoes of the great siege of 1570: to the north the crescent of Turkey flies from the Roccas Bastion, while the Greek cross is displayed to the south with blue-bereted UN soldiers (usually French Canadians) squeezed into the middle. The **Holy Cross Catholic Church**, a bulky basilica in yellow stone, remains accessible, though officially it is within the UN zone. The Franciscan Order has recalled the four centuries of its medieval presence in the city by incorporating a few chosen Latin tombstones and heraldic shields, but otherwise only the bullet holes in the ceiling of this 19th-century hall catch your attention. Just to the south, the old police barracks top the wall opposite, where a Romanesque-looking zig-zag arch leads into a compound around a recently restored 14th-century hall. Just up Favierou street is an anarchist-Lebanese café beside the tall modern belltower of the **Maronite Cathedral of Our Lady of Graces**, which has fine contemporary mosaics in its apse to redeem its interior of acrylic painted ferroconcrete.

Follow Regaena street, which skirts along the walls for about 600m until it reaches Plateia Eleftheria—perhaps a misleadingly grand description for the section of road which enters into the walled city. It is, however, undeniably central and is overlooked to its east by the colonial-classical town hall and post office which sit on D'Avila bastion. North of Eleftheria square stretches the newly pedestrianized **Ledra street**, one of the principal shopping arteries of the city. During the Independence struggle of 1955–9 it was nicknamed murder mile after the many EOKA assassinations of British soldiers. Now it is seldom without a few carefree tourists browsing past displays of Lefkara lace, who may experience a slight frisson on seeing the dilapidated tower of the Olympus Hotel capped by its UN post and the Green Line barricade that seals the northern end. On the way back down Ledra street pop down Nikokleus street to 28 October Square, overlooked by the 19th-century Church of Phaneromeni (the Revealed). Beside it is the marble mausoleum of Kyprianos, the archbishop martyred in the terror campaign of 1821. Just northeast of here is the intriguing exterior of the small **Arablar Mosque**, which stands like a battered composite of history. A stumpy minaret projects from a Byzantine dome, while Gothic gutters protrude from the walls.

Leventis Museum, Laiki Yitonia and the Tripiotis

The network of alleys to the east of Eleftheria square lying between the D'Avila Bastion and Hippokrates street are collectively known as **Laiki Yitonia**. They have been cleaned up to form a tourist zone, but outside of a shopping trip (*see* below) or an urgent desire for food this area can be avoided. Head instead for the **Leventis Municipal Museum of Nicosia** which is halfway along Hippokrates Street at No. 17, © (02) 451475 (*Open every day except Mon, 10–4.30; free*). Go upstairs and turn left at the top for a corridor journey through the city's history, walking past well lit reproduction costumes, objects, photographs and maps all accompanied by a multilingual text. The experience is more educational than aesthetic, as there are comparatively few genuine antiquities from before the 19th-century period on display. The trench in the hall exposes the foundations of the medieval building which formerly stood on this site. There is a café in the basement, a gallery for temporary exhibitions on the second floor, and a shop on the ground floor which stocks good reproductions, some in silver.

Just east of the Leventis Museum take the Solon street turning and walk 150m to **Tripiotis**, the most handsome Orthodox church in Nicosia, built by Archbishop Germanos in 1690. The round stone columns, the Romanesque arches, clean barrel vaults and plain stone walls conspire to give the triple-aisled nave a pleasing monolithic mystery. A richly gilded iconostasis marches across the whole width of the church, shielding the three separate apses and contrasting with the dark recess of the dome which rises directly above. Because of the close proximity of the street, no narthex was built to the west though there was space to construct an arcaded porch against the south wall. As you walk around the church you may notice odd fragments of medieval carving set as random decoration in the exterior walls or used as lintels over all three principal doors.

Costanza Bastion and the Omerieh Mosque

The western edge of the **Costanza Bastion** supports the small, modern mosque of Bayraktar, which stands beside the tomb of the heroic Turkish standard bearer who first planted the Ottoman flag on the walls of Nicosia in 1570 but was promptly cut down for his pains.

100m west of the bastion, Canning bridge and Trikoupis street mark the way north to the **Omerieh/Omerye Mosque** (*open around the hours of Muslim prayer; no adm but donations expected*) around which a weekly market spreads itself every Wednesday. The outer porch and the light Gothic tracery that survives around the west door of the mosque reveals an earlier role, when it served as the great Augustinian Priory of St Mary's. It was badly damaged by cannon fire during the siege, and the broken stumps of the nave columns were embedded into the wall during the Turkish restoration. So now, as you step inside, instead of soaring vaults you contemplate heavy protruding piers that carry the wide low arches and barn-like roof typical of indigenous Cypriot architecture. The church was a favourite burial place of the Latin nobility, and a number of fine gravestones were recovered this century which can be seen in Limassol castle and the Bedesten in North Nicosia. Some original vaulting and a fine rose window survive in the square side chapel which was added about a century after the church was finished around 1340. The octagonal turret in the corner of this chapel once gave access to the roof, and later provided a convenient foundation for a circular minaret. In exchange for a donation the custodian allows visitors to climb up and enjoy the view from the two balconies. From here you can look across the Green Line to the monuments in the North and admire the immediate precincts of the mosque. To the west are the glass pierced domes of a Turkish Hammam, a steam bathhouse theoretically open from 8–2.30, though you might check in advance, ✆ (02) 77588. On the ground the hammam is screened from view by a corner café. The tables of this café have a fine view across to the Omerieh mosque with its sturdy minaret set amongst palms, while just to the north stands an outer wall pierced by empty renaissance windows, the remains of the Venetian-built hospice.

The Konak of Hadji-Georgakis Kornesios

Open Mon–Sat 8–2; adm.

This Konak, or mansion house, is the finest secular building to survive from the Ottoman period. The front door of the mansion is on Patriarchis Gregorios street, 150m east of the Omerieh Mosque.

The building was constructed at the end of the 18th century by the Dragoman Hadji-Georgakis Kornesios. Dragoman, from the Turkish Tardjaman, literally means 'interpreter', but in this context is better translated as First Minister. It was a post that Kornesios occupied, at great profit to himself, for 30 years, aided by a convenient marriage to the archbishop's niece and a well-oiled friendship with the Grand Vizier in Istanbul. A surviving folk-ballad, *The Song of Hadji-Georgakis*, records his fall from power, a long-winded affair which began in 1804 with a tax revolt supported by the local garrison. A lynch mob burnt down the front door of the mansion, but the Dragoman escaped to Turkey from where he promptly returned with 2000 troops at his back. After restoring order he sailed to Istanbul but became emeshed in court intrigue, which resulted in his execution in 1809. His family, after a period of disgrace, were able to buy back the mansion, which was willed to the nation by one of his descendants in 1979.

The yellow stone exterior has a fortress-like severity with its high vertical wall filled with barred windows. It is also deliberately assertive: there are three ranks of windows outside but only two storeys within, and strong relief carving emphasizes the central pointed arch doorway which is overlooked by a handsome kiosk. Below the kiosk a marble plaque has been set into the wall, bearing self-invented heraldry, an ingenuous mix of Gothic tendrils, a double-headed Byzantine eagle and a cat-like Lion of St Mark from Venice.

There is a delightful contrast as you step inside into an open courtyard overlooked by a stone-flagged colonnade with a marble fountain, marking the transition into the walled garden shaded by palms. The ground floor and garden were the working areas of the house that held the storerooms, cisterns, stables, kitchens and a steam bathhouse. The upper storey was the formal part of the house, designed for entertainment, receptions and semi-official business. The Dragoman's family lived in a cottage at the far end of what was originally a much longer garden. The first floor of the mansion is approached by an outside staircase which leads directly into a broad open hall, spanned by a wide low arch—one of the most characteristic features of traditional Cypriot architecture. From the hall (furnished with late 19th-century pieces enlivened by one or two cabinets of

Damascus glass, medieval sgraffito bowls and Turkish metalware), a corridor leads south to the **oda**, the main reception room. This is a fine example of 18th-century Ottoman taste and has been sympathetically refurnished with a kilim and long divans. It achieves a strictly regular proportion by the use of a slight external cantilever. The built-in cupboards of the north wall are another typical feature, though they conceal the very personal addition of a secret escape way to the roof. The apse above is painted with a great domed seaside palace lined with cypresses, a form of decoration which made subtle reference

ng. House of Hadji Georgakis

to the Dragoman's contacts in the capital. The richly carved ceiling is also original and is dominated by a gilded spiralling wheel set against a star-flecked blue sky. On the south wall two portraits allow us to look into the worried but stern face of the Dragoman, who is depicted in both pictures clutching a document bearing the Tugra, the unmistakable formalized signature of the Sultan.

Ayios Antonios and the Podocataro Bastion

The streets around the church of **Ayios Antonios (St Anthony)** were inhabited by many of the richest Greek families during the Ottoman period. Though there is nothing that can compete with the grandeur of the Konak of Hadji-Georgakis Kornesios, the façades and balconies along Athens Street (off Patriarchis Gregorios street) are amongst the finest in the city. The Church of Ayios Antonios is usually only noticed for its delicate late 19th-century carved belfry, though the narrow 18th-century nave, supported by a line of yellow stone buttresses with a Gothic like array of protruding gutters, is not without a certain charm.

From the church cut along Ayios Antonios street to the public garden established around the **Liberation Monument** on **Podocataro Bastion**. Liberty stands on her plinth and watches approvingly as EOKA fighters lift a portcullis and allow the people of Cyprus out into the bright light of self-determination. It is a sad commentary on the post-independence troubles that most of the bronze life-size figures, including Liberty herself, have been neatly punctured by bullet holes.

The Archbishop's Palace Complex with Ayios Ioannis

Koraes street, which contains some fine late medieval carved stone doors such as the one at No. 14, leads up from the Podocataro bastion to a statue of Makarios III which stands before the brand new **Archbishop's Palace**. Both the statue and the palace are impressive, owing to their size rather than their artistry. Apart from the imperial purple marble by the main gilt door and the mix of Ionic and Byzantine capitals, it is directly modelled on a Venetian palace. It was badly damaged during the Samson coup of July 1974, when the Greek-officered National Guard reduced it to a burnt-out shell in their attempt to kill the Ethnarch. The northwestern wing of the palace houses the Makarios III Cultural Foundation, which runs a library and research centre as well as the public art galleries and the Byzantine (Icon) Museum. Amongst the palace railings stand the busts of Archbishops Kyprianos and Sopronius. The former was hanged in the terror campaign of 1821; the latter presided over the transformation from Ottoman to British rule and was the first to formulate the request for *enosis*, the union of Cyprus with Greece. Directly east of the palace stands the Neoclassical Pancyprian Gymnasium, the sixth-form college whose students played such a key role in the 1955–9 EOKA struggle.

Ayios Ioannis (Cathedral of St John the Evangelist)

Open 9–12, 2–4 Mon–Fri, 9–12 Sat; offerings accepted.

This modest chapel, which stands just to the north of the new palace, was built in the Ottoman period, and despite the rise in fortune of the Orthodox Church continues to serve as the cathedral church of Cyprus.

A dilapidated medieval monastery originally stood here, built by Benedictine monks who dedicated it to St John of Bibi, but this was replaced with the existing barrel-vaulted nave in 1662. Forty years later Archbishop Silvester turned this monastic chapel into his cathedral, and it was subsequently embellished by his successors with a wonderfully ornate gilded iconostasis, mother-of-pearl inlaid furniture, icons and frescoes. The 18th-century paintings are crude, especially in comparison with what can be found in the hills, but seen in the flickering half-light of a candle-lit Orthodox service they can still express mystery, majesty and a sense of awe. Start from the west end and advance towards the altar. The 5th bay is covered with a dozen, rather faded, scenes of the miracles of Christ; the 4th bay depicts the Tree of Jesse, while opposite is a picture of the whole world praising the Lord; the 3rd bay reminds us of the Last Judgement at the end of the world, with a dozen scenes of the Risen Christ above the Holy Handkerchief depicted on the lintel. Just beside the episcopal throne are four scenes showing the miraculous discovery of the tomb of St Barnabas (*see* p. 384). The 2nd bay is covered with 18 scenes from the life of Christ culminating in a large Crucifixion; the 1st bay depicts Christ in majesty surrounded by the hierarchy of heaven.

The Byzantine (Icon) Museum

Open Mon–Fri 9.30–1, 2–5.30 and Sat 9–1; adm; © (02) 456781.

This gallery of 150 icons, which occupies part of the northern wing of the Archbishop's palace, has been gathered from the collections of parish churches. It is one of the richest public collections of icons in the world—the museum acknowledges second place only to the collection in St Petersburg. It includes imported as well as Cypriot icons created within an artistic millennium that stretches between the 8th and the 18th centuries. Within the essential boundaries of the Byzantine tradition, there are subtle variations and degrees of skill to be found in each period. After an initial tour of the highlights, read the background piece before returning for a second look. Icons stand apart from the mainstream of Western art history, characterized by their mostly anonymous creators and continuous themes. All the ones shown here are worthy of contemplation, expertly restored and catalogued by Father Dionysios and Athanasios Papageorghiou, the Abbot of Khrysorroyiatissa Monastery and the Ephor of Ancient Monuments.

Go straight to the centre of the room to no. 66, a 12th-century Comnenian Christ. It is rendered for maximum impact in the dark interior of an Orthodox church; its gilded reflective background and the exaggerated shadows of the face are bordered by colours that would glow in candle-light. The eyes look out with the disarming power to gaze an inch above your head. Notice the clumsily painted blue cloak, a victim of a near-disastrous restoration job. From the same mountain church, is the Virgin Mary of Aracas (no. 69), whose face masterfully expresses our own puzzled humanity, touched with dreadful intimations for the future, but yet pointing out the world's only hope. Of equal power, and from the same period, is the small icon of St John and the Virgin of Khrysaliniotissa (no. 16 and 17), who is depicted with big Levantine hooded eyes, dark eyebrows and a long thin mournful nose. The pair of two-sided processional icons (no. 65 and 70), both bearing the Virgin and a Crucifixion-Deposition on the other side, are precious examples of the Palaeologue Renaissance developed in late medieval Constantinople. The plank icons (no. 46, 47 and 48) are also from this period, with their attenuated shape and the careful, sympathetic depiction of their western donors on the icons themselves. A fine example of the polish and cultural flexibility of the Cretan school in the 17th century is the group on the end wall: the orthodox imagery of no. 126, the virgin flanked by St Nicholas and St George, is in dramatic contrast to the Italianate portrayal of the donors.

Icons—Origins to Iconoclasm

An icon (from the Greek *eikon*) literally means an image, and by usage denotes a sacred image of the Orthodox Church. This may appear in any one of a dozen media, typically worked from either a glittering glass mosaic, inlays of precious metal, carved ivory, on a frescoed wall or on a wooden board—though unless otherwise specified the word 'icon' now usually refers to just the latter. The earliest surviving examples of paintings on wooden boards come from Fayum at about the time of Christ. In this town in the Nile delta, it was customary for vivid idealized portraits of the dead to accompany the body into the grave. It was a tradition whose proximity, portability and funeral associations gave it an immediate appeal to the early persecuted Church. However, there are only a handful of icons, mostly held in St Catherine's Monastery at Mount Sinai, that date back to before the 9th century. The reason for this is that from 725 to 842 AD a vicious civil war was waged, between the image haters (iconoclasts) and image lovers (icon-odules), which effectively purged the Byzantine Empire of its religious imagery.

9th-century Renewal

The iconodules emerged triumphant, but were careful to protect against future abuses and renewed strife by introducing a precise definition: icons might be venerated but not worshipped. The honour done to the icon does not rest in the image but is considered to pass to the original. It acts as a sacred window into the spiritual world, a special boon to the illiterate and hard-worked masses who lack the leisure or education for a religious life. Just as no variety is tolerated in copying the gospels, there could be no discordant variety in images, many of which are believed to be based on an unbroken chain of descent from St Luke. In the Constantinople of the 9th century a canon of iconography was formulated in total harmony with the liturgy, traditions and councils of the church. The relatively few surviving icons allowed for a codification that defined characteristic features, gesture, dress, symbols and deportment. Painting schools, established in the monasteries of Constantinople, dispatched finished images and masters to enrich the spiritual life of imperial provinces such as Cyprus. The wooden board of an icon was usually at a 5 to 4 vertical proportion, planed to create a natural frame around the sunken central surface. The board was treated with gesso before wax-based paints or sheets of gold leaf were applied.

Five Eras

From the **9th to the 10th century** sacred figures were depicted with a didactic, hieratic formality. They float without weight or consideration for the third dimension, and are set in almost abstract positions against a gold or plain background. They are depicted in a full frontal position which allows the eyes especial dominance. Indeed, the searching spiritual quality of a pair of eyes is an absolute characteristic of all Byzantine sacred art, and the impact of the gaze emitted from an icon is the single sure sign of its quality. Hands, especially those of Jesus, are also given an attenuated prominence and elegance. The best succeed in suggesting a state of serenity, a hidden order and quiet calm that is quite beyond one's own pudgy digits. In the **11th and 12th century (the Comnenian era)** a more emotional tone was added, giving a warmer and more approachable sacred image. This is at its most apparent in the various depictions, and numerous variations, of the Virgin and Child. It was also a most productive age, and icons were exported beyond the Empire to Serbia, northern Russia and Italy, where they acted as seeds from which grew distinctive provincial schools. During this period, Cyprus was directly in tune with Constantinople, and developed a special affinity with, and loyalty to, the art of this era. The island and the Byzantine capital shared similar fates, for Cyprus fell to Western Crusaders in 1191, only a decade before the devastation of Constantinople by the

Fourth Crusade in 1203. Though Cypriot icons were to be influenced by Western tastes, there was also a marked tendency to return again and again, right up until the Ottoman conquest, to the purity of Comnenian art. This can make the dating of Cypriot frescoes especially difficult, though icons are often much easier to date as they were quickly affected by the western habit of adding portraits of the donors. These diminutive side figures give a fascinating insight into the changing habits of dress and the inter-marriage between the Greek and Frankish cultures. Lusignan rule kept Cyprus isolated from the mainstream of Byzantine culture and the island was only slightly affected by the **Palaeologue Renaissance** (1271–1453), which produced a delicate, intimate religious art during the last two cultured, but doomed, centuries of Byzantine Constantinople. In the 15th century the island's artists, sometimes collectively known as the Cypriot School, either stayed true to their older Comnenian tradition or indulged in elements of the classically inspired naturalism that emanated from the great Italian city states. This can easily be recognized from a new sense of drama, of weighted figures set in a unified composition and in an increasingly realistic and three-dimensional landscape.

However, by the mid-16th century the artistic leadership had passed to neighbouring Crete, which was also under Venetian authority. The **Cretan School** was the only foreign guild of painters permitted in Venice, and from this commercial base it developed a Europe-wide reputation. The painters worked with equal skill in both Orthodox and Latin traditions in response to the demands of different markets. The Ottoman conquest of Cyprus in 1572 further confirmed this Cretan dominance, which nevertheless produced many substantial, polished portrait-like icons, seen at their best in the richly carved and gilded iconostases that are also characteristic of the period. By the 18th century there was a sharp decline in standards, Orthodox traditions were neglected to be replaced by cheap and debased versions of Italian art with a chap book-like uniformity that reflects the age of printing. The tacky *ex voto* icons and cheap reproductions produced in the 19th and early 20th centuries are only just now being superseded by a new confidence in Orthodoxy matched by a return to origins.

The upstairs **Western Art Galleries** are a famous anti-climax, and, apart from a smile at the 19th-century Orientalism of P. Bouirote, the dubious attributions that line the second floor can be totally ignored. The third floor has some prettier things: ink sketches, romantic watercolours and heroic oils, all concerned with the struggle for Greek Independence.

Folk Art Museum

The attractive old monastic outbuildings that survive just north of the cathedral have housed this folk art collection since 1937. However, the museum has been closed for renovations and has been collecting dust for a number of years, ✆ (02) 463205 for more information. Similar but accessible collections exist at Limassol, Paphos and Yeroskippos.

Museum of the National Struggle

This three-room collection of photographs, documents and militaria, records the EOKA struggle of 1955–9. It is just north of the Archbishopric complex on the corner of Apostolos Varnavas street and Ayiou Ioannou street. The voluble curator welcomes all, though the evidence of the British denial of popular will—blue traitor hoods, photographs of bomb victims and the shrine for those hanged—can make it a harrowing experience.

The Famagusta Gate (Porta Giuliano) and the Taht-el-Kaleh Quarter

Gatehouse open Mon–Sat 10–1, Mon-Fri 4–7; free; ✆ (02) 430877.

Famagusta was the chief port of medieval Cyprus, and the strongpoint of Venetian authority on the island. The eastern entrance into Nicosia was therefore designed to be the largest and most elegant of the gatehouses. Constructed in 1567, it was officially named after Count Giuliano Savorgnano, the chief architect, who modelled it on the Lazaretto Gate built two years earlier by the Venetians in Crete. In common parlance it became known as Porta di Sotto (the lower gate), which survives in Turkish as Taht-el-Kaleh, the general name for this quarter of the old city.

At first sight the round arch of the gateway does not seem worth all the fuss, even when you include the pair of flanking round windows, rough pilasters, surrounding palm trees and temple-like roof-line. All becomes clear, however, when you step inside. A barrel-vaulted masonry tunnel slopes down through the thick earth embankment of the walls to an innocuous door in the wall of the moat. The immaculate masonry conceals a gradual diminution in height and width that serves to create a double intensification of perspective. In the centre of this subtly tapered tunnel there is a great domed round chamber, illuminated by a circular skylight in a deliberate reference to the Pantheon in Rome. At each side a pair of fountains trickled audibly into drinking troughs for animals. The walls are pierced by four dark window frames through which two detachments of the watch could survey the passing traffic, as on either side of the tunnel a pair of vaulted chambers were constructed for the permanent use of the garrison. Since the 1981 Nicosia Festival the gatehouse has doubled both as a monument and a fully functioning cultural centre (*see* below for details).

The streets around the **Taht-el-Kaleh** mosque, on the western end of Famagusta street, have been denied to traffic and provided with benches, making the area into a calm spot, suitable, out of school hours, for a quiet picnic and a read. The 15th-century church of **Panayia Khrysaliniotissa** (The All Holy [Virgin] of the Golden Arms) with its low domes is 150m north of the mosque. It is the oldest Orthodox church in the city and is believed to have been built under the patronage of Helena Palaeologina, the Byzantine princess who married John II. At its southern wall are the remains of a Gothic cloister, with a Romanesque doorway and windows framed with foliate carving, including green men entangled in vines. It used to be visited for its rich collection of icons, rescued from the Cathedral of St Nicholas when it was converted into the Bedesten after the Ottoman conquest. They are now held in the Byzantine (Icon) Museum, though there are still a quantity on display in the barrel-vaulted chamber to the south. The key holding custodian currently lives at No. 2. The surrounding streets, overlooked by the Green Line, contain some fine traditional courtyard town houses in a state of picturesque decay, although there have been some recent restorations.

Walking Around the Venetian Walls

There are places other than the traffic-ridden centre of a capital city in which to find serenity and fresh air, but few walks can so vividly combine the passionate nationalism of the 20th century with the great clash of mediterranean empires in the 16th. The two-mile route outside the walls takes you from the eastern Flatro Bastion to the western Ledra Palace Crossing (from Green Line to Green Line).

The Making of the Walls

The Venetians had always realized that the medieval curtain wall that straggled for 9 miles around Nicosia was quite indefensible. Improving it would consume a fortune. Yet Nicosia, isolated on a flat waterless plain, would always remain vulnerable and a strategic liability to a naval power like Venice. Savorgnano, the military engineer commissioned to draw up plans for a concentric defence of the city, also insisted on including a separate report discouraging its implementation. Despite this good counsel, work began the next year with the demolition of all buildings outside the newly-defined defensive circle. Such famous landmarks as the convents of La Cava and Beaulieu, the frescoed Orthodox monastery of Mangana, St Dominic's filled with royal tombs and the Lusignan Gothic palace were all flattened. The fine carvings were reduced to rubble and used to fill the new 3-mile-long circular embankment. This was faced with stone and protected by 11 arrow-shaped artillery bastions that protruded from the walls to provide flanking fire. The embankment was pierced by only three tunnel-gates, named after the ports of Paphos, Kyrenia and Famagusta. Work finished just a few months before the Ottoman army landed at Larnaca on 3 July 1570.

The Great Siege of 1570

By the end of July an Ottoman army of 70,000 was camped to the south of the city, with its headquarters established on St Marina hill, where the Hilton stands today. The siege began with the digging of a network of trenches that zigzagged their way towards the southern walls, protected from Venetian cannon fire by mole-like earthworks stiffened with wood. As it was summer, the moat was bone-dry and the bastions, though admirably designed to provide each other with flanking fire, proved to have a blind spot at their apex. The noses of the four southern bastions—Tripoli, D'Avila, Costanza and Podocataro—were tunnelled away and slowly converted into entry ramps. Fifteen assaults were launched through August, attacking first one bastion, then two, then all four at once, but they were all beaten back. Then, in the beginning of September, a fresh draft of troops arrived from Istanbul bearing secret reports that the Venetian fleet and relief expedition had still not left Crete. The Ottoman commander, Mustafa Pasha, felt free to commit his entire army to one massive assault on the morning of 9 September. A standard was briefly planted in Costanza, its place now marked by the Bayraktar Mosque, before a Venetian counter-attack reclaimed control of the bastion. A similar pattern of events occurred at the Podocataro Bastion where the fate of the city wavered in the wind, but the Venetian commander suffered a crisis of confidence and withdrew to the palace while Mustafa Pasha rushed in reinforcements. The bastion was stormed and the neighbouring curtain wall and bastions fell like dominoes as they were outflanked. The Venetians fought on for another eight hours, and took their last stand in a desperate defence of the palace, which was only subdued by point-blank cannon fire. The siege ended with a farcical scene in the palace courtyard when a drunken Cypriot shinned up the flagpole. He threw down the tattered banner of the Lion of St Mark and replaced it with a fresh standard, the triple crescent on green of the Ottomans. After the habitual three days of licensed rapine, murder and plunder, discipline returned to the troops on the dawn of the fourth day. The walls were restored, the thousands of dead buried, the siege trenches filled in, and the Catholic cathedral converted into a mosque. Ten days later, on 22 September, the kettle drums led the Ottoman army out through the east gate towards Famagusta.

State Collection of Contemporary Art

Open Mon-Fri 10–5, Sat 10–1; adm; © (02) 302951.

This small gallery is just south of the Costanza bastion. Don't be put off by the slightly shut-up look: walk up the outside stairs to the green door of this yellow stone villa on the corner of Kritis street and Leoforos Stasinou. There is usually a temporary exhibition here, as well as the permanent collection of over 80 Cypriot and Greek artists, which includes such favourites as Glyn Hughes' split archetype head, no. 119, and Makariou Andreas' *Meze at Kato Paphos*, no. 58.

There are two good commercial galleries a short walk south. Follow Kritis street down past the gleaming Woolworth store at the crossroads, go straight over, passing through a pleasantly shaded Orthodox cemetery (whose funerary chapel and grandiose tombstones are eclipsed by a meadow of wild flowers in the spring), and in the streets just to its south you will find Gallery Gloria and Apocalypse Gallery (*see* below for addresses).

Nicosia Outskirts

Kaimakli was once the home of the island's stone carvers, and is one of the oldest of the city's satellite villages extending immediately northeast of the city walls. It is now an isolated lobe that stretches out through the entanglements of the Green Line, but its fine turn-of-the-century stone houses and churches can be admired in a guided walking tour that leaves every Monday at 10am from the tourist information office in Laiki Yitonia.

The village of **Strovolos** lies on the west bank of the Pedhieos river bed, about 3km southwest of the city walls. It has been surrounded by housing developments, but retains much of its old atmosphere and some small furniture workshops. However, it is not for these that this suburb receives a steady trickle of Western European pilgrims, but for the house and lecture hall of the disciples of Daskalos, the Magus of Strovolos. It is advisable to read Kyriacos Markides' study of this spiritual teacher and healer (*see* 'Further Reading', p. 418) before making enquiries.

The medieval **Castle of La Cava** stands on a high ridge at the southeast edge of the city, and is currently inaccessible as it is occupied by the Cypriot military. To the west of the castle the high ground of Athalassa has been planted with young Aleppo pine trees to make a future park. This was the work of the UN forces who marked two decades of duty in Cyprus by presenting a gift of lasting value to the citizens of Nicosia.

The palm-shaded monastery of **Arkhangelos Mikhail** (Archangel Michael) stands on the north bank of the Pedhieos river bed, just off the new main road to Peristerona. The yellow stone church, with its heavy buttresses and its monolithic-looking drum and dome, is one of the most handsome buildings from the Ottoman period. It was built in the mid-17th century by Archbishop Nicephoros, who was buried in the elaborate tomb in the porch, and who was also responsible for the purchase of the grey marble Islamic fountain that stands in the garden. It has recently been restored by the Kykko Monastery, who have converted the old outbuildings into a theological study centre. It used to be surrounded by vineyards, but these have been profitably converted into suburban housing estates.

The municipal food **market**, on the corner of Digenis Akrita and Leoforos E. & A. Theodotou, is open every morning, while near the Omerieh Mosque every Wednesday is a more varied and colourful street market.

The Laiki Yitonia quarter is stacked with **bazaars** selling Greek, Egyptian and home-grown tourist tack, while the more original shops are to be found along Aristokyprou street. The **House of Glass Blowing**, at No. 43, ✆ (02) 467785 is the most upmarket of the tourist bazaars, with a glittering magpie nest of imported damascene dishes, brass coffeepots, wood inlays and stone carvings and its own range of coloured glass scent bottles and ampoules. The **Diachroniki Gallery** at No. 2B, ✆ (02) 467257, which displays original Cypriot landscapes in pastels, oil and watercolour amongst antique prints and cheaper reproductions. **Symbolo** at no. 20A, ✆ (02) 453244, stocks a good selection of contemporary island **pottery**. At No. 13 is **MAM**, PO Box 1722, ✆ (02) 472744, a clearing house for all manner of Cyprus-related publications where you can browse, buy or order. MAM also manage a display in the

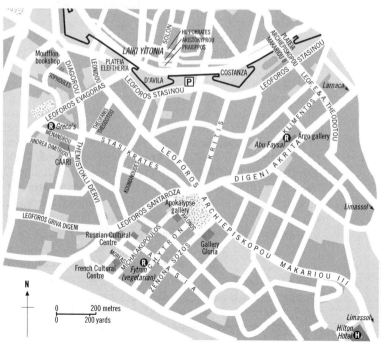

Phaneromeni Library at 46 Phaneromeni street. The **Collector** at 13 Praxippos street, Laiki Yitonia, ✆ (02) 461980, deals in original batik prints, maps, and cheaper reproductions as well as coins and stamps. The **gift** shop on the ground floor of the **Leventis Museum** at 17 Hippokrates street stocks reproduction Byzantine silverware, ranging from an expensive copy of the Lambousa plates to cheaper crosses and rings.

Moving out of the tourist area and south from the walled city there are two good **bookshops**: **Bridgehouse** on the corner of Leoforos Vryonos (Byron) and Leoforos Griva Digeni and the **Moufflon Bookshop** at 1 and 3 Sophoules street. The latter is run by Kevork K. Keshishian, the author-publisher of all 16 editions of *Romantic Cyprus* and the two editions of *Nicosia*. Evelyn Christodoulou runs **Karma** at 2 Koumanoudes street, PO Box 4582, ✆ (02) 457807, which is stocked with her personal selection of **weaves** and **sandalwood carvings** from India and Peru. **Fieros Antiques** is stuffed with Eastern pots and ex-colonial possessions, and is found at the corner of Stasikrates and Theofanis Theodotou street, with **Divas Antiques** nearby at 122 Statiskrates street.

Commercial Art Galleries

The embroideries, ceramics, wood carvings and especially the icons and frescoes seen in museums and churches throughout the island testify to a consistent artistic tradition. By the early decades of this century Cyprus was also producing artists influenced by developments in Western Europe. Few could find a market or a sympathetic audience at home, but since Independence this has been rapidly corrected. After a visit to the permanent collection at the State Gallery you can witness the explosion of artistic life which has occurred on the island by touring Nicosia's commercial art galleries: **Apokalypse** in Tofarco House on the corner of Avlonos and Chytron street, ✆ (02) 447231; **Argo** at 64E Digeni Akrita, ✆ (02) 444009; **Diaspora Art Centre** at 18 Evanthus street, ✆ (02) 450577; **El Greco** at 97 Limassol avenue, ✆ (02) 31432; **Gallery Gloria** at 3A Zenon Sozos street, ✆ (02) 452605. There is also **Alinea Gallery** at 23 Navarino street, ✆ (02) 4567654; **Opus 39** Gallery on Kimon street off Acropolis avenue and **Revolution Gallery** on St Helena street.

Cultural Centres, Theatres and Libraries

The Famagusta Gate Cultural Centre has a lively and varied programme with lectures, art exhibitions, films and debates throughout the weekend. They are usually held in one of the vaulted chambers that flank the tunnel, or in summer at the open-air theatre tucked into the corner of the bastion.

In addition to foreign theatre companies on tour during the summer festivals, there are three theatres in Nicosia which switch freely between Greek and English performances. The state-subsidized Municipal Theatre is on Museum street, ✆ (02) 463028; ENA is just north of the Famagusta Gate at 4 Athinas street, ✆ (02) 348203 and Satirico is out in the suburb of Strovolos at 3 Serrae street, ✆ (02) 312940.

The Russian Cultural Centre is at 16 Alasia Street, Ayii Omoloyitae, ✆ 441607, and usually has something worthy on Wednesday at 8pm, while the Film Society borrows the screen on Mondays and Tuesdays and shows European and American arthouse movies at 8.30pm. The British Council is in a grey and white apartment block two doors from the Cyprus Museum at 3 Museum street, ✆ (02) 442152. They run a library (open every morning except Sun 9–12 and 3–5.30 except Wed and Sat), with a lecture or video once a week which usually starts at 7.30pm. The French Cultural Centre at 3 Moreas street, off Michalakopoulos street, ✆ (02) 443071, runs a more varied programme of music, art and film.

If you wish to deepen your knowledge of Cyprus, two good starting places are: the Phaneromeni Library, 46 Phaneromeni street, PO Box 1722, ✆ (02) 464698, and CAARI, the Cyprus American Archaeological Research Institute, 11 Andrea Dimitriou street, ✆ (02) 451832.

Church Services

The **Tripiotis** and **Ayios Ioannis** churches are the best places to witness the haunting services of the Orthodox Church. At a lesser level of grandeur and mystery you could attend the **Holy Cross Catholic Church** by the Paphos Gate. It is run by Franciscan Friars, ✆ (02) 462132, who celebrate mass on Saturday evening at 6 or 7pm and on Sunday at 8am in Greek and at 9.30am in English. Nearby is the **Maronite Cathedral of Our Lady of Graces**, which has services in Aramaic, the language of Christ, at 7.30am, 8.30am and 10am. The **Anglican Church of St Paul**, a typical bit of rough stone 19th-century parish Gothic, stands amid a cluster of trees on the corner of Byron avenue and Grigori Afxentiou street.

Sports

Nicosia is not a sporting resort, though there are facilities for squash, tennis, bowling and swimming. For **squash** there is the Eleon Sports Centre on Ploutarchos street in Engomi, ✆ (02) 449923 and the Lyras Centre on Leoforos Griva Digeni in Engomi (behind the Ledra Hotel) ✆ (02) 351200. The Hilton Hotel has a sports club, membership of which allows use of its **tennis** courts, and partners can be found through the local tennis club, ✆ (02) 366822 in the morning. For **bowling** go to Kykko, behind the Ledra Hotel in Engomi on Leoforos Griva Digeni, ✆ (02) 350085. Apart from the pool at the Hilton you can also **swim** in the municipal pool at 8 Leoforos Louki Akrita, Ayios Dhometios, ✆ (02) 464155 and the Eleon on Ploutarchos street in Engomi, ✆ (02) 449923. For the more sedentary there are late afternoon games of cards at the Bridge Club at 6 Mykonos street, ✆ (02) 459220 and the weekend Horse Races. The race course with its tote betting offices is 3km west of the Venetian Walls. Sunday afternoon racing is from September to April, with Saturday events taking over in May, June and July. Ring the Race Club on ✆ (02) 497996 for more information.

Where to Stay

expensive

The six storey **Hilton**, off Leoforos Archiepiskopou Makariou III, PO Box 2023, ✆ (02) 464040, stands on a hill a mile south of the city walls, in its own grounds with a garden, tennis court and pool. It is large and efficient but not much of a base for exploring old Nicosia, though it has a reasonably lively lobby life with its buffet lunches, ice cream teas by the pool terrace and live music in the bar.

moderate

The **Kennedy Hotel** at 70 Regaena street, PO Box 1212, ✆ (02) 475131, fax 473337, has been completely refurbished and enjoys one of the best positions in town, just above the walls and west of the red-light district. On the ground floor is a crêperie and the Café Opera, where afternoon tea is served between 4.30–6 and music is played by Russian pianists from 9pm–1am. A double room is at the top of this price range (currently around CY£40), but if this is too much use the nearby **Venetian Walls Hotel** on the corner of 80 Regaena street and 38 Ouzounian street, ✆ (02) 450805, which is under the same ownership, but is simpler and about half the price.

cheap

The **Lido Hotel** on the corner of Phylokyprou and Passicratous street (just north of Eleftheria square), ✆ (02) 474351, is a central, unpretentious apartment block with 40 bedrooms. **Capitol Hotel** at 94 Regaena street, PO Box 1758, ✆ (02) 462465, is a functional boarding house with an institutional feel from its use in term time by High School students. Don't move much further down the price range for, despite its promising looking yellow stone and green balconied façade, the Nicosia Palace is just the wrong side of seedy and the Regina Palace has perhaps too much character and too many occupants for a good night's sleep. There are a growing collection of rooms to rent in Laiki Yitonia, such as **Tony's,** ✆ 466752, **Sans Rival,** and **Peter's** above the restaurant of the same name.

Eating Out at Lunch

moderate

The Laiki Yitonia district, a small grid of narrow streets due north of D'Avila Bastion, has been tarted up with new paving and turned into a picturesque tourist zone. There you can eat lunch outdoors at one of half a dozen taverna, such as **Royiatico** at 32A Ippocratous street, ✆ (02) 455081, that cater for jovial groups of day-glow day trippers.

Peter's House, ✆ (02) 463153 is the oldest, cheapest and least affected cafe-restaurant in the area. Moving out of this zone, try the **Propylaea** on the ground floor of the old Alexander hotel at 15A Trikoupis street.

South of the Venetian Walls the **Athineon Restaurant** occupies an old villa opposite the Finnish consulate at 8 Archiepiskopou Makariou III avenue, ✆ (02) 444786. It has a club-like atmosphere with rooms off the main staircase where you will be served heavy traditional stews and grills. **Event 3**, on the junction of Grivas Digenis avenue and Grigori Afxentiou street, is a modern building with a glitzy café-restaurant and roof garden.

If you are looking for something more individual, but still central, there is the **Ranoush Syrian-Arabic Restaurant** at 54 Regaena street, ✆ (02) 366523, which is directly below the Eonikon taxi kiosk. It is busiest in the evening when you can watch the paseo of street walkers which begins punctually at 8pm. Do not be put off by the Coca-Cola machine—the chef takes pride in cooking from an extensive menu which includes roast lamb testicles, chicken Jews mallow and Kabseh, a Saudi dish of rice with meat. Alternatively there is the **Ayios Georgios Demos Ionannou Taverna**, a quiet family-run place tucked away near the Green Line, halfway along Plateia Dimarchias which is off Eptanisos street. For vegetarian food use the **Fytron** counter at the Health Food Store, located about 1km south of D'Avila Bastion at 11 Chytri/Chytron street, ✆ (02) 461466.

Eating Out in the Evening

Practically all the more interesting places in Nicosia open only in the evening, usually somewhere around 8pm.

expensive

Abu Faysal is an acclaimed but reasonably pricey Lebanese restaurant tucked away in a villa at 31 Klementos street, ✆ (02) 360353. **Kavouri** at 125 Leoforos Strovolos, ✆ (02) 425153, is currently the city's most popular fish restaurant. Reservations are often required. Begin with home-made taramosalata, soup or fish cakes while your fish, chosen from the cabinet in the hall, is grilled and dressed with lemon, olive oil and spices.

moderate

In the old town there is the celebrated **Antonaki's Tavern**, near the offices of the Cyprus Mail, at 18 Germanou Patron street, ✆ (02) 464697, with its meze, music, Armenian specialities and boozy bottle-lined interior. **Greco's** is a more intimate tavern in an old yellow villa marked by a palm tree at 3 Menandrou street, ✆ (02) 474566. It is highly esteemed for its traditional vegetable specialities such as broad beans with aniseed, spinach and cumin seed sauce, lemon artichokes and cauliflower with mustard sauce. The suburbs hide some distinguished places worth a short taxi ride from the city centre, such as the **Mandri Tavern** opposite the old town hall at 27 Archiepiskopou Kyprianou avenue, Strovolos, ✆ (02) 497200, which has one of the island's richest assortments of *meze*.

Bars and Nightlife

South of the city walls there are a number of bars, such as **Mythos** beside the Athineon Restaurant on Theofanis Theodotou street, ✆ (02) 452010; **Romylos** at 4 Zena de Tyras street, ✆ (02) 445376, and the **Corner Pub** at 48 Dem. Severi avenue, ✆ (02) 465735; after which you could drift down and listen to the bouzouki music played at **Issadoras Night Spot** on the same street at No. 3, ✆ (02) 477387, or else take a taxi out to **Mikis Tavern** in Macedonitissa at 58 Leoforos Oktovriou 28, where you can listen to live music while you eat. For a club with floor shows, artistic tableaux, expensive drinks and bar flies head to **Crazy Horse** on Pantelis Katelaris street, ✆ (02) 473569.

To enjoy music in a slightly more serene atmosphere head for the streets around the Famagusta Gate, a little bohemia of theatres, music bars and cafés. It only comes alive in the evenings and is at its busiest in the summer, especially during the festival. Walk north from Famagusta Gate and its associated **Bastione Bar**, along Leoforos Athina to check out the bars on the way to the **Green Line Pub**. The **Nicosia Music Club** is south of the Famagusta Gate at 37 Heracles street, ✆ 435705, and is open throughout the year. A bottle rises in a magical greeting in the entrance hall, after which you can consume savoury pies and plates of sliced fruit washed down with wine on tables made from bicycle wheels, whilst listening to local musicians play jazz or folk. Walking back along the inside of the walls takes you through Regaena street, which becomes a red-light area at about 8pm though it remains friendly and unthreatening.

The Mountains

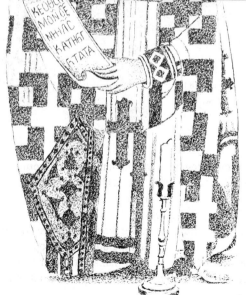

16th century fresco of St. Spyridon

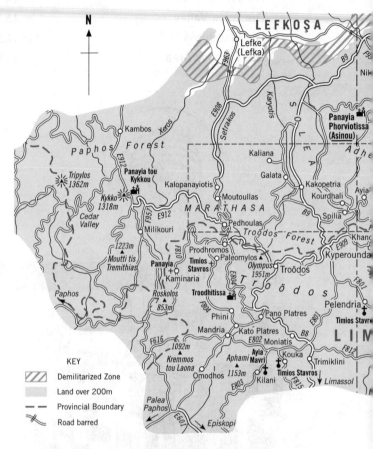

KEY

///// Demilitarized Zone

▨ Land over 200m

– – – Provincial Boundary

⤨ Road barred

The mountain region is the hidden jewel of Cyprus, occupying the centre of the island, both physically and spiritually. By most social or economic standards it is, however, a poor and backward region, which in the last half-century has witnessed a haemorrhaging of its working population, who have moved to Nicosia or Limassol. Many of the villages are running out of old people and have become dependent on holiday-makers for their survival. Fortunately, much of the terraced strips of farmland and the hill-

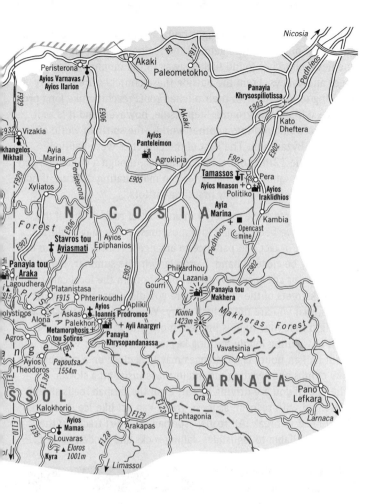

side orchards remain worked, even if the descendants of the old families now commute in half-tracks from the suburbs.

It is not so much the landscape that draws the visitor, for though the summits are high, the hills rise in slow, measured graduations with few of the dramatic peaks, escarpments and clear views found along the Gothic Range. Nor is it especially the fauna, for though the lower valleys can be dressed with a beautiful combination of vines and fruit, the mountains, when not scarred by open-cast mines, are usually either rough scrub or clad in recent plantations of Aleppo pine. The true gems of the region are the painted medieval churches found tucked away in the mountain slopes, villages and valleys. From the outside these churches are not very exciting to look at, with their pitched roofs reaching like long protective skirts to the ground. Step inside, however, and it is as if you have wandered into another world—the spiritual world of medieval Byzantium. The best of the churches were painted between the 12th and the 16th centuries, though a deliberate concern to maintain traditional styles can make dating difficult, if not actually irrelevant to many first-time visitors.

It is not an area to be explored in any sort of rush. None of the churches have been turned into museums, and it may require a fair amount of tact and patience to arrange a visit. A custodian or priest may be close at hand, particularly in the summer, but equally he or she may have to be sought out in the local café or in the backstreets of the village, before you discover, after all your efforts, that you are not in luck today. When you do get inside you may find that your time is limited; most church guardians have a habit of yawning loudly, rattling keys or tapping their watches after about half an hour. The distances may look close on a map but the slow climbs and twisting mountain roads insist on a slower schedule. If you are driving by car, even the tarmac roads should be treated with respect, as loose gravel can act like ice if you suddenly need to break. All roads, especially the dirt tracks in the spring, are liable to landslides, falling rocks and eroded verges.

The Five Mountain Areas

The mountainous centre of Cyprus is often simply referred to as the Troödos, though the Troödos is only the highest and best known of the five regions into which the mountains are customarily subdivided. The pine-wooded **Makheras**, centred around the famous monastery of the same name, occupies the far eastern range of the mountains. **Pitsilia**, a largely treeless region, is immediately to the west, but, despite its beautiful churches, is the most diffuse and least visited area. To the northwest is **Solea**, most of whose churches are concentrated in the twin villages of Kakopetria and Galata in the Karyotis valley. The **Marathasa** valley, where you will find the villages of Moutoullas, Kalopanayiotis and Pedhoulas, is due west of Solea. To the south of these two valleys, in the heart of the **Troödos** region, rises Mount Olympus, whose southern and western slopes can be explored from the old hill station of Pano Platres.

The mountains are an awkward area about which to give useful advice on restaurants. In the summer months numerous seasonal tavernas open up near practically every place of interest. In the evenings these tavernas are usually closed; in any event, you are unlikely to want to travel, and especially to return after consuming the village wine, along the twisting mountain roads. In practice, your choice is often restricted to your hotel dining room.

Getting Around

There are no service-taxi routes nor car hire agencies in the mountains, and only the major routes to and from Limassol and Nicosia are served by bus. Though a car makes things much easier, it is possible to explore the mountains without hiring a car. You can reach a resort village by bus (or private taxi) from Limassol or Nicosia, walk to all the surrounding sites and then take a rural taxis (operating out of the villages of Pano Platres, Agros, Kakopetria and Pedhoulas) on to your next destination.

By bus: The bus services from Limassol and Nicosia can take you up the main roads to the principal villages, but after that you are on your own. Agros, Pano Platres and the villages of the Marathasa valley (such as Pedhoulas and Kalopanayiotis) can be reached from Limassol. Kakopetria, the villages of the Karyatis valley and Pano Platres can be reached from Nicosia. *See* 'Limassol' and 'Nicosia' chapters for relevant information.

By taxi: Though there are no service-taxi routes from Limassol or Nicosia into the mountains, there is nothing to stop you taking a private taxi. It will cost around C£12 to get from Nicosia to Kakopetria, slightly more to the Marathasa villages and not much short of C£20 to Pano Platres. From Limassol, Pano Platres and Agros would be around C£11, and Kakopetria or the Marathasa villages about C£16.

Car and bicycle hire: There are no car hire firms in the mountains but plenty in Limassol and Nicosia. Bicycles can be rented in Pano Platres from **Tophill Souvenirs** which is beside the Splendid Hotel on the main street.

Tourist Information

The Cyprus Tourism Organization runs a booth in the centre of Pano Platres in the summer season from April to October, © (05) 421316.

The **Pano Platres** festival is held in mid-August and includes agri-cultural and folk-craft exhibitions as well as a cultural repertoire of music, dance and theatrical performances. For programme information ✆ (05) 421722.

The *panayiria*, the local two-day festivals that commemorate an important religious feast day or anniversary of a patron saint, can be held throughout the year in coastal Cyprus, but in the mountains the weather restricts them to the summer months. 14 and 15 August are important dates, indeed almost national holidays, when the three mountain monasteries of Kykko, Makhera and Troödhitissa all celebrate the **Dormition of the Virgin Mary**. The **Birth of the Virgin**, on 7 and 8 September, is also celebrated by Kykko, as well as the famous Asinou church outside Nikitari village and the celebrated Panayia tou Araka church outside Lagoudhera village. **The Raising of the Cross**, on 13 and 14 September, is celebrated at Omodhos (in the foothills to the south of Pano Platres) and at Stavros tou Ayiasmati church in Platanistasa village. The village of Kalopanayiotis commemorates **St John Lambadhistis**, its patron saint, in the monastery of the same name on 3 and 4 October. Akaki village (down in the Mesaoria plain to the east of Peristerona) celebrates **St Demetrios** on 25 and 26 October. The **Presentation of the Virgin to the Temple** on 20 and 21 November, celebrated at Panayia tou Makhera and Troödhitissa monasteries, brings the festival season to a close.

The Makheras Region

The Makheras area, unlike all the other mountain regions, has no hotels of its own. It can be approached from Pitsilia, to its west, or the hill town of Lefkara to the southeast (in Larnaca District), but is more often explored as a day trip out from Nicosia. This route from the capital also has the advantage of climbing up through the foothills, where you can find the cave-chapel of **Panayia Khrysospiliotissa** (on the edge of Kato Dheftera village), the monastery of **Ayios Iraklidhios** (St Herakleidios) and the **Royal Tombs of Tamassos** (on the edge of Politiko village). The mountains to the south feature only the monastery of **Panayia tou Makhera** (just to the east of Lazania) and the preserved highland hamlet of **Phikardhou**.

The Cave-Chapel of Panayia Khrysospiliotissa at Kato Dheftera

Kato Dheftera straddles the E902 road from Nicosia, but can also be reached from a signposted turning off the main B9 road to Palekhori. The ancient cave-chapel of

Panayia Khrysospiliotissa is set into an escarpment of golden rock overlooking the usually near-dry bed of the Pedhieos river. It is about 600m northeast of the village centre, approached along a tarmac drive that is found between the parish church and the bridge over the Pedhieos. A modern stairway now gives easy access to the chapel, which originally served as an inviolate sanctuary that could only be approached up a precarious ladder of rock-cut footings. The original fresco-lined interior has now almost entirely rotted away, but the two cave-chapels, connected by three side-tunnels, still retain an air of mystery. When the rains have fallen the cave echoes to the sound of the gurgling stream, which may have helped it become a particularly efficacious place to pray for rain. Nowadays the Virgin is requested to provide husbands, and a collection of bridal crowns and wedding wreaths deposited by grateful supplicants testify to her success.

The Royal Tombs of Tamassos

Open in summer every day except Mon 9–12 and 4–7; in winter (Oct–May) 9–1, 2–4.30; adm.

This pair of Archaic subterranean tombs are in the small archaeological enclosure just to the northeast of the village of **Politiko**, which stands on the west bank of the Pedhieos riverbed, directly opposite the larger village of Pera. They are the finest of their period in Cyprus, built from massive blocks of limestone, but with their plan and decorative scheme directly based on contemporary wooden constructions. They were built during the mid-6th century BC in the Cypro-Archaic II period, and, though smaller than those at Salamis, have much finer carved details. A slender stepped passage, known as a *dromos,* leads down to a porch (the *propylaeum*) set before the entrance. The flanking pilasters of the porch bear proto-Ionic capitals formed from an equilateral triangle flanked by curling scrolls of vegetation out of which protrudes an hibiscus-like tongue. It is derived from Assyrian prototypes, and provides graphic evidence of the eastern origins of what is too often sold to the world as classical-Greek architecture. The frieze above the doorway is clearly based on projecting wooden rafters, the origin of the dentil frieze, another regular feature of the classical order.

The **first tomb** is the most elaborate. It has an antechamber with blank vaults on its side onto which have been carved bolts in imitation of contemporary wooden structures. The five niches above the entrance door are filled with Archaic sacred carvings, including a central winged goddess flanked by composite symbols formed from an all-seeing eye, the altar-like horns of consecration and further floral variations of the proto-Ionic capital. The actual tomb chamber is dominated by a sarcophagus which stands on a raised plinth, to conjure up even in death the image of a royal throne.

Just to the south there is a confused area of excavations which includes the site of the temple of Aphrodite that stood at the centre of the Archaic city. There was also a third tomb of royal proportions nearby, but this was quarried in the mid-19th century for building stone. A similiar fate befell an exquisite bronze 5th-century statue of Apollo that was found in the riverbed in 1836 and was hacked into pieces to be sold for scrap. The head was retained, and, after a period at Chatsworth House, now rests in the British Museum. Fortunately, buried inscriptions and ancient poetry have proved more durable, and allow echoes of Tamassos's ancient identity to survive.

The Golden Apples of Aphrodite

Due to the presence of copper mines in the surrounding hills, Tamassos has a rich and long history stretching back to the Early Bronze Age (2700–1900 BC). It was an important late Bronze-Age town that was separate from the powerful harbour towns, and appears to have been in direct communication with the Hittite Empire. Like the rest of the island it declined during the Iron-Age invasions of the 11th century BC, but due to its mineral resources it was quick to revive and was well known to Phoenician merchants as early as the 9th century BC. Even then it was famous as an ancient religious centre with a temple that contained a monolithic shrine to the 'mother of the gods', who from surviving inscriptions was addressed as both Cybele (the ancient goddess of the Anatolians) and Astarte (the Syrian goddess), whose identity merges freely with that of Aphrodite. Sacred barbers were attached to the shrine and the hair clippings of worshippers were presented to the goddess in elaborate, inscribed dishes (a rite that Lucian describes in his 2nd-century AD account of the worship of the Syrian goddess). A smaller side altar was reserved for offerings to the male fertility god of the Cypriots. He was addressed as the god of cattle, and later equated with Phoenician Reshef or Greek Apollo, though his peculiar island identity was stressed by the epithet 'Alasiotas', from Enkomi-Alasia where the idol of a bronze-horned god was found in a temple. Beside the Tamassenian temple were forges, a familiar Cypriot juxtaposition of religion and metallurgy, which helps explain the unlikely marriage between Aphrodite and Hephaestus, the lame smith god.

Tamassos prospered during the Archaic era, as the royal tombs attest, but its wealth brought it nothing but trouble during the stormy politics of the Classical period. Its fortunes were similar to those of Palea Paphos; like Tamassos, it had joined the Ionian revolt of 499 BC and was reduced to a second-rate power after being sacked by the Persian army. By manipulating the rivalry between Salamis and Kition it maintained a precarious independence, though Tamassos was the first city to feel the effects of the new Hellenistic order. **Alexander the Great** gave the mines of Tamassos to King Pyntagoras of Salamis in return for his naval help during the siege of Tyre. These were then sold to Kition, which reaped small reward from its new suzerainty, for all the mines on the island were soon to be annexed to the privy purse of the Ptolemies, the Hellenistic monarchs of Egypt. The town, however, remained busy, and 500 years later, deep in the Roman period, it was still catalogued as one of the dozen cities of the island. Its ancient shrines and reputation for wealth continued to inspire poets. Claudian, (AD 370–404)—who was born an Egyptian, educated as a Greek and won renown as the last great Latin poet of a still pagan Rome—set Aphrodite's legendary twin fountains of love at Tamassos:

> Hence flow two fountains, sweet of taste the one
> The other bitter, and of poisonous taint,
> Whence Cupid tinged, as fame reports, his darts.

Ovid (43 BC–AD 18) saw Tamassos as the home of the sacred tree of Aphrodite which fruited golden apples:

> The Cyprian lands, though rich, in richness yield
> To that surnamed the Tamassenian field
> That field of old was added to my shrine
> And its choice products consecrated mine
> A tree there stands, full glorious to behold,
> Gold are the leaves, the crackling branches gold.

It remained a prosperous centre until the Saracen invasions of the 7th century AD brought mining to a complete halt, but by then it had a new spiritual identity established around Ayios Iraklidhios and Ayios Mnason.

The Monastery of Ayios Iraklidhios (St Herakleidios)

Usually open during daylight hours, but always at the discretion of the nuns, who firmly shut the doors 12–3, mid-May–September.

St Herakleidios stands on a slight hill just to the south of the village of Politiko, some 20km southwest of Nicosia. It is an old Christian pilgrimage centre that became a monastery in the 18th century, and, since 1962, has held a community of nuns. The exterior walls hide a range of ground-floor cells that look out through a wooden colonnade across a garden courtyard filled with the chatter of birds and the quieter resonance from a scattering of antique carvings. In the centre stands an 18th-century church with a small medieval chapel beside it, below which is a larger area of ruins from an early Byzantine basilica.

The shrine of St Herakleidios is acknowledged to be one of the earliest centres of Christianity in Cyprus, for Tamassos had a large, partly Hellenized, Jewish community. This was just the sort of audience that **St Barnabas** and **St Paul** would have wished to address in their missionary journey across the island. The Jews had come here as miners in the 1st century BC, when Herod the Great had leased the mines from the Ptolemaic kingdom. However, it was **Herakleidios**, the son of a pagan priest, who proved to be their most notable convert. He was later ordained the first bishop of Tamassos by Barnabas, and his active ministry is remembered in a catologue of miracles, stirring battles with devils and the foundation of numerous churches. He was martyred in the first public persecution of Christians, but his tomb, and that of his sister Herakleidiana and fellow martyrs Theodhoros and Macedonius, remained honoured by the undergound Church. These later became the focus of a pilgrimage centre when the Church became official, fashionable and well funded in the early 4th century.

The **medieval chapel** and **ancient tomb** are approached through the outer arched colonnade of the main church; from there a covered passageway, with a brand-new mosaic floor, leads around the side of the church to the domed medieval chapel that was carefully built over the cave-tomb of St Herakleidios. The presence of an early church on this spot (a large three-aisled basilica stood here from the 4th century until its destruction by the Saracens in the 7th) can be detected from the worn opus sectile floor, formed from distinctive golden hexagonal tiles interspaced with white marble. This was only laid in the 6th century after the original geometric mosaic floor had become worn away by two centuries of shuffling pilgrims. This aura of historical layers of devotion is further enhanced by the simple carvings on the stone iconostasis, a complete classical sarcophagus in the higher chapel and a trap door in the floor. This gives entrance to the cavernous hermitage of St Herakleidios, who used to meditate beside his rock-cut tomb. Just to the south lie the preserved foundations, crumbling mosaic floor and sarcophagi of another part of the 4th-century basilica.

The **main church** is composed of two barrel-vaulted aisles that were originally separate chapels. The southern one was built in the 15th century, and the northern chapel, originally dedicated to the Trinity, in the 16th century. They were joined together in 1759 by Bishop Chrysanthos when he established a monastery here. On the far south wall a frescoed group of saints, painted in the 11th century, survive on the strong stone-built piers of an earlier church. The dark interior is dominated by the richly gilded and carved iconostasis, divided by a pier into two halves. Most of the icons (apart from the finer central panels of the *Virgin, Christ* and *St John*) are believed to have been painted by the monk Pliaetos, who set up a productive but short-lived icon school here in the 18th century. The skull of St Herakleidios is displayed in a jewelled casket that stands on the carved reliquary table between the two iconostasis screens. On your way out you can buy produce from the nuns' shop by the gate, which usually includes some tempting pots of rose and almond jam.

The Chapel of Ayios Mnason and the Copper Mines

About 450m northwest of Politiko village stands the 18th-century chapel of **Ayios Mnason**, undistinguished apart from an Archaic capital built into the north wall. Mnason had a very similar career to Herakleidios, for he too was born of a local pagan family, became bishop and was martyred here. The traditions recall that he was one of the earliest converts, who had received instruction in Jerusalem from St John the Divine, before hurrying back to his homeland to help St Paul and St Barnabas on their journey through Cyprus. One of his more showy miracles was the public cursing of the local temple of Asklepios, which fell crashing to the ground before its astonished worshippers. Mnason was nearly lynched, but he miraculously blinded the town mob and only released them from their darkness on condition of a mass baptism.

A dirt track starts just south of the monastery and leads after 4km to **Mathiati South**, a great **open-cast crater** where ancient shaft openings can be seen burrowing their way down to the rich ores. The last copper mine in Cyprus closed down in the 1970s so you will not be in anyone's way and the old workings are gradually being repossessed by scrub. If you head 1.5km due west of the mines you will reach the hamlet of Philani and the chapel of Ayia Marina, from where you can follow the bed of the Pedhieos river back to Politiko. If you are too hot or tired you can drive to the mine; look out for the east turning found 3km south of the hamlet of Kambia on the E902 road.

Panayia tou Makhera Monastery

The monastery of Makheras, though of ancient foundation, is an unattractive turn-of-the-century building that is halfway to being transformed into a nationalist shrine. It does, however, enjoy a fine view north, and offers easy walking through the surrounding pine woods and a café-restaurant operating in the summer months. It is a 16km drive southwest from the Politiko turning at Pera village.

Four kilometres before you reach the monastery, you pass the charming 15th-century roadside chapel of **St Onoufrious**, which has recently been equipped with some new frescoes in its dome. St Onoufrious was one of the more heroically mad of the early Christian ascetics, who lived on the fringes of the Egyptian desert in the 4th century. His nakedness, devotion and solitude was so total that at his death his only companions were lions. These mourning beasts scratched a shallow grave for his thin corpse from out of the desert sand.

The miracle-working icon of the *Virgin Mary of Makheras* is preserved in the monastery's church, but is hidden from view by an encrustation of embossed silver. The icon was found by a pair of 12th-century hermits, Neophytus and Ignatius, hidden in a cave with a sword buried before it, as if in lone and miraculous guardianship. The hermits petitioned Manuel Comnenos (1143–80) for support in founding a monastery, and the distant emperor was pleased enough with the flattering analogy of himself to the miraculous sword to grant them money and a charter of liberties. Sadly, the old buildings were entirely destroyed by fire in the 16th century, rebuilt and destroyed again in 1892. Within Greek Cyprus it is now doubly famous through the martyrdom of **Grigoris Afxentiou**, one of the more youthful and better-looking leaders of the EOKA movement. Gregory the Eagle is now commemorated by an enormous bronze-winged statue on the monastery viewing terrace. He operated from the monastery where he maintained a disguise as one of the monks until a security leak brought Makheras under constant watch by the British forces, which eventually tracked Gregory down to a cave below the monastery. Though cornered and faced with certain death he heroically refused to surrender and was burnt out with a combination of petrol and grenades. His simple cave has been preserved as a national shrine and is found some 1 km along the signposted back road to Politiki. Some photographs, press clippings and charred relics are proudly exhibited opposite the west door of the monastery church.

Phikardhou (Fikardhou) Hamlet

A twisting mountain road continues west to pass Lazania, an attractive cluster of red-tiled roofs that hugs the mountain slopes, and Gourri, which is increasingly being colonized by weekenders, before reaching the almost deserted hamlet of Phikardhou, some 9km northwest of Panayia tou Makhera monastery. Phikardhou has no great antiquity or historical monument, but by a welcome decision of the government it has been preserved as a typical example of the indigenous architecture of the mountains. Two of the preserved houses in the hamlet are now open to the public; ask for the custodian in the house of I. Dimitriou Yiannakos, which is the attractive taverna overlooking the small village square, with its fountain, old schoolhouse and church dedicated to St Peter and St Paul. The village probably took its name from the wide-ranging estate of the Ficardi family, which produced powerful courtiers like Sir Thomas Ficardo, the chancellor to James II, the last Lusignan king. Until the latter half of this century it survived from the produce of its vineyards which allowed it to export wine, raisins, rosewater and zivania (a powerful marc-like spirit distilled from the pressed grapes left after wine-making), whilst herds of goats and carefully worked strips of terraced land allowed each family to be almost self-sufficient in food. The village houses are largely two-storey with the byres, winepresses and storehouses located on the ground floor and family accommodation in the upper storey. The walls of the ground floor are solid dry stone structures which, with the assistance of wooden beams and rafters, support a lighter mudbrick upper storey roofed with terracotta tiles. This upper storey might overlook a stone courtyard on one side and open onto a wide verandah formed from the flat roof of an attached barn on the other. Many of the wooden front door frames are decorated with hatching, though only the more prosperous villagers could afford stone window arches or lintels, which often bear a good-luck symbol such as a head or cross.

The Houses of Katsinioros and Achilleas Dimitri

Open all year Wed–Sun 10–1; 4–6 in midsummer; 3–5 the rest of the year; adm.

These two houses, preserved and carefully equipped with handlooms, wine-making equipment, primitive stills and village-fashioned wooden furniture, act as museums, where a new generation of Cypriots can contemplate the fast-disappearing peasant culture of their grandparents. It is good to see the gourd containers, earthenware storage jars, carved wooden bowls, dower chests, gypsum shelves (*souvantzes*), threshing boards (*doukani*) and corner fireplaces (*tsimines*) in their original context. It takes the tweeness out of folk art, but gives it a form of designer purity that it could never have aspired to in its heyday. The natural harmony of wood, terracotta, polished stone and home-woven linen has now acquired an intense retrospective glamour, though it is also still possible to imagine why these communities used to lap up the tackiest splashes of bright colour offered by printed nylon and moulded plastic.

Eating Out

The taverna in the mountain hamlet of **Phikardhou** serves a very good *table d'hôte* lunch, usually a pork-based stew with beans accompanied by olives, fresh local bread and wine.

The Pitsilia Area

The Pitsilia area occupies the eastern width of the central mountain belt, with Makheras in the foothills to its east and the Solea valley and the Troödos to its west. It is, with the exception of Agros, still largely unprepared for foreign tourists, though it remains the most heavily populated of the mountain regions, with the scattered agricultural settlements propped up by a generous system of government grants. Apart from almond and fruit groves around the villages, some indifferent vineyards and the odd pine plantation, it is an almost treeless zone with the highlands dominated by a goat-grazed scrub of rockrose, pistachio and golden oak. The principal attractions of the area are the mountain churches, especially the exquisite 12th-century frescoes in the **Panayia tou Araka** church near Lagoudhera. The frescoes from the later periods are undeniably cruder but have a compensating charm and variety. You should certainly not miss the late 15th-century frescoes in both **Stavros tou Ayiasmati**, outside the village of Platanistasa, and **Ayios Mamas** at Louvaras. A look at the 16th-century chapel of **Metamorphosis tou Sotiros** in Palekhori village and the 14th-century church **Timios Stavros** (of the Holy Cross) at Pelendria would complete a tour of the major sites, though there are another half-dozen lesser chapels and a few suggested walks for the more enthusiastic travellers.

The Pitsilia area can be approached from virtually all points of the compass, but is here described as if approached from Nicosia on the E903 road to Palekhori, from where the attractions of this region are described in an anticlockwise circuit. The village of Agros, 13km east of Palekhori, stands plum in the centre of this circuit and, though not a place of beauty, is perfectly sited as a base. It has a small—and virtually the only—choice of hotels, restaurants and banks in the area.

Nicosia to Palekhori

There is little to delay your journey out from the suburbs of Nicosia. The 18th-century convent of Ayios Panteleimon, 4km outside Agrokipia, might appear an inviting detour on your map, but to view its glittering iconostasis you will have to cross a land scarred with mine workings. South of Ayios Epiphanios the landscape improves as you climb up into the hills along the Maroullenas valley. The hamlet of Apliki, with its new lake formed by damming the Kambi stream, marks the start of the real mountain road that twists its way southwest to Palekhori.

Palekhori (Paleochoria)

The large mountain village of Palekhori, draped over both banks of the steep Palekhori stream, is some 44km southwest of Nicosia. It is a busy, self-contained place threaded with narrow mule-track alleys that twist down through the confusion of rustic cottages. It has a rough charm fully in keeping with its name, 'the old place', but apart from its churches, marked by half a dozen steeples protruding above the skyline, there are only a few cafés to delay the visitor.

The 16th-century church of **Panayia Khrysopandanassa** stands on the east bank of the village. It is the main church of the village, so it will often be found open. A number of frescoes are conserved on the central arcades, many of them obscured by soot and sealed in with a later coat of varnish. The four double scenes of *St Helena's Discovery of the Cross* are worth attention. (For the outline of the plot of this celebrated archaeologist *see* 'Stavros tou Ayiasmati', p. 146.)

The small chapel of **Metamorphosis tou Sotiros** (Transfiguration of the

Saviour), stands high up on the west bank of the village just off the Agros road, and has recently been awarded a signpost. The chapel is kept locked so you will need to inquire for the priest. Its interior is furnished with a complete cycle of early 16th-century frescoes from the Cretan school. These show the characteristic fusion of Italian artistic influence with that of Byzantium. The figures have a natural humanism and are arranged in harmonious compositions with a muted pallet to give a sense of calm order. They are, however, almost too familiar and serene, having lost the heightened spirituality, the glearing eye contact and hieratic distance of the earlier Byzantine traditions. They were painted around 1520, which reveals the dominance of Crete some 50 years before the Ottomans can be considered to have had any effect on Cyprus.

The decorative scheme follows the traditional arrangement. Amongst the more charismatic is the *Sacrifice of Isaac*, with its vividly portrayed grip of Abraham on his son's hair, the alarming proximity of the knife and the raging fire of the round altar. The *Communion of the Apostles* is depicted in its customary place below the calmly confident figure of the *Virgin* that dominates the apse. Christ, shielded by angelic deacons bearing fly swats, dispenses bread and wine to the whole company of the apostles in two scenes. In the far left, Judas spits out his bread as he leaves, a common habit amongst the worst sort of villains, who were believed to sell the hosts to sorcerers for use in black magic. In the recess of the south wall are the colourful figures of *St George* and *St Demetrius*. Though they are the familiar heroes of many an Orthodox church in Cyprus, this depiction of them riding together, arm on shoulder, is an imported tradition from Crete.

Around Palekhori

A short climb due east of Palekhori, or a short detour back on the Nicosia road, will bring you down to the head of the Maroullenas valley, where the small 16th-century chapel of **Ayii Anargyri** sits among poplars and fruit trees. Another possible destination for a short walk is to the picturesque village of **Askas**, which is about 4km from Palekhori along the Platanistasa road. The steep-pitched wooden roof of **Ayios Ioannis Prodromos** (St John the Baptist) stands on the southeast edge of the village. This small three-aisled mid-16th-century basilica is occasionally found open, as it serves as the parish church. It retains its original iconostasis but only those frescoes in the apse and the south arcade survive. The latter are dark with age but give us the only surviving cycle of the Baptist's life in Cyprus.

Another 3km to the west of the village, along the Platanistasa road but before the village of Phterikoudhi, is the small mountain chapel of **St Paraskevi/ St Caterina**. It is diminutive, but another charming example of the Cretan school of painting, which has been accurately dated to 1518 from the inscription that can be seen below the *Holy Handkerchief* over the door. *St Mamas* is easily recognizable riding his lion, whilst *St George* is depicted with his young Ottoman page, who rides pillion and bears a napkin and a fresh pot of coffee. Beside him *St Christina* is accompanied by the pious chapel donors, Madeleine and Constantine Mardaki.

Ayia Paraskevi

St Paraskevi the martyr is a popular patron saint for many a Cypriot church. She was born in the 2nd century AD of a well-established Roman family. After the death of her Christian parents, when she was 20 years old, she distributed her inheritance to the poor and became a missionary who attracted a growing number of converts. Despite the orders of the Emperor Marcus Aurelius she refused to betray her faith by sacrificing to the old gods. After horrible tortures she was executed on 26 July 180.

The Church of Stavros tou Ayiasmati outside Platanistasa Village

This gorgeous 15th-century mountain church, perched alone on the fringe of a forest of pine and surrounded by the light-dappled shade of an almond grove, is approached up its own drive which is found 3km north of Platanistasa village on the E906 road. You will need to have a car, not least to ferry the key-carrying custodian from the café in Platanistasa village up to the church, though on a summer day he might already be up there. The village of Platanistasa itself has a number of churches, of which the Arkhangelos Mikhail (Archangel Michael) attracts a few visitors who come to admire the ceramic plates recessed into its walls. If you are coming directly from Nicosia, Platanistasa is 27km south of the Peristerona turning; from Troödos it is 30km east; and from Palekhori 3km west.

The church is a completely undisturbed relic from the end of the 15th century. It has a simple rectangular nave with a high-pitched roof enclosed within the wider protection of barn-like eaves. It retains its complete body of frescoes, its dedication inscription and, on the outside of the south wall, a portrait of its alliterative founders, the priest Peter, son of Peratis and his wife Pepani. Local tradition recalls that they were refugees from the town of Ayiasmati in Anatolia, which fell to the Ottomans in the wake of the fall of Constantinople in 1453—though 'Holy Well', as Ayiasmati translates, is a more likely alternative origin. It was decorated by Philip tou Goul (who we know from his other surviving work of Ayios Mamas at Louvaras), who finished his work in 1494. Tou Goul, 'of the Red', may have been an affectionate nickname which he certainly earned here for the liberal use of warm ochre in the faces of his figures. Philip was a product of his age in producing a synthesis of Western and Byzantine traditions. He has his own informal style that, while respecting the traditions, is at times touched by a deliberate rustic naïveté that seems to be based on direct observation. Some of the scenes bring to mind faint echoes of a Stanley Spencer or a Beryl Cook, with their cheerful, rather solid and very human figures. The narrative scenes also express something of a slowly staged dance of unfolding reality which the Stylianous (the reigning scholars on Byzantine Cyprus) have suggested might have been influenced by touring Passion plays.

A complete cycle of 30 scenes, starting just to the south of the iconostasis with the *Birth of the Virgin Mary* and ending with her *Dormition*, takes us through the New Testament story. The saints, depicted on the ground floor of the nave, are much more conventionally portrayed and may be considered by some to have greater presence. This is especially true of the powerful *St John the Baptist* and those ubiquitous Cypriot heroes, *St George* on his white horse and *St Mamas* on his lion. The *Virgin Mary* stands dominant in the apse with her warm human face contrasting agreeably with the exaggerated 'acid' glimmer of her robes. The four Evangelists stand on either side of the original iconostasis whose cornice is decorated with circular medallions of saints, including a number of popes—a rare gesture of ecumenism. Perhaps the church's most famous frescoes are the group in a recess of the north wall, celebrated as much for their icon-like arrangement around a cross, as for their painterly qualities. They tell the story of St Helena's discovery of the True Cross, with various historical references to her son Constantine and some Old Testament analogies. Helena began by interrogating the Palestinian Jews and heard that one Judas (no relation to Iscariot) knew a thing or two but wouldn't tell; so she had him confined in a dry well for three days to soften him up for some intensive questioning. After this rather rough proof of the dowager empress's determination, Judas spent a night in prayer on the hill of Golgotha, and was told the location of various precious relics in a visionary dream. The crosses were unearthed and Judas was converted to Christianity, changing his name to Cyriacus and promptly being made bishop of Jersualem. St Helena, to sort out which was which, tested each cross for miraculous powers on a dying woman. She then had a number of adventures before safely returning to Constantinople, laden with her precious relics which helped protect the Byzantine Empire for over a thousand years. Philip must have painted these scenes in the hope of a new miracle, to reverse the recent conquest of Constantinople. Even today, Greeks may toast each other, 'Next year in Constantinople.'

The Church of Panayia tou Araka at Lagoudhera Village

This church, dedicated to the Virgin Mary of the Pea, is just to the west of the small village of Lagoudhera on the road to the hamlet of Sarandi. It is an isolated, almost awesome spot overlooked by a steep peak, skyward-pointing rocks and a scattering of pines. It sits on the flank of Mount Adhelphi just above the substantial pine forest that covers the foothills to the north. Access is easy as the key-holding custodian, a priestly refugee from Morphou, lives with his wife in the attractive double-arcaded monastic range just beside it. In the summer months, two tavernas and a pottery shop on the edge of Sarandi open up for trade.

Coming direct from Nicosia (a journey of about 35km), take the E906 road that turns south just before Peristerona and turn off for Ayia Marina to approach Lagoudhera via Xyliatos village; alternatively join the Palekhori road at Alona village and approach via Polystipos. If you are coming from Agros it is only an 8km drive north; from Limassol it is 65km; and from Troödos it is a 25km drive east—in all three cases you approach Lagoudhera via the village of Khandria.

The form of this church, a single aisle capped with a high dome, is obscured from view by the protective covering of an additional tiled roof, to give it an even more than usually barn-like exterior. This overhanging tiled roof extends almost to the ground, and, with the addition of a wooden lattice wood wall, has created a shady covered walkway all around the church. The church was painted in 1192, right at the end of the Byzantine period, when Richard I of England and the Knights Templars were in the brutal process of conquering the island. Lord Leon, the noble Greek patron of the church, left two dedicatory inscriptions: the first was formal and brief, as befitted the well-connected son of an *Authentis*, a title of honour that was often bestowed upon Byzantine provincial governors; the second was a desperate cry of supplication to the Virgin, from a man who had witnessed the destruction of his society and feared for the safety of his exile in a lone mountain monastery.

Nothing of this disturbing history is reflected in the painted interior. It is a jewel of the late 12th century, a supremely elegant example of the art that emanated from the Comnenian court at Constantinople. Apart from those on the west wall (demolished during the building of the extension which bears some damaged 14th-century paintings), they are complete and virtually untouched by later generations. The frescoes, expertly cleaned in 1973, still glow with colour 800 years after their creation. The figures have a calm grace, a princely serenity and an attenuated dignity that has invited comparison with the works of Giotto. This is not such a bad analogy, for it was the same rediscovery of classicism that influenced the unknown artist of Panayia tou Araka, just as it would, centuries later, affect the first artists of the Italian Renaissance such as Giotto. It is one of the tragedies of history that the early Greek revival of classical knowledge in the Constantinople of the Comnenian emperors was to be so totally destroyed by the Christian knights of the Third Crusade.

The interior is dominated by the central dome which bears Cyprus's most majestic portrayal of *Christ Pantocrator*. The power of this image has been eloquently summarized in the description by an illiterate parishioner: 'He looks away from our sins, to allow time for repentance.' Beneath the medallions of angels are depicted a dozen prophets, who stride around the window-pierced drum of the dome in unusual animation, brandishing their prophecies of the coming of Christ. The classicism of 12th-century Comnenian art has turned these most Semitic and gloomy of men into a celebratory chorus, whose movement is emphasized by the baroque billowing of their clothes. David in the east is easily recogizable from his royal robes, while to his right stands Isaiah, then Jeremiah, Solomon, Elijah, Elisha, Daniel, Gideon, Habakkuk, Ezekiel and Jonah, before we reach full circle with Moses.

The painter has skilfully subdivided the surface area of the aisle and has not fallen into the trap of crowding in too many scenes. The arched recesses on the north and south walls have been used to great effect, and bear gorgeous renditions of the major feasts of the Church. The seven daughters of the Hebrews led by Jaochim and Anna, in the scene of the *Presentation of the Virgin to the Temple,* could be the Graces themselves. Beneath this stands a moving portrayal of old *St Symeon* hugging the young Messiah. In the *Dormition of the Virgin* the apostles crowd mournfully around the bier and the hunched figure of St John, whilst Christ holds the saddled soul of his mother. Though this latter detail is comparatively crude, it is a poignant psychological image, a longed-for reversal of the love between a Mediterranean mother and son.

Kyperounda

Three kilometres east of Khandria, the village of Kyperounda, 'the Cypress Tree', does not altogether live up to the elegance suggested by its name. Of the three village churches, the steep-pitched chapel of **Timios Stavros** (Holy Cross) retains some 16th-century frescoes, copied from nearby Stavros tou Ayiasmati, in the arched recesses on the north and south walls. The *Archangel Michael* dominates the southern wall, with scenes from *St Helena's Discovery of the Cross* on the north recess. There is a cheap hotel and a taverna in the village, which could make an alternative base for some local walks. Walk across the valley to the neighbouring village of Khandria where a forestry track north of the village takes you up to the treeless slopes of **Mount Adhelphi** (1612m). From there you keep your height and the view by following the escarpment west for 1.5km to Madhari, where you can descend to the track that leads back to Kyperounda.

A less arduous walk is to take a track that branches off to the west just outside the village, on the Pelendria road. This loops around the scrub and wooded slopes of the Moutti tou Dhia hill before rejoining the Troödos road into the village.

The Church of Timios Stavros (The Holy Cross) in Pelendria Village

The village of Pelendria is on the southwestern edge of the Pitsilia area. It is overlooked by a ring of slight summits to its north, while to the south the broken scrubland of the Ayios Mamas hills stretches to the south, before giving way to the vineyards of the Limassol foothills. Pelendria is easily accessible from the E801, the Limassol-to-Kakopetria road, or along roads from Kyperounda or Agros.

The church of the Holy Cross stands on the southern edge of the village, from where paths wend their way into the hills. This squat triple-aisled basilica capped with a dome appears quite distinct from other mountain churches. It was not always so for the church began life as a typical single-aisled chapel surmounted by a dome, but in the 14th century the north aisle was added, and two centuries later the south aisle was tacked on. This southern aisle, apart from a large *St George*, is empty of the 14th-century frescoes that elsewhere cover the interior walls. They appear to have been commissioned for Prince John of Antioch, who, as well as being uncle and regent to Peter II, was the lord of the Casale of Pelendria. They are not all in the best condition and show a remarkable range in quality, ranging from the frankly rustic *Virgin* in the apse to the elegant *Ascension* (on the north face of the east vault of the dome), which clearly reveals that the artist had been exposed to the influence of the Palaeologue Renaissance. The western vault is filled with 14 scenes from the *Life of the Virgin*, and excludes anything from the New Testament, a revealing insight into the growing devotion to the Virgin Mary in the late medieval period. In a customary vignette, within the scene of the *Presentation to the Temple*, the youthful Mary is shown on the temple rooftop receiving food from an angel. New iconographic ground is broken in the meeting between Mary and Elizabeth, with the portrayal of the unborn babies of Jesus and John within their bellies.

The church is also famous for its various donors shown kneeling before the saints: there is one either side of St John the Baptist, the priest Basil and his wife Nengomia in the central north recess, and two donors by the fine *Doubting Thomas* scene on the south wall of the north aisle. There is no identifying inscription for this last pair, and though they are often taken to be Prince John and his wife, some critics consider that the details of their dress are not sufficiently grand. The *Tree of Jesse* (the genealogy of Christ's descent from King David as given in the Gospel of St Matthew) stands on the west wall of the north aisle, and might have been considered a suitable topic of contemplation for a Lusignan prince.

The Chapel of Ayios Mamas in Louvaras Village

The village of Louvaras is 8 km south of Agros as the crow flies, but about 16km as the mountain road wanders. Louvaras can also be quite easily approached from

Limassol, which is 28km away. Take the E110 north from Limassol and just before the village of Kalokhorio (where there is a taverna) take the turning for Louvaras, which is 4km to the southeast.

The small steep-pitched chapel of Ayios Mamas is found at the eastern end of the village in the more attractive old quarter, near the more prominent modern parish church, across from which lives the key-bearing custodian. The chapel was built in 1455 and decorated in 1495 at the expense of John and George, a pair of village notables, who can be seen kneeling with their wives on either side of the inscription above the wooden west door. They employed Philip tou Goul, who had only just finished working on the frescoes at Stavros tou Ayiasmati near Platanistasa a year before. A comparison between similar scenes in the two churches shows that for all their shared spiritual purpose there was no pattern-book monotony, and that the same artist in exactly the same period could produce a happy, almost playful variety in detail. Philip divided the small interior space of the chapel into three zones, keeping the saints in the lower zone, but packing in an almost bewildering number of scenes into two rows in the upper area. There are 27 assorted images from the New Testament, and the lack of space has compressed many of them into a crude, almost cartoon-like simplification. This paring down has, however, also generated in the scenes a quite animated progression, a narrative-like vividness, when they are seen as a whole series. There are a number of fairly unusual episodes from Christ's ministry on the southern wall, which you may have problems identifying. In the middle zone the familiar *Empty Tomb* is followed by the *Healing of the Cripple by the Pool of Bethesda*, then there is the *Judge Not, That Ye Be Not Judged* scene, followed by *Christ Talking to the Woman of Samaria at the Well*, the *Healing of the Blind Man* and then the typically medical attitudes of the protagonists in the *Healing of Peter's Mother-in-Law*. Amongst the saints on the ground level dado are the personifications of three of the Christian virtues—Faith, Hope and Love (Pistis, Elpis and Agapi)—which stand to the left of the west door with their mother, Holy Wisdom (Ayia Sophia), just around the corner. A later tradition turned these moral graces into actual martyrs who were horribly killed in the arena at Rome during the reign of the Emperor Hadrian. Just before the iconostasis, on the north side, *St Mamas* can be easily identified riding his lion, while standing to the south is a very confident, almost imperial *St John the Baptist* with none of his usual air of being either the wild, doomed prophet, the mystic contemplative or the patient intercessor. This disturbingly vivid portrait is a fitting object for a last reverential contemplation before lighting a candle and fumbling for a donation as you leave.

At the less attractive western edge of the village a road heads south to climb the wooded slopes of the Eloros escarpment 2km away. The forestry service has established a picnic spot along the track ending at the pilgrimage chapel of Kyra.

Agros

Apart from a few surviving old balconied houses the straggling village of Agros is not especially attractive, though this is more than made up for by its position. It stands at the head of the Agros valley surrounded by almond groves and pine-wooded hills. To the northeast the village of Alona is hidden from view by an escarpment, punctuated by the summits of Pltys (1475m) and Alourdotrypes (1475m), that marks the watershed and the border between the Nicosia and Limassol districts. It is, however, the twin peaks of Mount Papoutsa (1455m and 1554m) some 4km to the southeast (and easily approachable from the pass on the Palekhori road) that offer the finest views.

None of the village churches in Agros are very old: both the long nave of **St John's** and the **Panayia Eleousa Agrou** are products of the 19th century. The latter is named after its precious icon of the Virgin, which has fortunately (unlike many of the Cypriot icons attributed to St Luke) not yet been wrapped up in silver. Local traditions recall that it was brought to the safety of Agros by 40 monks who fled from the monastery of Kisikos in Anatolia in the 9th century.

Where to Stay in the Pitsilia Area

Agros

With three varied hotels, a post office, a couple of banks, tavernas and shops, Agros is the most convenient base for exploring the area.

The Rodon, ✆ (05) 521201, is perched on the hill above the village, with two tiled wings containing 60 rooms, a bar and restaurant. Despite its aloof position, it is moderately priced and the manager, Lefkos Christodoulou, is knowledgeable and wonderfully enthusiastic about the opportunities for walks in the surrounding area.

Of Agros's cheap hotels, **Vlachos**, ✆ (05) 521330, is your first choice, well placed on the high street and with its own restaurant, which is kept competitive by the neighbouring taverna. If it is full or you are hard up try the **Meteora**, ✆ (05) 521331, also on the high street, with nine very basic rooms and one bath.

Kyperounda

Livadhia Guesthouse, ✆ (05) 521311, has only nine rooms, but it serves meals, which can be varied with those at the **Amazel** taverna. It is an unlikely base for a holiday, but can make a useful stopover for a walking tour.

The Solea Valley

In addition to the Solea valley this section also takes in the area along and off the approach road from Nicosia. This allows for a passing look at the villages of **Peristerona** and **Vizakia**, though it is the painted church at **Asinou**, one of the great treasures of Cyprus, that should be your central objective.

The Solea valley, dominated by the almost continous hill resort village of **Galata-Kakopetria**, is deservedly famous for its fresh-grilled trout and the entrancing frescoes in the church of **Ayios Nikolaos tis Steyis**. The half-dozen other painted churches in this area, especially **Ayios Sozomenos** and **Panayia Podhitou** in Galata, all have their various charms and interest, but cannot compete with the interior of St Nicholas's, which has the added advantage of maintaining regular opening hours.

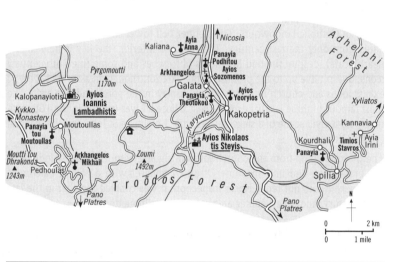

Peristerona and the Church of Ayii Varnavas and Ilarion

Peristerona has recently been bypassed off the main B9 road and stands 27km west of Nicosia. It is one of the largest of the dozen villages scattered over the flat plain of the western Mesaoria, which has been unequally divided between Greek and Turkish Cyprus. It is saved from the usual listless lassitude of the Mesaoria by a group of three historic buildings that sit beside the wide gravel bed of river. The old Venetian bridge, the yellow stone of the multi-domed medieval church and a nearby mosque used to form a celebrated view that symbolically expressed the juxtaposition of cultures in Cyprus. Since the bloody division of the island in 1974 it has lost its role as a visual symbol of cultural coexistence, but it retains its attraction particularly when contemplated in the evening light from a table at the nearby café-bar.

The church of Ayii Varnavas and Ilarion (Saints Barnabas and Hilarion), with its cluster of yellow stone drums and domes, forms an attractive mass overlooking the riverbed. It is one of the oldest surviving domed churches on the island, built in the 10th century, within a few years of the Byzantine reconquest of the island. Despite the fame of the two island saints, it was not raised in their honour but dedicated to two of the favourite patrons of the Byzantine army: a pair of 5th-century soldier saints, who, after an honourable career, retired to a life of piety in their homeland of Cappadocia. The church is a formal, though rather clean and undecorated, example of the style then popular in the capital. Its cross plan of five domes is imposed on a triple-aisled basilica, which has a characteristically undulating eastern wall formed from the row of three apses. The narthex, or western porch, is a recent addition that replaced a decayed chantry chapel built for a local family of Catholic landowners. The slender bell tower, like all such structures, dates from only the last century. The restored interior (the key is held in the nearby café), despite the odd fragments of frescoes and some fine 16th-century icons, doesn't live up to the promise of the exterior, though an assorted gallery of excess icons and church treasures are on display in the porch and side aisle. The most famous of these is a handsome chest whose lid was painted in the 16th century with a vivid scene of a siege between the Knights of St John and the 'general enemy Ottoman'.

The mosque uphill from the church looks intriguing with its Gothic windows in the prayer hall and its handsome Ottoman minaret with a pair of balconies. However, it does not repay closer inspection; it was cobbled together in the late 19th century, and is best appreciated as a distant silhouette.

The Chapel of Arkhangelos Mikhail at Vizakia Village

About 5km west of Peristerona along the main B9 road a side turning leads 4km due south to the village of Vizakia. The steep-pitched roof of the chapel is found to the west of the village beside the Nikitari road, just beyond the bridge over the stream. The key can be tracked down in the café or from the corner grocery store north of the parish church.

The simple nave of the chapel, with its high-vaulted wooden roof, rough river stone and mudbrick walls, is a perfect example of traditional architecture. This sort of structure has been in use in the mountains for thousands of years and served as the model for the 6th-century BC Royal Tombs that can be seen at Tamassos. Standing in the small 20-ft nave you could be a religious supplicant from almost any era of Cypriot history, until you gaze more closely upon the south and west walls which are covered with frescoes from the 16th century. These scenes from the *Life of Christ* were painted in the Venetian period, though there is little identifiably Italian in these most striking examples of naïve art. Bold red and black outlines define the two-dimensional figures, many of which have been deliberately distorted to evoke an emotional and deliberately human element in these epic but familiar scenes. In the *Birth of Christ*, a rather bored Joseph is depicted chatting to a shepherd in a sheepskin coat; in the *Betrayal*, Jesus and Judas exchange an almost sensual kiss in the garden, surrounded, as if an attentive audience, by ranks of big-nosed, gnome-like soldiers. An added solemnity and grief has been given to the *Crucifixion* by the darkened and greatly exaggerated bowed head of Christ. For all their rustic crudity these images have a disturbing power, and recall something of the spiritual vision of a Hieronymus Bosch.

Byzantine Frescoes

Orthodox religious images are to be venerated but not worshipped; the theologians explained them as windows to the divine and assured the pious that the honour done to an image would pass to the original. This image of the church as a spiritual window is a useful concept to remember when you stand in the interior of a church. Forget the exterior structure and imagine the painted images as the real body of the church looking in at you from another dimension. For a believer it has a dynamic tension, acting as both a comforting communion and a recurring reminder of the mute witnesses to your moral indiscretions.

At the ground level of the **nave** stands a long gallery of saints, those heroic fellow mortals who through their piety, bravery and spirituality show that godly life is possible. They are exemplars, possible allies and also stern critics. Above them, on the upper walls or vaults, there are likely to be uplifting scenes from the Life of Christ. In a large church there may be room for his principal miracles, scenes from his ministry and the Tree of Jesse (which traces Christ's descent from the line of David). Even the smallest chapel will usually make room for a portrayal of scenes relevant to the major festivals of the Church (like Christ's Baptism or the Assumption of the Virgin Mary) and the dozen events leading up to the Crucifixion.

If there is a central dome above the nave, the four squinches may bear the Evangelists or at least the tetramorphs, the familiar symbols of the winged lion of St Mark, the eagle of St John, the ox of St Luke and the man of

St Matthew. The lowest circle of the dome may be filled with Old Testament prophets bearing scrolls containing prophetic references to Christ. Above them will be the hierarchy of heaven, with an assortment of ranks and colour-coded angels, led by St John the Baptist and the Virgin Mary who approach the empty throne. In the centre of the dome will be a large powerful bust of Christ Pantocrator, staring down in stern judgment over the congregation.

Looking through the iconostasis, if you can, the lower back wall of the **apse** will carry a converging group of up to a dozen officiating prelates, almost as if they are assisting the priest in the liturgy and miracle of the mass. There is no strict list defining the order or number of bishops, but it will probably include **St Epiphanius** and **St Spyridon** who are not only celebrated saint-bishops of Cyprus but were also major figures from this period. St Epiphanius the Great, the celebrated archbishop of Constantia-Salamis (368–403) is also known as 'Our Defender' from his stringent defence of Orthodoxy. St Spyridon is usually depicted with a basket cap as befitting the humble shepherd who rose to become bishop of Tremithus. He is often shown holding the burning tile by which he helped prove the Trinity at the First Council, at Nicaea in 325 and condemn Arianism. As he miraculously crushed the tile, water trickled downwards, fire flickered upwards and earth remained in his hand to show 'three persons in one essence'. Above them will be the Virgin Mary either standing or enthroned with the Christ Child in a central medallion, but almost always flanked by the archangels Gabriel and Michael in the dress of Byzantine court ushers. If there is space the apse will also carry a long scene of the apostles receiving the first Communion at the Last Supper. There may also be some scenes from the Old Testament which were all understood as prophetic analogies of the New Testament. Four of the most popular Old Testament scenes would include Abraham and Sarah entertaining three angels, which was considered to presage both the Holy Communion and the doctrine of the Trinity; the sacrifice of Isaac by Abraham, which prefigures the Crucifixion; Moses receiving the Commandments, which was compared to the new covenant of Christ; and Moses loosening his sandle before the vision in the burning bush, which often bears a medallion of the Virgin and Christ Child.

The Church of Panayia Phorviotissa tis Asinou outside Nikitari Village

Asinou is one of the most entrancing churches in Cyprus. The church of Panayia Phorviotissa tis Asinou (The Virgin Mary of the Euphorbia of Asinou) stands alone in an isolated pine-clad valley on the edge of the forest of Adhelphi. It is a small enough building, but its rich interior, completely covered with 12th- and 14th-century frescoes, places it amongst the half-dozen most important painted churches on the island.

Asinou is 5km south of the village of Nikitari, which is approached via the village of Vizakia from a turning off the main B9 road, about 32km west of Nicosia. The priest-custodian lives in Nikitari and can be found by inquiring at the central café beside the parish church. You will need a car in order to take him up to Asinou and back to the village, though during holidays and summer weekends he may already be found up at the church, which can get quite crowded with visitors. In midsummer a couple of seasonal tavernas function to supplement the extensive family picnics spread out under the shade of the pines.

The church was built as a family chapel by **Nicephorus the Strong**, a senior Byzantine official. After the death of his wife, Yephrya, in 1099, he turned it into a monastery where he remained until his own death 16 years later. Asinou was not then such a reclusive place, but a small town traditionally considered to have been founded by settlers from Argos. The appellation 'Phorviotissa' (of the Euphorbia) seems an unlikely title for the Virgin, but all over the island the Madonna has inherited vegetable titles that were once borne by the old pagan goddesses. Euphorbia is, in any case, a powerful and prolific plant (there are over 30 species in Cyprus), whose toxic sap was used in antiquity for medical preparations.

After a first inspection of the dazzling frescoes, cleaned to reveal their original colours, it is possible to stand back from their spiritual role and see them as date-able works of art. Most of them belong to distinct eras, either to the original 1105 decoration of Nicephorus the Strong or to a restoration undertaken between 1330 and 1350. The major 12th-century scenes are in the west bay of the nave: the *Dormition of the Virgin*, the *Triumphal Entry into Jerusalem*, the *Last Supper* and the *Forty Martyrs of Sebaste* (*see* p. 162); or in the apse: the *Birth of the Virgin*, the *Presentation of the Virgin*, the *Annunciation*, the *Presiding Prelates* and the *Communion of the Apostles*. These all share the classicizing and expressive spirit that was emanating from the sophisticated court of the Comnenian emperors in this period. This is particularly marked in the latter scene; the twisting animated forms of the apostles have been compared to so many toga-dressed senators before their emperor. They are complemented by the frowning row of judge-like prelates below them, who are set against a light-blue background and depicted full frontal rather than in the usual converging circle.

The *Virgin* in the conch of the apse and all the other scenes in the church were painted in about 1350, apparently by the same artist who decorated the church of the Holy Cross at Pelendria. They are, in comparison, decidedly cruder, with rustic faces and less controlled features, but they do also have a certain vivacity. There is a deliberate concentration on extremes of light and dark, mixed with an exuberant depiction of brightly coloured clothing covered with a lace-like pointillism. The figures have, however, lost some of that extraordinary Byzantine spiritual quality. We look at the 14th-century figures, whilst the earlier ones look at us.

The frescoes in the porch belong to a slightly different period and were painted around 1330. The *Pantocrator* surrounded by groups of apostles looks down from the shallow dome, whilst a *Last Judgement* scene is depicted on the upper zone of the walls. This, for all its incidental detail of the saved in paradise and the damned in hell, takes second place to the striking depiction of various saints on the ground level. There is a fine *Deesis* to the right of the door, the gentle figure of *St Anastasia* the poison-curer with her vial of serum, and a dazzling *St George* in the south apse. His galloping white horse, scarlet cloak, serene features and sky-coloured shield, emblazoned with stars that include the cross-on-crescent of Byzantium, announce an unvanquishable celestial knight. He alone of all the figures in the narthex was painted in the 12th century, at the charge of one Nicephorus son of Kallias the horse breaker.

Kaliana

The fruit trees and olive groves in the lower reaches of the Solea valley make a pleasant place for a picnic and a stroll, though they cannot hope to compete with the attraction of the painted churches scattered around Galata and Kakopetria. However, if you have time for a fuller exploration of the area you could turn off the main road, about 2km south of Evrykhou, and head further down the valley to look at the Kaliana Khan, an old caravanserai, or rural inn, that has been preserved in the Karyotis valley amid millraces and two old chapels.

The actual village of Kaliana is situated 2km up the side valley to the west. The village church, dedicated to Saints Joachim and Anna, retains a fine 12th-century depiction of the *Forty Martyrs of Sebaste* in a recess on the northwest wall (this martyrs' tale is told below; *see* 'St Nicholas of the Roof', p. 162). There is a taverna in the village, and an appetite can be worked up by following the path that follows the valley to the west. This climbs up towards the twin hills of Moutti tis Khalepis and the higher Ayios Lazaros, whose wooded slopes separate the Solea and Marathasa valleys.

The neighbouring villages of Kakopetria and Galata are about 60km from Nicosia on the B9. They dominate the upper reaches of the Karyotis stream, standing on the transition zone between the pine-forested slopes and the cultivated valley whose small fields are shaded by apple trees, clumps of walnut and shimmering poplars. The twin villages have long since outgrown their role as agricultural settlements, to become bustling hill resorts for the population of Nicosia. They alone, of all the mountain villages, are well connected to the capital by bus, and have streets dotted with small hotels, shops and cafés, as well as restaurants serving fresh trout. The villages have expanded out from their original centres and in the process have almost imperceptibly merged together.

Old Kakopetria, a handsome but decaying collection of mudbrick and stone houses ornamented with terraces, is perched on a narrow rocky escarpment that stands between the Karyotis and Karvouna streams to the west of the valley. It is gradually being restored, assisted by a generous system of government grants, and a pair of traditional inns now sit at either entrance of the sinuous main alley of the old village.

Three Painted Churches in Galata: Ayios Sozomenos, Panayia Podhitou and Arkhangelos

The caretaker-priest who holds the keys to all three churches can be found by inquiring at the modern parish church or the café in the centre of Galata. It is an easy walk to Ayios Sozomenos, though for the other two he will need to be driven.

The church of **Ayios Sozomenos** stands in the middle of the old village in the street just above the large modern parish church. It is a typical steep-pitched mountain chapel of the 16th century that later assumed an outer wall. The church was built by a committee of 13 villagers, and decorated in 1513 at the expense of John the lawyer, a wealthy lay reader who had been born in the nearby village of Tembria. Almost the complete body of frescoes in the church are by Symeon Axenti, a Cypriot artist whose work, whilst undeniably provincial, is capable of reflecting a certain spirituality. This is particularly true of the confident portrayal of the saints and the Virgin, but less so of the small pictorial panels on the upper walls. These, with one or two exceptions such as the cleaned *Betrayal of St Peter*, are obscured by the smoke of centuries of incense and candle vapour. They are, however, a valuable yardstick of indigenous art with which to compare the works of imported Cretan and Italian artists.

The most unusual cycle, from the point of view of subject matter, are the scenes painted on the outside of the north wall showing the seven councils of the

Church, concluding with the large *Triumph of Orthodoxy*, the decision in favour of icons in AD 843. The interior has a conventional arrangement with the upper walls filled with blackened but still identifiable scenes from the *Life of Christ* and the *Life of the Virgin*. Concentrate your attention on what Symeon Axenti did best, the fine gallery of saints on the lower walls. At the west end of the south wall stand four female martyrs, *St Paraskevi, St Kyriaki, St Barbara* and *St Catherine*, whose identities are all touched by the creative web of invention and mythology. The martyr St Kyriaki is a Christianized embodiment of the week, but still looks remarkably Hellenistic with medallions of the seven days strung about her dress like a pagan deity. Another especially fine group are the soldier saints portrayed on the north wall: there is a mounted *St George, St Mercurius, St Theodore* the general with his forked beard, the youthful *St Nestor, St Demetrius* and another *St George*, before we reach *St Andronicus* beside the door. The *Virgin* in the apse has been cleaned, and appears very matriarchal and confident above the presiding prelates, who have been all but obscured by children's graffiti scratched into the blackened wall.

The chapel of the **Arkhangelos** (the Archangel Michael) is also locally known as Panayia Theotokou. It stands about 100m away from the church of Panayia Podhitou, in the valley fields just to the north of Galata, and can be approached along a rough track running parallel to the main road. The small low Arkhangelos chapel, simply constructed from stone, timber and daub, was built by the Venetian family of Zacharia in 1514. They had been established on the island for three generations, but had obviously fallen under the spell of Orthodoxy by the time they came to build this family chapel. They commissioned Symeon Axenti to create a cycle of frescoes bearing Greek inscriptions in the Byzantine tradition. Orthodox saints on the ground floor are succeeded by panels depicting scenes from the *Life of Christ*. The family group of donors can be seen above the north door, where Zacharia's French wife can be seen playing out her rosary.

The church of **Panayia tis Podhitou** (the Virgin Mary of Podhitou) is a more substantial building. It was built by Demetre de Coron, who came from a well-established but increasingly Hellenized, Crusader family. He was an active participant in the war between Queen Charlotte and her brother James in 1461, but by 1502 his mind had moved on to higher things, for this church was originally designed to serve a monastery. The silhouette of its single nave and high steep-pitched roof was later softened by the addition of an enclosing outer wall and a second roof. A skilful painter, deeply imbued in both the Italian and Byzantine traditions, was employed, but the work was never finished and to this day only the eastern apse, the western wall and the upper side walls are furnished with frescoes. You may need to take time to accustom your eyes to the dim interior, for the church is not currently in use and there are no lights.

The outer pediment of the western wall bears a depiction of *From Above the Prophets have Heralded Thee*, which has the enthroned Virgin with Christ in her lap surrounded by 10 prophets bearing their relevant predictions of the Incarnation. High up on the inner western wall is a *Crucifixion,* a very crowded and dramatic depiction whose very vividness distracts from its central message. It is full of acute human observation with details taken from contemporary life, such as the Turkish-looking figures in fluffy busbies and a crescent banner fluttering amongst the Italian-looking soldiers. The eastern end bears one of the most successful fusions of Italian and Byzantine art on the island. There is a splendid representation of the *Virgin* flanked by archangels, in her customary position on the conch of the apse. The *Communion* below it is another powerful creation, with the curious heavy thighs and rolling gait of the disciples naturally drawing your eye towards the two sacraments. On the right-hand side St Paul, an honorary disciple, takes the wine, followed by the beardless St John, James, Mark, Thomas and Simon. Moses is depicted in his customary roles on the pediment of the apse and there are scenes from the *Life of the Virgin* on the side walls.

Panayia Theotokou and Ayios Yeoryios Perachoritis

The old cemetery chapel of **Panayia Theotokou** stands on the northern edge of Kakopetria. It is on the right as you come from Galata along the old village road beside the BP station, whose manager holds the keys.

This simple single-aisled mountain chapel, built from timber and sunbaked mudbricks perched on stone footings, was constructed in 1520. It was the pious work of a mixed marriage, between the Greek Leontius and the Venetian Lucretia, but despite this mix of cultures the internal frescoes reveal a conservative Byzantine taste relatively unaffected by the 16th-century developments seen elsewhere. The frescoes are not all in good condition; under half remain but typically those in the apse have survived best. Here an *Ascension*, the *Sacrifice of Isaac* and the *Entertainment of Abraham* flank the *Virgin Blacherniotissa* in the conch.

Close by is another cemetery chapel, dedicated to the martyr Ayia Paraskevi, that preserves some fragments of frescoes in its apse. It is crude stuff, seemingly dashed off without too much effort by the painter Symeon Axenti in 1514.

The even smaller chapel of **Ayios Yeoryios Perachoritis** stands on the eastern edge of Kakopetria just above the main turning into the village from the new road. It is also a product of the early 16th century, but apart from the saints only one row of paintings survives on the side walls. They are touched with a rustic home-grown naïveté, but the relatively simple hues of flesh, the attenuated forms and the deep dark emphasis given to the eyes comes across rather powerfully to our late 20th-century Picasso-trained eyes.

Open Tues–Sat 9–4, Sun 10.30–4.

The gorgeously rich and colourful interior of Ayios Nikolaos tis Steyis (St Nicholas of the Roof) is upriver from Kakopetria. It is easily found by walking up the Karyotis stream, though if you want to drive (about 5km) take the main road south and look out for a signposted turning to the west which gradually deteriorates to bump you along through woodland towards the church. Andreas Georghiou, the knowledgeable resident guardian, is on permanent duty and seems to know as much about the church as any man. Apart from festivals the church is not in regular use, though from the 11th to the middle of the 19th century it was the centre of a small monastic community. At the extinction of this community it passed into the hands of the archbishops, who turned the surrounding area into a summer camp for city kids.

This small church, on the classic medieval plan of a cross in a square surmounted by a central dome, dates from about 1025. About a century later a domed porch was tacked onto the west end, and an additional steep-pitched roof placed over the protruding domes and Mediterranean pantiles. The interior, completely covered in frescoes, is a rich, inspiring internal space which, like a spiritual tardis, far exceeds the modest suggestion of its exterior. The frescoes have a remarkable homogeneity, particularly when you realize that they were all painted between the 11th and 17th centuries. Here, perhaps more than anywhere else on the island, you can relish the essential continuity of Byzantine art. Frescoes of all ages are placed in their customary position to create a seamless whole. The 11th-century *Virgin* is in the apse, the 14th-century *Pantocrator* is on the dome and a 12th-century *Last Judgement* is in the narthex. A veiled sun and moon can be seen in the 14th-century *Crucifixion* on the north wall, whilst the *Nativity*, of the same period, shows the Virgin suckling the Christ Child. This type of depiction is known as *Galaktotrophousa* (milk giving), and seems to have been directly based on the popular Egyptian image of Isis nursing Osiris.

The vigorous row of saints on the ground floor, except when they are accompanied by a dedicatory inscription, are almost impossible to date. Ask the custodian to point out a few of the island saints, such as *St John the Almoner* (beside *St John the Baptist* on the southwest pier of the dome), the original patron of the Knights Hospitallers, and *St John Lambadhistis Maratheftis* (on a small pier on the west wall) whose monastery-shrine is in the next-door valley. The life-size *St Nicholas* and the *Forty Martyrs of Sebaste* are the church's most celebrated frescoes, and are both 12th-century products of the Comnenian period. The story of the Forty Martyrs was beloved by the Byzantine army and imperial establishment, as it stressed the virtues of group loyalty and fortitude in adversity. The

Martyrs of Sebaste in Armenia were a body of soldiers persecuted for their Christianity in the late Roman period. They were stripped and forced into a freezing lake, around which the pagans arranged tempting warm fires and kitchens to reward any who cared to revert to the old religion. The 40 steadfastly refused and later the order was given to stone them to death. This drove one of their number to break ranks and desert, but his place was promptly assumed by one of the punishing soldiers who had been so impressed by their bravery. The heavens were opened and 40 martyrs' crowns sent down to relieve their suffering.

Below the left foot of *St Peter*, who appears on an east pier of the dome, you can see some graffiti scratched in 1735 by the Russian pilgrim Basil Barsky, whose account of his visits to the famous shrines of Cyprus, published after his death, are one of the great historical sources of the period.

There are two possible walks from St Nicholas. About 200m uphill from the church the track divides and then reunites; at this second junction the left-hand fork begins a slow, twisting 9km ascent that will bring you out at the tarmac road immediately below Mount Olympus and the Khromion trail. The right-hand fork, which can be cautiously driven along in good weather, leads 5km west to a forest station at a junction. From here you turn left and head south on a fairly level track through more pinewoods for about 8km to emerge by the Pinewood Valley Hotel, on the main road halfway between Pedhoulas and Prodhromos.

Two Painted Churches near Spilia: Panayia at Kourdhali and Timios Stavros at Ayia Irini

These two small 16th-century churches are only of secondary interest, though the journey into the hills and the opportunity for a walk is reason enough for going. About 5km up the Karvouna valley from Kakopetria is the trout farm that provides the local restaurants with their supplies of fresh fish. Just before the farm a turning to the east leads to the mountain village of Spilia with the ruined chapel of Ayios Yeoryios halfway along the road. East from Spilia is a forestry road that soon divides and subdivides to provide half a dozen tracks leading to some of the island's most dazzling treasures, such as the churches at Asinou and Lagoudhera.

The hamlet of **Kourdhali** is just over 2km northwest and downstream of Spilia, though it is approached by taking the eastern road. About 300m east of Spilia you reach a junction; take the left fork and 200m later turn left at another junction. Kourdhali is a 1.5km stroll from here. The 16th-century church of **Panayia** stands in an attractive position on the other side of the stream bed, linked to the village road by a small hump-backed bridge. It was originally built to serve a monastery, which you would not expect in such an isolated hamlet, but this does account for the width of the church and its three aisles. Only the frescoes in the apse and west wall have survived, though these are enough to show the different styles that could emerge within one modest early 16th-century commission. The paintings in the apse are an accomplished and balanced fusion of Greek and Italian influences. Those on the lower west wall (such as the *Deposition* and the *Lamentation*) are more conventionally Byzantine in form, whilst the *Crucifixion* up on the pediment is totally Italian in its mood of emotional humanism. The low-cut dress of the *Virgin Mary* is an almost unthinkable detail for a painter brought up in the Orthodox tradition.

The hamlet of **Ayia Irini** is 5km northeast of Spilia. At the junction 300m east of Spilia take a right turn, then 300m later turn left onto the track that twists over the wooded slopes of the Pervolia hill. Ayia Irini and its larger neighbouring village of Kannavia is surrounded by almond groves. The attractive exterior of the parish church of Ayios Dhimiytrios, with a nearby cypress tree in use as its belfry, stands to the southwest of the hamlet. The chapel of **Timios Stavros** (Holy Cross) is perched on the hillside to the north of the village. Only a small proportion of its fairly rustic and naïve 16th-century frescoes survive, mostly in the apse, where there is an unusual depiction of the *Trinity*: God the Father sits on a throne and supports the crucified Christ, whilst the Holy Ghost hovers above.

Where to Stay in the Solea Area

Kakopetria and **Galata** have a wide choice of cheap hotels supplemented by rooms to rent in the summer months. They are, however, all in the streets of the new village and tend to be a bit sparse and functional.

The moderately priced **Hellas**, © (02) 922450, with 30 bedrooms, is one of the more efficient hotels in Kakopetria, but can be closed during the winter. The **Hekali** (cheap), © (02) 922501, at 22 Georgiou Griva Digeni, is a functional place with a bar, restaurant and 30 rooms, some of which overlook the old village. The **Kifissia**, © (02) 922421, newly restored with 37 rooms, is the next budget choice, though if it is full you could try the **Romios**, © (02) 922456, and the nearby **Zoumos**, © (02) 922154, which, though principally restaurants, also have some rooms upstairs. They are both down by the stream at the northern edge of the old village.

Eating Out

In **Kakopetria** you should dine off fresh local trout at the **Maryland at the Mill** restaurant, © (02) 922536, which rises like a medieval château to the north of the old village. It is the creation of John Aristides, a local architect, and though you might have to reserve a table, it is, like most good restaurants in Cyprus, quite moderately priced.

In **Kakopetria** there is the **Clarian Disco Bar**, © (02) 923181, which is just downriver from the Maryland at the Mill restaurant.

The Marathasa

Apart from Kykko monastery, which is easily the most visited church in all the mountains, the Marathasa still remains pretty much off the tourist map. It cannot compete with the attractions of the famous Byzantine churches in the Solea and Pitsilia areas, though it has one exceptional 16th-century chapel. The dreamily picturesque monastery of **Ayios Ioannis Lambadhistis** hides a Latin chapel covered with the finest Italian frescoes found in Cyprus. The Marathasa, which is named after the wild fennel, does, however, have a gentle unhurried charm of its own. The villages remain reasonably well populated and have two fine painted churches: the 13th-century **Panayia tou Moutoulla** and the 15th-century **Arkhangelos Mikhail**. These, whilst not of the highest quality, are both possessed by a distinctive and enduring character.

Kalopanayiotis Village and the Monastery of Ayios Ioannis Lambadhistis

The church is nominally open 8–12 and 1.30–6, though in practice you may have to hunt down the village's busy, and often elusive, caretaker-priest in one of the cafés or other churches in the village.

The village of Kalopanayiotis lies beside some sulphur springs and is about 70km from Nicosia. It has a few cheap and characterful hotels on the roadside, but the prettiest part of the village is to the east of the main road. Here a picturesque muddle of houses are perched on a steep succession of terraces overlooking the Setrakos riverbed which is spanned by a bridge. The monastery of Ayios Ioannis (St John) Lambadhistis is the sole occupant of the east bank, and is the single great treasure of the Marathasa valley.

St John Lambadhistis

St John grew up in this valley in the late 11th century, and was torn between a desire both to serve the church and to obey his parents. He was forced to make a decision when a marriage was arranged for him with a local girl, which he renounced in order to become a monk at the monastery of St Herakleidios. Unfortunately, the scorned girl and her family were powerful sorcerers and they blinded and then poisoned the devout young monk with their magical enchantments. He died before he was 23 and his tomb was forgotten until an epileptic, accidentally stumbling upon his tomb during a fit, was miraculously cured. As the nearby sulphur spring was already well established as a medical cure, a steady trickle of afflicted and disabled visitors stopped by at this miraculous tomb. A proportion were cured and the fame of the saint spread, allowing for the gradual growth of the monastic church into an important shrine. St John is either portrayed as an attractive fair-headed young deacon holding a cross in his hand or as a young tonsured monk.

The Buildings

The single barn-like roof of the monastery's church obscures its division into four component parts. The first church to be built here, in the 11th century, was dedicated to St Herakleidios. This building still stands and is composed of three aisles arranged in a cross-shaped plan. It comprises the southern half of the present church and is directly entered through the south door that functions as the present entrance. About a century later a chapel to St John Lambadhistis was added (though this actual structure was to be replaced in the 18th century by the present barrel-vaulted nave). In the 15th century the popularity of this local saint led to the construction of a large vaulted porch to the west of the two churches, and soon afterwards the so-called Latin chapel was tacked onto the north end. This curious composite church of five aisles is given an apparent unity by the outer roof, though the frescoes within stress the different eras.

Some of the frescoes in the church of St Heracleidios date back to the 13th century, such as the *Christ Pantocrator* in the dome, the Ascension on the south vault and *Christ's Triumphal Entrance into Jerusalem* on the west arm of the church. They belong, as one would expect, to that troubled era of Byzantium, and are slightly crude and provincial copies of the Comnenian art of the previous century. The rest of the church is decorated with a second series of paintings executed around 1400. Rather than follow the previous spacious arrangement, the upper vaults were packed with over 30 small scenes from the New Testament, whilst the arrangement of the saints on the ground floor indicates a lack of planning and a Catholic presence. There are repetitions, obscure saints and even a number of popes, which, with the exception of St Peter, make only the rarest appearance in Orthodox churches. This unusual doctrinal balance between Orthodoxy and Catholicism is continued in the decoration of the medieval iconostasis, where the arms of the Lusignans and other leading Crusader families are interchanged with Byzantine eagles.

The adjacent chapel of St John, having been rebuilt in the 18th century, is empty of decoration. The only portion of the original chapel left standing is the northeast pier containing the **saint's tomb** and skull, exhibited in a silver reliquary for the attentions of the devout.

The vaulted porch or **narthex** served both churches and was built in the mid-15th century by a Catholic family. It was painted by a man from Constantinople, who produced not the cosmopolitan art of the capital, but the popular, undistinguished art one would expect in the most distant provinces. The porch was used by sick pilgrims as a lodging room where they could camp out for prolonged prayer vigils to invoke the healing powers of the saint. It is appropriately painted with scenes of Christ's miracles, his divine appearances on earth after the Resurrection, a *Last Judgement*, as well as long and accurate quotations from the Gospels, a reflection of the increasing literacy of the period. Standing against the west wall of the porch is a 15th-century iconostasis, taken from the nearby chapel of the Panayia Theoskepasti, that bears a gallery of two dozen gospel miniatures.

The **Latin chapel** is the finest and most complete example of the art of the Italian Renaissance in Cyprus. The chapel was built and decorated around 1500 by an artist trained in Italy, but deeply imbued in the traditions of Orthodoxy. The whole decoration of the chapel is based on the *Akathistos* (like the Katholikon at St Neophytus), that celebrated hymn to the Virgin composed by Patriarch Sergius in thanksgiving for the deliverance of Constantinople from the siege of barbarian Slavs and Avars in 626. The panel of scenes from the *Life of the Virgin* that covers the south and north walls follows the 24 stanzas of the hymn, one for each letter of the Greek alphabet. They are all executed with a delicacy, elegance and force that is quite breathtaking. The painter's spirit is perhaps best encapsulated by his image of the *Three Kings* following their star, accompanied by a winged angel on a white horse. In the foreground a pair of unconcerned wayfarers stride by in Phrygian caps, looking for all the world as if they have strayed across from a secular wall painting from 1st-century Pompeii. A *Tree of Jesse* fills the west wall, busts of the apostles framed by the painted ribbing fills the vaulted roof, and the *Virgin Mary* reigns from her apse. She is flanked by the customary Orthodox scenes such as the *Hospitality of Abraham, Moses Receiving the Ten Commandments* and *Moses Before the Burning Bush.* In the background of the latter two scenes some very Western-looking Gothic towers and abbeys have been included. A much more blatant piece of symbolism is the pair of popes that crowd the enthroned *Virgin Mary* in the northeast corner, though the painter's ultimate sympathies might be revealed by the faintly pushy and aggressive expressions he has given them.

The U-shaped open courtyard of the **monastery buildings** lies just to the south of the church. It is one of the very few such domestic ranges to have survived and has been carefully restored. The courtyard gives a delightfully Arcadian view of monastic life in the timber-rich mountains, with its wooden stairways, erratic balconies, barns and traditional olive- and winepresses. It is a valuable image to store in your mind if you wish to imagine how many of the island's old monasteries, so often reduced to a lone chapel, once looked in their original state.

In the summer months a café operates from out of the monastery buildings and the village's famous sulphur spring can be found beside the pretty old stone bridge that crosses the river. On the west bank of the river, just upstream from the monastery, sits the chapel of Ayios Andronikos, which conserves a dramatic fresco of the *Crucifixion and* a few saints.

To the east of the monastery a 200m track leads to the chapel of the Panayia Theoskepasti, which is shaded by an enormous holm oak from which the church bell is hung. The chapel contains only a small portion of a fresco, and a beautiful icon of the *Virgin and Child.* Her quiet impassive face leans to the left as she holds the playful struggling infant now half worn away by kisses.

Moutoullas Village and the Chapel of Panayia tou Moutoulla

The stilted, layered houses of Moutoullas village, 2km south of Kalopanayiotis, stand above the Marathasa valley, draped in vines with their corrugated iron roofs glinting in the sun. The village, strung along a bend in the road halfway between Kalopanayiotis and Pedhoulas, is now famous for its bottled mineral water, though it used to be renowned for its craftsmen. Many of the distinctive long plank bread boards, known as *sanides,* that hang from the walls of folk museums and tavernas will have been made here from local pine. The village, as well as its 19th-century parish church of St Paraskevi, is surrounded by attractive old chapels such as St Mamas, the ruined St Basil, St Sotiros and Prophitis Elias, which is perched on the summit of the hill to the east of the valley.

The unaltered 13th-century chapel of **Panayia tou Moutoulla** (The Virgin Mary of Moutoullas), with its damaged but still intact painted interior, is a precious survivor from a relatively impoverished period of Byzantine art. It was the time when both the capital and the richest provinces of the Byzantine Empire were groaning under the alien rule of French or Italian Crusader dynasties.

The chapel is a typical product of the mountains with a steep-pitched, barn-like roof covering a simple nave built from stone and mudbricks. This has been enclosed by another wall to create a covered walkway around the exterior of the chapel, which has itself been partly painted. The chapel is rather difficult to spot from the road, as it is tucked away on the hillside to the north of the village. The steep path up to the chapel (whose key is held in the neighbouring house) is just 50m beyond the village's blue-balconied café-bar.

The frescoes in the close space of the interior are impressive for their antiquity and rarity, though compared to the products of the 12th century the figures appear rather squat and rigid. However, the exuberant colours of the clothes and the unearthly stare of their round eyes aspire to give them a spiritual presence beyond the clumsy style. The painter has also added light personal touches that have further animated many of the scenes. In the *Crucifixion* St John is comforted by the good soldier whose shield bears a Crusader heraldic device, while in the *Raising of Lazarus* one can almost whiff the smell of the grave, in sympathy with the grave digger who muffles his nostrils with his sleeve. Beneath the *St George* on the north wall he has changed the nature of the dragon by giving it a human head. In the *Nativity* his depiction of Joseph looking rather out of sorts is a common theme, but he has given it a local touch by placing him on a donkey saddle. The *Three Kings* have been given an added complexity by being portrayed as the three ages of man. In the *Annunciation* in the apse there is a deliberate echo of Constantinople, with the Virgin standing before a snake-headed fountain just like the famous device that still stands in the centre of the Hippodrome race track. On the north wall of the apse there remains a very sketchy linear portrait of the two founders, John of Moutoullas and Irene his wife, who commissioned the chapel to be built and decorated in 1280.

The frescoes on the outer walls were added in later centuries. *Christ* and *St George*, with his turbaned pageboy, stand guard on either side of the west door. They may have been painted in the 18th century, whilst the *Last Judgement* on the north wall, with its diabolic punishments contrasting with a heavenly palmery garden, is from the 15th century.

Pedhoulas Village and the Church of Arkhangelos Mikhail

The mountain village of Pedhoulas is about 5km up the Marathasa valley from Moutoullas, by the turning to Kyyko monastery. It is largely overlooked by bare hills, the pines being restricted to the slopes of the north shoulder of Mount Olympus, some distance to the southeast. The largest village in the valley, Pedhoulas is a tightly packed settlement draped over a hill with an attractive confusion of contours, split-level houses, vine-shaded terraces and an Australian array of rust tones on the corrugated iron roofs. Within the island it is celebrated for its cherry orchards, found mainly to the east and north of the village on the valley floor. In high summer it functions as a hill resort for Nicosians, since at 1100m the village is noticeably cooler than the coast or the central plain. The village, which has a choice of hotels and restaurants as well as a bank, post office and a statue of Archbishop Makarios, is the obvious centre from which to explore the Marathasa.

The small 15th-century painted chapel of **Arkhangelos Mikhail** (the Archangel Michael), with its steep-pitched roof and rough-hewn stone walls, is tucked away in the middle of the village, the least conspicuous of the half-dozen churches in

Pedhoulas. However, it can be quite easily found by taking the track downhill from the prominent modern parish church. The key-holding caretaker lives just two doors up the street from Arkhangelos Mikhail, in the house with green doors.

The chapel was painted in 1474 by a local Marathasa man working for Basil the priest, who can be seen in his vestments with his wife and two daughters by the dedicatory inscription above the north door. The frescoes have survived the five centuries well, though some fading may account for the strong red hues that now dominate. As is customary in Cyprus, the lower row of saints stare impassively at the congregation and stress the unchanging nature of Byzantine art over the centuries. The scenes in the upper vaults reflect more the spirit of the painter and his age. Here the figures in the New Testament scenes (beginning with the *Birth of the Virgin Mary* and ending with her *Dormition*) are possessed with an almost rustic gaiety, with comparatively cheerful faces, kind eyes and plump cheeks. In the *Nativity* the Virgin is positively smiling with joy as she looks at the Three Kings, whilst Joseph looks his usual desolate self. This is also very noticeable in the *Baptism*, where Christ and St John, usually depicted with the gaunt asceticism suitable to dwellers in the wilderness, are given plump bodies and carefully plaited hair. The exuberantly painted iconostasis is also from the 15th century and bears the Lusignan arms (the southern Marathasa was a crown estate), as well as the double-headed eagle of Orthodox Byzantium. It is known as a *temblon*, after the original low altar screen of the Early Church, since it does—especially when compared to the gilded, icon-studded walls erected during the 16th and 17th centuries—allow the sanctuary to be viewed by the congregation.

Panayia tou Kykkou (Kykko Monastery)

Open daily all year during reasonable visiting hours, with a small admission charge to the museum.

Kykko is 19km west of Pedhoulas along a twisting, but entirely tarmac, mountain road. The monastery of Kykko is famous for its wealth, its power within the island, its imperial foundation, its ancient icon of the Virgin Mary by St Luke and its isolated location in the pine-wooded hills of Marathasa. Though an ancient foundation, the monastery has been burned to the ground four times—in 1365, 1542, 1751 and 1813—so that the actual church and the multiple courtyards of the surrounding monastery date only from the 19th century. Recent construction beyond the walls has added hostels (for the use of genuine Orthodox pilgrims, not tourists on a tight budget), school buildings, a coach park, a bland restaurant and a small hamlet of gift shops and stalls selling a good selection of preserved and dried fruit. If you are coming for a sense of history or spiritual calm, Kykko will be a big disappointment. It is an extremely popular destination, busy in midweek with coach tours of foreigners, often looking slightly at a loss, and in total contrast to the animated parties of Cypriots who come on a Sunday. Weddings, blessings and baptisms are continually and cheerfully performed by the monks, who, unlike many of their kind, seem to welcome the stream of chattering day-trippers.

The Byzantine Monastic Tradition

There is an admirable fluidity in Orthodoxy between a parish church, a chapel at ease, the cave-chapel of a hermit and the 'abbey' of a monastery. The name of a monastery or a hermitage is often retained centuries after its original use has disappeared, which may be initially frustrating to those brought up within the legal precision of Roman Catholicism and its Protestant offshoots. There is, however, no exact Orthodox equivalent to the Benedictines, Franciscans or Dominicans, though many writers have talked loosely about the Orthodox monasteries of St Basil. Orthodox Monasticism has stayed true to a much older, flexible tradition that, though it acknowledged the safety net of a community, has never lost sight of the heroic individual search.

Christian Monasticism came into fashion as soon as the era of martyrdom ended with the legitimization of the Church by the Emperor Constantine at the beginning of the 4th century. Hermits established themselves away from the everyday compromises of human life: in deserts, huts, mountain caves, tombs, trees and (like the famous stylites) on the top of columns. The first monastery was a community of hermits, pioneered by **St Pachonius of Egypt** (286–346) in order to check the strong danger of insanity, possession by an evil spirit, heretical doctrines and suicidal mortifications that a solitary mystic is liable to. These communities were later championed by **St Basil the Great**, who is erroneously considered to have established the 'Order of St Basil'. He merely left a well-structured code of conduct which most communities are happy to accept as the starting point for their own spiritual venture. Orthodoxy has never established a doctrinal blueprint for monasticism, and though there are imposing well ordered communities, such as Kyyko, there is also considerable flexibility. This includes an acknowledged middle way, known as the semi-enemetic, of small, loosely knit communities under the spiritual tutelage of a Hesychastic, a respected father figure.

The Holy Icon of St Luke

The Greek Orthodox world only acknowledges three icons of the Virgin Mary to have been painted from life by the Evangelist, St Luke. These three—one in Athens, one at Megaspelion in the Peloponnese and the one in Kyyko—are taken to be the root source of all the other myriad images of the Mother of God. They were some of the most treasured relics of Byzantium, but an 11th-century emperor, in gratitude for the miraculous cure of his daughter by the hermit Isaiah and out of respect for his holy entreaties, bestowed the icon into the hermit's care. The monastery, apparently named after the distinctive black wood of the ebony tree, called *koukkos*, rapidly grew in fame and power. Over the centuries it was given property by the pious from all over the Orthodox world; as well as its extensive holdings in Cyprus, it once managed a portfolio of property stretching from Russia to Syria. Like most of the monasteries, Kykko was actively involved in the EOKA struggle (General Grivas's hideout was nearby), and its land-holdings, carefully watched over and augmented by Makarios, have allowed it to more than share in the profits of tourism. The monastery is now a well-established power in the land, and from its own resources finances seminaries, theological study centres, museums, church restoration programmes and clerical salaries.

The Monastery Buildings

The courtyards and church of the monastery have been furnished with mosaics and frescoes created by contemporary artists working within the Byzantine tradition. They are colourful but not uplifting, and can be admired in the way one cherishes an illustrated book or a strip cartoon. The story of the icon of St Luke can be seen at the gatehouse, while the *Old Testament Creation* and the *Life of the Virgin* are illustrated in a number of brightly coloured, labyrinthine passageways leading down to the lower courtyard. Here you will find the monastery treasury museum filled with jewelled reliquaries, silver crooks, mitres, pearl-embroidered cloaks, silver repoussé crosses and Bible covers. Most of it dates from the 19th century, though there are some fine 17th-century pieces and a 12th-century manuscript Bible.

The interior of the church is famously opulent with its painted walls, ornate furniture, highly polished granite floor and a bizarre and astonishing collection of old and electric candelabra presented to the church in acknowledgement of answered prayers. Only at the east end, with its impressive triple iconostasis hung with row upon row of silver oil lamps and ostrich-egg pendants, does the spirit of mystery overwhelm this near *nouveau riche* farce. Here you may approach the icon of the Virgin painted by St Luke and enclosed in repoussé silver, framed in mother-of-pearl and near-obscured in embroideries. Either keep your distance or kiss the icon; merely to stare at close range is discourteous.

Throni

A 2km walk or drive to the west of the monastery will take you towards Throni or Kykko hill. The summit bears an open-air *copula* where the holy icon of St Luke (represented by a small mosaic panel) is exhibited at the winter-rain-summoning festival on 7 and 8 September and in times of drought. Beside it the wind tugs at the handkerchiefs tied to a prayer bush, their fluttering a reminder to the petitioned saint of the original supplication, which is believed to be granted when the cloth finally blows free. **Archbishop Makarios III**, abbot of Kykko and first president of Cyprus, chose to be buried nearby. You can pay your respects at his black marble tomb which sits in a natural open-air cave guarded by soldiers.

Kambos and the Cedar Valley

Just before the monastery, a signposted road heads north for 9km to the isolated village of **Kambos** which, with its simple hotel and taverna, could offer a few days of serenity or act as a walking base. The forestry track that climbs to the west of the village, past the ruined chapel of Ayia Anastasis, makes a long twisting 12km circuit of the partly-wooded Prophitis Elias and Moutti tis Lajeris hills, and returns at the hamlet of Chakistra 2km south of Kambos.

A more celebrated destination is the **Cedar valley**, some 18km from Kykko monastery. Watch out for a left turn about 4km north of Kykko on the Kambos road, then about 5km later take the left fork at a junction; the forestry track then twists 9km southwest to reach a valley on the southern slopes of Mounts Tripylos and Tremithias. This is Cedar valley, the last natural reserve of Cyprus cedar (*cedrus brevifolia*), which, with that of the Himalayas, the Atlas and Lebanon, is one of the world's four subspecies of cedar. It is believed to have once covered most of the mountains, and fortunately the Paphos forestry service is gradually expanding the stock by selective planting.

Prodhromos, Kaminaria and Paleomylos

Prodhromos is a small and not particularly attractive village situated just to the southwest of the road between Pedhoulas and Troödos. It stands at the edge of the Marathasa beneath the gathering height of Mount Olympus, and, at 1400m, has the distinction of being one of the highest villages on the island. Prodhromos boasts the convenience of a combined bank and post office, as well as a small cheap hotel called the Atlas. It is the epicentre of a number of tracks and roads that can take you to some minor but little-visited sites in unspoilt mountain villages.

About 2km along the road leading south directly to Pano Platres, you pass the old convent of Panayia Trikoukia now in the grounds of an agricultural research station. The church of Timios Stavros is found in the hamlet of **Paleomylos**, which is 5km southwest of Prodhromos on the road to Phini, and conserves some 16th-century frescoes on the north and east walls. The long drawn-out village of

Kaminaria, some 10km southwest of Prodhromos at the end of the road, is an even more reclusive destination. The journey is really its own reward, though the diminutive Panayia chapel standing on the hillside to the west of the village contains some 16th-century frescoes: apart from the saints there only is room for one *Crucifixion.* Another destination is the chapel of Ayios Vasilios, with its smoke-blackened frescoes. About 2km to the north of the village, look out for a path climbing to the lone chapel perched on the southern slope of the Ayios Elias hill.

Where to Stay in the Marathasa Area

Pedhoulas

With its choice of hotels and restaurants, Pedhoulas is the obvious base for this area. The isolated **Churchill Pinewood Valley Hotel,** © (02) 952211, has 30 moderately priced rooms, but was roofless and under restoration at the time of writing. Some of the charm of its position amongst the pine woods is lost by the proximity of the tin shacks of the British army. In town, outside of the summer season, you may choose from either **Jack's Hotel,** © (02) 952350, which has 23 moderately priced rooms, or its modern near-neighbour on the high street, the **Two Flowers,** © (02) 952372, which is principally a restaurant but has a dozen pristine rooms downstairs. In summer a number of smaller, cheaper hotels with vine-shaded terraces open up in the village back-streets, such as the **Central,** © (02) 952457, **Christy's Palace,** © (02) 952655, **Kallithea,** © (02) 952294, as well as the increasingly dilapidated but charming **Elyssia,** © (02) 952659.

Kalopanayiotis

Kalopanayiotis has a choice of cheap, slightly run-down but friendly places that are mostly strung along the main road. The **Kastalia,** © (02) 952455, run by Avraam Georgiou, is probably the first choice, followed by either **Drakos,** © (02) 952651, **Helioupolis,** © (02) 952451, **Loutraki,** © (02) 952356 or **Synnos,** © (02) 952653.

Kambos

The **Kambos guesthouse,** © (02) 942320, offers meals as well as one of its five simple rooms in this isolated village north of Kykko monastery.

Yerakies

Treetops, © (02) 952667, is a moderately priced modern hotel, with a dining room and 20 rooms. It is located in the village of Yerakies, which stands above the Kalopanayiotis dam just west of Nikos.

In **Pedhoulas** at lunch time avoid the high street dining rooms and take the back road to find the **Vryssi Spring Water restaurant** (also known as **Harry's**), ℂ (02) 952240, or its neighbour also called the **Vryssi**, ℂ (02) 952420, down towards the bottom of the valley.

The Troödos Area

The Troödos area contains two ex-colonial hill stations, some impressive stands of pine forest and Mount Olympus, the highest point in Cyprus. In places of interest it cannot compare to any of the other four mountain areas but it is easily the most popular. A steady flow of coaches from the beach resorts on the southern coast takes day-trippers on an itinerary that seldom strays much beyond Pano Platres, Troödos, Mount Olympus and Kykko monastery. There is no need to follow them nor to totally avoid the area. Villages and paths off from the principal road remain surprisingly tranquil and there are some additional destinations listed in 'Walks in the Limassol Foothills' on p. 206.

Troödos and Mount Olympus

Troödos is of little or no interest. It is not a village but a dank collection of souvenir stalls, snack bars, two hotels and a petrol pump scattered around a central mountain crossroads. It is an unlikely, though popular, stopping point for all the coach tours through the mountains, but there is absolutely no need to join the desultory groups of day-trippers browsing the pavement. To the west rises the wooded slopes of Mount Olympus; to the east is the enormous messy workings of the old Amiandos asbestos mine; while to the north lie a military camp and the presidential palace. The latter, a sadly inappropriate Scottish shooting lodge, is closed to visitors. It was built in 1878 as the summer residence for the British colonial governor, but is only of interest due to its connection with a French poet. Rimbaud oversaw some of its construction while working his passage down towards Abyssinia where, like a hero from Evelyn Waugh, he rose to become a chieftain and lived in a palace at Harrar, before returning to France to die in squalor.

Skiing on Mount Olympus

Troödos becomes almost attractive after a winter snowfall when the corrugated-iron huts are camouflaged under a dusting of snow and the place turns into a small resort for those wishing to ski down the slopes of Mount Olympus. No one comes to Cyprus specifically for the skiing, as the snow cover is much too unreliable and covers too limited an area. The runs on Mount Olympus tend to be used by locals and foreign residents popping up from Nicosia or Limassol for the day, rather than by tourists. Sufficient snow can fall here any time in the winter, though February and March are the most reliable months. Conditions tend to be Scottish—that is icy in the morning and slushy in the afternoon, with the chance of low cloud cover.

About 1.5km along the Prodhromos road from Troödos there is a tarmac turning that cuts through the pine-wooded slopes of Mount Olympus and climbs to the café and club shed. Nearby are three T-bar lifts: Northern Face, Hera and Sun Valley, of which the latter is more suitable for learners. A day-pass for the lifts and the hire of equipment for a day will cost under C£20 per person. The lifts only operate if there are more than 10 skiers, and close down at 4.30pm in February and 5pm in March. To check on current conditions ring the Cyprus Ski Federation in Nicosia on ✆ (02) 365340.

Mount Olympus (sometimes referred to as Troödos), is the highest mountain in Cyprus at 1952m, and enjoys a splendid prospect over the island. The unique spirit of this mountain has, however, long since been banished by the road access, the ski lifts littering its lower slopes and the enormous white telecommunication globes that stand just to the west of the summit. A shrine to Aphrodite Acraiea once stood at the summit of this breast-shaped mountain, though it is only the slight earth bank of a Venetian fort that can be discerned today.

Pano Platres and Around

Pano Platres is a summer hill resort of a dozen hotels, a couple of English pubs and one disco. It stands in an attractive position overlooking Cyprus's only perennial stream and surrounded by hills covered in pine and golden oak. It was created by the British in the 19th century to remind them of 'home', and, like a lot of ex-colonial hill stations, is still possessed by a bland aura of suburban conformity. The village high street, the quiet winding backstreets lined with brick villas, and the approved walks through the surrounding pine woods can be almost insufferably reminiscent of the duller parts of Britain. It remains popular with British expatriates and is an almost compulsory stop for the coach tours that rattle through the mountains.

For the first half of this century it used to attract a ritzy Levantine clientele that included King Farouk of Egypt, but this set have long sinced moved on. For over pine woods there is a sharp division in taste: to the Mediterranean soul they can summon up images of long lazy Augusts spent in a succession of family picnics, festivals and amorous weekends scented by a cool sap-flavoured breeze. While to the northern soul pine woods have all the glamour of a commercial crop touched by the cloying romanticism of respectable 19th-century taste and the creeping malevolence of a Grimm's fairy tale.

Nature Trails around Pano Platres

The CTO (Cyprus Tourism Organisation) has established a number of nature trails in the area, with leaflets describing the routes, signposts marking out points of interest, and wooden archways marking the start and finish. You might consider this either helpful or twee, but do not allow yourself to be discouraged from walking the rewarding Khromion trail.

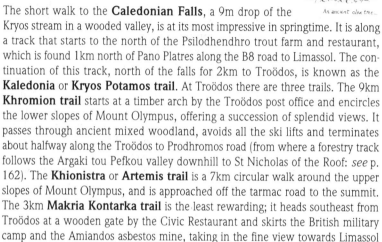

An ancient olive tree.

The short walk to the **Caledonian Falls**, a 9m drop of the Kryos stream in a wooded valley, is at its most impressive in springtime. It is along a track that starts to the north of the Psilodhendhro trout farm and restaurant, which is found 1km north of Pano Platres along the B8 road to Limassol. The continuation of this track, north of the falls for 2km to Troödos, is known as the **Kaledonia** or **Kryos Potamos trail**. At Troödos there are three trails. The 9km **Khromion trail** starts at a timber arch by the Troödos post office and encircles the lower slopes of Mount Olympus, offering a succession of splendid views. It passes through ancient mixed woodland, avoids all the ski lifts and terminates about halfway along the Troödos to Prodhromos road (from where a forestry track follows the Argaki tou Pefkou valley downhill to St Nicholas of the Roof: *see* p. 162). The **Khionistra** or **Artemis trail** is a 7km circular walk around the upper slopes of Mount Olympus, and is approached off the tarmac road to the summit. The 3km **Makria Kontarka trail** is the least rewarding; it heads southeast from Troödos at a wooden gate by the Civic Restaurant and skirts the British military camp and the Amiandos asbestos mine, taking in the fine view towards Limassol from the east end of the south shoulder.

Phini (Fini)

Phini is a refreshingly normal Cypriot village just 4km to the west of Pano Platres with its own trout farm and taverna. It was the birthplace of Archbishop Sopronius (1825–1900), who welcomed the British with an address that also adroitly framed the first request for eventual union with Greece. Phini is one of the ancient centres of island pottery (*see* 'Ceramics', p. 405), and though the 6ft-high *pitharia* storage jars are no longer produced commercially here, you can still acquire some plain earthenware pots or distinctive fritted figures from the couple of potters still functioning in the village. These and other craft traditions of the area, such as the village's famous holm-oak chairs, can be further investigated in the small folk museum run by, and in the house of, Theofanis Pivlakis.

About 2km to the west of the village, just south of the road to Ayios Dhimitrios and Prodhromos, is the haunted monastic church of **Ayii Anargyri** dedicated to St Cosmas and St Damian. It contains late frescoes of *St George* and the

Archangel Michael on the north wall. Be careful to be out of the area before dusk on Saturdays, as this is the time, according to the local legend recorded by Gunnis in the 1930s, when a dark-complexioned youth mounted on a horse can be seen to issue from the great Gothic doorway on the west wall and ride out in the night.

Troödhitissa Monastery

Open daily 6–12 and 2–8.

The handsome 18th-century monastery of Troödhitissa, with its high wooden gables and walls built from local grey mountain stone, is 10km north of Pano Platres on the direct road to Prodhromos. The monastery, surrounded by trees overlooking the terraced gardens, enjoys a splendid view down the steep valley towards Phini. It is the third monastery to stand on this site. The previous buildings, like so many of the medieval wooden churches of the mountains, burnt down, but fortunately each time the precious icon of the *Virgin Mary of Troödos* was saved from the flames. The monastery's church has an especially magnificent iconostasis, enhanced by the contrasting bare white walls and simple, high-pitched wooden roof. A double row of votive silver oil lamps and ostrich eggs hang from projecting eagles and dragons before the line of 16th-century Italianate icons. For 200 years the ancient icon of the Virgin has been sheathed from profane eyes by a covering of repoussé silver. Traditions record that it had been hidden by a devout monk during the iconoclastic period and was rediscovered two centuries later by a pair of mountain shepherds. The monastery shop has plenty of copies of the original, where the Virgin, clothed in a brilliant robe of red and gold, holds the learned Christ Child in his toga of blue and gold.

The monastery is also famous for its fertility belt which has enabled numerous childless couples to conceive. In previous centuries a male child conceived with the aid of the belt was returned to the monastery as a novice. This is a tradition that harks back to the mysterious temple boys of Aphrodite. It is perhaps just a coincidence that the old name for the monastery is Panayia Aphrodotissa.

The Chapel of Ayia Mavra near Kilani Village

Ayia Mavra (St Mavra) is a lone 15th-century chapel, though a small monastery was still functioning here in the 18th century. It is made exceptional more from its setting beside a taverna in the Kryos valley and its position astride a stream, than from the quality of its frescoes.

South from Pano Platres the Kryos stream leaves the pine-wooded hills behind to flow through a broader valley overlooked by limestone hills covered either in a rough maquis or small, terraced vineyards. Three villages, Perapedhi, Kilani and Vouni, occupy a succession of outlying spurs to punctuate the valley with attractive knots of stone-built houses capped with red tiles. Between Perapedhi and

Kilani (about 1km east of the latter) you can find the small chapel of Ayia Mavra beside Yiannis Frixou's seasonal taverna, which is shaded by an enormous plane tree. Ayia Mavra has the distinctive high-pitched roof of the mountains, but has been built directly over a spring whose gurgling waters make an attractive cacophony within the single-domed nave.

The chapel maintains most of its 15th-century frescoes, though many have been damaged over the centuries. They are crude but still powerful, particularly in the confined space of the chapel's sonorous interior. Aside from the traditional scenes there are some rarer representations. In the north recess above the door the Old Testament prophet *Ezekiel* has his vision of Mary and Jesus, flanked by matching prophets on either side of the window. *St Augustine*, the great theologian of the Early Church, is usually only honoured in Western Europe, but can here be found with a beard and white hair on the northeast pier looking south to *St Theodosius*. In the south recess below the *Dormition of the Virgin* stand *St Timothy* and *St Mavra* surrounded by side panels depicting their martyrdom. Little is remembered about them apart from that St Mavra was the niece of St Barnabas, and St Timothy was her husband. This gap in knowledge has been filled by a local legend.

St Mavra was a pious Christian girl who wished to enter a convent, but her father instead forced her into a loathsome marriage with a rich neighbour. On the night of the wedding feast, just before being taken to bed, St Mavra escaped and fled down the valley pursued by her father and her new husband, both drunk with wine and heavy with rich food. She was at last cornered at the site of this chapel where she fell on her knees and beseeched the aid of the Virgin Mary, as her spouse, with a belch and a lecherous leer, advanced towards her. The Madonna heard her prayer, the rock wall behind her instantly opened and St Mavra disappeared for ever. In her place a spring of fresh water flowed and the chastened men dedicated the rest of their lives to prayer, building this chapel where the sound of the spring would constantly remind them of St Mavra and their sins.

Timios Stavros, the parish church of the mountain hamlet of Kouka is about 3km southeast of Parapedhi on the road to Silikou village. It will only appeal to those who have gone quite mad on frescoes, and would enjoy identifying small patches of 15th- and 12th-century frescoes in the dark T-shaped interior.

Where to Stay in the Troödos Area

Pano Platres

Though it can be slightly depressing during the day, Pano Platres can work well as a touring or walking base. The hotel restaurants are not great generally, so be sure to eat well during the day.

The isolated **Forest Park** (expensive), © (05) 421751, used to be the height of exclusivity, but its 80 rather gloomy rooms and hallway wear an increasingly forlorn air despite some good period props. The **Minerva**, © (05) 421371, is a clean, moderately priced establishment that is open all-year round. It has a bar and tea garden, but only serves breakfast to its guests. The hotel is run by Yiannis Christofides, who is a mine of geological, botanical and historical information about the mountains. If the Minerva is full, you could stay just across the road at the moderately priced **Edelweiss**, © (05) 421335. Going out towards the Psilodhendhro trout restaurant is the **New Helvetia**, © (05) 421348. It is a well-established old colonial hotel with a restaurant and 17 moderately priced rooms, and is efficiently managed by Ms Lido Matheou.

The **Pafsylipon** (cheap), © (05) 421738, is a rambling old colonial place with an enormous sitting room, off which is a bar, restaurant and a balcony with a view down to the Kryos stream. If this is full you could try the slightly more expensive **Lanterns**, © (05) 421434, which has 15 rooms and serves only breakfast.

Troödos

Like Pano Platres, Troödos is only irritating by day. In the evening, when the coach tours have gone, it can become almost endearing, and it is well placed on a central mountain crossroads for you to explore a wide area.

The moderately priced **Jubilee**, © (05) 421647, with its large barn-like red corrugated-iron roof, is surrounded by pine trees. It has fires in the winter, cane furniture, a summer tea garden, 37 rooms and a restaurant that serves village wine. The **Troödos**, © (05) 421635, has quite a similar atmosphere but is smaller and slightly cheaper.

Perapedhi

Just to the south of Pano Platres, Perapedhi offers two cheap alternatives: the **Paradisos**, © (05) 421539, and **Pera Pedhi**, © (05) 432152, both guesthouses with a dozen simple rooms; only the latter serves meals.

Eating Out

If you are in **Pano Platres** at lunchtime try the fresh trout served at the **Psilodhendhro restaurant** just to the north of the resort.

Nightlife

Andy's Satisfy Disco in **Pano Platres** operates at weekends and in the summer. It is just uphill from the Lanterns hotel on the main street.

An octopus-decorated Mycenaean crater

Limassol

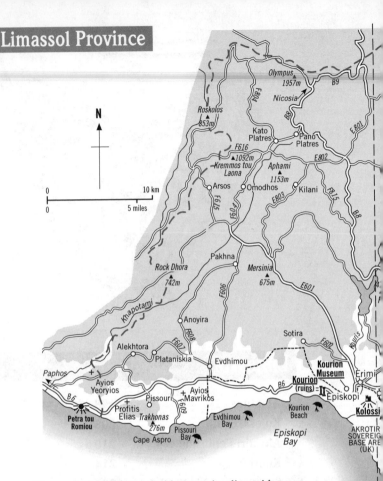

Limassol, Cyprus's second largest city, lies midway
along the southern shore, which it dominates like a
modern Mycenaean octopus, with tentacle-like motorways,
a deep-water harbour and a 16km-long strip of hotels to its
east. To the west of Limassol the Akrotiri Sovereign Base acts
as a break to coastal development, an unexpected but welcome
side effect of the British military presence. To the north, the land
rises up towards the Troödos massif, and after a light dusting of
suburban villas the dry limestone hills shake themselves free of the
city. Vineyards cover the slopes of the more northerly of these pale

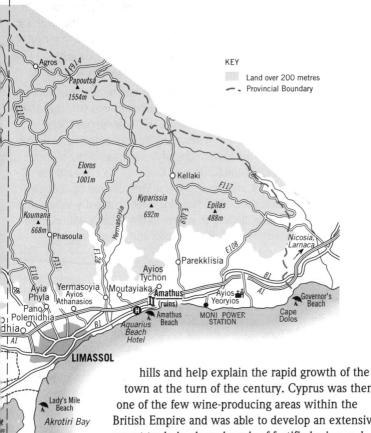

hills and help explain the rapid growth of the town at the turn of the century. Cyprus was then one of the few wine-producing areas within the British Empire and was able to develop an extensive export trade in cheap brands of fortified wine and brandy. The recent tourist boom has brought greater profits yet. Limassol remains the centre of the Cypriot wine trade which celebrates the annual harvest with a festival in early September.

Despite an initially off-putting image, Limassol does have redeeming features. Apart from the stream of midday browsers, it is curiously unaffected by the hundred-odd hotels just to its east. Begin by staying in the town centre, with its unpretentious but quietly agreeable turn-of-the-century streets which contain some of the island's best shopping. There are a few quiet, old and individual hotels, and the local cafés, bars and fish restaurants are still genuinely Cypriot. The ancient castle, with its Crusader connections, combines with the town's three other principal attractions—the Archaeological Museum, Art Gallery and Folk Museum—to give a powerful insight into the culture of Cyprus.

Apart from a walk round ruined Amathus and the odd nightlife trip in the evening, the self-sustaining beach-world that stretches to the east of the town can be left entirely alone. Instead head west to explore the unexploited beaches along the coast, and monuments such as the celebrated ancient city of Kourion, a colony of sacred cats and the castle of the Knights at Kolossi. This can easily be done from Limassol, though Pissouri makes an even better base. After these major sites, leave time for walks in the dry valleys and hills of the interior, finding your way to the island's unexplained and unique menhirs, its ruined chapels and quiet villages.

History

The small harbour at Limassol was overshadowed for centuries by its powerful neighbours, the ancient cities of Amathus and Kourion. Only after they were destroyed by the Saracens in the 7th century did it have a chance of emerging into the limelight of history. After the Dark Age ended with the Byzantine reconquest of the island in the 10th century, three small towns emerged along this coast. Episkopi, the heir of Kourion; medieval Amathus, which still squatted amongst its classical ruins; and Limassol, then known as Limezun, a walled town beside the Garyllis stream. The latter remained equal to its neighbours until a new era was born, one dark stormy summer night in 1191.

The Crusader Kingdom

A Crusader army under the command of King Richard I of England (Richard the Lionheart), having terrorized their hosts in Sicily, sailed east. The fleet was split up by a storm and the ship carrying Queen Joanna and Princess Berengaria, the king's beloved sister and his future wife, was driven to take shelter on this coast. Isaac, the despotic ruler of Cyprus, invited these eminent ladies to land, but reports on his conduct had reached their ears and they firmly declined. Isaac tried to insist, but just before his galleys could enforce his invitation the rest of the Crusader fleet appeared on the horizon. King Richard, who was always on the lookout for some easy looting and the chance of a fight, widened the misunderstanding by an exchange of insults which escalated into a satisfactory pretext for war. His English bowmen cleared the beach at Amathus with showers of arrows to allow for an armed landing that developed into a two-day running battle. The Cypriot levies proved no match for the experienced Crusader army. King Richard left Amathus a smoking and uninhabitable ruin and moved west to Limassol. At Limassol on 12 May, 1191 he celebrated his marriage to Berengaria, who was then crowned and later presented with the captive daughter of Isaac as lady-in-waiting. However, his wife was neglected, as King Richard seems to have preferred the company of soldiers for both his battles and his bed.

These events established Limassol as an early centre of Crusader power. A Byzantine tower was occupied and enlarged into the royal castle where another Crusading king, St Louis, stayed in 1248 en route to the Near East. The fall of Acre in 1291, the last outpost of the Crusaders in Palestine, brought a stream of refugees to Cyprus, most of whom settled in Famagusta or Nicosia. The two rival military orders, the Templars and the Hospitallers, both chose to settle in Limassol, which soon boasted four priories and two cathedrals. None of these fine Gothic buildings has survived, though the Grand Mosque and the Katholiki basilica mark the site of the old cathedrals. In 1303 the last Grand Commander of the Templars took ship from Limassol to France to answer the growing opposition to his order. On Friday 13 October, 1307 he and his knights were all summarily arrested and charged with heresy. This allowed the French King to seize the rich estates of the Templars. Despite enduring seven years of torture and state tribunals the Grand Commander protested the innocence of the Templars at his last trial. He was burnt as a heretic the same day on a small island on the Seine.

A Castle Surrounded by Ruins (1373–1878)

The Genoese, who devastated the island in 1373 with three successive invasions, paid particular attention to ruining Limassol, which was regularly raided to prevent its becoming a rival port to their Famagusta base. James I (1382–98), during his long campaign to expel the Genoese, constructed the existing castle from the ruins of a 13th-century church. A succession of earthquakes and invasions kept the town a ruin, so that when 10 corsair galleys raided Limassol in 1538, the castle was defended by a tiny garrison composed of just the governor, his wife and daughters. During the Ottoman period a garrison was based in the castle, but trade was deliberately discouraged by a punitive harbour duty, in order to concentrate all trade and customs collection in Larnaca.

A Century of Growth

The British occupation led to the contruction of a network of inland roads and a harbour pier in 1881, which combined with a vast new market for Cypriot wine and brandy within the British Empire. By the turn of the century Limassol had transformed itself from a village of mud houses to a prosperous harbour town.

Ironically, the division of the island in 1974 has served only to accelerate its steady growth. Despite the emigration of its Turkish population, the overall population trebled to reach 120,000, whilst the loss of Famagusta has allowed it to emerge as the undisputed first port and second city of Cyprus. It was also bolstered by a second batch of skilled refugees fleeing from the civil war in Beirut, which had hitherto acted as the financial and service centre of the Middle East.

Getting Around

By Ferry

A weekly ferry runs year-round between Limassol, Rhodes and Piraeus (the port of Athens). This currently departs on Friday at 12 noon, arriving in Rhodes at 9am on Saturday and in Piraeus at 7.30am on Sunday. In midsummer there is a more frequent service and a connection to Crete. The cheapest single ticket to Piraeus (sleeping on an aircraft-type seat) is about C£40.

By Bus

The Nicosia and Paphos route is covered by **KEMEK**, ℭ (05) 354394, whose bus stop is by the Bishopric at the corner of Enoseos and Eirinis streets. They run nine departures every weekday to Nicosia, between 5.45am and 6pm, and six to Paphos, between 6.30am and 5.30pm. A smaller, parallel service is offered by **Costas** at 9B Thessalonikis street, ℭ (05) 354394. For Larnaca catch the **Kallenos Bus**, ℭ (05) 362670, which leaves from the corner of Spyrou Araouzou and Hadjipavlou streets, near the castle, seven times a day between 6am and 5.30pm in winter and 6pm in summer.

By Local Bus

The no. 30 bus is the most efficient service, with frequent buses running from 8am–11.30pm between the new harbour on the far western edge of Limassol to the Méridien Hotel on the far eastern end of the beach strip. Another useful service is the Episkopi village bus, which connects Limassol castle to ancient Kourion; it departs at 9, 10, 11 and 12 noon and returns at 11.50 and 2.50. There are also four departures from the covered market bus stop to Kolossi castle, departing at 9.15, 10.45, 3.30 and 5, and returning at 8.45, 10.15, 3 and 4.30.

Going north into the hills (an area covered in the Nicosia chapter), the daily bus to Agros leaves opposite the central post office on Gladstonos street at 11.45am, leaving Agros the next day at 7am. For Pano Platres and all villages en route to Kalaopanayiotis there is a daily bus at 1pm from the KEMEK stop which leaves from Kalaopanayiotis the next day at 5.15pm. For Pano Platres only, there are two buses: the 12.45pm **Karydas** bus, ℂ (05) 362061, leaving from 21 Thessalonikis street, and the 2pm **Platres** bus, ℂ (05) 362907, leaving from 50 Eleftherias street. The former leaves Platres the next day at 7am, the latter at 6.45am. In high summer there are three additional Karydas bus departures to Platres, the Solea bus to Kakopetria and a 1pm Lefkara bus from the KEMEK stop.

By Taxi

Conventional taxis are useful for dropping you off at your hotel at night, or taking you to a nearby coast or hill village; they will seldom cost more than C£5 a trip. There is no need for a taxi any further afield, except during national holidays. A taxi ride to Larnaca or Paphos is currently about C£15 (including tip), a bit more for Nicosia and over C£20 for Polis or Ayia Napa.

By shared taxi: This is the most convenient way to the five towns, with departures every half hour from 6am–6pm (or 7pm in the summer), though you will have to change at Paphos for Polis and at Larnaca if you want to go east to Ayia Napa. The three Ks run the Nicosia and Paphos routes: **Kypros**, ℂ (05) 363979, are well placed at 49 Spyrou Araouzou (the seafront promenade); **Karydas**, ℂ (05) 362061, and **Kyriakos**, ℂ (05) 364114, are both at 21 Thessalonikis street, 700m inland by the Othello cinema. For Larnaca use either **Acropolis**, ℂ (05) 366766, which operates out of the Kypros office, or **Makris** at 166 Hellas street, ℂ (05) 365550.

Car Hire

Ring around for the best deal from some of the following local firms: **Saint George's** at 62 Leoforos Archiepiskopou Makariou III, ℂ (05) 336077; **KyproCars** at 57 Spyrou Araouzou, ℂ (05) 374180; **Europcar** at 4B Blue Sea House, Leoforos Octovriou 28, ℂ (05) 324025; **Eurodollar** at 24 Leoforos Archiepiskopou Makariou III, ℂ (05) 346020; or **Andy Spyrou** at 38040 Leoforos Omonia, ℂ (05) 371441.

Boat Trips/Cruises

In summer there are daily boat trips leaving at 10am from the beach opposite the Kanika Beach Hotel, 400m east of the municipal gardens, which motor west across to Lady's Mile beach. There are also shorter night cruises leaving at 9pm, ℂ (05) 382912. Another boat runs from out of the old harbour in high season on Wed, Fri and Sun (check availability on ℂ (05) 327342).

Sail Fascination offer sailing trips out of old Limassol harbour. They rent or skipper either Sun Fizz, a 40-ft sloop, or Gin Fizz, a 37-ft ketch, for a variety of destinations for up to 10 people. A simple day trip could take you to Lady's Mile and Cap Gata; a two-day trip might go further along the coast to anchor off Evdihmou Bay overnight, while in three days you could pass Paphos and sail right round the Akamas peninsula to Latchi harbour. Prices include drinks and snacks and range between C£40 for joining a day cruise to C£280 per day for hiring the yacht with skipper. For bookings, write to PO Box 257, Limassol, ☎ (05) 364200, fax (05) 352657, or visit their office at 27 Nikiforou Foka street.

Boat Cruises to Egypt and Israel

Mini-cruises from Limassol to **Egypt** and **Israel** are enthusiastically advertised by travel agents all over the island. Two shipping companies provide a busy schedule from the new harbour, with at least one departure a day. These cruises last two days and three nights, and are often tightly packed, with a stress on noisy entertainment, casino evenings, discos and floor shows. Coaches and guides await at Port Said to provide a whistle-stop tour of Cairo, the Pyramids, a papyrus factory and oriental bazaar. At the docks at Ashdod or Haifa another team awaits to conduct a day-long coach excursion through the major sites and souvenir shops of Jerusalem and Bethlehem. In TinTin terms it would tickle the soul of Jocelyn Wagg but disgust Captain Haddock. Prices include transfer from hotel, accommodation, meals and coach trips, and vary from around C£50 for an aircraft-type seat to around C£150 for the most spacious cabin. Bookings can be made through hotels, travel agencies or by telephoning directly; ring (05) 369000 for a reservation on **Ambassador Cruises'** *Romantica* and (05) 327342 for a berth on the *Princessa Cypria*, the *Princessa Marissa* or the *Princessa Amorosa*, run by **Louis Cruise Lines**, 158 Fragklinou Rousvelt street.

Tourist Information

The tourist information booths freely dispense maps and a glittering range of leaflets, as well as providing updates on the timetables of local bus services, churches and festivals. There is an office in the ferry terminal of the new harbour, ☎ (05) 343868, and another on the seafront in the centre of town at 15 Spyrou Araouzou, ☎ (05) 362756. Travel agents and hotel receptionists can usually arrange car hire, cruise and excursions bookings, as well as providing useful practical information.

The museums of Limassol and its other landmarks are described in a long loop of a walk beginning at the castle, going east along Ayiou Andreou (St Andrew) street to the municipal gardens and returning back along the seafront promenade.

Limassol Castle and Medieval Museum

Open every day except Sun 7.30am–5pm; © (05) 330419; adm.

The castle, sometimes known as the citadel, is 250m inland from the old harbour, on the west face of Eirinis street. The rectangular exterior presents the firm, rather forbidding silhouette of a Venetian artillery fortress, later put to use as a barracks in the Ottoman period, and a prison during the British rule. The interior, particularly the Gothic rib-vaulted lower hall, suggests an older and more complicated history. The lower hall is believed to have been built by the Knights Templars around 1300, but fell into neglect after the ruin of both the order and the town. It was given a new lease of life as the foundation of a new castle built by James I at the end of the 14th century, which was itself wrapped in stout walls a hundred years later by the Venetians. Local gossip has placed the marriage of Berengeria and Richard the Lionheart in the castle, though unfortunately this event predates the foundation stones by a century.

Talking Heads

Another, but this time historical, story recalls an oracular brass head hidden in a chamber of the castle. This tale has a curious link with the occupation of the castle by the Knights Templars. During the dissolution of the order the knights were charged with embracing heretical practices, like worshipping secret idols and talking heads. Under torture some of the knights identified this talking idol as the demon Baphomet whose preferred shape was that of a cat. The last person to have seen the talking head was an Italian visitor in the 16th century though his description fails to record the location of the secret chamber.

There is a fine view of the town from the battlements, which vies for your attention with the castle's medieval museum, housed in two storeys of cells to the east of the hall. The Gothic tomb-slabs were recovered from the floor of the Omeriye mosque in Nicosia, which had been an Augustinian abbey before the Turkish conquest of 1571. During its conversion into a mosque the tomb-slabs were all turned upside down, which has preserved the crisp incised lines depicting Eschive d'Ibelin, Aumauri de Montfort and Heyde de Vis. The ceramic display is dominated by brighter imports from Italy and Ottoman Turkey, which separately

Limassol

N

| 0 | 500 metres |
| 0 | 500 yards |

St George

Pattiheion Theatre

AYIAS ZONIS

VASILI MICHALIDI

THESSALONIKIS

GLADS

Karydas shared taxis **T**

Kyriakos shared taxis

Troödos, Paphos

ARCHIEPISKOPOU LEONTIOU I

Central Post Office ⊠

POL

St Barnabas

GLADSTONOS

AYIAS ZONIS

ANEXARTISIAS

Makris shared taxis **T**

Urban Buses

Municipal Market

NAVARINOU

ELLADOS

KANARI

SARIPOLOU

EIRINIS

ENOSEOS

Kemek Buses

Bishopric

Katholiki

EIRINIS

⊠

9

8

H

8

7

Garyllis

YILDIZ

ELEFTHERIAS

EIRINIS

Ayia Napa

Ayios Mamas

ISMET PASA

Cami Djedid

ANKARA

H 5

Cami Kebir

GENETHLIOU MITELLA

T 1

AR

6

SPYROU

P

10

Castle and Medieval Museum

EIRINIS

ℹ

3

DJELAL

BAYAR

KÖPRULUZATE

Ayios Antonios

Reptile House

FRAGKLINOU ROUSVELT

Keo Winery

AYIOU ANTONIOU

R Glaros Fish Tavern

Old Harbour

Paphos, New Harbour

KEY

1	Acropolis shared taxis	6	Kypros shared taxis
2	Aquamarina Hotel	7	Lefkaritis buses
3	Bedestan	8	Luxor Guest House
4	Continental Hotel	9	Metropole Hotel
5	Hellas Guest House	10	Turkish Bathhouse

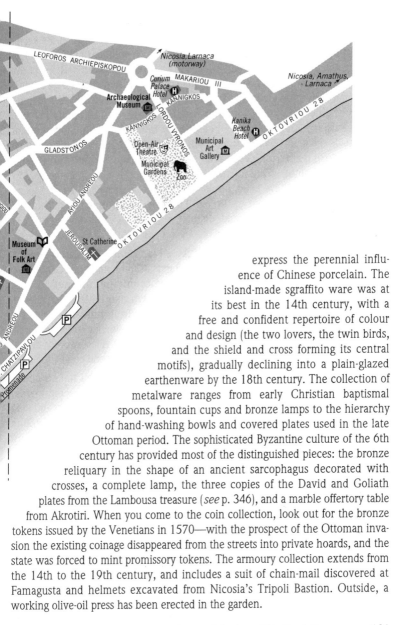

express the perennial influence of Chinese porcelain. The island-made sgraffito ware was at its best in the 14th century, with a free and confident repertoire of colour and design (the two lovers, the twin birds, and the shield and cross forming its central motifs), gradually declining into a plain-glazed earthenware by the 18th century. The collection of metalware ranges from early Christian baptismal spoons, fountain cups and bronze lamps to the hierarchy of hand-washing bowls and covered plates used in the late Ottoman period. The sophisticated Byzantine culture of the 6th century has provided most of the distinguished pieces: the bronze reliquary in the shape of an ancient sarcophagus decorated with crosses, a complete lamp, the three copies of the David and Goliath plates from the Lambousa treasure (see p. 346), and a marble offertory table from Akrotiri. When you come to the coin collection, look out for the bronze tokens issued by the Venetians in 1570—with the prospect of the Ottoman invasion the existing coinage disappeared from the streets into private hoards, and the state was forced to mint promissory tokens. The armoury collection extends from the 14th to the 19th century, and includes a suit of chain-mail discovered at Famagusta and helmets excavated from Nicosia's Tripoli Bastion. Outside, a working olive-oil press has been erected in the garden.

The Cami Kebir (Grand Mosque) and Turkish Quarter

The Cami (pronounced Djami) Kebir of Limassol stands 100m east of the castle tucked behind a proctective enclosure of shops off Genethliou Mitella street. The old mosque, which was destroyed in the flood of 1894, conserved portions of the 14th-century Gothic cathedral; the existing building, with its horseshoe arches, onion-dome derived windows and vulgar new marble inlay, is a pastiche of quite separate traditions of Islamic architecture. However, in the evening it has a delightful aspect—the muezzin call echoes out from the minaret and a pair of palms beside the fountain canopy are floodlit. The mosque was once the centre of the old Turkish quarter; the vegetable market remains in use just to the south whilst the old booths of the artisans beneath the pointed stone arches of the **Bedestan** enclosure have been turned into a tourist bazaar. Further east along the street is a turning down to the old **Turkish bathhouse**, its dilapidated changing-hall, sunken walls and distinctive glass-flecked dome seemingly oblivious to the expensive office developments to the west.

The heavy turn-of-the-century church of **Ayia Napa** (the Holy Handkerchief), with its high dome and double bell tower, stands at the junction of Genethliou Mitella and Ayiou Andreou streets. The covered **municipal market** is 300m north of the Ayia Napa church, up Saripolou street, which is dotted with cafés. A morning coffee and a stroll to admire the cascades of fresh fruit and vegetables make a good start to the day, even if you are not assembling goods for an out-of-town picnic. At the entrances are a number of stalls run by village women selling home-cured ham, goats' cheese, mountain honey, dried fruit and confections.

The **Katholiki basilica** overawes the administrative palace of the Orthodox bishop of Amathus and Limassol, which is 200m west of the covered market along Kanari and Enoseos streets. This building is in the slow process of being fitted with frescoes, and though there is much that is wonderful about the 20th century, there is also much that has been lost. The round, brown eyes of *Christ Pantocrator* look down from the dome in an even and bored gaze.

Ayiou Andreou (St Andrew) street runs east of the Ayia Napa church for 1.5km, passing the Folk Museum and rococo library on its way up to the municipal gardens and Archaeological Museum. It is also a place to dawdle, as it passes by some of the more interesting bars and shops (*see* 'Shopping and Nightlife' below).

The Museum of Folk Art

Open weekdays 8.30am–1.30pm; Mon, Tues, Wed and Fri 3–5.30pm; 4–6.30 in summer; © (05) 362303; adm.

The museum, halfway along Ayiou Andreou street at No. 253, is housed in a handsome square town house embellished with an ornate frieze that is fully in keeping with the objects stored within. Each room has been fitted with a *souvatnza*, a head-height wall shelf considered one of the glories of a traditional house. It stored and proudly displayed the wealth of the house as expressed in plates, baskets, gourds, cutlery and glass. The *souvatnza* was often dressed with embroidery and could be supported by a plaster cornice, impressed with an interlinked design, typically of vines and erotes The hall of the museum is furnished with four finely carved chests, known as *kasella* or *sentouki*, made from cypress or walnut wood, and raised above the dampness off the floor on heavy block feet. The chests held the dowery of household linen prepared by a bride before her marriage, and thus had both a practical and symbolic role within the house. The best chests were traditionally made in the Byzantine hill village of Lapithos (Lapta).

The traditional costume of a peasant villager, enlivened by the glamour of a *sclavouniko* waistcoast, is displayed in rooms **3** and **4**. Purple, red and black were the preferred colours, decorated with rich embroidery. The latter room has some spectacular pieces of local Fiti terracotta, the blossoming towers resembling miniature models of a Gaudí tower. The crisp whiteness of the bedroom (room **6**) is enhanced by bridal wreaths of cotton and wax.

Room **8** is furnished as a tool-strewn country kitchen. Here, the essential continuity of a village culture, melting away before our eyes, is revealed: the *voukami* board, used for crushing grain, the woven-grass cheese baskets and especially the black-on-red decoration of the gourds (strikingly similar to the Stone-Age ceramics in Nicosia's Cyprus Museum). The bread seal that impresses a cross into each loaf is in pleasing contrast to the pagan motifs on the carved board used for impressing plaster cornices. The 10-holed *yastra* planks are still being produced, though now mostly as bar-room and taverna décor. These allowed the dough of round loaves to rise before baking, and helped keep the various households' bread separate at the communal oven. There is also a rustic *anathrica* stool, a delightful hermit-like perch of bound and nailed rough branches.

Rooms **2** and **5** are dedicated to the second great industry of the island performed by women: the transformation of flax canes, fluffy seed pods and cocoons of mulberry-eating worms into fine embroidered linen, cotton and silk. The narrow two-foot widths of a house loom were joined to make broader bolts of cloth. Bright red stripes frame quieter bands of coloured lozenges and geometrical designs to create a markedly Levantine look, in harmony with the jewellery created from filigree twists and arabesque curls.

In the central ticket office there are some fine Iznik plates behind glass. Do not be confused by the Hellenic claims of the staff—these are the products of Ottoman Turkey, though due to the activity of merchants from Lindos on the island of Rhodes they are also misleadingly known as Rhodian ware.

The Library and Municipal Gardens

About 200m east of the Folk Museum is a rococo mansion which now houses the municipal library. Its playfully excessive exterior is a carved mass of yellow stone swirls, swags and capitals dripping in wreaths. The heads of the Pilavachi family extrude from window capstones, like a petrified version of Happy Families, with the smiling Miss P on the right, Mrs P on the left and Mr Anthony P above them on the top floor.

Five hundred metres east of the library are the **municipal gardens**, featuring an open-air theatre and a children's zoo (*open 9am–12 noon, 2–5.30pm; adm*) as well as fountains, ponds, promenading paths and a café.

The Archaeological Museum

> *Open Mon–Fri 7.30am–5pm, Sat 9am–5pm and Sun 10am–1pm;*
> *℘ (05) 330132; adm.*

Due north of the municipal gardens on the corner of Kannigkos and Lourdou Vyronos (Lord Byron) streets, stands the colonial residence of the District Commissioner and the Archaeological Museum. The Museum houses objects discovered at Amathus, assisted by the rich discoveries from the nearby Neolithic-Chalcolithic sites of Erimi and Sotira. The exhibits are well labelled but rather haphazardly arranged. (For an introduction to the shifting patterns of ancient art, *see* 'Cypriot Ceramics', p. 405.)

A Roman mosaic of Aphrodite and Cupid bathing is the star exhibit among the statuettes in the lapidary garden and the architectural fragments ranked in the sketching shelter at the rear. It is matched by the 5th-century BC Phoenician sarcophagus in the hall, with its classical female head carved onto otherwise plain white stone.

In the **first gallery** a new case displays findings from the contentious Akrotiri cave, occupied in 8000 BC. It is the earliest evidence of man on the island of Cyprus, which appears to coincide with the extinction of indigenous species like the pygmy hippo and dwarf elephant. The cave was found in 1961 by a 14-year-old English schoolboy on holiday. Ten years later he sent photographs of his finds, along with his own expert opinion and a map to the Cyprus Museum; however his submission was ignored. Fortunately the cave was rediscovered and excavated in 1988. Other principal attractions include the Chalcolithic stone idols, an enormous Bronze-Age jar, Phoenician devil masks, breast-clutching divinities and four bread makers. Among the rich collection of Archaic clay models is a pair of terracotta chests decorated with chevrons and hatches, displaying striking similarities to contemporary folk art. The six capitals at the far end of the gallery summon up that shadowy era when Cyprus acted as a bridge between the highly developed culture of Egypt and the emerging identity of Greece. The formation of the familiar classical orders can be recognized in the fronds surrounding the triangle-centred proto-Ionic capital. The dizzy opulence of the lotus capital with its Hathoric head decorated a palace in the Hellenistic era. Retain it in your mind's eye as a totem to dispel the Palladian complex, that temptation to see the ancient world like a monochrome Paestum or Parthenon print, without their garish red and blue paintwork, the stink of sacrifice and their largely unacknowledged debt to the cultures of the Near East.

The **second gallery** contains cases of pottery, jewellery and metalware, a jumble of chronology and cultures that nevertheless stresses the essential unity of all material culture. Amongst the gold, silver snake bracelets and Phoenician beads with eyes of Horus is a bronze coin minted during the reign of Caracalla (AD 212–7), which displays the island's prime attraction, the temple of Paphian Aphrodite. The gold *solidi* (coins) of Heraclius and his son Constantine (c. 613–39) bear witness to the last few decades of Byzantine prosperity, before the Saracen raids emptied the ancient cities.

The **third gallery** is dominated by the enormous statue of Bes, carved in the 3rd century AD, the height of the Roman period, but in a deliberately Archaic style, with stumpy horn, flat nose and full 'Assyrian' beard. He was known by the Greeks as 'Ptah Pataikos', the Phoenician dwarf who was carved on innumerable ships' figureheads. A Falstaff-like buffoon, Bes was also a popular confident who could help with childbirth, a woman's toilet and navigation; he could also chase away evil spirits, snakes and poisons. Bes is flanked by a pair of crudely carved heads of Zeus Lambrasianos, from the 4th and the 6th centuries AD. Whatever their artistic contribution, they provide graphic evidence of the continuation of pagan cults deep into the Byzantine period. Shrines to Lustral Zeus have been identified just outside the villages of Phasoula and Chandria. Descending dramatically in scale are 7 terracotta Tanagra figures, recalling the passing fashions in coiffure. There is also a cabinet filled with a fine display of Phoenician and Roman glass, blue ware amulets, and intricate bubble-beaded glasses set off in contrast to the clean lines of funerary urns.

The Municipal Art Gallery and the Sea Front

Open all weekday mornings 8.30am–1.30pm and 3–5.30pm (4–6.30pm in summer) except Thurs; adm.

The Municipal Art Gallery houses one of only two permanent collections of modern art on the island. It was opened in 1988, and is located in the distinctive white villa of Hypatia Pavlides on Oktovriou 28 street, 150m east of the municipal gardens. Amongst the more recognizably Cypriot canvasses is the steep-roofed upland chapel in the *Broken Cross* by C. Savva (no. 20), Sergis Sergious's mono-chrome secular icon (no. 37), Spyros Demetriades' wry and luminous street scenes (no. 56), and the heroic stature of A. Asproftas's country women. *A Demonstration* by Takis Frangandes recalls the passionate demonstrations of college students in the late fifties, hurling bricks in angular explosions of Hellenic blue and white.

The twin bell towers of the Franciscan church of **Ayia Ekaterini** (St Catherine) overlook Oktovriou 28 street, 500m west of the municipal gardens. The three-arched colonnade is ornamented with the quartered Red Cross of the Catholic patriarch of Jerusalem, familiar from the Gothic heraldry that litters the island. The clean stone interior of the nave is complemented by the contemporary frescoes in the apse, which feature both eastern and western saints. This attempt to bridge the gap between the Catholic and Orthodox Churches is also reflected in the use of the Uniate rite. This has all but died out in its original homeland of Ukraine and Rumania, where the Uniate Church accepted the leadership of the papacy but maintained its ancient Byzantine liturgy.

Just west of St Catherine's the shore pavement widens into the 1km-long **seafront promenade**, with its fountains playing amid palms and ornamental beds. It is at its best in its illuminated state in the quiet of the evening, when the moon's reflection joins those of the freighters floating patiently offshore.

The turn-of-the-century harbour, now used only by fishing boats and the Cypriot navy, is at the western end of the promenade. The wide road runs between the harbour gates and the castle to form the heart of a small quarter of restaurants and cafés. Amongst the taverna signs is one advertising the **Reptile House**, a private snake museum run by a family from Pakistan (*open daily 9am–5pm; adm*) with two dozen cabinets displaying such international stars as the green mamba, puff adder and saharan kufi, as well as a few locals such as the very rare *mauremis caspica*, the stripe-necked terrapin.

West of the castle, on the way to the KEO winery, you cross over the usually dry riverbed of the Garyllis, overlooked by the Cami Djedid (the mosque on the corner of Ankara and Köpruluzate streets) and the small modern chapel of **Ayios Mamas** (on Ismet Paşa street). The latter houses two-thirds of an exquisite 17th-century iconostasis with its gilded flowers and scalloped niches picked out on a red and blue background. This gorgeous frame was originally carved for the church of Ayios Antonios, which was demolished at the turn of the century .

The Limassol Wineries

There is currently only one daily tour of the KEO works, leaving at 10am promptly every weekday morning. Visits at other times or to other wineries are only available by prior appointment.

To the west of Limassol, between the castle and the new harbour, is an industrial quarter dominated by Cyprus's four big drinks companies. Along, or just off, the inland Fragklinou Rousvelt (Franklin Roosevelt) avenue are the offices, warehouses and factories of KEO, ✆ (05) 362053; ETKO, ✆ (05) 373391; LOEL, ✆ (05) 369344; and SODAP, ✆ (05) 364605. These four Limassol-based companies have long moved on from being just wineries. They produce a full range of products: beer, cordials, brandies, spirits, concentrated fruit juice, ouzo and sherry—in fact whatever the export market requires. Though free sampling is always a welcome inducement, the actual tour of a modern winery, with its laboratories, hygienic stainless steel vats and quality-control staff, can shatter many a romantic illusion.

If you have time and sufficient interest you can arrange a visit to one of the growing bands of independent wineries that have been emerging since the 1980s. There are now over a dozen regional wineries scattered amongst the inland hills, whose premises, barrels and scale of operations remain satisfactorily picturesque and personal. Amongst these are Ayia Mavri at Kilani, ✆ (05) 432870; Laona at Arsos, ✆ (05) 243200; and Nicoliades at Anoyira, ✆ (05) 221709. In the Paphos District there is Pecris at 3 Hadjistephanou street in Yeroskipos, ✆ (06) 237971, and the Khrysorroyiatissa monastery outside Pano Panayia village.

Commandaria—the Oldest 'Appellation'

The southern slopes of the Troödos mountains have been covered in vineyards for thousands of years. The vine was dispersed from its homeland in the mountain valleys of the Caucasus and Central Asia, and the first grape pips appear to have arrived in Cyprus by about 3000 BC, viticulture and wine-making developing some time later. These vital techniques allowed for a new form of inebriation, and are remembered in the triumph of Dionysus, vividly expressed in a mosaic floor at Paphos. This triumph is both an analogy of spiritual liberation and a historical record of the replacement of beer by wine. Though the Greek myth reverses the direction of conquest, so that instead of conquering the West from the East, Dionysos appears to us like an early prototype of Alexander the Great. Euripides mentions the drinking of Cypriot *Nama* at the festival of Aphrodite, which, though now known as Commandaria, survives as the sacramental wine of the Cypriot Orthodox Church. It was traditionally made by selecting the juiciest, ripest grapes from the vineyards, which were then laid out in the sun to bake for 10 days. A rapid fermentation in open tanks produced a strong sweet wine, which was then mixed in with the dregs of a previous batch—known as the *mana*, or mother—in order to teach the new vintage through its long maturity. On the birth of a baby boy, a barrel was buried to be ready for drinking two or three decades later at his wedding.

It was a robust wine that survived, indeed even improved during transport, and locally produced cane sugar could be added to make it a commercial winner for the sweet tooth of the Middle Ages. The Crusading orders, who had a well-developed banking and communications network, also controlled most of the vineyards around Limassol. These were administered in the mid-13th century by the *Grande Commanderie of the Knights Hospitallers* at Kolossi castle. The wine was shipped out by Venetian and Genoese merchants as Commandaria, and the name soon caught on even amongst the Cypriots. The dangers of Mediterranean piracy and the imitations that were developed at Madeira, Marsala and Malaga conspired to cripple the European trade in the 16th century. It has survived our neglect and is still made in a dozen villages and by all four of the big companies. LOEL's Alasia Commandaria, ETKO's Grand Commandaria, KEO's St John Commanderie and SODAP's St Barnabas Commandaria (who also market Extra, the 12-year-old brand leader), can be tasted, tested against each other and at least one bottle brought back to be drunk as pudding wine or with a slice of cake during tea breaks.

Amathus

Open daily; adm free.

The site of this ancient city is 10km east from Limassol town centre along the beach strip coast road. If you are coming from Larnaca or Nicosia take the Moni turning and approach Amathus from the west.

Amathus has surprisingly little to show for all its fame and longevity, due to the enthusiastic stone robbing and quarrying that took place in the 19th century. Approach the site as much for an opportunity for a walk as for its scattered and slight archaeological remains. It is best appreciated when decked with spring flowers or in the diffused gentle light of the morning.

History

Amathus was established as a refuge of the indigenous islanders whose Bronze Age civilization was destroyed by the invasion of the Dorian Greeks in the Iron Age. The acropolis has been crowned by a citadel since 1000 BC, but it was the arrival of Phoenican traders, who had established a port here by 800 BC, that assured its development. The twin sanctuary to Aphrodite and Melkarth, the patron god of Phoenician Tyre, reflects the partnership between the indigenous Cypriots and its mercantile colony. The city was named after Amathus, the son of Melkarth (known by the Greeks as Hercules), but it also remained a bastion of the aboriginal culture of the island where the Eteo-Cypriot (True Cypriot) language and the Cypro-Syllabic alphabet proudly remained in use until the 3rd century BC.

It was one of the dozen city-kingdoms that feuded for a controlling influence over the island in the Classical period, whilst copper mines in the hinterland assured its continual prosperity. Politically, like many of the Phoenician-influenced cities, it favoured the Persian rather than the Greek alliance. Despite the valuable naval assistance that Androcles, the last king of Amathus, gave to Alexander the Great, the city fell under the heavy hand of Hellenistic rule at the end of the 4th century BC. Ptolemy I symbolically destroyed the old royal palace on the acropolis, and proscribed the use of the old language. However the same period was marked by the repair of the harbour and the construction of elegant Greek temples and baths. The city expanded to fill 3 sq km in the Roman period, and was made one of the three regional capitals of the island. St Tychonas, the second bishop of Amathus who was appointed by the great St Epiphanios of Salamis, apparently had a difficult job in this city, which was still largely pagan in the 4th century AD. The inland village of Ayios Tychon was named after the tomb-shrine established at the place he was killed. In the 7th century the flourishing and by now thoroughly Christian city was destroyed by raiding armies of Muslims. By the end of the 12th century it had achieved a partial revival, but was finally destroyed when that Royal gay English terrorist, Richard the Lionheart, sailed over the horizon.

The Site

From the coast road a driveway approaches the ruins of the **Hellenistic baths** of the lower city which has only recently been opened to the public. Beneath the shed a piece of Doric entablature has been reassembled, allowing visitors to envisage the colonnade that once encircled the *palaestra*. This open-air gymnasium is neatly marked out by the stumps of bases and a few re-erected columns. To the south a semicircular row of seats in the companiable public latrines can be recognized. To the north, much altered by later restorations and alterations, stands a series of half-excavated pools, fountains and cisterns, fed by a subterranean aqueduct which can be seen disappearing into the hillside.

To approach the *kastros*, the old walled acropolis area of the city, take the path above the entrance drive. This allows a good view over the excavated foundations of a **5th-century Byzantine church** standing just above the main road. The broad central nave can be clearly discerned, the narthex, or entrance lobby, to its west and two narrow aisles to the south. The thin outer passage, known as the exonarthex, was for the use of catechumens, trainee Christians who were permitted to observe but not attend the mystery of the Mass. St John the Almoner, who was born in Amathus in AD 609, must have attended services here. The son of Duke Epiphanios, the Byzantine governor of the island, he rose quickly within the Church hierarchy to become a famous patriarch of Alexandria. In the dark years of the Persian wars of the early 7th century the patriarch virtually assumed the governance of the Christian East, though he is chiefly remembered for his charity to the poor and the aid he offered to Palestinian refugees from Jerusalem. Centuries later he was chosen to be the patron of a military order of Catholic Crusader-monks, thereafter known as the Knights of St John of Jerusalem or the Hospitallers, who coincidentally were later to build a castle nearby at Kolossi.

Rough goat tracks climb up the **Kastros hill**, which is still guarded by a clearly exposed circuit of walls. On the easternmost spur of the summit of the hill, excavations have revealed the foundations of a triple-naved Byzantine chapel. Beside it are the foundations of the ancient temple precincts jointly dedicated to Aphrodite and Melkarth, as Hercules was first known by the Phoenicians of Tyre. The new blocks of stone belong to an ambitious and contentious scheme to 'restore' the shrine as an attraction. In the courtyard before the temple stood two great lustral stone jars, one of which was taken to decorate the Louvre in 1865. In its northeast angle a Hellenistic chapel to the female trinity of Isis, Aphrodite and Serapis was added. It was one of the island's three great sanctuaries, and as such was demolished by the Christians who then covered the sacred site with their own, now vanished, buildings.

As you walk back down towards the inviting sea-view terrace of the Old Limassol Bar, the western extent of the city is marked by a few tombs and lime kilns that can be seen in the valley beneath Kastros hill. Finish off by picking your way along the rock-cut beach below the coast road. Passing through the walls that extend down to the sea, you return back into the lower city, marked by a deep bank of debris and shards above the beach. Foundation footings and old drain courses emerge from the rock; now lapped by the sea, they reveal the shifting levels of inhabitation. The ancient port was due south of the area occupied by the small basilica and Hellenistic baths.

Ayios Yeoryios Alamanou and Governor's Beach

The monastery of Ayios Yeoryios Alamanou (St George of the Germans) is 19km east of Limassol off the Nicosia to Limassol motorway. It was founded in the 12th century, though both the church and the blue and white monastic range that encloses it are modern. A small shop and studio exhibits *ex voto* icons (priced from C£30–50), painted by a venerable monk who moved here from St Barnabas after the Turkish occupation of the North. The greater attraction is the rough track leading south from the monastery to a small quiet pebble beach overlooked by the seasonal Napaliakon taverna. Coastal tracks travelling both east and west give access to a series of rocky coves, natural sunbeds of polished white stone, quiet sea-lapped caves and odd patches of sand hidden behind promontories. A 4km walk to the east (also signposted off the main road) takes you to **Governor's beach**, a grey sand-filled cove overlooked by the terraces of four beach-front tavernas providing meals, drinks and umbrellas to a slightly alternative crowd.

Despite the grandeur of its name, it is an endearingly scruffy place that looks east to a horizon filled by the radar aerials, works and pier of Vasilikos. The white rocks of Cape Dolos to its west provide innumerable picnic sites and natural diving platforms. If you have fallen for the place, you can catch a daily bus in the summer leaving Limassol at 9.50am and returning at 4.30pm Alternatively, ask around the tavernas (such as Andreas or Melani) for local rooms to rent

Festivals

Limassol is famous for its Wine Festival in early September and its Carnival parades. *Apokreo*, or Carnival, is a 10-day period of parades, parties and picnics over the Meat and Cheese weeks, which ushers in the period of lenten fasting before Easter. The calendar of events changes slightly each season and the dates depend on the timing of Easter, though generally the festival is inaugurated with a parade along the seafront on the Thursday, when King Carnival is welcomed into town. That Sunday a big children's parade, largely confined to the Lanition stadium, is orchestrated and televized. Fancy-dress balls, choirs and traditional poetry recitals are held during the week, with the more musical and risqué serenaders' parade staged on Saturday. The grand parade takes place on Sunday, followed by Green Monday, a quiet national holiday of family picnics.

The Wine Festival usually occurs during the first fortnight of September. It was invented in the sixties as a promotional event by the four big wine companies, to coincide with the beginning of the grape harvest. A variety of parades, traditional dances, demonstrations of traditional wine-making techniques, open-air banquets, vineyard tours and tastings are staged.

In addition the Cyprus Tourism Organization and Limassol Municipality organize a summer season of cultural events, ✆ (05) 357745. The open-air theatres at Kourion and Limassol's muncipal gardens, the library on Ayiou Andreou street and the Pattiheion theatre on Ayias Zonis avenue are the principal venues for a varying festival of classical drama, music, dance and art exhibitions. On the last Sunday of every month there is a concert staged by visiting soloists at Dr Nefen Michaelides' music school, ✆ (05) 335795.

Shopping

A stroll along **Ayiou Andreou** (St Andrew) street takes you past the island's most distinctive concentration of **pottery** and **craft shops**. Thesis is on two floors of an attractive old balconied town house at 217 Ayiou Andreou street, ✆ 369765, and is stocked with arts, crafts and eccentricities from India and Indonesia, as well as **island-made candles** and **furniture**. Ermis pottery is run by Rena Aristou, who produces **terracotta** casts of heads and masks including Athena and the sphinx, priced from C£8–80. She also produces **traditional wall plates** with her distinctive twin bird design, painted either in blue and white or poly-chrome. The Moustakis pottery and Libra studios, at 332 Ayiou Andreou street, specializes in the creation and design of composite sets of *meze dishes*, as well as turning out moulded figures which are fired and painted in the studio. Skaraveos, at 236 Ayiou Andreou street, stocks a range of **imported glass** and **ceramic**, with a strong house taste for mottled light- and bright-blue glazes. Amongst the imported textiles is a clever adaptation of the traditional Coptic embroidery strip on white. Mermaid, at 277 Ayiou Andreou street, is run by Anne Marie Constantinou and her astrologist husband, Dinos. It is filled with hand-printed T-shirts, Matisse-like papier-mâché pots, paintings and ceramics. Alia arts and crafts shop has the best selection of **raffia** and **basketware** on the island, amongst its other stock of brass pots, pottery and local watercolours.

For **book binding** in textile or leather go to Lellos Constantinides at 211 Ayiou Andreou street; for **antiques** try Portobello Antiques further along the street at 294–6. Kyriakou is an **English-language bookshop** in a pedestrian lay-by behind the Bank of Cyprus. Al Khayyam, a **carpet** and **kilim** dealer, is in the Hawai Royal Gardens on the seafront promenade.

Moving out from the Ayiou Andreou street area there are three well-established **galleries** exhibiting the work of contemporary artists: Gallery Morfi is at 8 Othonos and Amalias street, Peter's Gallery is out on Ioannis Polemis street (north of the Leoforos Archiepiskopou Makariou III inner ring road) and Rogmi Gallery is on Mesolongiou street.

Religious Services

There are four large turn-of-the-century Orthodox churches where you can witness the intoxicating romance of an evening service. Listen to the liturgy amongst flickering candles at the Katholiki by the Bishopric, at the church of Ayia Napa on Ayiou Andreou street, at Ayios Antonios (St Anthony's) near the seafront, or at Ayia Triada (where there is a school of Byzantine music) by Linonos off Ayiou Andreou street. The Roman Catholic church of St Catherine, ✆ (05) 362926, is on the corner of Jerousalim street and the seafront Oktovriou 28 street. Weekday Mass is celebrated at 6.30pm; on Sunday services begin in Arabic at 8am, followed by the Uniate Greek rite at 9.30am and the English service at 6.30pm. There is also the Anglican church of St Barnabas at 177

Archiepiskopou Leontiou I street, ℭ (05) 362713, an Evangelical church at 10A Platonos street, ℭ (05) 342731, and the Armenian church of St George on Vasili Michailidi street.

Sports

Limassol has the largest choice of qualified **subaqua** schools. Shop around to check the rates and a sympathetic atmosphere. The Aquarius Diving School, ℭ (05) 326652, at the Aquarius Beach Hotel makes a good first call. They are a friendly, family-run outfit who provide detailed price lists and a tempting summary of their two dozen most popular diving spots. They also operate a morning 'Try Dive', a comparatively cheap introduction before committing yourself to the expense of a three-day training course. Amongst other schools and equipment rental agencies there is the PADI Dive Centre at the yacht marina gates, ℭ (05) 326576; Nikos in the centre of town at 47 Spyrou Araouzou street, ℭ (05) 372667, fax (05) 352870; and Mercury Divers by the old harbour.

Most of the large beach-front hotels have watersports centres offering water-skiing, paragliding, sailing, canoeing, pedaloes, sea scooters, sailboards, knee boards and self-drive speed boats. In the unlikely event that you have difficulty finding an establishment, go to the new yacht marina, below the Sheraton or Crest watersports centres at the Elias Beach Hotel.

Limassol also has the best opportunities for **riding**, with a choice of three centres all established in villages beyond the outer edge of the town. The Amathus School at Parekklisia is available in the evenings only, ℭ (05) 327302; then there is the Elias Horse-Riding Centre, ℭ (05) 329444 or 325000, also at Parekklisia (*open Tues–Sun 9am–12 noon and 2–4pm*); and Safari Don Christo at Moutayiaka village, ℭ (05) 325030.

Limassol also has one of the island's only two **bowling** alleys, at 4 Argyrokastrou street, ℭ (05) 370414. If you want to stray outside your hotel for **bridge** partners ring the Limassol Bridge Club, ℭ (05) 327231 or 331162. Badly behaved children can be bribed into a reasonable attitude by promises of frequent trips to the Disneyland **dodgems** and **water slide** beside the Romios Hotel Apartments on the beach strip.

Where to Stay on the Beach Strip

luxury

On the far eastern edge of the beach strip, between the Amathus ruins and the Moni power station, is a new development of plush hotels set in their own gardens, with all the pools, tennis courts, sports and choice of restaurants a hard-working executive could require. Even if you are not normally given to conspicuous consumerism, the **Elias**, ✆ (05) 325000, **Sheraton**, ✆ (05) 321100 and **Le Méridien**, ✆ (05) 327000, are all worth a visit. Dress up as smartly as the locals, and enjoy tea or cocktails as you gaze around. From the Sheraton you can walk down to the new yacht marina or merely sit and admire the lifts in the vast red marble foyer. Le Méridien has the best foyer art and afternoon teas. The **Churchill-Limassol**, at Oktovriou 28 street, PO Box 1626, ✆ (05) 324444, fax (05) 323494, is on the other side of the beach strip closer into town. It is older, noisier and has much less extensive grounds. A standard-sized double room in summer with a sea view in any of these hotels is currently around C£100 a night.

moderate

The **Aquarius Beach Hotel** is an exception amongst the many over-large and shoddy establishments on the beach strip. It is an intimate but moderately priced place beside the Pebble Beach restaurant, with only 36 bedrooms and its own beach front. It is halfway along the strip on Amathus avenue, just east of the turning inland to Moutayiaka village; PO Box 1748, ✆ (05) 322042, fax (05) 384801.

Where to Stay in Town

expensive

The **Curium Palace Hotel** is directly opposite the Archaeological Museum on Lordou Vyronos (Lord Byron) street, PO Box 48, ✆ (05) 363121. It has a comfortable, tranquil and established atmosphere with a number of well-furnished public rooms, including a turn-of-the-century games room complete with green baize card tables, lace dollies and aspidistra. The hotel is surrounded by a mature garden and has its own pool, bar and restaurant.

moderate

The **Continental** is a dignified three-storey hotel whose shuttered and balconied façade overlooks the seafront promenade at 137 Spyrou Araouzou street, ✆ (05) 362530. It is well positioned to explore Limassol, and even better placed for a leisurely view of the city's street life from the tree-shaded tables of the downstairs café-bar. Do not, however, be tempted into eating anything more complicated than a cake. The rooms are worn but spacious and the hotel is busy throughout the year, used as much by passing businessmen as tourists. If you are looking for something a bit snappier and more expensive try the nine-storey **Aquamarina**, with its plate-glass bedroom windows, 100m east at No. 139, ✆ (05) 374277.

The **Hellas Guest House** occupies a central position, and has a delightful baroque exterior set off by its light-blue shutters. The entrance is just behind the Cami Kebir (Grand Mosque) at 9 Zik Zak street, ✆ (05) 363841. Most rooms have three beds in them costing C£3 each. In the same price range but with the added attraction of its own low-life bar is the 20-bedroom **Metropole**, whose light-blue balcony overlooks Ayiou Andreou street, though the entrance is at 6 Iphigenias street, ✆ (05) 362330. The **Luxor Guest House** at 101 Ayiou Andreou street, ✆ (05) 362265, is even smaller, and manages the difficult art of being both shabby but clean and dead central but quiet.

Eating Out

expensive

The restaurant in **L'Onda Beach Hotel**, ✆ (05) 321821, is one of the beach strip's best-kept secrets, with live music at the bar and dignified four-course à la carte meals for around C£10 a head (not including wine). Reservations and dressing up advised. If you are into less formal but still gutsy tea and coffee breaks, head straight for the hotel's Swiss pâtisserie.

moderate

The **NOA Nautical Club** is on the town end of the beach strip, past the Churchill Hotel and on the edge of the Dhassoudi eucalyptus woods. It is well placed for a long lunch with its own sea frontage, summer watersports, a moderately priced fish *meze* and a popular Sunday buffet.

The **Seamen's Club** is just to the east of the old harbour on the edge of the seafront promenade. This trade-union-affiliated restaurant serves good traditional fare in an unpretentious dining hall or outside on its terrace.

The **Glaros** fish taverna is open in the evening to the west of the old harbour, and so will probably only appeal to those already staying in the centre of town. From the old harbour walk west for about 400m along Köprulozate street, then turn left at the mosque and wind down the dark and unpromising-looking Ayiou Antoniou cul-de-sac. The taverna, managed by M. Papaiacouou, is suspended on stilts above the water's edge and serves a memorably diverse fish *meze*, ✆ (05) 357046 for reservations. Other pleasantly unspoilt but more easily approachable tavernas on this side of town include **Ismet's** and the **Britannia** restaurant, the latter often featuring live music. They are neighbours, just past the KEO brewery on Fragklinou Rousvelt street.

Kyanhakth, ✆ (05) 322495, serves baskets of bread and prawns, its pleasantly dilapidated air and position overlooking the sea justifying the stiff prices.

Bars and Nightlife

The **Mairoza Hotel Apartments** mark the nucleus of the beach strip's neon-lit nightlife. The massed outdoor tables of the **Cheers** and **Unicorn** bars stand outside the **Whispers** and **Caribbean Disco**, with the **Hippodrome** and **Hollywood** cocktail bars ticked up in the pool-equipped Maniata Centre.

Moving west towards the town end of the beach strip, opposite the Dhassoudi eucalyptus woods, is **Koutouki**, and 100m further east, the pine- and vine-shaded **Dhelos**, two traditional tavernas offering live folk music from 8pm–midnight most nights.

In the town centre is the **Echo 75 Boite**, which serves as both an artists' café featuring live music and a centre for the island's green movement (irregular opening times). It is run by Gregoraides Goris (creator of the double portrait of Zeus-Jesus decorating the door), and is located at 259 Ayiou Andreou street, ✆ (05) 369595. Further west is the **Jazz Bar** (beside the Angels Pub) at 217 Ayiou Andreou street, featuring live music every Friday and Sunday night 9am–11pm (cover charge), ✆ (05) 342650. **Cuckoo's restaurant**, at 224 Ayiou Andreou street, has a snug little bar suitable for lunch-time drinkers.

Yermasoyia village provides an alternative out-of-town selection with the **Blue Lantern Bar** on Americana street, ✆ (05) 323181, and the **Flogera** taverna at 25 Patra street, ✆ (05) 325751, which boasts a singing architect. The **Sala Mandra Nightclub** in Polemidhia village, ✆ (05) 334200, is recommended for those interested in contemporary Cypriot music. It is a good taxi-ride away from the tourist strip, northwest of the motorway ring road.

Walks in the Limassol Foothills

Inland from Limassol the limestone foothills of the Troödos range rise up to dominate the northern horizon. This is the area of the **Krassochoria**, characterized by vineyards and villages, harmonious but dwindling settlements built from local stone. The houses, packed around a prominent parish church, are partly lime-washed, giving a bicolour flicker beneath the burnt-red of the terracotta-tiled roofs. Surrounding the villages are plantations of olive or carob; the broad, sunbaked terraces of the hills are filled with vineyards, whilst the craggier summits are lightly clad with scrub and outcrops of pine. It is an open, unspoilt area, offering innumerable walks along its undulating hills and dry valleys, but, despite the apparently timeless views, it is a region undergoing rapid change. It has only been intensively settled since the Byzantine period and since independence the young working population of the villages has been drawn to the higher wages, busier and more sophisticated lifestyle offered by the big coastal towns. The vineyards and fruit groves are still maintained, but, apart from during the summer holidays and the harvest, only foreigners and old people inhabit these handsome villages. There is a growing quietness spreading through the hills.

Omodhos, 35km northwest of Limassol along the E601, boasts an old winepress, exhibited in the restored house of Linos. The modern parish church in the centre of the village stands on the site of the famous Byzantine monastery of Timios Stavros. It contains a fragment of the True Cross, the hempen ropes that bound the hands of Jesus, and a reliquary containing St Philip's skull. A modest **Folk and Enosis Museum** is housed in the old outbuildings. The neighbouring villages (as the crow flies, rather than as the mountain roads wander) of **Kilani** and **Arsos** are traditional centres of the wine region, and have recently seen the establishment of several small wineries (*see* 'Limassol Wineries' p. 196).

Kellaki, a 15km drive north up the E109 from junction 21 of the Limassol–Nicosia motorway, is another possible destination, offering a taverna and a number of short walks in the surrounding hills. Three kilometres due east of the village a road leads up to the hamlet of **Prastio**, with its early 18th-century chapel of the Virgin. To the west a 5km track leads to the hamlet of **Klonari** with its frescoed chapel of Ayios Nikolaos (St Nicholas) before ending, about 2.5km later, at abandoned **Vikla**. About 700m south of Kellaki on the Limassol road is a turning west leading to a modern nunnery established beside the shrine of Panayia tou Glossa (The Virgin of Glossa)—known for her sympathy for the deaf and dumb. A *paniyiri* (festival) is held here in spring, usually the first weekend after Easter.

The hamlet of **Phasoula** is just 10km north of Limassol, approached from the western of the two Ayios Athanasios roundabouts on the motorway ring road. The medieval but much-restored church of Panayia Khryseleousa stands above the stream on the western edge of the village. Southwest of the village, towards the hill known as Kastron Ayiou Ioannou (the castle of St John), lie the tomb of St Rheginos, the 5th-century archbishop of Cyprus, and the site of an ancient temple to the Shining or Lustral Zeus, still in frequent use in the 6th century AD. It is a fascinating juxtaposition that hints at the complex and hidden continuities between the pagan and Christian eras.

The picturesque village of **Sotira**, 25km west of Limassol, is approached on a back road just after the village of Kandou on the E601. Follow the track leading up to the small 17th-century church of the Transfiguration, and about 100m beyond on the left, is a fine example of a *tripimena petres*, the standing stones that are unique to Cyprus. Little is known about these menhirs with a hole in the middle, and even their accepted dating to somewhere around the 1st century AD rests on quite slender evidence. Over 50 have been found on the island so far, and most have an east–west or north–south alignment and are reasonably close to some chapel—but then what isn't in Cyprus? They average just over six feet in height, and the holes are large enough to allow all but a large adult to squeeze through. The lack of polish or bruising would seem to discount any industrial application, whilst surviving folk customs recall a variety of uses—to cure barrenness in women, to cure sickness, to solemnize an engagement or to detect a cuckold whose metaphorical horns would presumably bar free passage.

If you continue along the same path for 200m there is a fork; turn right to reach some rock-cut tombs 100m further on, or left and left again to reach the round hilltop summit overlooking Sotira. Here there are traces of the excavations that unearthed a village of round huts from a pottery-using Neolithic village, dating from around 4500 BC.

Kolossi Castle

Open daily 7.30am–7.30pm; adm.

Kolossi is 16km west of Limassol. Rather than approaching it from the motorway, take the road leading past the docks, which sweeps through the Phassouri plantations, a romantic vista of citrus groves surrounded by cypresses.

An old cypress stands as a lone sentinel beside the sunbaked machicolated battlements of the 15th-century tower of Kolossi. Its dark stone halls now often ring with the excited cries of children who can, perhaps, more easily catch the echoes of its past; of its garrison of Crusader knights sworn to a life of military service, monkish celibacy and obedience. Against the background of these chivalric virtues come the sounds and smells of fortunes being made at their sugar mill.

The Knights of St John at Kolossi

The Lusignan king Hugh I bestowed the manor of Kolossi on the Knights of St John in 1210 as a princely act of piety. At first it was just one of their many valuable properties on the island, but with the fall of Acre in 1291 (the last Crusader-held port in Palestine), the two military Crusading orders moved their headquarters to Limassol. It was a curious decision, for the Knights Templars and the

Knights of St John had been fierce rivals for centuries, but by then, like many a stormy marriage, they derived such continual emotional satisfaction from their mutual hatred that they could not think of parting. In 1302 the Knights of St John decided to build Kolossi up into the chief fortress of the order, but typically were ousted from possession a few years later by an intrigue of the Templars. It was their last victory, for in 1307 the Templar order was accused of heresy by the king of France. After a seven-year investigation its tortured leaders were burnt, its knights incarcerated, its property confiscated and its charter revoked by the pope. The Knights of St John took quiet warning of the fickleness of princes, and in the midst of the affair moved to the island of Rhodes, which they ruled as lone sovereigns. Their scattered estates in Cyprus, richly augmented by the sequestered Templar possessions, were administered by a Grand Commander based in Kolossi, assisted by branch offices in Paphos and Gastria. The Grand Commander ran virtually a state within a state, controlling some 60 villages, a chain of urban priories, a string of castles and a permanent military force known as the Commanderie. The Knights shared in the devastation caused by the Genoese, and especially that of the Mameluke invasion of 1426. The old castle was shattered, to be replaced in 1454 by the present square keep which survives today in near-perfect condition.

The Site

The castle's entrance is on the first floor and is approached across a drawbridge overlooked by a projecting gallery. This is a feature of practically all late-medieval towers in Cyprus, as can be seen elsewhere at Pyla, Kiti and Alaminos. The interior has an impressive and earthquake-resistant solidity, the two upper storeys composed of pairs of vaulted chambers resting on a triple-bayed basement whose foundations are set directly into bedrock. Its internal air of functional military simplicity is broken only by the window seats and **carved fireplaces** whose rope-work motif will be familiar to those who have admired the Knights' possessions in Rhodes. On the south wall by the entrance are the remains of a **fresco** of the *Crucifixion*, with Christ flanked by the Virgin and St John the Baptist. The machicolations on the summit, many of which were restored during this century, frame a number of fine views. To the north you look over the village and the nearby 12th-century chapel of St Eustathios, and to the south, the Phassouri plantations and Salt Lake beyond.

Immediately around the castle are the ruins of the first fortress mixed in with later outbuildings. The well in the centre of the old east tower makes an easily recognizable feature amongst the confused walls.

High up on the east wall of the castle is a large cruciform marble panel decorated with four **coats of arms**. The central shield bears the 15th-century Royal Arms of the Lusignans divided into quarters: the original Lusignan lordship in Poitou is represented by the lion on bars (top right); the kingdom of Cyprus by a red lion on gold (bottom right); the kingdom of Armenia by a red lion on silver (bottom left); and the kingdom of Jerusalem by the distinctive Cross of Jerusalem (top left). It is flanked by the arms of Jean de Lastic and Jacques de Milli, a pair of Grand Masters of the Knights of St John in the middle of the 15th century, whilst below, and tactfully smaller, are the fleurs-de-lys of Louis de Magnac, the Grand Commander in Cyprus who directed the building of the castle.

To the east of the castle is an aqueduct formerly used to divert water from the Kouris river to power a **medieval sugar mill**. The millstone remains in place, though it has not mashed up sugar cane since the early 17th century, when cheap imports from the Caribbean islands ruined the market. The vaulted stone building below, resembling an empty chapel, was in fact a factory where the black treacle racked off from the mill was boiled up in cauldrons. When it was reduced to the required purity the molten sugar was poured into pots and shipped out by Italian merchants as either cones or loaves. It was a highly profitable and much-coveted business. In 1488 it passed from the Knights of St John into the hands of the Cornaro, a powerful Venetian family, and it is no surprise to find that Murad Paşa, the second Ottoman Governor of Cyprus, concerned himself with its repair.

Akrotiri Peninsula

The flat Akrotiri peninsula stretches southwest from Limassol. It is composed of a Salt Lake surrounded by marshland that is framed by a pair of beaches to west and east and a rocky headland to the south. The peninsula is part of the Akrotiri Sovereign Base, but apart from the southern headland, which is occupied by an RAF airfield and barracks, you are free to wander at will.

The **Salt Lake** expands and contracts with the seasons, but is usually at its most extensive during the winter, when thousands of ducks, coots and pink flamingoes migrate here. To observe the birds you will need a pair of powerful binoculars, as the fringe of lakeside marsh keeps all but the most ardent twitcher (ornithologist, usually English with tripod) at a fair distance. Unlike Larnaca's lagoon, it was never lined with evaporation pans for the extraction of salt. Here it was the marsh itself that was quarried. The mud and light gravel were components in the thick grey plaster used to seal the flat roofs of traditional houses, which because of its high salt content was virtually weed-proof. A channel, no longer visible, once pierced the eastern shore to allow for the movement and convenient trapping of mullet in the Venetian period. This may have been the remains of an ancient canal system through, or at least into, the lake, as there have been some chance discoveries of old trading objects embedded in the mud. There was good cause for a canal—the innocent-looking eastern shore of Akrotiri hides a series of offshore reefs, that, combined with prevailing westerly winds and an onshore swell, claim a steady toll of shipwrecks.

Leaving Limassol from the southwest turn south just after the hamlet of Asomatos, which is nestled in the neat cypress-enclosed citrus groves of the Phassouri plantations. The road skirts the western edge of the Salt Lake to reach the village of **Akrotiri**, lined with pubs serving thirsty British troops from the Akrotiri Sovereign Base.

The Monastery of Ayios Nikolaos ton Gaton

The Hi Spot bar-restaurant in Akrotiri has a good view over the lake from its terrace. Below it is the lakeside track leading to the monastery of Ayios Nikolaos ton Gaton (St Nicholas of the Cats). This monastery, celebrated for its feline staff, has recently been restored to a spiritual life by a community of nuns who are currently pushing ahead with a building programme. There are currently no organized visiting hours and access can periodically be limited, either by the surrounding citrus farm, a security alert or by the nuns themselves who get especially bored of visitors during the summer.

The monastery buildings date from around 1400. There is a finely carved Gothic arch above the north door of the church with a bug-eyed St Peter emerging from floral swirls on the right-hand finial. Carved into the lintel are four heraldic shields around a chipped central cross, considered to be those of a noble patron, and crude versions of the royal Lusignan arms. The north door, the unlucky entrance, is usually closed, with the south door providing access to the barrel-vaulted nave. The latter has a certain dignity, with its rough stone providing a strong contrast to the fine icons produced by the sisters of the convent. A portion of the old arcade survives in the cat-overrun courtyard, where a row of antique capitals have been reused low down in the row of Gothic pointed arches. These may have been recovered from an earlier structure, whose foundations amidst an old well can be traced just to the north of the church.

Two kilometres to the east of the monastery the track reaches the 6km-long strip of pale grey sand known as **Lady's Mile beach**. For once this is neither a reference to the Virgin nor the goddess—the beach is named after the favourite mare of a British polo-playing major who used to be seen galloping along this stretch of sand every morning. Stay on the southern two-thirds of the beach, for as you approach the Limassol docks the marshland deteriorates into a refuse tip.

Sacred Cats

Duke Calocer, the governor of Cyprus appointed by Constantine, the first Christian emperor, is the traditional founder of the monastery. He brought with him from Constantinople some cats given to him by St Helena, who soon increased their population several times over. Calocer, in his turn, bequeathed away his excess cats, and specified in the foundation charter that the monks of St Nicholas should support a feline population of at least 100. Their descendants were much commented on by medieval pilgrims, who observed the cats being summoned to their meals by the tolling of a bell, and then being duly discharged by another bell, whereupon they would devote themselves to an unceasing war against the many snakes of the peninsula.

It is a delightful story which runs concurrent with another tale that whispers of a much, much older sanctuary dedicated to Bastet, the Egyptian cat-headed goddess. Her worship originated in the third millenium BC, in a similar landscape in the Nile delta, but like many local deities she was associated with the central cycle of Osirian myths, where she is depicted as a cat defending Ra from the serpent Adep. Cats were treated as sacred at her temples, and their virility, strength and agility honoured. No one knows how long the lighthouse-guarded headland has been called Cape Gata, the Cape of Cats.

Episkopi Village

The village of Episkopi, 20km west of Limassol, sprawls over the west bank of the Kourion river. The busy coast road (one day to be superseded by a Paphos to Limassol motorway) cuts through the old Turkish quarter at the foot of the village. Turn uphill from the petrol station, left at the mosque and up about 700m to the cafés and inn in the village centre. From here, continue west for about 350m to reach the modern church of St Paraskevi, opposite which is the **Kourion Museum** (*open weekdays 8am–2pm; adm*), an attractive building with traditional Cypriot arches, a verandah and a central paved courtyard shaded by cypress trees. It was built by George McFadden of Pennsylvania University in the 1930s as a hospitable centre for archaeologists, and after he accidentally drowned off these shores two decades later the house was given to the nation by his family and turned into a local museum.

A visit to the left-hand gallery allows you to furnish the bare ruins of the city of Kourion (Curium). A worn marble statue of Bacchus stands one-legged and flirtatious, his ringletted hair and leopard skin casually exposing his beautiful bottom. He could have been illuminated by the soft glow of the six-wicked bronze lamp and surrounded by the sound of trickling water from a fountain decorated by the pair of marble lions. The headless statue of Hermes Pastor, dating from the 2nd century AD, is in the classic good-shepherd pose, later to be taken over by Christian iconography. The most vivid, if gruesome, exhibits are the bones and objects recovered from a farmhouse destroyed in an earthquake during the night of 21 July in AD 365. A 25-year-old man, wearing a Christian monogrammed ring, arches his body protectively around his 19-year-old wife, who herself seeks to shelter her 18-month-old baby. Rats chewed up the hands of both adults and crunched up the baby—one hopes after all three were securely dead.

The right-hand gallery is dominated by a collection of Archaic terracotta figurines from the temple of Apollo Hylates. The various male worshippers, knights and charioteers sport a dazzling variety of hats and caps. Other exhibits come from a group of nearby digs that provide an unrivalled, continuous record of prehistoric Cyprus. The Kourion valley contains a Neolithic settlement at Sotira, a Chalcolithic village at Erimi, Middle Bronze-Age Phaneromeni, the Late Bronze-Age city at Bamboula and the Iron-Age cemetery at Kaloriziki. All the more aesthetically pleasing objects, like the Mycenaean pots, gold amulets, fine moulded pottery and carved ivories, were discovered at Bamboula.

Serayia

The museum curator also possesses the keys to the Serayia (from the Turkish for palace) complex, which is 150m south of the garage and shop by the crossroads on the main road. Excavations have revealed an early Byzantine church with an opus sectile pavement incorporating pieces of carved marble rescued from the ruins of the old cathedral-basilica. The various outhouses were greatly extended in the Crusader period to form a substantial manor house with its own sugar mill.

The Serayia appears to be the seed from which Episkopi grew. Traditions recall that the village was founded after the destruction of Curium in the 7th century. The local bishop, the *episkipos*, gathered together the tattered survivors of urban civilization onto a nearby hill, which was thereafter known as Episkopi. Due to its sugar and banana plantations it grew into an important and wealthy medieval town. It passed, almost symbolically, from the possession of the Orthodox Church to the d'Ibelin and then the Cornaro, two western noble families who provided Cyprus with some of its near-legendary queens. The Cornaro were in constant dispute over water rights with the Knights of St John at Kolossi, a legal battle they eventually won, prior to losing their entire estates during the Ottoman conquest. Until the recent archaeological activity a Turkish family remained in occupation.

Ayios Ermoyenis and Kourion Beach

> *'Under the trees by Ayios Ermoyenis chapel I gave you golden trinkets and you were giving me kisses.'*

—from a local ballad

Just east of Episkopi village the taverna of Ayios Ermoyenis marks the turning down to Kourion beach. Beside the taverna a eucalyptus grove shades the small, ancient chapel of Ayios Hermogenos whose feast day is enthusiastically celebrated on 5 October—as well as some miraculous instances of healing, the saint is also watches over courting lovers. He was the saintly bishop of Samos, who was tortured and martyred in the last great persecution of Christians in the early 4th century. His shattered corpse was placed in a coffin and pushed out to sea to spare it any further indignities. It was washed ashore here, and his tomb was later decorated with *cippi*, the cylindrical gravestone-altars of the pagan world that once covered this area, one of the graveyards of ancient Curium. Up above the chapel some surviving tombs can be seen cut into the rock face.

The broad beach, dotted with summer tavernas such as the Kourion, Blue Beach and Sunshine, is overlooked by cliffs that once defined the ancient city of Curium. The shore is pebbly at the east end, gradually becoming greyish-yellow sand at the west end. Keep an eye out for weak swimmers, as there is a mild but persistent offshore undertow.

Kourion (Curium)

> *Open daily 7.30am–7.30pm; adm, with a separate ticket required for the temple of Apollo.*

Kourion, from the Greek, or Curium in Latin, is the third of Cyprus's three great archaeological sites, but takes first place for its superb position. It is perched alone on a dramatic escarpment with exhilirating, breezy views over its cliffs out to sea and over the flat Akrotiri peninsula. The site is approached from its west end, where there is a tourist café beside the entrance gate, useful for drinks and its loo, though a meal would be more enjoyable on the beach or at Ayios Ermoyenis.

History

Kourion was traditionally founded by Greek refugees from Argos. In the anarchy of the Iron Age a strong defensive site was required, and this natural escarpment defended by its 300 foot sea cliffs, proved secure. Quarrying into the sandstone soon improved the landward defences, and a warren of underground cellars and cisterns (there was no natural spring) helped secure the city against siege. It is first mentioned in an inscription from Nineveh, when King Erhaddon in 673 BC boastfully listed the 10 sub-kings subject to his orders, including Damasos of Kourion. The city preserved its independence by a quick-footed foreign policy, shifting its alliance between Amathus and Palea Paphos, its two powerful neighbours. This policy was at its most mercurial and ruthless during the Ionian revolt of 499 BC, when Kourion shifted sides in mid-battle, deserting the pro-Greek league and assuring the success of Persia. By such craft the city retained its independence, its distinct dialect and pre-alphabetic script until Ptolemy I annexed the whole island in 318 BC. It declined into a small provincial town, but remained stable and quietly prosperous with a population of under 20,000 during the calm centuries of Hellenistic and Roman rule.

The savage earthquake of AD 365, felt in Greece and Egypt, but with its epicentre only 30km away, graphically marked the transition from the pagan classical world to that of Christian Byzantium. Its central monuments like the theatre, stadium and temple of Apollo were left in ruin and later quarried to build the cathedral and At Meydani basilica. The 5th century witnessed a revival in the city's fortunes, boosted by its strong standing in the local church and accredited visits by St Barnabas, its own martyred bishop, St Philoneides (who in keeping with local spiritual traditions jumped over the cliff), and Zeno, the celebrated local bishop who made the Cypriot church independent from Antioch in AD 431. The Saracen invasions destroyed these promising developments, and by AD 670 the plundered city, with its drains and water supply ruined, was deserted. A few stones were symbolically moved from the cathedral altar, down to the new church built at Episkopi.

The Forum Area

The northern area of the city, to the left of the ticket office, has been under excavation since 1975, and is closed to the public. It is hoped this rich monumental area will soon be accessible, as it includes the remains of the forum, the town hall, baths, a *nympheum*, a number of private houses and some fine mosaics including the *Gladiators* and *Achilles*.

The Cathedral

The ruins of the cathedral, sometimes referred to as the basilica of Kourion, are just to the right of the entrance gate. It is one of the largest and oldest Christian sanctuaries on the island, built around AD 430, possibly by bishop Zeno. It was built on the cheap, on a plot of land in the city centre made available by the earthquake damage, carefully reusing the existing foundations and stone salvaged from nearby ruins. In common with much early Christian architecture it follows the plan of a Roman basilica, the apsidal law courts that were a familiar feature throughout the empire.

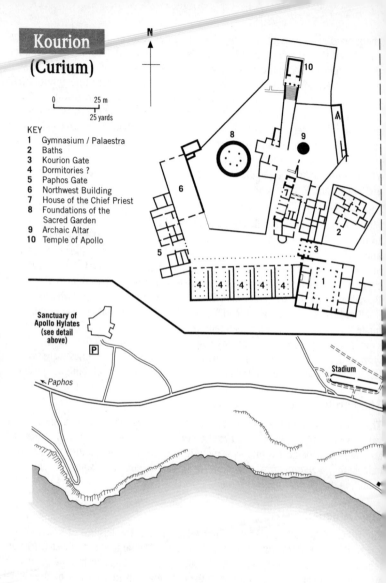

Kourion
(Curium)

0 ——— 25 m
0 ——— 25 yards

KEY
1 Gymnasium / Palaestra
2 Baths
3 Kourion Gate
4 Dormitories ?
5 Paphos Gate
6 Northwest Building
7 House of the Chief Priest
8 Foundations of the
  Sacred Garden
9 Archaic Altar
10 Temple of Apollo

Sanctuary of
Apollo Hylates
(see detail
above)

P

← Paphos

Stadium

0 ——— 500 metres
0 ——— 500 yards

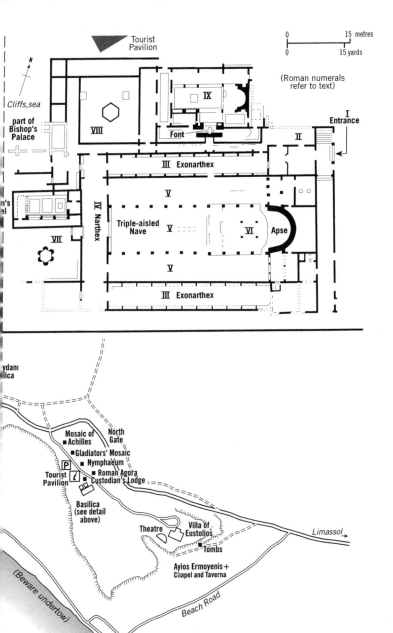

Tourist Pavilion

0   15 metres
0   15 yards

(Roman numerals refer to text)

N

Cliffs, sea

part of Bishop's Palace

IX

Font

I Entrance

II

VIII

III Exonarthex

IV Narthex

V

Triple-aisled Nave

V

VI

Apse

V

VII

III Exonarthex

ydanı lica

Mosaic of Achilles

North Gate

Gladiators' Mosaic

Nymphaeum

P

Roman Agora

Tourist Pavilion   i

Custodian's Lodge

Basilica (see detail above)

Theatre

Villa of Eustolios

Tombs

Limassol

Ayios Ermoyenis + Chapel and Taverna

(Beware undertow)

Beach Road

Enter through the pair of granite columns (**I**) and across an outer passageway into the first of a series of halls. On your right (**II**) is the old offertory chapel, once furnished with wall mosaics, where you would leave your donation before strolling down the exonarthex, a long bench-lined, paved passageway (**III**) to the narthex (**IV**), paved with black and white mosaic, with its three doors into the west end of the cathedral. This was as far as the catechumen, the unbaptized but aspiring Christian, could go, though a northern passageway decorated with a fine marble floor of golden hexagons and marble inlay allowed for a complete perambulation.

The interior of the church (**V**) was originally divided into three aisles by a pair of colonnades. Now there is but a single standing column to represent the two dozen columns that once stood here. Four small column bases (**VI**) mark the site of a canopy that shielded the altar in the early centuries before the development of the iconostasis screen. Behind it is the apse, much altered by the various doctrinal changes to the clerical seating arrangements, where the bishop would have sat on a throne surrounded by his staff, in the same position as a Roman judge sat in his basilica.

Due west of the narthex (**IV**) was a handsome domed room (**VII**), which still retains its hexagonal well. This unusual structure may have been incorporated from an earlier building. Beside it is a pink-paved chapel used by the deacon-accountants, as testified by its mosaic inscription: 'Vow, and pay to the Lord your God'. To the north of the narthex, beyond the two standing arches and directly below the tourist café, stands the ruins of the bishop's palace. This clutch of assorted offices and storerooms was arranged around a courtyard (**VIII**), with a hexagonal pool and one grey column still standing from its original colonnade. East of the courtyard is the baptistery chapel (**IX**), with much of its original mosaic floor still in place. The early church, which only numbered a small percentage of population amongst its congregations, put a great stress on adult baptism. To the south of the chapel lobby a ramped passage lead the catechumen up to the cruciform font, lined with grey marble, where the bishop presided over the three immersions. The newly baptized continued along the passage encircling the chapel, receiving a white robe and a candle before proceeding en masse to the cathedral for their first communion.

The Theatre

The existing theatre was built in 1963 over the foundations of the city's late Roman theatre. It is a partial job, lacking the colonnade that enclosed the curved auditorium of seats, the stage and the high, elaborate scene building that rose behind it. It is, however, useful for staging summer festivals of drama and the performance of classics like Shakespeare and the Greek tragedies. Every age has shaped the theatre to its use. It was first constructed in the 2nd century BC, in the

Greek fashion by cutting back into the hill. This was remodelled in honour of Nero, enlarged in the 2nd century AD, turned into a mini amphitheatre for the hunting of wild beasts a century later, then turned back into a theatre and improved. At its height it could seat 3500, a modest enough audience compared to Salamis's 15,000 (see p. 378, where productions and design are discussed at greater length). It was thrown into ruin by the 4th-century earthquake and never restored, which was just as well for within a few decades Theodosius had closed down all the theatres in the empire.

The Villa of Eustolios

Just uphill from the theatre the mosaic floors of an excavated villa can be admired from a wooden walkway. A succession of palaces have stood here, though the visible ruins date from a complete restoration by the builder Eustolios in the 5th century. The rooms are arranged around two courtyards with a bath annexe situated uphill so that its overflow could feed pools and water the gardens in the courtyards. After a century of private use it seems to have ended its days as a public guesthouse.

The house is approached across the western (servants') outer courtyard, with a welcoming inscription: 'Enter and good luck to the house' in a lobby overlooking the inner courtyard with its central pool and surrounding portico. Turn left up to the baths, where the hypocaust heating system is exposed beneath the floors of the hot rooms. Beside it is the long rectangular *frigidarium* with its geometric mosaic decoration containing a medallion of Ktisis, the founding spirit of the baths, admiring her measuring stick. The cold plunge bath with its stylized wave-pattern mosaic is one of the most successful designs, its geometric ripples awaking comparisons with Bradford's most famous artist.

The walkway then runs alongside the portico, which separates the inner courtyard from the large *triclinium*, a dining room with a crude and damaged mosaic. Just to the east is a small area of Hellenistic black and white pebble mosaics, where a wave pattern encloses a water jar and a mother dolphin with her pup. It is about 700 years older than the rest of the villa and is believed to be a *heroon*, a place to celebrate the feast of the dead and pour libations into the tomb below.

The southeast corner of the portico retains the most impressive mosaic, with birds and fish set into rectangular panels and four stylized crosses set in a dazzling variety of geometric designs and trick perspectives. The red-lettered inscriptions set a very pious tone that one hopes was ignored: 'The sisters' Reverence, Temperance and Obedience to the law tend this exedra and the fragrant hall' is matched by 'In place of big walls and solid iron, bright bronze and even adamant, this house has girt itself with the much venerated symbols of Christ'.

The Stadium and At Meydanı Basilica

Open all hours; adm free.

The stadium is 300m west of the Kourion entrance gate and just to the north of the coast road. It is the only one known in Cyprus, sited halfway between the city and the temple of Apollo. The massive stone structure, with its 6m-thick walls, was built in the middle of the 2nd century AD, the heyday of the Roman Empire when great rulers like Hadrian and Marcus Aurelius encouraged the spread of Greek customs. It was equipped with seven rows of seats, allowing a crowd of up to 6000 to watch naked athletes competing at games held in honour of the Gods, or the victories, jubilees and birthdays of the emperor. It is too narrow for chariot races ever to have been staged here. Foot races were run from the straight east end to the rounded west end and there would also have been boxing, wrestling, discus-throwing and javelin-hurling. The stadium remained in use for about two centuries, but was never restored after the earthquake of 365, when the increasingly Christian city had no time for body-proud athletics. This stance was upheld by a tradition that St Barnabas had been shocked by the nudity and merriment at the Curium stadium. The internal dimension of the track is exactly one stadium (184m), the Greek measure of length after which all our crowd enclosed playing fields and athletic tracks have been named.

Two hundred metres east of the stadium are the fenced-in ruins of the **At Meydanı basilica**, crowning the spur of a hill and enjoying fine views over the city and the Akrotiri peninsula. This is believed to have been the site of an ancient temple to Demeter, the goddess of the Earth, and her daughter Kore. In the late 5th century, when the Cypriot Church had just gained its independence from Antioch, it was replaced by a church which was perhaps dedicated to an early martyr. Much of the stonework, like the dark-grey twisted columns, would have been taken from disused Roman buildings, though the basket-shaped and increasingly stylized Byzantine capitals in the atrium would have been freshly carved. Here it stood conspicuously alone outside the city walls surrounded by a large graveyard, until it was destroyed by the Saracens in the 7th century.

The most noticeable feature of the ruins is the spacious and well-paved outer courtyard, the atrium, which probably survives from an earlier pre-Christian building. It is surrounded by column stumps that once supported a colonnade, and there was a cistern below it, fed by a sacred spring with a wide access well in the centre. The three-aisled church is comparatively small, the apse in the wider central nave preserving part of the *synthronon*, the semicircular bench for the clergy. On the north face of the church complex the original entrance gatehouse stood among the row of office buildings, the tomb-shrine and offertory chapel.

Open daily 7.30am–7.30pm; separate adm.

The ruins of the sanctuary of Apollo Hylates, God of the Woodland, are 1.5km west of the main Kourion (Curium) entrance, well marked off the coast road. The sacred precincts contain the ruins of over a dozen different buildings. There are slight traces of the earliest Archaic shrine, but practically all the existing stonework dates from an extensive Roman restoration that took place after an earthquake in AD 77. Three hundred years later another earthquake shattered the shrine to coincide with the triumph of Christianity in the 4th century.

He of the Woodland

The sanctuary of Apollo Hylates functioned as a pilgrimage centre for at least 1000 years and perhaps twice as long again if some fragments of Bronze-Age pottery are accepted as a temple deposit. Over 10,000 figurines have been discovered within the sanctuary whose changing symbolism chronicles the changes in patterns of belief. The temple at first honours a nameless young god who represents the cycle of annual death and rebirth, expressed by the miracle of the seasons and recurring crops. Like the corn that must be cut and the cattle that must be slaughtered, the god is honoured, cared for and loved, but ultimately doomed. The bull and the snake, seen entwined in some early figurines, were his symbols. The bull is one of the most heroically male of creatures, and is still bred for a form of sacrifice in Spain and Portugal. The snake remains feared and mysterious in dreams as well as life, and had an obvious symbolism in Cyprus with its hibernation in winter and reappearance each spring. Strabo (a geographer writing in the 1st century BC) tells the story of the sacred altar of Apollo Hylates, those who dared to touch it being flung from the cliffs of Kourion. This is but a half-remembered tale of the sacrifices of young men, who were dedicated at the shrine before being offered to the great goddess. Throughout the Aegean world there are numerous sacred precipices where men and male beasts were driven over cliffs into the sea as a gift to the goddess. In the 6th century BC offerings to the deity of the shrine were still being addressed as just 'to the god'. The first association with the wild, woodland aspect of the for ever young Apollo comes 100 years later. There are many aspects of this most Greek of gods, and the local Cypriot worshippers were keen to stress the essential continuity of their particular deity by defining him as 'our' or 'winepress' before settling on 'Hylates' which can be translated as 'He of the Woodland'. This name became established in the 3rd century BC when the religious life came under the control of the Hellenistic governor.

The Sanctuary

The sanctuary site is approached through a pleasant garden, an echo of the inviolate woodland filled with wild deer that surrounded the temple in antiquity. Turn right off the path to enter the gym, or **palaestra** where the stumps of a columns mark out the former colonnade. This open-air courtyard, dating from the 1st century AD, was surrounded by substantial rooms which would have looked onto scenes of wrestling and routine exercise. The corrugated barn, due north, protects the **baths** which are still in the process of being excavated, though they are easily recognizable from the brick stacks of the hypocaust heating system.

The pilgrim, now thoroughly cleansed, would then enter the sanctuary proper. Ascend up the 14 steps, between the gym and baths, which would originally have been framed by the arch of the **Kourion gate**. Ahead are five standing columns, the remains of a colonnade which once lined the barrack-like row of five dormitories. Each of these five buildings is fitted with a bench-lined walkway encircling a raised platform lined with Doric columns. Their exact function is not known, but they are presumed to be dormitories where the pilgrims slept, possibly amongst votive statues, carved oracles and arcane symbols. Here, having spent a day in contemplation at the sanctuary, they would await a visit from Apollo in their dreams. At the west end of this row of dormitories is the remains of the **Paphos gate**, flanked by outbuildings and cellars with patches of pebble mosaic from the Hellenistic era. To the north of the Paphos gate, a flight of steps leads up to the **northwest building**, a large rectangular structure fitted with a double walkway. This is likely to have been an additional, somewhat showy new dormitory, built on the orders of the emperor Augustus who liked to be seen to be pious.

From here, the neatly paved Sacred Way leads directly to the temple of Apollo. On your right stood the temple kitchens, the treasury and the apartment of the chief priest. To your left a fence protects the curious **circular monument** with the bedrock pitted with holes. This was the sacred garden of the god, which may have looked like a Chinese garden with a formal arrangement of charismatic stones around the carefully tended, gnarled, ancient trunks of myrtle and laurel. A reservoir beside the outer wall watered the enclosed area from underground pipes. One can imagine this lush oasis filled with dancers performing ritual circular movements, as depicted in contemporary terracotta figurines.

To your right just before the temple a pile of stones in an open space is all that remains of the 7th-century BC **Archaic altar**—the one which you were hurled off the Kourion cliffs for touching. Excavations revealed a vast quantity of votive figurines buried during different eras when the sanctuary was periodically cleared of its surplus statuettes. These statues were left by worshippers as a reminder to the god of their supplication mumbled as they offered the right back leg of a young male goat to the fire that raged in the circular altar.

The partly restored **temple**, approached up a flight of 12 stairs, dominates the site. Though Roman, it seems from its simple, slender proportions and curious Archaic capitals that it was a deliberate reconstruction of an older shrine. A worshipper, having made a sacrifice, would approach the temple and make an obeisance in the *pronaos*, or columned porch. The *cella*, the actual interior of a temple containing a cult statue of the deity, would never usually be entered, though the college of priests would assemble here to partake of a sacred meal on great festivals. Fragments of *pithoi*, or large jars, were found during excavations, which may have been filled with gifts of olive oil to feed flickering lamps. The temple was not destroyed by fanatical monks, but by the great earthquake of AD 365; the neat rows of stone lay undisturbed until reassembled in 1979.

Beaches and Walks around Pissouri

As you move west from Kourion the coast road passes through Episkopi cantonment, a veritable suburban Camberley in the sun, which could not be anything other than part of the British Sovereign Base at Akrotiri. The road sweeps past the polo fields of Happy Valley, watered by garrison sewage and the Symvoulos stream.

About 5km later look out for the turning to Evdhimou Bay, approached along a 3km track that twists through vineyards to a sand- and pebble-strewn beach. A single pier and a pair of ruinous mud and stone warehouses stand beside the seasonal Kyrenia bar-restaurant. A headland to the east separates you from another beach guarded by the palm-shaded Melanda taverna with its wooden balcony. Fortunately this tranquil stretch of coast should remain safe from development, as it is situated within the territory of the British base.

West along the main road there are separate turnings south to the mini-resort of **Pissouri** village and (4km on) Pissouri Bay. The roadstead beside the latter turning, halfway between Limassol and Paphos, is a long-established truck stop with a number of pleasantly rough cafés, bars, tavernas and fresh fruit stalls. The village itself is perched on a rocky summit with views east over the surrounding vineyards. It has one registered hotel, supplemented by a growing number of rooms to rent, a few tavernas, a bakery and a car and bicycle hire agency called Xantris Nicos, © (05) 21010. Despite the recent growth of villa apartments, it has maintained a calm, alternative character to the beach resorts.

If you are setting out from Pissouri village, you can either walk 4km southeast to Pissouri Bay (passing a few rock tombs on the way), or alternatively go north for 1.5km, across the main road and along the back road to Aekhtora, to reach the smoke-blackened murals in Ayios Yeoryios. There is also a road due south to the aerial and the view from the summit of Cape Aspros, and some lesser tracks west which could take you all the way down to the Petra tou Romiou beaches 6km away, or, more modestly, to the Prophitis Elias chapel with some remaining murals beside a rock-cut tomb overlooking the main road 1.5km west of Pissouri. Another destination for a stroll are the ruins of Ayios Mavrikos, 3km due west of the village, which was converted from the Catholic chapel of St Maurice.

Those with transport or firm thighs could venture further afield to the villages north of the coast road, which formed a small Turkish enclave until 1974, and are now inhabited by Greek refugees from the North. There is the empty monastery of Timios Stavros (Holy Cross), a late Byzantine church built beside the foundations of a small Roman temple. It is 5km north of Evdhimiou and outside Anoyira village, from which half a dozen tracks spread out into an untouched hinterland. Plataniskia hamlet, about 6km west of Evdhimiou, offers a stroll north, uphill to the ruins of Ayios Yeoryios on the way to the view from the Laona hilltop, with a chance to continue northwest for 2km to the ruins of Ayios Kassianos.

Where to Stay in Pissouri and Pissouri Bay

Pissouri is well placed to be the central base of a Cypriot holiday. It offers unspoilt beaches, the quiet of the surrounding countryside and easy access to some of the island's principal sites. The **Bunch of Grapes Inn** is tucked away in the centre of **Pissouri village**, at the end of a paper chase of discreet signs. It has an English pub-like bar and restaurant, and 10 rooms arranged around a courtyard with a 300-year-old mulberry tree in the middle. It is moderately priced and deservedly popular, but is often booked up by guests returning season after season. It is usually possible to find a cheaper room from neighbours, such as the **Victoria** on the corner, who have become used to picking up the surplus trade. For reservations at the Bunch of Grapes Inn, write PO Box 41, Pissouri or ✆ (05) 221275.

Pissouri Bay can be approached on a tarmac road directly from the main coast road or on a 4km dusty track leading down from the village. It is still a quiet place despite the villas that have grown up around the beach tavernas and the lone **Columbia Pissouri Beach Hotel**, ✆ (05) 221201, fax (05) 221505. It is large and expensive (currently around C£60 for a double), but, unlike so many similar places in Cyprus, worth it. It has recently undergone a complete refit, though the marble lobby still takes second place to the hotel's large pool, its terraced views toward the pale cliffs of Cape Aspro and its virtually private beach. If you are looking for something cheaper ask around the tavernas for flats to rent, and especially at the Pialio Limaniki supermarket.

Eating Out in Pissouri

Though there are now four restaurants in the centre of Pissouri village, including the **Lemon Tree** fish taverna, those down at the bay still win with their combination of beach sounds, wading opportunities and cheap traditional *meze* meals. Choose between the **Monte**, the **Vineleaf** and **Yialos taverna** with its sea view, ✆ (05) 221747.

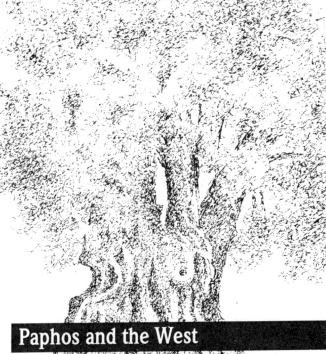

Paphos and the West

And I would be there;
Love hath an island,
And nurtureth there
For men the delights
The beguilers of care,
Cyprus, Love's island;
And I would be there.
At Paphos she dwelleth,
And I would be there.
At Paphos she dwelleth
And wealth cometh there

Euripides, *The Bacchae*

Paphos, the westernmost district of Cyprus, has always been the
most undeveloped area of the island. It was known for its wild
coast, its vineyards stretching over empty limestone hills, the
forested mountainous hinterland and the rustic, almost Arcadian
life of its villages and hamlets. Much of this idyllic landscape
remains; however Paphos has always enjoyed much greater fame
as the birthplace of Aphrodite, goddess of love and sexual desire.
The sanctuary sites of her once all-powerful cult stand to the east
of Paphos, though they are now little more than place names upon
which to hang anecdotes. Despite the efforts of archaeologists and
poets, only the faintest last ripples of the goddess can be found in
this Christian land.

Immense changes in the last two decades have transformed the
sleepy, somewhat backward provincial town of Paphos into a full-
blown tourist resort. It is now inaccurate to describe the coast
around Paphos as anything other than a package resort dominated
by over-large hotels, discotheques, fast-food counters, milling
groups of day-glo tourists and roads spattered with hired cars. It is
a surprising place to site a beach resort, in view of the astonishingly small area of beach—and one hopes the lack of this basic
amenity will act as a natural break to future investors.

Fortunately the upper town of Paphos, whilst benefiting from the
prosperity and hidden conveniences of this boom, remains almost
untouched by this transition. It is easy to stay in a calm environment in Paphos, and to eat in local tavernas all within easy reach

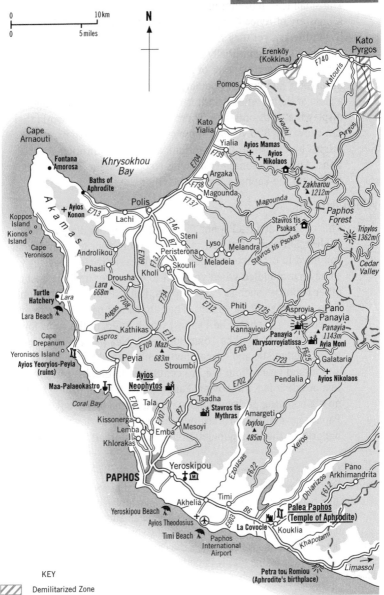

0   10 km
0   5 miles

N

KEY

▨ Demilitarized Zone

Cape Arnaouti

Fontana Amorosa

Baths of Aphrodite

Khrysokhou Bay

Ayios Konon

Koppos Island

Kionos Island

Cape Yeronisos

A k a m a s

Turtle Hatchery

Lara

Lara Beach

Cape Drepanum

Yeronisos Island

Ayios Yeoryios-Peyia (ruins)

Maa-Palaeokastro

Coral Bay

Kato Yialia

Pomos

Erenköy (Kokkina)

Kato Pyrgos

Yialia

Ayios Mamas

Ayios Nikolaos

Argaka

Magounda

Zakharou 1212m

Paphos Forest

Polis

Lachi

F713

F704

F739

F738

F737

Steni

F746

Peristerona

B7

Androlikou

F709

Phasli

Drousha

Lara 668m

F108

F734

Kholi

Skoulli

Meladeia

Lyso

Melandra

Stavros tis Psokas

Tripylos 1362m

Cedar Valley

Magounda

Phiti

F725

Asproyia

Pano Panayia

Panayia 1143m

Panayia Khrysorroyiatissa

Ayia Moni

Galataria

Ayios Nikolaos

Kathikas

E711

Mazi 683m

E709

Peyia

Stroumbi

Kannaviou

E703

F723

Pendalia

Ayios Neophytos

Tala

B7

Tsadha

Stavros tis Mythras

Kissonerga

Lemba

Emba

Mesoyi

Amargeti

Axylou 485m

Khlorakas

Yeroskipou

PAPHOS

Akhelia

Timi

Yeroskipou Beach

Ayios Theodosius

Timi Beach

Paphos International Airport

La Covocle

Kouklia

Palea Paphos (Temple of Aphrodite)

Petra tou Romiou (Aphrodite's birthplace)

Khapotami

Limassol

Pano Arkhimandrita

E701

E702

F622

E703

Xeros

Dhiarizos

F612

B6

E503

F622

Aspros

Aspros

Livadhi

Katouris

F740

Pyrgos

Stavros tis Psokas

of the astonishing collection of treasures in and around the town. The small icon museum in Paphos and the frescoes at the Monastery of Ayios Neophytos contain but a fraction of the island's Byzantine art, yet they make the best introduction into this entrancing though initially alien world. The cyclamen-flecked subterranean architecture of the Hellenistic Tombs of the Kings is deservedly famous and popular, while the mosaics of Paphos are in a class of their own. Again it is not the quantity but the range on display that is astonishing. There are few places in the world that can show you 800 years of mosaics, from their pebble-pavement origins to the fringes of Byzantium, and all in their original positions. After the Monastery of Ayios Neophytos, the Tombs of the Kings and the Paphos Mosaics the other sites pale.

Which Paphos?

This chapter divides Paphos town and the surrounding district of Paphos, between what you can walk to from your hotel and what you need to organize transport for. This easy division may get somewhat muddled when you start to encounter a whole host of other Paphoses such as Palea Paphos, Ktima Paphos, Pano Paphos, Kato Paphos and Nea Paphos. They are all just parts of the town, except Palea Paphos (Old Paphos) which refers to the ruins found in the village of Kouklia 16km southeast. Nea (New) Paphos refers to the Hellenistic and Roman town which stood by the harbour for a thousand years, from the 3rd century BC to the 7th century AD. Just beside it is Kato (Lower) Paphos, once a small fishing village, now a booming package-holiday resort. Ktima or Pano (Upper) Paphos covers the northern two-thirds of Paphos town, where the majority of the local population lives undisturbed by tourists.

History

Paphos was founded right at the end of the Classical period, when Cyprus was still divided between a dozen city states who manipulated the rivalry between Persia and Greece, the great powers of the day, in an attempt to achieve mastery of the whole island. The westernmost part of Cyprus, removed from the trade routes, the corn-growing plain and the rich copper mines, was on the edge of this struggle, dominated by the locally important cities of Marion (modern Polis) and Palea Paphos (modern Kouklia).

At the end of the 4th century King Nicocles of Palea Paphos, of the Kinyrad dynasty of high priests of Aphrodite, ruled over a conservative, inward-looking city which still used the native Cypriot syllabary rather than switch over to the Greek alphabet.

King Nicocles' New City

Halfway through his reign, King Nicocles decided to move his capital from its position beside the ancient temple of Aphrodite and plant it on an empty coastal promontary. This dramatic move to Nea Paphos marked a complete reversal in policy, as Nicocles attempted to catch up with the political realities brought on by Alexander the Great's astonishing conquests. He had missed the opportunity to assist the young Alexander on his way up, but did his level best to win the approval of his successors. He rushed through an intensive Hellenization of his state, founding temples to very Greek deities, such as Zeus and Artemis of Argos, and laying out Nea Paphos in the approved Greek fashion with a rigid grid of streets, a commercial sector around the agora square, a theatre and a new harbour. He even introduced the worship of the Greek goddess Hera to Palea Paphos where she received equal honours with Aphrodite.

The succession struggle after the death of Alexander in 323 BC divided the dozen cities of Cyprus into two factions. Nicocles risked everything in his determined support of Menelaus, brother of Alexander's general Ptolemy. By 312 BC the rival city of Marion had been razed to the ground, and its captive population transferred to Paphos. Nicocles did not enjoy his enhanced regional status for long, for within two years the city was placed under direct Ptolemaic rule. Nicocles was faced with a trumped-up treason charge but he and his entire family escaped the dishonour of a public execution by turning their palace into a royal funeral pyre.

The Capital of the Ptolemies

Of all their Cypriot possessions, the Ptolemies favoured Nea Paphos as it was the closest port to Alexandria, the new capital they constructed to rule over Egypt. It was also well sited as a naval base from which to patrol the western approaches to Cyprus from rival Greek states. Even more important to the Ptolemies were the local supplies of timber for shipbuilding, for it was one of the established inbalances of ancient history that Egypt produced no wood but required a strong navy for its defence. During the struggle for the mastery of Cyprus against Antigonus, 306–294 BC, (a rival heir of Alexander) it served as the principal Ptolemaic base. When the Ptolemies finally triumphed in 294 BC, the city's star was set firmly in the ascendant, and it soon replaced Salamis as the administrative capital of the island. The Strategos, the governor, resided here with his staff of specialist officials seconded from Alexandria. He was invariably a well-connected member of the royal family, such as Ptolemy II Philadelphos (285–246 BC), who when he ascended the throne founded two new towns in the Paphos area, both named Arsinoe in memory of his beloved sister-wife. The first Arsinoe was built over the ruins of Marion, the other less successful foundation stood halfway between Paphos and Palea Paphos.

Rome and St Paul

Apart from the suicide of the last Ptolemaic ruler, the transformation to Roman rule in 58 BC was almost entirely a peaceful process. Paphos remained the seat of the island's governor and reaped the benefit of the mythical relationship between the goddess Aphrodite (Venus) and both Aeneas, the founder of the city of Rome, and Julius Caesar, the founder of the Roman Empire. As proof of its new popularity the Emperor Augustus even paid for the city's restoration after heavy earthquake damage in 15 BC, and it became known as the sacred metropolis of all the towns in Cyprus.

The missionary journey of St Paul and St Barnabas into Cyprus (chronicled in the *Acts of the Apostles*, chapter 13, verses 4–13) was directed at well-established Jewish communities within the island. At Paphos they were summoned to speak before the Proconsul Sergius Paulus who kept a Jewish sorcerer, a certain Bar-Jesus also known as Elymas, at his court. The session dissolved into violent disagreement but St Paul triumphed when he called upon the power of the Holy Spirit to blind Elymas for a season. The astonished governor, when he saw this done, believed. Despite this prestigious convert, no cult centres have been identified from before the 4th century, when the Emperor Constantine legalized and supported Christianity. A bishop from Paphos is recorded in the lists of the first Church Council at Nicaea in 325, after which work must have begun on Paphos' church of Khrysopolitissa.

An Elegant Backwater, AD 365–653

Paphos was destroyed in AD 365 by a savage earthquake whose epicentre was only a few miles south of the traditional birthplace of Aphrodite. In the aftermath of the earthquake destruction the government was moved to Salamis-Constatantia and Paphos, deprived of its reason for existence, declined into an elegant provincial backwater. A number of gracious villas were gradually restored to use, their privileged inhabitants maintaining a preference for the old pagan deities, deep into the 6th century of the Christian era. In AD 653 a Saracen army raided and destroyed the city. In the succeeding centuries the harbour gradually silted up: the area around it degenerated into a malarial marsh and the surviving inhabitants retreated out of harm's way into the hills.

An Outpost in the West

After the Byzantine Empire reconquered the island for Christianity in the 10th century, a fortified outpost was established here. On the strength of its connection with St Paul, the coastal hamlet of Kato Paphos rose around the ancient ruins to become an established stop on the medieval pilgrimage route to Jerusalem. However, from the surviving reports, it seems to have been a big disappointment to most of its visitors, many of whom were stricken with marsh fevers.

Paphos was certainly considered obscure enough to be used as one of the places of exile by the Catholic Crusaders, who banished one of the four Orthodox bishops here in the early 13th century. His palace, chapel and *ktima* (private estate) became the nucleus of the inland village of Pano (Upper) or Ktima Paphos. In the late 14th century the Lusignan king, James I, during his long campaign against the Genoese, fortified the harbour with a castle whose foundations are partly embedded within the existing 16th century Ottoman artillery fort. Deep into the present century Paphos, sometimes referred to as Baffo, remained a sleepy pair of villages pursuing the traditional occupations of fishing and farming, with a small export trade in carob pods, dried fruit and products of the vine. It, like Polis and many of the poorer villages in the Akamas, had a markedly Turkish-Cypriot identity prior to the division of the island in 1974 when the Turks fled to northern Cyprus. In the last decade Paphos has been transformed by the rapid growth of the tourist industry, and its undreamed of opportunities for work and wealth. It now has a resident population of around 25,000, which is back up to Roman levels.

Getting Around
By Air

Paphos Airport, ✆ (06) 236833, is 14km southeast of Paphos town. It has been in operation since 1984 and remains a secondary landing strip to the main airport at Larnaca, most of its business being charter planes during the summer months. There are also a number of scheduled flights, once or twice a week, to Paphos from Heathrow and Gatwick, plus (summer only) Manchester by Cyprus Airways, ✆ (06) 236814. No buses or service taxis work from the airport. Regular taxis into town cost around C£4.

By Bus

The **Costas Bus Company**, at 2B Nikodimou Mylona street, ✆ (06) 241717, provides a direct service to Limassol and on to Nicosia, leaving at 8 and 9 on Mon, Tues, Thur and Fri but just at 8 on Wed and Sat. They charge C£1 for a single fare to Limassol, C£2 to Nicosia. More regular services to Limassol are run by the Kemek Bus Company, ✆ (06) 234255.

They leave from Leontiou street at 6.30, 8.30, 10, 12.30, 3 and 5.30, Mon–Sat. Buses to Polis are run by the **Amoroza Bus Company**, ✆ (06) 236740, leaving from near the main square at No. 79 Leoforos Evagora Pallikaridi at 6.45am and then hourly from 9 to 6 or 7 in summer, Mon–Sat. The bus for Kato Pyrgos leaves behind the Zena Cinema, off Evagora Pallikaridi avenue, at around 12.30 and 4 Mon–Fri, but just at 12.30 on Sat. The bus back from Kato Pyrgos departs at 5pm. Village buses to Kouklia and Peyia operate weekdays from the Pervola car park, off Nikodimou Mylona street. Departures to Kouklia are at 7 and 4, to Peyia at 10 and 4.

Within the conurbation of Paphos, bus no. 2 serves Yeriskopou village and leaves every half hour between 8am and 7pm from the main post office on Nikodimou Mylona street. Travel is easy along the coast road northwest to Coral Bay or southeast to Yeroskipou beach, the two extremities of current hotel and villa development. **Alepa Ltd**, ✆ (06) 234410, runs daily buses from Pervola car park every half hour between 8.30 and 5.30, for 30c. Out of season, between November and mid May, the service is reduced to 9, 10 and 11 departures to Coral Bay, returning at 3 and 5.

By Taxi

Taxi rides to Limassol cost around C£13, C£15 to Kato Pyrgos and C£7 to Polis, Pano Panayia or Palea Paphos. Shorter trips, to Coral Bay, Ayios Neophytos, Yeroskipos cost between C£3–5.

By service taxi: Service taxis only operate the run from Paphos to Limassol. If you want to go to Larnaca or Nicosia you must first go to Limassol, though you can speed up the process by being booked into a seat on the next leg of the journey by radio telephone. All four operators are near the main square on Pallikaridi avenue. **Karydas** and **Kyriakos** are at no. 9E, ✆ (06) 232459 and (06) 233181, **Kypros** and **Nea Paphos** are at no. 21, ✆ (06) 232376 and (06) 332132.

Car Hire

A. Petsas, ✆ (06) 245146 and **Budget**, ✆ (06) 245146, both operate rental counters at the airport. In town the majority of car hire firms are found along Apostolou Pavlou (St Paul's) avenue. **Avis** is at no. 87, ✆ (06) 243231, **Hertz** at no. 54a, ✆ (06) 233985, **Thames** at no. 62, ✆ (06) 244569. Budget and A. Petsas, which are both under the same management, are at no. 86, ✆ (06) 235522. For terms and prices, *see* Larnaca.

Tourist Information

There is a **tourist information office** at Paphos Airport, ✆ (06) 236833, and in Ktima Paphos at 3 Gladstone street, ✆ (06) 232841.

The main **post office** is on Nikodimou Mylona street, ✆ (06) 232241 though it may increasingly be superseded by the new district post office on the corner of Venizelou avenue and Constantinou XII street. For international **telephone** calls use the booths outside the telecommunications building east of the municipal gardens on Yeoryiou Griva Digeni avenue.

Banks and **travel agents** are found along Makariou III avenue and along Apostolou Pavlou (St Paul's) avenue,. the road down to the harbour.

Details of **chemists** on all night duty are published in the weekly *Cyprus Mail* or can be obtained by dialling 192.

For the **police** ✆ (06) 232352, for the general **hospital** ✆ (06) 232364, all emergency services can also be reached by dialling 199.

Festivals

Local *paniyiria* include: St Neophytus' Day celebrated at his monastery, 9km outside Paphos, on 24 and 25 January and again on 13 and 14 September; the Presentation in the Temple, on 1 and 2 February at the monastery of Khrysorroyiatissa; St Constantine and St Helen's Day, on 22 and 23 April, at Tsadha village; St Peter and St Paul's Day, on the 28 and 29 June, in Paphos; St Paraskevi's Day, on 25 and 26 July, at Yeroskipou; the Dormition of the Virgin, on 14 and 15 August, at the monastery of Khrysorroyiatissa; and St Demetrius's Day, on 25 and 26 October, at Phiti village.

August is the month of village harvest festivals celebrated with agricultural tableaux, dances, folk music and family picnics that provide a good opportunity for local families and émigrés to reunite.

In addition to the *paniyiria,* Paphos has its own celebrations organised by the municipality, ✆ (06) 232804. The *Anthistiria* is a flower festival that is usually held in mid-May. It recalls the celebrations held in honour of Dionysus with its procession of children and flower-decked chariots. In the same month, there is also a May Fair held in the municipal gardens. In the summer months performances of ancient Greek drama take place on one or two evenings, in the restored theatre of Nea Paphos. Dates are flexible as this is usually part of an island-wide tour by visiting theatre companies. In August the *Pampaphia* is staged, a festival of folk songs, dancing and craft exhibitions is staged; followed by the smaller Palouze (grape sweet) festival held before the floodlit fort in early September. Later in the month the grape harvest and the new vintage of wine is honoured with the Paphos Bacchus Festival whose dates may coincide with the more serious lectures and exhibitions of the Paphos Cultural Festival.

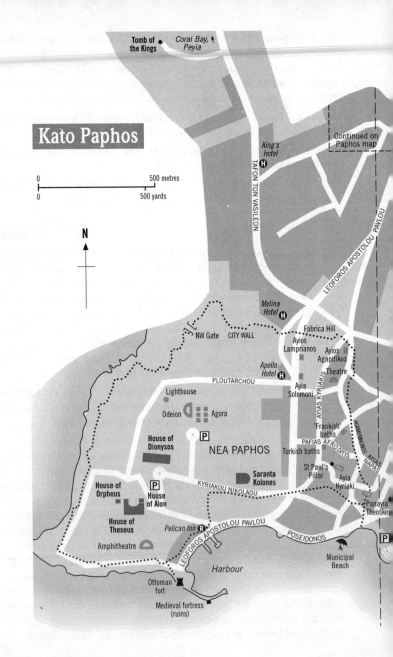

Kato Paphos

Tomb of the Kings

Coral Bay, Peyia

0   500 metres
0   500 yards

N

Continued on Paphos map

King's Hotel (H)

TAFON TON VASILEON

Melina Hotel (H)

NW Gate   CITY WALL

Fabrica Hill

Ayios Lamprianos

Ayios Agapitikos

LEOFOROS APOSTOLOU PAVLOU

Apollo Hotel (H)

Theatre

PLOUTARCHOU

Ayia Solomoni

AYIAS KYRIAKIS

Lighthouse

Odeion   Agora

'Frankish' baths

House of Dionysos

(P)

PAFIAS AFRODITIS

NEA PAPHOS

Turkish baths

AGAMEMNONOS

AYIAS NAPAS

St Paul's Pillar

Ayia Kyriaki

House of Orpheus

(P)

House of Aion

Saranta Kolones

KYRIAKOU NIKOLAOU

House of Theseus

Panayia Theoskepasti

Amphitheatre

LEOFOROS APOSTOLOU PAVLOU

POSEIDONOS

(P)

Pelican Inn (R)

Municipal Beach

Harbour

Ottoman fort

Medieval fortress (ruins)

The Tombs of the Kings

Open every day 7.30am–7.30pm, closing at dusk in the winter; adm.

The entrance to the Tombs of the Kings complex is found on the west side of Taphon Ton Vasilieos (Tomb of the Kings) Road, some 2km north of Nea Paphos. Throughout the winter and spring the hard-carved stone is flecked with wild flowers, particularly cyclamen, which hang in supremely decorative sprays over every tomb. It is by far the most impressive relic from the Hellenistic period to have survived on the island, but also gives pleasure way beyond its cultural importance. Groups of children and amateur scholars can be seen sharing the same joys of personal exploration, clattering down rock-cut stairways, tiptoeing into dark tomb recesses and blinking up to stare at carved details of Doric architecture bathed in bright sunshine. The more substantial tombs are numbered, from one to eight, but one or two may be closed for archaeological work.

The tombs, though of unmistakable opulence, were not built for kngs. They were carved out of the living stone for the ruling families of Macedonian officials who governed Cyprus from Paphos. They were appointed by the monarchs of the Lapid dynasty (that confusion of incestous Ptolemies and Cleopatras), who after the death of Alexander the Great, ruled over Egypt. The *strategos*, the governor, was usually a close member of the royal family on a short tour of duty who is unlikely to have died or been buried here. The tombs were constructed for career officials and their families, men like the Grammateis, the principal naval and military commanders, or the Antistrategos who controlled all the copper mines. There are a large number of small slots for infants who were often buried inside a terracota pipe.

The sunken stairway to the subterranean chamber, the dromos, is a well-established and ancient feature of Cypriot tomb architecture. The open subterranean courtyard with its ring of columns was an entirely new feature that deliberately imitated the houses of the living. It is Egyptian in inspiration, though the architecture and details are all Greek (particularly tombs No. 3 and No. 4, the stars of the show at the end of the tarmac drive). The peristyle courtyards are ringed with Doric columns that seem to support the immaculately carved entablatures.

The detailed carving causes you to forget that this is carved bedrock, seeing instead a metamophosed building. It would, however, have originally looked much more distinctive, as it was all plastered and painted (like all Greek temples) with a bright colour scheme of blue, red and yellow. Off the courtyards are chambers lined with rectangular openings, known as *loculus*, for individual burials.

Of the 18 burials discovered, only two were found undisturbed by generations of tomb robbers. They were accompanied by two amphorae from Rhodes, an unguentarium, and were covered in a linen cloth and a gold myrtle wreath worn on the brow. A number of carved fragments suggest that the courtyards may have been decorated with statues as well as with tubular *cippus* and more elaborate altar niches, like the 'horns of consecration' in tomb No. 2. They acted as both a headstone and an offertory table, where family picnicing parties could pour libations and place prized portions of the meals that were consumed at the death anniversaries of their ancestors and at the communal festivals of the dead. This air of domesticity is further enhanced by the careful carving of a number of replica wooden doors. Most of the large tombs have their own well, which may have supported a garden or been used for ritual washing.

They continued in use, with the addition of various chambers, until the destruction of the city in the 7th century AD, though this area was just a small portion of the necropolis that spread all around the city. There is plenty of evidence of medieval occupation, both by squatters who added a chimney at No. 3, and workmen who used No. 5 as a pottery. The Gothic arch inserted into No. 6 reveals its use as a chapel.

The Paphos Mosaics

Open 7.30am–7.30pm every day in summer, closing at dusk in the winter; adm.

The mosaics are housed in three separate shelters, at the end of Kyriakou Nikolaou road which branches west from Apostolou Pavlou (St Paul's) avenue 250m before the harbour.

The Paphos mosaics are one of the aesthetic highlights of a trip to Cyprus. They have an intriguing variety of style and quality, varying from clumsy reproductions to the sublime artistry of the Theseus medallion. They also range astonishingly in age, encompassing almost the whole artistic history of mosaic design, from its pebble origins in the 3rd century BC to the thresholds of Christian Byzantium. They are also quite new to our world. Though a British military trench-digging detachment first stumbled across them in 1945, they have all been excavated, and stabilized in their original positions for public viewing, since Independence.

House of Dionysos

The mosaics in this house reveal a fascinating, almost discordant range of tastes, as if the owner had flicked through a pattern book and jabbed his pudgy finger as he asked for one of each. There is a plain black and white floor as used in Roman Italy, a vivid hunting scene that could have come from North Africa, various set mythological pieces of Hellenistic taste, a geometric design from the northwest of the Roman Empire and various patterns that remind you of a knotted eastern carpet. The house was built at the end of the 2nd century, and is one of a succession of spacious mansions that occupied this block of the city centre. It stood in active use for 200 years before it was destroyed in the 4th-century earthquake. Its walls have long since been quarried for building stone but plaster fragments indicate that it was once furnished with frescoes as rich as the surviving mosaics.

The **Scylla mosaic** (1), made from black and white beach pebbles, is the oldest in Cyprus. This delightful depiction of 'greedy Scylla, girdled with savage dogs barking in the depths of the Sicilian waves' and holding on to the mast of a ship that she has sunk, was laid in the 4th century BC. The technique, known as *chochlaki*, survives on the Dodecanese islands, though there they use long as opposed to round pebbles.

Narcissus (2) is here depicted with a wispy youthful moustache, cocked back hat and blond sun-streaked hair (blonds appear always to have been considered attractive) in an attitude of doomed youth, worthy of an anti-heroin poster. He is admiring himself in the pool, 'at once seeking and sought, himself kindling the flame with which he burned'.

The **Four Seasons** (3) mosaic covered the floor of the entrance chamber and bears the welcoming inscriptions 'You Too' and 'Rejoice'. The floor was badly damaged and has been clumsily repaired. The seasons surround a youthful deity who personifies the life of the year. Spring holds a shepherd's crook, Summer sprouts corn and holds a sickle, Autumn grasps a knife and Winter, depicted with a shaggy beard, pours rainwater from a jar. The dentil frieze around the panels was probably designed to imitate the cornice of the ceiling, though not all the perspectives work.

The **peacock** (4) mosaic achieves a special dominance in this room, by its use of glittering blue and green glass. It is a fine example of an *emblamata*, a small detailed composition made from small pieces, known as *opus tessalatum*, set into a simpler floor, in this case of six white petals formed from normal-sized *tesserae*.

This room (5) is covered with a colourful but discordant array of geometric panels, like a sampler piece of embroidery, that is known as '**Décor multiple**'. It was a style that was very popular in the northwest of the Roman Empire, in France and Britain, but rare outside this region.

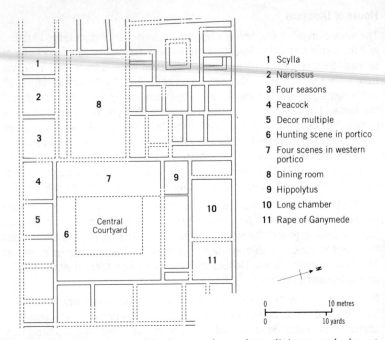

1 Scylla
2 Narcissus
3 Four seasons
4 Peacock
5 Decor multiple
6 Hunting scene in portico
7 Four scenes in western portico
8 Dining room
9 Hippolytus
10 Long chamber
11 Rape of Ganymede

This brings us to the centre of the house, where a large dining room looks out over a central courtyard which was once surrounded by a covered portico. On three sides of this shaded cloister (6) is a **hunting scene**, a well-established theme for this part of the house. The North African provinces of the Roman Empire specialized in producing these vivid scenes drawn from life not mythology. Against stylized rocks and trees, hounds drive wild animals towards various waiting huntsmen. The moufflon depicted here are part of the island fauna, though the presence of big cats like the tiger, leopard and lion, place it firmly outside the experience of an island where the largest predator is the fox. In the eastern portico there is a grisly scene of a leopard holding the head of a donkey in its jaws while the body bleeds before a city gate.

The **western portico** (7) of this colonade is filled with four mythological panels. The panel of *Pyramus and Thisbe*, prototypes of the doomed-lover story more familiar as Romeo and Juliet, is a bit misleading. Thisbe looks distraught enough as a wild beast tears her lovers clothes but Pyramus has been depicted as a river god, probably a clumsy confusion with the river Pyramos in neighbouring Cilicia. The longer panel tells the story of Icarios, who was told the secret of wine making by Dionysos. The god is here depicted drinking with the nymph Akme, a cellar maid who watched over wine until it reached its perfection—its Akme—of age.

The stout, balding figure of Icarios with his wine-skin-laden ox cart was torn apart by a pair of shepherds in their first frenzy of drunkenness. It was an obvious moral for both guests and hosts as they stepped into the dining room. The next panel shows Neptune advancing to ravish a compliant Amymone, who receives a gift of a spring for her drought-stricken homeland in return. Beside it the naked figure of Apollo advances towards Daphne, who is saved from rape by being turned into a laurel tree by her father, the river god Peneius.

The large **dining room** (8) is set off centre to give a pleasantly asymetric view of the courtyard. The outer fringe, of red swastikas on white, acted as a passage for servants; while the plain U-shaped geometric mosaic would have been covered with couches and tables during a meal. The dinner party would then be free to overlook the playful, half-fantasy scene of the grape harvest, its vines filled with winged erotes, peacocks, birds, rabbits and a snake. The entrance panel depicts the *Triumph of Dionysos* who is seen returning from the East in his leopard-drawn chariot, led by Silenus, whilst Pan abuses the Indian captives. These are both well-developed and popular themes which have been found throughout the Hellenistic East. On either side of the long Dionysos panel are two military figures with horses, the heavenly twins Castor and Pollux, also known as the Dioscouroi. They are totemic figures of good fortune that came to be especially associated with the Roman army and its emperors, which kept barbarians away from the civilized urban world of the Mediterranean. Their images and attributes were assimilated in the Christian era by St George, who is depicted with a white horse, and St Demetrius with a brown one.

Here in room (9) there is another mythological scene concerned with whether to love or to love not. Fair headed **Hippolytus**, depicted naked but for some hunting boots and a precarious cloak, looks in disgust at the amorous advances of his step-mother and strides off, accompanied by a faithful hound, for the celibate joys of the chase.

The floor of the **long chamber** (10) is filled with a geometric mosaic, where intertwined circles of rope and wave motifs frame a number of symbolic objects such as a plate of three pomegranates and a silver mirror and jug. This is a good example of the style that appealed to the Early Church and was used to decorate the floors of the nearby basilica.

The **Rape of Ganymede** (11) is a dramatic scene, but has been clumsily composed for the size of this room, for the eagle's wings have had to be cropped to fit the frame. Zeus, metamorphosed into an eagle, digs his claws into the thighs of the beautiful shepherd boy Ganymede, who has symbolically dropped his red shield to hug the neck of his predator. As well as expressing the joys of homosexual sex, it can also be read in a spiritual context, signifying the apotheosis of a mortal into heaven or the possession of a worshipper by the spirit of his divinity.

The House of Aion

The present building, 200m south of the House of Dionysos, encloses three rooms of a substantial villa discovered in 1983. The two geometric mosaics represent the porch and entrance lobby which preceded the main hall, whose floor is covered with an elaborate scheme of five mythological scenes. The mood here is quite different from the jocular, almost brash eclecticism of the House of Dionysos. The mosaics were laid in the middle of the 4th century AD when the great Christian basilica stood just half a mile to the east. Clearly the old religion was still alive and well in this period, openly supported by rich and influential patrons. The mosaics all feature a scene from classical mythology, not as some dead piece of decoration, but with an elegant, if somewhat scholarly, serenity that shows the pagan gods as a living religion. The apparently random selection of mythological incidents in the mosaics hides a single theme. For in this period the familiar old deities could all be worshipped under a single embodiment, as the syncretic cults of the Unconquered Sun, Thrice Great Hermes and Dionysos all taught.

The top right-hand panel shows the haloed Baby Dionysos in the lap of an imperious Hermes, as he is presented to his tutor and the various nymphs of Mount Nysa. The two nymphs preparing to wash the baby are strikingly similar to the ladies in an Orthodox nativity scene. Hermes is surrounded by three personifications: Theogonia (Birth of God), Nectar and Ambrosia, the foods of immortality.

To the left is a scene of divine conception, where Leda, Queen of Sparta, is bathing and about to be approached by Zeus in the guise of a swan. A wild-looking man from the hills adds a Dionysiac touch to the magical proceedings.

The large but damaged central panel shows the divine selection of the most beautiful woman in the world. To the left Cassiopeia, Queen of Ethopia, wins the contest against Thetis, Doris and Galatea, three Nereides who display their charms in their marine element. In the clouds above them, and applauding the choice, are Zeus and Athena.

The bottom right-hand panel illustrates the terrible punishment awaiting those mortals who lack a proper sense of humility towards the gods. The satyr Marsyas, having failed in a musical contest against Apollo, is shown being dragged away to be hung by the heels and skinned alive. Apollo looks fetching in the dress of a kithara (lyre) player, whilst beside him is the stern, female personification of wrong-thinking. Enough remains of the bottom panel, including Silenus and a pair of centaurs, to know that it shows the triumphal procession of Dionysos.

Villa of Theseus

Behind the house of Aion a wooden walkway crosses a public street of Nea Paphos to enter the House of Theseus. Though there is no definite proof, this large spacious mansion is almost certain to have been the administrative palace of the Roman governor, and the probable site of St Paul's famous interview. The wooden walkway crosses over the remains of a wide vestibule, a double-colonnaded pool and alongside a long portico to reach the **Theseus** mosaic. This is the finest mosaic on the island, created around the end of the 3rd century for the floor of a privy audience chamber once lined with marble. From its curved apsidal wall one can imagine the seated governor looking down the length of the portico to observe the respectful advance of his secretary escorting a nervous supplicant.

The central medallion is dominated by the heroic figure of Theseus, whose victory over the (damaged) minotaur has all the assurance of pre-ordained fate. The deity of the Labyrinth reels back to one side while Ariadne and the goddess of Crete look on with impassive approval. If you look carefully at the faces of Theseus and Crete you will notice a difference from the others, for they were remade at the end of the 4th century. Their eyes in particular have the dark, accentuated stare that is the hallmark of Byzantine art, while the earlier Hellenistic faces, for all the technical proficiency of colour and shading, have a comparatively inanimate look. Around the medallion spin decorative geometrical bands, the labyrinth, and through them you can trace Ariadne's thread which Theseus trailed behind him. The triangular corners of the room are filled with a sumptuous design, a floral weave of lilies set against purple stone.

The baths, sheltered by a large hangar are not yet open, so follow the walkway to the comparatively crude mosaic of the **First Bath of Achilles**, sited in the middle of the south wing of the palace. It is one of four scenes from the life of Achilles that originally filled the centre of this room. It was made in the middle of the 5th century AD, and provides more evidence of the slow transformation from the pagan world to that of the Christian Empire of Byzantium. The similarity of this scene (repeated elsewhere in the life-cycles of Dionysos and Alexander the Great) with the Nativity of Christ is quite apparent. A reclining Thetis and King Peleus watch the ritual bathing of their baby in the miraculous waters of the Styx, which bring invulnerability, watched by the three Fates: Clotho with her spindle, Lachesis with her diptych (two-leaved notebook) and Atropos with her open scroll. For all its clumsy artistry and pagan theme, the heavy eyes, the full frontal portrayal of faces and the stiff hieratic pose of the fully-clothed figures place it firmly in the world of Byzantium.

The **House of Orpheus** stands to the west of the Villa of Theseus. Excavations have not been completed but three fine late 2nd century mosaics will soon, no doubt, be opened to the public. They show Orpheus surrounded by a dozen beasts, an Amazon with her chestnut horse set against a blue background and Hercules about to wrestle with the Nemean lion. The mosaics in the House of Four Seasons which were only unearthed in 1992 will in due course be opened to the public.

Kato (Lower) Paphos and the ruins of Nea Paphos

The lesser sites of the ancient city of Nea Paphos are all of secondary interest. They are also open to the wind and can be admired without paying for any admission tickets, at any time you feel like a walk. They are described in a rough progression, from the north end of Nea Paphos to the harbour in the south.

Fabrica Hill and the Catacombs of Ayia Solomoni

Fabrica Hill is 1.5km downhill from Ktima Paphos, on the east side of Apostolou Pavlou (St Paul's) Avenue. This distinctive outcrop of rock, dusted with pockets of cyclamen, was first quarried for building stone at the end of the 4th century. The unweathered core was valued most, so many of the quarry workings take the shape of an internal pyramid, buttressed by supporting columns of rock with a sky hole at the apex through which the cut stone blocks were hauled to the surface. Many of these chambers were then put to a second use as burial places, and gradually furnished with a number of individual tomb chambers cut into the rock wall. Some of the richer tombs were embellished with frescoes, a habit that was absorbed into the Christian tradition. Only the names of the caves, Ayios Lambrianos, Ayios Misitikos (the patron saint of hatred), the hermits Ayios Themistos and Ayios Agapetos, remain to enliven them.

The catacombs of **Ayia Solomoni** have more substantial relics, and remain a place of active devotion. The entrance is well advertised by a tree whose branches are heavy with handkerchiefs tied up with seven knots. Steps cut into the rock lead down into the chapel, where blackened fragments of fresco remain in the sanctuary apse. A further flight of steps leads down to a Stygian holy well, whose water used to be efficacious against malaria.

Tying prayer rags around a tree associated with the shrine of a patron saint is an ancient tradition, found in Islamic, Christian and Buddhist cultures. It is like leaving one of the votive figurines seen in every archaeological collection in Cyprus, a reminder to the spiritual power of the original supplication. The prayer is repeated as it waves in the wind, and some believe that only when it disintegrates or flaps free is it answered.

The Catacombs of Ayia Solomoni are named after a Jewish heroine, from the pre-Christian era, who was brought into the fold of popular Christianity by an early canonisation. She and her seven sons, the Seven Maccabee brothers, were tortured and slain for refusing to eat pork on the order of Antioch Epiphanes, the Seleucid ruler of Palestine. Antioch Epiphanes briefly seized control of Cyprus from the Ptolemies in 164 BC, so it is possible that these Jewish martyrs could have executed and buried at Paphos. The seven Maccabee brothers are often confused with the seven sleepers of Ephesus, whose traditional burial place (amongst many other rival sites) is elsewhere on the island, at Hazreti Omer Tekkesi outside Kyrenia.

On the west side of the road stands a conical hill, visible in the gap between the Apollon and Melina hotels. Its summit has been excavated to reveal the low walls of the city's **North gate** which provides a good vantage point to survey the traces of Nea Paphos to the south. Nearby are a pair of connected underground rock-cut chambers, the so-called 'guards' camp', which may be the basement sanctuary of a Hellenistic temple. From literary sources we know of at least four temples, to Zeus, Artemis, Aphrodite and Apollo Hylates, of which only the last has been positively identified.

Returning to Fabrica Hill, there are some rock-cut foundations to be found on its eastern side (but do keep a watch out for quarry holes). This is thought to belong to the chapel of Ayios Agapitikos, the patron saint of love whose shrine replaced an earlier one to Aphrodite. On the southeastern face of the hill an archaeological trench has exposed seven rows of stone seats from a **Hellenistic theatre**.

'Frankish' and Turkish Baths

Halfway between this theatre and Ayia Kyriaki are the so-called Frankish baths, on the corner of Minoos and Agamemnos streets, whose three domes, surrounded by a scattering of foundations, make an attractive group. You can explore the empty chambers lit by bolts of sunlight streaming in through the lightholes pierced in the domes. There is of course nothing Frankish about them. They, like another similar complex on the corner of Ayias Kyriakis Asandrou and Paphias Aphroditis streets, are monuments of the Ottoman era and Paphos's old Turkish-Cypriot population.

The latter group, known as the Turkish Baths, are an even more romantic picture of decay with the roots of a dead tree gripped into the larger of the two domes. (To experience a working Turkish bath you will have to travel to Northern Cyprus and visit the Büyük Hammam in Northern Nicosia.) Just the other side of Paphias Aphroditis street from the baths stand the damaged remains of a mosque built on the foundations of a medieval chapel. Beside it is an elegant, though sadly empty, public fountain, made from classical capitals with an old sarcophagus for its bow.

Ayia Kyriaki, 'St Paul's Pillar' and other Christian relics

The small 15th-century church of Ayia Kyriaki (also known as Panayia Khrysopolitissa, 'Our Lady of the Golden City') is approached from the north down a turning off Paphias Aphroditis street. The large sunken area that almost surrounds it is an archaeological enclosure with no public access.

Soon after Christianity had become legitimate, and fashionable, due to the patronage of the Emperor Constantine in the 4th century, a gorgeous **seven-aisled**

cathedral was built here to the plan of a Roman basilica. The granite and marble columns capped with corinthian capitals and the red, black and white geometric designs of the mosaic floor belong to this early church, which had an enclosed fountain courtyard to its west and a bishop's palace to the south. It was repaired in the 6th century, its seven aisles reduced to five and its triple apse converted into a single one. Thus it stood for a 100 years before it was totally destroyed by Saracen raiders in AD 653, as recorded by some Arabic graffiti scratched on to one of the pillars. A pair of Orthodox chapels were built over the ruins in the 10th century, when the island returned to Christian rule under the Byzantine Empire. One was converted by the Catholics into the simple, vaulted chapel of Ayia Kyriaki around 1500. It has a dignified stone interior with a dome and incorporates several of the original columns within its structure. The church was given to the Greek Orthodox Church after the Ottoman conquest of 1571 but, by a happy and recent ecumenical decision of the bishop of Paphos, it is now used by both the Roman Catholic and Anglican communities for their services.

In the late 13th century the **Franciscans** built a church just to the northwest of the ruins, perhaps encouraged by the tradition that St Francis passed through the island in 1219. The plan of this three-aisled church can be easily traced round the two rows of yellow stone, the Gothic piers and doorway with its zigzag Romanesque moulding. There are two other Gothic buildings recorded by medieval travellers: an Augustinian chapel and a cathedral. Only the southwestern corner of the latter can be identified, on the west side of Apostolou Pavlou (St Paul's Avenue) about 150m south of the Apollon Hotel.

The actual site of **St Paul's Pillar**, where the apostle was said to have been tied and lashed 39 times, is open to a lively variety of local opinions. Nor is there even any mention of this whipping in the Acts of the Apostles. The incident at Caesarea, where Paul was about to be 'examined by scourging', but was unbound by an apologetic chief captain after he revealed himself a free-born Roman citizen, seems to have been the source of this confused tradition. However the story has an enduring resilience and the broken free standing column to the west of the basilica was long venerated as St Paul's Pillar. An additional degree of credulity is required to associate part of a 4th-century ruin with an event set three hundred years before.

Due east of Ayia Kyriaki is the parish church of Kato Paphos, **Panayia Theositedasti** (The Madonna Covered by God), perched prominently above the busy streets of the village on an outcrop of rock. Traditions recall a series of miraculous mists that hid this church from the destruction of seaborne Saracen raiders. The mists failed to protect it this century when this ancient shrine was demolished and replaced by the present edifice. Close by, on Ayiou Antoniou Street, is the diminutive but still intact medieval chapel of St Anthony.

The Castle of Saranta Kolones (Forty Columns)

These open-air ruins, 200m up Sophias Vembo street from Apostolou Pavlou (St Paul's) avenue, seldom fail to intrigue visitors, who can clamber over the towers, and try to work out the relationship of the defences to the various cellars, drains and tombs that have since been exposed.

The castle was built from the ruins of the city of Nea Paphos, with a ruthless utilitarian use of columns and finely carved capitals as mere building material. At first it looks a classic example of the sort of structure thrown up by the embattled Byzantine Empire in the 6th century, but recent excavations have pinpointed it to the first decade of Crusader rule, at the end of the 12th century. Even taking into account the abundant local building stone, it was an ambitious undertaking. A moat encircled an outer wall studded with eight towers, whose foundations reveal a playful experimentation with triangular, round, square and octagonal shapes. Within this enclosure stood an enormous keep with outlying corner towers and a round gatehouse. Inside, nine strong piers and two surviving vaults allow you to imagine the great basement of the keep. It was fitted with a number of water troughs (made from classical columns), and no doubt acted as a secure stable for the patrols of mounted knights who held the newly conquered island for their Lusignan lord. It did not function long, as the whole edifice was toppled by the earthquake of 1222.

Odeion, Agora and Northwest Gate

This cluster of three sites, approached up a track heading north between the Paphos mosaic buildings and the Castle of Saranta Kolones, are the only substantial public buildings of Nea Paphos to have been identified.

The **Agora** or forum is a dusty, flat sun-scorched wasteland with little to show for its past role as the centre of urban life. It was originally enclosed by a colonnade of grey granite columns with white marble Corinthian capitals, deeply cut in the baroque style popular in the 2nd century AD.

The **Odeion**, a small informal theatre, was built in the Roman period, but it uses the contours of the hill in the Greek style of construction. The seats all belong to a modern restoration and the orchestra floor has been raised above its original level. Here, no doubt, a sympathetic local audience would have heard the productions of Sopatras, a native Paphian playwright. For us his collected wit has been condensed down to only 25 surviving lines, in which he ridicules the philosopher Zenon, a fellow Cypriot but one who hailed from Kition (Larnaca).

Beside the Odeion is the remains of a sanctuary, just a simple apse flanked by two square rooms, that was dedicated to **Asklepion**, the son of Apollo and the god of healing. The island was reknowned for its doctors in the ancient world and produced such eminent figures as Onasilos Onasikyprou, Apollonious of Kition, Synessis the Cypriot as well as Zeno of Kition who founded a famous medical school at Alexandria in the 4th century AD. Galen (130–201) the greatest medical writer of the ancient world who was also the personal physician and confidant to a succession of Emperors, came to Cyprus on a fact-finding mission in AD 166. Excavations in Nea Paphos have revealed two other testaments to the islands medical life: a surgeon buried with all his instruments, pill boxes and powders and a unique cache of hot water bottles moulded to fit the human body (displayed at the archaeological museum).

The **lighthouse** just to the north occupies the site of an old temple whose steps can still be recognized. From here you can follow the line of the old city wall north to the **northwest gate**, a subtle blend of masonry and natural features. A ramped approach road enters the city under a natural stone arch once guarded by a pair of towers. A moat of sorts was formed by quarrying the ground outside the city, and the escarpment wall is dotted with the openings of a number of ancient drains and eroded tombs.

A coastal path allows you to walk around the headland, following the eroded traces of the old city wall, to approach the harbour from the west. About 150m before you reach the harbour a depression to the north of the path has been tentatively identified as the site of an amphitheatre. The area just north of the harbour row of bars and restaurants is the site of the early Byzantine church of Panayia Limeniotissa (Our Lady of the Harbour).

The Harbour and the Ottoman Fort of Paphos

The harbour is home to a few dozen fishing boats and a number of speedboats. Even with the assistance of various watersport craft, the marine activity seldom equals the busy passeo-life of the quayside. The harbour was once lined with shabby carob warehouses, but they have been replaced by a neat pavement and a cheerful line of restaurants and bars.

The harbour was first formed at the end of the 4th century BC by converting a natural reef into a breakwater. In the Hellenistic period it was a great naval and shipbuilding base for the Ptolemaic kingdom. A series of offshore reefs, noticeable from tell tale splashes of distant foam far out to sea, still provide an outer ring of defence against unwary shipping. Halfway along the mole are the stumpy remains of the east tower of a castle, built by King James I in 1391. This medieval fortress survived until it was slighted by the Venetians in the 16th century.

Since then the harbour has been dominated by the squat mass of the **Ottoman Fort** (*Open 7.30–2.30 Mon, Tues, Wed, Fri, 7.30–6 Thurs, adm*). This artillery fortress, battered by the wind and surf rather than any human enemy, is still surrounded by its moat and is approached across a drawbridge. The Arabic inscription above the doorway records its construction in 1592 by Ahmed Pasha, who incorporated the ruins of the old west tower of King James' Castle into its foundations. The interior hall is formed from four barrel vaults whose simple lines have been confused by a cascade of arches added during the construction of the flanking wings. There are a pair of cellars below, and a little mosque among the three rooms in the windblown upper gallery, where rusty cannon sit among the eroded, sea-etched golden stone of the walls.

Tombs along Poseidonos Avenue and the Temple of Apollo

The only tomb that preserves its original paintwork is found in the grounds of the Annabelle Hotel. You can visit it and then have tea or a cocktail in the hotel's lavish garden. The tomb is tucked away behind the false waterfall flowing from the water garden into the serpentine swimming pool. There are two more ancient tombs to be seen in the courtyard of the Alexander the Great Hotel, one of which has a well-preserved chamber with three sarcophagi.

Inland from the Alexander the Great Hotel, about 500m up Kleiou street, are the slight remains of a sanctuary to **Apollo Hylates**. A rectangular subterranean chamber leads into a circular room with a domed roof, dated to the 4th century BC by Syllabic inscriptions found here. It is, however, only for enthusiasts as the woodland site is partly used as a rubbish dump and is guarded by two dogs.

Ktima or Pano (Upper) Paphos and the Museums

The broad green triangle of the Municipal Gardens, overlooked by a row of neo-classical public buildings, forms a distinctive civic centre to the town of Paphos. Its northern corner, distinguished by the tall Corinthian column of the town war memorial, is known as Octovriou 28 square. Southwest of this column a broad avenue leads you the 400m towards the Byzantine Museum at the Bishopric and the neighbouring Eliades Ethnographic Museum. Southeast of the column stretches the road to Limassol, Georgiou Griva Digeni Avenue, 800m along which sits the archaeological museum. Just northwest of the column is the junction for the roads to Kato Paphos, to the hill village of Peyia and the town of Polis.

Before inspecting the museums of the upper town, walk due northwest of the column, along Makariou III and its continuation Agora street to the **Covered Market**. The market is only fully functional on Saturday mornings. The narrow streets of the commercial centre around it are lined with 19th-century houses, local shops, cafés and bars. They have their own quiet charm, especially when compared to the tourist-ridden coast. Before 1974 the market marked the transition from the Greek part of town to the Turkish. The narrow alleys and rustic houses of the old Turkish quarter stretch to the north of the market where you

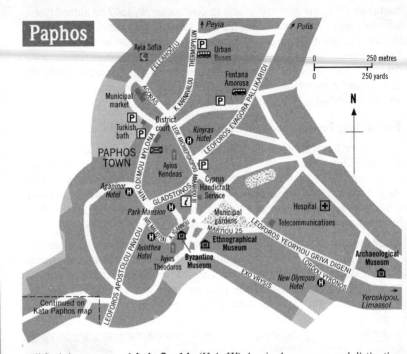

will find the mosque of **Ayia Sophia** (Holy Wisdom) whose name and distinctive Orthodox dome betray its origin as a 15th century church. Another Turkish relic, approached by steps near the parking place on Nikodimou Mylona street, is the domed bath house which has been recently restored. A mosque used to stand beside it, but this was destroyed in the communal fighting of the sixties. The neo-classical courthouse stands further down this street and enjoys a good view west over the coast. Almost opposite the junction of Nikodimou Mylona and Gladstonos streets is a calm, shaded public garden backing onto an escarpment pitted with ancient tombs and cellars. From here a stepped passage, Ivis Maliotou takes you directly up to the Bishopric, its associated chapel of Ayios Theodoros and the Byzantine Museum.

Byzantine Museum

> *Open 9–1, 4–7 Mon–Fri, 9–1 Sat in summer, in winter the afternoon hours change to 2–5; adm.*

This museum is justly celebrated for its small but superb display of icons, the island's second most important collection after that in Nicosia. It is housed in a couple of rooms within the Bishopric, © (06) 232092, on Ilysion/Elysee street, 400m due southwest of the war memorial column. There is a rich display of ecclesiastical vestments, jewels, documents such as the Ottoman firman from the Sultan that confirms the rights of the bishopric of Paphos, early liturgies, an illustrated 17th-century gospel and a 15th-century manuscript bible. Though worthy of attention these pale beside the icons (for an introduction to icons *see* p. 118).

The icons are constantly being rearranged, lent to exhibitions or cleaned. The best way to get your eye in is to find the cracked *Virgin Eleousa* from the monastery of St Sabas tis Karonos. This is the oldest icon in the collection and, despite being damaged, it is still the most powerful. The eyes of the Virgin look out with a dark, mournful intensity full of suppressed passion, recalling a world of absolute faith. The 13th-century double-sided icon from Philousa with its dark outlines is a naive, if venerable, curiosity. Next in age and intensity are three icons from the early 15th century: the *Crucifixion* on a green background from Panayia Khryseleousa at Kato Arkhimandrita; the splendidly spiritual other-worldly *St John the Baptist* from Ayios Epiphanios with its powerfully shaded facial features, and the *Virgin.* There is a dynamism, poise and balance in these three icons which reflect the influence of Constantinople, where the Palealogue Renaissance was introducing some of the spirit of heroic classicism to religious art.

The rest of the icons belong to the productive period of the 16th century, when the Cypriot school of artists were at work on the island. Some of their work stays true to Byzantine traditions (such as the *Virgin Hodegetria* from Trakhypedhoula by the painter Titus and the dark *Christ Pantocrator* from the church of St Constaine and St Helen at Tsadha), whilst others show a moving synthesis with Italian influences (such as the *Virgin Philochiotissa* from Ayia Marina in Philousa by the painter Silvester). These western influences can be seen more markedly in the *Virgin in Prayer* from Kato Arkhimandrita and the *Virgin of Kykko* from Ayios Nikolaos both of which have acquired an emotional and human quality at the expense of spiritual intensity. This trend was further exaggerated by the exodus of artists to Venice after the Ottoman conquest, where polished icons were exported to Cyprus until the 18th century.

Eliades Ethnographic Museum

Opening hours and days can vary though it is usually open from around 8–1, 3–6 © (06) 232010; adm.

The private ethnographical collection of George Eliades and family, who sometimes take visitors on a personal guided tour, is one of the most delightful and idiosyncratic museums on the island. It is found on Exo Vryisis street, just east of the Bishopric.

The 19th-century house is set in a pebble-paved yard, shaded with figs and dotted with cyclamen. The basement, with its cruciform open passage and four dusty rooms, holds the bulk of the exhibits. In the Villagers' Room the machinery of the islands' most famous cottage industry, now quiet dead, is preserved. A cotton spinner, a pair of thread separators, a gin to separate fibres from seed, a loom and branch-stools allow you to imagine the laborious process of cotton manufacture. On the wall hang tasselled purses and knapsacks, lovingly hung with cowrie shells. The bedroom is furnished with lace and clothes, including the traditional baggy black trousers (*vrakes*) that were worn with wasp-waisted striped waist-coats. The central hallway is filled with a delightful clutter of artefacts including bottles, once a scarce resource, hung securely and decoratively from the walls. The cart, pack saddle, potter's wheel and hand mills are instantly recognizable, but the distinctive flint-studded threshing sledges, the Y-shaped wooden vine-planter, the hollowed bread-making planks (*pinakotes*) and the various tools for making rope may be new to you. The long, bamboo-like canes of hemp were soaked for 40 days, stretched, pounded and then plaited into rope on the artists-eazel like structures. The archaeological room has a dusty hoard of Neolithic axe heads but this takes second place to the collection of 19th century island pottery, assembled when the traditional production centres, such as Kornos, Phini, Varosha and Lapethos, were still in active operation (*see* p. 409).

Around the museum garden are arranged a 19th-century kitchen, laundry, a communal oven filled with individual bread racks, an olive press and a mill. In the rock face a Hellenistic tomb has been excavated to reveal its two side chambers, complete with rock-cut sarcophagi and amphorae. Another cave has been turned into a chapel with a niche put aside for Venus. Ascend to the main hall of the house to find two finely carved wooden chests from Lapethos, and cabinets filled with antiquities, silverware, coins and a fine collection of obsidian and stone arrowheads, all knowledgeably explained by the curator.

Paphos District Archaeological Museum

Open in summer Mon–Sat, 7.30–1.30, 4–6, Sun 10.–1: in winter Mon–Fri 7.30–2, 3–5, Sat 7.30–1, 3–5, Sun 10–1: © (06) 240215; adm.

The archaeological museum is a modern structure surrounded by a small garden decorated with architectural fragments and carved tombstones. It has a neglected feel, tucked out from the centre of town, some 800m east of the war memorial column along Leoforos Yeoryiou Griva Digeni. Few of the exhibits would excite the average tourist but if you get a feel for the ruins of the area you will find they take on a life of their own.

Room I is dominated by the Chalcolithic discoveries made in the villages just to the north of Paphos: Mosphilia, Kissonerga and especially Lemba. The latter was destroyed by an earthquake in 2500 BC, trapping and preserving an unusual number of household objects such as a green stone idol, beads, pendants, some vivid red painted bowls (decorated with zig-zags, spirals and boxes within boxes) and a crouched pottery figure. This figurine with hands on breasts provide us with an intriguing insight into the culture of the 20-year-old girl who lies crouched in the position that she was buried some centuries before the village was destroyed by the earthquake. There is hardly any Early Bronze Age ware displayed but this gap in the record is made up for by a good selection of Middle and Late Bronze Age ceramics (*see* pp. 406–7 for details). The cabinet of metalware contains only a few relics from the Tombs of the Kings which have been thoroughly looted over the centuries. The Eros ring and a gold laurel wreath were worn by a Hellenistic official in his grave and give an idea of the town's prosperity in the 3rd century BC.

Room II has some vivid examples of Archaic painted pottery, which always looks particularly attractive placed beside the dull ring-decorated plates churned out in the preceeding Geometric era. The two-handled, urn-shaped pot, decorated with bull, lion, bird, dog and boar, is one of the best of these, exceeded only by the leopard-headed jug with its Mesopotamian scene of horned goats feeding from the tree of life.

Alongside the distinguished red-figured Attic ware, all imported from Greece, are a distinctive collection of jugs, with spouts formed from modelled female figures, that were produced by the potters of Marion, modern Polis, at about the same time. The collection of votive Archaic figurines come from three local sanctuaries: from Pomos (halfway between the rival city-states of Marion and Soli); from the nearby garden of Aphrodite at Yeroskipos: and from the great sanctuary of Aphrodite at Palea Paphos.

Room III holds a rich assortment of Roman and Hellenistic glass and ceramic objects. The delicate scent ampoules, tear pippets, moulded lamps and figurines help you to imaginatively furnish the empty mosaic-floored rooms of the villas in Nea Paphos. The House of Dionysos produced many of the small carvings in the cabinet including a striking lionskin-wearing Amazon, a young satyr with curvaceous torso, a graceful Dionysos with grapes and a stout Hercules. The matching pair of black and white goddesses are considered to be Persephone and Demeter, or the personifications of Night and Day, as the cloak of the black figure is speckled with stars. The most curious of the exhibits is the unique cache of medical hot water bottles, all shaped to cure different organs of the body.

Room IV and **V** conclude the museum with pieces from the late Roman, Byzantine and medieval era. There is a fine selection of glazed sgraffito ware with its distinctive quick drawn fluency of line, sketchy lines of hatched decoration and central animal motifs set amongst floral geometry. The Italian majolica and gold-painted glass bottles were imported, but the four large angels carrying the classical roof of a tomb could have been carved on the island. They are not Roman but Venetian, a 16th-century Renaissance addition to the Franciscan church at Kato Paphos, which was to be destroyed shortly afterwards by the Ottoman invasion.

Shopping

The *covered market* in Ktima Paphos is the first port of call for traditional baskets and produce. It is fully open only on Saturday morning though there are a number of stalls and shops in the surrounding streets open throughout the week. Up towards the mosque of Ayia Sophia is **Mikis antique shop** at 6 Fellahoglu street, © (06) 234464. It is full of turn-of-the-century junk and pieces of rural equipment with which to start your own ethnographic collection. **Axel Books** is the best bookshop in town, on the corner of Makariou III and Ayiou Kendeou streets.

Going south out of Ktima Paphos towards the harbour you pass the **Cyprus Handicraft Service** at 64 Apostlou Pavlou Avenue, © (06) 240243. **Seaworld**, beside the prominent Kings hotel on Tomb of the Kings road, stocks everything you might possibly need for watersports, swimming and sunbathing. **Kyklos Gallery** is well placed on the road to the ancient mosaics, to catch those interested in the work of local artists, shown in season from 9–12, 3–6 every day.

Out of town you will find one of the largest selections of traditional basketwork, raffia bags, split cane boxes and red earthenware terracotta (amongst piles of neatly wrapped boxes of Turkish delight) in the dozen or more shops that line the main road as it passes through the centre of Yeroskipou. For a different order of artistic commitment and imaginative interpretations of traditional ceramics, visit the **Lemba Pottery**, run by George and Sotevoulla Yeoryiades in Lemba village, © (06) 243822.

Church Services

Orthodox mass can be heard every Sunday morning, between 6.30 and 9 in any of the churches of Paphos: Ayios Theodhoros beside the bishopric; Ayios Kendeas, off Makariou avenue; or the big, modern, domed church of Ayios Pavlos on the road to Polis. A Roman Catholic priest comes over from Limassol to celebrate mass on Sunday at 12 noon in the Church variously known as Ayia Kiriaki, St Paul's Pillar or Panayia Khrysopolitissa. Anglicans also use the same historic church.

Sports

Paphos has three well-established **scuba diving centres** where you can hire equipment and sign up for a training course. Aloe Divers operate out of the Aloe Hotel, ✆ (06) 234000 and Paphos harbour; Cy-Dive Diving Centre, which remains in operation throughout the year, has its office well sited at 1 Poseidonos street, ✆ (06) 234271. The Annabelle Diving Centre operates from the Paphos municipal beach, PO Box 136, Kato Paphos, ✆ (06) 233091.

Although a number of hotels operate their own **water sports** centres you may find it more convenient to use the easily accessible facilities at Paphos harbour, the public beach at Coral bay or Latsi harbour outside Polis.

Fishermen work from the harbours at Paphos, Latsi, Pomos and Kato Pyrgos. An enjoyable day out **sea fishing** can be had on board 'Charlie's Angel', ✆ (06) 247924/248447 which operates out of Paphos harbour between April and November. A two-hour trip costs C£8 if you are fishing, half if you are not, with a bottle of champagne for the best catch of the day. The waters round the island have been seriously over-fished but locals continue to trawl for small, red mackerel with fine nets. There is an off chance of catching swordfish, but you will need to be about 30 miles out from the shore and lucky to be amongst them when they are moving.

The inland dams and reservoirs are much more promising territory for **angling** as they have been stocked with an assortment of American and British fish. Carp are found in healthy numbers, alongside roach, catfish, bass, eel and tench. Cyprus Angling Holidays, based outside Larnaca at 5 George Sefferis street, Aradippou, ✆ (04) 631802; can provide guides, maps, tackle and a fishing licence. The latter can also be acquired from the Fisheries Department, 13 Aiolou street, Nicosia ✆ (02) 303526.

The Cyprus **Bridge** Club has a Paphos branch organised by Jeremy Seavers, ✆ (06) 242597 or (06) 244689.

Excursions and Walks

Exalt runs a number of well-organised walks, treks and expeditions along the coast and into the lesser known valleys, gorges, and forested hills of the interior. The two managers, David Perlman and Zenon Zenonos are a fount of local knowledge. They keep group numbers small, arrange traditional Cypriot meals and are passionately involved in the island's archaeology and beleaguered conservation movement. The three most popular walking trips are the Peyia Forest (northeast of Ayios Yeoryios/ Cape Drepanum), the Akamas peninsula and the Xeropotamos valley. The latter two can also be done by jeep which is also the only way to get upto the Stavros Tis Psokas forest station in one day. There is a busy weekly schedule with morning departures from the office between 8.30 and 10;

prices run around the C£20 mark. Trekkers are usually divided into German or English speaking groups though they will also arrange private trips for up to six people and week-long treks for a minumum of eight. Their office, decorated with a large scale map of Cyprus, is at 24 Ayios Kyriaki street, Kato Paphos, © (06) 243803, is near a traditional boat builder and just north of St Paul's Pillar.

The **Louis Tourist Agency** at 117 Makarios avenue, © (06) 233320, amongst many others, can book you onto a whistle-stop coach tour from Paphos to the major nearby sites. They can also book a place on M.S. *Zeus Xenios* which is moored in Paphos harbour. It cruises north to Lara Beach on Tues, Wed, Thurs and Fri and around the Akamas peninsula to Fontana Amorosa on Sat and Sun, 9–4.30. The boat was badly bashed around in a winter storm but should now be running again. C£15 tickets include lunch and local wine.

Where to Stay in Kato (Lower) Paphos

expensive

The Paphos coast is now as brash and full of day-glo package tourists as any of the other big beach resorts. There are some astonishingly luxurious new hotels on the coast, furnished with a glittering prospect of pools, enclosed gardens, and a multiple choice of bars and restaurants. They are also touched by a suburban banality, strung in a row along Poseidonos street. They have plenty of secluded sunbathing terraces, but despite the cunningly tinted brochure photographs the actual shoreline, a predominantly rocky coast dusted with annual lorry loads of sand, is all a public beach. The **Annabelle Hotel** on Poseidonos street, PO Box 401, © (06) 238333, is the most elaborately appointed, with a water garden that cascades over a false rock wall into a serpentine swimming pool. A double bedroom with a sea view is not much short of C£100 a night.

moderate

At the top of this price range is the large **Paphos Beach Hotel** on Poseidon street, PO Box 136, © (06) 233091. It has been in operation for 15 years, and has one of the best positions, directly behind the municipal beach with a good view towards the harbour. The **Dionysos Hotel** at 1 Dionysou street, © (06) 233414; is right in the middle of Kato Paphos. It has its own pool and small but adequate rooms and is well placed for a holiday centred on the nearby bars and nightclubs.

Just west of the main Leoforos Apostolou Pavlou (St Paul's avenue) there is a choice of three medium-sized hotels directly overlooking the ruins of

Nea Paphos. The ornate stonework and the historical fantasy of the interior decoration in the **Roman Hotel**, PO Box 118, ℂ (06) 244400; and its even more bizarre neighbour, the **Melina Hotel**, PO Box 118, ℂ (06) 245411; seems either to appal or delight. If you are looking for something a bit more sober try the **Apollon Hotel**, PO Box 219, ℂ (06) 233909. It is opposite the Ayia Solomoni catacombs with a west facing sun terrace and a fine view through various antique altars and pillars.

Where to Stay in Ktima/Pano (Upper) Paphos

moderate

The entrance to the **Axiothe Hotel**, PO Box 70, ℂ (06) 232866; is at 2 Ivis Maliotou. This road goes under a variety of names (such as Eves or Hebes) and can be elusive, as it is a stepped passageway that links Apostolou Pavlou (St Paul's) avenue with Andrea Ioannou street, the road that goes past the bishopric. It is best approached, particularly when carrying luggage, from the latter. The hotel lobby with its cool stone clad floor is something of a local institution, presided over by Andreas Georghiou, wife and family. Through the hotel's portals pass a continous trickle of scholars, amateur specialists and friends, masquerading as guests, whilst various clubs and societies, oiled with brandy sours, assemble in odd corners amongst pictures by local artists which are for sale. There are 36 bedrooms, a buffet breakfast in the morning and other meals by arrangement. If you plan a longer stay you could ask about hiring an apartment in the **Ambassador** opposite.

The **New Olympus Hotel** occupies an imposing three-storey building which is tucked off the main Limassol road at 12 Lordou Vyronos (Byron street), PO Box 115, ℂ (06) 232020. It has a calm atmosphere, is close to the archaeological museum and well placed as a touring base. The reclusive but well appointed **Park Mansion**, ℂ (06) 245645, which used to be known in its scruffier days as the Phidias Guesthouse, is tucked down on Pavlou Mela street, off the roundabout junction between Makarios and Martiou 25 streets.

cheap

There are two fine hotels just within this price bracket, though they can both get filled pretty quickly. The **Kinyras Hotel** has 18 rooms and occupies an attractive old building with its own bar and open air courtyard. It is in the centre of town at 91 Archiepiskopou Makariou III avenue, ℂ (06) 241604. The **Agapinor** is a more conventional modern hotel with 25 rooms looking out southwest from a fine position on the edge of the old town. The entrance is along Nicodimou Mylona street, though its address is given as 24–26 St Paul's Avenue, PO Box 215, ℂ (06) 233926.

Eating Out in Lower Paphos

The harbour front is lined with a string of bars and restaurants, including the famous **Pelican** which once sat alone on this shore. It has a presence the others can't quite match, and despite accusations of living off its reputation you can still dine well on its outside tables. Try a meal of grilled prawns followed by a swordfish fillet or a full fish *meze* for two.

The outdoor taverna of the **Apollon** hotel, ℂ (06) 233909, on Apostolou Pavlou (St Paul's) avenue, has an open-air charcoal grill and ovens. It is well placed for a lunch break with a view over Nea Paphos, open from 12.30–2.30 and after 7pm.

The **Alakati Tavern**, ℂ (06) 238860, is a lively, boisterous place on Tafon Ton Vasileon (Tomb of the Kings) road that is run by its two resident managers, Loizou Nicos and Christoforou Christakis. There are over 20 different traditional dishes served here, including suckling pig plus live music on Saturday nights.

Avgerinos run by John Joannides and family at 4 Minos street, ℂ (06) 232990 is one of the more individual restaurants in this area, offering meals of freshly grilled fish and meat, without concessions to the prevailing package holiday atmosphere.

L'Ambiance Tavern, ℂ (06) 235001, run by chef Leonard Donnington, takes pride in its menu which includes Cypriot specialities, international dishes and charcoal-grilled steaks and fish. It is halfway up Thalias street and marked by a green neon sign on Poseidonos street after the Alexander the Great hotel. The **Carob Tree**, ℂ (06) 233654, is a near neighbour, just one block west on Kleios street with a mixed menu of international and Cypriot dishes.

The municipal **Plage Restaurant**, ℂ (06) 233745, used to be known as the Nautical Club when it stood beside the Customs post on the harbour. It has now moved 2km east to larger premises, the entrance drive emerging just beyond the Alexander the Great hotel on Poseidonos street. It has a smart look with its smoked glass, crisp blue tablecloths and prompt service though it is not expensive. Try the slow-roasted chicken and keep a look out for Cypriot specialities on the menu. The Plage is primarily used by locals, especially on weekends, who come here not just for a meal but for the day. It has its own car park and a range of facilities including a beach bar, sun-beds, water sports centre, changing rooms and showers.

Sunday lunch for the family is as much an institution in Cyprus as it is in Britain. The Paphos Beach Hotel on Poseidonos street has a regular Sunday buffet in its **Mosaic Restaurant**, decorated with a contemporary wall mosaic in pebble and rough stone tesserae.

For a formal evening meal from a largely international menu try the **Fontana Amorosa Restaurant** in the downstairs of the Annabelle Hotel on Poseidonos street. The four-course menu of the day gives you two choices per course and is consumed to the sound of a piano.

Eating Out in Ktima/Pano (Upper) Paphos

The **Paphos Grill House** is at 139 Makariou III avenue, ✆ (06) 34041, on a street corner opposite an illuminated municipal fountain. Allow the commanding presence of the patron Andreas to suggest what's best or tuck into a mixed kebab and salad.

The **Greek Tavern**, ✆ (06) 235856 (open from 10am to 1am), beside the junction of Makariou and Martiou 25 streets, is a small but distinctive place with a loyal following of customers. Try their spicy chicken kebab, called *Morea-itiko*, accompanied by a Lebanese tabouleh salad with spring onions, parsley and cracked wheat.

Cafés

For a taste of colonial Britain, take tea or breakfast in **Peggy's Miranda Café** on Makariou III avenue, ✆ 232188. This is the unofficial club house of the expatriate community, with notices for various amateur theatrical, library, social and church events, amongst a selection of imported kitsch to outdo Jeff Koons.

For a more creamy, upmarket experience dress up a bit for afternoon tea in the hall of the **Annabelle Hotel** on Poseidonos street. Or for a more casual but still filling engagement with gateau-life stop at the Café Vienna directly outside the Annabelle Hotel on Poseidonos street.

Nightlife

Paphos was long mocked by its neighbours as the sleeping town. This however is quickly changing, and a nightclubbers' zone has developed in Kato Paphos around the triangular garden framed by Ayia Napa, Constantinas and Klitemnistras streets. This is easy to find as it just 100m north of the village church of Theoskepasti, perched up on its conspicuous rocky eminence. An assortment of two dozen cocktail music-bars are assisted by a lesser number of disco-nightclubs, such as Samba, Acapulco or Eros on Ayia Napa street and Rainbow on Ayiou Antoniou street. Thai girls do cabaret turns in **La Grotte de Paphos** opposite the little 10th-century church of St Anthony on Ayiou Antoniou street. Showtime starts at midnight, a quarter bottle of whisky costs C£10 or C£15 when you buy it for an artiste.

La Boite 67, The Artists' Pub, on the harbour front, © (06) 234800, is Andreas the patron's tribute to the heady days of student-run Paris in the late sixties. A decaying mural, a shifting selection of locals and passing drinkers and live music from 9pm–1.30am, Wed, Fri, Sat and Sun makes it one the most individual bars in Paphos.

The **Plage** is about 2km east of the Ottoman Fort, just beyond the Alexander the Great Hotel on Poseidonos (Poseidon) street. It has live bands playing contemporary and traditional folk music to a principally Cypriot audience Thurs, Sat and Sun nights. It is often taken over for parties and weddings, so it might be worth booking a table in advance, © (06) 233745.

Paphos District

Most places of interest within the district of Paphos can be conveniently visited in a day trip from the town. However, if you prefer a quieter atmosphere and are interested in some gentle walking (particularly in the cooler hours of the early morning and late afternoon), you might consider shifting your bags to a village with a hotel, such as those found at Drousha, Ayios Yeoryios near Peyia, Pano Panayia or Kato Pyrgos. The town of Polis, which still remains just the right side of development, is another option.

The area around Paphos has been divided into six sections which follow each other in a roughly clockwise direction to make an introductory exploration of the countryside. The first trip follows the coast due north, passing the cutter of Ayios Yeoryios, the hamlet of Lemba and Coral Bay on its way to Cape Drepanum (Ayios Yeoryios near Peyia) a base for a number of walks in the Akamas. The second trip takes you just outside Paphos to the nearby monastery of Ayios Neophytos and the village of Emba. The third trip covers the northern coast, and includes Polis as well as some of the more interesting inland villages and the coast road east to Kato Pyrgos. The fourth trip heads northeast from Paphos to Pano Panayia village, the nearby monastery of Panayia Khrysorroyiatissa and the forested hills. The fifth trip goes east to Yeroskipos village and then on to the ancient city of Palea Paphos (at Kouklia village), with its ancient shrine of Aphrodite, before finishing at the birthplace of the goddess amongst the rocks of Petra tou Romiou.

In Kato Paphos take the Tafon Ton Vasileon (Tomb of the Kings) road, which leads you out of Paphos along an increasingly built-up coast road. About 3km north is the coastal hamlet of **Ayios Yeoryios**, now embellished with a gleaming new church to match the modern hotel. By the shore a large boatshed has been built to preserve *Ayios Georgios*, a coastal cutter used to smuggle arms to Cyprus right at the beginning of the EOKA (National Organisation of Cypriot Fighters) campaign for union with Greece. It was seized by the British in January 1955, who captured the all-Greek crew with a party of seven villagers from nearby Khlorakas, as they were unloading Greek military munitions. It had important repercussions at the time, though few could have been greatly surprised at the direct link between Greece and EOKA. The organiser of EOKA, Colonel Georgios Grivas (code-named Dighenis, after a Byzantine folk hero) though born on the island, had spent the bulk of his life as an ardent right-wing officer in the Greek army and had been deeply involved in the murderous fighting of the Greek Civil War. He trained the first EOKA fighters in the hilly Athenian suburb of Ekali, who were ferried secretly to Cyprus from the Greek islands. Dighenis himself took a boat from Rhodes and landed here on 10 November 1954 to direct the EOKA struggle which was unleashed by simultaneous bomb explosions on 1 April 1955.

From Ayios Yeoryios a road goes inland to the village of **Khlorakas** where you can stop for a drink in the village centre, at Nicos's bar which stands by the tree of idleness and the two parish churches. The smaller church of Panayia Khryselousa is medieval, with the coat of arms of its Byzantine patron above the west door.

The hamlet of **Lemba** is 2km north of Khlorakas, off the main Peyia road. This scattering of attractive cottages, beneath a rocky prominence and beside a stream-fed gorge, was primarily Turkish Cypriot before 1974. It has since been preserved and colonised by a mixed group of artists and archeaologists. The Cyprus College of Art, © (06) 245557, surrounded by vividly coloured sculptures, stands just above the village spring, that tinkles from out of a grotto-like crevice. As well as its formal three-year courses, it runs a summer school from June to September, bringing together an international mix of students. There are occasional exhibitions of work for sale, but visitors are also welcome at a number of studio-shops in the village: try the Lemba pottery of George and Sotevoulla Yeoryiades, the studio of Thraki draped in morning glory, or take tea at the Jones' residence.

Follow the tarmac road to its end and turn right; this will take you to the fenced excavation site of a Chalcolithic village, to which have been added the experimental structures of the **Lemba project**. Dr Edgar Peltenburg and his team from the University of Edinburgh have constructed three round huts using the available information from excavations here, as well as from Kalavassos, Khirokitia and especially the neighbouring site of Mosphilia-Kissonerga. Their shape, plan, post location, stone post plinths, myrtle thatch, stone footings and east-facing doors are based on hard evidence, as is the bold red ochre design on the internal walls. It is only in the upper walls, roof-structure, chimney vent and guttering that the team have had to be truly experimental. By observing the weathering of the huts, and comparing it to the slight but crucial remains they can test the effectiveness of current ideas. It is already clear that there was an intricate technology for the composition of the different mud daubs, lime mortar and plasters required for walls, roof and floors. Even the pre-ceramic cultures must have been familiar with the practice of lime, burning in crude kilns and annual replastering jobs. These allied skills offer a possible avenue with which to explain the invention of pottery in the early Neolithic period.

The aquamarine seawater, sheltered by rock escarpments of **Coral Bay**, some 12km north of Paphos remains a crisp and clear as ever, but the shore is being rapidly transformed into a mini-resort. There are actually two bays: the northern one has a fishing harbour now dominated by a new hotel complex: the southern one offers a fine stretch of sand, a colourful assortment of umbrellas, sun-beds, water sports (such as the Corallia Bay Watersport Centre) and snack bars. For a proper meal you should either head 3km inland to the attractive and restaurant filled hill village of Peyia, or to the nearby Tsolias Taverna on the promontory seperating the two bays. The outside tables of the taverna look directly over **Maa-Palaeokastro**, a fenced in archaeological site from the Late Bronze Age. Maa was enclosed by a land wall built by barbarian invaders from the north around 1200 BC. Fragments of copper slag, droplets of lead and bronze reveal that this alien colony was able to trade or collect tribute from the mines of the interior. The foreigners stayed here for only 50 years, for by 1150 BC the settlement was in ruins. It is tempting to see this as the protective action of a powerful Late-Bronze-Age city-state from the east of Cyprus such as Engomi or Kition, though ultimately the civilization of the island was fated to be destroyed 200 years later by other barbarians sailing down from the north.

A left turn off the road from Coral Bay to Peyia village leads through the maquis of the coastal strip to the settlement of **Ayios Yeoryios** (near Peyia), sheltering on the northern edge of Cape Drepanum, 20km north of Paphos. It is a charming windblown place consisting of little more than a chapel, fishing shelter and three restaurants. A Neolithic settlement has been found on the offshore island of Yeronisos, which is also littered with shards from the Hellenistic and Roman town of Drepanum that formerly once stood here. Over a dozen tombs await to be explored in the crumbling escarpment below the St George Taverna. The ancient undertakers of Drepanum may have benefited from a tradition that connects the town, or at least its namesake in Sicily, with the burial place of Adonis. The rock-cut tombs, believed to be from the Roman period, have carved door portals leading into a central hall, flanked by individual niches for the dead, some of which have been annotated with crosses. Just uphill from the modern chapel of St George is a fenced area of excavation, first dug in 1949 by a British archaeologist who has yet to publish his findings (who guards the guardians?). His digging has revealed the foundations of three Byzantine churches, two of which were added to the ancient town in the 6th century, little more than a 100 years before it was destroyed by seaborne Saracens. The arrangement of the largest church (the cathedral) is reasonably clear: five rows of seats in the central apse, the synthronon, were for the assembled clergy, whilst the altar, then unobscured by an iconostasis, stood in the nave protected by a canopy marked out by four Corinthian capitals. To its west was an outer porch opening onto an open courtyard for washing, beyond which was a baptistery chapel. A passage leads east from this group, past a half-exposed villa and bath complex, to a much smaller chapel whose distinctive basket-shaped Byzantine capitals, ornamented with a cross, hint at a much later date of construction, perhaps in the 10th century AD.

Walks in the Akamas

The Paphos-based Exalt Excursions (*see* 'Excursions and Walks' p. 253) runs a series of Jeep trips and walking tours, which explore hidden portions of this wild coast, whose future hangs in the balance between tourist development and preservation as a national park. Respect the peace and current limits of development and leave your vehicle at Ayios Yeoryios.

Just outside Ayios Yeoryios a dirt track branches off to rattle north up the wild and still unexploited coast of the Akamas peninsula. As you potter along it keep an eye out for an outcrop of limestone into which has been dug a dozen underground tombs, approached down rock-cut stairways. About 1km on, the track dips down the side of the Aspros valley whose pebble beach is overlooked by white cliffs. A shepherd's hut is tucked into the northern face of the escarpment with that mingling of natural grace and excitement that you expect from an Andy Goldsworthy sculpture. You can follow the bed of the stream for 6km as it twists inland and from where the more ambitious walkers can clamber up to a path that heads 4km due east to Kathikas and its restaurant.

Another day can be spent exploring the pair of gorges whose entrance is just 1km north of Aspros valley. Follow the Kalamouli stream inland for a 1km to the meeting of the Avgas and Kouphon streams, which have cut their way through the rough, maquis-covered hills of the Peyia 'Forest'. The track continues beyond Kalamouii to take you up to the sands of Lara Beach (where the turtles lay their eggs) overlooked by the white cliffs of the hammer-headed Lara promontory.

Open in daylight hours, usually seven days a week but always at the discretion of the monks.

The Monastery of St Neophytus is one of Cyprus's most precious treasures. Despite the steady trickle of visitors, it is still redolent with the spirit of its 12th century founder and has a small but exquisite selection of frescoes. It is 6 miles/9km north of Paphos and is easily reached from the Polis road, where the side turning is signposted opposite Mesoyi village. The monastery complex is approached through a high, terraced valley of fruit trees, and is found tucked away on the side of the pale limestone slope of the Melisosovonous hill. Modern residential blocks enclose the 16th-century church in a sheltered courtyard, while in a cliff just to the west a stone stairwell allows access into the original 12th-century hermitage of the saint. Between the two a shaded café-terrace sits below the level of the drive beside a spring that trickles into a cool rectangular pool. Aside from the historic interest of the site there is a small number of superb frescoes in both the hermitage and church.

St Neophytus the Recluse

The life of St Neophytus neatly straddles the transition of Cyprus from a Byzantine province to a conquered territory of the Crusaders, though no mere political catastrophe was responsible for his earlier decision to dedicate his life to God. At the age of 18 the young Neophytus, threatened with an early marriage, left his poor but pious parents in their mountain village near Lefkara and entered the monastery of Chrysostomos, that sits below the Castle of Buffavento in the Gothic Range. Here he tended the vines and studied for eight years, broken only by a pilgrimage to the Holy Land. A second trip planned for Mount Latmos was frustrated by his arrest at Paphos harbour and imprisonment by the local police, as in medieval society and particularly late Byzantium the difference between a fiery monk in search of spiritual enlightenment and a political activist was not always easy to judge. This injustice further confirmed Neophytus's disgust for the ways of the world, and he retired to the Melisosovonous hill above Paphos. By 1159 he had enlarged a cave into a two-room hermitage, complete with chapel and tomb in his living room. His strong youthful faith and impassioned learning soon attracted casual visitors and earnest followers who clustered around the hill in a semi-permanent encampment. This group formed the nucleus of the monastery, officially founded in 1170, that was under the control of its 36-year-old abbot. However Neophytus in order to distance himself from the distracting hum of community life withdrew to another *enkleistra* (hermitage) further up the rockface. This hermitage he named New Zion, and it served as his oratory where he could pray, meditate and write hymns, biblical commentaries, letters of spiritual advice. He also wrote a chronicle entitled 'Concerning the Calamaties that have befallen on Cyprus', an acute observation of the conquest of the island by that freebooting adventurer, Richard the Lionheart. Neophytus witnessed the first two decades of rule by the Lusignan Crusader state and died in 1219. His spirit, and the relics of his body, rediscovered in 1750, still preside over the monastery.

The Enkleistra

The original hermitage is now fronted by an arcaded terrace, and approached up a stone stairway. The left-hand doorway leads into the cave chapel (known as the church of the Holy Cross) composed of nave and sanctuary. A low doorway leads through the rock wall into the cell of Neophytus complete with its rock-cut tomb, table, desk, chair and quill niche. The upper enkleistra is retained as a working retreat for the monks, and is not open to the public.

The frescoes in the **nave** of the chapel date from two periods. The lower wall is lined with a superbly stern series of saints in dark robes, who stare out at the onlooker with unflinching conviction. These (and the exquisite face of Christ on the right of the door) were painted in the lifetime of Neophytus and are powerful examples of the artistic style of the Comnenian period. They are securely dated, to 1185, and we even know the name of the artist, one Theodoros Apseudes. Above them the scenes of a greener hue, that fill the bulging cave wall in two series, were painted in the 16th century. They have their own naïve charm and uncomplicated directness, particularly the scene of Abraham and Sarah entertaining the three angels, and that of Christ washing his disciples' feet.

Look into the **sanctuary, the bema**, of the chapel to admire the 12th-century frescoes depicting a row of saints, prelates bowing to the Virgin and *Christ Pantocrator*. On the western part of the cave roof the grey-bearded Neophytus is being escorted by a pair of angels on the dreadful day of judgment. Though the saint has been given a pair of wings, there is still doubt in his eyes and in the accompanying inscription: 'O holy twain, I fervently pray that this image should come true.'

The **cell** also retains its original frescoes with fragments of generous blue framing the saints, the *Crucifixion* and *Resurrection*. On the wall Neophytus, no doubt painted from life, prays on his knees before the stern image of the Deesis: a representation of Christ Enthroned flanked by the Virgin Mary and St John the Baptist interceding for mankind.

The Katholikon

The large church, dedicated to the Virgin Mary, stands in the centre of the monastery. It was built in the 16th century, in that period when the architectural traditions of the Catholic and Orthodox churches had begun to fuse. It has a high

Byzantine dome and triple apse, with a Gothic doorway and wide spacious nave whose vaulted roof is carried on capitals carved with acanthus leaves. The gilded wooden tomb and the silver-encased skull of St Neophytus stands before the splendidly carved iconostasis, whose upper rows of icons are characteristic examples of the polished, idealized art of the 16th century produced by the Cretan School. Once you have become accustomed to the dark you can appreciate the fine frescoes that survive in the apse and the north and south aisles. They also date from the 16th century and are charged with movement, decorative colours, and a concern for depth and plasticity that reveal the growing influence of the West. Here the art of the West has been harmoniously combined with traditional Orthodox scenes, details and inscriptions from the Acathist Hymn to the Virgin Mary (see the Latin chapel p. 167) to create a moving cycle of incidents from the life of the Virgin. The image of the *Conception*, rendered as the Virgin being wrapped in a cloth of gold, as well as the fresco depicting her meeting with Joseph are both touched with great tenderness and emotional power. Another favourite pair of scenes is *The Astonishment of the Angels* (at the news of the Annunciation) followed by *The Failure of the Four Wise Orators*, who stand speechless with empty scrolls before the Virgin on her golden throne.

Leaving the monastery there is a road south to Paphos that could take you through the villages of Tala and Emba. **Emba** has a number of chapels but the principal church, the 12th-century Panayia Khryseleousa, is easy to identify, as it stands in the centre of the village with a distinctive pair of domes and a slender bell tower. It retains elements of its impressive 16th-century interior, with a fine gilded iconostasis hung with a number of contemporaneous icons, but is more celebrated for the powerful fresco of the *Pantocrator* looking down from the dome. Below this stern representation of *Christ in Judgment* is a circle of angels, and beneath them, on the level of the windows in the drum, an assortment of prophets. Most of the lower scenes have been damaged by a clumsy, though well-intentioned, restoration job.

Polis and Khrysokhou Bay

The small market town of Polis, 34km/21 miles north of Paphos, sits on the east bank of the tou Stavrou tis Psokas valley. Though set back 1km from the sea, it is right in the centre of Khrysokhou Bay and makes a good centre for touring the surrounding area. It is a calm unpretentious town, which since the exodus of its largely Turkish-Cypriot population, has acted as a cheap alternative to the formal beach resorts. The post office and covered market on the high street have been joined by a number of bars, cafés and taverna whose tables spill out over the pebble pavement. There are few permanent hotels, but a large and shifting selection of rooms to rent in the backstreets.

The easiest route to the **beach** is along a track to the camping site, which winds north from the village centre, past the Gold Mine Disco and an orange grove to reach the eucalyptus wood that stands by the mixed sand and pebble shore. You can use the snackbar of the camping site, or march out with your own picnic east towards the old Limni mine jetty. The beach also stretches 2km west to Latchi/Lachi, a village whose identity as a quiet fishing shelter has recently been buried under a rash of new apartments and restaurants. Water sports and scuba diving have now taken over from fishing boats. Atlantic Diving, ✆ (06) 321656, operates from here, though its future is less certain since its manager Hans Roelofs got the bends.

There are a number of small, temporary excavation sites scattered around the town though as yet no substantial buildings have been discovered to excite the public interest, and most of the tombs have been long since despoiled. Polis stands over the ruins of **Marion**, one of the dozen ancient city-states of Cyprus that struggled with its neighbours, Palea Paphos and Soli, for regional dominance in the 4th and 5th centuries BC. Marion chose the losing side in a war between the Diadochi, 'the successors' of Alexander the Great, and was, with unaccustomed savagery, completely destroyed by Ptolemy I in 312. A generation later Ptolemy Philadelphus founded the town of Arsinoe just to the west of the ruins, which prospered in a quiet way until the 7th century.

Baths of Aphrodite

The so-called Baths of Aphrodite are 9km west of Polis along a coast road full of eating and drinking possibilities. From the recently established tourist pavilion at the end of the tarmac, a 200m signposted path leads to a small pool, fed by a dripping moss-covered rock face, that is shaded by a canopy of wild fig trees. The Baths would make a dazzling discovery if you happened upon them during a walk and could take a secluded bath with a loved one (like that Aphrodite is considered to have enjoyed here with her lover Akamas) though they are not equal to the current level of publicity. No nymph, however brazen, could possibly disport herself now before the trickle of gawping, slightly disappointed visitors and the ultimate indignity of a 'Do not drink the water' sign.

The coastal path beyond the Baths is a much more rewarding proposition. It leads through quiet woods, flower-strewn pastures, goat-grazed maquis and a succession of empty coves with small patches of sand amongst the eroded, puckered rocks of the limestone shore. It can make for a perfect day's walking, especially when combined with swims, sunbathing and a shady picnic. From the Baths this path stretches 8km northwest to finish at the **Fontana Amoroza**, a muddy spring with the grand title of the 'Fountain of Love'. The connection of Aphrodite with both the spring and the baths appears to have been a Renaissance fiction of

Lodovocio Ariosto (1474–1533), who visited the island in search of the haunts of Venus. In his epic poem *Orlando Furioso* he has left a charmingly romantic evocation of this shore.

> *Stands on a beauteous hill a verdant wood*
> *Where cedars, myrtles, bays and organe grow,*
> *With various plants that graceful scent bestow.*
> *Wild thyme, the lily, crocus and the rose*
> *Perfume the air, while every wind that blows*
> *Fresh from the land, far o'er the surgy main*
> *Wafts the sweet gale to greet the sailor train,*
> *Clear from a spring a murmuring rivlet pours*
> *Its winding tribute to the mead and flowers.*
> *Well may this spot be named the favourite soil*
> *Of lovely Venus, where with roseate smile*
> *Each dame, each virgin shine in bloomy pride*
> *Of charms unequalled through the world beside,*
> *Whilst the soft goddess youth and age inspires*
> *And even in life's last stage maintains her amorous fires.*

Cape Arnauti stretches north of the spring but 20th-century realities intrude upon the poetic idyll, for the area continues to serve as a military firing range.

Villages Inland from Polis

The quiet hill village of **Drousha** lies 10km south of Polis, signposted just off the E701 road to Paphos via Peyia. It is well placed for a walking holiday or a few days of quiet pottering along paths stretching out north and west of the village along the rocky spine of the Akamas peninsula. A particularly fine 6km stroll, heading west out of the village, then twists north to the deserted hamlets of Phasli and Androlikou, emptied of their Turkish Cypriot population during the events of 1974. A taverna, café, a few artisan shops and the accommodation on offer in the modern Droushia Heights hotel ensure a steady trickle of visitors.

If you have been walking in the hills of Cyprus and have not succeeded in spotting any snakes, then head for the village of **Skoulli** just 4 miles/6.5km south of Polis on the main B7 road where throughout the summer there is a live exhibition of amphibians and reptiles *(open from 9am–dusk; adm)*. You might also care to walk to the neighbouring hamlet of Kholi to visit the church of Arkhangelos Michael, whose structure incorporates a medieval watchtower with a number of 16th-century frescoes surviving in the interior.

Of the dozen or so attractive hill villages to the southeast of Polis, **Lyso** (at the end of the Steni-Peristerona-Meladeia road) has long been considered the prettiest, with its fine medieval church, Panayia Khryseleousa, retaining pieces of Gothic carving and vaulting that date from its origins as a Catholic church. There are plans to open a small folk museum in the village to conserve the memory of the traditional industries of the area such as spinning, weaving and embroidery. Just 2km to the east of Lyso a track allows you to walk up to the abandoned Turkish Cypriot hamlet of Melandra.

The Coast East to Kato Pyrgos

To the east of Polis stretches the predominantly rock and pebble shore of the Khrysokhou Bay. The pier, reservoir and industrial residues at nearby Limni make a messy introduction to the area. Copper and sulphide ores are no longer carted out to waiting freighters and while industrial activity has ceased this coast has yet to be exploited by tourism. The narrow strip of red soil by the shore is an intensely worked area of market gardens, banana and fruit plantations. Settlement used to be restricted to a dozen poor villages scattered out of harm's way in the pine-forested hills. The majority of the population has now moved down to the coast, but the forestry tracks into the interior offer a number of quiet walks.

Promos point marks the edge of the Khrysokhou Bay and from here you can look east to the **Kokkina Enclave**. The road twists through the rough hills in a mad confusion of hairpin bends to avoid this tiny Turkish-Cypriot enclave which is now an exclusively military zone filled with Greek, Turkish and UN outposts quietly observing one another. As well as serving as a bargaining counter, Kokkina also has a symbolic value, as it was here that the Turkish Cypriots received shipments of arms from the mainland of Turkey and the regional population congregated to protect themselves from Greek Cypriot attacks. Supplied by sea, they withstood a sniping siege, but almost fell to a determined attack led by Grivas in 1964. This was only broken by the intervention of Turkey and the carpet bombing of the surrounding wooded hills. Ten years later, this was repeated and the hills are only very slowly recovering.

Most maps draw in a scattering of Greek villages around Kokkina, though this is more a declaration of political will than objective reality. Settlement is concentrated in the village of **Kato Pyrgos** situated on the edge of the Green Line which doubles as a garrison post and small summer resort. The fishing harbour with its grey-green boulder breakwater overlooked by a couple of small taverna-hotels and flanked by odd patches of sand, maintains the quiet charm of the Cypriot coast which has almost disappeared elsewhere in the South. The citrus orchards surrounding the village are watered by two streams, the Katouris and Potamos tou

Pyrgou. The latter is out of bounds but a 2km/1½ mile stroll south beside the former brings you past the pretty domed Byzantine chapel of Panayia Galoktisti (The Nursing Virgin) and halfway to the Pyrgos dam.

To Panayia Khrysorroyiatissa Monastery and Pano Panayia

The monastery buildings of Panayia Khrysorroyiatissa are not of any antiquity, nor do they shelter any great treasure, aside from its cellars of award-winning wine. It has a fine position and a pleasant air of untroubled calm, but it is the journey there, more than any specific monument, that makes this such a delightful destination. The road quickly sheds the busy coast and climbs into soft, rolling, pale hills, clad with a patchwork of vineyards, fruit orchards and olive groves. It is an entrancing landscape and the monastery marks the northeastern edge of this agricultural zone, above which march the pine-clad hills of the central mountains. The villages of Kannaviou and Pano Panayia offer a choice of tavernas where long lunches, and local wine can be enjoyed in the shade of trees. A few simple rooms are available in Pano Panayia for those with time for a more leisurely exploration. If you are approaching by car take the Limassol road out of Paphos, turning off at Timi, and climb northeast to the monastery and Pano Panayia. On your way back take the E703 which brings you back onto the Paphos–Polis road at Tsadha.

Though there is no evidence now, **Amargeti** village, about halfway from Timi to the monastery, was the site of an opium cult centred on the aspect of Apollo as the god of healing. A crude mudbrick temple, built during the classical era, was found filled with crude pottery and stone votive figures dedicated to Apollo of the Melanthium Poppy, known to modern botanists as *nigella sativa*. There are other references to opium in ancient Cyprus, such as an opium pipe found in a temple at Kition and the thousands of poppyhead opium flasks that were exported from Cyprus to the Near East.

The turning to the hamlet of **Galataria** is about halfway between Pendalia and the monastery of Khrysorroyiatissa. It conserves a pretty 18th-century church in its centre, but about two miles/3km to the southeast of Galataria is the lone stone chapel of St Nicholas. It sits like an inanimate disciple amongst vines at the foot of a prominent outcrop of rock, overlooking the upper reaches of the Xeropotamos valley. It is a scene worthy of an Old Testament prophet or a fiery Byzantine hermit. The floor of the chapel is formed from the bedrock floor, and some 16th-century frescoes remain in its apse.

The small monastery of **Ayia Moni** is just 1.5km south of Panayia Khrysorroyiatissa. Recently restored it sits beside a vine planted combe surrounded by the wooded hills, its large 19th-century stone church and detached side chapel partially wrapped in cloisters. Traces of a much older apse with a crypt can be seen on the exterior of the eastern apse dating back to a 6th-century basilica. This was built over asanctuary of Hera (the Juno of the Romans).

Panayia Khrysorroyiatissa

The temple to Hera, and the memory of the goddess's epithets may account for the distinctly pagan flavour of the various translations of **Panayia Khrysorroyiatissa** such as the 'Golden Nipples of the Virgin Mary' or 'Our Lady of the Golden Pomegranate'. The monastery has had a cyclical history of decline, fall and restoration, fully in keeping with its maverick 12th-century founder. The present buildings, with their handsome white stone walls, protruding balconies, carved wooden screens, steep red-tiled roof and Gothic pointed arches have an almost Central European look. They date from the mid-19th century, the 18th-century monastery having been destroyed by the Turkish terror campaign of 1821. The monastery is now under the sure direction of Abbot Dionysos, Cyprus's leading specialist in the conservation of manuscripts of icons, who is also responsible for the monastic winery, which under the 'Monte Royia' label produces the award-winning dry white 'Ayios Andronicus' wine.

The church has a richly carved and gilded iconostasis, where its icon of the Virgin by St Luke stands encased in silver and draped in curtains. Beside it is the reliquary of St Ignatius, a hermit who lived in the forests but was drawn down to the shore by a fierce white light that shone in the night. On the night of 15 August, 1152 the light reappeared, allowing Ignatius to discover this precious icon which had been washed across the sea from Isauria. He tried to take it up the mountain to his hermitage, but on his way back he fell asleep under a pine tree below Mount Royia, whereupon he was told in a dream to establish this monastery.

The village of **Pano Panayia** is famous for its wine and as the birthplace of Makarios Mouskos, the monk from Kykko who was appointed Archbishop Makarios III in 1950, and who subsequently led the struggle for enosis which resulted in his election as the first President of the Republic of Cyprus in 1960. The simple village house of his parents, where he spent his childhood before entering Kykko monastery as a 13-year-old novice, has been preserved and is open to the public. It has an Arcadian simplicity and dignity with a single principal room and simple outer courtyard with tree and oven. The nearby Makarios III Cultural Centre, with its statue and display of clippings and memorabilia is interesting but less moving. In an early pose in episcopal robes Makarios bears an uncanny likeness to Peter Sellers.

Walking around Pano Panayia

East of Pano Panayia a forest track enters the pine-clad hills of the Paphos forest. In the summer the comparatively cool and resin scented breezes make the village an attractive walking base. There are plenty of tracks for some light walks but for those who like a mission there is the possibility of a 21km hike across the hills to Kykko monastery. This can be varied and lengthened by taking the track that swings around Mount Tripylos and dips down into Cedar valley, the principal island stronghold of the indigenous *Cedrus brevifolia*, or Cypriot cedar.

West of Pano Panayia, the E703 road passes through Asproyia before reaching the hamlet of **Kannaviou** ,where a couple of taverna sit in the shade beside the Ezousas stream. Kannaviou also marks the starting point of one of the easiest, and signposted, 19km-long tracks to the forestry station of **Stavros tis Psokas** established beside an old monastery by the British in 1884. This was the principal base for the long war waged by the forestry wardens to deny the area to goatherds who had inherited the right to pasture their flocks in the denuded hills. The current state of the Paphos District Forest, which contains two-thirds of Cyprus's forestry stock, is one of the proudest and most enduring achievements of the British colonial administration. The forest shelters both the indigenous cedar (Cedrus brevifolia) and the Cyprus mouflon (Ovis ophion). The mouflon is a wild mountain sheep whose rarity and sweet tasting flesh made it the number one quarry for medieval huntsmen, who used trained leopards for the chase. It was driven near to extinction in the late 19th century, but it has since recovered its position amongst the lonely hills. A herd is kept for breeding and viewing purposes in an enclosure by the forestry station, the only place you are likely to see this shy and reclusive beast. The Forestry Department also runs a picnic site, canteen and a small hostel with a dozen beds. A place in the hostel should be booked well in advance of your arrival, © (06) 722338.

Southwest from Kannaviou, the road rattles through a string of quiet, agricultural villages in a sea of vineyards before regaining the main B7 Polis-to-Paphos road outside **Tsadha**. The village has a fine view over the coast and used to serve as the residence of the Bishop of Paphos. Two miles/3km southeast of the village stands the monastery of Stavros tis Mythras which preserves a holy cross, now encased in silver, in its 18th-century church. Two 16th-century doorways are all that remain from the Gothic abbey that once stood on the site.

Yeroskipou (Geroskipos)

The village of Yeroskipou is 4km southeast of Paphos, astride the main road to Limassol. Ribbon development, along both beach and roadside, has now left only a stream bed to divide Paphos from Yeroskipou. The latter, for all its initial impression as a dusty, roadside suburb lined with souvenir shops selling assorted flavours of *loukoumia*, Turkish delight and local craft has yet managed to retain its own distinctive history and identity. The church in the centre of the lively village square is surrounded by a number of cafés and bars. By dusk the last coachload of tourists has departed and you can settle down to a drink and a plate of nuts whilst you imagine the past glories of this once-sacred place.

Hiero Skepos

The name Yeroskipou recalls its origin as the Hiero Skepos, the Sacred Gardens, of the patron goddess of Cyprus. It was an established staging post for the pilgrims landing at Paphos and journeying out to the shrine at Palea Paphos. This famous garden is one of three known sites on the island dedicated to the sexual rites of Paphian Aphrodite that has helped give the monotheistic world its image of paradise. The Hiero Skepos was a walled sanctuary, watered by its own sacred springs and filled with flowers, vines and venerable trees under whose shade devotees honoured Aphrodite with random sex. From the surviving descriptions it is not clear if the temple prostitutes were ordinary island women doing temporary duty or professional priestesses. The role played by the bejewelled temple boys (known from a number of reclining statues) is also a mystery.

Yeroskipou is also the traditional site of the biblical vineyard of Engadi, as referred to in the 'Song of Songs': 'my beloved is unto me as a cluster [of Cyprus grapes] in the vineyard of Engadi.' This initially confusing cross-reference between the pagan and Judaic worlds makes abundant sense if you accept the reading of the 'Song of Songs' as no mere piece of secular semitic eroticism but as verses from the tragedy of Adonis where Aphrodite goes in search of her dead lover. This annual festival was held in spring, but fortunately the long days of mournful search were followed by a riotous celebration of his return, which one can only picture as a combination of Easter, a teenage toga party and Mardi Gras in New Orleans.

The sacred garden of Engadi was last seen by Rudolph von Suchen in 1340, who reported that its like is nowhere to be found, for it was wonderfully fruitful, four square miles in expanse and hidden within mountain walls. Rudolph had perhaps crossed over that delicate frontier between mythology and mythologizing, but lovers of *arcana* will be relieved to hear that it was safely in the hands of the Knights Templars, who are seldom far from a good mystery.

Ayia Paraskevi

In the centre of the village square stands the whitewashed stone cruciform church of Ayia Paraskevi, with its celebrated, and much-sketched, silhouette formed from five nipple domes and a slender 19th-century bell tower. Beneath the tower stands the curious little *martyrion* or reliquary annexe tacked onto the church. Though the western end is modern, the bulk of the church dates from the early 9th century when Cyprus was still a no-man's-land between Byzantium and the Islamic caliphate. It is an extremely rare example from this Dark Age period, that extended from AD 649–965, and is made even more precious by the discovery, during restorations, of a simple geometrical decorative scheme dating from the iconoclastic period. Well into this century the churchyard was surrounded by architectural fragments from an old Roman temple to Venus. Just 6m from the southwest corner of the church, now blocked, is the entrance to a large cave. Out of this cave flowed the spring of Aphrodite which watered her sacred gardens.

The interior of the church has been recently restored, and most of the furniture and icons are modern. One well-worn exception is the double-faced icon of the Virgin Mary Yeroskipiotissa (usually hung behind glass on the northwestern corner of the iconostasis) found hidden in a nearby field. It is contemporary with the church's surviving body of frescoes, which mostly date from the 15th century. Scenes such as the *Baptism of Christ* (complete with classically derived personifications of the river Jordan and the sea in her coracle), the *Raising of Lazarus*, the *Washing of the Disciples' Feet* and the *Judgement of Pilate*, (who is depicted as a young man turning to wash his hands) are all vivid expressions of faith. They have a vitality and fluency drawn from both the classicism of the late Paleologue period and the Italian Renaissance, though in scenes like the *Betrayal*, the former has become dominant. The active gestures of the soldiers surrounding Judas, as he plants a kiss of treachery on Christ, are undeniably Western. In the centre of the *Crucifixion* scene an earlier 12th century frescoe (depicting the *Dormition of the Virgin*) has been exposed, allowing you to compare the calm certainty of an earlier period of Byzantine art with the increasingly frenetic realism of the 15th century.

The church's most famous fresco is the well-preserved *St Paul*, on the northeast pendentive of the western dome. The saint's head is portrayed with his customary bald brow and earnest expression, but his position, bent double in urgent proximity to a seated scribe, is outside the accepted canon of iconography. It works well, however, and the intensity of this little scene reaffirms our faith that every syllable of the Epistles was intended. St Paul could write but his style was so peculiar that he used it sparingly, and more as a signature of authenticity than for practical communication.

Yeroskipou Folk Art Museum at the House of Haji Smith

Open 7.30–2.30 Mon, Tues, Wed and Fri, 7.30–2.30, 3–6 Thurs, closed Sat and Sun, © (06) 240216; adm.

The museum, established in the 18th-century stone house of Haji Smith in Athens street, is just a short stroll east of the village church. The Department of Antiquities manages this rich collection of traditional tools, household implements and clothing arranged over two storeys. (For an explanation of the more idyiosncratic implements, *see* either the Eliades collection in Paphos on p. 249 or the

Limassol museum on p. 192.) Haji Smith began life as an intelligent youth by the name of Andreas Zimboulaki. He so impressed Sir Sydney Smith with his wit and local knowledge (in 1800 the quixotic Sir Sydney was then visiting Paphos in the full flush of victory, with the captive Marshal Junot aboard his ship), that he was appointed Vice Consul for Great Britain. Nowadays it is an honour that an Andreas could gracefully decline, but then it was a valuable privilege that granted virtual immunity from Ottoman jurisdiction. In gratitude he took the name of his patron and became known as Haji Smith.

East to Kouklia

On the road east from Yeroskipou to Kouklia there are two possible stops. Just a mile south from the roadside hamlet of Akhelia is the small cruciform Byzantine chapel of Ayios Theodosius, containing smoke-blackened remnants of its original body of frescoes, painted in the 13th and 16th centuries. Just east of the turning to Timi village is the road to Paphos Airport which takes you past Timi beach. This is pebble not sand, but has some usefully sited tavernas for those about to catch a flight or awaiting the delayed arrival of friends.

The Temple of Aphrodite at Palea Paphos (Kouklia Village)

> '*And laughter loving Aphrodite went to Paphos in Cyprus where she has her sacred precinct and fragrant altar*'

> Book VIII of Homer's *Odyssey*

The turning to Kouklia is 16km southeast of Paphos along the main road to Limassol. Kouklia is a quiet, almost subdued village that stands over the centre of the ancient and once-extensive city of Palea Paphos. Few visitors seem to stray outside the temple-museum area. A quick visit to the attractive little 14th-century church of Panayia Katholiki just to its east would allow you to see the fresco of *Christ Pantocrator* in its dome.

The Temple Site

Open every day 7.30am–7.30pm closing at dusk in the winter; adm.

Though the ancient city of Palea Paphos and its temple of Aphrodite have been well dug over, researched and written up over the last century, the actual visible remains are disappointingly slight. Nothing remains standing from the once-extensive walled city, a leading power throughout the Archaic and Classical periods.

The fenced **temple site** (just uphill and north from the Manor House Museum) is an area of sun-bleached bedrock, shards and low foundations. As you walk up, you will see an L-shaped group of massive grey limestone blocks, mysteriously drilled with holes. They are easy to identify and all that remain of the Late Bronze Age sanctuary that stood here in the 11th century BC. There is not enough evidence for any certain reconstruction, but these blocks are believed to have been part of the **temenos**, the monolithic perimeter wall which enclosed the sacred precinct. From descriptions and coins it appears that the actual altar was a tripartite shelter, that allowed the holy black stone of Aphrodite to stand in the open air. This was the final destination for pilgrims who through clouds of incense offered bloodless sacrifices of precious oils, fragrant flowers or released caged doves sacred to the goddess. In return they received symbolic gifts such as salt and *Pyramos*, sacred cake, from the priests.

Further north you can, with relative ease, trace the foundations of the sanctuary's wide **outer courtyard**. These ruins are not particularly ancient; they belong to an ambitious 1st-century Roman rebuilding that took place after extensive damage from an earthquake in 77 AD. In form they were probably very similar to what can still be seen today at the shrine of Apollo Hylates outside Kourion. The courtyard was entered through processional side gates and surrounded by long halls, where the votive statues and long-winded pompous inscriptions so beloved by the Romans could be displayed amongst the benches where the pious, having sacrificed, would recline in the hope of receiving divine instruction in a dream.

The sanctuary flourished deep into the Christian era. It appears to have been restored after more earthquake damage in AD 323 but was formally closed down by the Emperor Theodosius at the end of the 4th century. There is no way of knowing if the shrine was allowed to gradually decay or was deliberately destroyed after local resistance (as was recorded occurring elsewhere in the empire). The city, deprived of its ancient temple, the profits of the pilgrim trade and the protection of its patroness, rapidly withered away. By the Byzantine era the once-proud walled city of Palea Paphos had degenerated into a mere village.

The Royal Manor House

The ruins of Palea Paphos were extensively quarried, not least in the 13th century by the Lusignan kings who built the Castle of Conuclia here, also known as the Chateau de Covocle. This edifice was wrecked during the Mameluke invasion of 1426, though the hall of the old castle was used as the nucleus for the Royal Manor House. It operated as a centre for a very profitable sugar-cane plantation, similar to that of Kolossi Castle (*see* p. 208). After the Ottoman conquest of 1571, it was turned into a Chiftlik, an hereditable estate, and the manor house was enlarged with the addition of the gatehouse and the north and west wings with their elegant arched arcades. This attractive and historic complex has proved an irresistible base for archaeologists, who have been coming here since 1888. A recent restoration has repaired the old medieval hall and two rooms in the east wing now house a small museum.

The museum's principal exhibit is a **polished black phallic stone** that was found locally. It has been identified as the altar of Aphrodite, and certainly looks similar to the lingams that are still honoured in the temples of Hindu goddesses in India. Black phallic stones were widely associated with the cult of Cybele, the ancient fertility goddess of Anatolia, though none of these has survived. The Kaaba, in the centre of Mecca, houses a similar stone (though it is dark green not black) venerated by centuries of pagan Arabs before the Prophet Mohammed identified it as the altar of Abraham.

The fine **Archaic limestone head** of one of the high priest-kings of the city was just one of many objects found embedded in an ancient siege mound. The remnant of this mound can be seen 600m out from the village on the road to Archimandrita. It was built in 498 BC by a Persian army besieging Palea Paphos after it had joined the Ionian revolt against the Persian Empire. The besiegers used the spoil from cemeteries and sanctuaries outside the city to build the mound whilst the besieged dug no less than three tunnels into it, in an attempt to undermine the mobile siege towers that threatened their walls. They failed, the city fell and was sacked. Its chastened Kinyrad dynasty of high priest-kings (who claimed descent from Kinyras, the father of Adonis, most beautiful of men, who was the beloved of Aphrodite) then followed a strictly conservative and unadventurous foreign policy until Nikokles founded Nea Paphos in 321 BC.

Other objects on display include fine ivories, jewels and ceramics unearthed from the string of cemeteries surrounding the city, dating from the Late Bronze Age through to the late Roman period. Most of the excavated tombs have been covered up again, but the Hellenistic tomb of '*Spilaion tis Regis*' (the cave of the Queen) can be located 700m southeast of the museum.

An easier walk from the museum is along a 200m path to the northwest of the museum, to look at some 1st century AD mosaics from a Roman house. The *Leda and Swan* floor is a copy (the original was stolen and then later recovered in London and is now safely displayed in Nicosia's Cyprus Museum).

Palaea Enkleistra and Arkhimandrita

About 4km northeast of Kouklia on the road to Arkhimandrita, look out for a cave-chapel in the escarpment overlooking the usually dry riverbed. The hermitage of **Palaea Enkleistra** was believed to have been used by St Neophytus but the soft pastel colours of the frescoes, much mutilated by iconoclastic shepherds, have been dated to the 15th century. A fresco of St Onoufrius the hermit guards the entrance while the flat roof of the cave chapel carries an unusual fresco: a depiction of the Trinity (the image of Christ being used for both Father and Son) enclosed in an eight-pointed star surrounded by angels and an outer circle of the four evangelists. Amongst a number of damaged saints, St Anastasis, the poison curer can be recognized on the south wall with her bottle of snakebite serum and cross.

The village of Pano Arkhimandrita, about 13km northeast of Kouklia, is surrounded by vine-covered hills. A signposted path just south from the village leads down to the small rock cut shrine of **Ayii Pateres**, an ossuary of martyrs' bones, belonging to a group of 318 Syrian Christians who fled the turbulence of their own country and sought refuge in Cyprus. As this unhappy band landed on a nearby shore they only had time to give thanks to God for their deliverance before being massacred by Saracen pirates.

Petra tou Romiou (Rock of the Romans)

From Kouklia the B6 road from Paphos to Limassol heads down towards the long, and still completely undeveloped, pebble beaches of this part of the Cypriot shore. As you approach the white cliffs of Cape Aspro, about 25km east of Paphos, a group of high, pale rocks, known as Petra tou Romiou, stands just offshore. The surrounding pair of coves is the legendary birthplace of Aphrodite, the foam borne. It is an irresistible place for a baptismal bathe, and a pedestrian tunnel under the main road now allows you to do this without the risk of being run over. In bad weather you can give up the idea and drive up to have a drink at the restaurant-cum-viewing pavilion.

Botticelli's *Birth of Venus* has forever colonised the Western mind with his image of this graceful nativity, though the Homeric Hymns summon up a more regal and dramatic event: 'The moist breeze of zephyr brought her there on the waves of the sea with a noise of thunder among the soft foam, and the gold-clad Horae received her with joy. They decked her with precious jewels and set her immortal head a beautiful crown of gold, and in her ears ear-rings of copper and gold.'

It is curious that the legends should have chosen this region of Cyprus, the last to be settled by man, as the birthplace of the patron deity of the island whose cult directly descends from the age-old fertility rituals of the Mother Goddess. It is easier to see it, not as the birth of the goddess, but as a memory of the arrival of new cult practices from the sophisticated palace culture of Minoan Crete. This form of enlightened worship, rich in analogy, poetic liturgy, sexual liberty and processional rituals, would have soon overshadowed the fierce old seasonal sacrifices that must have soon appeared rustic and clumsy by comparison. The bloodless nature of the sacrifices of Paphian Aphrodite were a well noted feature and may alone have helped the quick spread of the new cult. However in other shrines on the island, such as that to Aphrodite Acraea at the Klihdes, the old ways may have continued deep into the classical period.

Ayios Yeoryios (near Peyia)   *moderate*

There are three small, relaxed places to stay and eat in the coastal hamlet of Ayios Yeoryios (St George) which stands beside Cape Drepanum. The **Yeronisos** hotel, © (06) 621078 has a dozen rooms; **Saint George**, © (06) 621306 (which is the closest to the sea and run by the affable Nicos Theodosiou) has five double rooms; whilst the **Macarthur** fish restaurant has a few more.

Polis-Lachi   *moderate/cheap*

The Marion, PO Box 29, © (06) 321216, is a moderately priced hotel, cast in the familiar unforgiving concrete. It contains 50 rooms and a swimming pool, and stands by itself on the road east from Polis. Just to the west of Lachi harbour, above its own gritty pebble beach, is the kinder silhouette and smaller size of the Souli hotel-restaurant, © (06) 321088, which lets out a dozen cheap rooms. Other even cheaper possibilities include the dowdy Akamas hotel in the middle of Polis, or the camp site on the beach. You can also check out the rooms to rent in the back streets as well as the purpose-built apartments found along the Polis beach track, such as Sea View or Vougenvilea, © (06) 321684.

Kato Pyrgos

There are no hotels on the coast east of Polis until you reach Kato Pyrgos. The **E J Pyrgos Bay** hotel which overlooks its own sandy bay just to the west of the village of Kato Pyrgos, is the most comfortable but this moderately priced hotel is only open in the summer. By the fishing harbour are two cheap hotels: the **Tylos**, © (06) 522348, and the **Pyrgiana**, © (065) 22322, which both run their own restaurants overlooking the fishing boats and patches of well-groomed sand. In addition there are plenty of rooms-to-let signs, such as that of Andreas Drakos, © (06) 22347, and there is a well stocked supermarket for picnics by the Ayia Irini church.

Pano Panayia   *cheap*

The **Romantika Restaurant** on the high street of the village, © (06) 722434, has half a dozen rooms to rent which cost only C£7.50 per person. If they are full you could also try the Oak Tree restaurant and bar. If you are staying any length of time you can vary your meals by eating in one of the nest of three tavernas in the shade of trees in the neighbouring village of Kannaviou.

Droushia

The **Droushia Heights**, ✆ (06) 332351, is a moderately priced hotel with 30 bedrooms and a swimming pool. It stands just to the east of the village with a magnificent view north taking in the wide span of Khrysokhou Bay. The hotel shares the calm atmosphere of the village (it was built and is run by a committee of prosperous village émigrés) and makes a perfect base for walking in the Akamas. The hotel's kitchen can be varied by trips out to the café and taverna in the village.

Eating Out in Paphos District

moderate

Polis-Latchi

There are a growing number of tavernas popping up on the coast west of Latchi. **Ttakkas Bay Restaurant** about 250m east of the Baths of Aphrodite car park, is run by a refugee family from Rizokarpaso (Dipkarpaz). It is unlikely to be improved upon with its charmingly shabby air, private pebble beach and charcoal-grilled fish. **Psaropoulos Beach**, ✆ (06) 321069, is another well-established restaurant just west of Latchi, with a more varied menu and daily specials including traditional vegetable dishes.

Kathikas Village

Araouzos is a handsome taverna, built and decorated with traditional materials, and which looks out over its own courtyard. The kitchen delights in using home grown local products and recipes as well as serving two village wines, Demetra red and Argyro white, produced by Yiannoula Pana Retou. It is a model of its kind, funded by the Laona project, who are attempting to conserve the buildings and traditions of the Akamas.

Peyia Village

The hill village of Peyia enjoys a fine view over the coast around Coral Bay and out into the Mediterranean where you can watch the sun sinking each evening. There are over half a dozen good tavernas established in the village all of which provide a good meal, though **Michaelis's Peyia Tavern** (on the right hand corner as you go into the village) is possibly the best of the bunch.

Kissonergha Village

Try the **Apothiki**, 'the barn' taverna, for a full-blown Cypriot *meze* served in an old Carob warehouse.

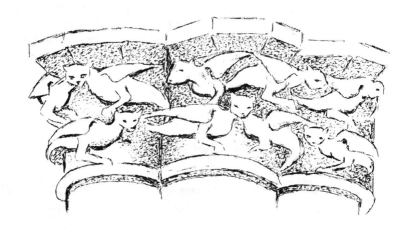

Northern Nicosia and West Coast

Northern Nicosia is markedly poorer and quieter than its bustling Greek neighbour to the south and has a much smaller population. The Turkish half of the old walled city contains the towering Gothic cathedral-mosque, and more than its share of the lesser medieval and Ottoman monuments. They are surrounded by quiet, dusty streets, blown with a matt layer of genteel dilapidation. It is a pleasant area to walk through, for the streets are virtually empty of traffic and it has retained much more of its traditional architecture than the south. However, it also has a corresponding lack of

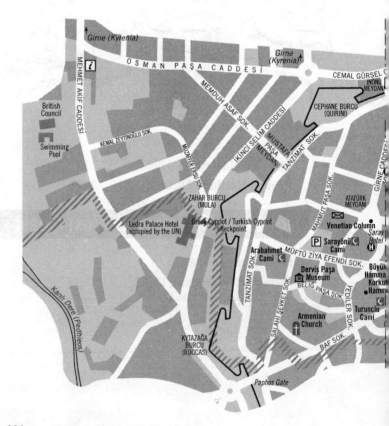

urban vivacity. It is low on that mixture of careless browsing, bar cruising, window-shopping and taverna-hopping that makes a city just as much as do its monuments.

The Green Line splits both the city and the province of Nicosia in two, leaving all the mountain valleys and painted churches in the Greek half. The most attractive parts of the Turkish province are all along the west coast. There you will find the monastery of Ayios Mamas, the pretty village of Lefke and the ruins of Soli and Vouni.

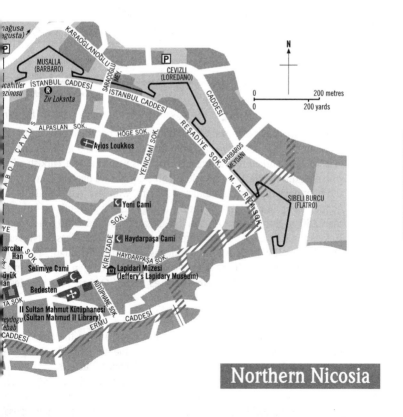

Northern Nicosia

The City of Northern Nicosia (Lefkoşa)

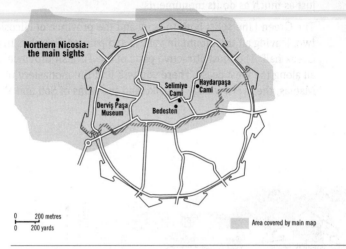

Northern Nicosia: the main sights

Haydarpaşa Cami

Selimiye Cami

Derviş Paşa Museum

Bedesten

0   200 metres
0   200 yards

Area covered by main map

Getting Around

By Air

The old Nicosia airport, to the west of the city, is occupied by UN forces. Ercan airport, a 23km-drive east from the city, was an old military airstrip that has been turned into a civil airport and is named after a Turkish pilot who died during the 1974 invasion. Three companies operate from Ercan and offer daily flights to Istanbul and Ankara, with less frequent flights to Adana, Izmir and Antalya. A return flight to Istanbul, Izmir or Antalya costs £80, slightly less for Ankara or Adana and around £250 to London. Tickets can be brought either from the airport or from offices in Nicosia. The **Cyprus Turkish Airlines** office is on Atatürk Meydanı, ✆ (020) 73821, **Istanbul Airlines** is at 3–4 Mirata Apts, Osman Paşa Caddesı, ✆ (020) 77140 and **Turkish Airlines** at 32, Osman Paşa Caddesı, ✆ (020) 71061.

By Bus

The main terminal for the city and North Cyprus is on the crossing of Atatürk Caddesı and Kemal Asik Caddesı. On the nothern side of the terminal are half a dozen ticket offices, around which cluster stalls of fruit and nut salesmen with more substantial meals available from a *lokanta* on the first floor terrace. A *dolmuş* minibus departs for Girne (Kyrenia) every 20 minutes. There are fourteen buses a day east to Gazimağusa

(Famagusta) and about the same number west to Güzelyurt (Morphou), running between 6.45am and 5.15pm. Lefke is served by six direct buses, Dipkarpaz (Rizokarpaso) by one which currently leaves at 11.30am.

By Taxi

During the daytime taxis can be found in profusion just inside the Kyrenia Gate in İnönü Meydanı. They do not cruise the streets much and at night it is often easier to call up a cab: try either Ankara on (020) 71788, Izmir on 78242, Nato on 71556, or Yilmaz on 73036. They do not have meters but rely on officially monitored printed tariffs, which you may ask to see before settling your fare. The journey to Girne (Kyrenia) is about £5, to Gazimağusa (Famagusta) about £10, while a full day tour for up to four people, lasting from 9am–6pm, will be around £35.

By shared taxis: A place in a shared taxi (which can take the shape of a minibus or a large car, known affectionately as a *dolmuş*—a sandwich) is a fraction of the cost of a regular taxi but they only go to the four major towns and might involve a half-hour wait. Ring Kombos first, ✆ (020) 72929 or walk to their office which is on a side street off Girne Caddesı behind the Sarigizmeli Lokanta restaurant at no. 174.

By Car

Capital Rent-a-Car, ✆ (020) 78172, is in the Firko building on Sehit Uluşamgil Sokağı at the northern end of Bedrettin Demirel Caddesı just beside Sabri's Orient Hotel. Elite is within the walls at 103, Girne Caddesı, ✆ (020) 73175. For rates and terms *see* 'Kyrenia (Girne)' p.317.

Tourist Information

The **tourist and public information office** is tucked safely out of the way of casual visitors on 95, Mehmet Akif Caddesı, ✆ (020) 75051 while its sub-office, well placed in the Kyrenia gatehouse, is seldom manned. Use the Saray Hotel in Atatürk Meydanı instead, which is admirably sited as a rendezvous point with telephones and lavatories. Buy a balcony ticket from the reception desk, which gives you a tea, coffee or beer whilst you take in the panoramic view from the eighth floor to provide a perfect introduction to the monuments and streets of northern Nicosia.

If you have come across from the south there is no special need to **exchange** money, as shops and restaurants will freely accept Cyprus pounds or any major European or American currency. There are three **banks** to be found along Girne Caddesı and in Atatürk Meydanı as well as the much faster service offered by currency exchange bureaux. The central **post office** is also on Atatürk Meydanı, ✆ (020) 73754.

Most visitors come for just one day, returning over the border or to the Kyrenia coast by dusk. In order to make good use of this time, a full day's itinerary is given below. If you prefer to wander at will, make sure you don't miss the Selimiye mosque (the old Gothic cathedral of St Sophia), the old Haydarpaşa mosque (the medieval church of St Catherine) or the mansion of Dervish Paşa.

Enter the old city and its circuit of Venetian walls beside the stumpy Girne Kapısı (Kyrenia Gatehouse). Pop into the Mevlevi Tekke museum, the old monastery of the whirling dervishes, on the way down to Atatürk Meydanı (Atatürk Square) where you can enjoy a coffee at the top of the Saray Hotel, followed by a browse in Rustem's bookshop. Then book a bath at the Büyük Hammam before admiring the two caravanserais, the Kumarcılar Han and the Büyük Han, on your way to the Selimiye mosque. Take in the nearby Bedesten with its medieval tombstones, before examining the calligraphy in Sultan Mahmut Kütüphanesi (Sultan Mahmud's library) and the fine stonework in the Lapidari Müzesi (Lapidary Museum). Shopping is best done in the covered market and down Araşta street; the café on the south side of the Selimiye mosque makes a useful rendezvous point. Walk up to the Gothic Haydarpaşa and from there cut back through the Ayios Loukkos back streets for lunch, at the Saray or Sarigizmeli Lokanta. After lunch saunter down to the Arabahmet mosque and branch off from a promenade down Salahi Şevket, old Victoria street, to visit the Mansion of Dervish Paşa. Experience the Green Line along Tanzimat street, followed by a sweat in the Büyük Hammam or a beer outside the Kyrenia Gate before dusk.

The Venetian Walls

Northern Nicosia holds five and a half of the eleven bastions that protrude like blunt arrowheads from the city walls. They were hurriedly built by the Venetians in the mid-16th century (*see* p. 122). All of the bastions are inaccessible as they are occupied by the Turkish army. For the Green Line sensation take a walk along Tanzimat Street, the section between Kaytazağa (Roccas) bastion and Zahra (Mula) bastion, which overlooks the Ledra Palace crossing. The road is still protected as if from 1974 sniper fire by a continuous line of earth-filled oil drums that becomes a green and yellow line when the weeds sprout in spring. A late afternoon stroll around the exterior, through the various parks, pitches and playgrounds provides a much better view of the stone-dressed earth walls and ramparts. Stop at a table in the tree-shaded area outside the Kyrenia Gate, where you can order beers from the Mucahitler Gazino kiosk. The cannons in this park are mostly English, and were used by the quixotic Sir Sidney Smith (founder of a short-lived order of chivalry to combat slavery) in his successful defence of Ottoman Acre against Napoleon's Egyptian expedition.

Girne Kapısı (Kyrenia Gate)

This modest Venetian gatehouse stands at the intersection of Girne Caddesı and Cemal Gürsel Caddesı. It is now stranded in a sunken position in the middle of the road that the British punched through the old walls in 1931. For centuries it commanded one of only three entrances into the city that were approached from roads from the island's chief ports: Famagusta, Paphos and Kyrenia. The stonework would originally have been largely hidden in the bulk of the earth filled wall. The Turks added the dome in 1821 in order to cast extra light into the dark passageway. Above the portcullis gate on the south face are three inscriptions: a piece of Koranic verse and the initials of George V are combined with a re-erected Venetian tablet bearing the date MDLXII (1562). To the north of the gate stands a statue of Kemal Atatürk, the heroic commander at Gallipoli and founder of the secular Turkish Republic. Just within the gate to the east is a statue of Dr Fazil Kutchuk, the Turkish Cypriot community leader who was elected Vice President at the time of Independence in 1960.

Mevlevi Tekke

Open 9am–1.30pm, 2.30pm–5pm Tues-Fri and on Sat 9am–1pm; adm; the entrance is 100m south of the Kyrenia gate on Girne Caddessi.

The Tekke, the Muslim equivalent to a monastery, was built for the Mevlevi or Whirling Dervishes, a religious brotherhood which followed the teaching of Mevlana Jelaledin Rumi, the mystical poet and great Sufi master who died at Konya in Turkey in 1273. It was built in the early 17th century with a fountain at the entrance gate, lodging rooms, a kitchen and a central hall. It remained in use until Independence, when it was converted into a museum of Turkish Folk Art. The displays of traditional arts and crafts takes second place to the building itself, with its wooden dancing floor furnished with a niche for the presiding sheikh and a gallery for musicians. The disciples aspired to a glimpse of the divine through the ritual of sacred dance, known as sema. The various dances and their musical scores, of which 50 have been recorded, combined with a tradition of learning and calligraphy, to make the tekkes a lodestone of Ottoman culture.

Whirling Dervishes

The dancers wore a distinctive high felt hat made from camel hair, symbolizing a tomb, while their long pleated white skirt was compared to a funeral shroud. One hand pointed to the sky and one to the earth to indicate the hopeless predicament of mankind, aspiring to heaven but destined for the earth. The ritual began with a prayer to the prophet, the silence broken by a drumbeat commanding 'Be!', succeeded by a flute solo suggesting the breath of life. The dance began with

greetings and a circular walk before culminating in four spinning whirls. The first was conceived as a meditation on knowledge,
the second on the wonder of the created world, the third a desire for
the rapture of divine love and with it the submission of the mind,
while the fourth was a meditation on mortality and subservience to
revealed religion. The session concluded with a reading from the Koran.

The Mausoleum of the Sheikhs leads off from the hall, and consists of a long row
of domed tomb chambers filled with row upon row of white-turbaned headstones
on green felt-draped catafalques. To stroll through the tombs of the 16 successive
sheikhs of the Tekke, from its foundation to its demise in the 20th century, is like
stepping into a recurring image formed by opposing mirrors.

Atatürk Meydanı (Square)

Atatürk Meydanı looks rather drab initially but it is worth a second look. It was
the political centre of Cyprus for centuries, for the northern face of the square
(now filled by ex-colonial police barracks) was once filled by the 'Saray', the
Gothic palace of the governor throughout the Frankish, Venetian and Ottoman
periods. In 1904 an unimaginative British administration demolished this 700-
year-old complex with its fine apartments, arcaded courtyard and throne hall.
Only a hexagonal Ottoman fountain survived, to which a colonial review stand
was added in the 1920s.

In the centre of the square stands the **Venetian Column**, which was crowned
by the lion of St Mark until toppled by the victorious Turks in 1570. This granite
column, traditionally believed to have been quarried from the temple of Jupiter at
Salamis, lay in the grounds of the Saray mosque for several centuries. The British
re-erected it during the First World War, when they were at war with the
Ottoman Empire. They decorated the new plinth with the two dates of the
column's erection, 1550 and 1915, by a pair of maritime Empires that were each
fated to rule Cyprus for exactly the same period, 84 years.

The original **Saray önü mosque** was demolished at the turn of the century and
but for its minaret, replaced by something moorish. Horseshoe arches were used
freely both within and without, by an English architect who ignored Cyprus's visible Ottoman, Byzantine, Gothic and vernacular traditions in favour of his
inadequate recollection of Andalucia. It is no longer used for prayer, and its
shaded outdoor benches make an inviting place for a quiet read.

Büyük Hammam

A finely carved medieval round arch, half obscured by the modern street level,
creates the distinctive entrance to the Büyük Hammam, the great bath. It is the

largest Turkish bath on the island, and a valuable working example of a once ubiquitous element in the urban landscape of Cyprus. It is also the perfect place to while away the forbidding heat and glare of an afternoon in Nicosia, *see* p. 296. The sunken entrance arch recalls medieval street levels and the site of the 14th-century church of St George of the Latins that once stood here. The church gained notoriety as the meeting place for a group plotting to assassinate King Peter I, on 17 January 1369. It later became known as St George of the Poulains, the half-castes, when the area was settled by the offspring of Christian Arab and Frankish marriages.

Büyük Han

This elegant courtyard, on the southwest corner of tatty Asmaalti Square, is the earliest and one of the finest monuments from the Ottoman period. It was used by the British as a prison, and since 1960 has been in an intermittent state of repair. During weekday work hours one of the two gates is likely to be open.

A Han, or caravanserai, was designed for the use of merchants and passing travellers. They were built along the trade routes and in all the principal towns of the Ottoman Empire. The Büyük Han, or Great Inn, was commissioned by Muzaffer Paşa, a general who remained on the island after the initial campaign of conquest to serve as the first Ottoman Governor of Cyprus. He raised a levy of two paras a head in order to build the han, but this small unsanctioned tax was considered to exceed his grant of authority and led to his recall to Istanbul and execution.

The severe exterior walls are breached by a pair of strong lateral gates, to reveal an elegant courtyard lined with a double verandah of carved stone. The round arches of the ground-floor arcade give birth to slender columns that support the higher pointed arches of the upper gallery. It has a very Western look to it, for the good reason that it was largely assembled from the remains of a number of Catholic churches. The ground floors of hans were often used for stabling, but at Büyük animals were tethered outside, except along the east wall which was lined with 10 shops. Rooms were available free of charge for the first three days but could be rented for longer terms by artisans or traders. The upper storey was more desirable, as its chambers were equipped with built-in wall cupboards and fireplaces. The rows of octagonal chimneys topped with a pointed pyramidal cap are a distinctive addition to the Nicosia skyline. They were developed by Mimar Sinan, the celebrated 16th-century architect of Ottoman Istanbul, and may have been brought to Cyprus by one of his pupils. In the centre of the courtyard is an octagonal kiosk which stands over the communal water tank, supported by eight white marble columns. The domed upstairs room is decorated with a carved mihrab niche to indicate the direction of prayer. The forgotten benefactor of this Islamic chapel lies in the grave below.

Kumarcılar Han

The 17th-century Kumarcılar Han, the Inn of the Gamblers (also known in its time as the Han of Fiddlers or the Caravanserai of Travelling Minstrels), is on Asma Altı Street, 50m north of the Büyük Han. Kumarcılar is easy to miss, as only its grilled entrance gate is free from the shops and booths that cluster around its outer walls. The Antiquities Department, © (020) 72916, care for it but it is unfortunately rare to find it open to the public, though a key may be found by inquiring at the local café.

The Han consists of an intimate courtyard overlooked by the solid arches of the ground-floor arcade and a lighter upstairs verandah whose tiled eaves are supported by wooden beams and stone columns. It began life as a number of separate structures that were united to create a single courtyard in the Ottoman period. This initial variety has been further exaggerated by centuries of slight alterations, repairs and improvements, such as the marble paving on the first floor and a scattering of Roman spoliae embedded in the walls.

Selimiye Mosque (Cathedral of St Sophia)

The Gothic Cathedral of St Sophia stands pre-eminent on high ground in the centre of old Nicosia. It is built from the pinkish golden limestone of Kyrenia, ringed with flying buttresses and crowned by two Turkish minarets that proclaim its conversion to a mosque in 1570. It was renamed 'Selimiye' in 1954 in honour of Sultan Selim II, and remains a place of Muslim prayer, being especially popular for funerals. Visitors are welcome though the western entrance may be found locked outside the hours of prayer. You should wait until the actual prayers are over and remove your shoes before entering. Men are expected to wear trousers, women skirts though there are usually some wraps available at the entrance to correct any sartorial shortcomings.

Architectural History

Work began on this site in 1193, in the first year of the rule of the French Lusignan dynasty, but only a few reused fragments remain from this abortive first building. The existing cathedral was started in 1209 and progressed under the enthusiastic direction of Eustorgius of Montaigu, the Archbishop of Nicosia who later was to die in the Egyptian crusade led by the saintly King Louis IX of France. The plan, a nave of five bays flanked by aisles with transepts and concluding at a single ambulatory apse, was directly based on such classic early French Gothic structures as Sens and the choir of Nôtre Dame de Paris. There are some slight adaptations, such as a flat roof and the low, almost chapel-like transepts, which can be explained on the grounds of economy and climate. The vaults of the nave slowly advanced westwards as the century progressed, and the elaborate porch, in the distinctive 'Decorated Gothic' style, was added in the early 14th century. St Sophia was consecrated in 1326 but it was never properly finished. The great flood of 1330, the triple sacking by the Genoese in 1373, the Mameluke devastation in 1426 and the 1490 earthquake created higher priorities than the completion of the twin bell towers. Contarini, the Venetian bishop of Paphos, presided over the last Christian service here on 9 September 1570 when he preached an impassioned sermon to a packed congregation of the besieged. By the first Friday after the Turkish conquest it had been cleansed of its Christian furnishings and inaugurated as a mosque. Gypsum screens replaced the stained glass windows and the corner stairwell towers were extended into a pair of 49m-high minarets. Before the microphone era reached Nicosia in 1949, the muezzin had to climb 170 steps five times a day in order to issue the call to prayer.

The Porch

Immediately in front of the three superbly decorated Gothic doors of the western entrance stands a sadirvan, a covered booth for ritual washing before Muslim prayers. The great porch (variously referred to as a galilee, parvis or narthex) was built in the early 14th century, probably by the same team of Rhineland masons who worked on the cathedral of St Nicholas in Famagusta. The central door is twice the width of the flanking entrances, above which a pair of bell towers were to rise but only the first storey of the north tower was ever completed. The marble sculptures decorating the central door were destroyed, except for the pair of angels with censors, whom Muslims also honour. Similar angelic couples survive in converted churches in Famagusta, Rhodes and Istanbul. The clematis capitals and small figurative carvings under the canopies in the north door have survived well, for they were covered in plaster. On the south door bored pageboys and armigerous 16th-century travellers have carved graffiti and coats of arms while sitting out a long service.

The Interior

Shafts of light pierce through the breaks in the tall gypsum window screens to illuminate cascades of worn Turkish carpets. These are orientated towards the various angled mihrabs on the south wall that indicate the direction of prayer towards Mecca. Scattered in the nave are raised platforms for Koranic reciters and the stepped minbar for the Friday sermon, while in the north transept is a blue-painted gallery for female worshippers.

The plain whitewashed walls, marred only by green paint splashed on the capitals, serves to highlight the austerity of the early Gothic columns and their simple pointed arches. The four columns around which the high altar would have sat are antique granite columns that may have stood in a pagan temple, while the early Byzantine capitals must once have graced a 4th-century church.

The wooden choir, the marble altar screen, silk hangings, gilded altar pieces, tapestries, carved tombs, stained glass and blue-painted vaults sprinkled with gold stars of the Christian period survive only in the descriptions of medieval chroniclers. They were all swept aside when the Turks arrived in 1570 and the building was converted into a single Muslim prayer hall. There were five distinct side chapels before the Turkish conquest. On the south side the Lady chapel occupied the transept; a square chantry chapel lit by round windows was added two bays to the west a few centuries later. This chantry chapel has been identified with the De Pins family from the punning three pine-cones on a surviving stone coat of arms. Beside it was the chapel of St Thomas Aquinas, the great medieval synthesist of philosophy and theology, who dedicated his *De Regimine Principum* to his friend Hugh III of Cyprus in 1275. The chapel and altarpiece were decorated with appropriate quotations. The north transept, now filled by the women's gallery, was dedicated to St Nicholas. East of this is the two-storey (and usually locked) treasury, whose upper floor is equipped with a window seat that stares directly at the altar and is identified as the oratory of St Thomas à Becket.

The Precincts

Most of the external door on the north face of the Selemiye mosque survives from the original 12th-century building and it later communicated directly with the extensive palace of the archbishops. This was later burnt down by Greeks enraged at the financial exactions of the Catholic clergy.

No cloister was ever constructed, but in its heyday the cathedral precincts housed 24 canons, three archdeacons, 32 chaplains, a school of theology and one of grammar. By the 16th century the archbishopric had become a sinecure for absentee Venetian nobles and the institutions had all fallen into decline. By 1547 this great church had sunk into such a state of neglect, that the Governor had to send specially for a priest in order to hear mass in St Sophia.

The **Zeyno Banko Café**, on the south side of the mosque, makes a delightful viewing point for Gothic finials. The café's tables are scattered in a rough garden amongst 13th-century piers and flying buttresses that were added in the 14th century. An eroded figure holding a sundial can be identified on the second flying buttress. The medieval façade of the chapterhouse also overlooks the café though the interior now houses nothing more glamorous than the communal bedrooms of the Selimiye Pansiyon.

Bedesten (Orthodox Cathedral of St Nicholas)

Open daylight hours, seven days a week.

The half ruined Orthodox Cathedral of St Nicholas stands just a street's width to the south of the Selemiye mosque's porch. The repetition of tower-like buttresses and extending animal gargoyles gives a fortified if not fearsome aspect to its exterior. Orthodox churches were generally left undisturbed by the Ottoman conquest, unlike the Roman Catholic ones, which were all confiscated. St Nicholas was an exception, presumably because it was too close to the new principal mosque, and so it was converted into a *bedesten*, a smart covered market, a shopping mall for textiles, before later serving as a barn for government tithes.

It had only become established as an Orthodox cathedral during the period of Venetian rule, in about 1500, when the nave and the northern aisle were built. They were tacked onto the side of an existing 14th-century Gothic church which, despite its architecture, may have been an Orthodox chapel built by one of the succession of strong-willed Greek queens who helped their church regain its independence and position.

The original chapel, which was turned into the south aisle is the most ruinous and retains a quite different look. It was formed from two long and narrow aisles, and its vertical dimension was emphasized by slender columns and carved drum capitals. The 16th-century nave and north aisle is a more solid and pragmatic structure, based on sturdy piers which carry lower arches, simple vaulting and the drum of a small dome. The church's great showpieces are the **three north doors**, which have survived almost intact despite facing the mosque and its iconoclastic worshippers for over three centuries. The largest door is modelled on the central entrance gate of St Sophia. The marble lintel bears an image of St Nicholas supported by the arms of six Italian families, who must have had strong Orthodox affiliations. The central 'blocked doorway' was never an entrance but served as a decorative frame for an external icon. The grey marble lintel of the Dormition of the Virgin is considered to be too fine to be the work of 16th-century Cypriot carvers, and may have once decorated the original chapel.

Two ground-floor rooms of an old house (just to the east of the south aisle, but within the Bedesten fence) are used to exhibit a dozen **medieval tombstones**. These were taken from the floor of the Omeriye Mosque, the old Augustinian monastery in Southern Nicosia, and depict with economical line the privileged population of Frankish Cyprus: ardent young knights, wealthy widows, proud clerics and a pair of prosperous burgesses. In the second room, look up at the fine if dilapidated Ottoman marquetry ceiling, a geometrical grid of red and white roses around a central boss.

Sultan Mahmut Kütüphanesi (Sultan Mahmud II Library)

Open 8am–1pm, 2–5pm, Mon–Sat.

Just to the east of the Selemiye mosque stands a small koranic library built by Sultan Mahmud II in 1829. He was an energetic, reforming ruler, and the library

was an important addition to the island's principal Muslim college of higher education which once stood nearby. It is a simple but dignified example of classical
Ottoman architecture, though dating from a time when Istanbul itself had long
discarded restraint for the wilder side of Baroque grandeur. The square library
chamber is capped by a hexagonal drum that supports the central dome, while a
pair of lower domes create an open-air and interior porch. Inside the domed hall
there is a display case for Korans and the original bookcase, whose frieze unites
with that on the walls to envelop the room in gold calligraphic lettering on a blue
background. Hilm Effendi, the Mufti of Cyprus, composed the couplets in praise
of the Sultan's generosity and was rewarded for his eulogy with an invitation to
the palace, where he was decorated, 'King of Poets'.

On a street corner about 70m due east of the Selemiye mosque is a stocky 15th-
century Venetian house, **Lapidari Müzesi (Jeffery's Lapidiary Museum)**.
Named after the first British custodian of antiquities, it has become a scrapyard for
medieval stone carving recovered from demolitions and casual excavations
(*access at the discretion of the custodian of the Sultan Mahmud II Library*).
Amongst the worn tombstones, shields, gargoyles, capitals and friezes is a marble
sarcophagus and a fine flamboyant Gothic window from the Saray, the Lusignan
palace that stood in Atatürk Meydanı. The building is managed by the Antiquities
Department, ✆ (020) 72916.

Haydarpaşa Mosque (St Catherine's Church)

Open 9am–1pm, 2.30–5pm Mon–Fri and Sat 9am–1pm.

Nicosia's most complete, elegant and mysterious Gothic building is on Kirlizade
street, 150m northeast of the Selemiye mosque. This medieval chapel, which was
converted into a mosque after the Turkish conquest of 1570, now houses an art
gallery which welcomes visitors.

The church was constructed in the flamboyant style (also known as perpendicular
or rayonnant) and must have been completed by the end of the 14th century. It
has remained virtually unchanged since, apart from the addition of a minaret and
the replacement of its great fields of stained glass by a monochrome gypsum
screen. Nothing is known of its early history, and its connection with St Catherine
is based on 19th-century street opinion. The exterior face of this single-aisled
church is dominated by high windows flanked by tower-like buttresses which are
pierced by beheaded gargoyles. The two entrances are embellished with heavy
but finely carved canopies. The west door, currently closed, has opposing dragon
and mermaid corbels and an intriguing marble lintel decorated with two roses surrounded by six dragons. The three shields on the lintel of the south door would
once have clearly announced the chapel's patron but they were defaced by
the Turks. These three shields have led to a tentative association with James I

(1382–98), the first Lusignan monarch to claim the crown of Armenia in addition to those of Cyprus and Jerusalem.

The interior is in superb condition. Engaged columns, composed of five rods, rise between the high windows to sprout from floral capitals into ribbed vaults that join an opposing span or support one of the three central bosses. The three-sided apse once nurtured an altar beside the piscina that is set into the wall. This is equipped with a special flue for conveying the washed traces of the holy sacrament into a hidden reservoir, rather than into the common drain. To the north of the apse is a vaulted sacristry, now used as an office, which once supported a secretive loft with a lower window looking into the church and an upper window surveying the outside. Four centuries of Muslim worship are recalled by a gallery that leads to the minaret, a gypsum mihrab, and an antique capital with steps that once acted as a minbar.

Yeni Cami and Ayios Loukkos

The slight medieval remains of Yeni Cami (New Mosque) and the dilapidated church of Ayios Loukkos (St Luke's) are of secondary interest, but provide an opportunity to walk the quiet streets of this quarter.

The old corner tower and minaret stand beside the modern prayer hall of Yeni Cami, 150m north of the Haydarpaşa mosque. This is all that remains of a 14th-century church which was admiringly referred to as Kuchuk Ayasofya, 'little St Sophia', by the Turks. It was demolished in 1772 by Mentesh Hadji Ismail Aga, the Ottoman governor, in his quest for elusive buried treasure. He hurriedly built another mosque to atone for his desecration but this failed to protect him from the Sultan's justice. His headless body lies buried in the grounds of the mosque.

Walk 150m further north and take a left turn into Alsancaks Lates (Apostolos Loucas) street. On the right, 200m along, is an 18th-century Orthodox church with a simple bell tower. It once housed a distinguished collection of icons but since the partition of the city has lain gutted.

Arabahmet Mosque and the Armenian Church

On the corner of Müftü Ziya Efendi street and Salahi Şevket (Victoria) street is the Arabahmet mosque. The low dome and contrasting minaret is set in a shaded garden filled with carved marble tombs, an archetypal vision of provincial Ottoman taste. Though it was built in 1845 it follows the rigorous classicism perfected in 16th-century Istanbul with its single minaret, three-domed porch and a simple square prayer hall covered by a dome. The transformation from the square walls to the circular base of the dome is achieved through an external hexagonal drum and by an internal 'choraic' ring of eight columns. It may seem a world removed from the Greek churches of Nicosia, but both are equally the heirs of medieval Byzantium. The principal elements of Arabahmet can be recognized in 10th-century churches such as Antiphonitis, the chapel ruins at St Hilarion or Abscithi (all are in the Beşparmak/Pentadaktylos mountain range to the north).

The flaking whitewashed interior, with its stone-paved floor covered by a contrasting collage of coloured carpets and kilims, is usually locked. The floor incorporates Frankish tombstones from an old church on this site which was converted into a mosque and named after a philanthropic 16th-century Paşa of Cyprus. Ahmed Kamil (1833–1913) is buried in the garden, a native Turkish Cypriot from the village of Pyroi who rose to become Grand Vizier of the Ottoman Empire on three separate occasions. He was deposed by the coup d'état of the Young Turks but died much honoured in Nicosia in 1913.

The 19th-century townhouses that line **Salahi Şevket (Victoria)** and **Tanzimat streets** create one of the most distinctive and elegant quarters of Nicosia. The deep eaves, shutters, latticed windows and the covered balconies projecting out into the street are all typical aspects of Ottoman domestic architecture. The carved decoration of the stone doorways is more characteristically Cypriot. The island's golden limestone was shaped by masons from the outlying village of Kaimakli, who drew freely on the island's history for their eclectic references.

The **Armenian church** is off a side street, close to the Green Line, and it is occupied by the Turkish army and inaccessible to the public. It was originally the chapel of the Benedectine Nunnery of Our Lady of Tyre, which with its surviving cloisters and dormitories was rebuilt by King Henry II at the end of the 14th century. It was given to the Armenian community in 1570 for their assistance in the Turkish conquest of the island. An outside altar beside the vaulted northern porch of the church has been created from the tombs of two abbesses.

Derviş Paşa Museum

Open 9am–1pm, 2.30–5pm Mon–Fri and on Sat 9am–1pm; adm.

The konak of Ahmed Dervish Paşa, a traditional Nicosia mansion, is on Beliğ Paşa street which is off Salahi Şevket (Victoria) street. It houses the island's richest collection of Ottoman artefacts. It is little visited and one of the hidden treasures of the city. Ahmed Dervish Paşa was a leading figure of the Turkish Cypriot community and a member of the small assembly that rubber-stamped the decisions of the British administration. His mansion is a fine example of Ottoman domestic architecture. The whitewashed walls, plain yellow stone arches, terracotta-tiled roof and blue-stained woodwork reveal a disciplined restraint and classical love of order. The house is L-shaped, with a sturdy stone arcaded basement which combines neatly with the arcade that defines the walled garden. The ground floor was devoted to the practical working of the household and spilled out into the shaded garden which contained a well, washroom, outdoor oven and bathhouse.

At the entrance door is a linen-lined café which has been made from the external roadside room traditionally used to entertain male visitors at a distance from the family compound. The first ground-floor room is arranged as a simple kitchen and displays Turkish metalware and plain glazed ceramics. The second room is furnished with a central charcoal brazier, a household loom, a hand mill and a carved and painted dower chest. In the open downstairs hall are agricultural tools from the surrounding Mesaoria cornlands (*see* 'Limassol Folk Museum' p. 192). The third room contains items relating to the wider culture of the Ottoman Empire: scribes tools, mother-of-pearl inlaid work, 19th-century glassware, metal tableware, curved swords and two Iznik dishes from the Arsenal Tower excavations at Famagusta (*see* p. 358).

The private rooms of the family are all located in the wooden and plaster built first floor, approached up a formal exterior stairway leading directly into a cool, hall-like, verandah. On the first floor, care was taken to ensure that the rooms enjoyed harmonious rectangular proportions. The upstairs verandah is devoted to island embroidery, including a gorgeous deep red velvet waistcoat, patterned with silver and gilt floral devices, and a handkerchief stitched with poppies and pomegranates, the very image of Desdemona's fatally lost hanky. The Turkish costume room contains three richly coloured and embroidered wedding dresses as well as the formal kaftan of Ali Rifat Effendi, the last Cadi (judge of traditional Islamic law) of Cyprus. There are two furnished bedrooms, both hung with the yellow shade of Cypriot cotton beloved by the Turks, as well as local woodwork and embroidered covers mixed with imported carpets, braziers and inlaid boxes. The house tour concludes at the formal reception room with its painted ceiling. It has a sparse Oriental elegance with its minimal furnishings of light coffee-tables, charcoal burner and hubbly bubbly pipes for the smoking of water-cooled and filtered tobacco. An Ottoman gentleman took pride in his heritage of Turkic nomadic mobility, and traditionally could be on the road with all his possessions packed within a few hours of receiving a summons from his sultan.

The Museum of Barbarism

Open 9am–1pm, 2.30–5pm Mon–Fri; adm.

Outside the walled city and just west from the road to Girne/Kyrenia in the Kumsal area there is a dull suburban villa at 2 Irfan Bey, off Mehmet Akif street. It is not for casual visitors unless they want a disturbing insight into the emotional background to Cypriot politics. Officially known as the Museum of Barbarism, it is more usefully considered a memorial to the Turkish victims of inter-communal violence. Photographs in the hall recall terrible scenes from the massacres at the villages of Ayios Vasilios and Ayios Sozomenos in 1964. The bathroom and toilet have been left untouched since an attack by Greek gunmen on Christmas Eve

1963. Mrs Ilhan and her three children Murat, Kutsi and Hakan were gunned down in the pathetic shelter of their bathtub while a neighbour, Feride Hassan, hiding in the toilet, was shot in the head.

Hammams (Public Baths)

The Büyük Hammam is open from 7am–10pm and mixed sex or female groups are welcome by appointment, ✆ Kasim Yilmaz on (020) 71740. A simple self-wash steam bath costs £2.50, whilst the complete body service with manipulation, massage, shampoo and a glove-washed scrub costs £10. Changing booths line the sides of the great entrance hall whose beam and cane ceiling is supported by two arches that tower above the central fish pond. Bathers wrapped in the traditional cotton sarong, which must remain firmly on male users, pass through two small and smelly lobbies before reaching the steam rooms. A large central dome rises above the raised octagonal massage platform, with a nest of smaller domes over the hot bench and side wash-rooms. The domes are pierced with dozens of small glass skylights which allow shafts of sunlight to cut through the warm humid air, and chronicle the afternoon with their drifting spotlit illuminations. Fresh towels and cups of tea are provided back in the entrance hall where you readjust your body to a normal atmosphere to the lush sound of Turkish music.

Korkut Hammam is Northern Nicosia's other working Turkish bath, at No. 16 Beliğ Paşa street, near the Turunclu Mosque. It is open from 8am–10pm and is much cheaper than the Büyük Hammam (about £1.50 a wash); however it is exclusively, if not enthusiastically, male and makes no concessions to tourists. It has a smaller steam room, but a more expansive hall ringed with comfortable open beds.

Shopping

Nicosia is still the principal shopping centre in the north, with a covered market for food, though it is mostly the imported Turkish goods, like cheap jeans, kilims, brassware and Iznik pottery that appeal to visitors.

Kemal Rustem presides over North Cyprus's most distinctive bookshop at 26 Girne Caddesı. Do not be put off by the grimy windows, the dusty towering shelves of unreachable stock, the indifference of the elegant proprietor or his policy of never marking a price. Rustem's bookshop is worth your support, as half of the books on Cypriot culture and politics sold here have also been single-handedly published here, ✆ (020) 71418.

For glossier foreign magazines and newspapers try Hazim Remzi on the groundfloor of the Saray Hotel on Atatürk Square, ✆ (020) 72553.

For cheap imported Turkish leather and denim jackets, brand-name jeans and cotton shirts browse amongst the stalls along Araşta street, downhill from the Selemiye mosque. For wicker baskets and piles of fresh and dried fruit, nuts and Turkish Delight look into the covered market south of the Bedesten. Just north of the Selemiye mosque stand a couple of junk shops and Cyprus Copper, ℂ (020) 71187, a more conventional souvenir shop.

Imported Turkish kilims, metalware and Iznik pottery can also be acquired from a couple of shops established in Ikinci Selim street as it approaches the Ledra Palace checkpoint. One of the best of these is Hicsonmezg, ℂ (020) 84553, a shop which has ignored centuries of carpet-dealing tradition by labelling their prices and adopting a charming soft-sell approach to the passing day-tripping trade.

Art Galleries and Libraries

The HP Gallery (*open 9am–1pm, 2.30–5pm Mon–Fri and on Sat 9am–1pm, ℂ (020) 81771*) is a commercial concern that has taken a long lease of the medieval Haydarpaşa Mosque from the government. It organizes a number of annual exhibitions and principally concentrates on bringing Turkish artists to North Cyprus. Exhibitions, films and lectures are also staged at the state-managed Atatürk Cultural Centre at 7 Kardesler Pasaji off Yediler Sokağı.

The British Council runs a library and reading room in the elegant old High Commission. It has a scandalously slim section on Cyprus, but a good selection of current British papers and magazines. (*Open from 7.30am–1.30pm Mon–Fri and, except Wed, in the afternoon from 2.30–5pm at 23 Mehmet Akif Caddesi, ℂ (020) 74938.*) American periodicals and newspapers can be read at the American Centre at 20 Guner Turkmen Sokağı, ℂ (020) 72443 (*open Mon–Fri 8am–5pm*).

Sports

There is a squash club with one court at Bahadir Sokağı, ℂ (020) 74064 where non members are welcome. Equipment can be hired and the court costs £1.50 an hour. The one tennis court in town is marooned in the Green Line and the laborious process of acquiring a military pass (with the help of Ilter Sanel, ℂ (020) 71313) is for residents not visitors.

Where to Stay

Very few tourists stay even one night in Northern Nicosia. Visitors from the south have to be back across the border by teatime and holidaymakers in the north return to their hotels on the coast.

The Saray on Atatürk Square, © (020) 83115, fax 84808, is really the only choice. The building and its interiors are unimaginative but this is mitigated by its central position and superb views. The restaurant does a good lunch, but eat out in the evening.

cheap

There are dozens of very cheap pensions with delightful looking exteriors that hide some pretty bleak bedrooms. One of the cleanest, with only 10 rooms, is the Antalya Aile Pansiyonu, © (020) 77396, which is just down from the Büyük Hammam.

Eating Out

moderate

For a formal lunch with a magnificent view over Nicosia, go to the top floor of the **Saray Hotel** which has a good menu of the day for £6 per person. The **Zir Lokanta** is a small, local restaurant on Istanbul Caddesı that obstinately resists commercial possibilities and only opens in the quiet of the evening. **Yakamoz** on Bedrettin Demirel Sokağı, © (020) 71728, serves a varied *meze* followed by grilled fish for £5. **Kibris Asevi**, the Cyprus Kitchen, is at 39A Atatürk Caddesı, Gönyeli (Geunyeli), © (020) 31751. It is on the left as you approach the old village of Gönyeli from the signposted turning off the main Nicosia-to-Güzelyurt (Morphou) road, some 5km from the city centre. Although a modern building, it has been decorated with such a rich collection of traditional furniture, tools, embroideries and kitchenware that it looks like a working museum. Equal attention is paid to the repertoire of Cypriot dishes; you will need to order the pot roasts, which are cooked outside in a traditional clay-sealed oven, in advance. Open for lunch and dinner and a favourite with visiting delegations and local politicans. Dinner for two with wine about £10.

cheap

The corner **Sarigizmeli** at 174 Girne Caddesı, © (020) 73782, is one of the best lokantas in the centre of Nicosia. Choose your composite meal from any of the dozen freshly cooked trays. A filling lunch for two is to be had for under £5.

The **Guneydogu Kebab ve Lahmacun Salonu** , © (020) 81271 is a small but popular lunchtime kebab house that backs onto the Green Line with tables overlooking the bazaar street-life. From the Bedesten, walk downhill along the main shopping thoroughfare and take the fifth turning on the left. A mixed plate of kebabs with salad for two costs £7.

Seven is an enormous and boisterous restaurant designed for groups and family parties, with cabaret and belly-dancing turns. It is off the Girne (Kyrenia) road and is open from 8pm, ✆ (020) 78458/78469. A reasonably indulgent night will set you back about £15 for two. An alternative evening could begin at the **Music Bar**, halfway up Bedreddin Demirel Caddesı, before concluding at the casino at **Sabri's Orient Hotel** at the northern end of this avenue, near the government ministries. It is open between 9.30pm and 3am, ✆ (020) 78234. There is also a disco in town, the **Picnic Night Club** on Sehit Sener Enver Sokağı, ✆ (020) 72122.

Around Northern Nicosia

Ortaköy (Orta Keuy) and Gönyeli (Geunyeli)

A mess of five-storey apartment blocks sprawls beside the main road out of Northern Nicosia, obscuring the old villages of Ortaköy and Gönyeli that once commanded the way to Kyrenia. It was a bitterly contested zone during the inter-communal violence of this century, with the Turks in possession of Gönyeli while the Greeks held Ortaköy. In 1958 a British patrol foolishly released a group of Greek detainees outside Gönyeli. This body of unarmed men was mistaken by the Turkish villagers for an Eoka group and lynched. Nine men were hacked into pieces and many more mutilated. This appalling incident was capped by a piece of black comedy worthy of Evelyn Waugh. His son Auberon, then a young cavalry officer, managed to riddle himself with six bullets from the machine gun of his own armoured car. In his long convalescence in Nicosia he was visited by Lady Foot, the Governor's wife, who inflicted additional torture by reading aloud from *Bitter Lemons*. 'Nothing could have been more kindly intended, but I conceived a great hatred for Lawrence Durrell...this has never left me, and embraces the entire school of expatriates who write sensitively about sunnier climes than our own.'

Değirmenlik (Kythrea)

If you are looking for a break on the way from Northern Nicosia to Gazimağusa, the Değirmenlik (Kythrea) turning has the best cluster of roadside cafés. Değirmenlik, which is about 15km northeast of old Nicosia, is the largest of half a dozen mud-brick villages that cluster around a perennial stream that flows from the Kephalovryso mountain spring. Until the last century it had a vital strategic role, for the valley ground all of Nicosia's flour at its three dozen mills. Now there is just one mechanized flour mill at Baspinar, at the head of the valley, though picturesque stone arches of the old mill-races punctuate the villages. In summer the valley has the additional charm of being a fertile oasis in the midst of mud-brick houses, barren hills and the scorched fields of the Mesaoria plain. The springs have assured a continuous history of settlement: archaeologists have identified Copper Age sites, the Iron Age citadel of Chytri and a sanctuary at Gökhan (Voni), though it was a local ploughman who unearthed the famous bronze statue of the Roman Emperor, Septimius Severus, which now stands in the Cyprus Museum.

West from Nicosia: Güzelyurt (Morphou), Lefke, Soli, Vouni

The province of Nicosia, like the city, was divided in two during 1974. The old B9 road to the unfashionable pebble-strewn shores of the west coast passes beside the airport, which is now within the UN buffer zone. The new northern thoroughfare, off the Gonyeli roundabout to the northwest of Nicosia, now bypasses the sleepy villages of the undulating dust-brown agricultural plain. This area, the western Mesaoria, is of no interest for everything memorable is near the coast.

The hilltop palace of Vouni ignites the imagination like no other archaeological site on the island. It alone justifies a trip to the western corner of Nicosia province, and there is also the medieval tomb-church of Ayios Mamas, the Güzelyurt Museum, the village of Lefke and the ruins of Soli. If you are coming across the Green Line from South Cyprus it is possible to squeeze it all into one day, though the Soli Inn makes an ideal base for a gentler exploration, with a swim at Yeşilırmak and an evening at a fish restaurant.

Güzelyurt (Morphou)

This market town is 30 miles west of Nicosia, beside the Serrakhis riverbed, entirely surrounded by orange groves and five miles inland from the sea. Güzelyurt (Morphou) was a Byzantine foundation, the western headquarters for the Akrides anti-pirate patrols established in the 10th century. This base, embellished by the famous tomb of St Mamas, grew into one of the principal medieval baronies. It is now a simple market town with a population of around 11,000 and a bypass. Follow signs to 'city centre' for the Monastery of St Mamas and the museum which is opposite the brand-new mosque and Atatürk Park.

Monastery of Ayios Mamas

The keys are held by the custodian of the neighbouring museum. Though empty of monks and worshippers since the Turkish occupation in 1974, the monastery is yet fortunate, for it has been meticulously preserved down to the last vestment, and is one of only six Orthodox churches in North Cyprus not to have been desecrated and robbed. The antique marble sarcophagus of St Mamas is the core around which the monastery was established, but from the beginning it was built over, not around, and so appears on both the inside and outside of the church. This seems entirely suitable treatment for one of Cyprus's most idiosyncratic and venerated saints, who appears in icons as a young man carrying a lamb and happily riding a ferocious lion. This is explained by two different tales.

The most popular has St Mamas as a local hermit who lived in a cave in such abject and holy poverty that he refused to pay the poll tax. The Byzantine Duke of Cyprus sent soldiers to arrest the hermit but on their way back to the capital the way was barred by a lion who was about to eat a lamb. St Mamas just had to raise his hand for the lion to release the lamb into his care and humbly offer its back as a mount. St Mamas then rode lion-back right into the Duke's courthouse in Nicosia, where the Duke was so impressed and alarmed, lions being quite unknown on the island, that he immediately granted St Mamas a pardon and a lifelong tax exemption. In the second tale St Mamas was a Syrian hermit who milked lions and prepared cheese for the poor, until he was martyred by the Saracens. His parents were forbidden to bury him, and so they launched his coffin out to sea where it floated to Cyprus. It was then carried inland until it reached its current site in Morphou, after which it could not be moved. His icon is associated with miraculous cures throughout the island, and the moisture that oozes from his tomb is considered to be highly efficacious against disease and storms, but evaporates when the wearer enjoys any form of sex.

The **Monastery Buildings** have been constantly updated and enriched over the last 500 years. The dome and the high, pointed, barrel-vaulted roof were added in the 18th century. An imposingly simple yellow stone cloister, equipped with a wooden gallery, also dates from this period, though it is believed to follow closely the original medieval structure. A belfry and arcaded porch were added at the turn of the century.

The interior stonework was executed in the early 15th century when the separate Crusader and Byzantine traditions of church architecture had begun to fuse. This shrine to the most Cypriot of saints is decked with Gothic carving which would not have been out of place in Northern Europe. This union of cultures was symbolized by the marriage between King John II and Helena Palaeologina. This redoubtable Greek princess must have visited this shrine, for she first landed in Cyprus at a nearby beach. The aisles are separated by two rows of round columns with Gothic octagonal capitals. The most distinct pair are under the dome and feature a bearded green man and a sprouting vine, and garlanded women.

The celebrated tomb is against the north wall, the Roman marble sarcophagus enveloped by a crudely painted but finely carved flamboyant Gothic arch of the 14th century. It frames an icon screen filled with 38 scenes of miracles and martyrdom ranged above the three larger icons: St George on his white horse and St Demetrius on his brown horse flank the central icon of St Mamas on his lion.

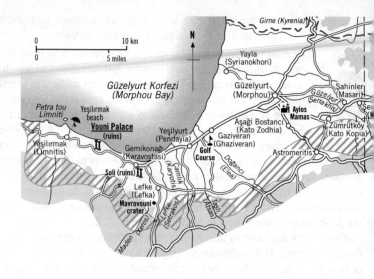

The iconostasis is a particularly fine and complete example of the rich Venetian-influenced carving of the 16th century, the gilded floral motifs and grotesques set against a background of deep blue. The sumptuous church furniture, the gilded and painted pulpit, icon stand and throne, are 18th century and contemporary with the elegant upper layer of seven icons. Peek through the iconostasis at the altar canopy which incorporates pieces of 12th-century Byzantine carving.

Güzelyurt Museum of Archaeology and Natural History

Open 9am–1pm, 2.30–5pm Tues–Sat, adm.

The Güzelyurt Museum is housed in the old palace of the bishop of Morphou which stands beside Ayios Mamas.

The ground floor of the museum is devoted to natural history and holds cabinets of geological samples, stuffed fish, mammals and birds native to Cyprus. Exotic breeding migrants are represented by the elusive Eleonora's Falcon, the bright plumage of the bee-eater and pink flamingos from the salt lakes. There is also a pair of mutant lambs. A more symbolic age would have read the fate of Cyprus from these twins with two heads on one body and two bodies on one head. Upstairs there is a small archaeological collection with the island's best display of Late Bronze Age white slipware (*see* 'Cypriot Ceramics' p. 407) and the recently discovered Ephesian Artemis.

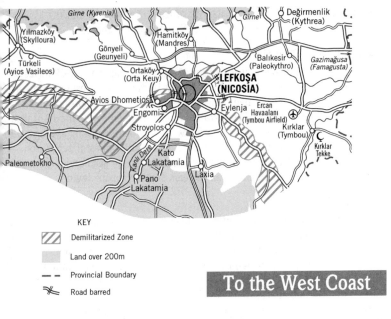

KEY

▨ Demilitarized Zone

░ Land over 200m

- - Provincial Boundary

✳ Road barred

To the West Coast

Rooms II & III house pieces from the Toumba Tou Skourou excavation, mostly base ring-ware and very fine examples of the white slip 'milk bowl' ware, with its distinctive tattoo-like designs dated 1600–1500 BC.

Room V is filled with artefacts from the Classical to Byzantine period, including two fine black on red Attic Lekythos vases, Hellenistic tableware, Roman glass and yellow-glazed, medieval sgraffito pottery. The room is dominated by the statuette of Artemis of Ephesus carved in the 2nd century AD. The weathered white body of the goddess, whose black face bears remnants of a tidy coiffure, was discovered in the Bay of Salamis in 1980. Thirty-six nipples protrude from her tightly bound dress embroidered with five rows of hieratic wild things, the guardian sphinxes and griffins customarily associated with the Great Goddess. Her protruding bottom echoes the ancient pose of the fertile mother goddess, who is flanked by two crouched guardian creatures.

Due west of Güzelyurt a road winds through orange groves to **Yayla (Syrianokhori)**, a hamlet with a café which can make an intoxicatingly odoriferous destination during the spring orange blossom season. Beyond Yayla dirt tracks lead out to a long, curving grey pebble beach, entirely deserted except for the occasional gravel-hunting lorry. Military encampments have made most of the area to the north of Güzelyurt (Morphou) out of bounds. Accessible spots of interest such as the Maronite village of Koruçam (Kormakitis) and the Myrtou Bronze Age sanctuary are described in the Kyrenia (Girne) chapter.

Gemikonağı (Karavostasi)

The humble pier and coastal warehouses of this ancient anchorage—Karavostasi translates as the mooring place of the ships—is 10 miles southwest of Güzelyurt. In the 1920s it was transformed into a great processing and exporting centre for Cypriot copper and asbestos. These works were abandoned during the 1974 invasion, and now a lone caretaker keeps a few ghostly lights burning amongst the ore-washing ponds, marine conveyor belts and rusting piles of scrap iron. A couple of curtained bars and a red-lit den, patrolled by an aged and elegant pin-striped proprietor, recall the more raffish years of this company town.

Lefke (Lefka)

The village of Lefke is a couple of miles inland of Gemikonağı, though with its palms and orange groves fed by the gurgling current of numerous irrigation trenches it could almost be an oasis in the Levant. This is further emphasized by the surrounding desert, created by decades of mining and inter-communal warfare. A cemetery of 'martyrs' at the foot of the town holds the local militiamen killed during Eoka B attacks in the sixties.

Lefke was an important medieval barony but received its current identity when it was extensively settled by Turks. Within three years of the Ottoman conquest of 1571, Lefke boasted the first purpose-built mosque and medersa, for the higher study of the Koran, on the island. The main street is dominated by handsome colonial public buildings to which a pillar-box fountain was added in 1937 to commemorate the coronation of King George VI. A stroll through the back streets and orchards reveals the town's rich heritage of traditional architecture. There are Turkish mansions, some complete with the glass-pierced domes of private bath houses, arched aqueducts of old mill races and three mosques. The latter are supposedly on the site of old churches but were restored in the 19th century using traditional techniques. The whitewashed prayer halls are formed from high, round arches that are linked with simple beams, covered in cane matting and protected by terracotta tiles. The market mosque is in the centre of town, beside the bullet-spattered wall of the Direk Hotel. The carpet-strewn floor of the Makheme Mescidi is on the northern edge of Lefke, just uphill from the blue-shuttered house of the Sufi Sheikh Nazim. On the southern edge of Lefke is the mosque of Piri Osman Pasha, its terracotta-tiled roof and freestanding minaret framed against a backdrop of palms and poplars. Its green-latticed arcade faces a garden overlooking an elegant hitching post formed from an antique marble column and the elaborately carved rococo marble tombs of Vezir Osman Paşa and the son of Veli Ağa, who rebuilt the town's aqueducts in 1818.

To visit the **Mavrovouni** mine crater, take the UN road south of the town. It is an ancient area of mining, though the modern open-cast methods have scoured out the old shafts to create an inverted step pyramid. The terraces recall the grades of hell from Dante's *Inferno*. Its lips are a bed of iron ore nuggets and historic slag. Grey terraces shift to darker grey against white, before descending to red and ferrous orange set against a livid green lake of copper sulphate.

Soli

> Open 9am–5pm, adm. On the western edge of Gemikonağı, look out for a small battered signpost indicating the track to the archaeological site.

Soli was one of the most famous of the dozen city-kingdoms of Cyprus but has retained few of its monuments. The temples, porticoes and triumphal arches reported by 18th-century travellers like Pococke have all been quarried away. A complete tour begins at the Byzantine cathedral with its famous mosaic floor, then passes a reconstructed Roman theatre before finishing with the view from the Acropolis hill.

History

This coastal plain was settled by Greek-speaking seaborne invaders in the 13th century BC. Soli emerges into the light of history in 700 BC as 'Sillu' in an Assyrian tribute list. This contradicts the tradition that the town was named after Solon, the Athenian philosopher and political reformer, who advised King Philocyprus of Aepea to move here in 580 BC. Whatever the hidden truth of this legend, Soli occupies a site worthy of a sage. It was defendable, removed from malarial marshes, well supplied with water from two mountain streams yet close to a safe anchorage. Situated at the intersection of three economic zones, it acted as the natural marketplace for the irrigated orchards of the Solea valleys, the corn land of the Mesaoria plain and the mixed forest and pasture of the Tilliria highlands. The nearby copper mines of Mavrovouni and Skouriotissa assured its position amongst the dozen kingdoms that jockeyed for dominance in ancient Cyprus.

King Aristocyprus of Soli took a leading role in the coalition of Greek cities which revolted against the Persian Empire in 499 BC. He died fighting the Persian army, but his city withstood a five-month siege before submitting. The fortress-palace of Vouni was built to watch over the city. However, it was not the Persians but the triumph of Hellenism, in the wake of Alexander the Great, that ended Soli's independence. The mines were seized by the Ptolemaic dynasty and from there passed into the privy purse of the Roman and then the Byzantine emperors. Soli remained a prosperous but provincial city, until it was damaged by barbarian pirate fleets in the 5th century and finally destroyed by Saracens in the 7th century.

The Byzantine Cathedral

The entrance path drops the visitor into the half-excavated outer courtyard. It was ringed with colonnades like a cloister, which can be recognized from the opus sectile pavement, the marble carpet of geometrical patterns formed from precisely cut and fitted sections of grey, golden and red marble. The steps of the original oblique entrance gate can be seen on the north face. In the centre of the courtyard are fragments of animal mosaics. These would have shone beneath the water splashed from worshippers washing at the central marble basin.

The customary three doorways into the triple-aisled basilica can be identified from the low walls. Only the bases and a few capitals remain of the two rows of enormous columns that once supported the wide roof of the central aisle. The columns were constructed from drums of locally cut yellow stone, as complete marble columns of this size would have to have been specifically cut and imported from Imperial quarries on the mainland.

Unbaptized worshippers were restricted to the lobby (narthex) and outer aisles (exonarthex), here distinguished from the mosaic of the central nave by a stone and opus sectile pavement. The nave is covered in a variety of geometrical designs like some enormous patchwork quilt. There is no overall design, nor do the floors reflect the architectural divisions of the basilica, for this charming mosaic floor was laid down piecemeal, by individual members of the congregation, as two damaged inscriptions attest. The red tesserae are cut from terracotta, a bright, local product that was a much cheaper alternative to importing red marble from the porphyry quarries of Egypt. The most celebrated individual design is of a white swan cornered by lotuses, a favourite motif of Cypriot Archaic art.

The eastern end of the central aisle is covered by a raised floor of brick and mortar. This belongs to a 12th-century Byzantine chapel which reoccupied the holiest portion of the old cathedral some five centuries after its destruction. It returned to its cathedral status when the Orthodox bishops of Nicosia were exiled to Soli by the Roman Catholic hierachy from the 13th to the 15th centuries.

The Theatre and Acropolis Hill

The restored theatre is uphill, with room for an audience of 3500. There is nothing antique to be seen, for it was entirely re-created in the 1930s. The original was built in the 2nd century AD, the golden age of the Roman Empire. It uses the contours of the hill in the Greek fashion rather than relying on free-standing masonry as does the typically Roman theatre at Salamis (*see* p. 378 for information on ancient drama and design).

A hole in the wire perimeter fence allows for an easy ascent to the Acropolis hill. This was both the city's citadel and its temple quarter. Its former role is much in evidence from the recently abandoned military slit trenches, while only slight depressions reveal the sanctuaries excavated and neatly reburied by a Swedish expedition in the 1930s. They unearthed the famous statue of Aphrodite Soli, hidden by a devotee in her temple outbuildings, which is now on permanent display in the Cyprus Museum in Southern Nicosia. There were also separate shrines to Apollo, Isis and Serapis. The latter was built in the 6th century AD, after the Byzantine cathedral, and reminds us of the long survival of pre-Christian deities.

The Palace of Vouni

The approach road that twists up to Vouni is 6km west of Gemikonağı. The custodian's office is seldom manned and the ruins are open at all hours.

This ancient palace perches on the summit of a cliff-guarded conical hill. Its low walls, unearthed by the Swedish archaeologist Gjerstad, would excite slight interest but for their dramatic position, which commands an imperious view over the Cypriot shoreline and deep out over the bay. A walk among the ruins is like stepping into the pages of one of the novels of Robert Graves or Mary Renault, though the present division of the island provides a powerful enough analogy to the time when Cyprus was riven into pro-Greek and pro-Persian factions.

History

The palace of Vouni was a hated symbol of the dominance of the neighbouring town of Marion, and the citizens of Soli burnt it down before it was 100 years old. It was built in the aftermath of the failed Ionian revolt against the Persian Empire in 499 BC. Soli had been a leading member of this coalition of rebel Greek cities and was punished by being placed under the suzerainty of Marion (modern Polis), her old rival who was naturally a strong supporter of the other side. Vouni was the residence of a tribute-collecting governor from Marion, and its plan reflects the Oriental and Phoenician culture of many Cypriot cities. The palace was altered a generation later when a nominee of the Athenian Empire, one Stasioikos, was placed on the throne of Marion. This coincides with the building of a temple to Athena and the remodelling of Vouni, which more than doubled in size in this second period. Another revolt against Persia, in the 380s BC, provided the opportunity for Soli to regain her independence from Marion and destroy the palace, but not before one of its doomed inhabitants hid the household treasure. Swedish archaeologists discovered a blackened pot out of which flowed a cascade of chased bowls, gold Persian bracelets and silver coins from the leading pro-Persian cities of Cyprus.

The Palace Site

Three suites of three rooms (A) lay at the heart of the original palace. These nine interconnecting rooms, variously screened with doors, curtains and doormen, were the administrative centre for the kingdom of Soli, and were used for ceremonial receptions and as courts for local arbitration. Seven steps lead down into the inner courtyard (B) which functioned as the private quarter. Nine column bases remain to suggest the colonnade which once screened the three rooms lining this enclosure. Something of this courtyard's original opulence can be imagined from the Hathor capital, which was later placed by the cistern and used as a well head. There was also an upper floor and a terrace to catch the pine-scented evening breeze while watching the busy streets of Soli to the east or the billowing sails of merchant ships as they rounded the cape to the north.

In the eastern corner there is a bathhouse (C) with its accompanying pointed-arch tunnel for servicing the heating flues. The lower levels to the west (D) are marked by flights of interconnecting stairs. This is the area of the kitchens, service quarters and store rooms (E), whose floors are fitted with holes to hold upright rows of amphorae filled with oil, corn and wine.

The Athenian-backed transition of governors in 449 BC was marked by a change in doors. The new principal entrance (F) at the north turned the inner courtyard into the entrance hall, and so changed the layout from Oriental to typically Greek. A light mud-brick second storey was added and a new range of storehouses and kitchens (G) was built to the east, forming a separate enclosed courtyard which has been seen as a guard barracks or tribute storehouse.

Above the palace, immediately below the modern breeze-block walls, is the site of the temple of Athena. The reddish stone of the foundation walls marks out a 20m-long rectangular court with a shrine to the west beside an excavated pit on the precipice edge. The foundations of a smaller temple with a triple shrine are due east on the cliff edge. A number of bronzes were found amongst the mass of terracotta offerings, including a cow based on the famous lost statue by Myron and a bull being savaged by lions, a recurring image for an acceptable sacrifice.

Yeşilırmak (Limnitis) Beach

Off the coast road west of Gemikonağı there are a number of pebble beaches with seasonal restaurants and offshore rafts where the UN forces practise their water sports. Yeşilırmak, 'green river', is the only one of half a dozen villages west of Vouni to have survived the intercommunal fighting. It is also the furthest removed from the pollution of the old mine workings. For the beach, turn right just beyond the bridge in the middle of the village. There are four vine-shaded restaurants along this stretch of pebbles and a fishing shelter below the eucalyptus-lined river bank. Even at the height of summer menus can be limited; out of season only the pool table and indoor bar of the Mlicahitler Gazinosu stays open. To the west of the beach is the steep-sided offshore island of Petra tou Limniti, which harboured a neolithic settlement but is inaccessible even to strong swimmers as it is just within a Turkish military zone.

Vouni Palace

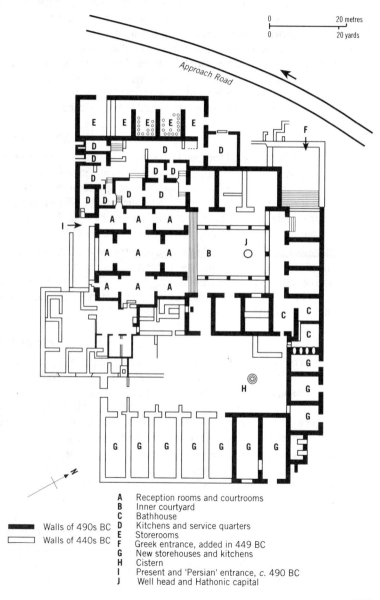

0 _____ 20 metres
0 _____ 20 yards

Approach Road

A Reception rooms and courtrooms
B Inner courtyard
C Bathhouse
D Kitchens and service quarters
E Storerooms
F Greek entrance, added in 449 BC
G New storehouses and kitchens
H Cistern
I Present and 'Persian' entrance, c. 490 BC
J Well head and Hathonic capital

■■■■■ Walls of 490s BC
▢▢▢▢▢ Walls of 440s BC

Sports

Just west of the village of Yeşilyurt, look out for a turning marked '*Cengiz Topel Hastanesi*', which leads to a nine-hole golf course built by the Cyprus Mines Corporation. The Turkish army have entrenched themselves in bunkers around two holes and reduced the course, which is maintained by Ian Cooper, an ex-employee of the Mines, and a small club of British expatriates who play on Tuesday, Thursday and Sunday mornings. Visitors are welcome and some battered clubs can be borrowed. Beer, sandwiches and anecdotes are available in the clubhouse.

Where to Stay

The white-arcaded **Soli Inn**, run by the former head mining engineer and his English wife, has recently expanded with eight bungalows and a pool added to the five suites that occupy the roof terrace of the restaurant. Even at £22 for a suite it is to be much preferred to the **Güzelyurt hotel**, an unexceptional apartment block a mile along the Aşağı Bostancı (Kato Zodhia) road from the Güzelyurt bus station, © (072) 43412.

Mehmet Karyagdi, 'No Rain' who organized the 1948 miners' strike, runs one of the island's most characterful bar-hotels, perched with its tattered terraces above the sea in Gemikonağı, © (077) 17371. The bar is dominated by three yellow fridges of beer, six massed ranks of local whisky, craftwork, assorted *objets trouvés* and erotic driftwood.

Eating Out

There are over a dozen restaurants at bathing places along the coastal road. The most sophisticated and popular of these is the **Mardin Aile Gazinosu**, © (077) 17439, a fish restaurant run by Süleyman Oral, offering a rich selection of vegetable *meze*, spiced baked fish as well as charcoal-grilled. The Mardin is tucked down a turning on the west side of Gemikonağı, which leads to a pebble beach before the second mine pier.

Café Pastane Akpinar on the Gemikonağı shore, © (077) 17643 makes a good stop for a Turkish coffee and sticky honey and almond cake served on gingham tableclothes in a large dining room complete with a fireplace and collection of traditional copper and tin kitchenware.

Nightlife

Lefke has its own nightclub, the Tropicana, a dancing bar fuelled by local musicians, students and teachers of the Lefke University (*open 8pm–3am, adm*).

View from St. Hilarion Castle

Kyrenia and the Gothic Range

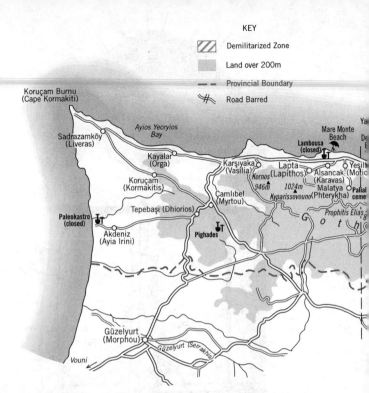

Koruçam Burnu
(Cape Kormakiti)

Sadrazamköy
(Liveras)

Ayios Yeoryios Bay

Kayalar
(Orga)

Koruçam
(Kormakitis)

Karşıyaka
(Vasilia)

Kornos 946m

Lapta (Lapithos)

Mare Monte Beach

Lambousa
(closed)

Alsancak
(Karavas)

Yeşil (Motic

Çamlıbel
(Myrtou)

1024m
Kyparissovouno

Malatya
(Phterykha)

Palial
ceme

Paleokastro
(closed)

Tepebaşı (Dhiorios)

Akdeniz
(Ayia Irini)

Pighades

G o t h

Prophitis Elias

Güzelyurt
(Morphou)

Güzelyurt (Serakhis)

Vouni

With its intimate horseshoe harbour overlooked by massive castle walls,
Kyrenia has drawn visitors since the 17th century. Girne, the official
Turkish name for the town, is a recent variant that sits unhappily even on
the lips of locals. The jagged silhouette of the Gothic Range of mountains
seals the horizon to the south to enclose a verdant coastal strip, never
more than three miles in depth. A number of sheltered sandy bays are
etched into the predominantly rocky shore. The clarity of the sea is like a
continuous invitation for a swim, which makes up for a foreshortened
dusk, as the sun passes early behind the mountains. The sea-tempered
climate and a succession of spring-fed irrigation streams have coloured
this littoral with a generous concentration of Mediterranean plants. Salt-
tolerant succulents on the limestone headlands give way to wind-whipped
maquis broken by patches of intensely farmed gardens and corn fields.
Climbing slightly, you pass into irrigated groves of citrus, olive and carob

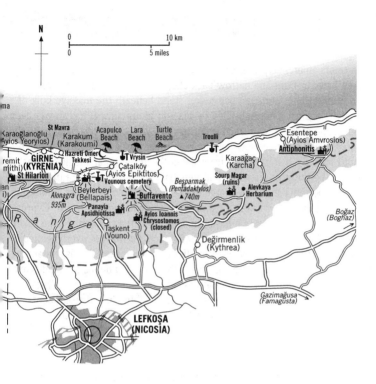

which give way to dense scrubland of juniper, lentisk and wild olive and finally the Aleppo pine woods of the peaks.

Flecked within this landscape are some of the most memorable and evocative monuments of Cyprus. The fragile genius of Byzantine art flowers in two isolated chapels: Antiphonitis monastery hidden in a mountain valley and the diminutive St Mavra concealed in a quarry. The three centuries of the crusader kingdom are irresistibly recalled by the mountain-top castle of St Hilarion, the palatial abbey of Bellapais and the ruinous prison eyrie of Buffavento. All three are bordered by the barracks of the Turkish army, who are a prominent part of the provincial landscape. The armed guards, barbed wire and 'keep out' notices are initially disturbing but you'll find they soon recede into the background as you settle into the easygoing lifestyle of North Cyprus. The big daily decisions slowly retreat as you nose out your favourite swimming place or pine-scented walk and become adopted by a taverna.

Kyrenia offers an archetypal vision of the eastern Mediterranean with its restaurant-lined harbour front and narrow back alleys. The contrasting silhouettes of a Muslim minaret and Christian bell tower stand beneath the massive bulk of a castle, all set against a horizon filled by sea and mountains. It has always been considered one of the most attractive corners of Cyprus, and can claim to be the oldest continually inhabited town on the island. The castle is the town's chief testament to its long history and encapsulates the three great medieval eras of Byzantium, the Lusignan kingdom and Venetian sovereignty. Before the division of the island, Kyrenia sheltered a large expatriate British community amongst its mixed population, and was one of the two acknowledged centres of Cyprus's small tourist trade. Since 1974 it has been eclipsed by the creation of large resorts in the south. As a result it retains a happy balance, for it is not overwhelmed by tourists, but is sufficiently developed to offer a wide range of hotels, restaurants and something of a nightlife. There is rock bathing in town but all the sandy coves are some distance along the coast. Bathing and eating places within a half-hour drive of the town have been listed under Kyrenia. All the inland monuments, villages and undeveloped coast are described in the Gothic Range section.

History

Kyrenia is associated with Mount Kerynia of the Peloponnese, on the Greek mainland. This is the traditional place of origin for the Greek-speaking invaders who settled this area at the beginning of the Iron Age. They merged with the earlier Bronze-Age culture, as excavations into the two important hillside cemeteries of Vounous and Karmi have revealed. Phoenician merchantmen appear to have been the first to establish a permanent settlement at the harbour in the 9th century BC. In the 6th century BC after Cyrus II conquered the island, the settlement was remodelled to become the principal Persian base. Thereafter it ruled the surrounding hinterland and was one of the dozen city states that jockeyed for the dominance of ancient Cyprus. The loss of liberty in the Hellenistic period was offset by increased stability, a growing population and trade which culminated in the Roman era, when the city was known as Corineum. It was an early centre of Christianity, the seat of a bishopric and the traditional birthplace of Simon of Cyrene who carried the Cross for the exhausted Jesus up the hill to Calvary. The piratical raids of northern barbarian tribes, beginning in the 5th century AD, weakened the city, which was finally destroyed by the Saracens in the 7th century.

A Medieval Fortress

The city lay neglected for 300 years before the ruins were quarried to build a rectangular fortress. This was on the orders of Nicephorus Phocas (AD 963–9), the emperor who re-established Byzantine rule over Crete and Cyprus. Kyrenia castle was designed to be one of the strongest links in the island's defence, for it guarded the pass through the Gothic Range and one of the narrowest crossing points to Anatolia. Its strategic situation was recognized by the Lusignans, who immediately reinforced the walls. Later monarchs added the royal apartments and a curtain wall to protect the town which had grown around the harbour. Kyrenia castle was the centrepiece around which a dozen princely feuds, succession struggles and betrayals were staged. On two crucial occasions, the Genoese invasion of 1373 and the Mameluke devastation of 1426, it alone of all the coastal towns stood firm when the rest had fallen to the invaders. The Venetians completely overhauled the defences in 1554, in order to bring them up to date with new developments in artillery power. However, an agreement appears to have been made between the Venetian governor and the Ottoman besiegers to go slow on local fighting and await the result of the siege of Nicosia. After the fall of the capital, the heads of the Venetian commanders were collected in a bag and taken at a gallop over to Kyrenia Castle. The governor, on inspecting these grim trophies, accepted the result and promptly arranged amicable terms of surrender.

Ottoman and Anglican Kyrenia

Kyrenia declined in importance as the Ottoman war zone moved west and the old trade routes of the eastern Mediterranean were diverted around Africa by the Atlantic powers. There was a flurry of excitment in 1765 when Khalil Bey, the local Ottoman commander, used a tax strike to mount his own coup against the governor in Nicosia, but he ended up decorating the castle gallows. There was no dramatic breach between the Ottoman and British administrations of the late19th century, which both used the castle as a prison. The former added the Cafer Aga mosque, the latter the Anglican church of St Andrew, to the nearby streets.

By 1950, Kyrenia and its surrounding villages were home to a community of 2500 British expatriates served by an Anglican church, a cemetery and the Dome Hotel. Despite the presence of Lawrence Durrell it was not a markedly hedonistic or artistic colony, but a scattering of pensioned military and colonial officers who had become too fond of the sun to relish retirement in Tunbridge or Hove. The local community, although predominantly Greek, was well integrated and tolerant. As communal violence escalated in the sixties, the Turkish Cypriots established their hold over the hills to the south and periodically shut the road to Nicosia. The first objective of the Turkish army which landed here in 1974 was to link up with this strategic enclave. The Greek Cypriots who fled from the fighting were replaced by Turkish Cypriots from Limassol.

You can get around Northern Cyprus quite easily without hiring a car. There are buses to other large towns, minibuses along the immediate coast road, shared taxis to Nicosia and regular taxis which will take you anywhere. A car is worth hiring if you want to go for isolated picnics in the hills or to distant and empty beaches.

By Boat

There are two small car-ferries, the **Erturk** and the **Fergun,** which operate throughout the year between Kyrenia (Girne) and Taşucu. Travel on the *Erturk*, the faster of the two, which takes just under six hours for the crossing in good weather. There are five sailings a week arranged on a varying timetable of days. The *Erturk* has reclining aircraft-type seats in the lower deck for a snooze, and a snack bar on the upper deck selling cold beer, toasted cheese sandwiches and freshly brewed hot drinks. You are supposed to buy your ticket at least two hours before departure at 11, either at the harbour itself or from agencies in the town. A single costs around £10 plus another £6 worth of local taxes. Other expenses can be incurred at the terminal café, which sells jumbo packs of tea and distilled spirits from Famagusta.

On landing at Taşucu, British passport holders will need to pay £5 for a Turkish visa, acquired at a separate desk from the main queue. There are hotels to suit all pockets in the small resort port of Taşucu. The bus station is 100m beyond the ferry building, from where you can travel along the Cilician coast road to Anamur, or to the nearby towns of Silifke or Mersin which have better inland bus connections.

The return ferry from Taşucu to Kyrenia (Girne) leaves at midnight five times a week, to give plenty of time for a late dinner at the Balik or Istanbul restaurants which are just by the port. You will arrive at Kyrenia shortly after dawn has lit up the castle and mountains with its rosy fingers.

In the high summer months—late June, July and August—there may be a hydrofoil service to Taşucu (which though noisy and virtually viewless does take half the time) and a weekly boat to Alanya. The timetables and boats change each year so inquire first at the tourist office in the harbour.

By Bus

The official bus terminal is along Bedrettin Demirel Caddesı, which is off the Nicosia road. However, the town square and the park to its east function as the starting point for most journeys. The minibus to the main

Nicosia bus station, where you can pick up all sorts of connections, runs every 20 minutes, from dawn to teatime. There is a bus service west along the coast and then southwest to Güzelyurt (Morphou) but no regular service along the coast east to Boğaz (Boghaz). The coast roads are also plied by assorted minibuses, run by the large out-of-town hotels. The timetable changes every season, but as an example the Acapulco Bay hotel runs half a dozen journeys to and from Kyrenia between 9am–7pm.

By Taxi

The main taxi rank is just beside the Dome Hotel on the waterfront, with another stand along Atatürk Caddesı. There is no meter but a printed list of tariffs is usually available on request. The inflation of the Turkish lira does however require that these lists are constantly having to be updated. The journey to Nicosia (Lefkoşa) is about £5; to Güzelyurt (Morphou) about £9; Gazimağusa (Famagusta) is about £14; Ercan airport about £8. To hire a taxi for a full day, from 9am–6pm, for up to four people costs around £35. For collection from a hotel or restaurant ring either: Liman on ☎ (081) 53395, Jet on ☎ (081) 54943, Kombos on ☎ (081) 52317, Dome on ☎ (081) 52376 or Güven on ☎ (081) 53172.

By shared or service taxi: The only regular route for shared taxis is to Nicosia, which is a tenth of the price of hiring a regular taxi. Ask at the **Kombos** office on the town square or ☎ (081) 52317.

By Car

Kyrenia has about half a dozen rival car hire firms. **Atlantic** is the best established, while **Canli Balik** usually offers the cheapest rates. Both companies offer a friendly service with occasional discounts and cups of coffee as well as doubling up as foreign exchange offices. The Atlantic office, which also runs a booth at Ercan airport, is just to the left of the Dome hotel's front door, ☎ (081) 53053/52986, fax (081) 52772. You can also reserve a car through their London office ☎ (071) 700 5551, fax (071) 700 5557. Canli Balik, which means 'fresh fish' in Turkish, grew out of the harbour restaurant of the same name and their office overlooks the marina office, ☎ (081) 52182.

The price of a rented car includes an empty petrol tank, comprehensive insurance over a £150 threshold and unlimited mileage. Vehicles are available for a minumum of three days. Domestic or international driving licences must be produced and a deposit, currently set at £50, left at the office. Prices range from £8 a day for a Renault 12 in low season to £20 a day for a four-wheel-drive jeep in high season. Open-air jeeps look the glamorous choice, but their worn suspension can negate the effects of a through breeze and prove especially uncomfortable for the back-seat passengers. Tyres are often well worn, and their reduced grip should be borne in mind when executing sharp turns on the gravel-strewn hairpin bends of the mountain roads.

Tourist Information

The **tourist information office**, ℭ (081) 52145, is at 30 Kordon Boyu, on the harbour front. On either side of the office there are places where you can rent a car and exchange money.

The main **banks** along Hürriyet Caddesı and in the town square are much slower, and you should allow at least half an hour for a transaction.

Newspapers can be bought opposite the entrance to the covered market and along the main street.

The **post office**, ℭ (081) 52108, is just to the east of the town square on Mustafa Cagatay Caddesı. Its tree-shaded forecourt, with its battered yellow telephone kiosks and noticeboard, functions as the expatriate gossip zone. The parcels office is downstairs (*open 9.30–11.30 Mon, Wed and Fri*). Stamps and telephone tokens are bought upstairs (*open 8am–1pm, 2–5 Mon–Fri and 9–1 on Sat*).

The **British Residents' Society** runs an office behind the post office which is open between 10am and 12pm on Sat.

For **medical care** telephone either Dr Hakan Ataker, ℭ (081) 52065 at 101 Kordon Apt which is opposite the Dome Hotel or the Akçiçek Hospital on Cumhürriyet Caddesı, ℭ (081) 52254.

The **police station** is beside Kyrenia Castle, ℭ (081) 52014.

Festivals

Parades along Kyrenia's seaside Esplanade culminate in an exhibition of Turkish folk dancing at the harbour front to celebrate the opening of the tourist season on **1 April** and to commemorate the landing of the Turkish army on **20 July** 1974. These events are eclipsed by the dancing and live music to be found in a restaurant on Saturday nights.

Harbour

A century ago the harbour front was lined with narrow warehouses from where fresh lemons and carob pods were shipped to Syria and Egypt. It was a functional wharf directly facing the open sea. The warehouses were unadorned, apart from the odd hoist and mooring ring. They took the full blast of the winter storms and helped shelter the houses in the upper streets. The construction of an outer mole by the British in 1891 allowed for the development of the harbour area. Balustrades, terraces and windows were then gradually added to the bleak façades as they were converted first into houses and later into shops, restaurants and apartments. The harbour area is now given over to the feeding and accommodating of visitors, but there is little to regret in the addition of cane chairs, flowery cushions, candle-lit tables and the gentle enticements and banter of waiters. Spare scraps also support a small drifting community of cats and dogs.

The lighthouse tower, on the eastern promontory of the old harbour, has been much restored but was originally a Byzantine structure. In times of danger a chain was suspended across the harbour, to where the Customs House now stands. The half-ruinous wharf connecting the lighthouse to the shore is made from *cippi*, tubes of carved stone which served as gravestones and altars for celebrating the feasts of the dead in the necropolis of Roman Corineum.

Two round towers are all that survive from the walls that originally enclosed the medieval town. The larger tower, just below the town square and beside the covered market, guarded the southwest corner. The smaller tower, just up from the tourist information office, guarded the western Lapta gate. There are also some fine carved doorways to be found in the back streets, dating from the 15th century. The **Cafer Aga mosque** looks venerable but has been rebuilt twice this century, the last reconstruction in response to an EOKA-B bomb.

Kyrenia Castle

Open Mon–Sat, 8–1, 2–5; adm.

The castle stands to the east of the harbour, approached across a modern arched bridge which spans a moat.

History

The castle belongs to three eras. The first stage was the construction of a rectangular Byzantine fortress from the ruins of the classical city in the 10th century. The harbour lighthouse which stands at the end of a small pier was probably contemporary to this and gave some shelter to passing shipping, though the fortress was itself equipped with a broad sea gate to allow the safe berthing of a couple of galleys. It was reinforced by Guy de Lusignan soon after he acquired control of Cyprus in 1192, but the second stage of building occurred a century later in 1290. The seaward towers were remodelled and the moat extended, while gracious apartments and serviceable barracks were fitted within the central courtyard. It was this castle that, under Prince James, successfully resisted the siege of the Genoese in 1373 and two generations later, under the command of Cardinal Hugh de Lusignan, that of the Egyptian Mamelukes. The Venetians undertook the final shaping in the mid-16th century: a west and south wall were added, like a thick outer skin, to the old castle, and three new artillery bastions protruded from the corners. This last remodelling was achieved with sympathy for many of the old structures, which were encased rather than destroyed.

The Northwest Bastion and St George of the Castle

The entrance ramp was designed for the quick manoeuvring of artillery. It passes diagonally through the thickness of the Venetian walls to emerge into an irregular courtyard formed from the space left between the medieval and 16th-century walls. From here the ramp bends to approach the squat north-western bastion with its view over the harbour. The rest of this corner of the castle is a delightful confusion of stairs, darkened passages, ramps, blind tunnels and converging walls with some Hellenistic terracotta tombs currently resting in an open-air casemate. To the left of the gatehouse a passageway leads to a 12th-century Byzantine domed chapel, now somewhat damp. This building was originally detached from the castle, on an exposed site between the sea and the outer walls. The chapel was annexed by the Lusignans, who named it St George of the Castle, before it became inextricably embedded within the walls by the Venetians. The cruciform barrel vaults and four reused late Roman capitals help date it. Another clue to the chapel's age is provided by the patch of opus sectile floor, of white octagons picked out with triangles of green in the right hand of the three apses. To the east it is connected to a square Lusignan corner tower which is built around the circular core of a Byzantine tower.

The tomb of Sadik Paşa lies in the medieval gatehouse beside the portcullis and the restored arms of the Lusignan kings. Sadik was the Ottoman commander responsible for the bloodless capture of the castle in 1570, though he died later in the campaign.

The Courtyard

The castle's large inner courtyard is partly covered by a garden flecked with pieces of ancient statuary,

Ottoman tombs and Byzantine capitals. The courtyard reflects the plan of the original Byzantine fortress, except for the south wall which now stands a considerable way further inland.

The west range of buildings, capped by a roofless medieval hall with a window seat by its north-facing Gothic window, is the most satisfyingly picturesque ruin. Beneath it are the vaulted chambers of the Lusignan royal apartments, now occupied by offices. The north range of buildings is composed of a double row of stone-built prison cells with brown bolted doors. Peep through the warden's

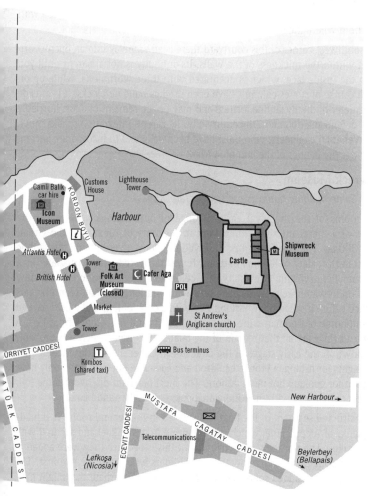

observation holes to watch boxes filled with excavated antiquities slowly gathering dust. The castellated north wall and the northeast tower date from the late 13th century. The Venetians were sure in their sea power and consequently never got round to upgrading this section. The protruding northeast tower contains two high arched halls, pierced by eight portals to provide a firing gallery. A similar but smaller version of this tower can also be seen at Kantara Castle.

The bulky southern landward wall, against which the brunt of any siege was likely to be directed, is entirely Venetian, with a great round tower on the southeast corner and an arrow-shaped bastion on the southwest. If you have a torch or stick you may descend into the basements of both towers, which are pierced with portals from where the moat and ground could be swept with grapeshot.

In the southwest corner of this courtyard there is an archway into an open courtyard set within the thickness of the walls. Its antiquity is not apparent until you look on the inside face, which is decorated with three worn lions, while up on the17th course of stones columns have been used as building blocks. It is outside the perimeter of the Byzantine fortress and may be the remains of a fort hurriedly built to defend the doomed 7th-century city. Its careful integration speaks much for the Venetian engineers, who must have been delighted to incorporate ancient lions under the banner of the lion of St Mark.

Shipwreck Museum

Same opening hours as castle; separate adm.

Three rooms of the medieval eastern range of outbuildings now house the remains of a merchant ship which sank in the time of Alexander the Great, around 300 BC. The wreck was first observed by a local diver in 1965, just a mile north from the safety of Kyrenia harbour. It was recovered a few years later by a team from Pennsylvania University in a celebrated demonstration of the new skills of underwater archaeology. The boat was 14m long and had seen 80 years of service before it sailed on its last journey with a crew of four and a hold packed with amphorae of Rhodian wine, sacks of almonds and mill stones from Kos. A pile of lead rings are all that remain of the boat's single sail, which was probably taken down in the early stages of the fatal storm. Other discoveries include 300 lead weights for fishing, a bronze cauldron and casserole pot that could only have been used for cooking hot meals ashore. The most poignant discovery is the four mess sets of the crew with their individual cups, salt cellars and oil jugs.

A reconstructed segment of the boat is displayed in the second room. It is made from planks of Aleppo pine, which were built up from the keel and secured with copper spikes. The ribs look a bit chaotic, but this is because they were added at the end, in contrast to contemporary boat builders who fitted the ribs first. The lead sheathing was added some decades later during an overhaul that might have coincided with a change in ownership. The black-treated remains, preserved in the darkened, humidity- and temperature-controlled environment of the third hall, are an initial anti-climax. However, the background hum of machinery and the hospital-like quiet of the gallery allows you to imagine the boat as a frail 2300-year-old patient lying helpless in an operating theatre, who may yet awaken and speak in the voices of the old sea.

Khrysokava, the Rock-cut Chapel of St Mavra

On Iskerendum Caddesı, the road east out of Kyrenia, turn left for the new port, signposted 'Turizm Limani'. Just before the harbour gates turn left again—you'll see a university apartment block behind which stretch three quarries, filled with vegetable gardens and joined by tunnels cut into the rock. Smile at the usually unwelcoming gardeners as you walk along the beaten paths of this hidden Eden. The second quarry has a large tomb cave now in use as a barn for animals. The third quarry is entered through a low tunnel. As you emerge blinking into the sunlight, turn sharp left to face an open-air altar shaded by an overhanging rock. Rock-cut benches flank a recessed apse, above which are the long attentuated fingers of the hand of Christ in the traditional Greek blessing, with third finger and thumb joined in the ancient symbol of unity. On an overhanging ledge Christ ascends into heaven within a mandala supported by four angels. The collapse of the surrounding walls has left only six haloed heads of apostles and angels as witnesses of this extraordinary event on Mount Sinai.

St Mavra was an early Christian martyr whose burial place in one of the many quarries surrounding the late Roman city became a place of reverence. Three layers of frescoed plaster reveal it to have been in use since Roman times, though the existing fragments date from the late 10th century. They are among the earliest to survive in Cyprus and were probably painted when the castle was built.

Museums

The **Icon Museum** is above Kordon Boyu, the seafront promenade. (*Open office hours; adm.*) It is housed in the 19th-century whitewashed church of Archangelos which stands with its carved belltower on a rocky eminence. The original church furniture, iconostasis and icon collection have been preserved, but apart from a small 17th-century woodworm-eaten panel of *Christ Entombed* there is nothing of historical or artistic interest. Just to the east, beneath the church, are a few late Roman tombs carved into the rock face. The **Decorative Arts Museum** (Guzel Sanatler Muzesi) is a1930s red-tiled villa filled with watercolours, colonial and oriental bric à brac which has a certain neglected charm. It is on the west side of Paşabahçe Avenue, opposite a military hospital and just before a barracks. (*The official opening hours are 8–1, 2–5 Mon–Sat though it can sometimes be found* locked up, in which case you can make an appointment with the custodian, © (081) 52142.) The **Folk Art Museum** is housed in a converted 18th-century granary in a back street behind the harbour front. It houses a small collection of domestic and agricultural equipment, Cypriot embroidery and kitchen tools (*see* pp. 192 and 295). (*It has been closed for years but is supposed to be reopening for business from 8–1, 3–5 Mon–Sat, © (081) 52142.*)

Swimming within 20km of Kyrenia

In the centre of Kyrenia you can swim from the harbour mole or from the stone wharf below the east wall of the castle which has iron steps and a summer café. These areas are free, basic, and popular with local boys. For more serenity and the use of a sunbed, showers and a bar buy a day ticket for the use of the bathing pier of the Dome Hotel, © (081) 52453. Out of town the coast is rocky but punctuated by a number of sand-filled coves. Some of these have been occupied by the Turkish military since 1974 and are therefore inaccessible. The most inviting sandy bays are managed, so prepare to buy a day ticket, currently around £1.50 for an adult, for which you get a sun-bed, changing room, shower and access to a café-bar. The largest stretches of sand are managed by the Mare Monte, Denizkizi and Acapulco hotels, who also provide water sports facilities and a regular Kyrenia bus service (*see* 'Where to Stay' and 'Eating Out' sections below).

The Coast West of Kyrenia

About 4km west of Kyrenia there is a turning to a small beach below the Hotel Riviera Mocamp which is on the eastern edge of **Karaoğlanoğlu** (Ayios Yeoryios) village. On the other side of the village look out for the exuberant stone carvings that advertise Ali Nasni's workshop. Shortly afterwards the brutalist freedom monument emerges, opposite a military cemetery where Turkish soldiers, who died during the July 1974 landings here, are buried. Beside it, a collection of war photographs and damaged Greek military material is known as the Peace and Freedom Museum, a misnomer which could almost have been taken from George Orwell's *1984*. Just beyond is the Altinkaya Fish Restaurant from where steps and a dirt track (just to the west) leads down to the **Yavuz Cikarma Plaj** with its split-cane-shaded parking around the Sunset bar. It is also known as Five Mile, Bambi or Golden Rock Beach after the small rocky island offshore. About 1500m west along the coast road a knot of apartments and hotels marks the turning to the **Denizkizi Beach**, turn right just before the Denizkizi Hotel entrance to reach this rock-girt sandy cove. The **Mare Monte** Hotel controls a similar sandy cove, which is another kilometre further along this coast (about 12km west from Kyrenia). **Lapta**, alias L.A. Beach, can be overcrowded as it is just in the lee of the Celebrity, Marmaris and Château Lambousa hotels. An alternative is to use the small pool and rock bathing accessible from the roadside Rita on the Rocks restaurant, 1500m further west along the coast road.

The Coast East of Kyrenia

Going east, you pass through Karakum (Karakoumi), now virtually an eastern suburb of Kyrenia. Turn left at the Hong Kong Restaurant and then right when you reach the shore to reach the small sandy cove of **Karakum**. After Karakum you pass through an area famed for its olive groves before passing north of the whitewashed village of **Çatalköy** (Ayios Epiktitos) which is 6km east from Kyrenia. Just after the first turning to Çatalköy there is a road marked 'Hz (Hazreti) Omer Tekkesi' leading to a small Muslim **shrine** by the sea. This mausoleum was built out from a cave that held the tombs of seven holy men. A shaded terrace overlooks the rocky cove. It was also venerated by Greek Cypriots who referred to it as Ayii Phanontes. Though no traditions survive it is likely that it is another of the many Mediterranean shrines dedicated to the Seven Sleepers. During the persecution of the Emperor Decius seven brothers hid in a cave and fell asleep for 200 years, waking only when Christianity had become the official religion. What makes this legend so widepsread is that it is corroborated by a verse from the Koran.

On the other side of Çatalköy, the turning by the Happy Valley restaurant leads down a tarmac road to the town beach, **Belediye Plaji**, a pair of coves with a terrace, a summer bar and a 50m strip of sand.

Acapulco beach is 7 miles (11km) east of Girne (Kyrenia). It is a 500m-wide strip of golden sand framed by rocky outcrops that is wholly contained within the grounds of the Acapulco Bay Hotel, ✆ (081) 535110 but is accessible for a daily entrance fee. The café-bar on the rocky height to the east stands beside a wired enclosure containing half a dozen excavated stone huts. These belong to an early pottery-using Neolithic village, named **Vrysin** and dated between 4–3000 BC. The litter-strewn floors of the huts were constantly replastered with clay, forming fascinating layers filled with evidence of everyday life which were dug away by archaeologists in 1969. From the litter evidence we know that the dead were buried beneath the floors in close contact with the living. The inside walls were plastered and the windowless interiors were lit by lamps. The hearth fire and a nearby bench were slightly raised above the floor, which was covered with rush mats. Polished stoneaxes, hand mills, figurines, bone needles and fragments of boldly decorated white pottery suggest a high level of culture. Fish, sheep, goat and pig bones indicate a varied diet. Cat bones have also been found, perhaps less for the cooking pot than for the early human need for 24-hour rodent patrols to protect stored corn. It was at first presumed that the circular huts may have supported a beehive-shaped dome like the Troulli houses of southern Italy, but it now appears that the walls, though thick, are still not strong enough. They may have borne a flat roof of timbers and daub or a pitched thatch of reed like that of a bothy in the Scottish Highlands. A short walk east from Vrysin is **Baris Plaji**, a long pebble beach dotted with foxholes and used by soldiers and youth camps.

One km east of the Acapulco gates is the turning for the scruffier but more tranquil **Lara Beach**. There is a comparatively small strip of sand in front of the taverna but this is compensated by a long shelf of smooth rock to the west which is ideal for sunbathing and rock diving. A short stroll along the pebble shore to the west brings you to a ruined whitewashed cave-chapel.

The 2km-long **Turtle Beach** collects nicknames as freely as the rubbish that is washed up on its shore. Save for the billowing plastic, it is a deserted shoreline enclosed by sand dunes, rocky outcrops and orchards, variously known as Ayia Ekaterini, 12-Mile Beach, Alkadi, Daoud and St Kathleen's. The west end of the beach is the easiest to get to take the dirt track just after the bridge to the east of the roadside St Kathleen taverna. At the far east end of the beach there is the distinctive rock-capped **Troulli peninsula** littered, like so many Cypriot headlands, with pottery shards from a vanished city. Troulli can also be reached about 5km along the twisting road from the St Kathleen taverna, where a dirt track follows the Alakation stream through a quiet valley, filled with the collapsing dry stone walls of an old farming hamlet. It is 7km further east from this turning to Troulli before you reach the inland turning for Esentepe (Ayios Amvrosios) and the monastery of Antiphonitis. For Esentepe and the coast east to Karpas, *see* p. 342.

Shopping

Ibrahim Dündar presides over **Aladdin's**, one of the most individual and imaginative shops in North Cyprus, which is found behind the round tower by the covered market on Attila Sokağı, ℭ (081) 53886. It is hung with scarfs, embroidered handkerchiefs and strewn with kilim cushions, gilt-stitched waistcoats, woven hats and slippers. The postcard selection includes some sketches by Sheila Aitken, a local artist, made all the more delightful in contrast to the unappealing images displayed elsewhere. Just above Aladdin's is a shop devoted to coffee with a proprietor happy to explain the art of making a decent cup of Turkish coffee.

For a souvenir made in North Cyprus rather than imported from mainland Turkey the best place to go is **Dizayn '74 pottery**, ℭ (081) 52507. It is beside the road 3km west of Kyrenia, outside Karaoğlanoğlu village. The painting desks, kilns and pottery wheels can be peeked at from the salesroom, which furnishes all the local hotels with decorated brown slipware. Dizayn also produces a range of white slipware decorated with boldly painted fruits as well as delightful one-off designs, such as brightly glazed fish plates and small hyacinth pots. They also sell traditional dark Cypriot earthenware; plain, fritted or with applied animal reliefs.

On Kordon Boyu, the esplanade running from the Dome Hotel to the harbour, there are a few gift shops. **Bahri**, ✆ (081) 53604 stocks imported Turkish pottery, metalware and sheepskins amongst the less desirable piles of imitation jade and onyx ashtrays. They also have trays of blue glass evil-eye pendants and a basket of Iznik-ware eggs.

On the corner of the modern shopping precinct at the turning to Bellapais Abbey is **Nihans** who deals in Turkish kilims and carpets, ✆ (081) 54468. On the opposite side of the road have a quick glance through the small stock at the **Merdiven bookshop**, ✆ (081) 51502. Basic supplies, like vegetables, fruit and eggs, can be bought at the **municipal market** near the medieval round tower below the town square. For a more elaborate picnic and a good choice of Turkish and imported wines, shop at **Barbaroslar**, ✆ (081) 53272, on the western end of Hürriyet Caddesı.

Religious Services

An easy introduction into the expatriate community is to attend **St Andrew's Anglican Church** which overlooks the southwest bastion of Kyrenia Castle. It is served by a resident vicar, ✆ (081) 54329, who presides over Sunday services starting with Holy Communion at 8am, followed by Matins at 8.45 and a longer Parish Holy Communion at 10.15. There is also a **Roman Catholic Chapel** on Ersin Aydın Caddesı, the street that leads south from the Dome Hotel, where Mass is celebrated on the first Sunday of each month at 5.30pm by the Papal Nuncio who drives across from Southern Cyprus especially.

Sports

Dolphin Sailing (open daily 10–5, Apr–Oct, ✆ (082) 18720) is at the beach below the Denizkizi hotel. They offer the most comprehensive water sports in North Cyprus with a team of qualified British instructors, largely recruited from the Cockshott family. They hire out windsurfing boards and sailing dinghies and tow water skiiers, parasailors and water toboggans as well as providing lessons. Other centres operate from Acapulco Bay, Lambousa and Mare Monte hotels from mid April to October. Prices are established at around £4 a water-ski tow or for half an hour's windsurfing.

There is no qualified diving school but for those who are already trained the **Dive Marine shop**, ✆ (081) 51189, between the police station and the Cafer Aga mosque, will be able to provide equipment and organise boats for a morning dive.

The Mare Monte, Celebrity, Jasmine Court and Acapulco Bay hotels all have **tennis courts** which are freely hired for about £2.50 an hour.

The village of Karaoğlanoğlu, on the road west of Kyrenia, has two **riding** schools. The **Tunaç**, ✆ (081) 52855, is the larger, older and cheaper of the two, open 6.30–8am and 5–7.30pm, and charges under £4 an hour, with tuition offered at weekends.

Despite a succession of coves, empty beaches and a yachting marina in the old harbour of Kyrenia, the coast of North Cyprus is virtually empty of yachts, due to numerous no-go areas established by the Turkish military.

From May to October there are **boat trips** from Kyrenia harbour to the hotel-controlled beaches at Acapulco Bay or Mare Monte, leaving at 10.30am and returning by 4.30pm. The £15 ticket, which includes lunch and drink, can be brought from Nulisi Mûderisoiglu on the boat, or from the harbour front Café-Terrace, ✆ (081) 53708.

Where to Stay

For most visitors the choice is between the centre of the town, or somewhere out of town near a beach, though if you are an advance planner you could rent a flat or house in one of the inland villages.

expensive in town

The ex-colonial **Dome Hotel**, ✆ (081) 52453, on Kordon Boyu, still dominates Kyrenia's seaside esplanade, but is perhaps just a bit too dowdy, with its neglected pool and brown bedroom curtains, to justify the amount it charges for a double room. Its chief attractions are the casino and bathing pier, both of which are available to non-residents. If you do stay, tuck into the hotel's breakfast and tea, but eat out for all other meals. Those with expensive tastes are now drawn to the enclosed world of the **Jasmine Court Hotel**, just to the west of town at 20 Temmuz Caddesı, ✆ (081) 51540. White apartment blocks enclose a marina-like water courtyard and the dining rooms have a clear view out to the separate pool terrace. The simplest double room starts at £50.

The **Mare Monte Hotel**, ✆ (082) 18310, is well designed but with an isolated, somewhat enclosed atmosphere 7 miles/11km west of Kyrenia. The 80 odd rooms are distributed in bungalows scattered in the garden, exposing only the white central reception block. It has its own beach that is open to non residents which is overlooked by a terraced restaurant with views over the water sports by day and the open-air disco at night.

Denizkizi Hotel, © (082) 18710, is set in a terraced garden overlooking a rock-enclosed sandy bay 5 miles/8km west of Kyrenia. The 60-bedroom, four-storey block is unexceptional; however it is suffused with a friendly but courteous atmosphere overseen by its affable owner-manager. There is usually live music on Saturday night, a lamb roast for Sunday lunch, and in summer meals are served underneath the vine-clad terrace.

moderate

The **Atlantis** and the **British** (which used to be known as the Ergenekon) are two small, rival hotels set back one street from Kyrenia harbour. About half the rooms have balconies and breakfast is served in the lobby-bar. The Atlantis is at 4 Efdal Akça Sokağı, © (081) 52242 and the British which is just round the corner, on © (081) 52240.

There are also a number of hotels along Hürriyet Caddesı which are larger and have better facilities but not the intimacy or position of the Atlantis or British. Try the **Anadol**, © (081) 52319, which is off the road and has a small garden, followed by either the **Socrates** at No. 95 Hürriyet Caddesı, © (081) 52157 or the nearby **Dorana**, © (081) 53521.

Riviera Mocamp, © (081) 53369, is a tranquil enclosure 3km west of Kyrenia with a small sandy beach and two dozen suites and barrel-vaulted rooms scattered around a central restaurant. Camping is also available in the grounds of this low-key but popular family hotel.

cheap

The **Set Pension**, © (081) 53845, is a handsome building with its own terrace situated beside the Aga Cafer mosque. It has nine spacious bedrooms on one floor but don't accept the poky tenth room. The Byfaz pâtisserie occupies the downstairs of the building with some lesser pensions scattered around the nearby streets. There is also the ageing **Bristol Hotel**, © (081) 52321, now a pension on the north side of Hürriyet Caddesı. For a secluded beach-break try the isolated house overlooking Lara Beach which rents out a couple of rooms but has no telephone.

Villa Rentals Cerenia Ltd, © (081) 54934, is run by Mrs Audrey Ellison, an ex-Lebanon hand, who manages the rental of about two dozen distinctive villas and flats in and around Kyrenia. Prices currently average about £190 a week for two persons. Bookings should be secured well in advance, though there are occasional vacancies to be picked up at the last minute. For more information write to Cerenia Ltd, PO Box 520, Girne, Mersin 10, Turkey or fax (081) 53738.

Lapta Gardens at 2 Orhan Gazi Sokak also requires some advance organization. It is a traditional house at the top of the village of Lapta which has been converted into a five-room pension with two fountains and a swimming pool. It can only be booked in London through CTA, President Holidays or Elite Tours.

Eating Out

Friday and Saturday are the busiest nights for dining out, with the greatest chance of live music (see 'Nightlife' below), and reservations are required. The Cypriot Sunday lunch, involving at least three generations, is another well-established event. There are over 50 restaurants around Kyrenia. Fortunately there is no stability in reputation and no consensus of opinion with which to dispute this personal selection. There is no great differential in price between the moderate and cheap list.

expensive in town

The old Kyrenia harbour is ringed with rattan chairs where you can sip an aperitif before choosing from an outer circle of fish restaurants established in the old carob warehouses. Waiters from the Set, Vendelik, Canli Balik and Marabou restaurants stand ready to usher visitors into elegantly dressed candle-lit tables. The **Set** is currently the most esteemed for its steamed fish accompanied by vegetable and fish kebabs. At the eastern end of the harbour the red-railed **Harbour Club Restaurant**, ℂ (081) 52211, has the least impressive aspect but is considered by local residents to have the best kitchen (closed Tuesday).

The intimate **Efendi's House**, ℂ (081) 51149, with its mouthwatering and constantly changing menu, derived from traditional French and local cuisine, is tucked away in one of the backstreets at 6 Kamil Paşa Road, ℂ 51149. Lunch is served between 11.30–14.30 and dinner from 7.30. Reservations are advised; prices start from £15 for a set menu with wine.

moderate in town

Niazis, ℂ (081) 52160, is a long established kebab restaurant situated almost directly opposite the Dome Hotel on Kordon Boyu Caddesı. The kitchen prepares the meat, salads and bread but all the meat is grilled before your eyes in a large central hearth. Order a full kebab and taste the full range of house specialities (closed Wednesday).

The **Perge**, ℂ (081) 54629, sits on a high open terrace beside the Icon museum and the Roman tombs. It serves a traditional fish meze under the stars, accompanied by music some weekends.

The **Set Italian Restaurant**, ℂ (081) 53845, is tucked away in the streets behind the harbour and is best approached from the Aga Cafer mosque. The small courtyard garden, dominated by a swaggering stair-case, is a perfect setting for a candle-lit dinner. The food is recognizably Italian but not distinguished; pick simple dishes and lots of wine.

The **Dragon House**, ✆ (081) 52130 is opposite the uptown mosque with a tall minaret in Namik Kemal Caddesı. It has been vastly improved by the recruitment of a Cantonese chef and the witty gossip of Allan Cavinder, who presides over the bar at lunch.

cheap in town

The **Aydın Restaurant**, at 13 Canbolat Sokağı, ✆ (581) 52068, has a courtyard terrace at the back and is open all hours. It serves a classic Turkish menu of soup, kebab and cold vegetable *meze*. The latter comes in a star-shaped arrangement of six dishes and is a cheap and filling meal.

Ziya Baba, opposite the round medieval tower by the municipal market is a traditional Turkish lokanta with its visual menu of steaming trays of richly sauced beans, meat and stuffed vegetables.

The **Paşabahçe** or Kyrenia Tavern at 2 Türkmen Sokağı, ✆ (081) 52799, is a homely place filled with the sounds of taped opera. The terrace looks out over a garden where the dignified owners are bullied by their dogs. The menu of the day is reasonable and there is a good selection of wine.

expensive in villages or on the coast

The **Abbey House** in Bellapais village, ✆ (081) 53460, remains the most prestigious restaurant with its French cooking served in a secluded jasmine scented garden. There have been mutterings about it living off its reputation but it is nevertheless advisable to book in advance. It faces the east side of Bellapais Abbey off a discreet footpath without a whiff of advertising and is run by Graham Cousens and Bryan Hill (*open for dinner between 8–11pm, every day except Sunday*).

moderate in villages or on the coast

The **Kybele Restaurant**, ✆ (081) 55208 is perched in the corner of the abbey grounds of Bellapais with an unforgettable view into the cloisters and over the coast. It is open from 11am–11pm. If there are no tables or you are likely to be irritated by slow service try the **Huzür Ağaç**, the Tree of Idleness Restaurant, ✆ (081) 53380, beside the village coffee shop, where you can order a cheap and filling plate of cold vegetable *meze*.

The **Levante Restaurant**, ✆ (081) 55431 which occupies an old house in the centre of Karaman (Karmi) offers a Lebanese menu of freshly prepared soups, spiced chicken and lamb dishes with yoghurt. It has a small but well-furnished dining room sprinkled with backgammon boards and a fire in winter. There is also a terrace with a fine view of St Hilarion and a bar where the Anglo-Dutch proprietors preside over a mixed community, in contrast to the undiluted Englishness of Karmi's **Crow's Nest Pub** and the **Duckworth House Restaurant**, ✆ (081) 52880.

Gülers Restaurant, ✆ (081) 52267, is off the main road west of Kyrenia, beside the well-signposted Serif Hotel Apartments, but with a good position on the edge of a broad cove and directly above a 50m stretch of sand. Gülers is discreet and locally esteemed and is somehow considered to be able to acquire fresh fish.

Altinkaya Restaurant, ✆ (082) 18341, is just west of the concrete monument that commemorates the landing of the Turkish Army here in 1974. It is a large and often boisterous place, offering the essential Cypriot banquet of *meze*, followed by plates of grilled and fried fish which is more often accompanied by whisky than wine.

Rita on the Rocks, ✆ (082) 18922, is both a restaurant and a large, charismatic, dark-glass-wearing English woman with a genius for remembering her guests and making a party from a mixed crowd of diplomats, UN soldiers, expatriates and holiday-makers. This roadside restaurant is about 13km west of Kyrenia and has a pool, rock bathing, a busy open-air bar and an innovative menu designed by her husband Ergün. Try the curried *borek*, followed by the fish *kofte* or charcoal grilled tandoori chicken.

Sirin Yali, ✆ (082) 18583, is one of the three restaurants to be found amongst the ruinous warehouses in the centre of the coastal village of Karşıyaka (Vasilya). You can go rock-bathing off a deserted coastal walk to the east of the village, before sitting down to a meal of *meze* followed by fish. Sirin Yali is signposted off the main road by a bust of Atatürk at the Dörtyol Café (*open all year, closed Thursdays*).

The **Lemon Tree Restaurant**, ✆ (081) 14045, is on a terrace above the coast road, about 4 miles/6.5km east of Kyrenia, near Çatalköy. It serves typical Turkish Cypriot food, a selection of cold vegetable *meze*, followed by hot stuffed pastries which concludes with a choice of grilled fish or meat. Your meal will be observed by ornamental fish that swim seemingly unconcerned by all the cooking in a large tank in the dining room.

The **St Kathleen Restaurant**, ✆ (081) 52496, is on the west end of Turtle beach, 18km east of Kyrenia. The reclusive roadhouse exterior of the restaurant belies its warm chatty interior. It provides good traditional charcoal-grilled meats with fresh salads.

The **Courtyard Inn**, ℂ (081) 53343, is just off the coast road east of Kyrenia. It is unashamedly modelled on a convivial English pub, but rises above expectations with an imaginative menu and a good selection of Turkish wines. Try a spinach and apricot *borek* with the house speciality of fillet stuffed with pâté and prawns.

cheap in villages or on the coast

The bear-like Celâl, his wife and their beautiful daughters run the **Başpınar Restaurant**, ℂ (082) 18661, which stands beside a millrace fed by the spring at the summit of Lapta. Do not be put off by the tortuous approach road; the view (which on a clear evening can often takes in the Cilician mountains of southern Turkey) is alone worth the trip. The Başpınar has a high reputation for its *meze* and kebabs which are served without reference to menus or written bills.

The Old (olive) Mill in the centre of Ozanköy (Kazaphani) looks permanently closed but it shelters within its dusty exterior **Shenol's**, a small but lively bar and restaurant. The set menu which consists of *meze* followed by a choice of four meat dishes is extremely good value, though the bill is usually doubled by the freely flowing wine and brandy.

Bars and Cafés

The **Akpınar café** looks out over the seafront promenade by the Dome Hotel. It has the best selection of cakes, croissants and *baklava* served at a scattering of tables under an awning beside a homemade fountain.

The **Grape Vine** is tucked away from the street beside the Esso filling station on the Nicosia road. It is a popular meeting place for locals and expatriates with an attractive bar, old wooden benches and kilims.

Nightlife

Kyrenia is a small resort which manages to present an intriguing variety of nightlife in mid-summer. There are half a dozen casinos, hotel discos and a couple of nightclubs, as well as **live music** in local tavernas. **Zia's**, ℂ (081) 52927, **Paradise**, ℂ (081) 52356, and **Ali Paşa**, ℂ (082) 18515, are three of the most reliably boisterous and musical, particularly at weekends. They serve traditional *meze*, and seldom bother with menus or written bills. Zia's and Paradise are east of Kyrenia, signposted outside Çatalköy, Ali Paşa is west of Kyrenia, near Lapta, and is well-illuminated off the main road. In the evening the lobby of the Pizza Napoli on the harbour front echoes to synthesizer-backed melodies, but the music politely stops to give precedence to the muezzin call from the mosque.

The cluster of **casinos** in the central and adjacent **Dome**, ℂ (081) 52453, **Grand Rock**, ℂ (081) 52379, and **Limani**, ℂ (081) 52001 hotels are the most appealing for the social gambler (though there are gambling halls in some out-of-town hotels as well). They operate one-arm bandit galleries that are open throughout the day, as well as evening games rooms filled with green baize tables for roulette, vingt-et-un/pontoon and crap games. These open at 8pm and stay in business until between 3am and dawn. They are not exclusive and only the Limani insists on a small minimum entrance stake. There is no dress code, though most of the players are in a long evening dress or blazer and tie, while only the staff wear dinner jackets.

The **Mare Monte**, ℂ (082) 18310, and **Celebrity**, ℂ (082) 18751 hotels, which are between 11 and 14km west of Kyrenia, run **discos** for their guests in the summer months, which open at 10pm. For a more lively and mixed crowd try the **Tunnel Disco** on Ecevit Caddesı (the Nicosia road) or the **Hippodrome**, ℂ (081) 54932, in Karaoğlanoğlu village. For live **cabaret** acts with your dancing try **Club Golden Girl**, ℂ (081) 53512, which opens its doors at 9.30pm and is found off the road to the new harbour.

The Gothic Range and Cape Kormakiti

Other maps might label the narrow spine of mountains that run for a hundred miles along the northern coast of Cyprus either the Besparmark, Pendadhaktylos or the Kyrenia range. They are also known, due to the descriptions of Lawrence Durrell and Rose Macaulay, as the Gothic Range. It was Lawrence Durrell who made the famous analogy of this area with the world of the sixteenth-century print and who went on to add: 'It is par excellence the Gothic range, for it is studded with crusader castles pitched on the dizzy spines of the mountains...the very names smell of Gothic Europe: Buffavento, Hilarion, Bellapais.' This enthusiasm for the monuments of the Latin Crusaders should be tempered by a visit to the Byzantine monastery of Antiphonitis, though sadly the other great monuments from this era such as Lambousa on the coast and Ayios Ioannis Chrysostomos on the southern face of the mountains remain under military occupation and inaccessible.

The Abbey of Bellapais

> 'A most magnificent uninhabited convent, which is almost entire...'
>
> —Dr Pococke in 1738

The ruins of the abbey (*open daily 8–5; adm*) stand on a high terrace on the northern edge of the village of Beylerbey (Bellapais), 6km southeast of Kyrenia. From afar it looks like a great blockhouse, but Bellapais is the most delectable Gothic ruin in Cyprus. It has a near-perfect juxtaposition of a garden with a view, richly sculpted stone ornamenting a half-ruin which can all be appreciated for hours from the table of a licensed restaurant. The Abbey is also touched by a humanity missing from the island's other great Gothic monuments. Cyprus's Crusader castles, cathedrals and soaring chapels are glorious but they also seem imposed upon this landscape. This was perhaps deliberate, since they were powerful symbols of the separate culture and origins of the Crusader aristocracy. Bellapais is part of this imported northern genius, but it is also touched by the spirit of the eastern Mediterranean. It sits in the lee of a white-washed village, amongst cypresses, olives, oleanders and oranges. At Bellapais one can feel the cold northern soul of the Crusaders ripening and absorbing the spirit of the Levant.

History

The abbey began as a retreat for the Augustinian canons of Nicosia who, with the Franciscans and Dominicans, were one of the great teaching orders of the Catholic Church. Some time in the early 13th century the canons here were permitted to take on the austerities and seclusion of a rule established by St Norbert in 1120. This branch of the Augustinian family tree is known as the Premonstratensian or Norbertine. The abbey was named Abbaye de la Paix, the Abbey of Peace, but was nicknamed the White Abbey, after the white habits of the canons, or simply *Episcopia*, the church. It began to make a name for itself with its prickly, independent spirit. The abbey attracted bequests, mixed with requests for burial and masses from the Crusader nobility. However, it was the patronage of three Lusignan monarchs that was directly responsible for the magnificence of the monastic buildings. Hugh III (1267–84) granted the Abbot such special privileges as the right to wear a mitre during Mass and a gilded sword and golden spurs when outside the Abbey. His enthusiastic interest was matched by that of Hugh IV (1324–98) and Peter I (1358–69) who used the abbey as a spiritual retreat, though by now it was assuming more the aspect of a palace. The Genoese invasion of 1373 stripped it of portable treasures, and it sank into comparative obscurity. By the late 15th century its revenues were being diverted by a 'protector', and its name had been corrupted to Bellapais. It was not just the name that had changed; a report by the Venetian governor in 1565 speaks of the decay of both the building and its inhabitants. The former was in need of repair while the latter had furnished themselves with wives and mistresses, allowing only their offspring into the community. After the Abbey's sack during the Ottoman conquest of 1570, its empty buildings were taken over by Greek villagers, who put them to good use both as a parish church, school, stable and barn.

The Monastery Buildings

From the ticket office a path leads past a machicolated gateway, decorated with a dove of peace and a sphinx. The gateway is fitted with grooves for a drawbridge which would have crossed a moat surrounding the high walls of the abbey. Medieval visitors were permitted access to the church but only the most privileged would have been allowed into the enclosed world of the white canons. A breached wall, by the garden tables of the Kybele Restaurant, now allows direct access to the spectacular ruins of the cloister. The high-vaulted, cool cloister is decorated with vegetable bosses on the outside and human figures on the inside. It was carved in the late 14th century by locally trained masons, and though full of vigour and humour it lacks the technical excellence achieved by the Rhineland masons in Nicosia and Famagusta. Broken tracery and complete arches are punctuated by cypress trees beneath which sprawl low hedges of rosemary. In the northwest corner of the cloister a pair of antique marble sarcophagi are arranged to form a fountain where the monks could wash before meals. The upper sarcophagus is carved with a rich pagan decoration of erotes and sacrificed bulls' skulls supporting a heavy floral swag. A row of six holes was drilled in its base to allow water to trickle merrily and audibly into the lower basin before flowing out along the irrigation channels to water the courtyard garden.

An elaborately carved door, with Romanesque zig-zags framing three blank windows, leads from the cloisters into the magnificent high refectory. It was built a generation before the cloisters and is comparatively austere. Seven Gothic columns, composed of three rods, shoot up the long side walls before branching above their floral capitals into vaults which cross the ceiling in immaculate trajectories. The eastern wall is fitted with a rose window, but all attention is drawn to the six windows pierced through the north wall, through which shine spectacular views over the olive and orange groves right down to the coast. The windows are fitted with grooves to hold detachable frames of glass, and vents have been installed at floor level to allow the room to be washed clean. A staircase is cut into the thickness of the wall, leading up to a high pulpit, where passages from the rules, gospels or lives of the saints could be read to the monks during the otherwise silent meals. Beneath the refectory are two crypt-like cellars with rib-vaulted ceilings supported by pairs of strong octagonal columns.

On the east side of the cloister five steps lead down into the ruins of the common room. A single antique marble column stands in the centre of the chapterhouse, which occupied the southern end of this range. Stone benches still ring this once vaulted chamber, where the canons would assemble to discuss the day-to-day business of the abbey. A number of carved bosses remain on the wall. Some of the more disturbing, like the figure consuming his own hand, the youth between two mermaids and the fat faces restrained by garlands of olives, illustrated common proverbs now lost to us. The ruined upper storey housed the dormitory of the canons. Their cells are marked by a neat line of wall cupboards and a row of windows looking inwards over the cloister. The stairway to the dormitory is in the south wall of the cloister and leads up to the roof from where there is a magnificent but perilous view over the coast.

The church is kept locked but if you ask politely the custodian will probably open it up for you. The interior, blackened by three centuries of Orthodox candles and incense, remains just as its village congregation left it, filled by an indifferent iconostasis, melting candlesticks and brown varnished furniture. The church is the earliest part of the abbey and is surprisingly small and simple in comparison to the lavish monastery buildings beside it. It was erected in the early 13th century before Bellapais had attracted its wealthy royal patrons. It is composed of three aisles with the broad central nave supported by a double row of solid columns. The porch, which has a few surviving patches of wall painting, was added later in the century, probably after King Hugh III was buried here.

Bellapais Village and the Bronze-Age Cemetery at Vounous

The village of Bellapais is not only famous for its abbey, but also through Lawrence Durrell's book *Bitter Lemons*. The house occupied by Durrell from 1953–6, and around which the book is centred, stands in the upper part of the village. To examine its exterior, walk uphill from the Tree of Idleness café, take the first right, pass the post office and carry on uphill, to a white house with brown shutters on the left, marked by a yellow commemorative plate.

If you like walking and have seen some of the remarkable pottery in the Cyprus Museum in Southern Nicosia, you may be tempted to visit the Bronze-Age cemetery at Vounous, where much of it was discovered. The cemetery is about 4km from Bellapais. Walk downhill for 1.5km, along the track following the villages western river bed to reach Ozankoy (Kazaphani) village. From there take the dirt back road east to Catalköy (Ayios Epiktitos). About halfway along (another 1.5km), turn uphill, just before a deserted two-storey roadhouse marked 2391. Follow the track to an area of bulldozed hillside. This is Vounous, which in recent years has been so badly looted that the government decided to flatten the evidence of tomb-robbing. The obsessive tomb-spotter can then walk up into the pine-clad hills and spot the badger-like mounds of earth that indicate another plundered ancient grave.

> '*Twisting up and up into the sky, terrace above terrace,
> tower over tower, till it ends in an eyrie that surveys the
> world, it is a dramatic pile of ruin… a picture-book castle
> for elf kings.*'

—Rose Macaulay

The mountain-top castle of St Hilarion (*open daily 8.30–5; adm.*) is approached from the main Kyrenia (Girne)-to-Nicosia road. At the summit of the pass, about 10km from Kyrenia, turn right, to the west, up a narrow road that climbs the hillside. You will pass a Turkish army camp before reaching an Alpine meadow where knights used to joust and where soldiers now test themselves over an assault course. Come as early as possible, both to avoid the crowds and in order to enjoy walking in the cool of the morning. You will need stout shoes but there is no need to bring your own drink as there are two cafés.

The crumbling walls of St Hilarion Castle are draped over four levels of the partly wooded slopes of Mount Didymos in a spectacular vision of romantic ruin. It is deservedly the most popular site in North Cyprus, for it exceeds the most exacting Gothic imagination and has been credited with providing the inspiration for the creations of both King Ludwig of Bavaria and Walt Disney.

History

There are two St Hilarions who lived in Cyprus and their life stories have a tendency to become intertwined. The castle is named after the celebrated hermit or anchorite who was born near Gaza in 291. (His namesake lived a few centuries later and died in Episkopi in 731; he is known as 'the Great'.) St Hilarion was converted to Christianity whilst a student at the university of Alexandria. An early visit to the desert-dwelling St Anthony of Egypt introduced him to the ascetic life which he perfected in the wilderness outside Gaza. St Hilarion ate only 15 figs a day, consumed at sunset, and filled his days with prayer and basket-weaving. His fame spread, for he could perform miraculous cures and exorcisms, but the once empty desert became filled with an irritating number of pilgrims and potential disciples. Hilarion escaped his fans by taking a boat to Paphos but found this still pagan city spoilt by demons, and so he moved on. He established himself in a humble cave beside a neglected pagan temple high up in the mountains above the city of Kyrenia, where he stayed in prayer for the last five years before his death in 371. The memory of his holiness was still strong centuries later when the Byzantine Empire re-established its control over Cyprus in the 10th century. A monastery with a handsome octagonal church was built beside the hermit's cave, and the mountain summit was transformed into a fortified lookout post.

By the 13th century, if not before, this group of buildings had passed into the hands of the Ibelin, one of the most powerful and well-connected families of the Crusader nobility. Jean d'Ibelin, regent to the young Henry I, turned it into the fortress of Dieu d'Amour (the god of love) for the mountain was believed to have been sacred to Venus's Cupid. The castle was a key point of contention during the attempt by the Emperor Frederick II to seize control of Cyprus from the Lusignans between 1228 and 32. It was twice besieged, and in the aftermath of the Lusignan victory it was repaired and greatly embellished to become the fortified summer palace of the dynasty. Five Ibelin queens presided over St Hilarion/Dieu d'Amour in the golden hundred years of Lusignan Cyprus, between 1250 and 1350. In the hot summer months the court moved out from Nicosia to enjoy jousts, hunts, pageants and flirtations in the healthy air of the mountains and to dine, brushed by cool pine-scented breezes, in the evening.

The triple invasion of the Genoese in 1373 broke this halycon spell of courtly ease. While most of the family of the young Lusignan king Peter II were besieged in Kyrenia, his slightly mad uncle, the Prince Regent, John of Antioch, stayed on in the upper keep of St Hilarion, defended by his bodyguard of Bulgarian highlanders. By the 15th century the castle had began to fall into neglect and, rather than face repair bills, the Venetians, soon after they assumed control of Cyprus, dismantled it. It lay abandoned for centuries, but the overgrown ruins, tidied up by the British, were fought over again in the spring of 1964. Turkish Cypriot militia garrisoned the castle and fought off attacks led by the Greek Cypriot Minister of the Interior to keep control of the main Nicosia-to-Kyrenia road. Ten years later the Turkish army landed and remain in control of this strategic site.

The Site

The entrance to the castle is through a double gatehouse which is dressed with finely carved corbels that once supported an external gallery. This was designed to be the only entrance through the machicolated outer curtain wall, which, studded with round towers, encloses the scrub-filled outer bailey. The outer bailey is dotted with cisterns, modern barracks, old stables and ruined medieval outbuildings. The parapet and a number of the towers have been repaired to allow for a promenade before following a path up through fields of fennel to a second gatehouse which was originally approached across a drawbridge.

From this second gatehouse a vaulted tunnel passes directly to the palace apartments, but first climb up from this throughway to the low ruins of the original 10th-century Byzantine church. The stumps of eight restored columns, made from the typical Byzantium medium of alternate layers of brick and stone, would have risen into a connecting octagon of arches to support a central dome. This spacious single nave was a delightful variation on traditional design, but only occurs in two other Cypriot churches, Antiphonitis and Panayia Apsidhiotissa, both of which are situated in the Gothic Range. Tiny fragments from the original wall painting can be spotted, like the curtain dado at shin height on the south wall. To the left of the altar apse are two small chambers, thought to be either a sacristry or a pious reconstruction of Hilarion's hermitage.

To the east of the church is a café, restored hall and various lesser vaulted rooms of the summer palace. These extend out on a slip of narrow rock to embrace spectacular views and manipulate the breeze to create a cooling tower-of-winds effect. The near-vertical drops have been skillfully used in the placement of the latrine. Walk past the lesser ruins on the other side of the café towards a large buttressed water tank. It is tempting to imagine a Russell Flint tableau here, an arrangement of gypsies and princesses in wet damask, but this was the castle's vital water cistern collected from runoff, and not a swimming pool.

From the cistern an eroded path zig-zags up a steep slope towards an arched gate leading into the upper ward of the Castle. It is an enchanted place, a secret garden formed by a double set of medieval chambers that bridge the gap between two mountain peaks. This is believed to be the site of an ancient temple to the Lord of the High Places, the lover of the Goddess, which was established by the Phoenicians and recalled in St Hilarion's other name of Dieu d'Amour. It is now populated by cedars but is nevertheless easy to fill this space with a scene from a medieval illumination. Coiffured women, pale youths and strong knights saunter around a formal, scented garden of knot beds and stone seats arranged around a symbolic fountain. Tame partridges flitter through the herbs, bells tinkle in the wind, a lover sighs and a poet sings.

The kitchen stood to the north, eclipsed by the grandeur of the roofless two-storey Great Hall at the western end. In the upper hall is the Queen's View: Karaman (Karmi) and the receding coast are framed by three Gothic windows of carved stone. A path climbs up to the northern summit where you can rest amongst the remains of three watch towers. Just outside the gateway of the upper ward castle the path divides; turn right (if you are leaving the upper ward, left if arriving) for one more steep climb. This will take you up to the lone tower of Prince John of Antioch which stands on a rocky crag with sheer drops on three sides.

Eleanor, the Queen Mother, envied Prince John his position as the regent of young King Peter. She realised that Prince John was invulnerable in the upper castle of St Hilarion so long as it was garrisoned by his devoted bodyguard of wild Bulgarians. She managed to convince Prince John that they were planning his assassination, and so one night he called them up, one by one to this tower, where they were tripped headlong into the abyss. It was only when the last Bulgar, their commander, saluted before obediently walking off the parapet, that the misguided Prince realised the true depth of their loyalty.

St Hilarion to Lapta Walk

Get a lift up to St Hilarion soon after the road opens at 8.30, and ask to be dropped by the firm dirt road beneath the castle. This road carries on west along the crest of the mountains, to provide an almost level, sap scented stroll through pine woods with innumerable spectacular views both north and south. After about three hours, or 16km, having passed below the summits of Potamoudhia, Mazeri, Prophitis Elias and Gomaristi, you reach a forestry crossroads. Take the right turn for Lapta, winding downhill to pass the ruined chapel of Ayios Pavlos set in a small olive grove, beside a spring. Fragments of frescoes have miraculously survived the seasons and still adorn portions of the interior. The track then continues its descent for 4km and reaches the Başpinar Restaurant (*see* 'Eating Out' p. 333) at the summit of the sprawling village of Lapta. The Başpinar stands beside its eponymous spring and an old millrace, with meals and drinks to reward the walker and a telephone with which to call a taxi.

Monastery of Panayia Apsidhiotissa

The empty monastery of Apsidhiotissa stands high up on the southern slopes of the Gothic Range. At Taşkent (Vouno), which is 10km north of the Nicosia ringroad, take the rough dirt road uphill from the village shop and bear right at the first fork, weaving your way up past the quarry workings to approach the monastery half-hidden in a pine wood. The church, which was restored in the sixties, is a sophisticated example of 12th-century Byzantine architecture. The wide nave is formed from a circle of six arches which support a high, window-pierced drum and a generous dome. The arches have been cunningly placed to accentuate the eastern altar with a wide-open arch. This extra width has been compensated for by reducing the entrance to a narrow slit which also helps exaggerate the natural drama of the interior. Though all the paintings have disappeared, some of the dramatic effect of this single-domed nave remains. The large double-apsed western porch, known as a narthex, is supported by ribs of stone, the central span of which meets in a cross-decorated boss. This was added in the 15th century when the monastery was occupied by Catholic monks and known as the Abbey of Abscithi. After the Ottoman conquest it passed under the control of the Orthodox Church. Around the church stand numerous ruined outbuildings and to the north a curious single-naved refectory supported by five round brick arches. The interior is lit by long, narrow window slits to give it a markedly Russian look.

Uphill from the monastery the path leads through the ruined barracks of the Greek Cypriot army. Though Buffavento castle is just to the east, it cannot be approached from this direction as a Turkish paratroop regiment occupy the ground between. To the west of Taşkent (Vouno) village, the soldiers have laid out in stone one of Atatürk's most famous dictums, '*Ne Mutlu Türküm Diyene*'—

'Fortunate is the man who can declare himself a Turk'. This piece of unbridled nationalism is clearly visible from Greek Nicosia. It is also a linguistic landmark, for before 1920 it was a very fine thing to be an Ottoman, but a Turk was then a disparaging description reserved for Anatolian peasants. There is a small museum in the village which commemorates the massacre of the village's Turkish minority by EOKA B gunmen in December 1963, when Vouno was still a Maronite village.

Alevkaya Herbarium

This forestry station, plant nursery and herbarium (*open every day 8–4*) is on the southern face of the mountain ridge at Alevkaya (Halevaga) 11km north of Değirmenlik (Kythrea) on the road to Karaağaç (Karcha). It is surrounded by mountain tracks and has a small bar-restaurant and picnic tables under some mature pine trees which make it a popular day trip for Cypriot families. The forest guards are usually happy to give advice or even accompany walkers and Dr Deryck Viney, the resident botanist since 1988, shows interested visitors around the one-room herbarium with its growing collection of line drawings, bottled and pressed specimens covering 800 species, including 20 endemic to North Cyprus.

Antiphonitis Monastery

The empty Monastery of Antiphonitis lies 29km east of Kyrenia in the mountains southeast of the village of Esentepe (Ayios Amvrosios). In Esentepe take the Nicosia road out of the village and just as the road bends to the right take the first turning on the left. Follow this dirt road for 4km, passing through woodland and below the 16th-century Chapel of Panayia Apati, before turning left at a cross-roads and down a short but rough track.

The 12th-century domed church is tucked in a secretive valley, surrounded by empty outbuildings and a terrace to the north, with a good view over the nearby coast. Antiphonitis is the finest example of the octagonal nave, which can also be seen at St Hilarion and Panayia Apsidhiotissa. Rather than divide the interior into the customary three dark aisles, a ring of eight columns frames a single nave. This circle of columns have been described as choraic by some historians who see a reference to the slow, measured circular dances of ancient Greek religion. This design creates a spacious interior, given additional drama by a high drum carrying the irregular eye-shaped dome. The barrel-vaulted porch on the west end and the handsome arcade of pointed stone arches supported by octagonal columns to the south were both added in the 15th century.

The architectural features, however, take second place to the surviving wall paintings. The great glory of the church is the *Christ Pantocrator*, which, wounded by blasts of buckshot, stares down from the dome within a rainbow circle. There is a flicker of surprise, a hint of recognition in Christ's face, as if you might be yet another Judas coming to plant a fatal kiss in a garden. Below him a circle of winged angels and saints are led by the Virgin and St John in a procession before the empty throne. In the third circle the 12 apostles are seated on spacious thrones, an odd departure from their usual standing-only rule, and below them are pairs of prophets interspaced between the windows. The dome paintings date from the early 15th century. The posture of the figures and colours are typically Byzantine, but there is also a breath of the Renaissance about them, noticeable even in Christ's blue cloak which has an implicit sense of drama and movement.

The damaged *Virgin Blachernitissa* in the eastern apse, with its deep blue and old gold, is part of the original 12th-century decoration. She is flanked by two archangels, Gabriel in scarlet and Michael in green, both wearing the costume and carrying the red rods of ushers from the Comnenian court at Constantinople. There are only shadows to suggest the six prelates on the lower wall.

On the free-standing columns before the altar, Michael and Gabriel also reappear with scrolls appropriate to their other role as recording angels. These are also suitably decorated with Symeon Thaumatiges and Theodosios, a pair of stylites (hermits who spent their life perched on the top of columns) who peer across the central door at each other. An attractive portrayal of St Romanus, a celebrated Byzantine hymn-writer, can also be found on the inner face of the south column. Most of the 15th-century paintings in the nave have either faded, been scratched with 19th-century graffiti or stolen, like the large Tree of Jesse scene that has been chipped away from the southwest wall. There are three other fine scenes worth hunting out, an early *Baptism*, a *Transfiguration* and an *Entombment*.

Buffavento Castle

The ruined mountain-top castle of Buffavento, 13km southeast of Kyrenia, is accessible any time that you are prepared for a strenuous climb. It is not possible to approach the castle from the south, as this road passes beside the medieval monastery of Ayios Ioannis Chrysostomos, which is now a Turkish military training ground and a forbidden area. The only approach is off the Kyrenia/Girne-to-Değirmenlik (Kythrea) road. As this reaches the summit of the mountain crossing, there is a crossroads and a battered green sign which reads '*Karayollari Dairesi Tas Ocaklari*'. A track saunters 6km west through pine-scattered hills to the olive tree roundabout at the foot of Buffavento. It makes a pleasant hour-and-a-half stroll but is also passable in a rented car.

A path zig-zags up the mountain to approach the scattered buildings of the castle, which are erected on two levels and capped by a summit chamber and lookout post. The awesome view combined with the exertion of the climb is enough to silence most visitors. Nicosia, the Mesaoria Plain and the Ercan airport are laid out like a playground for the gods to the south, with all the hidden beaches and coves of the shore exposed to the north. There is also a melancholy air to the castle, in keeping with its use as a state prison by the Lusignan dynasty. Sir John Visconti had informed the Lusignan King Peter I (1359–69) that his wife had been having an affair with the popular Count Rochas while he had been on tour. The queen and her court, having more than one secret to protect, closed ranks in a conspiracy of silence that left Sir John alone. He was accused of malicious slander and locked away without trial. Later he was taken up to Buffavento and starved to death.

Buffavento, which means gust of wind in Italian, was also known as the Lions' or the Queen's Castle. It seems to have been first established in the 10th century as a Byzantine lookout tower which could signal directly to Nicosia. It was part of a chain of fortresses guarding the northern coast, and could receive messages from St Hilarion or Kantara and further down the line, Kastros and Kyrenia. Its position, defended by nature, never required a curtain wall or a strong gatehouse or allowed for much in the way of a concentric plan. The buildings, simple, vaulted rectangular rooms designed for storage and accommodation, are difficult to date, as they were all built from the mountain stone. The castle was slighted by the Venetians in the mid-16th century, who concentrated their resources on Nicosia and the coastal fortresses of Kyrenia and Famagusta.

The inaccessible Monastery of Ayios Ioannis Chrysostomos, St John of the Golden Mouth, can be glimpsed at from Buffavento. It is composed of the twin churches of the Holy Trinity and St Chrysostomos encased in a courtyard, with two ruined cemetery chapels, of the Saviour and Panayia Aphendrika, just to the south. The Holy Trinity and the Saviour were built by Duke Eumathius Philocales, the Byzantine Governor of Cyprus, at the end of the 11th century. They contain some of the island's most important wall paintings, of a similar age and quality to those that can be seen at Asinou, in the south.

Beşparmak (Pentadaktylos) Mountain

Take the track heading east at the dirt track crossroads which is on the summit of the tarmaced Girne (Kyrenia) to Değirmenlik (Kythrea) road, to reach the Beşparmak (Pentadaktylos) mountain. The 'Five-Fingered Mountain' has the most noticeable silhouette in Cyprus, and is often used to describe the whole northern mountain range. A peaceful alpine meadow lies in the southern lee of the five rippling summits which look more like knuckles than fingers. A number of tales are attached to the mountain, one of which involves a queen (all good Cypriot legends circle around a nameless queen) who tested a young ardent lover by sending him off to fetch a drink of water from a distant spring. By the time he had returned the queen had quite forgotten about either him or her drink. The exasperated young giant poured the precious spring water onto the ground and shaped a great mud ball which he hurled at the queen. It missed and landed on the mountains where it solidified into the five-fingered peak. Follow the track east though pine woods to re-emerge at the Alevkaya (Halevga) forestry station.

Karaman (Karmi)

The inconspicuous turning to Karaman (Karmi) is in Karaoğlanoğlu (Ayios Yeoryios) village. The road twists up through Edremit (Trimithi) before climbing further south to the mountains. Before you enter the village, turn left by the Duckworth House Restaurant sign, and follow the tarmac track down to the east slope of the hill, where a number of Bronze Age tombs from the Palialona cemetery have been excavated. Bedrock was cut away to create a sloping entrance-way down to the circular mouths of the tomb chambers which were sealed with stone slabs. The most substantial tomb, No. 6, is protected by a hut. Stairs have been carved into the entrance slope with a simple triangular frieze set into the lintel and the side walls decorated with crude columns. On the right-hand wall a female figure can just be discerned. This chthonic deity, with folded arms, breasts and staring eyes, welcomes the dead back to the earth from which all life comes and all returns.

Karmi is an attractive village of whitewashed houses, lodged beside a spring at the foot of the mountains. It is now exclusively inhabited by a colony of British and German expatriates which includes a couple of former British MPs, a few artists and a drifting quantity of potential novelists. The best time to visit is on Sunday morning when Farell Bevan opens her studio, Nadia Brunton presides over the old Orthodox church and the Levant Restaurant prepares Sunday lunch.

Farell Bevan's studio is on the right as you enter the village. Views of St Hilarion, Bellapais and Kyrenia are for sale with still-life paintings and some haunting sketches of olive trees. There are prints for around £10 while original water-colours, pastels and oils range from £45–120.

Nadia Brunton, the doyenne of Karmi, opens the old whitewashed Orthodox church at the centre of the village to visitors from 10.30–1 on Sunday. She is responsible for its preservation, and has maintained it since the exodus of the Greek community in 1974. This village church is undistinguished in architecture and decoration, but its heavy 19th-century carvings and crude *ex voto* icons have an increasing appeal when set against the devastation of so many church interiors throughout much of the north. An alien but welcome addition to the church is the icon of St Catherine, by Mary Walton, by the west door.

There are two walks west from Karmi to the coast that are best covered in two hours of the morning. The lower path drops down into a valley and skirts Edremit

(Trimithi) before joining a track to the coast road outside Karaoğlanoğlu (Ayios Yeoryios). The upper path keeps its height for 2km before descending to join the road leading uphill to Malatya (Phterykha). Turn right at this junction, down to Yeşiltepe and then take the farm road into the back of Alsancak (Karavas).

Lambousa

Lambousa, 'The Shining One', is currently inaccessible to the public. The area is occupied by the Turkish army, though it is hoped that the slow de-militarization of the north will soon renew access to this important site. A quick peek at Lambousa's three medieval churches can be had by taking the third turning on the right as you proceed west past the Mare Monte Hotel. Do not proceed beyond the military barrier at the end of the road.

Lambousa was founded by Phoenician traders in the 8th century BC and remained a quietly prosperous town until the Christian era, when groves of mulberries fed a highly profitable silk industry. The foundations of a lighthouse, sea-water fish-ponds and a portion of the city's wall survive from the 6th-century Byzantine town. A silver dinner service from this period was found here in the early years of this century, presumably hidden just before the Saracens sacked the city in the 7th century. It is the finest example of secular art from early Byzantium and is now split between the collections of the Metropolitan, British and Cyprus museums. Lambousa was revived as a port, though all that remains from this second period are three distinctive medieval churches. The 13th-century double-domed monastery of Akhiropietos, 'Built without Hands', was erected over the ruins of an old cathedral. Akhiropietos was enlarged in the 15th century, at the same time that the ancient shrine of St Evlalios was also completely restored. The curious rock hewn chapel of St Eulambios is the core remnant of an old quarry. It was turned into catacombs in the late Roman period, and is where the body of Eulambios, an early martyr, was interred.

Lapta (Lapithos)

This sprawling, diffuse hill village, 10km west of Kyrenia, is spread out over half a dozen levels. A number of springs from the Kyparissovounon mountain flow noisily out along irrigation channels to water the surrounding gardens and groves of citrus and olive. There are half a dozen attractive, decaying whitewashed churches scattered throughout the village, though none of them dates from before the 18th century. The village itself is much older, founded by refugees from Lambousa seeking safety in the high ground from pirate raids. Lapithos was the seat of an Orthodox bishopric, until it was suppressed by the Catholic Crusader state in the 13th century. Lapta contains one of the island's most handsome stone mosques, whose classical Ottoman silhouette of minaret, square prayer hall, hexagonal drum and dome can be seen in Dumlupinar Sokağı. The cliff-face by the town hall is enlivened by a waterfall fed by the *kephalovryson*, 'the ever-flowing spring' at the head of the valley. Follow signs to the Başpinar Restaurant in order to reach the source of the spring with its uplifting view. (This could make an alternative starting point for the St Hilarion–Lapta walk, *see* p. 341.) A shorter but still arduous walk begins along a back road, at town hall level, and passes below the old Ayia Varvara church on its way to the smaller village of Karşıyaka (Vasilia), 4km to the west. A dirt track to the left of the Karşıyaka café twists uphill to give an approach for the climb to the summit of Kornos, a distinctive 946m-high summit on the western edge of the Gothic Range.

The Koruçam (Kormakiti) Peninsula

The dank Club Güzelyali Hotel stands above a seaweed-rich pebble beach, 25km west of Kyrenia. It marks, for the moment, the furthest advance of development along this coast. Just to its west, the narrow road to Cape Kormakiti twists above cliffs and dips down to the sea to give access to a succession of sandy coves. A few fishing boats bob in quiet anchorages and goat tracks cut through the maquis. You will have no difficulty in finding an empty beach here for a day-long picnic.

After the rural village of Kayalar (Orga), there is a spectacular 3km drive west along the sea cliffs to reach Ayios Yeoryios bay where the empty chapel of St George and a carob warehouse are overlooked by a promontory. This natural eminence is dotted with massive boulders and wind-etched caves. The shards and a rock cut cistern on the summit remain from the Byzantine fort of Ghalala.

The church of St Helen and St Constantine stands empty in Sadrazamköy (Liveras) which has been settled by immigrants from Anatolia. The foundations of a Venetian watchtower can be found amongst sheep enclosures that embrace a line of rock-cut tombs just north of the hamlet. The road further west deteriorates, but the track cut through the wind-eroded bedrock makes a pleasant 4km walk to the low Cape Kormakiti with its battered lighthouse built on the site of an old temple. Treading on the odd patches of sand, it is possible to wade out 50m from the shore to reach the savagely eroded island of Kormakiti girt by the teeming sea.

The back road from Sadrazamköy (Liveras) leads up through a low forest and maquis-covered limestone escarpment to Koruçam (Kormakiti). There is a small barrel-vaulted chapel of the Virgin Mary on the way into the village which is dominated by the limestone basilica of St George, opposite which stands the Kotsiras tavern and a 15th-century chapel. All three churches are in use, as Kormakiti's population is Maronite, not Greek Orthodox. The Maronites are a sect of Eastern Christianity which first formed around Maron, a 4th-century Syrian hermit. They were persecuted in the 7th century by the Orthodox church, as they were considered heretical, and took refuge in the mountains of Lebanon. The Maronites supported the Crusader kingdoms, and at their fall many communities fled from the Muslim reconquest of Palestine. They settled along the north coast of Cyprus, which at the peak of their prosperity in the 16th century was peppered with 60 Maronite villages. They acknowledge the spiritual leadership of the Pope but retain their own Patriarch, traditions and ancient Syriac liturgy. This can be heard at St George's every Sunday amongst the dwindling population of the last Maronite community in the north.

The road southeast from the village cuts through the Mandres forest which is a military area. It is open to traffic passing out of the village but not in.

The Bronze-Age Sanctuary of Pigadhes

Halfway along the road from Kyrenia to Güzelyurt (Morphou), take the turning to Nicosia/Lefkosa beside the village of Çamlıbel (Myrtou). About 3 miles/5km on, after passing the Monastery of Ayios Pandelemon and a petrol station, look out for a right turn down a cypress-shaded road.

The double-horned altar of a Bronze Age sanctuary will have an irresistible fascination for those interested in mythology and ancient history. For others Pigadhes is a tranquil picnic site, sympathetically planted with cypress and cedar. The sanctuary's 12ft-high altar is raised on four steep steps capped with the Horns of Consecration. The exterior face of the altar platform is decorated with precise geometrical carving of four squares surrounding a cross. It now stands, as it did in the Late Bronze Age, in the open air, but it would then have been enclosed within a courtyard containing a sacred well. The low foundation walls of the various outbuildings range all around. These sacred precincts would also have probably been surrounded by woodland, thus closing all horizons save for the divine summits of Mount Olympos and the twin peaks of the Gothic Range.

Paleokastro, another celebrated sanctuary, is 20km due west of Pigadhes. In 1929 a Swedish expedition discovered over 2000 votive terracotta statues in this Archaic 7th-century temple, which are now exhibited in Nicosia and Stockholm. The road to the coast from Tepebaşi (Dhiorios) through the pine forest to the village of Akdeniz (Ayia Irini) is now open but the actual site of Paleokastro and most of the beach is still occupied by the Turkish army.

14th century chapel of Ayios Ephimianos

Famagusta, Salamis and Karpas

Eastern Cyprus is composed of two contrasting regions, the Mesarya (Mesaoria) plain and the Kirpaşa (Karpas) peninsula. The Mesaoria shore stretches in the great semicircular bay of Salamis, defined by Gazimağusa (Famagusta) to the south and the hamlet of Boğaz to the north. East of Boğaz stretches the rocky coast of the Karpas Peninsula, where a number of undisturbed sandy bays can be found along its attenuated shore.

The Karpas peninsula is a long skeletal finger of land jutting out northeast into a the Mediterranean like an abortive causeway to Antioch. It is flecked with quiet villages, small Byzantine relics from a richer past, and large areas of wilderness where only birds and braying donkeys are likely to disturb a walker. The Mesaoria, which trans- lates as 'Between the Mountains',

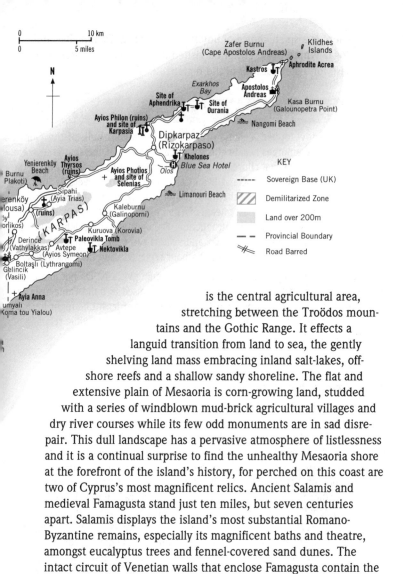

is the central agricultural area, stretching between the Troödos mountains and the Gothic Range. It effects a languid transition from land to sea, the gently shelving land mass embracing inland salt-lakes, offshore reefs and a shallow sandy shoreline. The flat and extensive plain of Mesaoria is corn-growing land, studded with a series of windblown mud-brick agricultural villages and dry river courses while its few odd monuments are in sad disrepair. This dull landscape has a pervasive atmosphere of listlessness and it is a continual surprise to find the unhealthy Mesaoria shore at the forefront of the island's history, for perched on this coast are two of Cyprus's most magnificent relics. Ancient Salamis and medieval Famagusta stand just ten miles, but seven centuries apart. Salamis displays the island's most substantial Romano-Byzantine remains, especially its magnificent baths and theatre, amongst eucalyptus trees and fennel-covered sand dunes. The intact circuit of Venetian walls that enclose Famagusta contain the richest array of Gothic architecture in the Eastern Mediterranean, which can be seen sprinkled amongst the quiet streets of a provincial backwater. It is an unsung magpie's nest of medieval buildings, which rivals Rhodes yet remains virtually neglected by tourists.

There is a small choice of hotels in Famagusta, Salamis Bay and Boğaz which could either be visited in succession, or used as a base for a general tour of the region.

Gazimağusa (Famagusta)

From the meadow-topped Venetian ramparts, the golden bulk of the Gothic cathedral-mosque emerges beside clusters of palm trees and the shattered skeletons of dozens of medieval churches. The walled town of Famagusta contains an astonishing collection of Gothic and Renaissance buildings that overawe the quiet modern streets. It has an even richer fund of stories to which the tale of an imprisoned prince, of an abdicating last queen, of a pair of spendthrift millionaires and of a returning goddess form just an introduction. Famagusta is also celebrated as the garrison port of Shakespeare's *Othello*, and visitors can pace through the original settings of Acts III to V: the citadel, the harbour esplanade and the palace square.

Famagusta is viewed by only a handful of day-tripping visitors. Do not join them; the cumulative midday glare from the golden stone used to build Famagusta can turn a treat into an exhausting ordeal. Allow yourself at least one night here, so that you can make the most of the morning and evening light, while relaxing on the beach at midday.

History

A 14th-Century Boom Town

At the beginning of the 13th century only a single tower stood at Famagusta to guard the reef anchorage used by pilgrims visiting the nearby shrines of St Barnabas and St Epiphanios. This obscurity ended in 1291 when Acre, the last Crusader-held port on the coast of Palestine, was recaptured for Islam. Famagusta was settled by sophisticated Christian refugees and almost overnight became the new entrepôt for the valuable trade between Islam and Western Europe. Its position was further reinforced by a papal ban on direct trade with Muslims, which placed the exchanges in the hands of the traditional Near Eastern trading communities: Greeks, Jews, Armenians and especially the Christian Arabs of Syria, who all settled here. The competitive Latin merchants, largely drawn from Catalonia, Pisa, Venice and Genoa, built separate bases to secure their lives and goods. Famagusta became a liberal free port and a boom town, a byword for opulent dress and extravagant entertainments. It was the cynosure of moralists and the envy of the world, loosely presided over by the Lusignan monarchy. Its wealth was reflected in its packed markets, palaces, hidden gardens, its magnificent cathedral and bewildering selection of community churches.

A Base for Genoa or Venice

This halcyon period of building based on mercantile prosperity lasted just 80 years. Famagusta, the golden goose of the eastern Mediterranean, was destroyed by the greed and fierce rivalry between Genoa and Venice. The conflicting ambitions of these two maritime powers were graphically expressed by their respective rights to hold the left and right reins of the monarch's horse during the coronation procession. In 1369 the accession of a new king precipitated a squabble over precedence which exploded into savage riots, dividing the city into two murderous factions. The Genoese were expelled, but returned in 1373 to sack the rich city before attempting to monopolise its business. The merchants and the trading routes rapidly returned back to Damascus and Alexandria, and Famagusta deteriorated into a dreary Genoese garrison town. Ninety years later King James II, 'the bastard', finally managed to regain control of Famagusta and preside over a brief revival. He was, however, soon in hock to Venice, and was dead within a year of celebrating his marriage to Caterina Cornaro. Her subsequent reign masked the gradual Venetian takeover of Cyprus. On Thursday 26 February 1489, Caterina, the last independent monarch of Cyprus, abdicated her authority to Venice in a solemn ceremony staged in the cathedral against the background din of the town's carnival. The Venetian Republic cherished Famagusta: it restored a number of churches, redeveloped the main square into a Renaissance piazza and spent freely on embellishing the defences as well as restoration.

The Thirteen-Month Siege of Famagusta

The battle for Famagusta is one of the most celebrated events in that great clash of cultures between the rival Christain and Muslim Empires that convulsed the Mediterranean in the mid-16th century. In its scale, longevity, range and effects it almost deserves to be considered a World War. Popular accounts of the siege of Famagusta were quickly translated into a dozen languages to become best-sellers throughout Europe. Shakespeare's London audience would have known all about Othello's Cyprus, and would have chilled to the phrase 'general enemy Ottoman'. However, unlike the successful defence of Vienna and Malta and the great naval victory of Lepanto, it was an Ottoman victory and, as such, has been allowed to recede from the collective European memory. It remains very much alive to Turkish Cypriots, who in the post-1974 negotiations turned down a generous cash offer by the USA, for their stake in the island had been won with the blood of 70,000 compatriots four centuries previously.

An Ottoman army landed on the south coast of Cyprus in July 1570, but it was not until October that this force of 100,000 men was camped to the south of Famagusta. An abortive winter blockade was replaced by greater militancy in the spring. On 19 May 1571 five Turkish artillery batteries began their bombardment, but the Venetian gunners proved equally destructive during the month-long cannon duel. Lala Mustafa, the Ottoman commander, then instructed his corps of Armenian engineers to dig mines under the key points of the southern wall, the Arsenal (Canbulat) and Ravelin bastions. The first series of mine explosions was sporadic and allowed the defenders to beat off individual attacks. This was followed by a co-ordinated detonation of half a dozen mines, combined with a bombardment and general assaults on 29 June. Though repelled, the Turks had severely weakened the walls and succeeded in constructing new artillery forts close to four breaches in the southern wall. A continuous bombardment provided cover to fill in the moat and to create trenches for the safe approach of troops.

On 9 July simultaneous attacks were launched. The seventh assault of the day succeeded in overrunning the outer bastion of the Ravelin, but a Venetian officer fired the emergency mine, at the cost of a hundred of his own men engaged in hand-to-hand fighting with a thousand Turks. A week later another Ottoman assault in this area was decimated by hidden Venetian mines. The Turks then cleared the area by rolling enormous faggots against the walls and igniting a three-day bonfire which melted the iron land gate. The defenders, by now reduced from 8000 to 500 active men, took council with their commander Mercatorio Bragadino. They agreed to hold out for two weeks, time enough for one last appeal for help to reach the Venetian forces in Crete. On 29 July 1571 the siege reached its appalling crescendo. Another series of mines further reduced the southern walls, while the besiegers mounted assaults through every hour of daylight for the next 60 hours. A respite on 1 August allowed for honourable articles of surrender to be agreed. The discovery of the corpses of a boatload of Mecca-bound pilgrims killed by the Venetians incensed the Ottoman commander, who broke the terms and took his revenge on the Venetian high command.

A Turkish Village

In the aftermath of the siege the fortress town was renamed Magusa. The largest churches were converted into mosques, the walls were repaired and Christians were forbidden to enter without a pass. Trade had long since moved to Larnaca, so the harbour silted up and Famagusta declined into a graceful Turkish village. It became a favourite place of banishment, with a shifting cast of imprudent poets, disgraced ministers and inconvenient religious leaders all pining to return to Istanbul. One of the more colourful 17th-century exiles was an early Ottoman aviator, whose series of gliding flights, launched from the summit of the Galata Tower in Istanbul, won him such wild popularity that a jealous sultan packed him off to Cyprus.

The Greek Cypriots lived in Maraş (Varosha), just south of the walls and this developed into the commercially active quarter of town. The harbour was only revived in 1906 when a railway line brought copper ore to the newly created docks. Famagusta and Varosha then gradually expanded to become the leading port, as well as the commercial and tourist centre of the island. This prosperity was broken by the partition that followed the Turkish invasion in 1974. It was renamed Gazimağusa, 'unconquered Magusa', and despite the port and a university it is now a sleepy provincial town, haunted by its empty half. The once bustling streets of Varosha are empty, overlooked by crumbling high-rise apartment blocks and acres of overgrown villas. Occasionally it crops up in the international press as a possible negotiating counter in peace talks, but otherwise it remains a ghost town enclosed in rusting wire and patrolled by the Turkish army.

Getting Around

By Boat

There is an all-year ferry service to the Turkish port of Mersin, though it is cheaper and quicker to use the ferry from Kyrenia/Girne to Taşucu-Silifke. Mersin is an unattractive modern city, while Taşucu is a small coastal resort and the neighbouring town of Silifke is an ancient town with a castle, museum and numerous small archaeological sites. If you still want to go to Mersin tickets for this state-run ferry link are available from Fergun Denizcilik Sirketi at 10 Fevzi Cakmak Bulvarı, © (036) 63412 or Kibris Turk Denizcilik at 3, Bulent Ecevit Bulvarı, © (036) 65995. Despite the enticing evidence on maps and what other guides might tell you, there is no longer a ferry service to Syria.

By Bus

Famagusta's bus terminal is 500m from the Ravelin Bastion on Gazi Mustafa Kemal Bulvarı. There are frequent morning services to Nicosia and the larger neighbouring villages; but check the last departure, currently at 5pm, and the much-reduced services over the weekend.

By Taxi

There are usually half a dozen taxis waiting beside the Renaissance façade of the Venetian palace on Namik Kemal Meydanı. Otherwise ring one of the local firms such as Salamis on © (036) 65555, Omur, © (036) 62233, Gocmen, © (036) 62323 and Istanbul, © (036) 64864.

By Car

A pick of the local car hire firms would include Atlantic on Sinan Paşa Sokağı, © (036) 63277 or Sur on Ismet Inonu Bulvarı, © (036) 65600. For conditions and prices see Kyrenia/Girne.

There is a **tourist information booth** at 5 Fevzi Çakmak Bulvarı, ℭ (036) 62864 though it is not always manned. If it is closed try the Canbulat Museum for cultural inquiries, and for practical information try the reception desk at the Palm Beach Hotel. There are a couple of foreign exchange booths and a number of banks around Namik Kemal Meydanı (the square before the cathedral-mosque) such as the Faisal Islam Bankasi, ℭ (036) 63263, which operates from the old domed Koranic school. If you need a doctor, ℭ (036) 62616 for Dr Aytekin Colakoglu at 2 Afrodit Sokağı or ℭ (036) 62876 for the local state hospital; for dental problems ℭ (036) 64896 for Dr Fehmi Tuncel at 3 Naim Efendi Yolu. For other emergencies the police are on ℭ (036) 67066.

Orientation

The town, with its rich collection of intact, ruined and half ruined buildings, is described in a walking tour that takes you through the most important sites first. This starts at the Ravelin Bastion, proceeds down the southern walls, descending down to the Arsenal/Canbulat bastion which contains a museum, then along to the Citadel before approaching the eminent and central cathedral-mosque. This area in the centre of the walled city then remains your base for a number of strolls out to the town's secondary monuments.

The Venetian Walls

The 16th-century ramparts of Famagusta are one of the most complete in all of the Mediterranean. The views over the town are entrancing, and the rampart summits are especially attractive in the spring when they are covered in wild meadow flowers.

The Land Gate, also known as the Limassol Gate, was designed to be the only landward entrance into the city. The gatehouse was designed as a miniature fortress overlooked by the massive walls of the Ravelin bastion. It was totally destroyed in the great siege, and after their victory the Turks opened up a new gate just to the east of the Ravelin. They added the narrow, arched bridge which crosses the moat and built an attractive guardhouse just within the walls, now functioning as a post office. In the Venetian period you would have entered the city through the high, pointed-arched tunnel beneath the Ravelin Bastion. It is decorated with faded heraldic frescoes and marble carvings but, like many a dark cul-de-sac, also reeks of urine. It gives access to the ruined ramps, stairways, cisterns and portcullis-guarded doorways of the old gatehouse, which is surrounded

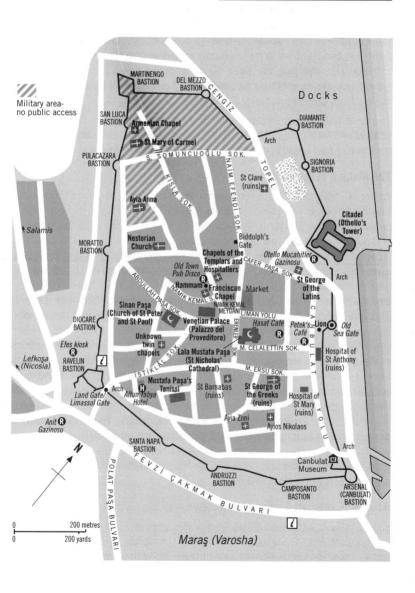

Gazimağusa Town

Military area–no public access

MARTINENGO BASTION

DEL MEZZO BASTION

CENGIZ

Docks

SAN LUCA BASTION

Armenian Chapel

DIAMANTE BASTION

St Mary of Carmel

Arch

PULACAZARA BASTION

S. SOMUNCUOĞLU SOK.

NAIM EFENDİ SOK.

TOPEL

SIGNORIA BASTION

St Clare (ruins)

KIŞLA SOK.

Ayia Anna

↑ Salamis

MORATTO BASTION

Nestorian Church

Biddulph's Gate

Citadel (Othello's Tower)

Chapels of the Templars and Hospitallers

CAFER PAŞA SOK.

Otello Mucahitler Gazinosu

Old Town Pub Disco

Hammam

ABDULLAH PAŞA SOK.

Franciscan Chapel

Market

St George of the Latins

Arch

NAMIK KEMAL S.

NAMIK KEMAL MEYDANI

Sinan Paşa (Church of St Peter and St Paul)

DIOCARE BASTION

Venetian Palace (Palazzo del Proveditore)

LIMAN YOLU

Hasat Café

Petek's Café

CANBULAT YOLU

Lion

Old Sea Gate

ERENLER SOK.

Unknown twin chapels

Efes kiosk

Lefkoşa ↑ (Nicosia)

RAVELIN BASTION

Lala Mustafa Paşa (St Nicholas' Cathedral)

M. CELALETTİN SOK.

Hospital of St Anthony (ruins)

İSTİKLÂL SOK.

Mustafa Paşa's Tanissi

Altun Tabya Hotel

Land Gate/ Limassol Gate

Arch

St Barnabas (ruins)

St George of the Greeks (ruins)

M. ERSU SOK.

Hospital of St Mary (ruins)

Ayia Zoni

Ayios Nikolaos

Arch

Anit Gazinosu

N

SANTA NAPA BASTION

FEVZİ ÇAKMAK BULVARI

Canbulat Museum

POLAT PAŞA BULVARI

ANDRUZZI BASTION

CAMPOSANTO BASTION

ARSENAL (CANBULAT) BASTION

| 0 | 200 metres |
| 0 | 200 yards |

Maraş (Varosha)

by its own moat. Even in peacetime the Venetians kept a company of 50 pikeman and gunners on permanent guard here. Another ramp invites you up to the upper terraces of the Ravelin, which has a fine view. From here you can stroll along the western ramparts, passing the Diocare, Moratto and Pulacazara bastions, though you will have to turn back at the latter to avoid entering the northwest military zone. You can climb up to the southern ramparts just to the east of the modern entrance gate and pass the Santa Napa, Andruzzi and Camposanto bastions (which took the brunt of the siege, as described in the history section), to descend down a flight of steps just beside the Arsenal/Canbulat bastion.

The moat walk, begun outside either the Arsenal (Canbulat) or Del Mezzo bastions, allows for a circuit of the land walls along a tranquil and partly pine-shaded track with a beer break at the Efes kiosk tucked below the Ravelin bastion.

The Making of the Walls

As late as 1560 the Venetian Senate was debating the need to defend Nicosia, but they never had any doubts over Famagusta. In 1492, within three years of the formal annexation of Cyprus, the Venetian Senate had voted a monthly income of 500 ducats for the continuous improvement of the Famagusta walls. A conscript labour force was raised, and one in every 30 Cypriot families had to provide a man. This was supplemented by specialist Venetian workmen employed to make lime mortar and cut into the solid bedrock. After 20 years of labour the flimsy land wall raised by the Genoese had been transformed into a 3.5km-long rampart. The 20m-high masonry outer wall rested on the firm foundations of the bedrock and was buttressed by 8m of packed earth and reinforced by 13 bastions. Beyond the walls stretched a 25m-wide moat which could be swept by cannon fire from oval portals set at bedrock level. Outside the moat the counterscarp, an angled bank of earth 11m high, acted as an absorbent cushion against all but the most accurate bombardment. In 1530 Sammichele, the greatest military engineer of his day, redesigned the two most vulnerable corner bastions, the Ravelin and Arsenal (Canbulat), turning them into elaborate strongpoints. Hercules Martinego designed the bastion in the northwest corner and was busy with his plans for an elevated central artillery fort when the Turks landed. All that was required to bring the defences into final order was the levelling of the suburban buildings and gardens to provide a clear field of fire.

Arsenal (Canbulat) Bastion and Museum

Canbulat Bey, the great Turkish hero of the siege of 1571, was buried at the centre of the Arsenal (Canbulat) Bastion after the capture of the city. His restored tomb is now the centrepiece of a small museum, with a dozen badly lit display cases arranged along both sides of the long barrel-vaulted entrance tunnel. The east wall is lined with some of the island's celebrated ancient pottery (*see* p. 109 and 405); the west wall with Turkish costumes, embroidery and period armour. The collection of Ottoman Iznik pottery is the finest in Cyprus, even though most of it has been carefully pieced together from refuse discovered during the restoration of the bastion. It provides a brief summary of Iznik ware, with a piece of the derivative blue and white Chinese style and six examples from the late 16th century. This was the period of classic Iznik, with its stylized carnations and tulips portrayed in distinctive hues of cobalt blue and brilliant red, combined with oriental motifs like the double lips or tiger lily. There is also a cabinet filled with blue-hued wall tiles, the lesser products of the 17th century. The early 19th-century stone epitaph by the stairs represents the poetic and calligraphic traditions of Ottoman culture. It was composed by a dervish from Nicosia in praise of the master of the Djalwatiya sufis who died in exile at Famagusta in 1691.

The green-shrouded catafalque of Canbulat Bey is surrounded by Turkish regimental flags and an old ensign of the Ottoman navy. The bastion used to be roofless and the tomb was open to the air, engulfed by a sacred fig tree hung with prayer rags from childless couples and pregnant mothers appealling for sons as brave as Canbulat. Canbulat was the Bey of the Anatolian province of Kilis, who was given command of operations against the great Arsenal bastion that was to be renamed in his honour. He detonated the first mine on 20 June 1571 and stormed the breach, holding the walls for five hours before being forced back. The Venetians subsequently defended this gap with a fearsome spinning wheel studded with blades. Canbulat determined to disarm this instrument at any cost and spurred his horse into a headlong gallop. The machine was destroyed but both Canbulat and his horse were torn to shreds. His sacrifice proved a crucial inspiration to the Ottoman army, which in the last three days of the siege was facing casualties of 5000 men a day.

The Hospitals of St Mary and St Anthony beside the Sea Wall

The wall stretching between the Arsenal (Canbulat) bastion and the Citadel was the weakest stretch, as it faced the secure harbour which was enclosed by reefs and a chain. Canbulat (Djamboulat) Yolu runs along the landward face of this wall which was later punctuated by dockyard arches. About 200m from the Arsenal (Canbulat) bastion, just to the west of the road, is a ruined chapel, which has been identified as the Hospital of St Mary run by the Teutonic knights. 100m north, squeezed between the walls and the road, are the ruins of the 14th-century Hospital of St Anthony, one of the earliest examples of a fusion of Byzantine and Gothic architecture. The nave is filled with the fragments of six grey granite columns, taken from Salamis, which once supported a typically Greek central dome, whilst Gothic carving can be seen on a surviving east wall.

A large antique marble lion decorates a bend in the sea wall and helps identify the Sea Gate, currently closed. This low gateway is tucked beneath the round tower in this dusty corner. The harbour face of the gate is decorated with a marble relief of the Lion of St Mark and an inscription recording Nicolao Priolo, the Venetian governor in 1496.

The Citadel, 'Othello's Tower'

Officially open daily 8am–5pm; adm, though it may equally be found closed or open without a custodian.

The Citadel is the oldest building in Famagusta. The northeast tower incorporates the single watchtower, which witnessed the arrival of the first refugees from Acre in 1291. Thirty years later the Prince of Tyre, the usurping younger brother of the melancholic King Henry II, transformed the area around the tower into a fortified palace. Strong outer walls enclosed a quadrangle of gothic apartments which over-looked an open courtyard. It was here in 1373 that the Genoese negotiating team overpowered the guards and opened the city to 80 years of alien rule. A hundred years later a local revolt against the growing influence of Venice swept through the town, halting only at the walls of the Citadel. Queen Caterina's uncle and cousin were caught the wrong side of the closing gates and lynched by the mob.

Within a year of the formal annexation of the island, the Venetians began the symbolic transformation of the Citadel into what we see today. The elegant but vulnerable upper storey was demolished, the lower walls were thickened and the four corners were defended by round, squat artillery towers. Further protection was provided by a sea-filled moat and the earth banks of the counterscarp. A pier supported on high arches was added to link the Citadel to the square harbour tower, from where a suspended chain could close the inner, naval docks. The finishing touch was the decoration of the gateway in 1492 with a marble relief of the lion of St Mark accompanied by the name of the governor, 'Nicolao F. Oscareno Cypri Praefecto', who presided over this first graphic demonstration of the power of Venice.

Aside from these powerful historical themes there is a good view over the town and modern harbour from the Citadel battlements, while the internal courtyard is littered with a discordant array of rusty armaments, stone cannonballs and pieces of Roman, Byzantine, Gothic and Venetian carving. An impressively dark and gloomy five-bayed medieval hall is preserved on the ground floor of the north range. Within the length of the south range of buildings is a dark cramped passage lit by melodramatic bolts of sunlight that flood through the skyholes. In such conditions, Peter Paul Scaliger, the last of the ruling family of Verona, was confined by the Venetians. After 11 years he was permitted a limited freedom within the Citadel. From his vantage point on the walls he fell in love with a concubine, and though forbidden to produce a legal heir he was allowed to set up house in some neglected apartments. In his old age Scaliger lived beside the Greek cathedral, cherished by the town for his unfailing kindness and cordiality despite a lifetime of imprisonment. He was also well cared for, as one of his illegitimate daughters had married Famagusta's Dutch doctor.

The Othello Connection

The Citadel became known as 'Othello's Tower' under the British administration, though there is no specific mention of Famagusta in the tragedy of Othello. Shakespeare refers only to 'a seaport in Cyprus', though his set directions, which require a Citadel, a harbour pier and a square, fit perfectly. The town was governed by the resident Castellani of Famagusta who was appointed for a two-year term. In peacetime he commanded two galleys and an 800-strong garrison, divided into seven companies of Italians and Germans, but deliberately excluding any Greeks. The soldiers were professional mercenaries who signed up for periods of five years and were paid 15 shillings every 45 days. There is no Castellani who can be identified as Othello, though the careers of two officers may have contributed to the fictional creation of the noble Moor. Francesco de Sessa provides some passion and mystery. He was a dark-complexioned Calabrian mercenary known as 'Il Capitano Moro' who was dismissed from the Venetian service in Cyprus in 1544 for an unknown offence. A sense of brittle honour can be derived from Christophoro Moro, a Venetian nobleman who served a two-year stint as lieutenant governor of Cyprus from 1506, returning home without his wife.

St George of the Latins

The medieval chapel of St George is just south of the Citadel at the junction of Djafer Pasha and Kapou streets. It stands in a spectacular state of romantic neglect, roofless and with only two standing walls. It was reduced to this state during the great siege by Turkish artillery fire from a fort temporarily established on an offshore reef. Even in its overgrown and perilous state it is easy to recognise that this is one of the island's most delicate and exuberant pieces of Gothic architecture. The chapel has a simple plan, consisting of a single nave of four bays ending in a three-sided apse. It was constructed by masons recruited from the Rhineland, who built it almost as a test piece before setting to work on the cathedral. The soaring upper windows of the north wall are raised on pointed arches, supported by elegant columns formed from triple rods which bud at their common capital to separate into the groins required for the high vaults. There is fine carving, including the four central bosses on the nave floor, the eroded splendour of the north gate, a lion lying down with a lamb on the northwest tower, a capital formed from a swarm of Cypriot dog-headed bats and the marble dragon and human greyhound gargoyles which projects above the eastern apse.

Lala Mustafa Paşa Mosque (St Nicholas' Cathedral)

The cathedral-mosque, on the east side of Namik Kemal Meydanı, is a great mass of carved golden stone that broods protectively over the town. It is especially magical in the diffused light of dusk or dawn, when the muezzin call ripples from out of the octagonal minaret that sprouts like some organic growth of measured stone from a medieval bell tower. The foundations were laid in 1300 and work progressed quickly despite one bishop's absconding with the entire building fund.

Famagusta in the early 14th century could afford the best. Architects and masons were recruited from the Rhineland towns where the newest advances in building techniques were being pioneered. The western façade, with its three great ornate doors flanked by two bell towers capped with decorated gable ends, was completely up-to-date for its period; it is early 14th century state-of-the-art. So are the carved buttresses (though many have been clumsily restored after an earthquake), and the flamboyant window frames of the protruding five-sided apse. The plan deliberately recalls that of Reims, where the kings of France were crowned. Famagusta was where the Lusignan kings were invested with the additional crown of Jerusalem after their coronation as kings of Cyprus in Nicosia. Jerusalem was an empty honour after the loss of Acre in1291 but not one without a heady mystique for most of medieval Europe. There are also a number of specific Cypriot modifications to the cathedral in keeping with the traditions of the island. There is no transept, just a simple three-aisled nave which is supported by columns rather than piers and which culminates with three apses at the east end.

Though it is not visible from street level, the roof is flat not pitched as is usual in northern Europe. The Cypriot climate also encouraged external balconies and silken banners that would float freely in the evening breeze. Remnants of the walkway and flagstaff supports can be seen around the outer walls and the central apse. The delicate carving around the western doors includes one specific Cypriot reference amongst the opulent medley of vegetable and geometrical motifs. Beside the doors are rows of empty statue canopies, whose capitals are decorated with the leaves of agnus castus convolvulus, an aromatic shrub common throughout the island.

The Interior

Open daily during Muslim hours of prayer; donation suggested.

The interior of the cathedral-mosque does not live up to the brooding, sunbaked majesty of its exterior. This is partly due to the use of columns in the central aisle of the nave rather than ornately carved piers. The two rows of big plain cylindrical columns make a clumsy, discordant introduction to the soaring pointed arches of the vaulted ceiling. The interior is also disappointingly empty of the glittering humanistic clutter of Catholic Christianity. This was removed during the Genoese conquest in 1373, and more thoroughly by the Ottomans after the conquest of 1571. Gone are the gloomy oil paintings in dark side-chapels, polished ornaments, ancient hangings and carved wooden screens, whilst the carved details in the stone vaults have been obscured by layers of purifying white paint. A much greater transformation is effected by the replacement of the original great fields of stained glass with carved gypsum screens which cast a diffused, almost other-worldly light across the aisles. Modern Islamic glass in the west window reminds you of the dramatic qualities of illuminated glass which was once a central aspect of the cathedrals interior, around which the web of Gothic architecture was spun.

The mosque furniture is of an unexceptional rustic simplicity. There is an elevated stool for the reader, a raised platform for the muezzin, the pulpit-like minbar for the Friday sermon and a screen in the north aisle for female worshippers. A grace-less mihrab arch reorientates the direction of prayer from the eastern alignment of a church to the southeast, in order to face towards Mecca. A recent addition is the fitted wall-to-wall carpet which adds a bizarrely inappropriate touch of aspira-tional suburbia.

The Cathedral Precincts

The piazza before the western doors of the cathedral has echoed to countless coronations, marriages and jubilees of the medieval Lusignan monarchy. It also witnessed the abdication of the last queen of Cyprus, the arrival of a goddess and the screams of the last Venetian governor as he was skinned alive before its doors.

The cathedral precincts, whilst full of history, are also somewhat pinched, for commercial Famagusta was already firmly established before the cathedral was commissioned. The cathedral was given a prime, but also a strictly defined, site between the two main covered bazaars that ran from the palace square to the har-bour. There was simply no room for the customary ecclesiastical sprawl of close, cloisters, chapterhouse and palace. The bishop's garden with its private chapel (now a public café) is due east of the apse. His apartments were arranged along a balconied corridor perched above the seven elegant medieval shop-fronts that still line Liman Yolu. The entrance hall of the episcopal apartments is now occupied by a complex of three domed buildings, which frame the north of the cathedral piazza. It is an attractive example of an Ottoman kulliye, a charitable complex of school and public fountain built around the founder's tomb.

Two antique granite columns emerge from these Islamic walls. These decorated the 16th-century tomb of Venus which was assembled by the Venetians in a remarkable instance of Renaissance spirit. It was a period when the classical gods were being enthusiastically rehabilitated into contemporary culture. Many were interpreted as heroic figures of the past who had been deified for their virtues. Venetian antiquarians discovered an ornate sarcophagus at Paphos in 1564 which was announced to be that of Queen Venus. It was carried in state to Famagusta and reverently placed before the cathedral.

The side chamber on the southern face of the piazza, currently used as a Muslim washroom, is another delightful relic of the Renaissance. It has a simple triple-bayed interior, but an extravagant and innovative exterior. Benches made from antique Roman carving sit below a pair of large oval windows separated by the flowing carved stone of the circular carriage arch.

The Venetian Palace (Palazzo del Proveditore)

The royal palace of the Lusignan kings was built on the west face of the central square as the cathedral was being raised on the east. This original rambling medieval palace has entirely disappeared and the present fragmentary ruins date from the Venetian rebuilding in the 16th century. The most impressive remnant is the outer façade, where three arches, fitted with granite columns taken from Salamis, once supported an elegant marble balcony. On the south side of the palace compound the Side Pansiyon occupies the attractive old guard house, while just behind the arches stretches the outer courtyard. This is now partly filled by a scruffy garden littered with broken columns but shaded by an ancient eucalyptus and also by a car park. In the ground floor of the old guard house there is a prison cell which has been restored and named after Namik Kemal. He was a celebrated free-speaking 19th-century Turkish poet and playwright who was locked up here between 1873–6. A bronze bust of the poet can be seen on the other side of the square that is named after him. Further to the west of the palace compound stand tall ruined Renaissance walls, the remains of the actual residence of the Venetian Governor which enclosed an internal courtyard.

The Franciscan Chapel and Turkish Hammam

At the corner of Namik Kemal and Kisla streets and just to the north of the ruins of the Venetian Palace stand the partial ruins of a Franciscan chapel. It was built in 1300 by Henry II, who succumbed to alternate bouts of depression and disease. The king later added a tunnel so that he could potter from his bedroom straight to the services of the friars. His nephew, Hugh IV, had no such needs and turned the tunnel into a crossbow range. It then developed into the parish church of the Genoese, whose factory communicated with the Franciscan cloisters. They added two mortuary chapels to the second bay to form a false transept. The Turks built a bathhouse immediately beside it, which is now occupied by the 'Old Town Pub

Disco'. After a drink in the hall the manager is usually happy to show visitors around the once hot rooms. For a working Turkish bath, go to Nicosia.

Sinan Paşa Camii (Church of St Peter and St Paul)

Occasionally open for concerts or exhibitions.

To the south of the palace ruins, at the corner of Istiklal and Sinan Paşa streets, stands the former Church of St Peter and St Paul. This large edifice was built in the 1360s by the merchant Simon Nostrano from a third of the profits of just one of his Syrian trading ventures. Its most impressive feature is the row of plain buttresses that rise from the side aisles to support the high roof of the nave. St Peter and St Paul's is often disparagingly compared to the highly decorated cathedral nearby, though this is to ignore what were concurrent and different traditions within Europe. It looks to the simple clean lines of the basilica of Provence and Catalonia, rather than to the highly decorative archetypes of northern Europe. The circular windows and the high functional western front with an open belfry are typical features of this alternative tradition. It also had a much simpler eastern face, as the three apses were originally hidden behind a covering wall.

The interior is more typically Cypriot, dominated by the massive columns and pointed arches of the nave. There is also a profusion of flagstaff holders, and evidence of a bridge-passage linking the palace and the church roof. Another royal connection is provided by the finely carved white marble north door, which was made deliberately ornate, for it faces the palace. This whole doorway must have been acquired from a much older church with its pair of flanking angels, one holding a censer, one holding souls wrapped in his shirt. On the southwestern octagonal turret there is a cracked stump of a minaret that testifies to its centuries of use as a place of Muslim worship. It was converted to a Mosque soon after the conquest of 1571 but later fell into disuse. The prosaic British administration used it as a potato store but it has recently acquired a more elevated role as an occasional venue for plays, concerts and exhibitions.

The Unknown Twin Chapels

Immediately south of St Peter and St Paul, on Ali Paşa Caddesı, are a pair of roofless and unidentified chapels. The northernmost has a magnificent eroded doorway and a wide nave flanked by a pair of tomb niches. Its most intriguing details are the seven carved heads of the arch springs. The double faces, the green men overwhelmed by their floral bract moustaches and the exaggerated bug-eyed features of Romanesque carving, combine to make a disturbing gallery. They are even more curious in an early 15th-century chapel and appear to have been a deliberately conservative detail.

St George of the Greeks and the Orthodox Chapels

Southern Famagusta was the medieval Greek quarter. Half a dozen of their chapels can be identified around the conspicuous ruin of the Church of St George, built as an orthodox cathedral in 1360 a block south of the towering Gothic cathedral of St Nicholas. Though now a roofless ruin (beside Mouzaffer Ersou street) it is easy to conjecture its original form, as it was architecturally a sister to the complete church of St Peter and St Paul. Even without this nearby protype the rose window above the west door, the triple aisles and the twin row of columns down the central nave give it a typically Cypriot Gothic aspect. The Byzantine influence is only marked in the eastern end. The central apse has the traditional three steps, and the walls have been kept as plain as possible to allow a generous field for wall paintings. Traces of these are discernible: there is a negative of the *Crucifixion* high up on the inner side of the west wall and a *Betrayal, Utter Humiliation* and *Entombment* on the left hand side of the south apse. Enough remains to show a strong Italianate influence in the action and positioning of the figures. A Gothic gate in the south aisle gave entrance to an older, twin-aisled Greek chapel, which, though remodelled in the 14th century, is believed to have covered the sarcophagus of St Epiphanios.

About 150m due south of St George of the Greeks is a picturesque pair of Greek chapels, framed by palms and surrounded by vegetable gardens. Ayios Nikolaos is a partial ruin. Its dome rests on an octagonal drum pierced by windows, which in turn sits on a cruciform of pointed arch vaults. Ayia Zoni is the simpler though better preserved domed chapel. Walking southwest of St George of the Greeks you may notice two other ruins buried amongst the modern housing: the 16th-century Greek chapel of St Barnabas and, a bit further along a mid-15th-century chapel, now known as Mustafa Paşa's Tanissi from its stint as a Turkish coffee house in the 19th century.

The Twin Chapels of the Templars and Hospitallers

The old chapel of the Templars now houses the Atatürk Cultural Centre (*open 8am–1pm, 2pm–5pm*) which stages exhibitions of local artists, occasional shows and runs a small café.

The twin chapels of these famous military orders of monks are 100m along Kışla Sokağı from the cathedral-mosque. The larger and northernmost of the pair is the dark three-bayed Templar Chapel, built around 1300. The Knights of St John of Jerusalem, alias the Hospitallers, added the smaller chapel a few years later but inherited the Templar Chapel in 1308 with the worldwide suppression of the order. Frescoes were added in the 14th century and a belfry in the 16th century. The Knights Hospitallers were a force to be reckoned with in medieval Cyprus, not only due to their rich estates and castles but also as a neighbouring power, the rulers of Rhodes and the Dodecanese, whose ambitions had to be watched.

Naim Efendi Sokağı

A walk along Naim Efendi Sokağı begins at the arcaded covered market just to the north of the cathedral-mosque. This street used to be one of the smartest addresses in Famagusta, lined with the palace-factories of all the merchant powers and jealous city states. None of these is now identifiable but there is an elegant late-15th-century walled compound and the ornate 'Biddulph's gate' to recall this area's former Renaissance splendour.

The cellar of the convent of St Clare is not currently accessible, though it is marked on the town map. A mass used to be held here once a year to give thanks to Ayia Fotou of Famagusta who drove off a medieval plague which she symbolically condensed and then petrified before sentencing this plague-rock to dwell for ever underneath the sea. The convents of the Poor Clares were usually renowned for their spiritual vigour but the Famagusta branch seems to have quickly deteriorated into a lodging house for unwanted mistresses. These ladies were maintained here at the expense of their seducer and the chronicles record nocturnal visits, intrigues, assignations and a constantly changing cast—enough to inspire a whole series of lush historical novels.

Nestorian Church (The Church of St George the Exiler)

Occasionally open as cultural centre of Eastern Mediterranean University.

Wealthy Syrian Christian traders occupied the high land in the northwest corner of the medieval town. In 1360 the fabulously wealthy Lachas brothers began work on a church for their fellow Syrians of the Nestorian Church. The result is suprisingly modest for this pair of brothers, whose daughters wore jewellery richer than that of the kings of France. It began as a single-aisled chapel, which was then doubled in size, a porch tacked onto the central nave and courtyards added to taste. This organic growth contrasts with the neat triple apse of the east end and the clean lines of the belfry façade with its pair of lancet windows. The interior retains only patches of its once rich and diverse frescoes, which were accompanied by Syriac script. Other peculiar features include the variegated stones of the altar arch and the Romanesque zigzag decoration cut into the arch of the original courtyard gate. It is tempting to see this as a deliberate archaic reference to the architecture common in the old Crusader states of Palestine.

The Nestorians, also known as the Chaldeans, were only one of several Semitic churches that had separated from Greek orthodoxy in the 5th century over the contentious issue of the mixture of God and man in the person of Jesus. During the Turkish period the church served as a camel stable, and gained an almost occult reputation as Ai Yorghi Xorinos—St George the Exiler. The interior was cleaned for an annual service, after which earth from the floor would be gathered and sprinkled over the portal of an enemy in order to send him into exile within the year.

Northwestern Famagusta

The northwestern corner of the old city is occupied by the military, which unfortunately puts three interesting churches and the Martinego bastion out of bounds. They can be appreciated at a distance, but not photographed or sketched, by strolling along S. Somuncuoğlu Sokağı.

Ayia Anna is the simple but graceful church situated 100m beyond the Nestorian church. It has a single Provençal-style nave, which has been given greater stature by the high western face with its acroter-tipped summit. A pair of pointed-arched windows act as a belfry, which was originally equipped with banners and a corbelled balcony. The church was once surrounded by a verandah-like porch which is believed to have once been connected with a passage that led to a nearby Maronite monastery.

Below the Pulcazarra Bastion and at the corner of the road you approach the ruins of **St Mary of Carmel** and a smaller Armenian chapel. St Mary's is a monument to St Peter Thomas, a devout and much-loved Carmelite friar who also served as Papal Legate, Latin Patriarch of Constantinople, and friend and adviser to King Peter I. The church was built from alms received by Peter Thomas from a tour of the royal courts of Europe preaching a new Crusade. He was buried here in 1366 and the church promptly developed into a pilgrimage centre after his rapid canonisation. The buttresses of this majestic roofless ruin still stand beside long-empty windows that stare sightlessly out from the four-bayed nave and three-sided apse.

The **Armenian chapel** has the characteristic solidity and cruciform plan of its own traditions, embellished by a slight pediment on the roof-line. It must have been built some time after 1346 when James Berne, a passing pilgrim, noticed the arrival of 1,500 starving Armenian refugees who had fled from Lajazzo.

The **Martinengo Bastion** was finished only a few years before the great siege but was largely untouched by the fighting. The Italian architect, Hercules Martinengo, fought in the siege but managed to avoid the general massacre by an opportune conversion to Islam. He travelled back to Istanbul, but after the peace treaty of 1573 was allowed to return to Venice, where he wrote his memoirs.

The Canbulat Museum may inspire the need for a souvenir from A.K. Petek, beside the corner café (marked on the map) of the same name, which has a good selection of Iznik style ceramics imported from Kutahya in Turkey. Hosgor Ticaret at 15, Mahmut Celalettin Sokağı, ✆ (036) 64572 (just uphill from the cathedral-mosque) has one or two antique pieces amongst its stock of well-executed reproductions of traditional Ottoman metalware. Venus, a junky antique shop, is just opposite the attractive old arched house (traditionally considered to be the house of Scaliger, the prisoner of the Citadel), along from the cathedral-mosque on Erenler Sokağı, ✆ (036) 67041. The Atatürk Cultural Institute, in the old Chapel of the Templars on Kisla Sokağı, often has work by local artists for sale (*see* p. 366 for opening hours.)

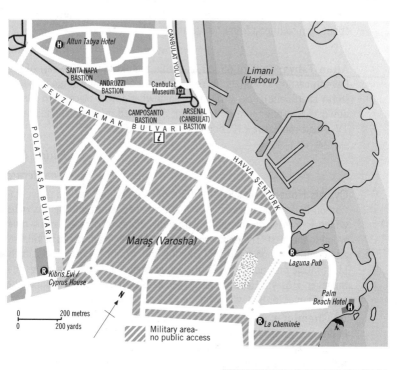

Maraş (Varosha)

Sports

There is a delightful stretch of golden sand designated as a public beach between the Palm Beach Hotel and the Varosha border. The hotel has an instructor in the summer who manages water-skiing, surfing and sailing from this beach. The hotel also runs a beach bar, hires sunbeds and operates changing rooms from its own beach strip, open to non-residents for the price of a day ticket.

Where to Stay

expensive

The **Palm Beach**, ✆ (036) 62000, is the most luxurious, animated and efficient hotel on the east coast. Even if you can't afford to stay here, you can still make use of its beach, or have tea in the lobby or a drink on the terrace bar from where you look out across the disturbing emptiness of Varosha. The pink hotel building is off the coast road, Havva Şentürk, about 1km southeast from the Arsenal (Canbulat) bastion.

moderate

Altun Tabya, ✆ (036) 65363, is within the old town, 50m east of the Ravelin bastion at 7 Kizikule Yolu, ✆ (036) 65363. It is a modern two storey apartment block, a friendly if somewhat dowdy place, with a large downstairs sitting room for breakfast, dominated by an inextinguishable TV. Single rooms are £10, doubles £15, triples £20.

Eating Out

moderate

Cyprus House, 'Kibris Evi', ✆ (036) 64845, occupies the old police station on Polat Paşa Bulvarı, a broad double avenue just outside the walls which is overlooked by old government offices to the east and a pine wood to the west. The dining room resembles a living museum of folk art, and combines good traditional cooking with erratic service. Zeki usually plays music on Friday and Saturday nights and on quieter evenings the manager, Huseyin Hepsoy, can be persuaded to read your fortune in the cards. Dinner for two with wine for £12, closed Sunday.

La Cheminée, ✆ (036) 64624, has an intriguing and serene position beside the Varosha boundary, 400m southwest of the Palm Beach Hotel. A dozen tables with red gingham tablecloths are arranged around the central fireplace. The French and Italian cooking has recently deteriorated, so choose the simplest dishes. It is open for lunch and dinner every day except Monday; dinner for two with wine costs around £20.

In the walled town there are half a dozen kebab houses along Liman Yolu Caddesı, of which the vine-shaded terrace of the Vilanya offers the best combination of cooking and view. All the kebab houses are fine and cheap places for lunch or high tea, but close too early for dinner.

Cafés, Bars and Nightlife

The Hasat Café occupies the old chapel and garden of the Catholic bishops just east of the great cathedral-mosque. You can either enjoy a game of backgammon in the sepulchral gloom of the interior or contemplate the carved golden stone of the Gothic apse from a table underneath the dappled shade that surrounds the fleur de lys pool. For a gutsier break go downhill to A.K. Petek's on the corner of Liman Yolu and Canbulat Yolu with its gâteau gallery, first-floor balcony and fountain courtyard café.

For a beer with a view there is the Efes kiosk in the moat or the Anit Gazinosu above the monument roundabout outside the Limassol or Land Gate. Alternatively there is the bar in the Old Town Pub Disco (the disco is seldom running) on Namik Kemal Meydanı, or the Otello Mucahitler Gazinosu, © 65520, which is just in front of the Citadel. The latter serves food and stays open late a couple of nights a week on music nights. The old town generally quietens down in the evening but there are livelier places beyond the walls. Try the Laguna Pub halfway between the Palm Beach Hotel and the Arsenal (Canbulat) Bastion, and Erich's pub-restaurant along Salamis Caddesı, © (036) 66214, open 12 noon–12 midnight.

Salamis Bay

Salamis Bay, 9.5km north of Famagusta, offers a mixture of beach life and antiquities. It has its own hotels, though it is probably easier to make either Boğaz or Famagusta your base and come here on a day trip. The ruins of the city of Salamis, especially the Roman theatre, baths and two early Byzantine churches, are the most immediately rewarding in Cyprus. There are three additional sites just inland. The half-dozen Royal tombs dating back to the 8th century, their approaches littered with the barbaric splendour of chariot sacrifices, are reached through a small explanatory museum. In a clump of trees just to their west stands the monastery and underground mausoleum of Ayios Varnavas (St Barnabas), the native apostle of Cyprus. Since the 1974 invasion it has been empty of monks and has recently been converted into a local museum. The third site, the excavations into the Bronze Age city of Enkomi/Alasia, lies 2km further inland.

Getting Around

There are two entrances to the ruins of Salamis. If you are arriving on a Gazimağusa (Famagusta)-to-Boğaz bus, you can ask to be dropped off at the west gate, beside the main road. If you are being dropped off by taxi you might ask for the north gate, which is right beside the sea, a restaurant and the ruins of the baths and the theatre. A stout walker can visit all the sites in one day, but should start early in the morning equipped with hat and dark glasses; those with less energy can arrange a taxi tour or hire a bicycle from the Salamis Bay, an unmissable high-rise hotel on the coast.

Where to Stay

expensive

Just off the Salamis road is the **Park Hotel**, © (036) 66511, an isolated two-storey, L-shaped villa with a terracotta-tiled roof and a near-Alpine interior of varnished wood. It has its own pool, beach front and tennis courts and is just a 300m stroll from the Salamis ruins.

moderate

The blue-shuttered **Mimoza**, © (036) 65460, is a medium-sized beach-front hotel of 50 rooms found just beside the Kocareis Restaurant. Some of its appeal is diminished by being overlooked by the twin towers of the neighbouring Salamis Bay complex though this does provide nearby facilities such as water sports, bicycle hire, supermarket, a disco and taxi rank.

Eating Out

The terrace of the **Bedis Bar Restaurant**, © (036) 65833, overlooks a wooden swimming pier and the back entrance to the Salamis ruins. It is perfectly situated for a post-ruin recovery: allow £5 a head for a long liquid lunch with fresh grilled fish and salad. If you are spending a night at Salamis, you can escape from the hotel bars by taking the inland road to the village of Yeniboğaziçi (Ayios Seryios) where you'll find the **Eyva Restaurant** and an exuberantly decorated bar, the Antik Gece Kulubu.

The Ruins of the City of Salamis

Open daily 8am–7pm and closing at 5pm in winter; adm.

Salamis lies 8km north of Famagusta between the road and the sea. It is one of the most celebrated coastal ruins of the Mediterranean and is easily the most impressive and important of the nine ancient Cypriot cities. Salamis is both an archaeological site and a sand-dune-covered coastal park, the ideal backdrop for a succession of picnics or lunches.

The two most substantial sites are the enormous public bath complex and the nearby theatre, which comprise the central nugget of visually impressive ruins. The more enthusiastic and energetic visitor will also want to wander amongst the network of tracks and find the remains of a Roman villa, the 4th-century Cathedral of Ayios Epiphanios, the overgrown forum and the beautifully positioned early Byzantine Kampanopetra Church.

History

Salamis was a coastal citadel established in the 11th century BC by iron-using, Greek-speaking invaders. They, or a preceding wave of immigrants, had destroyed

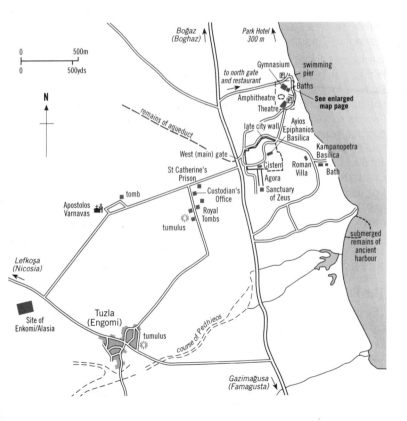

the sophisticated Bronze-Age city of Enkomi just 2km inland. Teucer, one of the heroes of Homer's *Iliad*, is the legendary founder, who named it Salamis after his father's island kingdom, from which he had been banished. Phoenician traders from the coast of Lebanon helped Salamis to emerge from the obscurity of the Dark Ages to become the most prosperous city on the island. The excavation of the Royal Tombs have revealed a chariot-using warrior dynasty who flourished during the 8th century BC, and who imitated the trappings of the great Near Eastern states, such as Egypt and Assyria, to whom they would soon be paying tribute.

The kings of Salamis are central figures in the maelstrom politics of ancient Cyprus, when a dozen cities jostled for dominance. Salamis, under such able rulers as Onesilos and Evagoras I, was the leader of the pro-Greek league, and led a number of near-successful revolts in the 5th century against Persian suzerainty. Ironically, it was the triumph of Greece, under Alexander the Great, that led to the eclipse of Salamis. When Ptolemy, one of Alexander's generals, won possession of the island, the last king of Salamis, Nicocreon, commited suicide, the city walls were levelled and Paphos was chosen to be the administrative centre for the province of Cyprus.

Salamis was denied a political role throughout the long period of Hellenistic and Roman rule but remained pre-eminent in size and commerce: a New York to Paphos's Washington. St Barnabas, a Greek-speaking Jewish tent maker, was a not untypical citizen of the cosmopolitan city. He returned to preach in his home town in AD 45 and again in AD 52, the traditional date for his martyrdom. One hundred years later, the city's large Jewish community revolted, but they were speedily suppressed and banished from the entire island. An earthquake in AD 342 entailed a wholesale reconstruction of the city, whose name was changed to Constantia in honour of the Emperor Constantine II. This was also the era of the first purpose-built churches, which collectively give a markedly early-Byzantine look to the surviving ruins. In AD 649 this city was destroyed by the army of Muawiya, the Muslim governor of Syria. In later centuries it was visited only by pilgrims and stone quarriers. Tomb-robbing in the 19th century gave way to more precise excavations, but great extents of the city still remain under a protective blanket of sand, shaded by eucalyptus, fennel, wild asparagus and mimosa.

The Palaestra and Baths

The **palaestra** (**I**), a great rectangular courtyard enclosed by standing marble columns, is the most photographed and celebrated part of Salamis. It provides a haunting image of urban elegance which still has the power to mock us with the lost pleasures of antiquity.

The courtyard was an open-air gymnasium, paved in precisely cut geometrical arrangements of marble, known as opus sectile. Patches of these disciplined swirls of orange octagons, squares and hexagons offset by triangular blades of red and

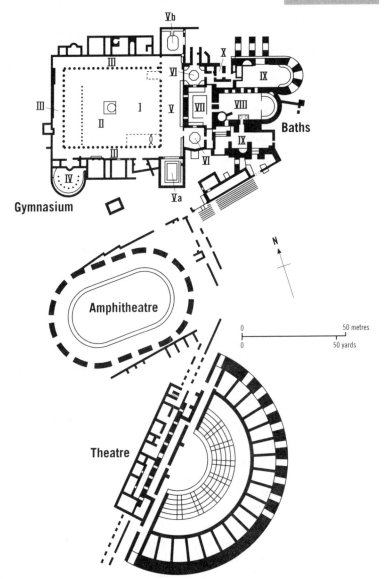

Vb

X

IX

II

VI

III

I

V

VII

VIII

II

IX

Baths

III

VI

IV

Va

Gymnasium

N

Amphitheatre

0   50 metres

0   50 yards

Theatre

The Ruins of the City of Salamis   375

white stone remain to be overwhelmed in spring by golden weeds. The rough looking **central plinth** (**II**) that supports a dark piece of fluted column was added in the 5th century AD to hold an imperial statue.

The grey and white columns originally supported a colonnade which provided a shady **cloistered walk** (**III**) around the sunbaked courtyard. A close look at the column bases, the carved Corinthian capitals and the candle-like tapering of the columns reveals a surprising lack of unity. In fact there is hardly a matching pair. This erratic display was assembled by sequestering those columns that had survived the 4th-century earthquake for the restoration of the baths. Surviving portions of marble bench can be seen against the interior walls. The baths formed a central focus of urban social life. The public would have thronged the colonnade to watch the glistening bodies of athletes working out, to greet friends, to '*passeo*', or visit the associated shops, latrines, libraries and shrines.

The **latrines** (**IV**) are entered directly from the colonnade, originally at the cost of one as, a trifling fee. Visitors entered into the outer porch where a fountain tinkled into a pool, and then took a right turn through the lobby to enter an apsidal chamber lined with a semicircular bench which could accommodate 44. Each place was sectioned off by metal brackets. An eight-pillar colonnade shaded the users and allowed for ample ventilation whilst a sewer ran below the benches. A trench of fresh water trickled by their feet where sponges would be dipped for bottom-washing. The walls above would have held niches filled with statues of heroes and suitable deities such as Hygeia and Fortune. The latrines were a mixture of delicacy and coarseness that has no modern equivalent, a place where people met, conversed and exchanged invitations without embarrassment. The three-niched chamber directly opposite has been identified as a shrine; beside it, with steps leading up to two sturdy columns, may have been a reference library with an entranceway on the corner.

The fluted columns on the eastern face of the palaestra courtyard are much higher, and originally enclosed the long nave of the **frigidarium** (**V**), the cold bath. Old proto-Ionic sandstone capitals can be seen that once capped the northern gateway. A number of Greek and Latin inscriptions and fluted pilasters in the worn grey marble paving testifies to the re-use of antique stone in the Byzantine opus sectile pavement. Halfway along, a missing section reveals an older area of Hellenistic pebble paving, probably dating to the 3rd century BC, though the practice still survives in some Greek islands.

The frigidarium was the centre of the bath ritual, a shaded area kept at normal temperature, which is here flanked by two large and ornate cold-water **pools**. The southern pool (**Va**) is embellished with pink and white columns, the northern (**Vb**) with nine headless statues found in excavations and added to the wall to suggest something of the original decoration.

Doorways in the east wall of the frigidarium lead into a labyrinthine, half-ruined network of hot rooms and passages. A few precious fragments of wall mosaic and fresco remain, which allow a tantalising glimpse at the vanished magnificence of the interiors. They have a symmetrical arrangement, but this duplication appears to have been aesthetic rather than practical, as it was different opening hours rather than walls that kept the sexes apart. A complex roof-line of domes, dependent half-domes and barrel vaults covered the rooms to produce an external roof-line not unlike a medieval Byzantine church. Buttresses, some of which are still standing, were later added to reduce the stress on the outer walls.

The bather entered one of the two frigidaria (**VI**), both of which retain their opus sectile flooring and central cold water octagonal pools, before passing through apsidal passages into the **tepidarium** (**VII**). This was a rectangular hall of mild humidity with underfloor heating, marble-clad massage benches and a pool fed by water cascading down from a channel on the far wall.

Above the south passage is a portion of a fresco which depicts Hylas refusing the advances of a braceleted water nymph with closed eyes and water dripping seductively through her fingers. The beautiful youth Hylas was one of the Argonauts and the beloved young companion of Hercules. Hylas was however deprived of his role in Jason's epic adventure by some water nymphs who lured him underwater to their enchanted grotto. The frontal depiction of Hylas and his accentuated, wide eyes gives it a very Byzantine look, though this fresco was made in the 3rd century AD. It is one of the earliest examples of the new artistic style that would transform the classical world into medieval Byzantium. Two doors connect the tepidarium to the **caldarium** (**VIII**), an even larger rectangular hall with a heated apsidal pool. On the soffit of the third northern arch is a fragment of mosaic, of floral wreaths around a damaged medallion. In the southwest corner stands a medieval kiln that used to burn the abundant supply of marble and stone to make lime mortar. Either side of the caldarium are the tangled ruins of the **sudatoria** (**IX**), the steam rooms. The southern sudatorium retains a pair of mosaic panels in two southern apses. The legs, dropped quiver, shield and bow are all that remain of a grim scene of the twins Artemis and Apollo shooting down the children of Niobe. The other panel shows two swans, the metamorphosed Leda and Zeus, taking off beside a river god, neatly labelled EBPΩTAΣ (Eurotas). You could explore the shitty-smelling **praefurnium** (**X**), the furnace cellars, from an entrance on the north face of the baths; watch where you tread.

Just west of the path running between the baths and the theatre is a partially excavated dip in the ground, the city's small amphitheatre which retains a few rows of stone seats on its north face. To the east of the path there is a much better preserved row of eight seats that rise up against the back of a water cistern, the purpose of which remains unknown.

The Theatre

The theatre at Salamis was built during the reign of Augustus (27 BC–14 AD), and gave a recognizably Roman stamp to the city centre. For it is a free-standing building, supported on massive masonry arches in the Roman manner, rather than using the contours of a hill in the time-honoured Hellenic tradition. In its heyday it seated 15,000 spectators in 50 rows of seats, divided into eight sectors by access stairs. Only the worn lower seats, the smart area then as now, are original, for the theatre was partially reconstructed by the Antiquities Department in the 1960s. Its original extent is revealed by the low outer segment-like foundations. It was severely damaged in a 4th century AD earthquake, and was subsequently used as a quarry for the Byzantine reconstruction of the city. By this stage, theatres with their strong pagan overtones were beginning to fall into official disfavour.

Salamis is an early example of Latin theatre design which only crystallized into its final form in about 80 BC. The Romans incorporated a number of improvements to Greek theatres and created a blueprint which served throughout their diverse empire. Seating (*cavea* in Latin, *koilon* in Greek) was defined within a strict semi-circle, and was no longer encroached upon by the wings of the stage. Roman entrance passages (known as confornicationes) faced each other directly across the front of the stage, and helped to define the component areas of the theatre. The circular Greek orchestra, where all the action used to take place, was trimmed to a semicircle which was then used only by the supporting choirs. The pulpitum wall, decorated with an undulating surface of niches, divided it from the stage. Salamis has eight rectangular and one central semicircular niche, which was dedicated to Apollo. The Romans also raised and deepened the stage (*proscaenium* in Latin, *skene* in Greek) which became a platform for the principal action of a play. They also greatly elaborated the backdrop (*scaenae frons*) into a magnificent three-storey façade of columned porches, furnished with statues of the muses, appropriate deities and deified emperors. The ground floor of the backdrop was pierced by three doorways and two side entrances. The central door, known as the royal, was reserved for the leading actor, the right-hand-side door for town characters, the left for those acting strangers and messengers.

The Roman theatre season began in April and ended with the people's games in September. There was a popular and flexible programme of debates, lectures, farce, pantomime, circus and comedy, in addition to the classical repertoire of Greek tragedies. For the latter, coloured masks hinting at the character's fate were worn: brown for men and white for women. Dress was also conventionally determined: a white robe signified an old man, yellow a courtesan, purple for the rich, red for the poor, multicoloured for uncertain youth, and a short tunic for a slave.

The Roman Villa

From the theatre, go back up the entrance road; take the left fork and 300m later turn left at the crossroads. Look out for an overgrown track on your right which leads to the ruins of a villa lying about 50m from the roadside.

This was a moderately prosperous household, paved in stone not mosaic, with a single reception hall and living rooms arranged around a small inner courtyard with a well in the corner. A corrugated iron shelter now protects the traces of fresco; decorated with a design of white bands enclosing areas of green, red and yellow, like a live-in Mondrian. The reception hall had an apsidal niche which was used in the medieval period as the foundations for a mill. The central grinding bowl, two millstones, drain and collecting pit have been left in place. Traces of the interior's original fluted pilaster decoration, made from plaster, can be seen at ground level. Only two steps survive from a staircase which led up to a first floor terrace from which the inhabitants could enjoy the sea view.

Kampanopetra Basilica

Continue along the road from the Roman villa, taking a left turn at the fork which leads down to the beach and the ruins of Kampanopetra, framed by the blue sea. The basilica is one of the earliest on the island, built in the 4th century AD when the reign of a single emperor, Constantine, raised the status of Christianity from that of a persecuted sect to the dominant cult of the empire. Kampanopetra is a purposely grand building with a spacious western courtyard. The column bases indicate an interior colonnade and in the centre stands a pink and white column which formed part of a circular canopy that shaded a well. This was for ritual washing, a common feature of Near Eastern religious life, and one which survives in Islam but has not been retained by the Orthodox Church.

Moving east, you pass through the porch before entering the central hall of the church, originally divided into a broad nave and two aisles by a double row of marble columns. The north and central apse were overbuilt by a later 10th-century Byzantine chapel which deliberately repossessed the holiest portion of this ancient church. A rough altar, or reliquary, made from half a grit sandstone sarcophagus, stands in the northern apse. Beyond the aisles are a pair of narrow flanking passageways, known as the exonarthex, which were for the use of the unbaptized members of the congregation who could look onto the mystery of the mass through windows. The southern passage is particularly well preserved, with a fine opus-sectile pavement that leads you down towards six marble sarcophagi of the good and the great.

To the east of the church is a second courtyard with more patches of mosaic and opus sectile flooring, which is thought to be the centre of the bishop's palace. The five standing marble columns are part of an arcade whose rounded arches reflect the broad Romanesque arches of the strong outer wall. The seaward columns are capped by early Byzantine capitals which are noticeably different from the re-used Roman Corinthian capitals. Byzantine carvers created a basket-shaped capital with increasingly stylized motifs from two-depth cutting. It was a move away from the full-blown classical idealism, concentrating on the effect of shadows and contrasts of light.

Immediately east, but lower-lying, is a suite of rooms and cisterns forming a small but luxurious bath, possibly part of the episcopal palace. The hall is furnished with an intact opus sectile floor whose centrepiece is one of the hidden glories of Cyprus. A circle filled by diminishing rings of coloured marble triangles flickers like the petals of a geometrical flower. Within this design swim red marble fish-like abstractions that are drawn to the missing centre.

The beach below provides a welcome break for swimming. Walk south along the sand and rock for about 450m, beside metre-thick residues of terracotta shards exposed by the sea, to the site of the ancient harbour sheltered by the southern lee of a headland.

Ayios Epiphanios Cathedral

Returning to the crossroads 300m south of the theatre, take the left-hand turning, which leads to the ruins of Ayios Epiphanios Cathedral and the Byzantine cistern.

The Cathedral, a massive but somewhat graceless structure, reflects the character of its creator. It was built by St Epiphanios, the obstinate, learned and controversial Palestinian-born champion of Orthodoxy who ruled the Cypriot church as metropolitan bishop of Constantia (Salamis) from his election in AD 368 to his death in 403. In 401 his life's work was crowned when a Council of the Church held in this cathedral irrevocably condemned the heretical doctrines of Origen.

The enormous rectangular floor of the metropolitan cathedral has been excavated from the surrounding scrubland. Archaeologists have indicated the ground plan by placing fragments of capitals on the bases of the double row of fourteen columns. The broad nave was bridged by an entablature which upheld a flat coffered ceiling. The flanking side aisles are also exceptionally wide, though they would have supported a lower ceiling, carried by a row of arched piers. The aisles both terminate at small double altars and vestries which helped to focus all attention onto the deep central apse. This retains its stepped semicircular bench, the synthronon, where the clergy would be seated to assist the presiding bishop in celebrating the mysteries. Beyond the aisles lies the exonarthex, an outer passage for committed but unbaptized Christians. Here it has been reduced to a tiny passage, a prelude to the gradual phasing out of this feature of early Christianity.

After the destruction of the city by the Saracens in the 7th century AD, a chapel was constructed in the precincts of the ruined cathedral, to the east of the south aisle. The six shoulder-high piers date from the 9th-century restoration, when three domes were raised above the nave. This improvement is traditionally associated with Emperor Leo VI, who built the monastery of St Barnabas and took the body of St Epiphanios to Constantinople for safe keeping. This chapel retained enough relics to remain an established port of call on the medieval pilgrimage circuit.

Forum Cistern

About 50m to the south of the cathedral are the ruins of the great water cistern of the city. Through the half-cleared debris of its floor emerge a regular grid of 36 piers which once culminated in round arches, supporting the concrete ceiling. A small stretch of the aqueduct which brought fresh water from Değirmenlik (Kythrea), 50km west of Salamis, survives nearby.

Only one column rises above the undergrowth, which is retaking possession of the enormous rectangular forum. This was the city's marketplace, flanked by a 700ft colonnade supported by 27ft-high Corinthian columns. The forum (or *agora* in Greek) was open to the south, facing Salamis's grandest and oldest temple, the sanctuary of Zeus, of which only a dug-over artificial mound remains. The temple was considered to have been founded by Teucer in the 11th century and was much visited by pilgrims. It was an inviolable sanctuary that was proudly depicted on the city's coinage with columns decorated with unique bull's-head capitals.

The Royal Tombs

Open daily 8am–4pm; adm.

The half-dozen Royal Tombs are all from the 8th century BC. They are the best of over 100 tombs that were systematically excavated during the 1960s in this area, which in antiquity formed the vast necropolis of Salamis. They are in a cluster beside a back road to Nicosia (Lefkosa) which leaves the main coast road almost directly opposite the west Salamis gate. Take the first left to reach the museum and custodian's office.

History

Most of the tombs have at some point been re-used or robbed, but collectively they give us a powerful insight into the burial customs of Archaic Cyprus. These have a close correspondence to the funeral of Patroclus, beloved of Achilles, held outside the walls of Troy. For it was at the time when these tombs were being sealed that the folk memories of the early Iron Age were being transformed by Homer into a polished saga. The 23rd song of the *Iliad* describes the funeral of Patroculus (on pages 412–19 if you have a Penguin *Iliad*).

The honoured dead were laid in a magnificently equipped war chariot before starting on their last journey to a hut-shaped stone tomb, filled with valuable weaponry, jewellery and furniture to match a king's ransom. An excavated processional way lined with large jars of oil and wine led the last hundred feet down to the tomb entrance where a funeral pyre consumed the body. This was accompanied on its spiritual journey by the sacrifice of the terrified pair of chariot horses and an additional human or two. The ashes were collected in an urn which was sealed and placed in the tomb with libations and a last meal. The tomb was then buried under a mound.

The Museum and Six of the Royal Tombs

The museum houses bronze casts and wooden reconstructions of the horse harnesses and chariots found at the mouth of all these tombs. Horses had a potent symbolism that was closely connected with the Indo-European male sky gods. In Persia their sacrifice was reserved to the Sun, in Greece to Poseidon. Horses had only been introduced into the Mediterranean world, from the Eurasian steppes, around 1200 BC, and their arrival is everywhere associated with violent conquest. The leather horse harnesses and iron bits are immediately recognizable, and even the bronze, crescent-decorated breastplate survives in the formal dress of contemporary cavalry regiments.

The museum also contains iron fire-dogs, a fasces formed from a bundle of rusted spearheads and fine Phoenician work: carved ivory plaques that were riveted onto a throne and bed, gilded metalwork and lotus capital censers. From the most militantly Greek city of ancient Cyprus it constitutes a heady Oriental cultural heritage. The classical clay portrait on display is not from this period, but from the 3rd-century-BC pyre of Nicocreon.

Tomb no. 47, by the museum, has a broad processional way, known as a dromos, which tapers down to a three-stepped terrace where the skeletons of a pair of slaughtered horses before the tomb-altar are set into a rock-carved niche. **Tomb no. 79** also has a pair of horse skeletons, now mildewy within their glass case, but a more impressive rock-cut tomb, decorated with flanking niches and the remains of a terracotta sarcophagus. This tomb revealed the richest cache of grave goods, including plates of chicken and fish, as well as the magnificent ivory-clad throne and bronze cauldron displayed in the Cyprus Museum in Southern Nicosia.

Tomb no. 50, better known as 'St Catherine's Prison', has easily the most impressive funerary chamber. It was originally conceived in the 8th century BC as an open U-shaped terrace before the tomb chamber, and was decorated with a bold cornice. In the Roman period it was enclosed by an east wall and the monolithic, barrel-vaulted roof. This within a few generations was broken into by tomb robbers who bashed a hole through the north wall. The monumental processional ramp of dressed stone with a pair of sacrificed chariot horses was left undisturbed until discovered by archaeologists in 1965. From an early medieval period to the 1950s the tomb was used as a chapel. Greek priests reopened the well and carved three crosses over the entrance into the original 8th-century-BC tomb chamber which is associated with an episode in the life of St Catherine, before her martyrdom on the wheel at Alexandria. It was here that she was hidden by her influential uncle, who wished to protect her, and his reputation, when Salamis was being scoured for Christians during the persecution of Diocletian.

Tomb no. 2 is on the other side of the track. It was fairly carelessly reassembled after the excavation, which revealed human bones amongst the team of sacrificed asses. It retains its impressive basic structure of massive stones, though the limestone frieze on the exterior now looks somewhat out of place.

Tomb no. 3 was deliberately buried off centre beneath an enormous earth mound to foil robbers and recalls the barrows of England and the Kurgan mounds of southern Russia. The subterranean hut-shaped tomb chamber is the most beautifully executed, formed from a few huge but precisely fitting limestone blocks. The last tomb is in a field to the east of the barrow and has a ragstone chamber recessed into a pale limestone wall capped with a lintel.

The Monastery of Apostolos Varnavas (St Barnabas)

Open daily 8am–6pm; adm.

The monastery of St Barnabas looks at its best from the near distance. The interior has been ruined by clumsy restorations and the atmosphere is disappointingly secular, the last monk having left in 1977. As you approach the monastery from Salamis, a cluster of eucalyptus trees casts dappled shade over the ancient exterior of the double-domed church, with its Italianate bell tower and fountain set before the rustic gatehouse. Beside the exterior wall of the eastern apse are two columns, a section of wall and an area of opus sectile paving from the original 5th-century church built by Archbishop Anthemios. The gatehouse and monastery buildings around the garden have been converted into a café and local museum. The museum exhibits some indifferent 19th-century icons and a representative collection of antiquities, mostly found locally at either Salamis and Enkomi, that range from the Early Bronze Age to the Ottoman period (*see* 'Ceramics' p. 405).

The church was remodelled in the 18th century and disastrously restored. It is possible however to visualize the original interior of this important early medieval building. There are a number of fine antique capitals, proto-Ionic as well as Corinthian, set into the walls. They now appear mere random decoration, but before the remodelling they acted as corner springs supporting the various barrel vaults and domes. An almost identical plan and construction can be admired in its original condition at Ayios Lazarus in Larnaca. Ayios Lazarus shares the same claim to have been constructed by Emperor Leo VI at the end of the 9th century.

In the south apse, a peeling 20th-century mural tells the story of the discovery of the tomb of St Barnabas. It was painted by Chariton, Barnabas and Stephanos, the three celebrated brothers all of whom were monks at the monastery, and who came from a family of exceptional longevity. The trinity of smiling, white-bearded faces was a familiar sight on generations of Cypriot postcards, brochures and photographs. They painted thousands of *ex voto* icons, particularly of St Andrew, St George and the Virgin Mary, as well as being much in demand for baptisms. A member of the family, now resident at the Monastery of St George Alaminos, outside Limassol, continues the tradition.

The Apostle's Tomb

In AD 477 Anthemios, archbishop of Constantia-Salamis, was under pressure from Peter Fuller, the new patriarch of Antioch, who was using his childhood friendship with the Emperor Zeno to further an old claim to exercise suzerainty over Cyprus. Just when Anthemios had reached the end of his legal tether he was instructed in a dream to dig under a distinctive old carob tree in the enormous necropolis of Salamis. He acted on this inspiration, and the next day discovered the sarcophagus of St Barnabas which revealed the bones of the apostle clasping his own handwritten copy of the Gospel of St Matthew, lovingly placed there by St Mark. Anthemios, armed with such irrefutable proofs of an independent apostolic foundation, hurried to Constantinople. He presented the gospel to the Emperor Zeno, who was so moved that he bestowed in return the right to use a sceptre and purple ink, which were both imperial prerogatives. He also arranged a synod which recognized Cyprus as the first autocephalous church, that is, fully independent and able to appoint its own archbishop but a step below the dignity of the historic patriarchs.

Ask the custodian for the key to the domed tomb chapel which is just outside the monastery. Stairs within lead down to a rock-cut twin chamber, the sarcophagus of St Barnabas is the first on the right and is seldom without a simple floral wreath. Literally 'son of consolation', St Barnabas was a Jewish native of Cyprus and by tradition a tent-maker. He is considered one of the apostles owing to the role he played in introducing St Paul to the Early Church. He later accompanied St Paul on missionary journeys which included his homeland of Cyprus. St Mark may have been his cousin. St Barnabas was the first bishop of Salamis and the founder of the independent Church of Cyprus, and was martyred by stoning. He is especially associated with the gospel of St Matthew, which he used in a number of miraculous healing ceremonies.

If you would care for a short stroll and some more tombs, follow the track imme-diately opposite the monastery of St Barnabas that leads to Tuzla (Engomi) village. About 200m along it, just past a young olive grove, a rusting wire fence encloses half a dozen rock-cut tombs.

The Bronze-Age Town of Enkomi/Alasia

Open during reasonable daylight hours; adm.

One mile southwest of the monastery of St Barnabas, on the other side of the T-junction, is a cluster of sheds that includes the guardian's hut. The Bronze Age town of Enkomi/Alasia, buried under three millennia of river silt, is one of the great archaeological discoveries of Cyprus. Its treasures are on display in the British as well as the Cyprus Museum, while the crumbling excavations (untouched since 1974), though extensive, have little to attract the tourist without archaeological interests.

History

Enkomi, also known as Alasia from a cryptic mention in the records of the Egyptian 18th dynasty, was occupied for at least 700 years. It was in existence by 1800 BC and was destroyed around 1050 BC, when most of the civilized, literate world disappeared during the anarchic first centuries of the Iron Age. Enkomi reached its apogee in the 16th century BC, when its streets covered over a square mile (2.5sq km) and it housed a population of 15,000. Its prosperity was firmly based on the smelting and export of copper, but by then it may also have con-trolled most of the agricultural wealth of Cyprus. Enkomi traded with the civilized Near East through Ugarit, the great Canaanite merchant city on the Lebanese coast, and at different periods sent tribute to Egypt and the Hittite Empire. There is increasing evidence of Mycenaean influence during the 14th century and the gradual settlement of these free-ranging warrior merchants from the coast of Greece. The city was destroyed by fire around 1200 BC and was then rebuilt on a rigid grid plan. It is mainly the remnants of this second city that we see today. Enormous resources were allocated for defence, and the city was protected by a complete circuit of monolithic walls, studded with watch towers. In the 11th cen-tury Enkomi was abandoned, and the hoards of hidden metal suggest that few of its citizens were able to return, though one can hope that some may have sur-vived to settle in Salamis.

The Site

A path leads downhill to the excavated town centre, an ordered area of paved streets within which fit a disciplined rectangular grid of foundation walls for courtyard houses, workshops and shrines fitted with drains, cisterns and well-heads. At the centre of the excavations is the sanctuary of the Horned God (on display in the Cyprus Museum in Southern Nicosia) which is identifiable from the skilfully cut and jointed stone blocks. For all its sophistication, which was not to reappear in Cyprus for centuries, Enkomi at first seems to be sited in a bafflingly dull location. It is plonked in an unexceptional portion of the wide Mesaoria plain, apparently devoid of natural facilities and now popular only with thunder flies. To see it through the eyes of its proud citizens, one must imagine thick belts of virgin forest clothing the plain and the island's largest stream running just to the south, whose estuary provided safe anchorage from the sea, which in those days was a mile/2km further inland.

Tuzla (Engomi)

In the village are a pair of antique carved lions, which once embellished an Archaic tomb and are now perched in the dust before the disused 18th-century Greek church. 100m east of the church is a crumbling earth mound, the funerary pyre of Nicocreon, the last of the kings of Salamis. He took his life in 295 BC after the triumph of general Ptolemy who ruled Cyprus as a province of Egypt. The mound had been much tunnelled by tomb robbers, in fruitless searches for the non-existent tomb, but when excavated it produced some astonishingly vivid clay busts, presumed to be ancestral effigies. They are on display in the Cyprus Museum in southern Nicosia with copies in the Royal Tombs Museum.

The Mesaoria

The Mesaoria (Mesarya in Turkish) is a flat agricultural plain, broken by eucalyptus windbreaks, threaded by dry water courses and dotted with dozens of villages. It is a dull, listless landscape, enlivened only in spring by thick gashes of red, blue and yellow, as weeds briefly dominate the young fields of corn. Many of the traditional mudbrick village houses are still standing, but since 1974 there has been a sad reduction in its few outstanding monuments. Practically all the churches have been gutted and their small treasures, the icons, Byzantine frescoes and odd pieces of antique carving have been either removed for safe keeping or stolen. These churches are locked or used as animal shelters, except the fortunate few which remain structurally sound, having been converted into mosques.

Akdoğan (Lysi) and Surroundings

This is the liveliest of the villages to visit as it has a café, petrol station and restaurant-bar. In the centre of the village is a wonderfully exuberant late-19th-century Orthodox church, covered in a thick layer of Gothic decoration copied from the great medieval cathedrals of Famagusta and Nicosia.

The diminutive 14th-century shrine of Ayios Ephimianos, 2km southwest of the village, enjoys a lonely position, shaded by a clump of eucalyptus just above a water course. The fresco of *Christ Pantocrator* in the dome and the *Virgin* in the apse were stolen, but later identified in Texas. They are now protected by an American court order, and are to be returned when a comprehensive peace agreement is signed.

West of the village, 2km along the tarmac road to Yiğitler (Arsos), there is a distinctive hillock capped with rounded boulders. Halfway down its southern face is an Archaic nympheum, a small natural cave that archaeologists found filled with votive statuettes. It has been romantically identified as the grotto of the Cypriot sibyl, whose holiness is immeasurably increased by approaching it along the Layline taken from the nearby sacred site of Ayios Ephinanios. From this approach the silhouette of the sibyl's hill hovers as a visual echo of the Five Finger Mountain on the northern horizon.

About 4km further west along this road, the other side of Yiğitler (Arsos), is the hamlet of Erdemli (Tremetousha), the site of Richard the Lionheart's victory over Isaac Comnenos. The ruinous church and buildings on the northern edge are the remains of an 18th-century rebuilding of the ancient monastery of St Spyridon. This very Cypriot saint, a shepherd turned local bishop and bulwark of Orthodoxy in the 4th century, lay buried here for a few centuries before being moved to Constantinople. Since the 15th century he has rested on the island of Corfu, of which he is the patron saint.

Boğaz (Boghaz)

Boğaz is a coastal hamlet on the southern edge of the Karpas peninsula, with half a dozen fish restaurants ranged round its harbour. It also has some pleasant patches of sandy beach and the only two large and reliable hotels in the area. The constant flow of customers to the village's restaurants also makes it an invaluable place to find a lift or taxi. Further up the coast, about 5km east, is a cement and oil terminal established beside the moat and foundations of Strongylos Castle, a Byzantine watchtower enlarged by the Knights Templar in the 12th century.

Where to Stay

Boğaz is well sited as a base to explore the region, only 25km north of Famagusta and on the edge of the Karpas. There are two hotels with identical prices run by one company. Hotel View, ✆ (090) 537 12651, fax (090) 520 82603, is the newer of the two, with 30 balconied rooms set back from the coast road, its own pool and two tennis courts. Hotel Boğaz, ✆ (037) 12659, is a simpler, three-storey building with 40 rooms right beside the beach and coast road. Choose a front room for the morning sun and sea view or a back room for tranquillity. A double room costs £25, a single £20.

Eating Out

It is difficult to choose from the restaurants above the Boğaz fishing harbour. Karsel, under the management of Hamdi'nin Yeri, currently has an edge on his rivals and provides an ample *meze*, enhanced by herbs cut freshly from those growing around the terrace, followed by grilled fish.

Iskele (Trikomo) and the Church of Panayia Theotokos

Open 8–4 every day, adm.

The church of Panayia Theotokos (The All Holy Mother of God) has been preserved as the Yeni Iskele Icon Museum. Iskele is 4km from the coast road between Boğaz and Salamis and the museum is tucked away on the western edge of the village, beside the road to Geçitkale (Lefkoniko).

The history of the church is best appreciated from the south side where you can separate the barrel-vaulted additions, a 15th-century north aisle and an extension to the nave, from the original 12th-century cruciform chapel. The former has plain buttresses; the latter is embellished with blind Romanesque arches and a dome with an unusually high drum, pierced by a dozen slender windows. The belfry was added in the 19th century, but incorporates a piece of carving from an early Byzantine stone iconostasis.

The interior is dominated by the *Christ Pantocrator* in the dome, painted in the early 12th century. Although touched by a certain naïvety of execution, it has undoubted power. Christ is depicted with thick dark outlines that stress a tightened neck, a downturned mouth and eyes that consistently avoid your glance. 'Mortals be fearful of the Judge' warns the inscription, and this spirit of dread is carried on into the circle of angels with bended head and knees, their arms hidden in cloaks as they approach the empty throne, where to one's relief stand our intercessors, John the Baptist and the Virgin.

Other notable 12th-century paintings include seven scenes from the life of the Virgin, four in the soffit of the south arch and three in the blind north arch, of which the former has an unusual depiction of Joachim in a tent of bent trees.

Above the altar is *Christ in Ascension*, enclosed in an aureola held by four angels; in the apse, apostles watch the Virgin reveal the Christ Child (with an unusual mane of long dark hair) with open arms. The Italianate medallions in the north were probably added in the 16th century.

There are five other churches in Iskele, of which the 15th-century chapel of Ayios Iakovos has acquired a certain fame: it has been duplicated by Queen Marie of

Romania as a private oratory on the shores of the Black Sea. It is also infamous as the birthplace of George Grivas, the leader of the EOKA struggle for independence in the 1950s and a prime fermenter of the inter-communal violence of the 1960s. His village is now largely populated by Turkish refugees from Larnaca.

Kantara (Kandara)

Kantara village, 12km northwest of Boğaz, is a small hill resort where a dozen or so terraced colonial bungalows shelter amongst pine woods, enjoying cool breezes and a fine view over the Mesaoria plain. It was the site of a medieval monastery, but now the bar/restaurant is its central attraction. Kantara Castle lies 3km northeast along a forest road that keeps to the high ground.

Kantara Castle

Open from dawn to dusk.

The castle perches on a mountaintop with an Olympian view through the pine strewn slopes. From its crumbling medieval walls is a superb vista of the Karpas peninsula stretching east, the spine of mountains to the west, the Mesaoria plain to the south and the narrow sea-wrapped foreshore to the north. The walls of Kantara Castle seem to grow out of the rocky summit. The dressed grey stone of its surviving towers melts into the orange-streaked natural outcrop. At dusk it has an added magnificence as the walls trap pools of light and cut spectacular silhouettes, while swallows flaunt their skill amongst the gathering pine-scented rustle of the evening wind. As a combination of nature and man it equals the dizziest fantasies of the Gothic imagination.

The first permanent watchtower was erected here in the 10th century, when the Byzantine Empire established the Atrides Garrison to defend the island from Saracen raids. The Kantara peak is offset from the central range of mountains, and can freely signal to Buffavento and St Hilarion as well as to Strongylos on the coast. Isaac Comnenus took refuge here, after his defeat by Richard the Lionheart, and before he moved east to try to catch a boat from his tottering state. It was a hotly contested stronghold during the struggle between the Lusignan and imperial parties, and by 1230 was in near ruin after a year-long siege.

The castle, then known as Le Candaire or Cantare, was completely rebuilt in the late 14th century to watch over the fabulously wealthy city of Famagusta, which in 1373 was seized by the Genoese. It was to the safety of this Lusignan stronghold that Prince John rode when he escaped from Italian captivity in Famagusta Castle, together with his old cook. The prince was blackened up like a scullery boy, piled up with broken old pots, his clanking leg irons hidden within a pair of high leather boots, and together they sauntered past the guards.

The Venetian Senate neglected the inland castles, ignoring the advice of a series of military experts, and allowed the walls to crumble. When the threat of Turkish invasion grew imminent in the 1560s they ordered the slighting of Kantara. A sympathetic restoration in the early decades of this century has secured the walls without destroying the romantic aura.

The outline of the summit has dictated the parallelogram shape of the castle, and that its entrance should be on the sloping ground to the east. This eastern face is the best preserved. The weak-looking gateway is protected by two higher towers, and especially by the extending arm of the northeast bastion, with its loop-holed passage and protruding firing gallery. The rounder southeast tower preserves vaulted two-storey chambers, though the old prison in the basement now serves as a cistern. Just beside the southeast tower is the garrison mess, and on the southeast corner is a barrack block of three vaulted chambers with an adjacent latrine tucked onto the edge for a clear drop. In the centre stands the watchtower, in lonely eminence but for the windblown young cedars growing beside it. It is known as the Queen's Tower, not from the residence of any historical queen, but in acknowledgement of the guardian spirit of Cyprus, an elusive fusion of the Virgin and half-remembered pagan goddesses. The north and south curtain walls have mostly fallen, but in the southwest corner there is a range of five surviving buildings hiding the secretive postern gate.

Ancient City Sites: Galounia, Pergamon and Aphrodision

The coast north of Kantara is a piece of unchanged Mediterranean littoral. A narrow road twists and bumps through mixed groves of carob and olive, past deserted coves and raw limestone uplands covered with the stumpy odiferous shrubs of goat-grazed maquis. One horizon is filled by the wine-dark sea, the other by the pine-clad peaks of the Beşparmak/Pentadaktylos mountain range. There is an endless choice of picnic sites, quiet walks and rock bathing, of which the half-dozen suggestions below are merely those with historical associations. The beaches are generally uninviting, for they are usually strewn with an impressive quantity of wind-ripped plastic rubbish thrown up by winter storms. There are two possible meal stops, at Kaplıca (Dhavlos) harbour and just west of Yali.

The sprawling village of **Büyükkonuk** (Komi Kebir), 13km north of Boğaz, is surrounded by olive groves, beneath the declining grandeur of the Pendadhaktylos range. Both the modern Turkish and the mixed Arabic-Greek of the old name translate as the 'The Big Here'. This is not from local pride but in response to the body of St Auxentios, a Roman soldier turned saintly hermit, who settled the dispute over his burial place by sitting up from the dead and intoning 'Komi'—here!

The coast road climbs uphill from the village, and as you descend and approach the shore, look out for a left turn. Walk 300m down this track to Yedikonuk

(Ephtakomi) and then turn coastward to stumble amongst the shard-littered site of **Galounia**, a city occupied throughout the classical period, whose anchorage is protected by an offshore reef.

The Kaplıca (Dhavlos) fishing shelter is set into the west face of a protective bay and overlooked by Mustafa Balikci's vine-shaded bar/restaurant shack. A pretty avenue of pines leads uphill to the village, which is now dominated by the brand-new gleaming domed, arcaded and illuminated Raif Denktaş Mosque.

The chapel of **Panayia Pergamintissa**, Our Lady of Pergamon, is 6km west of the turning to Mersinlik (Phlamoudhi) and 4km northeast of Tatlısu (Akanthou). The chapel is just visible from the road, framed by trees and shrubs on a low plateau of pale limestone. It has a characteristically medieval silhouette, with its high drum surmounting the crossing of the cruciform aisles, capped by a shallow dome. Despite attempts to seal the building, the best of the decaying interior frescoes have been stolen. A trench dug around the church has revealed the apse and some fallen capitals of a much larger 5th-century Byzantine structure. Other traces of ancient Pergamon can be found scattered in the surrounding acres, among them a profusion of terracotta shards, millstones, upstanding stones, cisterns and rock-cut footings. Between the church and the road is a tiny cave chapel cut out of the rock, complete with an iconostasis, looking like a three-bayed trough, hewn from the stone. The acropolis, the nucleus of the city, stood on the higher ground to the north of the road. There has been no change in the romantic desolation since Ross's first putative identification of this site in the 1840s.

Just west of the greenhouse-strewn hamlet of Yalı (Neriadhes) take a sharp turn inland to reach the gutted chapel of Arkhangelos Mikhail and a small fishing shelter. The peninsula beside the chapel, scarred with foundation footings, is the site of the ancient city of **Aphrodision**. It was at its most extensive in the Roman period, though tombs in the surrounding fields have revealed a much older history. The rare concentration of Hittite grave goods may indicate that Aphrodision was the administrative and garrison centre for this Bronze-Age Anatolian Empire in Cyprus. A scattering of shards amongst the tell-tale diggings reveals the work of recent tomb robbers. Inland, beside the turning to Tatlısu (Akanthou), there is a shack **café** which turns out a good plate of freshly grilled fish.

At the Esentepe (Ayios Amvrosios) turning are the remains of the old pattern of economy that survived into this century. The ruins of two mills can be identified, the one by the shore fed by an aqueduct and the other higher up by a mill stream tunnelled through rock. A line of five roofless warehouses stand before a tattered wharf with rear ramps for the use of carts. These stored all forms of exportable island produce but especially carob pods, which were shipped as fodder to Egypt and Syria. The village is inland, safely removed from pirate raids and perched beside a gorge on a naturally defensive site. The church, with its Gothic vaults crammed with pepper-pots, was built early this century and has been converted into a mosque. It occupies the central square, surrounded by a few dusty cafés, clubs and the Tumba Restaurant. For the Monastery of Antiphonitis *see* p. 342.

The Karpas Peninsula

On a map the Kirpaşa (Karpas) peninsula looks like a dramatic eastern projection of the Gothic (Besparmark/Pendadhaktylos) mountain range. The landscape is, however, quite different. The Karpas is filled with rough hills that never aspire to be mountains or boast much in the way of forest or woodland. These limestone uplands are covered in thickets of juniper, lentisk and wild olive. Cultivation is restricted to the coast or inner valleys where corn, tobacco and olive and carob groves are found. The climate has necessitated dry-farming techniques, such as naturally contoured wind-breaks of myrtle and wall-enclosed fields designed to retain flash-flood water and halt erosion. Set at random in many of the fields are square stone huts with just a window and a door, where the farmworker can rest in the middle of the day, store tools and camp out during the harvest. Traditional houses are scarcely more elaborate, though the odd upper room or arcaded balcony can be seen. The villages in this area do not have the concentric plan seen in the rest of Cyprus, and often appear more like a reluctant conglomeration of hamlets centred around a café, rather than a church or mosque.

There are a number of ruined churches to visit, and the sites of many a vanished city which, while not individually exceptional, add up to something memorable and distinctive. Another great attraction is the almost total absence of any military personnel and forbidden areas which elsewhere impinge upon the joys of walking in North Cyprus. There is also an abundance of bird life. Even those who are indifferent to ornithology will delight in the sound, colours, gait and explosive takeoff of the two types of Karpas partridge: Alectoris chukar and Francolinus francolinus. It is also home to a reclusive population of wild donkeys, who can be heard braying from the thickets but are seldom seen. After a recent demand for their culling by local farmers, a census established the herd at only 160. Plans to establish a natural park for their preservation remain on the drawing board.

Cape Elea and Bafra Beach and Sazlıköy (Livadhia)

These two areas of deserted coast are reached from separate turnings in Çayırova (Ayios Theodhoros) village, 10km east of Boğaz. Approaching the village from Boghaz take the first right turn, past an abandoned church, before twisting through 6km of scrubland to reach a small dune-shrouded beach in the lee of Zeytin Burnu (Cape Elea). A 1500m stroll west along an inland track brings you to the site of the classical city of **Knidhos**, the birthplace of Ctesias, a 5th-century BC historian.

The long, broad, sandy **Bafra Beach**, overlooked by a failed development and the Panoula peninsula, is 2km from the scruffy hamlet of Bafra (Vokolidha) which is reached by taking a right turn just as you leave Çayıvora to the east.

At Çayırova turn north for Zeybekköy (Ayios Eustathios) and then east to Sazlıköy (Livadhia). In the village, take the road to Mehmetcik (Galatia) (where you could stop off later at the bar) and turn left opposite the Turkish cemetery for the chapel of **Panayia Kyras**. Although the famous 9th-century mosaic of the Virgin has now totally disappeared from the apse, this tiny derelict whitewashed chapel remains a satisfying, spiritual place. An early Byzantine column is built into the north wall and the empty cistern echoes the tread of visitors. It is overlooked by outcrops of rock covered in smooth boulders which provide a fine view west towards Kantara.

Kumyalı (Koma tou Yialou)

Kumyalı is 23km east of Boğaz. Turn right just as you enter the village to reach a small beach beside a fishing harbour, further enhanced by the Pelican Restaurant. Kumyalı village was once a prosperous market town and a medieval centre of stone carving. Stone was quarried from the Kakozonora hills, which were last extensively worked to provide for the Venetian fortification of Famagusta. In its medieval heyday the village boasted 14 chapels, all of which are now either rebuilt or in total ruin. The most characteristic of the period, Ayios Solomon, stands on the high ground to the north of the village with an antique tomb for a crypt. Take any of the right-hand turnings in the village, most of which join a track running east and parallel to the shore for 4km. You will pass the ruins of Ayia Sophia before reaching the quarry chapel of Ayia Anna, which bears the Italian date, mdxxxiii die xii marzo, 12 March 1533.

The Church of Panayia Kanakaria

At the village of Ziyamet (Leonarisso) there is a back road that leads to the hamlet of Gelincik (Vasili) and on to the 12th-century church of Panayia (Our Lady of) Kanakaria on the western edge of Boltaşli (Lythrangomi). A key can usually be found through friendly but persistent enquiries at the café.

The walled monastic enclosure includes a small bell tower, a farmhouse with a delightful rustic arcade, an olive mill under a fig tree and some Byzantine capitals lying by the west door. An open porch was added in the 13th century to shelter the south door, thus adding to the confusion of barrel vaults, drums and domes covering this small church. The interior is subdivided into the traditional three aisles. The nave is given greater height and light by its two domes, in strong contrast to the dark side aisles which are dominated by piers, narrow wall-cut passageways and supporting arches. The four pendentives of the central dome each carry a 16th-century fresco of an Evangelist, but sadly the greatest treasure of the church has been stolen. Three holes in the plaster now mark the position of a wall mosaic in the central apse, which consists of a pair of archangels flanking an enthroned Virgin with Christ Child. It was the sole survivor of an earlier church generally considered to be 9th-century, though enthusiasts think the mosaic might be a rare example of pre-iconoclastic art from around AD 500.

The stolen mosaic eventually found its way to being offered to the Getty Museum but in 1991 it was recovered by the Orthodox Church of Cyprus in a successful legal action in the American. The mosaic is to be exhibited in the Byzantine Museum in Southern Nicosia.

Kuruova (Korovia): the Paleovikla Tomb

The Paleovikla Tomb is difficult if not actually dangerous to visit and can only be seen by a fit person looking for a challenge. From Boltaşli the road passes through the hamlets of Derince (Vathylakkas) and Avtepe (Ayios Symeon) before dropping down from the plateau to a wheat-growing valley overlooked by rounded hills. Stop at a stone bridge about 2km west of Kuruova (Korovia) village: the dark tomb entrance is on the other side of the valley, cut into the yellow stone rock face of the Paleovikla escarpment. There is no path, though it is possible to push through thorn thickets and scramble over gullies and fallen boulders to reach it. The ascent along a very narrow crumbling crawl-space cut into the weak strata of the cliff is made more hazardous by colonies of wild bees nesting in the eroded stone. Just within the rounded entrance of the tomb are a pair of observation chambers whose narrow window slits peer out from the rock face. The passageway then leads straight into the hillside, where a great triple-aisled hall has been hewn out of the living rock and equipped with a well. Around the hall are half a dozen burial chambers with niches carved into recessed beds of stone. Nothing has changed since Hogarth or Thubron enthusiastically described their visits in 1880 and 1960. Tales of robbers and hermits freely attach themselves to this extraordinary man-made cavern.

Kuruova (Korovia): the Nektovikla Ruins

All that remains of this square Bronze-Age fortress built with corner towers and fortified gateway, between 1800–1600 BC, are its excavated foundations. It may have housed a garrison from a powerful city like Enkomi-Alasia, or been the residence of some local lord. It is perched on a coastal escarpment a good 4km walk or jeep-ride south of Korovia. To reach it take the first, the westernmost, of the two tarmac roads going down into the Argaki Too Lachion valley and which deterioate into farm tracks. Keep left at both junctions to reach a dead end about 200km short of the sea between the Ayia Varvara hill to the west (with the ruins of a chapel dedicated to St Barnabas) and the Nektovikla ruins a 300m scramble uphill to the east.

From Korovia it is just 3km to Kaleburnu (Galinoporni), where this back road ends, though two tracks extend east and make an attractive walk to Dipkarpaz (Rizokarpaso). Kaleburnu is a rustic and pretty Turkish village wedged between the Vouno and Skoutelli hills. The eastern side of the Vouno is pock-marked with dozens of rock-cut tombs. The most extensive are by the ruined chapel of Ayia Anna, about 2km out of the village, for which you will need a guide.

Yassı Burnu (Cape Plakoti) Beach

This is one of the few accessible beaches on the north coast of Karpas, just outside Yenierenköy (Yialousa), 37km east of Boğaz on the way to Dipkarpaz (Rizokarpaso). Just east of the town take the first big track left, which bumps down to this long beach split in two by a sheltering rock. There are changing huts and ovens, but unless you have come well prepared you will need to drive 1.5km from this turning to reach the **Malibu Restaurant** by the fishing shelter.

Sipahı (Ayia Trias)

A 6th-century Byzantine church and baptistry have been discovered in a paddock surrounded by a grove of olive trees in the scattered hamlet of Sipahi. The easiest approach to the ruins is to take the coast road east of Yenierenköy (Yialousa) for 5km, then turn right and about 1km later stop by a derelict school bus on your right. The ruins are easier to understand by starting at the far corner of the excavations. Two town streets define the southern and western boundary of the town block occupied by the church. A suite of rooms surrounds an open hall, easily identified by its six standing columns. It is a cosy, almost domestic arrangement of rooms that may have been used as the bishop's residence. In the hall stands the offertory table, looking quite like a bird table, and an inscribed hollow column which served as a reliquary for the bones of a saint. Three eastern doors gave entrance to a wide mosaic-paved porch with an apsed side altar on its south wall. Another three doors led into the three-aisled interior of the church supported by two rows of five columns. The mosaic floor, unlike that at Soli, has been carefully composed in harmony with the architecture. There is no impious imagery, just a web of geometric fields with simpler designs for the side aisles. The nave is dominated by decorative bands surrounding a central walkway, which was enclosed by a low marble screen. The communicants processed up this passage, passing over two Greek inscriptions, to receive the sacrament at the foot of the raised altar. Beside the south aisle is the exonarthex, where the unbaptised catechists could watch but not partake in the mystery of the mass.

The baptistry is just to the southeast of the church. A central hall, once embellished with two pairs of columns, overlooks a large cruciform font. This was approached through a long passage where the initiate would be questioned before descending into the stepped font for the ritual three immersions of baptism. On the other side of the font are two lobbies where the new member would be symbolically clothed in white before being invited to partake of the Lord's feast.

Ayios Thyrsos and Ayios Photios

A derelict modern whitewashed church and the decaying Florya Restaurant stand 8km east of Yenierenköy (Yialousa) and serve as landmarks for the old stone chapel of Ayios Thyrsos on the other side of the road. It sits on a terrace beside the shore, filled with the sound of lapping waves. The dark interior is given a Stygian touch with its the sunken columns and pebble-paved floor from which a staircase leads down to a crypt, carved around an *ayiasma*, a sacred spring. Sufferers of skin diseases would seek a cure by washing first at this spring and then in the sea.

The chapel of Ayios Photios is 4km further east and a 200m walk uphill from the road. Traces of the Byzantine town of Selenias lie around the chapel, and antique columns, capitals and millstones have been built into the terraced walls of the surrounding fields. Only fragments of the original frescoes can be seen inside, apart from the prominent 17th-century wall painting of St Michael.

Dipkarpaz (Rizokarpaso) and Karpasia

At the centre of this sprawling farming village stand a brightly painted police station and separate Greek and Turkish cafés, overlooking the Church of Ayios Synesios and a new mosque. Dipkarpaz is the last area in North Cyprus to maintain a Greek community. It had once before served as a bastion of orthodoxy when the Greek bishopric of Famagusta was exiled to the Karpas by the Roman Catholic Church between 1222 and 1470. The bishops used Ayios Synesios as their cathedral, though only the eastern apses recall this period of exile. The bulk of the church, including the central dome, Gothic decoration and bell tower, was added in the 18th and 19th centuries.

From Dipkarpaz take the left turn uphill from the police station: pass under a house over the road and turn right at the Church of Ayios Trias before rattling downhill to the shore. Perched on the coast is the substantial ruin of the 12th-century **Church of Ayios Philon**. It sits amongst palm trees beside a dilapidated beach café, on the ruins of an early Byzantine cathedral and surrounded by traces of the ancient city of Karpasia. Ayios Philon is one of only half a dozen orthodox churches built in the Romanesque style (known as Norman in Britain). As these are only found in the Karpas, they were at first mistakenly thought to have been derived from the architecture of the nearby Crusader states in Syria.

The three-aisled interior of the church is divided by four central piers that once supported a dome-capped drum at the crossing. In the floor of the central apse a stairway leads down to a cistern filled by an *ayiasma*, a sacred spring. The exterior walls are decorated with blind arches recessed into the stonework. This is most complex at the south door, with five structural levels, and most playful on the triple apse, where blind windows flank the real apertures. The invariable proportion of the round Romanesque arch gives it a characteristic unity and dignity.

Outside the church is a scattering of Corinthian capitals and columns. These originally adorned the classical city but were reused in the 5th century AD to create a cathedral dedicated to St Philon, bishop of Karpasia and a noted biblical scholar. Philo was the chaplain to Pulcheria, the influential sister to the sibling co-emperors Arcadius and Honorius, and arrived in Cyprus in AD 401 to request that Epiphanios, the great bishop of Constantia-Salamis, might attend his sick mistress. Epiphanios at once recognized Philo's worth, appointed him his deputy and transported him to Karpasia before hurrying to the imperial court. The cathedral was burnt when Saracens destroyed the city in 802, but the site was reclaimed for Christianity 300 years later when the Romanesque church was built.

The 5th-century ruins to the south of the church retain a cut marble floor with a startling spiralling whorl, a design whose centrifugal pull must have had a striking resonance to those nervous catechumens who passed this way. The mosaic is set into the antechamber of the stepped baptismal font, which was overlooked by a rectangular marble hall. A circle within a square marks the position of the bishop's throne, which was flanked by pairs of columns. In plan it is almost identical to the other Karpas baptistry at Sipahı (Ayia Tria). The excavated passageway leads inland to the Bishop's Palace, where you can identify the remnants of a hexagonal pool that once stood in the central courtyard.

Shards and fragments of stone from the old city litter the surrounding fields. There are rock-cut tombs to be found in the hillface to the west, and the substantial eastern mole of the harbour extends 100m from the shore just to the north. This witnessed one of the more spectacular coups in the 4th-century BC wars for the control of Alexander the Great's Empire. Maverick Demetrius Poliorchetes, 'conqueror of cities', sailed his fleet straight into the harbour and subsequently used it as a base for his naval victory against Ptolemy, fought off Salamis, in 306 BC.

Aphendrika

About 7km east along the coast from Karpasia, the ruins of three churches mark the site of ancient Aphendrika, one of the six largest cities of Ptolemaic Cyprus. The small chapel of Ayios Yeoryios (St George) retains a fragment of its dome and an unusual double apse. Panayia Chrysiotissa, the seawards of the two larger buildings, is a simple 16th-century barrel-vaulted chamber built within the nave of a larger 12th-century church.

Panayia Asomatos is also a Romanesque church of the 12th century, but in slightly better condition. The sturdy round arches of the south aisle survive, their shape reflected in the blind arches set into the north and south walls. At first wood-roofed and tiled like the earliest churches (there are beam holes in the south aisle), it was later given barrel vaults when stone ribs were added to the piers. The triple apse has noticeably different stonework, which reveals its older origins. The toppled stone altar is an antique corded capital, a suitable architectural adaption for a trading city. Aphendrika had a harbour due north, and also made use of the port of Ourania in the western corner of Exarkhos Bay, which is about 2km east along a track leading past a few durable and reusable remains: rock-cut tombs, millstones and wells.

Panayia Apakou and Limanouri Beach

From Dipkarpaz a road leads southeast for 5km to a fishing harbour, the well-advertised Blue Sea Hotel (*see* p. 400) and the small chapel of Panayia Apakou. Just in front of the harbour stands an old carob warehouse, a fine example of traditional architecture with its wide internal arches set close together to provide a small span for the slight beams of the island. The knob of rubbish-strewn land to the east of the harbour was the site of the Iron-Age city of Khelones.

The dune-fringed empty beach of **Limanouri** is 5km to the south, and only accessible to walkers. About 800m along the road to Dipkarpaz from the hotel take a left turn onto a path (just after the sharp bend which crosses the gully of the Olos stream) before following the coastline. The central hillock of the three that overlook the beach is crowned by the ruined chapel of **Panayia Dhaphonda**, Our Lady of the Laurel, one of the many titles of the Virgin acting as a bridge between the classical and Christian eras.

Nangomi Bay

The most magnificent beach in Cyprus, a great crescent of clean golden sand surrounded by dunes and broken into two unequal parts by the Pakhyammos promontory, fills Nangomi Bay. The road passes Galounopetra Point, 4km short of the shrine of Apostolos Andreas, which gives a splendid view over the bay. It is inhabited by a virulent type of sandfly in high summer and is virtually undisturbed by humans, remaining one of the few secure nesting grounds of the turtle.

Apostolos Andreas

The pilgrimage centre of the Apostle Andrew is now in a mournful state of decay. It was once the Lourdes of Cyprus, served not by an organised community of monks but by a changing group of volunteer priests and laymen. Since 1974 it has been empty, maintained by distant gifts and the dwindling local Greek community. An enormous modern plaza of pilgrims' lodgings frames the slightly older monastery buildings wrapped around the church. This is now partly occupied by a police post where the passport details of all visitors are recorded. You are then free to find a caretaker, either Andreas or one of a shifting cast of old ladies who watch over a large pig, and pay your respects to the Virgin and the draped icon of St Andrew with its attendant collection of votive candles and trinkets. Below, the modern church steps lead down to a square, vaulted chapel, three baptismal basins fed by a sacred spring and an old wharf. It was on this site that St Andrew briefly landed in Cyprus on his final missionary journey back to his Palestinian homeland. His footfall revealed a spring whose waters miraculously healed the blind captain of his ship. A fortified monastery stood here in the 12th century, from which Isaac Comnenus negotiated his surrender to Richard the Lionheart, though the chapel built in the 15th century is the oldest surviving building.

Andreas

St Andrew was the brother of St Peter, who served John the Baptist and was

the first, 'O-Protoklitos', of the apostles to be called to the ministry by Jesus. Traditionally his missionary areas covered much of the medieval borderland of Byzantium, such as Macedonia and the Black Sea coast, with miraculous incidents set in Nicea, Thessalonica and Ethiopia. Images of his martyrdom depict him as a white-bearded old man of 80, tied to an olive-tree cross that stood by the sea-shore at Patras in the Peloponnese. He continued to preach for two days before he finally expired. He is the patron saint of Greece, Russia and Scotland, a protector of travellers and commander of winds. His feast day is celebrated on 15 August and 30 November.

The shrine only became a popular sanctuary with the miracle of Maria Georgiou in 1895. 17 years after the disappearance of her son, she received a dream in answer to her unceasing petitions to St Andrew, which instructed her to go from her native Cilicia to the neglected shrine of Apostolos Andreas at the tip of Cyprus. On the boat over she explained her journey to fellow passengers and particularly excited the attention of a young travelling dervish. He asked Maria how she would identify her lost son, so she told him of the peculiar pair of birthmarks he bore on his shoulder and chest. The dervish threw off his woollen cloak to expose the same marks and fell on his knees before his mother. He was then persuaded by the other tearful travellers to relate his own story: his kidnap by pirates, his sale in the slave market of Istanbul and his education as a devout Muslim. Within months the shrine received a stream of pilgrims which increased into a flood as the saint proved his power over a random tithe of supplicants, Greeks as well as Turks, sophisticated Athenians as well as local peasants.

Zafer Burnu (Cape Apostolos Andreas)

The cape, formerly known as Cape Dinaretum, the easternmost point of Cyprus, lies 5km up a dirt track from Apostolos Andreas through a haunted landscape of rocky coves and low maquis, with a propensity for damp sea mist. The Karpas peninsula terminates in a natural rock fortress known as Kastros. In the southern lee of this outcrop archaeologists have discovered and partially restored the circular stone huts of the oldest village in Cyprus. The inhabitants belonged to a pre-ceramic Neolithic culture (non-pottery-using farmers). It is a reclusive almost fearful location that invites some speculative imaginings—perhaps these first migrants were storm-tossed from Syria, which on fine days can be seen on the distant horizon.

On the northeast face of the outcrop stood the shrine of Aphrodite Acraea, whose rites were ancient and mysterious even in antiquity. No married woman was permitted into the sanctuary, but once in her lifetime a woman had to sit within its precincts with a plaited fillet in her hair, waiting for a man to throw a silver coin in her lap, saying 'In the name of the Goddess'. The coin then became sacred: it could not be refused and the man took the woman outside where they enjoyed each other.

The cape, its offshore reefs and ten islands, called the Klidhes, 'the Keys', were a notoriously dangerous area for early shipping, which relied on a coast hugging system of navigation. A lighthouse now operates on the largest of the Klidhes islands, sending out beams of light where once the headland of Cyprus was marked by a temple dedicated to the goddess of love.

Where to Stay and Eat

The Blue Sea Hotel, 5km southeast of Dipkarpaz (Rizokarpaso), is the traditional stopping-off point in the Karpas. It is run by a charming but shy family who catch fish, cook and look after the five bedrooms and one shared bathroom. There is no telephone and rarely any electricity. Prices can vary, depending on what they think of their guests, but a double room will usually cost £12 a night; dinner for two with wine about the same again. If the Blue Sea is full, there is usually a chance of a room at two seasonal restaurants just a few hundred metres further east, the Manastir and the Golden Beach. There are also rooms to rent in the villages of Dipkarpaz and Yenierenköy: look out for notices or ask in cafés.

In the Beginning

Cyprus is an island and a geological mass unto itself. The 'hard' Cypriot continental shelf is covered with molten rock that flowed out onto the deep ocean floor of the Tethys sea some 90 million years ago. This was covered in sedimentary deposits, formed from eons of dead sea creatures, which were compacted to form limestone as well as beds of clay and sand. These submarine layers were raised up from the ocean shore when the continents of Africa and Eurasia first began to grind together some tens of millions of years ago in the movement that formed the Alps. The Cyprus shelf was underthrust by Africa and lifted up 2000m. At first the Troödos mountains and the Gothic Range formed separate islands but these were united when the flat Mesaoria plain gradually emerged from the sea. Most of the island's surface is covered by limestone, except the central Troödos, where it has been eroded away to reveal the mineral-rich igneous core where the famous asbestos and copper ores of the island are found. Cyprus has always been an island, though at times only a strait some 20 miles wide has kept it apart from Syria or Turkey from where most of the island's indigenous flora and fauna derive.

For a long time her two mountain ranges formed separate islands, until the Mesaoria plain between them emerged about a million and a half years ago. Dense forests, wide deltas and lagoons were populated with a chance selection of mammals, which swam or were storm-tossed across on some natural raft. It was never home to the large carnivores, like lions or wolves, and remained a paradise for herbivores, which, free from predators, evolved a more appropriate size. Elephants had no need of their bulk and shrank to a mere yard high. The pig-sized Cypriot hippo spent less and less time in the water and learned to pick its way around the dry land on tiptoe. The dwarf deer could only amble, as, faced only with other herbivores like the wild boar, hare and moufflon it had forgotten how to run.

Predatory man poisoned this paradise in 8000 BC, destroying the island's unique fauna.

Trees

Cyprus is not a primary destination for a tree-man, though pleasure can be derived from the ancient groves of olive and carob in the foothills, the tighter ranks of citrus plantations in well watered valleys and the pine woods in the hills. The island was quantities of wood were also required for the charcoal needed to smelt the island's copper ore, an industry which was already well developed by 1600 BC. From the estimated 4 million tons of ancient slag found, economists have worked out that around 60 million tons of charcoal was required, which means that the island's entire stock of wood was burnt 16

Geology, Flora and Fauna

renowned for its forests in ancient times but, over more recent centuries, these have been destroyed for firewood and shipbuilding. Wood was a valuable export, especially to powerful but virtually treeless neighbours (if you exclude the palm) like Egypt. Vast times over. Clearly the ancient city states knew how to manage woodland efficiently. The damage seems to have been inflicted in the last five centuries. The healthy but destructive appetite of the goat, combined with a lack of management over the wild no-man's-land of the forested hills, had by the 19th century led to a seriously depleted stock. The British started re-afforestation, combined with protection from the goat herds, in the late 19th century. Though this has achieved impressive results in the Troödos and Paphos Forest districts, it was too late to save many varieties from extinction. Fortunately the indigenous Cyprus cedar (*cedrus brevifolia*), whose durable but lightweight wood was much in demand for ship construction, was saved but exists only on the slopes of Mount Tripylos and a valley, Cedar valley, just to its south. Forests in the higher altitudes are mostly composed of black pine, Aleppo pine, stone pine as well as Troödos pine (*pinus larico*) which are all suited to the Cyprus climate and can grow to considerable heights. Older patches of woodland may contain the smaller, alder-leafed or golden oak. In the river valleys are the usual planes, alders and maples; otherwise the lower land below the pine forest zone supports figs, olives (*olea europaea*), cypress, carob (*ceratonia siliqua*) and the eucalyptus of Australia. The larger shrubs such as tamarisk, lentisk (or mastic tree) and myrtle are fairly evenly distributed, as are the strawberry and turpentine trees.

Wild Flowers

Cyprus has a wealth and variety of wild flowers. There are about 1800 different kinds of flowering plants on the island, a bewildering assortment that ranges across European, typically Mediterranean and some exclusively Cypriot plants. What follows is a brief summary of some of the more interesting flowers which can be fairly easily discovered. The climate is hotter and drier than elsewhere in the Mediterranean and the soil is generally chalky. The flowering season is from autumn to spring.

In late September, when the first rains are due, one of the earliest flowers to push up through the dry ground will be the small mauve squill, shortly followed by the late-flowering narcissus found dotted around the coastal garigue.

As autumn moves into winter the small grape-hyacinths appear and one of the truly Cypriot flowers: the *cyclamen Cyprium*. This can be distinguished from other cyclamens present at the same time by its fragrant white flowers with purple blotches at the base. Both pink and white cyclamen are common from December to May. They were considered to have been engendered from the blood of Adonis when he was killed by the wild boar. In the depth of winter the Cape sorrell, that most invasive winter intruder imported from South Africa, carpets fields, orchards and roadsides with its bright yellow nodding flowers. The crown anemone is a sight to see in its many colours, white first followed by red, pink, lavender, violet and blue, in either its dwarf or normal form, from December through to the spring. It can be confused with the Turban buttercup, which comes out at the same time in deep red, yellow and white, but is distinguished by buttercup leaves.

In midwinter the scrubland near the coast will be lit up by the pretty pink Romulea flowers poking out of the bare ground before their leaves form. They are more difficult to find on cloudy days as they are only open in the sunlight. As elsewhere around the Mediterranean, asphodels which have been hiding all summer in any spare broken ground will spring up in the January rain, forming clouds of white with their tall wands of delicate flowers. The ancients held that they were the flower of Elysium, the resting place of the dead. The blue anchusas come out with the asphodels and can still flower as late as May on higher ground.

January is the time to see the greatest array of colour. The ground is covered in a myriad small flowers such as the blue pimpernel, the pale yellow euphorbia or sun spurge, the white wild garlic, hairy milk vetch, pale stars of Bethlehem, wild blue iris and the ugly and poisonous henbane clutching stone walls and ruins. The low, prickly, spiny burnet changes from brittle clumps of thorns to green glossy bushes with red fruits in February which brighten the lower treeless hillsides. The mandrake flourishes on hard dry wasteland and could be mistaken for African violets in flower. A member of the potato family, it is surrounded by superstitions because of its leg-like roots, and its propensity for shrieking when pulled up.

From February to April, a feature of the barren hillsides is the sage-leaved rock-rose or *cistus*. At Easter the French lavender conveniently flowers in time to decorate Orthodox churches on Good Friday. It thrives on rocky foothills and is abundant after rain. In central Cyprus the giant fennel can be seen by the roadsides and cannot fail to impress with its yellow umbrellas of flowers carried up to 10ft high. As spring progresses, wild purple gladioli can be seen in cornfields and scrubland together with wild peonies and blue tassel hyacinths. Wherever there is some dampness the butterwort can be found, looking like a white violet. In stony places, cracks in rocks or fissured walls the white-flowered caper will scramble, bearing the fruit in early summer which is pickled as an aperitif. When the oxalis are over, their place is taken by the brilliant roadside display of the golden crown daisy, whose flowers are gathered to dye hard-boiled eggs for Easter.

Cyprus abounds in small orchids which form a study in themselves. They are mostly to be found from April to May in the limestone hills of the Gothic Range. The largest and most easily seen orchid is the Anatolian with pale purplish pink, occasionally white, flowers borne on separate spikes. Unique to Cyprus are many insect orchids, so called because their flowers mimic various insects. Another indigenous flower is the Troödos alyssum which is found only on the northern slopes of the Troödos. It is not spectacular, but patches of its silvery leaves bearing tiny yellow flowers spread up the hillsides in cushion-shaped clumps.

In August the sea squill surprises with its tall, thin leafless stems bearing fronds of pinky grey florets above inhospitable rocky ground. The sea lily performs similarly at the same time but on coastal dunes. Its short-stemmed, white, daffodil-shaped flowers sweetly scent the evening air. As summer reaches its height the land is parched and only purple-headed thistles thrive on rough ground. Colour is provided through summer by the oleanders which are also commonly cultivated as ornamental shrubs, but can be found in the wild, following the lines of the remaining water courses or dried out ditches. It is a robust shrub with large sweet-smelling pink flowers above narrow grey-green pointed leathery leaves. Oleander is probably 'the rose growing by the brooks' of Ecclesiasticus.

Birds

Cyprus is a Mediterranean island, and as such remains a place where birds still exist to be shot at, netted and trapped, not spotted. Any person who has walked much on Cyprus can attest to the scattering of shot-gun cartridges found in even the most desolate corners of the island. Cypriots are near inured to the distress this causes to their northern European visitors. The different social values are summed up by the story of a sage Greek hostess who hurriedly removes a plate of tasty small birds her granddaughter has brought to the table of her English guests. In the kitchen she explains that it is taboo for the British as they believe that after death their souls are turned into little birds that fly south towards heaven.

Cyprus is on a north–south migration route and there are many birds in transit, some in vast flocks, some in small clusters. These migrating birds may only rest for a few days. March to May is the period of northward migration and August to October the southward. The list of resident birds has few surprises for those familiar with the general stock of European birds. The Griffon vulture is the largest and the most distinctive in flight due to its 8ft wing-span which sometimes encourages a mistaken identification as an eagle, but there are no eagles now in Cyprus. It can be spotted throughout the island but especially at the eastern edge of the Gothic Range, between St Hilarion and Kantara. Smaller resident raptors include the Scops and Little owl. Game birds are represented by the Francolin, similar to the English partridge, and the Chikor which is similar to the French partridge. They can both be seen throughout the island, but especially in the Kantara peninsula. On the coast you will see the lesser black-backed gull, the herring gull and Audoins gull as well as the common cormorant or shag. The black-headed gull is a winter visitor only. There are several resident warblers and tits and the island boasts an indigenous species, the Cyprus warbler, found only here in scrub and open woodland. It resembles the more widespread Sardinian warbler but without the red eye and with very strongly marked black and white underpants.

The most spectacular of the winter visitors is the flamingo which inhabits the salt lakes of Larnaca and Akrotiri sometime between October and March. Their arrival depends on the lakes' water levels and a sufficient food source. A lack of rain may delay their arrival to January but when they do come, with as many as 5000 birds at Akrotiri and 1000 at Larnaca, it is a sight not to be missed. Many types of duck—shelduck, mallard, teal, wigeon, pintails and shovellers—also visit the salt lakes, dams and coasts in winter.

The most beautiful of the summer visitors, between April and September, are the small colourful bee-eaters, the larger pale blue roller, the yellow and black golden oriole and the unmistakable hoopoe of pink plumage and black and white barred wings, body and tail.

Snakes, Moufflon and Wild Donkeys

The reclusive Cypriot moufflon, an indigenous wild mountain sheep that was hunted to the verge of extinction and now survives with an estimated 200 breeding pairs in the protected reserve of the Paphos Forest District, is much talked about but seldom seen outside the enclosure at the Stavros Tis Psokas Forest Station. There are a similar number of vocal but shy wild donkeys in the Karpas peninsula. The island is better known for its snakes, which can be seen moving purposefully through the undergrowth in spring and autumn. They hibernate in winter and are less active in summer though they feature in live exhibitions at Skouilli village and Limassol. The more common varieties include the pink worm snake (*typhlops vermicularis*), and the large whip snake (*coluber jugularis*) which has a long, thin body with a dark grey to mottled brown patterning. The coin snake (*coluber nummifer*) is dressed in leopard on a rock khaki camouflage background. The cat snake (*telescopus fallax*) appears very like the coin snake but is usually smaller with paler skin. The Cyprus whip snake (*coluber Cypriensis*) is a long dark green to black serpent while the Montpelier snake (*malopon Monspessulianus*) has a long dry-grey body and a narrow head. The blunt-nosed viper (*vipera lebetina lebetina*), alias *Saittaros*, has a broad head and thick body with even paler markings than the cat snake and a distinctive horny tail. It is one of only two poisonous snakes on the island but the only one whose bite can kill. It is not actively aggressive but will defend itself if disturbed.

Cypriot pottery offers an extraordinary cultural continuity. It connects, with disarming ease, the world of 4500 BC to that of our contemporary artists and artisans. It is a liberating, and also a sobering process, to glance back over the millennia of art and realise that, for all our other abilities, we in the 20th century cannot hope to match the inventiveness of the third millennium BC or the haunting sincerity of the images of the Archaic era.

Any short stroll through a local market, along the corridors of a museum, past the polished windows of a smart boutique or across the burnt acres of a ruined city, will reveal that the Cypriots have an exceptional affinity with pottery . If you have a secret weakness for picking up ancient shards, Cyprus can show you such a glut that you will be in danger of being bored by your destructive hobby. Shards are broken fragments of pottery that in the normal course of events are virtually indestructible. As each culture has shown marked preferences in its taste for pots, the ordered classification and dating of pottery has become one of the essential yardsticks of archaeology. Its importance is further stressed by the almost total decay of other household materials, such as wood, cloth, leather and painted plaster. Fortunately as an amateur one can ignore the academic battles over chronologies and admire them as precious remnants of 6000 years of plastic art.

The First Potters, 4500–4000 BC

Though we have the evidence of their clay-daubed huts and primitive lime kilns, the first Neolithic culture in Cyprus remained ignorant of pottery. The technique was imported into the island around 4500 BC with the second wave of settlers. This first pottery is consciously based on the shapes and textures of existing tools. Sturdy handles imitating leather or rope stress the need for containers that could be hung from the beams of huts, safely out of the reach of rodents and children, in the days before cupboards and shelves. Many of the pottery shapes are directly based on gourds (which still survive in use as containers on the island) and some even have been given gourd-like dimples. Other pottery shapes suggest themselves as copies of the low stone bowls carved from river boulders or those that were hewn from wood. Incised chevrons broken by lines are applied as decoration, perhaps inspired by decorative notchings cut into wood, gourd, or human skin as a tattoo.

Chalcolithic, 4000–2500 BC

In the Chalcolithic period these same shapes can be recognized, though the pale island appreciable delicacy developing in the thick-rimmed bowls, mugs, 'egg cups' and gourds.

Cypriot Ceramics

clay is often painted with a red slip. They may still appear somewhat crude and slightly bumpy in design but, even so, there is an This growing artistry reaches its culmination in egg-shaped vats, boldly decorated with red designs. Two forms of regional decoration emerged: comb brush-strokes in the south and rippled red on white in the north. However, aside from an unique pottery idol, in the Pierides museum in Larnaca, there is nothing to match the haunting mystery of the idols carved from grey-green stone in this period. These deities, with outstretched arms and crouched knees, are depicted in the attitude of a crucifixion. Some have blank 'Cycladic' faces; some have defined features; others wear a small crucifix. They almost certainly represent the annual sacrifices that early agricultural cultures considered necessary for the fertility of the fields.

The Age of Invention in the Early Bronze Age, 2700–1900 BC

The Early Bronze Age is one of the world's most inventive periods for modelled pottery. There is an explosion of shapes, textures and designs: bird-shaped pots, decorated loom weights, multiple bowls, triple cups, two-headed jars, double spoons and slender grebe-shaped jugs. The complete museum pieces should each be seen as a moulded sculpture and, though one can recognize types, there is no uniformity. The first applied decoration, groups of eggs and snakes, has an easily recognizable sexual and spiritual symbolism—and one that we still live with in the familiar egg-and-dart plaster cornice. In addition, they are the first modelled figurines, ranging from a familiar image of daily life—for example, butter-making—to powerful representations of religious life. The creations of this period were coated with a creamy mix before firing to give a distinctive polished finish in either red or black or both. The shards in the field are quite easy to recognize, with a pale inside face, a dappled polish on the exterior and a thick, grey, gritty texture on the broken edge. Vast vats and strainers suggest corn-fermented drinks, crude beers, that were prepared as part of ritual life. They were a form of communion with the young sacrificial god that, when assisted with music and dance, brought on the divine madness and delirium remembered in the natures of Apollo and Dionysus.

Middle Bronze Age, 1900–1600 BC

As we progress into the Middle Bronze Age, which compared with its predecessors is a brief period of 300 years, there is a settling down of shapes and forms which coincides with a growth in decoration and colour. **Black slip** was originally an accidental discoloration caused by sulphides burning out of the wood, but this was soon developed into a technique. It was used by itself to create a metallic burnish, or with red to suggest a ripening fruit. White-painted wares make their first appearance: the creamy white pots are covered in multi-coloured designs usually formed from chevrons, crisscrossings and tartan checks. Notice the arrival of single figurines such as a cow-shaped cream jug, celebrating the cattle and oxen which had been imported onto the island in the previous era.

The Late Bronze Age (1650–1050)

Though the first rectangular box-like rooms appear in the Middle Bronze Age, neatly dressed stone and the flat surface were developed in the Late Bronze Age. This led to the creation of **base ring ware**, a mysterious-sounding product which simply refers to the sausage of clay applied to the base of a pot in order to make it balance on a flat surface. This is mirrored by the so called **poppy-headed** pots which were exported to Egypt and the Near East and which may have contained opium. Alongside these functional developments was an even more refined decorative scheme with greater balance. This can be most easily appreciated on the elegant lightweight **white ware** with its characteristic dark brown hatchings composed of chains of crossed diamonds and chevrons—motifs that are still used in kilims, carpets and tatoos. The typical wide-bottomed pots with open handles and the shallow shape of the smaller bowls suggest a filling of porridge or some frothy brew of sweetened fermented milk. In the same period we also meet the first imports: the characteristic **crater pots** of the Mycenaeans who were merchant-warriors established on the Greek coast. These Mycenaean imports give us the first glimpse of the classic silhouettes of Hellenistic pottery but also of a stronger and more forceful decorative tradition. Interconnecting swirls, budding spirals, waves and fish scales frame bold images of bulls, charioteers, and octopi with enormous straddling tentacles. Some of these designs betray the influence of the sophisticated palace culture of Minoan Crete. At the same time there is also the red and black painted pottery coming from Syria-Canaa (and particularly from its main port of Ugarit). The shapes are dramatically different: fantastically elongated jars amongst more practical- looking unguent jars, hip flasks and small slender amphorae. Egyptian influences can be recognized here, although direct imports from the Nile tended to be stone, such as the instantly recognizable alabaster urns. Cypriot-produced pottery of the Late Bronze Age experimented with copies and new shapes as well as continuing with its own traditions.

The Dull Geometric of the Iron Age, 1050–750 BC

The Late-Bronze-Age civilization of Cyprus, having absorbed two waves of Mycenaean settlers, was itself destroyed by barbarian invaders who sailed down the north coast, in around 1050 BC. This wholesale destruction coincided with the spread of iron weapons, the horse and the pottery wheel. The latter produced uniform and utilitarian plates and bowls which are known as **geometric ware**. The fired clay is left pale and unburnished with decoration restricted to black lines, either perfect circles or hatching formed from straight lines. Despite the addition of red, the collections of geometric ware with their immaculately traced circles appear maddeningly uniform after the exuberant individuality of the earlier ages. There is also a style that has been burnished an ugly grey, presumably in imitation of the powerful new iron technology. Though there is no hard evidence, it has been suggested that this dramatic difference in style also reflects the change from women's individual modelled pottery to male team work.

The Phoenicians, who originated from six trading cities along the Lebanese coast, had begun to reopen the old trade routes in the 9th century and helped usher in the Archaic culture. Despite the magnificence of Phoenician imports—carved ivory, gems, jewellery, early glass and majestically wrought bronze—there is only a slow improvement in ceramics. Polished backgrounds and colour inversions are reinvented before we catch the first breath of life with the addition of plant motifs (typically a stylized palm, young wheat ear or lotus bud) to the austere bi-coloured geometric circles. Then suddenly in the 600s the potteries of eastern Cyprus produce

'free field' ware—

characteristic jugs bearing exuberant and imaginative creatures, bulls and especially the haunting sinuous birds. These fantastic creatures are often associated with swastikas and an arrow-fishbone device that expresses emerging vegetal growth. They are vivid expressions of a system of belief centred around a cyclical continuity based on a careful observation of nature. This is personified by an all-encompassing Mother Goddess whose relationship with her doomed brother-lover-son gives a recurring pattern to the otherwise anarchic flux of existence. Thousands of male clay figurines have been found from this era, piled up around the altars of forgotten rural sanctuaries, with especially rich collections unearthed at Ayia Irini and the temple of Apollo at Kourion. They represent the worshipper with his hand often raised in salute, a physical reminder to the young god of agriculture and war, of a past sacrifice—and its attendant request. They span many centuries and degrees of wealth, ranging from a crude tubular and almost faceless figures to figurines cast in moulds, and delicately crafted representations of mounted and chariot-riding warriors—and viewed collectively they sport a spectacular assortment of hats. Other shrines have produced scenes of childbirth, breadmaking and sea journeys. The city of Marion (modern Polis) developed a distinctive jug with its spout formed from an applied female figure holding a miniature jug. Side by side with these developments are the Archaic carvings in the pale local limestone. Both men and women share that hint of a smile that expresses calm serene confidence. They also share the attenuated, emphasised eyes of the Near East where you can almost catch a glint of kohl, colour and careful manicure from the carefully defined lids and eyebrows. Male facial hair is carved with a delight in decorative detail to almost equal the superbly dignified female busts: veiled, bejewelled, crowned, bare-breasted women of regal power. Some of the greatest examples from this era, such as the vast statues of the Eastern deity Bes, or the intimate and effeminate portraits of temple boys, are now housed in foreign museums.

The Triumph of Attican Imports

The 5th century BC witnesses the triumph of Greek art and the end of a distinctive Cypriot identity. Local pottery is brushed aside by the celebrated Attic ware imported from the great cities of Athens and Corinth with its masterly depiction of mythological and epic scenes. Local traditions in stone carving survive longer but eventually even religious sculpture follows that irresistible fusion of harmony, grace and movement invented by Greece. The taste for marble and the island's lack of this stone prohibits the development of any later local school. In the Hellenistic and Roman period (325 BC–325 AD) the high ground of artistic experiment is taken over by glass and silver-ware. Pottery becomes cheap, simple and standardized. Functional terracotta amphorae, storage jars and plain red slip table ware produced and traded all over the Mediterranean. Oil lamps, religious figurines and impressed table ware are churned out from stone moulds that were cut in Greece.

Medieval Sgraffito

Sgraffito ware was produced on the island between the 12th and 16th century, presumably in different shapes though only the bowls that have survived. It has a distinctive quick-drawn fluency of line with sketchy hatched decoration washed with casual tin and copper-oxide glazes, giving attractive sheens of green, yellow and brown. A youth,

a pair of lovers or birds are favourite early motifs, often set amongst swirls of floral geometry. In later periods, animals—birds, an eagle, fishes, a dragon or a goat—seem to take over the decorative repertoire, before giving way to an increasingly lifeless decorative scheme.

16th–19th Centuries

After the Ottoman conquest no sgraffito ware was produced and only small quantities of Iznik ware, characterised by gorgeous coloured floral patterns (exhibited in the Arsenal tower at Famagusta), were imported. However recent excavations at Lapithos (Lapta) have revealed furnaces, constructed in the 16th century, that carried on some aspects of the medieval sgraffito tradition and produced glazed and crudely painted decorative bowls well into the 19th century. Varosha, the Greek commercial quarter outside Famagusta, produced a plain yellowish glazed ware in this period. The Kouzarides guild at Varosha produced water vessels in a light clay with flat bottoms, made on pottery wheels. They would also decorate the vessels with moulded snakes, animals on shoulders and faces, in striking similarity to past eras. Otherwise the rural production centres turned out a traditional deep red earthenware that could almost belong to any historical age. It was made by hand on a primitive wheel (the *gyristari*) by guilds of village women who worked at home. Decoration was engraved or stamped on a variety of bowls, pots and jars, all of which have their proper descriptive titles: *kouzes* is a two-handled water jar, *botides* a one-handled jar, and *vatooes* a jar with no handles. In the countryside, pots with rounded bottoms which could be dug into the soil remained much more useful than those with flat bottoms. The Mastorises guild of Kornos, in the hills west of Larnaca, were the principal producers, matched by a group of three villages to the southwest of Mount Olympus: Phini, Ayios Demetrios and Kaminaria. The Koutzatzines, the female guild of Phini, were assisted by their men who made *pitharades*, large wine jars, from applied strips of clay over a 12-day period, a technique which has been traced back to 2100 BC.

Acropolis	The highest fortified hilltop of a Greek city which often developed into its religious centre.
Aga	Commander; Ottoman title of rank.
Amphora	Tall, long-necked jar which was the basic storage and transport unit of ancient trade. It had a pointed base which allowed for it to be dug securely into the earth and helped stop shifting in long boat journeys.
Amphitheatre	An oval arena surrounded by tiers of seating.
Apse	A semi-circular recess covered by an arch or dome. Apses were a feature of late Roman architecture, often used in baths and public halls, that were borrowed by the Church to emphasise the eastern end of churches. A row of three eastern apses is a distinctive feature of Orthodox churches.
Ashlar	Technical term for masonry of squared stones which first appeared in Cypriot buildings in the Late Bronze Age.
Bailey	The defended outer courtyard of a castle.
Barbican	Defensive works outside a gate.
Basilica	Originally a Roman law court and commercial exchange, whose one broad nave flanked by two side aisles was taken as a model for the first purpose-built churches of the 4th century.
Bastion	A defensive work, often used to refer to a fortified artillery platform that projected from the line of the walls.
Bema	Raised part of an apse in an Orthodox Church, whose original use was as a speaker's platform in the democratic assemblies of ancient Greece.
Buttress	A construction built to contain the lateral thrust against a wall, of which a flying buttress is connected to the wall by an arch.
Chiton	An ancient Greek garment; the short sleeveless (Doric) variety was used to depict lesser figures, the longer sleeved (Ionic) tunic used for saints, apostles and Christ.
Cippus	An ancient stone memorial, often tubular, inscribed and shaped like an altar for the offering of libations to the dead.
Crater/Kratir	Large two handled classical wine goblet used in the days when wine was always mixed with water.
Enkleistra	Hermitage.
Entablature	A decorated lintel, which in the classical scheme of architecture is divided into three: the upper portion is known as the cornice, the middle as the frieze and the lower third as the architrave.
Escutcheon	A decorative carved shield, or similar heraldic device.
Finial	Decorative ornament that crowns an arch or pinnacle.
Gargoyle	A water spout carved in the form of a grotesque face, mythical creature or savage animal.

Han	Ottoman term for a caravansarai or fondouk, an enclosed secure courtyard surrounded by simple apartments and workshops for the use of travelling artisans and traders.
Icon/Eikon	A portable panel painted with a religious image for veneration, *see* Icon Museums at Nicosia and Paphos, p. 117 and 248.
Iconostasis	The screen in front of the altar sanctuary in an Orthodox church. Originally low and built of stone piers, it slowly evolved into a magnificently carved and gilded wooden screen hung with precious icons.
Konak	Ottoman mansion.
Machicolation	Projecting wooden gallery of a fortification that was suspended from a wall by stone corbels. It was equipped with openings in the floor through which the approaches to a gateway could be swept with fire or noxious substances.
Mameluke	Officials who were acquired as child slaves and trained to fill high government posts in Muslim states. These officials assumed the sovereignity of Egypt in the medieval period and in revenge for the destruction of Alexandria invaded Cyprus in 1426.
Merlon	The upright portion, the teeth, of a crenellated battlement.
Mihrab	Arched niche in a mosque which indicates the direction of the holy town of Mecca for Muslim prayers.
Minaret	Tower attached to a mosque with external galleries from which the muezzin (or his loudspeaker) issues the call to prayer. In Cyprus the minarets follow the Ottoman tradition and are round with a *muquarna* supported balcony and a conical, now often metallic, summit.
Mimber/Minbar	Pulpit-like staircase in a mosque that is used for the noontide Friday sermon.
Muezzin	Muslim call to prayer, and also the caller.
Narthex	The lobby or outer porch on the west end of an Orthodox church, sometimes known as a galilee in western Europe.
Oda	Formal reception room of an Ottoman house.
Paşa/Pasha	Ottoman governor or high official, who were ranked into one, two or three horse tail banners.
Petra	Stone.
Pithos	Large terracotta storage jar for oil, wine or corn.
Pyxis	Cylindrical vase.
Quatrefoil	A decorative Gothic circle internally divided into four leaves.
Rhyton	A drinking horn.

Glossaries

Rose Window	A round window subdivided like the petals of a rose-flower with internal spokes.

Scarp & counterscarp	Defensive embankments for absorbing artillery fire on either side of a ditch or moat.
Spring	The point at which an arch rises from its supporting structure.
Synthronon	Semi-circular rows of seats for the clergy in the apse of early Byzantine churches.
Tchiflik	Hereditary estate from the Ottoman period.
Temenos	Sacred boundary wall.
Templon	Low marble screen that seperated the sanctuary from the nave before the development of the iconostasis.
Trefoil	Tracery divided into three leaves.

Glossary of Religious and Iconographic Terms

Achrastos	Immaculate, spotless; one of the titles of the Virgin Mary.
Aeiparthenos	Literally 'Ever Virgin', for in Orthodox doctrine Mary was a virgin both before and after the birth of Jesus.
Anargyri, Ayii	Literally the silverless saints, such as the physician saints, Cosmas and Damian.
Anastasis	Known as the Harrowing of Hell in the West, when the resurrected Christ shattered the gates of Hell and rescued the righteous. In Byzantine art this is symbolized by the dragging of Adam and Eve from the deep sleep of the grave, watched by the more alert figures of King David and Solomon.
Angelos	Angel: ranked, according to Dionysios the Aeropagite who recorded St Paul's vision of the third heaven, into three hierachies subdivided into three choirs. The angelic order of counsellors is composed of seraphim, cherubim (who have no bodies and are both depicted with just their heads enclosed by multiple wings), and thrones. All three are shaded red, the colour of love. The angelic order of governors is divided into the choirs of dominions, virtues and powers who are blue, the colour of light and knowledge. The angelic order of messengers is divided amongst the choirs of principalities, archangels (such as Gabriel, Michael and Raphael) and angels. The latter assumes a guardianship of every baptized Christian.
Antiphonitis	Respondent.
Athanasiotissa	Most Immortal (of mankind), a title of the Virgin Mary.
Ayia/Agia	Female Saint.
Ayii Pantes	All Saints.
Ayia Trias	Holy Trinity.
Ayios/Agios	Male Saint.
Blacherniotissa	A representation of the Virgin with raised hands in prayer and a medallion of the Christ Child superimposed over her chest.
Deesis	'The Supplication', which is depicted as Christ Enthroned,

flanked by the Virgin and St John the Baptist. The two outside figures are turned slightly inward, caught in the act of interceding with the stern direct gaze of Christ in Judgement. It is also a graphic demonstration of the link between the two scriptures, Mary the temple girl and John the last prophet are the fulfillment of the Old Testament. They close one story and introduce the greater revelation of Jesus.

Eleousa	Literally 'Merciful', an appellation for the Virgin when depicted holding Christ in her right arm.
Gabriel	One of the seven archangels, famous as the messenger who informed St Anne of the birth of the Virgin Mary, Zacharias that of St John, the Virgin that of Christ (an event known as the Annunciation) and who dictated the Koran to the prophet Mohammed. Often depicted with St Michael, with whom he guards the doors of a church against the devil and escorts the Virgin Blacherniotissa in the apse.
Hodegatria	Literally 'Conductress', a title of the Virgin when depicted holding Christ with her left arm.
Mandorla	Italian for almond and also an iconographic term for an almond-shaped aura of brilliant light that surrounds Jesus Christ in any scenes after the Resurrection. The mandorla is often enclosed in a multi-coloured border suspended by angels, and seems to have originated from a Persian device to denote supernatural powers.
Metamorphosis	Transfiguration.
Michael	Winged archangel often depicted as a warrior who commanded of the host of heaven against the rebel angel Lucifer. He ranks first amongst the seven great archangels and with Gabriel has the honour of escorting the Virgin Blacherniotissa in the apse of Orthodox churches.
Panagia/Panayia	'All Holy', first of the titles of the Virgin Mary and often used in isolation. In full, 'Our All Holy, Immaculate, Most Blessed and Glorified Lady, mother of God and Ever Virgin Mary.'
Pantocrator	Christ, depicted as the Ruler of the World, which is often painted on the central dome above the nave.
Prodromos	The Fore Runner, a title of St John the Baptist.
Stavros	Cross.
Theotokos	Mother of God, the title awarded to the Virgin Mary in the Third Council at Ephesus in preference to Nestorius's Mother of Christ, or Mother of Man.

Glossary of Common Greek Terms

Aloni	Threshing floor.
Argaki, Argakin	Stream.

Ayia, Agia	Saint, female.
Ayios, Agios	Saint, male.
Kato	Lower, often used to distinguish the lower part of a town or village, as in Kato Paphos and Kato Lefkara.
Khryso	Golden, as in the monastery of Khrysorroyiatissa.
Lakkos	Well.
Linos	Wine press.
Mandra	Sheepfold.
Megalos	Large.
Moni	Monastery.
Moutti	Summit.
Neos, Nea, Neo	New, as in (misleadingly) the Roman city of Nea Paphos.
Nisi, Nisos	Island.
Paleo, Paleos, Palea	Old, as in Paleo-Paphos and Palaeo-lithic.
Panayia, Panagia	Literally All Holy, first of the titles of the Virgin Mary.
Panayiri	Holy Day, a holiday linked to a religious festival.
Pano	Upper, as in Pano Lefkara.
Petra	Stone.
Potamos	River.
Stavros	Cross.
Vouni, Vouno, Vounon	Hill or mountain.
Xeros	Dry, as in the typically Cypriot river name, Xero-potamos.

Glossary of Common Turkish Terms

Ada	Island.	Kopru	Bridge.
Askeri Bölge	Military area.	Köy	Village.
Baghçe	Garden.	Kule	Tower.
Bedestan	Covered market.	Kücük	Small.
Belediye	Town hall.	Kütüphahe	Library.
Büyük	Large.	Liman	Harbour, cove.
Caddesı	Street.	Meydanı	Square.
Cami	Mosque.	Mukhtar	Village headman.
Çarşi	Market.	Müzesi	Museum.
Çesme	Fountain.	Plaj	Beach.
Dağı, Dağları	Mountain, mountains.	Şadirvan	Ablutions fountain.
Deniz	Sea.	Saray	Palace.
Girilmez	No entry.	Sokağı	Avenue.
Hammam	Bath house.	Tekke	Sufi monastery.
Hisar	Castle.	Tepe	Hill.
Kapi	Gate.	Türbe	Tomb.
Kilise	Church.	Yol	Road.

Greek Pronunciation Guide

Letter	Pronunciation		Letter	Pronunciation
Αα	*a*		Νν	*n*
Ββ	*v*		Ξξ	*ks* at begining, or *x*
Γγ	*y/g* before a, o and i; *y* before e		Οο	*o* as in cot
Δδ	*th* as in this		Ππ	*p*
Εε	*e* as in bet		Ρρ	*r*
Ζζ	*z*		Σσ	*s*
Ηη	*ee*		Ττ	*t*
Θθ	*theory*		Υυ	*ee*
Ιι	*ee*		Φφ	*f*
Κκ	*k/tsch*		Χχ	*ch* as in loch
Λλ	*l*		Ψψ	*ps*
Μμ	*m*		Ωω	*o* as in cot

Paired Letters	Pronunciation		Paired Letters	Pronunciation
ΑΙαι	*e* as in penny		ΓΓγγ	*ng*
ΑΥαυ	*av/af*		ΓΚγκ	*g/ng* mid word
ΕΙει	*ee*		ΜΠμπ	*b*
ΟΙοι	*ee*		ΝΤντ	*d/nd* mid word
ΕΥευ	*ev/ef*		ΤΣτσ	*ts*
ΟΥου	*ou* as in tour		ΣΙσι	*sh*

Turkish Pronunciation Guide

Letter	Pronunciation		Letter	Pronunciation
Cc	*j*		Iı (no dot)	p*u*t with a broad smile
Çç	*ch*		Jj	*zh* as in treasure
Gg	*g* as in bag		Öö	*ur* through pouting lips
–Ğ–ğ	silent and lengthens preceding vowel		Şş	*sh*
			Üü	*ew* through pouting lips
Hh	*ch* as in loch		Yy	lengthens preceding vowel

Basic Vocabulary

English	Greek	Turkish
Hello	*yá sou/khérete*	*merhaba*
Goodbye	*adío*	*allahismarladik* or *güle güle*
Please/thank you	*parakaló/efkharistó*	*lütfen/tesekkür ederim*
Yes/no	*neh/ókhi*	*evet/hayir*
Good morning	*kalí méra*	*günaydin*
Good evening/night	*kalí spéra/kalí níkhta*	*iyi aksamlar/iyi geceler*
How are you?/fine	*tí kánete?/kalá ímeh*	*nasilsinizi?/iyiyim*
I don't understand	*dhen katalavéno*	*anlamiyorum*
Excuse me	*signómi*	*pardon*
Do you speak English?	*mípos miláte angliká?*	*ingilizce biliyor musunuzi?*
Good/bad	*kaló/kakó*	*iyi/kötü*
How much does it cost?	*póso káni?*	*bu, ne kadari?*

A **paperback shortlist** includes Colin Thubron's *Journey into Cyprus*, Lawrence Durrell's *Bitter Lemons*, David Hunt's *Footprints in Cyprus* and Simon Raven's *The Judas Boy*.

There are three well established specialist **travel bookshops** in the centre of London which stock both new and out-of-print titles. Daunts, with its elegant chapel-like interior, is at 110 Marylebone High Street; the more cramped but chatty Travel Bookshop is at 13 Blenheim Crescent, W11, ℗ (071) 229 5260; and The Travellers' Bookshop with its ground floor packed with old Baedekers is off Charing Cross Road at 25 Cecil Court, WC2N 4E2. For an excellent selection of new titles and maps, try Stanford's, 12–14 Longacre, WC2E 9LP. For the more esoteric titles you will be better off at either Zeno at 6 Denmark Street, WC2, or in the Cypriot basement of the Hellenic Book Service which has moved to 91 Fortress Road, NW5 1AG.

If you live out of London use Books For Travel Ltd, PO Box 1397, SW6 1JQ , ℗ (071) 381 6838, fax 381 8356, a specialist mail-order firm that delivers promptly from its list of ten Cypriot titles. Eastern Books, 125a Astonville Street, SW18 5AQ, ℗ (081) 871 0880, is an antiquarian bookshop that will send a catalogue of their Cyprus stock on demand.

Travel

Giovanni Mariti, *Travels in the Island of Cyprus* (1760–7), translated by Cobham in 1909 and available through a 1971 Zeno reprint.

H.I.H. Archduke Louis Salvator of Austria, *Levkosia*, London 1881, available through a 1983 Zeno reprint.

D.H. Hogarth, *Devia Cypria; an Archaeological Journey in Cyprus*, London 1889, followed by *The Nearer East*, London 1902.

Henry Rider Haggard, *A Winter's Pilgrimmage*, London 1901.

Patrick Balfour, *The Orphaned Realm*.

Lawrence Durrell, *Bitter Lemons*, London 1957.

Colin Thubron, *Journey into Cyprus*, London 1975.

Art, Antiquities & Architectural Guides

The Royal Academy Catalogue for the *From Byzantium to El Greco* exhibition of frescoes and icons only included five from Cyprus, but the essays are all relevant.

A. & J. Styllianou capped a lifetime of study with their well-illustrated *The Painted Churches of Cyprus*, London 1985.

Desmond Morris's *Art of Ancient Cyprus* is informed with a stimulating passion not always apparent in the academic.

Major Tankerville Chamberlayne, *Lacrimae Nicossienses*, Paris 1894.

G. Jeffrey, *Historic Monuments of Cyprus*, Nicosia 1918.

Rupert Gunnis, *Historic Cyprus*, London 1936, available second hand or through a Rustem's reprint in North Nicosia.

Louis di Cesnola, *Cyprus: its Ancient Cities, Tombs and Temples*, 1877, reprinted by James Bendon, PO Box 6484, Limassol.

Further Reading

Wiktor Daszewsha & Demetrios Michaelides, *Mosaic Floors in Cyprus*, Ravenna 1988.

Camille Enlart, *Gothic Art and the Renaissance in Cyprus*, Paris 1899, translated from the French by David Hunt for a Trigraph, London reprint in 1988.

V. Karageorghis, *Kition, Salamis* and *Paphos* volumes (*see* 'History').

H.W. Swiny, *Ancient Kourion Area*, 1982.

General History

Footsteps in Cyprus is a well-illustrated discursive history written by a team of specialists under the editorship of **David Hunt**—and in a paperback edition.

Cyprus in History is an older, more detailed study by the Greek historian **Doros Alastos**, published by Zeno, London.

Going into even greater length and depth there is **George Hill's** authoritative life work *A History of Cyprus*, published in four volumes by Cambridge University between 1940 and 1952 and seldom seen far from a university library.

All historians are happy to acknowledge their debt to **Claude Deval Cobham** for his anthology of source material *Excerpta Cypria*, though only specialist libraries stock either the original Cambridge 1908 edition or the expensive 1969 reprint.

Archaeology and Ancient History

Vassos Karageorghis, who has recently retired from his long tenure as Director of Antiquities, has written a number of fluent histories of the ancient period that have kept fully abreast of the various archaeological discoveries. His *Cyprus; from the Stone Age to the Romans*, London 1982, accompanies and partly supersedes *The Civilization of Prehistoric Cyprus*, Athens 1976. His popular digests of the major archaeological sites are themselves an impressive body of work: *Salamis*, London 1969, was followed by *Kition, Mycenean and Phoenician Discoveries in Cyprus*, London 1976, and (with **F.G. Maier**) the well-illustrated *Paphos: History and Archaeology*, Nicosia 1984.

For a practitioner's update on the current developments in prehistory look at *Early Society in Cyprus*, published by Edinburgh University in 1989 and edited by **Edgar Peltenburg**, the Director of the Lemba project.

C. Vermeule has filled a noticeable gap with his *Greek and Roman Cyprus*, Boston 1976.

There is still no good study of the transition from the late Roman to early Byzantine period unless you go out to the broader Mediterranean view provided by **Robin Lane Fox** in his fluent *Pagan and Christians*, Penguin 1986 and **Peter Brown's** *The World of Late Antiquity.*

Medieval to Modern

Moving into the medieval period the trail picks up with **J. Hackett's** extremely rare *History of the Orthodox Church in Cyprus*, London 1901, **H.T.F. Duckworth's** *The Church of Cyprus*, SPCK 1900, and **R.J.H. Jenkins's** *Studies on Byzantine History of the 9th and 10th Centuries.*

Of **Steven Runciman's** three volume *History of the Crusades* Volume 3 is the most relevant, but they are best read in quick succession like a dazzlingly evil and name-filled adventure story. His *The Great Church in Captivity*, Cambridge 1968, is principally concerned with the patriarchate at Constantinople (Istanbul) but also provides a magisterial survey over Orthodox doctrine and Greek intellectual life up to 1821.

To continue the story of the Crusader states in the East look in on **W. Miller**, *The Latins in the Levant*, London 1908.

For the Venetian period there is **Jan Morris**, *The Venetian Empire*, London 1980—Cyprus is in Chapter 5.

David and Iro Hunt's *Caterina Cornaro*, Trigraph 1989, is a biography of the last Queen of Cyprus.

The Ottoman period is covered by **Sir Harry Luke**, *Cyprus under the Turks*, published in 1921 and recently reprinted by Rustem's in North Nicosia.

Ahmet C. Gazioglu, *The Turks in Cyprus*, London 1990, covers the same period.

For the solid period of British administration read **C.W.J. Orr**, *Cyprus under British Rule*, 1918.

20th-Century Politics

There is a thick stream of titles about the enosis struggle and the partition of 1974 but it is still too early to hope for a history. Most of the volumes begin with a declaration of impartiality and then quickly descend into polemics and partisan politics based on a selective summary of events. It is very much a case of one man's freedom fighter being another man's terrorist with the great CIA Plot shimmering on the horizon. Start with the 1985 *Minority Rights Group on Cyprus* by Keith Kyle which gives the most succinct and balanced coverage.

Micheal Attalides, *Cyprus Nationalism and International Politics*, Q Press, 1979.

Nancy Crawshaw, *The Cyprus Revolt*, London, 1978.

Rauf Denktas, *The Cyprus Triangle*, 1982.

C. Foley, *Island in Revolt*, London 1962.

P.N. Vanezis, *Makarios Faith and Power*, (biography).

Frank Kitson, *Bunch of Five*, Faber, London 1977—a record of five counter-insurgency operations by one of its leading exponents includes a section on Cyprus on pages 205–277.

Kyriacos Markides, *The Rise and Fall of the Cyprus Republic*, Yale 1977.

S.G. Xydis, *Cyprus Conflict and Conciliation*, and *Cyprus; Reluctant Republic.*

T. Ehrlich, *Cyprus 1958–67.*

Robert Stephens, *Cyprus a Place of Arms*, 1966.

Michael Harbottle, *The Impartial Soldier*, 1970.

P.G. Polyviou, *Cyprus: The Tragedy and the Challenge*, 1975.

J.T.A. Koumoulides (edited), *Cyprus in Transition*, 1960–85.

Anthropology & Social Histories

Kyriacos Markides offers a trilogy that observes a modern mystic and healer at work in his native Cyprus: *The Magus of Strovolos, Homage to the Sun* and *Fire in the Heart* are published in the green livery of Arkana Books.

Peter Loizos's *The Heart Grown Bitter*, 1985 and *The Greek Gift; Politics in a Cypriot Village*, 1975 with **J K Campbell's** *Honour, Family and Patronage*, 1964 are three of the best regarded and more conventional dispassionate social histories.

You could perhaps supplement these with **David Lavender's** *The Story of the Cyprus Mines Corporation*, Huntington Library, California, 1962.

Food and Wine

George Aristidou's *Cyprus Wine*, is a 130-pp booklet published in Nicosia, 1990.

Giovanni Maritis's 18th-century *Wines of Cyprus* was reprinted by Nicolas Books, Athens, 1984. For Cypriot cuisine, look at:

M. Mourtzis, *The Cypriots at Table.*

N. Nicolaou, *Cooking from Cyprus.*

Gilli Davies, *A taste of Cyprus, a seasonal look at Cypriot cooking.*

T. Ioannou, *Taverna Meze of Cyprus.*

Flowers, Birds and Country Walks

David & Mary Bannerman, *Birds of Cyprus*, London & Edinburgh 1958 and *Flora of Cyprus* by R. D. Meikle of Kew Gardens are the definitive works, but they are expensive, heavy and almost inaccessible to the mere amateur.

Two informative booklets have recently been published by the Laona Project: **Bill Oddie and Derek Moore**, *A Bird Watcher's Guide to the Birds of Cyprus*, and **Adrain Akers Douglas**, *Discover Laona: Walks, Strolls and Drives* (available from Laona Project (UK), Dudwick House, Buxton, Norwich NR10 5HX, £5.35 and £4.35 inclusive of post and packaging).

The Collins' *Bird Book of Britain and Europe with North Africa and the Middle East* and **Oleg Polunin and Anthony Huxley's** *Flowers of the Mediterranean*, London 1987 are good field guides which can be supplemented by more popular summaries which are available on the island. These include:

Sonia Halliday, Laura Lushington, *Flowers of Northern Cyprus*, Nicosia 1988.

P. R. Flint and P.F. Stewart, *Birds of Cyprus*, 1983.

J. M. E. Took, *Common Birds of Cyprus*, 1973.

Anne Matthews, *Lilies of the Field*, Nicosia, 1968.

Elektra Megaw, *Wild Flowers of Cyprus.*

Christos Georgiades, *Flowers of Cyprus: Plants of Medecine*, *Nature of Cyprus: Environment, Flora, Fauna* and *Trees and Shrubs of Cyprus.*

Fiction

Simon Raven set *The Judas Boy*, number six in his Alms for Oblivion, in the Cyprus of Grivas, foreign agents and international intrigue. It is one of his best thrillers with a particularly memorable execution matched only by the titillation torture of Angela Tuck, published by Granada.

M.M. Kaye (of *Far Pavilions* fame) used incidents from a 1949 Cypriot painting holiday to create *Death in Cyprus*, a romantic who-dunnit published by Penguin in 1984.

Arden Winch's spy thriller, *The Rape of Aphrodite*, was published by Headline books in 1988.

Index